Kaplan Publishing are constantly finding new ways to make a difference to your studies and our exciting online resources really do offer something different to students looking for exam success.

This book comes with free MyKaplan online resources so that you can study anytime, anywhere. This free online resource is not sold separately and is included in the price of the book.

Having purchased this book, you have access to the following online study materials:

CONTENT	ACCA (including FFA,FAB,FMA)		FIA (excluding FFA,FAB,FMA)	
	Text	Kit	Text	Kit
iPaper version of the book	✓	✓	✓	✓
Interactive electronic version of the book	✓			
Check Your Understanding Test with instant answers	✓			
Material updates	✓	✓	✓	✓
Latest official ACCA exam questions*		✓		
Extra question assistance using the signpost icon**		✓		
Timed questions with an online tutor debrief using clock icon*		✓		
Interim assessment including questions and answers	✓		✓	
Technical answers	✓	✓	✓	✓

* Excludes F1, F2, F3, F4, FAB, FMA and FFA; for all other papers includes a selection of questions, as released by ACCA

** For ACCA P1-P7 only

How to access your online resources

Kaplan Financial students will already have a MyKaplan account and these extra resources will be available to you online. You do not need to register again, as this process was completed when you enrolled. If you are having problems accessing online materials, please ask your course administrator.

If you are already a registered MyKaplan user go to www.MyKaplan.co.uk and log in. Select the 'add a book' feature and enter the ISBN number of this book and the unique pass key at the bottom of this card. Then click 'finished' or 'add another book'. You may add as many books as you have purchased from this screen.

If you purchased through Kaplan Flexible Learning or via the Kaplan Publishing website you will automatically receive an e-mail invitation to MyKaplan. Please register your details using this email to gain access to your content. If you do not receive the e-mail or book content, please contact Kaplan Flexible Learning.

If you are a new MyKaplan user register at www.MyKaplan.co.uk and click on the link contained in the email we sent you to activate your account. Then select the 'add a book' feature, enter the ISBN number of this book and the unique pass key at the bottom of this card. Then click 'finished' or 'add another book'.

Your Code and Information

This code can only be used once for the registration of one book online. This registration and your online content will expire when the final sittings for the examinations covered by this book have taken place. Please allow one hour from the time you submit your book details for us to process your request.

Please scratch the film to access your MyKaplan code.

Please be aware that this code is case-sensitive and you will need to include the dashes within the passcode, but not when entering the ISBN. For further technical support, please visit www.MyKaplan.co.uk

D1396017

Paper P2 (INT and UK)

Corporate Reporting

EXAM KIT

British Library Cataloguing-in-Publication Data

A catalogue record for this book is available from the British Library.

Published by:

Kaplan Publishing UK

Unit 2 The Business Centre

Molly Millar's Lane

Wokingham

Berkshire

RG41 2QZ

ISBN: 978-1-78415-700-5

© Kaplan Financial Limited, 2016

Printed and bound in Great Britain

Acknowledgements

The past ACCA examination questions are the copyright of the Association of Chartered Certified Accountants. The original answers to the questions from June 1994 onwards were produced by the examiners themselves and have been adapted by Kaplan Publishing.

We are grateful to the Chartered Institute of Management Accountants and the Institute of Chartered Accountants in England and Wales for permission to reproduce past examination questions. The answers have been prepared by Kaplan Publishing.

CONTENTS

Section

Key features in this edition

In addition to providing a wide ranging bank of real past exam questions, we have also included in this edition:

- An analysis of recent examination papers.

- Paper specific information and advice on exam technique.

- Our recommended approach to make your revision for this particular subject as effective as possible.

  This includes step by step guidance on how best to use our Kaplan material (Complete text, pocket notes and exam kit) at this stage in your studies.

- Enhanced tutorial answers packed with specific key answer tips, technical tutorial notes and exam technique tips from our experienced tutors.

- Complementary online resources including full tutor debriefs and question assistance to point you in the right direction when you get stuck.

You will find a wealth of other resources to help you with your studies on the following sites:

www.MyKaplan.co.uk

www.**acca**global.com/students/

UK GAAP Focus

The Examiner has indicated that, for the purposes of this exam, International Financial Reporting Standards (IFRS) are the main accounting standards examined in the preparation of financial information.

The majority of the UK syllabus examination paper will be the same as the international paper, which is based on IFRS. The UK paper will also test some differences between UK GAAP and the IFRS for small and medium entities. There could also be a focus on the requirements of Companies Act 2006. It is anticipated that the differences will account for no more than 20% of the UK P2 paper.

UK syllabus students should refer to the list of examinable documents for the UK examination which identifies the main areas of difference between the IFRS for small and medium entities and UK GAAP and the extent to which those differences are examinable at P2. This document is available on the ACCA web site at www.accaglobal.com

To assist UK syllabus students, additional questions and answers based on examinable UK content are included within this Exam Kit.

Quality and accuracy are of the utmost importance to us so if you spot an error in any of our products, please send an email to mykaplanreporting@kaplan.com with full details.

Our Quality Co-ordinator will work with our technical team to verify the error and take action to ensure it is corrected in future editions.

INDEX TO QUESTIONS AND ANSWERS

INTRODUCTION

Note that the majority of the questions within the kit are past ACCA exam questions, the more recent questions (from 2005) are labelled as such in the index.

Many of the old ACCA questions within this kit have been adapted to reflect the current style of paper and also the latest examinable documents. If changed in any way from the original version, this is indicated in the end column of the index with the mark *(A)*.

KEY TO THE INDEX

PAPER ENHANCEMENTS

We have added the following enhancements to the answers in this exam kit:

Key answer tips

All answers include key answer tips to help your understanding of each question.

Tutorial note

All answers include more tutorial notes to explain some of the technical points in more detail.

Top tutor tips

For selected questions, we "walk through the answer" giving guidance on how to approach the questions with helpful 'tips from a top tutor', together with technical tutor notes.

These answers are indicated with the "footsteps" icon in the index.

ONLINE ENHANCEMENTS

 Timed question with Online tutor debrief

For selected questions, we recommend that they are to be completed in full exam conditions (i.e. properly timed in a closed book environment).

In addition to the examiner's technical answer, enhanced with key answer tips and tutorial notes in this exam kit, online you can find an answer debrief by a top tutor that:

- works through the question in full

- points out how to approach the question

- how to ensure that the easy marks are obtained as quickly as possible, and

- emphasises how to tackle exam questions and exam technique.

These questions are indicated with the "clock" icon in the index.

 Online question assistance

Have you ever looked at a question and not know where to start, or got stuck part way through?

For selected questions, we have produced "Online question assistance" offering different levels of guidance, such as:

- ensuring that you understand the question requirements fully, highlighting key terms and the meaning of the verbs used

- how to read the question proactively, with knowledge of the requirements, to identify the topic areas covered

- assessing the detail content of the question body, pointing out key information and explaining why it is important

- help in devising a plan of attack

With this assistance, you should then be able to attempt your answer confident that you know what is expected of you.

These questions are indicated with the "signpost" icon in the index.

Online question enhancements and answer debriefs are available on MyKaplan:

www.MyKaplan.co.uk

SECTION A-TYPE QUESTIONS

SECTION B-TYPE QUESTIONS

ANALYSIS OF PAST PAPERS

The table below summarises the key topics that have been tested in the most recent P2 INT examinations.

Commencing September 2015, only selected questions will be released by ACCA every six months. The September/December 2015 questions and answers are included in Sections 3 and 4 of this exam kit.

	Dec 12	Jun 13	Dec 13	Jun 14	Dec 14	Jun 15	Sept / Dec 15
Group financial statements							
Consolidated SP/L				Q3			
Consolidated SFP	Q6	Q5			Q2	Q1	✓
Group cash flow statement			Q4				
Foreign subsidiary							✓
Complex group	Q6	Q5					
Step acquisition		Q5			Q2		
Loss of control in the year				Q3		Q1	
Equity transfer in the year				Q3			
Joint arrangement					Q2		
Reporting standards							
IAS 1							✓
IAS 2							
IAS 7	Q30						
IAS 8		Q28					
IAS 10		Q28			Q22		
IAS 12	Q30			Q24			✓
IAS 16		Q28			Q23		✓
IAS 17	Q31	Q29	Q26				
IAS 19							
IAS 20	Q30	Q28					
IAS 21	Q30			Q24			
IAS 23							
IAS 24					Q22		
IAS 27							
IAS 28							
IAS 32/IFRS 7/IFRS 9			Q27	Q24	Q22	Q21	✓
IAS 33							
IAS 36	Q31						
IAS 37	Q31	Q28		Q25			✓

	Dec 12	Jun 13	Dec 13	Jun 14	Dec 14	Jun 15	Sept / Dec 15
IAS 38				Q25		Q21	✓
IAS 40	Q31	Q29					
IAS 41						Q20	
IFRS 1							
IFRS 2						Q20/21	
IFRS 3 Revised			Q27		Q23		✓
IFRS 5		Q29	Q26	Q25			
IFRS 8		Q28				Q21	
IFRS 10/11/12	Q30				Q23		✓
IFRS 13		Q29				Q20	
IFRS 15	Q30	Q28	Q26	Q25			✓
IFRS for SME							
Entity reconstructions							
Group reorganisations							
Essay question							
Fair value (IFRS 13)	Q63						
Disclosures (incl. IFRS 7)		Q62					
Accounting policies (IAS 8)			Q61				
Debt or equity (IAS 32)				Q60			
Impairment (IAS 36)					Q59		
IAS 1 and <IR>						Q58	
Revenue (IFRS 15)							✓

EXAM TECHNIQUE

- **Divide the time** you spend on questions in proportion to the marks on offer:

  Whatever happens, always keep your eye on the clock and **do not over run on any part of any question!**

- If you **get completely stuck** with a question:

  - leave space in your answer book, and

  - **return to it later.**

- Stick to the question and **tailor your answer** to what you are asked.

  - pay particular attention to the verbs in the question.

- If you do not understand what a question is asking, **state your assumptions**.

  Even if you do not answer in precisely the way the examiner hoped, you should be given some credit, if your assumptions are reasonable.

- You should do everything you can to make things easy for the marker.

  The marker will find it easier to identify the points you have made if your **answers are legible**.

- **Written questions**:

  Your answer should have:

  - a clear structure, including headings and paragraphs to provide focus

  Be concise and stay on topic. You will score no marks if you do not answer the question.

- **Computations**:

  It is essential to include all your workings in your answers – method marks are available

  Many computational questions require the use of a standard format:

  e.g. standard formats for financial statements.

  Be sure you know these formats thoroughly before the exam and use the layouts that you see in the answers given in this book and in model answers.

- **Reports, memos and other documents**:

  Some questions ask you to present your answer in the form of a report, a memo, a letter or other document.

  Make sure that you use the correct format – there could be easy marks to gain here.

PAPER SPECIFIC INFORMATION

THE EXAM

FORMAT OF THE EXAM

			Number of marks
Section A: 1 compulsory question			50
Question 1:	Group accounts and discussion including ethics		
Section B: choice of two from three available questions @ 25 marks each			
Question 2:	Mixed transactional	(25)	
Question 3:	Mixed transactional	(25)	50
Question 4:	Essay style – discussion	(25)	
			———
			100
Total time allowed:	3 hours 15 minutes.		——

Note that:

- Question 1 will focus on preparation of group financial statements for 35 marks. The remainder of the question is likely to be discursive, perhaps based upon the appropriateness of a particular accounting treatment within the group accounts and will require application of ethical and professional principles to information within the question.

- Question 1 is also likely to require technical knowledge of reporting standards to be applied as part of the consolidation exercise.

- Questions 2 and 3 are likely to be multi-transactional questions. They will often be presented in the form of a scenario with an entity in the final stages of preparing their annual financial statements, with technical issues still to resolve. This may also include use of incorrect accounting treatments which will require identification, correction and explanation.

- Question 4 is an essay-style question, usually comprising a current issue or a theoretical or conceptual issue for discussion. This may include a relatively small computation element.

- In the P2 exam, marks are awarded for knowledge of key principles and also for the application of those principles to the scenario.

- Two professional marks are available for each question in section B of the examination. As only two from the three available questions must be attempted, a maximum of four professional marks are available per examination. You must answer each part of the question to be awarded the full two marks.

PASS MARK

The pass mark for all ACCA Qualification examination papers is 50%.

UK GAAP FOCUS

The Examiner has indicated that up to 20% of the P2 UK examination paper may comprise specific UK GAAP content. This could consist of an individual question or elements of more than one question from either or both sections of the examination paper. It may comprise of discursive and/or numerical content and requirements, and will test the differences between UK standards and IFRS for small and medium entities as well as some of the requirements of Companies Act 2006. Note that the UK syllabus examination paper will be denominated in dollars (identified as $); this Exam Kit adopts the same notation and style for UK syllabus content.

DETAILED SYLLABUS

The detailed syllabus and study guide written by the ACCA can be found at:

www.accaglobal.com/students/

KAPLAN'S RECOMMENDED REVISION APPROACH

QUESTION PRACTICE IS THE KEY TO SUCCESS

Success in professional examinations relies upon you acquiring a firm grasp of the required knowledge at the tuition phase. In order to be able to do the questions, knowledge is essential.

However, the difference between success and failure often hinges on your exam technique on the day and making the most of the revision phase of your studies.

The **Kaplan complete text** is the starting point, designed to provide the underpinning knowledge to tackle all questions. However, in the revision phase, pouring over text books is not the answer.

Kaplan Online progress tests help you consolidate your knowledge and understanding and are a useful tool to check whether you can remember key topic areas.

Kaplan pocket notes are designed to help you quickly revise a topic area, however you then need to practice questions. There is a need to progress to full exam standard questions as soon as possible, and to tie your exam technique and technical knowledge together.

The importance of question practice cannot be over-emphasised.

The recommended approach below is designed by expert tutors in the field, in conjunction with their knowledge of the examiner and their recent real exams.

The approach taken for the fundamental papers is to revise by topic area. However, with the professional stage papers, a multi topic approach is required to answer the scenario based questions.

You need to practice as many questions as possible in the time you have left.

OUR AIM

Our aim is to get you to the stage where you can attempt exam standard questions confidently, to time, in a closed book environment, with no supplementary help (i.e. to simulate the real examination experience).

Practising your exam technique on real past examination questions, in timed conditions, is also vitally important for you to assess your progress and identify areas of weakness that may need more attention in the final run up to the examination.

In order to achieve this we recognise that initially you may feel the need to practice some questions with open book help and exceed the required time.

The approach below shows you which questions you should use to build up to coping with exam standard question practice, and references to the sources of information available should you need to revisit a topic area in more detail.

Remember that in the real examination, all you have to do is:

- attempt all questions required by the exam
- only spend the allotted time on each question, and
- get them at least 50% right!

Try and practice this approach on every question you attempt from now to the real exam.

EXAMINER COMMENTS

We have included the examiner's comments to many examination questions in this kit for you to see the main pitfalls that students fall into with regard to technical content.

However, too many times in the general section of the report, the examiner comments that students had failed due to:

- "misallocation of time"
- "running out of time" and
- showing signs of "spending too much time on an earlier question and clearly rushing the answer to a subsequent question".

Good exam technique is vital.

THE KAPLAN PAPER P2 REVISION PLAN

Stage 1: Assess areas of strengths and weaknesses

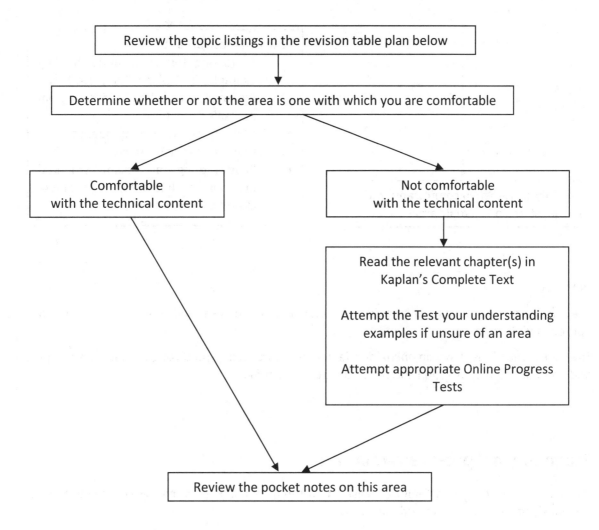

Stage 2: Practice questions

Follow the order of revision of topics as recommended in the revision table plan below and attempt the questions in the order suggested.

Try to avoid referring to text books and notes and the model answer until you have completed your attempt.

Try to answer the question in the allotted time.

Review your attempt with the model answer and assess how much of the answer you achieved in the allocated exam time.

Fill in the self-assessment box below and decide on your best course of action.

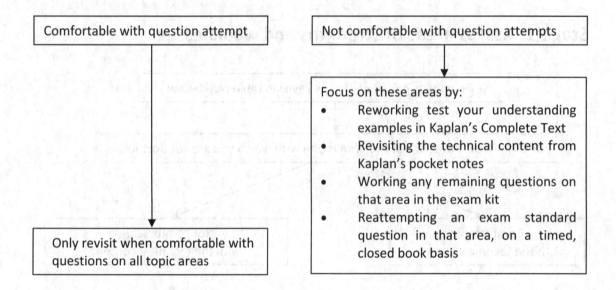

Note that:

The "footsteps questions" give guidance on exam techniques and how you should have approached the question.

The "clock questions" have an online debrief where a tutor talks you through the exam technique and approach to that question and works the question in full.

Stage 3: Final pre-exam revision

We recommend that you **attempt at least one three hour mock examination** containing a set of previously unseen exam standard questions.

It is important that you get a feel for the breadth of coverage of a real exam without advanced knowledge of the topic areas covered – just as you will expect to see on the real exam day.

Ideally this mock should be sat in timed, closed book, real exam conditions and could be:

- a mock examination offered by your tuition provider, and/or

- the exam paper in the back of this exam kit, and/or

- the last real examination paper.

KAPLAN'S DETAILED REVISION PLAN

Topic	Complete Text Chapter	Pocket note Chapter	Questions to attempt	Tutor guidance	Date attempted	Self assessment
The financial reporting framework	1	1	Q20 Q58 Q63 Q65(a) Q71	Ensure that you are able to define, discuss and apply the elements of financial statements as identified in The Framework. It is also important to know and be able to apply the rules and definitions in IFRS 13 *Fair Value Measurement*.		
The professional and ethical duty of the accountant	2	2	Q1(c) Q2(c)	Ensure that you can apply the ACCA Code of Ethics to a practical scenario.		
Appraisal of financial performance and position	3	3	Q5(b) Q60	This is likely to be asked as part of a question, and may also require consideration of other accounting issues.		
Reporting financial performance						
Performance reporting	3, 4	3, 4	Q26 Q28	This could include revenue recognition per IFRS 15, plus discontinued activities and non-current assets held for sale per IFRS 5		
Non-current assets	5	5	Q23 Q51 Q55	There are several reporting standards within this heading. In particular, the accounting requirements of IAS 16, IAS 36 and IAS 38 are regularly examined.		

Foreign currency transactions	6	Q24	Ensure that you know how to account for exchange differences arising on overseas transactions within an individual company's financial statements.	
Leases	7	Q29 Q32 Q65(b)	Ensure that you can classify and explain the differences between finance and operating leases per IAS 17 and that you can account for sale and leaseback transactions.	
Employee benefits	8	Q46(a)	Ensure that you understand how to account for defined benefit and defined contribution schemes per IAS 19.	
Share-based payment	9	Q38 Q53	Ensure that you understand how to account for both cash-settled and equity-settled transactions per IFRS 2.	
Provisions and events after the reporting period	10	Q46(b)	Ensure that you know when a legal or constructive obligation arises per IAS 37, and can apply the definition of an adjusting and non-adjusting event per IAS 10.	
Financial instruments	11	Q22 Q27 Q43	Ensure that you understand and can apply recognition, measurement and classification rules relating to financial instruments per IAS 32 and IFRS 9.	

Income taxes	12	12	Q40 Q52	The main focus is likely to be deferred tax, with recognition of temporary differences to create deferred tax assets and liabilities per IAS 12.
Segment reporting	13	13	Q45	Ensure that you can define a reportable segment per IFRS 8 and apply the definition to information provided.
Related parties	14	14	Q49	Ensure you can identify related parties per IAS 24, and the implications for any transactions which they may enter into.
Changes in accounting regulation and reporting	15, 17	15, 17	Q36 Q70	Ensure that you know how to account for the first-time adoption of IFRS. The growing importance of integrated reporting is also likely to be a key topic.
Specialised entities and specialised transactions	16	16	Q34 Q56 Q64	Ensure that you understand accounting issues associated with SMEs, as well as the reasons for, and the accounting treatment of, an entity reconstruction.
Current issues	18	18	Q68 Q69	Regularly review the IASB web site for current developments, together with the ACCA web site for articles relevant to paper P2.

Group financial statements				
Basic groups	19	19	Q1	Ensure that you understand the standard workings required for subsidiaries in group financial statements, as well as key definitions per IFRS 10, IFRS 11 and IFRS 12.
Complex structures	20	20	Q5 Q6	Ensure that you understand how control is exercised in complex structures, and the impact upon standard workings required.
Changes in group structure	21, 23	21, 23	Q3 Q7 Q12	Ensure that you know how to account for share transactions where control is either gained, lost or retained.
Foreign currency subsidiaries	22	22	Q9 Q17	Ensure that you know how to consolidate a foreign subsidiary in accordance with IAS 21.
Statements of cash flows	24	24	Q4 Q10	Ensure that you know the format of a statement of cash flows per IAS 7 and can deal with changes in group structure within the statement.

Note that not all of the questions are referred to in the programme above. We have recommended an approach to build up from the basic to exam standard questions. The remaining questions are available in the kit for extra practice for those who require more questions on some areas.

TECHNICAL UPDATE

Since 1 September 2014, which was the previous year's cut-off date for new examinable documents, there have been no major changes to the examinable IFRSs and IAS.

Section 1

PRACTICE QUESTIONS

SECTION A-TYPE QUESTIONS

GROUP FINANCIAL STATEMENTS

1   **KUTCHEN (JUNE 15 EXAM)** *Walk in the footsteps of a top tutor*

Kutchen, a public limited company, operates in the technology sector and has investments in other entities operating in the sector. The draft statements of financial position at 31 March 2015 are as follows:

	Kutchen $m	House $m	Mach $m
Assets:			
Non-current assets			
Property, plant and equipment	216	41	38
Investment in subsidiary			
Mach	52		
Finance lease receivables	50	14	8
	–––	–––	–––
	318	55	46
Current assets	44	25	64
	–––	–––	–––
Total assets	362	80	110
	–––	–––	–––
Equity and liabilities:			
Share capital of $1 each	43	13	26
Retained earnings	41	24	15
Other components of equity	12	5	4
	–––	–––	–––
Total equity	96	42	45
	–––	–––	–––
Non-current liabilities	67	12	28
Current liabilities	199	26	37
	–––	–––	–––
Total liabilities	266	38	65
	–––	–––	–––
Total equity and liabilities	362	80	110
	–––	–––	–––

The following information is relevant to the preparation of the group financial statements:

1   On 1 October 2014, Kutchen acquired 70% of the equity interests of House, a public limited company. The purchase consideration comprised 20 million shares of $1 of Kutchen at the acquisition date and 5 million shares on 31 March 2016 if House's net profit after taxation was at least $4 million for the year ending on that date. The market price of Kutchen's shares on 1 October 2014 was $2 per share and that of House was $4.20 per share. It is felt that there is a 20% chance of the profit target being met.

Kutchen wishes to measure the non-controlling interest at fair value at the date of acquisition. At acquisition, the fair value of the non-controlling interest (NCI) in House was based upon quoted market prices. On 1 October 2014, the fair value of the identifiable net assets acquired was $48 million and retained earnings of House were $18 million and other components of equity were $3 million. The excess in fair value is due to non-depreciable land. No entries had been made in the financial statements of Kutchen for the acquisition of House.

2   On 1 April 2014, Kutchen acquired 80% of the equity interests of Mach, a privately owned entity, for a consideration of $57 million. The consideration comprised cash of $52 million and the transfer of non-depreciable land with a fair value of $5 million. The carrying amount of the land at the acquisition date was $3 million and the land has only recently been transferred to the seller of the shares in Mach and is still carried at $3 million in the financial records of Kutchen at 31 March 2015. The only consideration shown in the financial records of Kutchen is the cash paid for the shares of Mach.

At the date of acquisition, the identifiable net assets of Mach had a fair value of $55 million, retained earnings were $12 million and other components of equity were $4 million. The excess in fair value is due to non-depreciable land. Mach had made a net profit attributable to ordinary shareholders of $3.6 million for the year to 31 March 2014.

Kutchen wishes to measure the non-controlling interest at fair value at the date of acquisition. The NCI is to be fair valued using a public entity market multiple method. Kutchen has identified two companies who are comparable to Mach and who are trading at an average price to earnings ratio (P/E ratio) of 21. Kutchen has adjusted the P/E ratio to 19 for differences between the entities and Mach, for the purpose of fair valuing the NCI.

3   Kutchen had purchased an 80% interest in Niche for $40 million on 1 April 2014 when the fair value of the identifiable net assets was $44 million. The partial goodwill method had been used to calculate goodwill and an impairment of $2 million had arisen in the year ended 31 March 2015. There were no other impairment charges or items requiring reclassification.

The holding in Niche was sold for $50 million on 31 March 2015 and the gain on sale in Kutchen's financial statements is currently recorded in other components of equity. The carrying value of Niche's identifiable net assets other than goodwill was $60 million at the date of sale. Kutchen had carried the investment in Niche at cost.

4   Kutchen has decided to restructure one of its business segments. The plan was agreed by the board of directors on 1 January 2015 and affects employees in two locations. In the first location, half of the factory units have been closed by 31 March 2015 and the affected employees' pension benefits have been frozen. Any new employees will not be eligible to join the defined benefit plan. After the restructuring, the present value of the defined benefit obligation in this location is $8 million. The following table relates to location 1.

Value before restructuring	Location 1 – $m
Present value of defined benefit obligation	(10)
Fair value of plan assets	7
Net pension liability	(3)

In the second location, all activities have been discontinued. It has been agreed that employees will receive a payment of $4 million in exchange for the pension liability of $2.4 million in the unfunded pension scheme. Kutchen estimates that the costs of the above restructuring excluding pension costs will be $6 million. Kutchen has not accounted for the effects of the restructuring in its financial statements because it is planning a rights issue and does not wish to depress the share price. Therefore there has been no formal announcement of the restructuring. The pension liability is shown in non-current liabilities.

5   Kutchen manufactures equipment for lease or sale. On 31 March 2015, Kutchen leased out equipment under a 10-year finance lease. The selling price of the leased item was $50 million and the net present value of the minimum lease payments was $47 million. The carrying value of the leased asset was $40 million and the present value of the unguaranteed residual value of the product when it reverts back to Kutchen at the end of the lease term is estimated to be $2.8 million. Kutchen has shown sales of $50 million and cost of sales of $40 million in its financial statements.

6   Kutchen has impairment tested its non-current assets. It was decided that a building located overseas was impaired because of major subsidence. The building was acquired on 1 April 2014 at a cost of 25 million dinars when the exchange was 2 dinars to the dollar. The building is carried under the cost model. At 31 March 2015, the recoverable amount of the building was deemed to be 17.5 million dinars. The exchange rate at 31 March 2015 is 2.5 dinars to the dollar. Buildings are depreciated over 25 years.

The tax base and carrying amounts of the non-current assets before the impairment write down were identical. The impairment of the non-current assets is not allowable for tax purposes. Kutchen has not made any impairment or deferred tax adjustment for the above. Kutchen expects to make profits for the foreseeable future and assume the tax rate is 25%.

No other deferred tax effects are required to be taken into account other than on the above non-current assets.

Required:

(a) **Prepare the consolidated statement of financial position for the Kutchen Group as at 31 March 2015.** **(35 marks)**

(b) When Kutchen acquired the majority shareholding in Mach, there was an option on the remaining non-controlling interest (NCI), which could be exercised at any time up to 31 December 2015. On 30 April 2015, Kutchen acquired the remaining NCI which related to the purchase of Mach. The payment for the NCI was structured so that it contained a fixed initial payment and a series of contingent amounts payable over the following two years. The contingent payments were to be based on the future profits of Mach up to a maximum amount. Kutchen felt that the fixed initial payment was an equity transaction. Additionally, Kutchen was unsure as to whether the contingent payments were equity, financial liabilities or contingent liabilities.

After a board discussion which contained disagreement as to the accounting treatment, Kutchen is preparing to disclose the contingent payments in accordance with IAS 37 *Provisions, Contingent Liabilities and Contingent Assets*. The disclosure will include the estimated timing of the payments and the directors' estimate of the amounts to be settled.

Required:

Advise Kutchen on the difference between equity and liabilities, and on the proposed accounting treatment of the contingent payments on acquisition of the NCI of Mach. **(8 marks)**

(c) The directors of Kutchen are considering the purchase of a company in the USA. They have heard that the accounting standards in the USA are 'rules based' and that there are significant differences of opinion as to whether 'rules based' standards are superior to 'principles based' standards. It is said that this is due to established national approaches and contrasting regulatory philosophies. The directors feel that 'principles based' standards are a greater ethical challenge to an accountant than 'rules based' standards.

Required:

Discuss the philosophy behind 'rules based' and 'principles based' accounting standards, setting out the ethical challenges which may be faced by accountants if there were a switch in a jurisdiction from 'rules based' to 'principles based' accounting standards. **(7 marks)**

(Total: 50 marks)

2   JOEY (DEC 14 EXAM) *Walk in the footsteps of a top tutor*

(a)   Joey, a public limited company, operates in the media sector. Joey has investments in a number of companies. Draft statements of financial position at 30 November 2014 are as follows:

	Joey $m	Margy $m	Hulty $m
Assets			
Non-current assets			
Property, plant and equipment	3,295	2,000	1,200
Investments in subsidiaries and other investments			
Margy	1,675		
Hulty	700		
	5,670	2,000	1,200
Current assets	985	861	150
Total assets	6,655	2,861	1,350
Equity and liabilities:			
Share capital	850	1,020	600
Retained earnings	3,340	980	350
Other components of equity	250	80	40
Total equity	4,440	2,080	990
Non-current liabilities	1,895	675	200
Current liabilities	320	106	160
Total equity and liabilities	6,655	2,861	1,350

The following information is relevant to the preparation of the group financial statements:

(1)   On 1 December 2011, Joey acquired 30% of the ordinary shares of Margy for a cash consideration of $600 million when the fair value of Margy's identifiable net assets was $1,840 million. Joey treated Margy as an associate and has equity accounted for Margy up to 1 December 2013. Joey's share of Margy's undistributed profit amounted to $90 million and its share of a revaluation gain amounted to $10 million.

On 1 December 2013, Joey acquired a further 40% of the ordinary shares of Margy for a cash consideration of $975 million and gained control of the company. The cash consideration has been added to the equity accounted balance for Margy at 1 December 2013 to give the carrying amount at 30 November 2014.

At 1 December 2013, the fair value of Margy's identifiable net assets was $2,250 million. At 1 December 2013, the fair value of the equity interest in Margy held by Joey before the business combination was $705 million and the fair value of the non-controlling interest of 30% was assessed as $620 million. The retained earnings and other components of equity of Margy at 1 December 2013 were $900 million and $70 million respectively. It is group policy to measure the non-controlling interest at fair value.

(2)   At the time of the business combination with Margy, Joey has included in the fair value of Margy's identifiable net assets, an unrecognised contingent liability of $6 million in respect of a warranty claim in progress against Margy. In March 2014, there was a revision of the estimate of the liability to $5 million. The amount has met the criteria to be recognised as a provision in current liabilities in the financial statements of Margy and the revision of the estimate is deemed to be a measurement period adjustment.

(3)   Additionally, buildings with a carrying amount of $200 million had been included in the fair valuation of Margy at 1 December 2013. The buildings have a remaining useful life of 20 years at 1 December 2013. However, Joey had commissioned an independent valuation of the buildings of Margy which was not complete at 1 December 2013 and therefore not considered in the fair value of the identifiable net assets at the acquisition date. The valuations were received on 1 April 2014 and resulted in a decrease of $40 million in the fair value of property, plant and equipment at the date of acquisition. This decrease does not affect the fair value of the non-controlling interest at acquisition and has not been entered into the financial statements of Margy. Buildings are depreciated on the straight-line basis and it is group policy to leave revaluation gains on disposal in equity. The excess of the fair value of the net assets over their carrying value, at 1 December 2013, is due to an increase in the value of non-depreciable land and the contingent liability.

(4)   On 1 December 2013, Joey acquired 80% of the equity interests of Hulty, a private entity, in exchange for cash of $700 million. Because the former owners of Hulty needed to dispose of the investment quickly, they did not have sufficient time to market the investment to many potential buyers. The fair value of the identifiable net assets was $960 million. Joey determined that the fair value of the 20% non-controlling interest in Hulty at that date was $250 million. Joey reviewed the procedures used to identify and measure the assets acquired and liabilities assumed and to measure the fair value of both the non-controlling interest and the consideration transferred. After that review, Hulty determined that the procedures and resulting measures were appropriate. The retained earnings and other components of equity of Hulty at 1 December 2013 were $300 million and $40 million respectively. The excess in fair value is due to an unrecognised franchise right, which Joey had granted to Hulty on 1 December 2012 for five years. At the time of the acquisition, the franchise right could be sold for its market price. It is group policy to measure the non-controlling interest at fair value.

All goodwill arising on acquisitions has been impairment tested with no impairment being required.

(5)   Joey is looking to expand into publishing and entered into an arrangement with Content Publishing (CP), a public limited company, on 1 December 2013. CP will provide content for a range of books and online publications.

CP is entitled to a royalty calculated as 10% of sales and 30% of gross profit of the publications. Joey has sole responsibility for all printing, binding, and platform maintenance of the online website. The agreement states that key strategic sales and marketing decisions must be agreed jointly. Joey selects the content to be covered in the publications but CP has the right of veto over this content. However on 1 June 2014, Joey and CP decided to set up a legal entity, JCP, with equal shares and voting rights. CP continues to contribute content into JCP but does not receive royalties. Joey continues the printing, binding and platform maintenance. The sales and cost of sales in the period were $5 million and $2 million respectively. The whole of the sale proceeds and the costs of sales were recorded in Joey's financial statements with no accounting entries being made for JCP or amounts due to CP. Joey currently funds the operations. Assume that the sales and costs accrue evenly throughout the year and that all of the transactions relating to JCP have been in cash.

(6)   At 30 November 2013, Joey carried a property in its statement of financial position at its revalued amount of $14 million in accordance with IAS 16 *Property, Plant and Equipment*. Depreciation is charged at $300,000 per year on the straight line basis. In March 2014, the management decided to sell the property and it was advertised for sale. By 31 March 2014, the sale was considered to be highly probable and the criteria for IFRS 5 Non-current Assets Held for Sale and Discontinued Operations were met at this date. At that date, the asset's fair value was $15.4 million and its value in use was $15.8 million. Costs to sell the asset were estimated at $300,000. On 30 November 2014, the property was sold for $15.6 million. The transactions regarding the property are deemed to be material and no entries have been made in the financial statements regarding this property since 30 November 2013 as the cash receipts from the sale were not received until December 2014.

Required:

Prepare the group consolidated statement of financial position of Joey as at 30 November 2014.   **(35 marks)**

(b)   The Joey Group wishes to expand its operations. As part of this expansion, it has granted options to the employees of Margy and Hulty over its own shares as at 7 December 2014. The awards vest immediately. Joey is not proposing to make a charge to the subsidiaries for these options.

Joey does not know how to account for this transaction in its own, the subsidiaries, and the group financial statements.

Required:

Explain to Joey how the above transaction should be dealt with in its own, the subsidiaries, and the group financial statements.   **(8 marks)**

(c) Joey's directors feel that they need a significant injection of capital in order to modernise plant and equipment as the company has been promised new orders if it can produce goods to an international quality. The bank's current lending policies require borrowers to demonstrate good projected cash flow, as well as a level of profitability which would indicate that repayments would be made. However, the current projected cash flow statement would not satisfy the bank's criteria for lending. The directors have told the bank that the company is in an excellent financial position, that the financial results and cash flow projections will meet the criteria and that the chief accountant will forward a report to this effect shortly. The chief accountant has only recently joined Joey and has openly stated that he cannot afford to lose his job because of his financial commitments.

Required:

Discuss the potential ethical conflicts which may arise in the above scenario and the ethical principles which would guide how a professional accountant should respond in this situation. (7 marks)

(Total: 50 marks)

3 **MARCHANT (JUNE 14 EXAM)** *Walk in the footsteps of a top tutor*

The following draft financial statements relate to Marchant, a public limited company.

Marchant Group: Draft statements of profit or loss and other comprehensive income for the year ended 30 April 2014.

	Marchant $m	Nathan $m	Option $m
Revenue	400	115	70
Cost of sales	(312)	(65)	(36)
Gross profit	88	50	34
Other income	21	7	2
Administrative costs	(15)	(9)	(12)
Other expenses	(35)	(19)	(8)
Operating profit	59	29	16
Finance costs	(5)	(6)	(4)
Finance income	6	5	8
Profit before tax	60	28	20
Income tax expense	(19)	(9)	(5)
Profit for the year	41	19	15
Other comprehensive income – revaluation surplus	10	–	–
Total comprehensive income for year	51	19	15

The following information is relevant to the preparation of the group statement of profit or loss and other comprehensive income:

1   On 1 May 2012, Marchant acquired 60% of the equity interests of Nathan, a public limited company. The purchase consideration comprised cash of $80 million and the fair value of the identifiable net assets acquired was $110 million at that date. The fair value of the non-controlling interest (NCI) in Nathan was $45 million on 1 May 2012. Marchant wishes to use the 'full goodwill' method for all acquisitions. The share capital and retained earnings of Nathan were $25 million and $65 million respectively and other components of equity were $6 million at the date of acquisition. The excess of the fair value of the identifiable net assets at acquisition is due to non-depreciable land.

     Goodwill has been impairment tested annually and as at 30 April 2013 had reduced in value by 20%. However at 30 April 2014, the impairment of goodwill had reversed and goodwill was valued at $2 million above its original value. This upward change in value has already been included in above draft financial statements of Marchant prior to the preparation of the group accounts.

2   Marchant disposed of an 8% equity interest in Nathan on 30 April 2014 for a cash consideration of $18 million and had accounted for the gain or loss in other income. The carrying value of the net assets of Nathan at 30 April 2014 was $120 million before any adjustments on consolidation. Marchant accounts for investments in subsidiaries using IFRS 9 *Financial Instruments* and has made an election to show gains and losses in other comprehensive income. The carrying value of the investment in Nathan was $90 million at 30 April 2013 and $95 million at 30 April 2014 before the disposal of the equity interest.

3   Marchant acquired 60% of the equity interests of Option, a public limited company, on 30 April 2012. The purchase consideration was cash of $70 million. Option's identifiable net assets were fair valued at $86 million and the NCI had a fair value of $28 million at that date. On 1 November 2013, Marchant disposed of a 40% equity interest in Option for a consideration of $50 million. Option's identifiable net assets were $90 million and the value of the NCI was $34 million at the date of disposal. The remaining equity interest was fair valued at $40 million. After the disposal, Marchant exerts significant influence. Any increase in net assets since acquisition has been reported in profit or loss and the carrying value of the investment in Option had not changed since acquisition. Goodwill had been impairment tested and no impairment was required. No entries had been made in the financial statements of Marchant for this transaction other than for cash received.

4   Marchant sold inventory to Nathan for $12 million at fair value. Marchant made a loss on the transaction of $2 million and Nathan still holds $8 million in inventory at the year end.

5   The following information relates to Marchant's pension scheme:

	$m
Plan assets at 1 May 2013	48
Defined benefit obligation at 1 May 2013	50
Service cost for year ended 30 April 2014	4
Discount rate at 1 May 2013	10%
Re-measurement loss in year ended 30 April 2014	2
Past service cost 30 April 2014	3

The pension costs have not been accounted for in total comprehensive income.

6   On 1 May 2012, Marchant purchased an item of property, plant and equipment for $12 million and this is being depreciated using the straight line basis over 10 years with a zero residual value. At 30 April 2013, the asset was revalued to $13 million but at 30 April 2014, the value of the asset had fallen to $7 million. Marchant uses the revaluation model to value its non-current assets. The effect of the revaluation at 30 April 2014 had not been taken into account in total comprehensive income but depreciation for the year had been charged.

7   On 1 May 2012, Marchant made an award of 8,000 share options to each of its seven directors. The condition attached to the award is that the directors must remain employed by Marchant for three years. The fair value of each option at the grant date was $100 and the fair value of each option at 30 April 2014 was $110. At 30 April 2013, it was estimated that three directors would leave before the end of three years. Due to an economic downturn, the estimate of directors who were going to leave was revised to one director at 30 April 2014. The expense for the year as regards the share options had not been included in profit or loss for the current year and no directors had left by 30 April 2014.

8   A loss on an effective cash flow hedge of Nathan of $3 million has been included in the subsidiary's finance costs.

9   Ignore the taxation effects of the above adjustments unless specified. Any expense adjustments should be amended in other expenses.

Required:

(a)   (i)   **Prepare a consolidated statement of profit or loss and other comprehensive income for the year ended 30 April 2014 for the Marchant Group.   (30 marks)**

(ii)   **Explain, with suitable calculations, how the sale of the 8% interest in Nathan should be dealt with in the group statement of financial position at 30 April 2014.   (5 marks)**

(b)   The directors of Marchant have strong views on the usefulness of the financial statements after their move to International Financial Reporting Standards (IFRSs). They feel that IFRSs implement a fair value model. Nevertheless, they are of the opinion that IFRSs are failing users of financial statements as they do not reflect the financial value of an entity.

Required:

Discuss the directors' views above as regards the use of fair value in IFRSs and the fact that IFRSs do not reflect the financial value of an entity.   (9 marks)

(c)   Marchant plans to update its production process and the directors feel that technology-led production is the only feasible way in which the company can remain competitive. Marchant operates from a leased property and the leasing arrangement was established in order to maximise taxation benefits. However, the financial statements have not shown a lease asset or liability to date. A new financial controller joined Marchant just after the financial year end of 30 April 2014 and is presently reviewing the financial statements to prepare for the upcoming audit and to begin making a loan application to finance the new technology.

The financial controller feels that the lease relating to both the land and buildings should be treated as a finance lease but the finance director disagrees. The finance director does not wish to recognise the lease in the statement of financial position and therefore wishes to continue to treat it as an operating lease. The finance director feels that the lease does not meet the criteria for a finance lease, and it was made clear by the finance director that showing the lease as a finance lease could jeopardise the loan application.

Required:

Discuss the ethical and professional issues which face the financial controller in the above situation. **(6 marks)**

(Total: 50 marks)

4   ANGEL (DEC 13 EXAM) *Walk in the footsteps of a top tutor*

The following draft group financial statements relate to Angel, a public limited company:

Angel Group: Statement of financial position as at 30 November 2013

	30 November 2013 $m	30 November 2012 $m
Assets		
Non-current assets		
Property, plant and equipment	475	465
Goodwill	105	120
Other intangible assets	150	240
Investment in associate	80	
Financial assets	215	180
	1,025	1,005
Current assets		
Inventories	155	190
Trade receivables	125	180
Cash and cash equivalents	465	355
	745	725
Total assets	1,770	1,730

Equity and liabilities

Share capital	850	625
Retained earnings	456	359
Other components of equity	29	20
	1,335	1,004
Non-controlling interest	90	65
Total equity	1,425	1,069
Non-current liabilities		
Long-term borrowings	26	57
Deferred tax	35	31
Retirement benefit liability	80	74
Total non-current liabilities	141	162
Current liabilities		
Trade payables	155	361
Current tax payable	49	138
Total current liabilities	204	499
Total liabilities	345	661
Total equity and liabilities	1,770	1,730

Angel Group: Statement of profit or loss and other comprehensive income for the year ended 30 November 2013

	$m
Revenue	1,238
Cost of sales	(986)
Gross profit	252
Other income	30
Administrative expenses	(45)
Other expenses	(50)
Operating profit	187
Finance costs	(11)
Share of profit of equity accounted investees (net of tax)	12
Profit before tax	188
Income tax expense	(46)
Profit for the year	142

Profit attributable to:

Owners of parent	111
Non-controlling interest	31
	142

Other comprehensive income:

Items that will not be reclassified to profit or loss

Revaluation of property, plant and equipment	8
Actuarial losses on defined benefit plan	(4)
Tax relating to items not reclassified	(2)
Total items that will not be reclassified to profit or loss	2

Items that may be reclassified to profit or loss

Financial assets	4
Tax relating to items that may be reclassified	(1)
Total items that may be reclassified subsequently to profit or loss	3
Other comprehensive income (net of tax) for the year	5
Total comprehensive income for year	147

Total comprehensive income attributable to:

	$m
Owners of the parent	116
Non-controlling interest	31
	147

Angel Group: Extracts from statement of changes in equity for the year ended 30 November 2013

	Share capital $m	Retained earnings $m	Other components of equity – financial assets reserve $m	Other components of equity – revaluation reserve $m	Non-controlling interest $m
Balance 1 December 2012	625	359	15	5	65
Share capital issued	225				
Dividends for year		(10)			(6)
Total comprehensive income for the year		107	3	6	31
Balance 30 November 2013	850	456	18	11	90

The following information relates to the financial statements of the Angel Group:

(i) Angel decided to renovate a building which had a zero book value at 1 December 2012. As a result, $3 million was spent during the year on its renovation. On 30 November 2013, Angel received a cash grant of $2 million from the government to cover some of the refurbishment cost and the creation of new jobs which had resulted from the use of the building. The grant related equally to both job creation and renovation. The only elements recorded in the financial statements were a charge to revenue for the refurbishment of the building and the receipt of the cash grant, which has been credited to additions of property, plant and equipment (PPE). The building was revalued at 30 November 2013 at $7 million.

Angel treats grant income on capital-based projects as deferred income.

(ii) On 1 December 2012, Angel acquired all of the share capital of Sweety for $30 million. The book values and fair values of the identifiable assets and liabilities of Sweety at the date of acquisition are set out below, together with their tax base. Goodwill arising on acquisition is not deductible for tax purposes. There were no other acquisitions in the period. The tax rate is 30%. The fair values in the table below have been reflected in the year-end balances of the Angel Group.

	Carrying values $ million	Tax base $ million	Fair values $million (excluding deferred taxation)
Property, plant and equipment	12	10	14
Inventories	5	4	6
Trade receivables	3	3	3
Cash and cash equivalents	2	2	2
Total assets	22	19	25
Trade payables	(4)	(4)	(4)
Retirement benefit obligations	(1)		(1)
Deferred tax liability	(0.6)		
Net assets at acquisition	16.4	15	20

(iii) The retirement benefit is classified as a non-current liability in the statement of financial position and comprises the following:

	$m
Net obligation at 1 December 2012	74
Net interest cost	3
Current service cost	8
Contributions to scheme	(9)
Remeasurements – actuarial losses	4
Net obligation at 30 November 2013	80

The benefits paid in the period by the trustees of the scheme were $6 million. Angel had included the obligation assumed on the purchase of Sweety in current service cost above, although the charge to administrative expenses was correct in the statement of profit and loss and other comprehensive income. There were no tax implications regarding the retirement benefit obligation. The defined benefit cost is included in administrative expenses.

(iv)   The property, plant and equipment (PPE) comprises the following:

	$m
Carrying amount at 1 December 2012	465
Additions at cost including assets acquired on the purchase of subsidiary	80
Gains on property revaluation	8
Disposals	(49)
Depreciation	(29)
Carrying amount at 30 November 2013	475

(v)   Angel has constructed a machine which is a qualifying asset under IAS 23 *Borrowing Costs* and has paid construction costs of $4 million. This amount has been charged to other expenses. Angel Group paid $11 million in interest in the year, which includes $1 million of interest which Angel wishes to capitalise under IAS 23. Ignore any deferred tax consequences of this transaction.

The disposal proceeds were $63 million. The gain on disposal is included in administrative expenses.

(vi)   Angel purchased a 30% interest in an associate for cash on 1 December 2012. The net assets of the associate at the date of acquisition were $280 million. The associate made a profit after tax of $40 million and paid a dividend of $10 million out of these profits in the year ended 30 November 2013. Angel does not hold investments in any other associate entities.

(vii)   An impairment test carried out at 30 November 2013 showed that goodwill and other intangible assets were impaired. The impairment of goodwill relates to 100% owned subsidiaries.

(viii) The following schedule relates to the financial assets owned by Angel:

	$m
Balance 1 December 2012	180
Less sales of financial assets at carrying value	(26)
Add purchases of financial assets	57
Add gain on revaluation of financial assets	4
Balance at 30 November 2013	215

The sale proceeds of the financial assets were $40 million. Profit on the sale of the financial assets is included in 'other income' in the financial statements.

(ix)   The finance costs were all paid in cash in the period.

Required:

(a) Prepare a consolidated statement of cash flows using the indirect method for the Angel Group plc for the year ended 30 November 2013 in accordance with the requirements of IAS 7 *Statement of Cash Flows*.

Note: The notes to the statement of cash flows are not required. **(35 marks)**

(b) The directors of Angel are confused over several issues relating to IAS 7 *Statement of Cash Flows*. They wish to know the principles utilised by the International Accounting Standards Board in determining how cash flows are classified, including how entities determine the nature of the cash flows being analysed.

They have entered into the following transactions after the year end and wish to know how to deal with them in a cash flow statement, as they are unsure of the meaning of the definition of cash and cash equivalents.

Angel had decided after the year end to deposit the funds with the bank in two term deposit accounts as follows:

(i) $3 million into a 12-month term account, earning 3.5% interest. The cash can be withdrawn by giving 14 days' notice but Angel will incur a penalty, being the loss of all interest earned.

(ii) $7 million into a 12-month term account earning 3% interest. The cash can be withdrawn by giving 21 days' notice. Interest will be paid for the period of the deposit but if money is withdrawn, the interest will be at the rate of 2%, which is equivalent to the bank's stated rate for short-term deposits.

Angel is confident that it will not need to withdraw the cash from the higher-rate deposit within the term, but wants to keep easy access to the remaining $7 million to cover any working capital shortfalls which might arise.

Required:

Discuss the principles behind the classifications in the statements of cash flows whilst advising Angel on how to treat the two transactions above. **(9 marks)**

(c) All accounting professionals are responsible for acting in the public interest, and for promoting professional ethics. The directors of Angel feel that when managing the affairs of a company the profit motive could conflict with the public interest and accounting ethics. In their view, the profit motive is more important than ethical behaviour and codes of ethics are irrelevant and unimportant.

Required:

Discuss the above views of the directors regarding the fact that codes of ethics are irrelevant and unimportant. **(6 marks)**

(Total: 50 marks)

5   TRAILER (JUNE 13 EXAM) *Walk in the footsteps of a top tutor*

(a)   Trailer, a public limited company, operates in the manufacturing sector. Trailer has investments in two other companies. The draft statements of financial position at 31 May 2013 are as follows:

	Trailer $m	Park $m	Caller $m
Assets:			
Non-current assets			
Property, plant and equipment	1,440	1,100	1,300
Investments in subsidiaries			
Park	1,250		
Caller	310	1,270	
Financial assets	320	21	141
	3,320	2,391	1,441
Current assets	895	681	150
Total assets	4,215	3,072	1,591
Equity and liabilities:			
Share capital	1,750	1,210	800
Retained earnings	1,240	930	350
Other components of equity	125	80	95
Total equity	3,115	2,220	1,245
Non-current liabilities	985	765	150
Current liabilities	115	87	196
Total liabilities	1,100	852	346
Total equity and liabilities	4,215	3,072	1,591

The following information is relevant to the preparation of the group financial statements:

(1)   On 1 June 2011, Trailer acquired 14% of the equity interests of Caller for a cash consideration of $260 million and Park acquired 70% of the equity interests of Caller for a cash consideration of $1,270 million. At 1 June 2011, the identifiable net assets of Caller had a fair value of $990 million, retained earnings were $190 million and other components of equity were $52 million. At 1 June 2012, the identifiable net assets of Caller had a fair value of $1,150 million, retained earnings were $240 million and other components of equity were $70 million. The excess in fair value is due to non-depreciable land. The fair value of the 14% holding of Trailer in Caller, which was classified as fair value through profit or loss, was $280 million at 31 May 2012 and $310 million at 31 May 2013. The fair value of Park's interest in Caller had not changed since acquisition.

(2) On 1 June 2012, Trailer acquired 60% of the equity interests of Park, a public limited company. The purchase consideration comprised cash of $1,250 million. On 1 June 2012, the fair value of the identifiable net assets acquired was $1,950 million and retained earnings of Park were $650 million and other components of equity were $55 million. The excess in fair value is due to non-depreciable land. It is the group's policy to measure the non-controlling interest at acquisition at its proportionate share of the fair value of the subsidiary's net assets.

(3) Goodwill of Park and Caller was impairment tested at 31 May 2013. There was no impairment relating to Caller. The recoverable amount of the net assets of Park was $2,088 million. There was no impairment of the net assets of Park before this date and any impairment loss has been determined to relate to goodwill and property, plant and equipment.

(4) Trailer has made a loan of $50 million to a charitable organisation for the building of new sporting facilities. The loan was made on 1 June 2012 and is repayable on maturity in three years' time. Interest is to be charged one year in arrears at 3%, but Trailer assesses that an unsubsidised rate for such a loan would have been 6%. Trailer recorded a financial asset at $50 million and reduced this by the interest received in the year. The loss allowance has been correctly dealt with.

(5) On 1 June 2011, Trailer acquired office accommodation at a cost of $90 million with a 30-year estimated useful life. During the year, the property market in the area slumped and the fair value of the accommodation fell to $75 million at 31 May 2012 and this was reflected in the financial statements. However, the market recovered unexpectedly quickly due to the announcement of major government investment in the area's transport infrastructure. On 31 May 2013, the valuer advised Trailer that the offices should now be valued at $105 million. Trailer has charged depreciation for the year but has not taken account of the upward valuation of the offices. Trailer uses the revaluation model and records any valuation change when advised to do so.

(6) Trailer has announced two major restructuring plans. The first plan is to reduce its capacity by the closure of some of its smaller factories, which have already been identified. This will lead to the redundancy of 500 employees, who have all individually been selected and communicated with. The costs of this plan are $9 million in redundancy costs, $4 million in retraining costs and $5 million in lease termination costs. The second plan is to re-organise the finance and information technology department over a one-year period but it does not commence for two years. The plan results in 20% of finance staff losing their jobs during the restructuring. The costs of this plan are $10 million in redundancy costs, $6 million in retraining costs and $7 million in equipment lease termination costs. No entries have been made in the financial statements for the above plans.

(7)   The following information relates to the group pension plan of Trailer:

	1 June 2012	31 May 2013
	$m	$m
Fair value of plan assets	28	29
Actuarial value of defined benefit obligation	30	35

The contributions for the period received by the fund were $2 million and the employee benefits paid in the year amounted to $3 million. The discount rate to be used in any calculation is 5%. The current service cost for the period based on actuarial calculations is $1 million. The above figures have not been taken into account for the year ended 31 May 2013 except for the contributions paid which have been entered in cash and the defined benefit obligation.

Required:

Prepare the group consolidated statement of financial position of Trailer as at 31 May 2013.   **(35 marks)**

(b)   It is the Trailer group's policy to measure the non-controlling interest (NCI) at acquisition at its proportionate share of the fair value of the subsidiary's net assets. The directors of Trailer have used this policy for several years and do not know the implications, if any, of changing the policy to that of accounting for the NCI at fair value. The fair value of the NCI of Park at 1 June 2012 was $800 million. The fair value of the NCI of Caller, based upon the effective shareholdings, was $500 million at 1 June 2011 and $530 million at 1 June 2012.

Required:

Explain to the directors, with suitable calculations, the impact on the financial statements if goodwill was calculated using the fair value of the NCI.   **(9 marks)**

(c)   The directors of Trailer are involved in takeover talks with another entity. In the discussions, one of the directors stated that there was no point in an accountant studying ethics because every accountant already has a set of moral beliefs that are followed and these are created by simply following generally accepted accounting practice. He further stated that in adopting a defensive approach to the takeover, there was no ethical issue in falsely declaring Trailer's profits in the financial statements used for the discussions because, in his opinion, the takeover did not benefit the company, its executives or society as a whole.

Required:

Discuss the above views of the director regarding the fact that there is no point in an accountant studying ethics and that there was no ethical issue in the false disclosure of accounting profits.   **(6 marks)**

(Total: 50 marks)

6   MINNY (DEC 12 EXAM)   *Walk in the footsteps of a top tutor*

   Timed question with Online tutor debrief

Minny is a company which operates in the service sector. Minny has business relationships with Bower and Heeny. All three entities are public limited companies. The draft statements of financial position of these entities are as follows at 30 November 2012:

	Minny $m	Bower $m	Heeny $m
Assets:			
Non-current assets			
Property, plant and equipment	920	300	310
Investments in subsidiaries			
Bower	730		
Heeny		320	
Investment in Puttin	48		
Intangible assets	198	30	35
	1,896	650	345
Current assets	895	480	250
Total assets	2,791	1,130	595
Equity and liabilities:			
Share capital	920	400	200
Other components of equity	73	37	25
Retained earnings	895	442	139
Total equity	1,888	879	364
Non-current liabilities	495	123	93
Current liabilities	408	128	138
Total liabilities	903	251	231
Total equity and liabilities	2,791	1,130	595

The following information is relevant to the preparation of the group financial statements:

(1)   On 1 December 2010, Minny acquired 70% of the equity interests of Bower. The purchase consideration comprised cash of $730 million. At acquisition, the fair value of the non-controlling interest in Bower was $295 million. On 1 December 2010, the fair value of the identifiable net assets acquired was $835 million and retained earnings of Bower were $319 million and other components of equity were $27 million. The excess in fair value is due to non-depreciable land.

(2) On 1 December 2011, Bower acquired 80% of the equity interests of Heeny for a cash consideration of $320 million. The fair value of a 20% holding of the non-controlling interest was $72 million, a 30% holding was $108 million and a 44% holding was $161 million. At the date of acquisition, the identifiable net assets of Heeny had a fair value of $362 million, retained earnings were $106 million and other components of equity were $20 million. The excess in fair value is due to non-depreciable land.

It is the group's policy to measure the non-controlling interest at fair value at the date of acquisition.

(3) Both Bower and Heeny were impairment tested at 30 November 2012. The recoverable amounts of both cash generating units as stated in the individual financial statements at 30 November 2012 were Bower, $1,425 million, and Heeny, $604 million, respectively. The directors of Minny felt that any impairment of assets was due to the poor performance of the intangible assets and it was deemed that other assets were already held at recoverable amount. The recoverable amounts have been determined without consideration of liabilities which all relate to the financing of operations.

(4) Minny acquired a 14% interest in Puttin, a public limited company, on 1 December 2010 for a cash consideration of $18 million. The investment was accounted for under IFRS *9 Financial Instruments* and was designated as at fair value through other comprehensive income. On 1 June 2012, Minny acquired an additional 16% interest in Puttin for a cash consideration of $27 million and achieved significant influence. The value of the original 14% investment on 1 June 2012 was $21 million. Puttin made profits after tax of $20 million and $30 million for the years to 30 November 2011 and 30 November 2012 respectively. On 30 November 2012, Minny received a dividend from Puttin of $2 million, which has been credited to other components of equity.

(5) Minny purchased patents of $10 million to use in a project to develop new products on 1 December 2011. Minny has completed the investigative phase of the project, incurring an additional cost of $7 million and has determined that the product can be developed profitably. An effective and working prototype was created at a cost of $4 million and in order to put the product into a condition for sale, a further $3 million was spent. Finally, marketing costs of $2 million were incurred. All of the above costs are included in the intangible assets of Minny.

(6) Minny intends to dispose of a major line of the parent's business operations. At the date the held for sale criteria were met, the carrying amount of the assets and liabilities comprising the line of business were:

	$m
Property, plant and equipment (PPE)	49
Inventory	18
Current liabilities	3

It is anticipated that Minny will realise $30 million for the business. No adjustments have been made in the financial statements in relation to the above decision.

Required:

(a) Prepare the consolidated statement of financial position for the Minny Group as at 30 November 2012. **(35 marks)**

(b) Minny intends to dispose of a major line of business in the above scenario and the entity has stated that the held for sale criteria were met under IFRS *5 Non-current Assets Held for Sale and Discontinued Operations.* The criteria in IFRS 5 are very strict and regulators have been known to question entities on the application of the standard. The two criteria which must be met before an asset or disposal group will be defined as recovered principally through sale are: that it must be available for immediate sale in its present condition and the sale must be highly probable.

Required:

Discuss what is meant in IFRS 5 by 'available for immediate sale in its present condition' and 'the sale must be highly probable', setting out briefly why regulators may question entities on the application of the standard. (7 marks)

(c) Bower has a property which has a carrying value of $2 million at 30 November 2012. This property had been revalued at the year end and a revaluation surplus of $400,000 had been recorded in other components of equity. The directors were intending to sell the property to Minny for $1 million shortly after the year end. Bower previously used the historical cost basis for valuing property.

Required:

Without adjusting your answer to part (a), discuss the ethical and accounting implications of the above intended sale of assets to Minny by Bower. (8 marks)

(Total: 50 marks)

 Calculate your allowed time, allocate the time to the separate parts

---

7   ROBBY (JUNE 12 EXAM) *Walk in the footsteps of a top tutor*

The following draft statements of financial position relate to Robby, Hail and Zinc, all public limited companies, as at 31 May 2012:

	Robby	Hail	Zinc
	$m	$m	$m
Assets			
Non-current assets:			
Property, plant and equipment	112	60	26
Investment in Hail	55		
Investment in Zinc	19		
Financial assets	9	6	14
Jointly controlled operation	6		
Current assets	5	7	12
	___	___	___
Total assets	206	73	52
	___	___	___

Equity and Liabilities:			
Ordinary shares	25	20	10
Other components of equity	11	–	–
Retained earnings	70	27	19
	–––	–––	–––
Total equity	106	47	29
Non-current liabilities	53	20	21
Current liabilities	47	6	2
	–––	–––	–––
Total equity and liabilities	206	73	52
	–––	–––	–––

The following information needs to be taken into account in the preparation of the group financial statements of Robby:

(i)   On 1 June 2010, Robby acquired 80% of the equity interests of Hail. The purchase consideration comprised cash of $50 million. Robby has treated the investment in Hail at fair value through other comprehensive income (OCI).

A dividend received from Hail on 1 January 2012 of $2 million has similarly been credited to OCI.

It is Robby's policy to measure the non-controlling interest at fair value and this was $15 million on 1 June 2010.

On 1 June 2010, the fair value of the identifiable net assets of Hail were $60 million and the retained earnings of Hail were $16 million. The excess of the fair value of the net assets is due to an increase in the value of non-depreciable land.

(ii)   On 1 June 2009, Robby acquired 5% of the ordinary shares of Zinc. Robby had treated this investment at fair value through profit or loss in the financial statements to 31 May 2011.

On 1 December 2011, Robby acquired a further 55% of the ordinary shares of Zinc and gained control of the company.

The consideration for the acquisitions was as follows:

	Shareholding	Consideration
		$m
1 June 2009	5%	2
1 December 2011	55%	16
	–––	–––
	60%	18
	–––	–––

At 1 December 2011, the fair value of the equity interest in Zinc held by Robby before the business combination was $5 million.

It is Robby's policy to measure the non-controlling interest at fair value and this was $9 million on 1 December 2011.

The fair value of the identifiable net assets at 1 December 2011 of Zinc was $26 million, and the retained earnings were $15 million. The excess of the fair value of the net assets is due to an increase in the value of property, plant and equipment (PPE), which was provisional pending receipt of the final valuations. These valuations were received on 1 March 2012 and resulted in an additional increase of $3 million in the fair value of PPE at the date of acquisition. This increase does not affect the fair value of the non-controlling interest at acquisition. PPE is to be depreciated on the straight-line basis over a remaining period of five years.

(iii)   Robby has a 40% share of a joint operation, a natural gas station. Assets, liabilities, revenue and costs are apportioned on the basis of shareholding.

The following information relates to the joint arrangement activities:

The natural gas station cost $15 million to construct and was completed on 1 June 2011 and is to be dismantled at the end of its life of 10 years. The present value of this dismantling cost to the joint arrangement at 1 June 2011, using a discount rate of 5%, was $2 million.

In the year, gas with a direct cost of $16 million was sold for $20 million. Additionally, the joint arrangement incurred operating costs of $0.5 million during the year.

Robby has only contributed and accounted for its share of the construction cost, paying $6 million. The revenue and costs are receivable and payable by the other joint operator who settles amounts outstanding with Robby after the year end.

(iv)   Robby purchased PPE for $10 million on 1 June 2009. It has an expected useful life of 20 years and is depreciated on the straight-line method. On 31 May 2011, the PPE was revalued to $11 million. At 31 May 2012, impairment indicators triggered an impairment review of the PPE. The recoverable amount of the PPE was $7.8 million. The only accounting entry posted for the year to 31 May 2012 was to account for the depreciation based on the revalued amount as at 31 May 2011. Robby's accounting policy is to make a transfer of the excess depreciation arising on the revaluation of PPE.

(v)   Robby held a portfolio of trade receivables with a carrying amount of $4 million at 31 May 2012. At that date, the entity entered into a factoring agreement with a bank, whereby it transfers the receivables in exchange for $3.6 million in cash. Robby has agreed to reimburse the factor for any shortfall between the amount collected and $3.6 million. Once the receivables have been collected, any amounts above $3.6 million, less interest on this amount, will be repaid to Robby. Robby has derecognised the receivables and charged $0.4 million as a loss to profit or loss.

(vi)   Immediately prior to the year end, Robby sold land to a third party at a price of $16 million with an option to purchase the land back on 1 July 2012 for $16 million plus a premium of 3%. The market value of the land is $25 million on 31 May 2012 and the carrying amount was $12 million. Robby accounted for the sale, consequently eliminating the bank overdraft at 31 May 2012.

Required:

(a) Prepare a consolidated statement of financial position of the Robby Group at 31 May 2012 in accordance with International Financial Reporting Standards.

(35 marks)

(b) (i) In the above scenario (information point (v)), Robby holds a portfolio of trade receivables and enters into a factoring agreement with a bank, whereby it transfers the receivables in exchange for cash. Robby additionally agreed to other terms with the bank as regards any collection shortfall and repayment of any monies to Robby. Robby derecognised the receivables. This is an example of the type of complex transaction that can arise out of normal terms of trade. The rules regarding derecognition are quite complex and are often not understood by entities.

Describe the rules of IFRS 9 *Financial Instruments* relating to the derecognition of a financial asset and how these rules affect the treatment of the portfolio of trade receivables in Robby's financial statements. **(9 marks)**

(ii) Discuss the legitimacy of Robby selling land just prior to the year end in order to show a better liquidity position for the group and whether this transaction is consistent with an accountant's responsibilities to users of financial statements.

Note: Your answer should include reference to the above scenario. **(6 marks)**

(Total: 50 marks)

8 TRAVELER (DEC 11 EXAM) *Walk in the footsteps of a top tutor*

Traveler, a public limited company, operates in the manufacturing sector. The draft statements of financial position are as follows at 30 November 2011:

	Traveler $m	Data $m	Captive $m
Assets:			
Non-current assets			
Property, plant and equipment	439	810	620
Investments in subsidiaries			
Data	820		
Captive	541		
Financial assets	108	10	20
	1,908	820	640
Defined benefit asset	72		
Current assets	995	781	350
Total assets	2,975	1,601	990

Equity and liabilities:			
Share capital	1,120	600	390
Retained earnings	1,066	442	169
Other components of equity	60	37	45
Total equity	2,246	1,079	604
Non-current liabilities	455	323	73
Current liabilities	274	199	313
Total liabilities	729	522	386
Total equity and liabilities	2,975	1,601	990

The following information is relevant to the preparation of the group financial statements:

1   On 1 December 2010, Traveler acquired 60% of the equity interests of Data, a public limited company. The purchase consideration comprised cash of $600 million. At acquisition, the fair value of the non-controlling interest in Data was $395 million. Traveler wishes to use the 'full goodwill' method. On 1 December 2010, the fair value of the identifiable net assets acquired was $935 million and retained earnings of Data were $299 million and other components of equity were $26 million. The excess in fair value is due to non-depreciable land.

     On 30 November 2011, Traveler acquired a further 20% interest in Data for a cash consideration of $220 million.

2   On 1 December 2010, Traveler acquired 80% of the equity interests of Captive for a consideration of $541 million. The consideration comprised cash of $477 million and the transfer of non-depreciable land with a fair value of $64 million. The carrying amount of the land at the acquisition date was $56 million. At the year end, this asset was still included in the non-current assets of Traveler and the sale proceeds had been credited to profit or loss.

     At the date of acquisition, the identifiable net assets of Captive had a fair value of $526 million, retained earnings were $90 million and other components of equity were $24 million. The excess in fair value is due to non-depreciable land. This acquisition was accounted for using the partial goodwill method in accordance with IFRS 3 (Revised) *Business Combinations*.

3   Goodwill was impairment tested after the additional acquisition in Data on 30 November 2011. The recoverable amount of Data was $1,099 million and that of Captive was $700 million.

4   Included in the financial assets of Traveler is a ten-year 7% loan held at amortised cost. At 30 November 2011, the borrower was in financial difficulties and its credit rating had been downgraded. At this date, the gross carrying amount of the loan asset was $30 million and the loss allowance was $1 million. Traveler has agreed for the loan to be restructured; there will only be three more annual payments of $8 million starting in one year's time. Current market interest rates are 8%, the original effective interest rate is 6.7% and the effective interest rate under the revised payment schedule is 6.3%.

5   Traveler acquired a new factory on 1 December 2010. The cost of the factory was $50 million and it has a residual value of $2 million. The factory has a flat roof, which needs replacing every five years. The cost of the roof was $5 million. The useful economic life of the factory is 25 years. No depreciation has been charged for the year. Traveler wishes to account for the factory and roof as a single asset and depreciate the whole factory over its economic life. Traveler uses straight-line depreciation.

6   The actuarial value of Traveler's pension plan showed a surplus at 1 December 2010 of $72 million, represented by plan assets with a fair value of $322 million and a defined benefit obligation with a present value of $250 million. The aggregate of the current and past service costs and the net interest component amount to $55 million for the year ended 30 November 2011. After consulting with the actuaries, the company contributed $45m into the plan on the last day of the year. No entries have been made in the financial statements for the above amounts. At the year-end, the fair values of the plan assets are $340 million and the present value of the obligation amounts to $288 million. At both the start and end of the year, the pension surplus falls below the asset ceiling.

Required:

(a)   **Prepare a consolidated statement of financial position for the Traveler Group for the year ended 30 November 2011.**   **(35 marks)**

(b)   Traveler has three distinct business segments. The management has calculated the net assets, turnover and profit before common costs, which are to be allocated to these segments. However, they are unsure as to how they should allocate certain common costs and whether they can exercise judgement in the allocation process. They wish to allocate head office management expenses; pension expense; the cost of managing properties and interest and related interest bearing assets. They also are uncertain as to whether the allocation of costs has to be in conformity with the accounting policies used in the financial statements.

Required:

Advise the management of Traveler on the points raised in the above paragraph.
                                                                                      (8 marks)

(c)   Segmental information reported externally is more useful if it conforms to information used by management in making decisions. The information can differ from that reported in the financial statements. Although reconciliations are required, these can be complex and difficult to understand. Additionally, there are other standards where subjectivity is involved and often the profit motive determines which accounting practice to follow. The directors have a responsibility to shareholders in disclosing information to enhance corporate value but this may conflict with their corporate social responsibility.

Required:

Discuss how the ethics of corporate social responsibility disclosure are difficult to reconcile with shareholder expectations.   **(7 marks)**

                                                                                    (Total: 50 marks)

9   ROSE (JUNE 11 EXAM)   *Walk in the footsteps of a top tutor*

Rose, a public limited company, operates in the mining sector. The draft statements of financial position are as follows, at 30 April 2011:

	Rose $m	Petal $m	Stem Dinars m
Assets:			
Non-current assets			
Property, plant and equipment	370	110	380
Investments in subsidiaries			
Petal	113		
Stem	46		
Financial assets	15	7	50
	544	117	430
Current assets	118	100	330
Total assets	662	217	760
Equity and liabilities:			
Share capital	158	38	200
Retained earnings	256	56	300
Other components of equity	7	4	–
Total equity	421	98	500
Non-current liabilities	56	42	160
Current liabilities	185	77	100
Total liabilities	241	119	260
Total equity and liabilities	662	217	760

The following information is relevant to the preparation of the group financial statements:

1   On 1 May 2010, Rose acquired 70% of the equity interests of Petal, a public limited company. The purchase consideration comprised cash of $94 million. The fair value of the identifiable net assets recognised by Petal was $120 million excluding the patent below. The identifiable net assets of Petal at 1 May 2010 included a patent which had a fair value of $4 million. This had not been recognised in the financial statements of Petal. The patent had a remaining term of four years to run at that date and is not renewable. The retained earnings of Petal were $49 million and other components of equity were $3 million at the date of acquisition. The remaining excess of the fair value of the net assets is due to an increase in the value of land.

Rose wishes to use the 'full goodwill' method. The fair value of the non-controlling interest in Petal was $46 million on 1 May 2010. There have been no issues of ordinary shares since acquisition and goodwill on acquisition is not impaired.

Rose acquired a further 10% interest from the non-controlling interest in Petal on 30 April 2011 for a cash consideration of $19 million.

2   Rose acquired 52% of the ordinary shares of Stem on 1 May 2010 when Stem's retained earnings were 220 million dinars. The fair value of the identifiable net assets of Stem on 1 May 2010 was 495 million dinars. The excess of the fair value over the net assets of Stem is due to an increase in the value of land. The fair value of the non-controlling interest in Stem at 1 May 2010 was 250 million dinars.

Stem is located in a foreign country and operates a mine. The income of Stem is denominated and settled in dinars. The output of the mine is routinely traded in dinars and its price is determined initially by local supply and demand. Stem pays 40% of its costs and expenses in dollars with the remainder being incurred locally and settled in dinars. Stem's management has a considerable degree of authority and autonomy in carrying out the operations of Stem and is not dependent upon group companies for finance.

Rose wishes to use the 'full goodwill' method to consolidate the financial statements of Stem. There have been no issues of ordinary shares and no impairment of goodwill since acquisition.

The following exchange rates are relevant to the preparation of the group financial statements:

	Dinars to $
1 May 2010	6
30 April 2011	5
Average for year to 30 April 2011	5.8

3   Rose has a property located in the same country as Stem. The property was acquired on 1 May 2010 and is carried at a cost of 30 million dinars. The property is depreciated over 20 years on the straight-line method. At 30 April 2011, the property was revalued to 35 million dinars. Depreciation has been charged for the year but the revaluation has not been taken into account in the preparation of the financial statements as at 30 April 2011.

4   Rose commenced a long-term bonus scheme for employees at 1 May 2010. Under the scheme employees receive a cumulative bonus on the completion of five years service. The bonus is 2% of the total of the annual salary of the employees. The total salary of employees for the year to 30 April 2011 was $40 million and a discount rate of 8% is assumed. Additionally at 30 April 2011, it is assumed that all employees will receive the bonus and that salaries will rise by 5% per year.

5   Rose purchased plant for $20 million on 1 May 2007 with an estimated useful life of six years. Its estimated residual value at that date was $1.4 million. At 1 May 2010, the estimated residual value changed to $2.6 million. The change in the residual value has not been taken into account when preparing the financial statements as at 30 April 2011.

Required:

(a) (i) Discuss and apply the principles set out in IAS 21 *The Effects of Changes in Foreign Exchange Rates* in order to determine the functional currency of Stem. **(8 marks)**

(ii) Prepare a consolidated statement of financial position of the Rose Group at 30 April 2011, in accordance with International Financial Reporting Standards (IFRS), showing the exchange difference arising on the translation of Stem's net assets. Ignore deferred taxation. **(35 marks)**

(b) Rose was considering acquiring a service company. Rose stated that the acquisition may be made because of the value of the human capital and the opportunity for synergies and cross-selling opportunities. Rose estimated the fair value of the assets based on what it was prepared to pay for them. Rose further stated that what it was willing to pay was influenced by its future plans for the business.

The company to be acquired had contract-based customer relationships with well-known domestic and international companies and some mining companies. Rose estimated that the fair value of all of these customer relationships to be zero because Rose already enjoyed relationships with the majority of those customers.

Required:

Discuss the validity of the accounting treatment proposed by Rose and whether such a proposed treatment raises any ethical issues. **(7 marks)**

(Total: 50 marks)

10 JOCATT GROUP (DEC 10 EXAM) *Walk in the footsteps of a top tutor*

The following draft group financial statements relate to Jocatt, a public limited company:

Jocatt Group: Statement of financial position as at 30 November

	2010	2009
	$m	$m
Non-current assets		
Property, plant and equipment	327	254
Investment property	8	6
Goodwill	48	68
Intangible assets	85	72
Investment in associate	54	
Financial assets at FV through OCI	94	90
	616	490
Current assets		
Inventories	105	128
Trade receivables	62	113
Cash and cash equivalents	232	143
Total assets	1,015	874

Equity and Liabilities	$m	$m
Equity attributable to the owners of the parent:		
Share capital	290	275
Retained earnings	351	324
Other components of equity	15	20
	656	619
Non-controlling interest	55	36
Total equity	711	655
Non-current liabilities:		
Long-term borrowings	67	71
Deferred tax	35	41
Long-term provisions-pension liability	25	22
Current liabilities:		
Trade payables	144	55
Current tax payable	33	30
Total equity and liabilities	1,015	874

Jocatt Group: Statement of profit or loss and other comprehensive income for the year ended 30 November 2010

	$m
Revenue	434
Cost of sales	(321)
Gross profit	113
Other income	15
Distribution costs	(55.5)
Administrative expenses	(36)
Finance costs paid	(8)
Gains on property	10.5
Share of profit of associate	6
Profit before tax	45
Income tax expense	(11)
Profit for the year	34

Other comprehensive income after tax – items that will not be reclassified to profit or loss in future accounting periods:	$m
Gain on financial assets at FV through OCI	2
Losses on property revaluation	(7)
Net remeasurement component gain on defined benefit plan	8
Other comprehensive income for the year, net of tax	3
Total comprehensive income for the year	37

Profit attributable to:

Owners of the parent	24
Non-controlling interest	10
	34

Total comprehensive income attributable to:

Owners of the parent	27
Non-controlling interest	10
	37

Jocatt Group: Statement of changes in equity for the year ended 30 November 2010

	Share capital	Retained earnings	Fin assets at FVTOCI	Revaluation surplus (PPE)	Total	Non-controlling interest	Total equity
	$m	$m	$m	$m	$m	$m	$m
Balance at 1 Dec 2009	275	324	4	16	619	36	655
Share capital issued	15				15		15
Dividends		(5)			(5)	(13)	(18)
Rights issue						2	2
Acquisitions						20	20
Total comp inc for year		32	2	(7)	27	10	37
Balance at 30 Nov 2010	290	351	6	9	656	55	711

The following information relates to the financial statements of Jocatt:

(i)   On 1 December 2008, Jocatt acquired 8% of the ordinary shares of Tigret. On recognition, Jocatt had properly designated this investment as fair value through other comprehensive income in the financial statements to 30 November 2009. On 1 December 2009, Jocatt acquired a further 52% of the ordinary shares of Tigret and gained control of the company. The consideration for the acquisitions was as follows:

	Holding	Consideration
		$m
1 December 2008	8%	4
1 December 2009	52%	30
	60%	34

At 1 December 2009, the fair value of the 8% holding in Tigret held by Jocatt at the time of the business combination was $5 million and the fair value of the non-controlling interest in Tigret was $20 million. No gain or loss on the 8% holding in Tigret had been reported in the financial statements prior to 1 December 2009. The purchase consideration at 1 December 2009 comprised cash of $15 million and shares of $15 million.

The fair value of the identifiable net assets of Tigret, excluding deferred tax assets and liabilities, at the date of acquisition comprised the following:

	$m
Property, plant and equipment	15
Intangible assets	18
Trade receivables	5
Cash	7

The tax base of the identifiable net assets of Tigret was $40 million at 1 December 2009. The tax rate of Tigret is 30%.

(ii) On 30 November 2010, Tigret made a rights issue on a 1 for 4 basis. The issue was fully subscribed and raised $5 million in cash.

(iii) Jocatt purchased a research project from a third party including certain patents on 1 December 2009 for $8 million and recognised it as an intangible asset. During the year, Jocatt incurred further costs, which included $2 million on completing the research phase, $4 million in developing the product for sale and $1 million for the initial marketing costs. There were no other additions to intangible assets in the period other than those on the acquisition of Tigret.

(iv) Jocatt operates a defined benefit scheme. The current service costs for the year ended 30 November 2010 are $10 million. Jocatt enhanced the benefits on 1 December 2009, however these do not vest until 30 November 2012. The total cost of the enhancement is $6 million. The net interest cost of $2 million is included within finance costs.

(v) Jocatt owns an investment property. During the year, part of the heating system of the property, which had a carrying value of $0.5 million, was replaced by a new system, which cost $1 million. Jocatt uses the fair value model for measuring investment property.

(vi) Jocatt had exchanged surplus land with a carrying value of $10 million for cash of $15 million and plant valued at $4 million. The transaction has commercial substance. Depreciation for the period for property, plant and equipment was $27 million.

(vii) Goodwill relating to all subsidiaries had been impairment tested in the year to 30 November 2010 and any impairment accounted for. The goodwill impairment related to those subsidiaries which were 100% owned.

(viii) Deferred tax of $1 million arose on the gains on the financial assets designated as fair value through other comprehensive income in the year.

(ix) The associate did not pay any dividends in the year.

Required:

(a) **Prepare a consolidated statement of cash flows for the Jocatt Group using the indirect method under IAS 7 *Statement of Cash Flows*.**

Note: Ignore deferred taxation other than where it is mentioned in the question.

(35 marks)

(b) Jocatt operates in the energy industry and undertakes complex natural gas trading arrangements, which involve exchanges in resources with other companies in the industry. Jocatt is entering into a long-term contract for the supply of gas and is raising a loan on the strength of this contract. The proceeds of the loan are to be received over the year to 30 November 2011 and are to be repaid over four years to 30 November 2015. Jocatt wishes to report the proceeds as operating cash flow because it is related to a long-term purchase contract. The directors of Jocatt receive extra income if the operating cash flow exceeds a predetermined target for the year and feel that the indirect method is more useful and informative to users of financial statements than the direct method.

(i) Comment on the directors' view that the indirect method of preparing statements of cash flow is more useful and informative to users than the direct method. **(8 marks)**

(ii) Discuss the reasons why the directors may wish to report the loan proceeds as an operating cash flow rather than a financing cash flow and whether there are any ethical implications of adopting this treatment. **(7 marks)**

(Total: 50 marks)

11 ASHANTI (JUNE 10 EXAM) *Walk in the footsteps of a top tutor*

The following financial statements relate to Ashanti, a public limited company.

Statements of profit or loss and other comprehensive income for the year ended 30 April 2010.

	Ashanti	Bochem	Ceram
	$m	$m	$m
Revenue	810	235	142
Cost of sales	(686)	(137)	(84)
	——	——	——
Gross profit	124	98	58
Other income	31	17	12
Distribution costs	(30)	(21)	(26)
Administrative expenses	(55)	(29)	(12)
Finance costs	(8)	(6)	(8)
	——	——	——
Profit before tax	62	59	24
Income tax expense	(21)	(23)	(10)
	——	——	——
Profit for the year	41	36	14

Other comprehensive income for the year, net of tax which will not be reclassified to profit or loss in future periods:

Gains (net) on PPE revaluation	12	6	–
Remeasurement losses on defined benefit plan	(14)	–	–
Other comprehensive income for the year, net of tax	(2)	6	–
Total comprehensive income for year	39	42	14

The following information is relevant to the preparation of the group statement of profit or loss and other comprehensive income:

1   On 1 May 2008, Ashanti acquired 70% of the equity interests of Bochem, a public limited company. The purchase consideration comprised cash of $150 million and the fair value of the identifiable net assets was $160 million at that date. The fair value of the non-controlling interest in Bochem was $54 million on 1 May 2008. Ashanti wishes to use the 'full goodwill' method for all acquisitions. The share capital and retained earnings of Bochem were $55 million and $85 million respectively and other components of equity were $10 million at the date of acquisition. The excess of the fair value of the identifiable net assets at acquisition is due to an increase in the value of plant, which is depreciated on the straight-line method and has a five year remaining life at the date of acquisition.

Ashanti disposed of a 10% equity interest to the non-controlling interests (NCI) of Bochem on 30 April 2010 for a cash consideration of $34 million. The carrying value of the net assets of Bochem at 30 April 2010 was $210 million before any adjustments on consolidation. Goodwill has been impairment tested annually and as at 30 April 2009 had reduced in value by 15% and at 30 April 2010 had lost a further 5% of its original value before the sale of the equity interest to the NCI. The goodwill impairment should be allocated between group and NCI on the basis of equity shareholding.

2   Bochem acquired 80% of the equity interests of Ceram, a public limited company, on 1 May 2008. The purchase consideration was cash of $136 million. Ceram's identifiable net assets were fair valued at $115 million and the NCI of Ceram attributable to Ashanti had a fair value of $26 million at that date. On 1 November 2009, Bochem disposed of 50% of the equity of Ceram for a consideration of $90 million. Ceram's identifiable net assets were $160 million and the fair value of the NCI of Ceram attributable to Bochem was $35 million at the date of disposal. The remaining equity interest of Ceram held by Bochem was fair valued at $45 million. After the disposal, Bochem can still exert significant influence. Goodwill had been impairment tested and no impairment had occurred. Ceram's profits are deemed to accrue evenly over the year.

3   Ashanti has sold inventory to both Bochem and Ceram in October 2009. The sale price of the inventory was $10 million and $5 million respectively. Ashanti sells goods at a gross profit margin of 20% to group companies and third parties. At the year-end, half of the inventory sold to Bochem remained unsold but the entire inventory sold to Ceram had been sold to third parties.

4   On 1 May 2007, Ashanti purchased a $20 million bond with annual interest of 8%, which is also the effective rate, payable on 30 April. The bond is classified as fair value through profit or loss. At 30 April 2010, the carrying value of the bond is $20 million and interest has just been received as normal, but there are reports that the issuer of the bond is in financial difficulty. The market rate of interest is now 10% and Ashanti estimates that the only amounts that will be received in settlement of the bond will be as follows: $1.6 million on 30 April 2011, $1.4 million on 30 April 2012 and $16.5 million on 30 April 2013. The only accounting entries made in the financial statements for the above bond since 30 April 2009 were to correctly account for the interest received.

5   Ashanti sold $5 million of goods to a customer who recently made an announcement that it is restructuring its debts with its suppliers including Ashanti. It is probable that Ashanti will not recover the amounts outstanding. The goods were sold after the announcement was made although the order was placed prior to the announcement. Ashanti wishes to increase the loss allowance against trade receivables by $8 million, of which $5 million relates to this sale.

6   Ashanti owned a piece of property, plant and equipment (PPE) which cost $12 million and was purchased on 1 May 2008. It is being depreciated over 10 years on the straight-line basis with zero residual value. On 30 April 2009, it was revalued to $13 million and on 30 April 2010, the PPE was revalued to $8 million. The whole of the revaluation loss has been posted to other comprehensive income. Depreciation has been charged for the year. It is Ashanti's company policy to make all necessary transfers for excess depreciation following revaluation.

7   The salaried employees of Ashanti are entitled to 25 days paid leave each year. The entitlement accrues evenly over the year and unused leave may be carried forward for one year. The holiday year is the same as the financial year. At 30 April 2010, Ashanti has 900 salaried employees and the average unused holiday entitlement is three days per employee. 5% of employees leave without taking their entitlement and there is no cash payment when an employee leaves in respect of holiday entitlement. There are 255 working days in the year and the total annual salary cost is $19 million. No adjustment has been made in the financial statements for the above and there was no opening accrual required for holiday entitlement.

8   Ignore any taxation effects of the above adjustments and the disclosure requirements of IFRS 5 *Non-current assets held for sale and discontinued operations*.

Required:

(a)   Prepare a consolidated statement of profit or loss and other comprehensive income for the year ended 30 April 2010 for the Ashanti Group.   **(35 marks)**

The directors of Ashanti believe that the rules governing the reclassification of financial assets, in IFRS 9, will give them the capability to reclassify loss-making financial assets and therefore will help them to smooth their income. They feel that there is no problem with managing earnings as long as the shareholders do not find out and as long as the accounting practices are within the guidelines set out in International Financial Reporting Standards (IFRS).

Required:

(b)   Describe the rules regarding reclassification of financial assets and discuss whether these rules could lead to 'management of earnings'.   **(8 marks)**

(c)   Discuss the nature of and incentives for 'management of earnings' and whether such a process can be deemed to be ethically acceptable.   **(7 marks)**

(Total: 50 marks)

12 GRANGE (DEC 09 EXAM) *Walk in the footsteps of a top tutor*

Grange, a public limited company, operates in the manufacturing sector. The draft statements of financial position of the group companies are as follows at 30 November 2009:

	Grange	Park	Fence
	$m	$m	$m
Assets			
Non-current assets			
Property plant and equipment	257	311	238
Investments in subsidiaries:			
Park	340		
Fence	134		
Investment in Sitin	16		
	———	———	———
	747	311	238
Current assets	475	304	141
	———	———	———
Total assets	1,222	615	379
	———	———	———
Equity and liabilities			
Equity share capital	430	230	150
Retained earnings	410	170	65
Other components of equity	22	14	17
	———	———	———
Total equity	862	414	232
Non-current liabilities	172	124	38
Current liabilities:			
Trade and other payables	178	71	105
Provisions for liabilities	10	6	4
	———	———	———
Total equity and liabilities	1,222	615	379
	———	———	———

The following information is relevant to the preparation of the group financial statements:

(i) On 1 June 2008, Grange acquired 60% of the equity interests of Park, a public limited company. The purchase consideration comprised cash of $250 million. Excluding the franchise referred to below, the fair value of the identifiable net assets was $360 million. The excess of the fair value of the net assets is due to an increase in the value of non-depreciable land.

Park held a franchise right, which at 1 June 2008 had a fair value of $10 million. This had not been recognised in the financial statements of Park. The franchise agreement had a remaining term of five years to run at that date and is not renewable. Park still holds this franchise at the year-end.

Grange wishes to use the 'full goodwill' method for all acquisitions. The fair value of the non-controlling interest in Park was $150 million on 1 June 2008. The retained earnings of Park were $115 million and other components of equity were $10 million at the date of acquisition.

Grange acquired a further 20% interest from the non-controlling interests in Park on 30 November 2009 for a cash consideration of $90 million.

(ii)   On 31 July 2008, Grange acquired a 100% of the equity interests of Fence for a cash consideration of $214 million. The identifiable net assets of Fence had a provisional fair value of $202 million, including any contingent liabilities. At the time of the business combination, Fence had a contingent liability with a fair value of $30 million. At 30 November 2009, the contingent liability met the recognition criteria of IAS 37 *Provisions, contingent liabilities and contingent assets* and the revised estimate of this liability was $25 million. The accountant of Fence is yet to account for this revised liability.

However, Grange had not completed the valuation of an element of property, plant and equipment of Fence at 31 July 2008 and the valuation was not completed by 30 November 2008. The valuation was received on 30 June 2009 and the excess of the fair value over book value at the date of acquisition was estimated at $4 million. The asset had a useful economic life of 10 years at 31 July 2008.

The retained earnings of Fence were $73 million and other components of equity were $9 million at 31 July 2008 before any adjustment for the contingent liability.

On 30 November 2009, Grange disposed of 25% of its equity interest in Fence to the non-controlling interest for a consideration of $80 million. The disposal proceeds had been credited to the cost of the investment in the statement of financial position.

(iii)   On 30 June 2008, Grange had acquired a 100% interest in Sitin, a public limited company, for a cash consideration of $39 million. Sitin's identifiable net assets were fair valued at $32 million.

On 30 November 2009, Grange disposed of 60% of the equity of Sitin when its identifiable net assets were $35 million. The sale proceeds were $23 million and the remaining equity interest was fair valued at $13 million. Grange could still exert significant influence after the disposal of the interest. The only accounting entry made in Grange's financial statements was to increase cash and reduce the cost of the investment in Sitin.

(iv)   Grange acquired a plot of land on 1 December 2008 in an area where the land is expected to rise significantly in value if plans for regeneration go ahead in the area. The land is currently held at cost of $6 million in property, plant and equipment until Grange decides what should be done with the land. The market value of the land at 30 November 2009 was $8 million but as at 15 December 2009, this had reduced to $7 million as there was some uncertainty surrounding the viability of the regeneration plan.

(v)   Grange anticipates that it will be fined $1 million by the local regulator for environmental pollution. It also anticipates that it will have to pay compensation to local residents of $6 million although this is only the best estimate of that liability. In addition, the regulator has requested that certain changes be made to the manufacturing process in order to make the process more environmentally friendly. This is anticipated to cost the company $4 million.

(vi)   Grange has a property located in a foreign country, which was acquired at a cost of 8 million dinars on 30 November 2008 when the exchange rate was $1 = 2 dinars. At 30 November 2009, the property was revalued to 12 million dinars. The exchange rate at 30 November 2009 was $1 = 1.5 dinars. The property was being carried at its value as at 30 November 2008. The company policy is to revalue property, plant and equipment whenever material differences exist between carrying amount and fair value. Depreciation on the property can be assumed to be immaterial.

(vii)   Grange has prepared a plan for reorganising the parent company's own operations. The board of directors has discussed the plan but further work has to be carried out before they can approve it. However, Grange has made a public announcement as regards the reorganisation and wishes to make a reorganisation provision at 30 November 2009 of $30 million. The plan will generate cost savings. The directors have calculated the value in use of the net assets (total equity) of the parent company as being $870 million if the reorganisation takes place and $830 million if the reorganisation does not take place. Grange is concerned that the parent company's property, plant and equipment have lost value during the period because of a decline in property prices in the region and feel that any impairment charge would relate to these assets. There is no reserve within other equity relating to prior revaluation of these non-current assets.

(viii)   Grange uses accounting policies, which maximise its return on capital, employed. The directors of Grange feel that they are acting ethically in using this approach as they feel that as long as they follow 'professional rules', then there is no problem. They have adopted a similar philosophy in the way they conduct their business affairs. The finance director had recently received information that one of their key customers, Brook, a public limited company, was having serious liquidity problems. This information was received from a close friend who was employed by Brook. However, he also learned that Brook had approached a rival company Field, a public limited company, for credit and knew that if Field granted Brook credit then there was a high probability that the outstanding balance owed by Brook to Grange would be paid. Field had approached the director for an informal credit reference for Brook who until recently had always paid promptly. The director was intending to give Brook a good reference because of its recent prompt payment history as the director felt that there was no obligation or rule which required him to mention the company's liquidity problems. (There is no change required to the financial statements as a result of the above information.)

Required:

(a)   **Calculate the gain or loss arising on the disposal of the equity interest in Sitin.**
    (6 marks)

(b)   **Prepare a consolidated statement of financial position of the Grange Group at 30 November 2009 in accordance with International Financial Reporting Standards.**
    (35 marks)

(c)   **Discuss the view that ethical behaviour is simply a matter of compliance with professional rules and whether the finance director should simply consider 'rules' when determining whether to give Brook a good credit reference.**   **(9 marks)**

(Total: 50 marks)

13 BRAVADO (JUNE 09 EXAM) *Walk in the footsteps of a top tutor*

Bravado, a public limited company, has acquired two subsidiaries and an associate. The draft statements of financial position are as follows at 31 May 2009:

	Bravado $m	Message $m	Mixted $m
Non-current assets :			
Property, plant and equipment	265	230	161
Investments in subsidiaries:			
Message	300		
Mixted	128		
Investment in associate – Clarity	20		
Financial assets at FV through OCI	51	6	5
	764	236	166
Current assets:			
Inventories	135	55	73
Trade receivables	91	45	32
Cash and cash equivalents	102	100	8
	328	200	113
Total assets	1,092	436	279
Equity and liabilities:			
Share capital	520	220	100
Retained earnings	240	150	80
Other components of equity	12	4	7
Total equity	772	374	187
Non-current liabilities:			
Long-term borrowings	120	15	5
Deferred tax	25	9	3
Current liabilities:			
Trade and other payables	115	30	60
Current tax payable	60	8	24
Total equity and liabilities	1,092	436	279

The following information is relevant to the preparation of the group financial statements:

(i)   On 1 June 2008, Bravado acquired 80% of the equity interests of Message, a private entity. The purchase consideration comprised cash of $300 million. The fair value of the identifiable net assets of Message was $400 million including any related deferred tax liability arising on acquisition. The owners of Message had to dispose of the entity for tax purposes by a specified date and, therefore, sold the entity to the first company to bid for it, which was Bravado. An independent valuer has stated that the fair value of the non-controlling interest in Message was $86 million on 1 June 2008. Bravado does not wish to measure the non-controlling interest in subsidiaries on the basis of the proportionate interest in the identifiable net assets but wishes to use the 'full goodwill' method. The retained earnings of Message were $136 million and other components of equity were $4 million at the date of acquisition. There had been no new issue of capital by Message since the date of acquisition and the excess of the fair value of the net assets is due to an increase in the value of non-depreciable land.

(ii)   On 1 June 2007, Bravado acquired 6% of the ordinary shares of Mixted. Bravado had treated this investment as far value through other comprehensive income in the financial statements to 31 May 2008 but had restated the investment at cost on Mixted becoming a subsidiary. On 1 June 2008, Bravado acquired a further 64% of the ordinary shares of Mixted and gained control of the company. The consideration for the acquisitions was as follows:

| | Holding | Consideration |
		$m
1 June 2007	6%	10
1 June 2008	64%	118

Under the purchase agreement of 1 June 2008, Bravado is required to pay the former shareholders 30% of the profits of Mixted on 31 May 2010 for each of the financial years to 31 May 2009 and 31 May 2010. The fair value of this arrangement was estimated at $12 million at 1 June 2008 and at 31 May 2009 this value had not changed. This amount has not been included in the financial statements.

At 1 June 2008, the fair value of the equity interest in Mixted held by Bravado before the business combination was $15 million and the fair value of the non-controlling interest in Mixted was $53 million. The fair value of the identifiable net assets at 1 June 2008 of Mixted was $170 million (excluding deferred tax assets and liabilities), and the retained earnings and other components of equity were $55 million and $7 million respectively. There had been no new issue of share capital by Mixted since the date of acquisition and the excess of the fair value of the net assets is due to an increase in the value of property, plant and equipment (PPE).

The fair value of the PPE was provisional pending receipt of the final valuations for these assets. These valuations were received on 1 December 2008 and they resulted in a further increase of $6 million in the fair value of the net assets at the date of acquisition. This increase does not affect the fair value of the non-controlling interest. PPE is depreciated on the straight-line basis over seven years. The tax base of the identifiable net assets of Mixted was $166 million at 1 June 2008. The tax rate of Mixted is 30%.

(iii)   Bravado acquired a 10% interest in Clarity, a public limited company, on 1 June 2007 for $8 million. The investment was initially accounted for as fair value through other comprehensive income and, at 31 May 2008, its value was $9 million. On 1 June 2008, Bravado acquired an additional 15% interest in Clarity for $11 million and achieved significant influence. Clarity made profits after dividends of $6 million and $10 million for the years to 31 May 2008 and 31 May 2009.

(iv)   On 1 June 2007, Bravado purchased an equity instrument of 11 million dinars which was its fair value. The instrument was classified as fair value through other comprehensive income. The relevant exchange rates and fair values were as follows:

	$ to 1 dinar	Fair value of instrument – dinars
1 June 2007	4.5	11
31 May 2008	5.1	10
31 May 2009	4.8	7

Bravado has not recorded any change in the value of the instrument since 31 May 2008.

(v)   Bravado manufactures equipment for the retail industry. The inventory is currently valued at cost. There is a market for the part completed product at each stage of production. The cost structure of the equipment is as follows:

	Cost per unit $	Selling price per unit $
Production process – 1st stage	1,000	1,050
Conversion costs – 2nd stage	500	
Finished product	1,500	1,700

The selling costs are $10 per unit and Bravado has 100,000 units at the first stage of production and 200,000 units of the finished product at 31 May 2009. Shortly before the year end, a competitor released a new model onto the market which caused the equipment manufactured by Bravado to become less attractive to customers. The result was a reduction in the selling price to $1,450 of the finished product and $950 for 1st stage product.

(vi)   The directors have included a loan to a director of Bravado in cash and cash equivalents of $1 million. The loan has no specific repayment date on it but is repayable on demand. The directors feel that there is no problem with this accounting entry as there is a choice of accounting policy within International Financial Reporting Standards (IFRS) and that showing the loan as cash is their choice of accounting policy as there is no IFRS which says that this policy cannot be utilised. The risk of suffering credit losses is immaterial and should be ignored.

(vii)   There is no impairment of goodwill arising on the acquisitions.

Required:

(a) Prepare a consolidated statement of financial position as at 31 May 2009 for the Bravado Group. **(35 marks)**

(b) Calculate and explain the impact on the calculation of goodwill if the non-controlling interest was calculated on a proportionate basis for Message and Mixted. **(9 marks)**

(c) Discuss the view of the directors that there is no problem with showing a loan to a director as cash and cash equivalents, taking into account their ethical and other responsibilities as directors of the company. **(6 marks)**

(Total: 50 marks)

14 WARRBURT (DEC 08 EXAM) *Walk in the footsteps of a top tutor*

The following draft group financial statements relate to Warrburt, a public limited company:

Warrburt Group: Statement of financial position as at 30 November 2008

	30 Nov 2008	30 Nov 2007
	$m	$m
Non-current assets		
Property, plant and equipment	350	360
Goodwill	80	100
Other intangible assets	228	240
Investment in associate	100	–
Financial assets at FV through OCI	142	150
	900	850
Current assets		
Inventories	135	198
Trade receivables	92	163
Cash and cash equivalents	312	323
Total assets	1,439	1,534
Equity and Liabilities		
Equity attributable to owners of the parent		
Share capital	650	595
Retained earnings	391	454
Other components of equity	25	20
	1,066	1,069
Non-controlling interest	70	53
Total equity	1,136	1,122
Non-current liabilities:		
Long-term borrowings	20	64
Deferred tax	28	26
Long-term provisions	100	96

Current liabilities:

Trade payables	115	180
Current tax payable	35	42
Short-term provisions	5	4
	____	____
Total equity and liabilities	1,439	1,534
	____	____

Warrburt Group: Statement of profit or loss and other comprehensive income for the year ended 30 November 2008

	$m
Revenue	910
Cost of sales	(886)
	____
Gross profit	24
Other income	31
Distribution costs	(40)
Administrative expenses	(35)
Finance costs	(9)
Share of profit of associate	8
	____
Loss before tax	(21)
Income tax expense	(31)
	____
Loss for the year from continuing operations	(52)
	____
Loss for the year	(52)
	____

Other comprehensive income for the year (after tax) which will not be reclassified to profit or loss in future years:

Financial assets at FV through OCI	27
Gains on property revaluation	2
Remeasurement component losses on defined benefit plan	(4)
	____
Other comprehensive income for the year (after tax)	25
	____
Total comprehensive income for the year	(27)
	____

Profit/loss attributable to:	$m
Owners of the parent	(74)
Non-controlling interest	22
	(52)

Total comprehensive income attributable to:	$m
Owners of the parent	(49)
Non-controlling interest	22
	(27)

Warrburt Group: Statement of changes in equity for the year ended 20 November 2008

	Share capital	Retained earnings	Financial assets at FVTOCI	Revaluation Surplus	Total	Non-controlling interest	Total equity
	$m	$m	$m	$m	$m	$m	$m
Bal at 1 Dec 2007	595	454	16	4	1,069	53	1,122
Share capital issued	55				55		55
Dividends		(9)			(9)	(5)	(14)
TCI for the year		(78)	27	2	(49)	22	(27)
Transfer to retained earnings		24	(24)				
Bal 30 Nov 2008	650	391	19	6	1,066	70	1,136

Note to Statement of changes in equity:

	$m
Profit/Loss attributable to owners of parent	(74)
Remeasurement component losses on defined benefit plan	(4)
Total comprehensive income for the year – retained earnings	(78)

The following information relates to the financial statements of Warrburt:

(i)   Warrburt holds investments in equity instruments. These financial assets are measured at fair value through other comprehensive income (FVTOCI). The following schedule relates to those assets.

	$m
Balance 1 December 2007	150
Less sales of financial assets at FVTOCI at carrying value	(38)
Add gain on revaluation of financial assets	30
	142

The sale proceeds of the financial assets at FVTOCI were $45 million. Profit on the sale of these financial assets is included within 'other income' in the financial statements. Deferred tax of $3 million arising on the revaluation gain above has been taken into account in 'other comprehensive income' for the year. The profit held in equity on the financial assets at FVTOCI that were sold, amounting to $24 million, has been transferred to retained earnings.

(ii) The retirement benefit liability is shown as a long-term provision in the statement of financial position and comprises the following:

	$m
Liability at 1 December 2007	96
Expense for period	10
Contributions to scheme (paid)	(10)
Remeasurement component losses	4
Liability at 30 November 2008	100

The benefits paid in the period by the trustees of the scheme were $3 million. There is no tax impact with regards to the retirement benefit liability.

(iii) The property, plant and equipment (PPE) in the statement of financial position comprises the following:

	$m
Carrying value at 1 December 2007	360
Additions at cost	78
Gains on property revaluation	4
Disposals	(56)
Depreciation	(36)
Carrying amount at 30 November 2008	350

Plant and machinery with a carrying amount of $1 million had been destroyed by fire in the year. The asset was replaced by the insurance company with plant and machinery which was valued at $3 million. The machines were acquired directly from the insurance company and no cash payment was made to Warrburt. The company included the net gain on this transaction in 'additions at cost' and 'other income'.

The disposal proceeds were $63 million. The gain on disposal is included in administrative expenses. Deferred tax of $2 million has been deducted in arriving at the 'gains on property revaluation' figure in 'other comprehensive income'.

The remaining additions of PPE comprised imported plant and equipment from an overseas supplier on 30 June 2008. The cost of the PPE was 380 million dinars with 280 million dinars being paid on 31 October 2008, and the balance was paid on 31 December 2008.

The rates of exchange were as follows:

	Dinars to $1
30 June 2008	5
31 October 2008	4.9
30 November 2008	4.8

Exchange gains and losses are included in administrative expenses.

(iv) Warrburt purchased a 25% interest in an associate for cash on 1 December 2007. The net assets of the associate at the date of acquisition were $300 million. The associate made a profit after tax of $24 million and paid a dividend of $8 million out of these profits in the year ended 30 November 2008. Assume a tax rate of 25%.

(v) An impairment test had been carried out at 30 November 2008, on goodwill and other intangible assets. The result showed that goodwill was impaired by $20 million and other intangible assets by $12 million.

(vi) The short term provisions relate to finance costs which are payable within six months

Warrburt's directors are concerned about the results for the year in the statement of comprehensive income and the subsequent effect on the cash flow statement. They have suggested that the proceeds of the sale of property, plant and equipment and the sale of financial assets at FVTOCI should be included in 'cash generated from operations'. The directors are afraid of an adverse market reaction to their results and of the importance of meeting targets in order to ensure job security, and feel that the adjustments for the proceeds would enhance the 'cash health' of the business.

Required:

(a) **Prepare a group statement of cash flows for Warrburt for the year ended 30 November 2008 in accordance with IAS 7 *Statement of cash flows* using the indirect method.** **(35 marks)**

(b) **Discuss, the key issues which the statement of cash flows highlights regarding the cash flow of the company.** **(10 marks)**

(c) **Discuss the ethical responsibility of the company accountant in ensuring that manipulation of the statement of cash flows, such as that suggested by the directors, does not occur.** **(5 marks)**

(Total: 50 marks)

15 RIBBY, HALL AND ZIAN (JUNE 08 EXAM) *Online question assistance*

The following draft statements of financial position relate to Ribby, Hall, and Zian, all public limited companies, as at 31 May 2008:

	Ribby	Hall	Zian
	$m	$m	Dinars m
Assets			
Non-current assets:			
Property, plant and equipment	250	120	360
Investment in Hall	98	–	–
Investment in Zian	30	–	–
Financial assets	10	5	148
Current assets	22	17	120
Total assets	410	142	628

Equity and liabilities:			
Equity shares	60	40	209
Other components of equity	30	10	–
Retained earnings	120	80	299
Total equity	210	130	508
Non-current liabilities	90	5	48
Current liabilities	110	7	72
Total equity and liabilities	410	142	628

The following information needs to be taken account of in the preparation of the group financial statements of Ribby:

(i)   Ribby acquired 70% of the equity shares of Hall on 1 June 2006 when Hall's other reserves were $10 million and retained earnings were $60 million. The fair value of the net assets of Hall was $120 million at the date of acquisition. Ribby acquired 60% of the equity shares of Zian for 330 million dinars on 1 June 2006 when Zian's retained earnings were 220 million dinars. The fair value of the net assets of Zian on 1 June 2006 was 495 million dinars. The excess of the fair value over the net assets of Hall and Zian is due to an increase in the value of non-depreciable land. There have been no issues of ordinary shares since acquisition and goodwill on acquisition is not impaired for either Hall or Zian. Goodwill is to be calculated on the proportion of net assets basis i.e. without allocating any goodwill to the non-controlling interest.

(ii)   Zian is located in a foreign country and imports its raw materials at a price which is normally denominated in dollars. The product is sold locally at selling prices denominated in dinars, and determined by local competition. All selling and operating expenses are incurred locally and paid in dinars.

Distribution of profits is determined by the parent company, Ribby. Zian has financed part of its operations through a $4 million loan from Hall which was raised on 1 June 2007. This is included in the financial assets of Hall and the non-current liabilities of Zian. Zian's management have a considerable degree of authority and autonomy in carrying out the operations of Zian and other than the loan from Hall, are not dependent upon group companies for finance.

(iii)   Ribby has a building which it purchased on 1 June 2007 for 40 million dinars and which is located overseas. The building is carried at cost and has been depreciated on the straight-line basis over its useful life of 20 years. At 31 May 2008, as a result of an impairment review, the recoverable amount of the building was estimated to be 36 million dinars.

(iv)   Ribby has a long-term loan of $10 million which is owed to a third party bank. At 31 May 2008, Ribby decided that it would repay the loan early on 1 July 2008 and formally agreed this repayment with the bank prior to the year end. The agreement sets out that there will be an early repayment penalty of $1 million.

(v) The directors of Ribby announced on 1 June 2007 that a bonus of $6 million would be paid to the employees of Ribby if they achieved a certain target production level by 31 May 2008. The bonus is to be paid partly in cash and partly in share options. Half of the bonus will be paid in cash on 30 November 2008 whether or not the employees are still working for Ribby. The other half will be given in share options on the same date, provided that the employee is still in service on 30 November 2008. The exercise price and number of options will be fixed by management on 30 November 2008. The target production was met and management expect 10% of employees to leave between 31 May 2008 and 30 November 2008. No entry has been made in the financial statements of Ribby.

(vi) Ribby operates a defined benefit pension plan. On 1 June 2007, Ribby improved the pension entitlement. This improvement applied to all prior years' service of the employees. As a result, the present value of the defined benefit obligation on 1 June 2007 increased by $4 million. Ribby had not accounted for the improvement in the pension plan.

(vii) Ribby is considering selling its subsidiary, Hall. Just prior to the year end, Hall sold inventory to Ribby at a price of $6 million. The carrying value of the inventory in the financial records of Hall was $2 million. The cash was received before the year end, and as a result the bank overdraft of Hall was virtually eliminated at 31 May 2008. After the year end the transaction was reversed and it was agreed that this type of transaction would be carried out again when the interim financial statements were produced for Hall, if the company had not been sold by that date.

(viii) All financial assets, with the exception of the loan by Hall to Zian, referred to in note (ii) above are correctly stated at fair value at 31 May 2008.

(ix) The following exchange rates are relevant to the preparation of the group financial statements:

	Dinars to $
1 June 2006	11
1 June 2007	10
31 May 2008	12
Average for year to 31 May 2008	10.5

Required:

(a) **Discuss and apply the principles set out in IAS 21 *The effects of changes in foreign exchange rates* in order to determine the functional currency of Zian.** **(8 marks)**

(b) **Prepare a consolidated statement of financial position of the Ribby Group at 31 May 2008 in accordance with International Financial Reporting Standards.** **(35 marks)**

(c) **Discuss how the manipulation of financial statements by company accountants is inconsistent with their responsibilities as members of the accounting profession setting out the distinguishing features of a profession and the privileges that society gives to a profession. (Your answer should include reference to the above scenario.)** **(7 marks)**

(Total: 50 marks)

 Online question assistance

16 ANDASH (DEC 06 EXAM)

The following group draft financial statements relate to Andash, a public limited company:

Draft group statements of financial position at 31 October

	20X6	20X5
	$m	$m
Assets		
Non-current assets:		
Property, plant and equipment	5,170	4,110
Goodwill	120	130
Investment in associate	60	–
	5,350	4,240
Current assets:		
Inventories	2,650	2,300
Trade receivables	2,400	1,500
Cash and cash equivalents	140	300
	5,190	4,100
Total assets	10,540	8,340

Equity and liabilities	$m	$m
Share capital	400	370
Other reserves	120	80
Retained earnings	1,250	1,100
	1,770	1,550
Non Controlling interest	200	180
Total equity	1,970	1,730

	20X6	20X5
	$m	$m
Non-current liabilities:		
Long-term borrowings	3,100	2,700
Deferred tax	400	300
Current liabilities:		
Trade payables	4,700	2,800
Interest payable	70	40
Current tax payable	300	770
Total equity and liabilities	10,540	8,340

Draft statement of changes in equity of the parent for the year ended 31 October 20X6

	Share capital	Other reserves	Retained earnings	Total
	$m	$m	$m	$m
Balance at 31 October 20X5	370	80	1,100	1,550
Profit for the year			200	200
Dividends			(50)	(50)
Issue of share capital	30	30		60
Share options issued		10		10
Balance at 31 October 20X6	400	120	1,250	1,770

Draft group statement of profit or loss for the year ended 31 October 20X6

	$m
Revenue	17,500
Cost of sales	(14,600)
Gross profit	2,900
Distribution costs	(1,870)
Administrative expenses	(490)
Finance costs – interest payable	(148)
Gain on disposal of subsidiary	8
Profit before tax	400
Tax	(160)
Profit for the year	240
Attributable to: Owners of the parent	200
Non-controlling interest	40
Profit for the year	240

There were no items of other comprehensive income.

The following information relates to the draft group financial statements of Andash:

(i)   There had been no disposal of property, plant and equipment during the year. The depreciation for the period included in cost of sales was $260 million. Andash had issued share options on 31 October 20X6 as consideration for the purchase of plant. The value of the plant purchased was $9 million at 31 October 20X6 and the share options issued had a market value of $10 million. The market value had been used to account for the plant and share options.

(ii) Andash had acquired 25 per cent of Joma on 1 November 20X5. The purchase consideration was 25 million ordinary shares of Andash valued at $50 million and cash of $10 million. Andash has significant influence over Joma. The investment is stated at cost in the draft group statement of financial position. The reserves of Joma at the date of acquisition were $20 million and at 31 October 20X6 were $32 million. Joma had sold inventory in the period to Andash at a selling price of $16 million. The cost of the inventory was $8 million and the inventory was still held by Andash at 31 October 20X6.

(iii) Andash owns 60% of a subsidiary Broiler, a public limited company. Goodwill, calculated on a proportionate basis, attributable to the parent company arising on acquisition was $90 million. The carrying value of Broiler's identifiable net assets (excluding goodwill arising on acquisition) in the group consolidated financial statements is $240 million at 31 October 20X6. The recoverable amount of Broiler is expected to be $260 million and no impairment loss has been recorded up to 31 October 20X5.

(iv) On 30 April 20X6 a wholly owned subsidiary, Chang, was disposed of. Chang prepared interim financial statements on that date which are as follows:

	$m
Property, plant and equipment	10
Inventory	8
Trade receivables	4
Cash and cash equivalents	5
	——
	27
	——
Share capital	10
Retained earnings	4
Trade payables	6
Current tax payables	7
	——
	27
	——

The consolidated carrying values of the assets and liabilities at that date were the same as above. The group received cash proceeds of $32 million and the carrying amount of goodwill was $10 million. The non controlling interest is not measured at fair value.

(Ignore the taxation effects of any adjustments required to the group financial statements and round all calculations to the nearest $million).

Required:

(a) Prepare a group statement of cash flows using the indirect method for the Andash Group for the year ended 31 October 20X6 in accordance with IAS 7 *Statement of cash flows* after making any necessary adjustments required to the draft group financial statements of Andash as a result of the information above.

(Candidates are not required to produce the adjusted group financial statements of Andash.)   **(28 marks)**

(b) Discuss how and why the cash flow provides useful financial information. Include in your answer ways of measuring cash flow performance.   **(10 marks)**

(c) Some companies 'window dress' their financial statements at the year-end. Explain what 'window dressing' is and discuss how it can be achieved and whether it is an ethical way of preparing financial statements.   **(12 marks)**

(Total: 50 marks)

17   PARSLEY

Parsley is a public limited company which has investments in a number of other companies. These companies prepare their financial statements in accordance with International Financial Reporting Standards. The draft statements of profit or loss for Parsley and its investments for the year ended 30 April 20X4 are presented below:

	Parsley	Sage	Saffron
	$m	$m	FRm
Revenue	143	68	210
Cost of sales	(61)	(42)	(126)
Gross profit	82	26	84
Distribution costs	(10)	(6)	(14)
Administrative expenses	(23)	(10)	(29)
Operating profit	49	10	41
Investment income	1	2	–
Finance costs	(2)	(4)	(3)
Profit before taxation	48	8	38
Taxation	(11)	(2)	(9)
Profit for the period	37	6	29

The following notes are relevant to the preparation of the consolidated financial statements:

1   Parsley acquired 70% of Sage's one million $1 ordinary shares for $6m many years ago. At the acquisition date, the carrying value of Sage's net assets was $5m, and this was deemed to be the same as their fair value. The non-controlling interest was measured using the proportion of net assets method. Goodwill arising on the acquisition of Sage has never been impaired. On 31 October 20X3, Parsley sold 300,000 of its shares in Sage for $6.5m. The fair value of the interest retained was $9.5m. The retained earnings of Sage were $9m as at 30 April 20X3. The only entry posted in Parsley's individual financial statements is to record the cash received and to credit these proceeds to a suspense account.

2   On 1 May 20X3, Parsley purchased 60% of Saffron's one million FR1 ordinary shares for FR71m. The non-controlling interest at acquisition was valued at FR29m using the fair value method. At 1 May 20X3, the carrying value of Saffron's net assets was FR60m but the fair value was FR70m. The excess in fair value was due to an unrecognised brand with a remaining useful economic life of five years at the acquisition date.

3   At 30 April 20X4, it was determined that goodwill arising on the acquisition of Saffron was impaired by FR4m. Goodwill impairments are charged to administrative expenses.

4   On 28 February 20X4, Sage paid a dividend of $1m to its ordinary shareholders.

5   On 1 May 20X3, Parsley signed a lease to use an item of machinery. The useful economic life of the machine and the lease term were both five years. The fair value of the asset was $5m. Parsley must pay the lessor $1.3m annually in arrears. The payment for the year ended 30 April 20X4 was charged to cost of sales. No other accounting entries have been made in respect of the lease. The interest rate implicit in the lease is 9.5%.

6   On 1 June 20X3, Parsley commenced construction of a new head office and financed this out of its general borrowings. The construction was completed on 30 April 20X4 at a total cost of $10m (excluding interest on borrowings). Parsley has had the following loans outstanding for the whole financial year:

	$m
10% bank loan	14
8% loan notes	6

All interest for the year has been expensed to the statement of profit or loss. None of the loan notes are held by any other companies within the Parsley group.

7   On 1 November 20X3, Parsley granted 10,000 share options to each of its 100 managers. These options will vest on 31 October 20X5 if the managers are still employed. Five managers had left the company by 30 April 20X4 and it is expected that another five will leave by 31 October 20X5. The fair value of the share options was $3.10 on 1 November 20X3 and $5.15 on 30 April 20X4. No accounting entries have been posted in relation to this scheme.

8   The following exchange rates are relevant:

	FR: $1
1 May 20X3	5.0
30 April 20X4	4.0
Average for year ended 30 April 20X4	4.6

Required:

(a) **Prepare the consolidated statement of profit or loss and other comprehensive income for the Parsley Group for the year ended 30 April 20X4.** **(35 marks)**

Related party relationships are a common feature of commercial life. The objective of IAS 24 *Related party disclosures* is to ensure that financial statements contain the necessary disclosures to make users aware of the possibility that financial statements may have been affected by the existence of related parties.

Required:

(b) **Describe the main circumstances that give rise to related parties and explain why the disclosure of related party relationships and transactions is important.**

(7 marks)

A public listed company, X, owns two subsidiary company investments. It owns 100% of the equity shares of A and 55% of the equity shares of B. During the year ended 31 May 20X6 B made several sales of goods to A. These sales totalled $15 million and had cost B $14 million to manufacture. B made these sales on the instruction of the Board of X. It is known that one of the directors of B, who is not a director of X, is unhappy with the parent company's instruction as he believes the goods could have been sold to other companies outside the group at the far higher price of $20 million. All directors within the group benefit from a profit sharing scheme.

Required:

(c) **Describe the financial effect that X's instruction may have on the financial statements of the companies within the group and the implications this may have for other interested parties.** **(8 marks)**

(Total: 50 marks)

18 MEMO

Memo, a public limited company, owns 75% of the equity share capital of Random, a public limited company which is situated in a foreign country. Memo acquired Random on 1 May 20X3 for 120 million crowns (CR) when the retained earnings of Random were 80 million crowns. Random has not revalued its assets or issued any equity capital since its acquisition by Memo. The following financial statements relate to Memo and Random:

Statements of financial position at 30 April 20X4

	Memo	Random
	$m	CRm
Property, plant and equipment	297	146
Investment in Random	48	–
Loan to Random	5	–
Current assets	355	102
	705	248

	$m	CRm
Equity and liabilities		
Equity shares of $1/1CR	60	32
Share premium account	50	20
Retained earnings	360	95
	470	147
Non-current liabilities	30	41
Current liabilities	205	60
	705	248

Statements of profit or loss for year ended 30 April 20X4

	Memo	Random
	$m	CRm
Revenue	200	142
Cost of sales	(120)	(96)
Gross profit	80	46
Distribution and administrative expenses	(30)	(20)
Operating profit	50	26
Investment income	4	–
Finance costs	–	(2)
Profit before taxation	54	24
Income tax expense	(20)	(9)
Profit for the year	34	15

There were no items of other comprehensive income in the financial statements of either entity.

The following information is relevant to the preparation of the consolidated financial statements of Memo:

(a) During the financial year Random has purchased raw materials from Memo and denominated the purchase in crowns in its financial records. The details of the transaction are set out below:

	Date of transaction	Purchase price	Profit percentage on selling price
		$m	
Raw materials	1 February 20X4	6	20%

At the year-end, half of the raw materials purchased were still in the inventory of Random. The inter-company transactions have not been eliminated from the financial statements and the goods were recorded by Random at the exchange rate ruling on 1 February 20X4. A payment of $6 million was made to Memo when the exchange rate was 2.2 crowns to $1. Any exchange gain or loss arising on the transaction is still held in the current liabilities of Random.

(b)   Memo had made an interest free loan to Random of $5 million on 1 May 20X3. The loan was repaid on 30 May 20X4. Random had included the loan in non-current liabilities and had recorded it at the exchange rate at 1 May 20X3.

(c)   The fair value of the net assets of Random at the date of acquisition is to be assumed to be the same as the carrying value. Memo uses the full goodwill method when accounting for acquisition of a subsidiary. Goodwill was impairment tested at the reporting date and had reduced in value by ten per cent. At the date of acquisition, the fair value of the non-controlling interest was CR38 million.

(d)   Random operates with a significant degree of autonomy in its business operations.

(e)   The following exchange rates are relevant to the financial statements:

Crowns to $	
30 April/1 May 20X3	2.5
1 November 20X3	2.6
1 February 20X4	2
30 April 20X4	2.1
Average rate for year to 30 April 20X4	2

(f)   Memo has paid a dividend of $8 million during the financial year.

Required:

(a)   **Prepare a consolidated statement of profit or loss and other comprehensive income for the year ended 30 April 20X4 and a consolidated statement of financial position, including separate disclosure of the group foreign exchange reserve, at 30 April 20X4 in accordance with International Financial Reporting Standards.**

(35 marks)

Memo is currently suffering a degree of stagnation in its business development. Its domestic and international markets are being maintained but it is not attracting new customers. Its share price has not increased whilst that of its competitors has seen a rise of between 10% and 20%. Additionally it has recently received a significant amount of adverse publicity because of its poor environmental record and is to be investigated by regulators in several countries. Although Memo is a leading supplier of oil products, it has never felt the need to promote socially responsible policies and practices or make positive contributions to society because it has always maintained its market share. It is renowned for poor customer support, bearing little regard for the customs and cultures in the communities where it does business. It had recently made a decision not to pay the amounts owing to certain small and medium entities (SMEs) as the directors feel that SMEs do not have sufficient resources to challenge the non-payment in a court of law. The management of the company is quite authoritarian and tends not to value employees' ideas and contributions.

(b)   **Describe to the Memo Group the possible advantages of producing a separate environmental report.**

(8 marks)

(c)   **Discuss the ethical and social responsibilities of the Memo Group and whether a change in the ethical and social attitudes of the management could improve business performance.**

(7 marks)

(Total: 50 marks)

19 ZAMBEZE

The following draft financial statements relate to Zambeze, a public limited company:

Draft group statements of financial position at 30 June

	2006 $m	2005 $m
Assets:		
Non-current assets:		
Property, plant and equipment	1,315	1,005
Goodwill	32	25
Investment in associate	270	290
	1,617	1,320
Current assets:		
Inventories	650	580
Trade receivables	610	530
Cash at bank and cash equivalents	50	140
	1,310	1,250
Total assets	2,927	2,570
Equity and liabilities:		
Share capital	100	85
Share premium account	30	15
Revaluation reserve	50	145
Retained earnings	254	250
	434	495
Non controlling interest	62	45
Total equity	496	540
Non-current liabilities	850	600
Current liabilities	1,581	1,430
Total liabilities	2,431	2,030
Total equity and liabilities	2,927	2,570

Draft group statement of profit or loss and other comprehensive income for the year ended 30 June 2006

	$m
Revenue	4,700
Cost of sales	(3,400)
Gross profit	1,300
Distribution and administrative expenses	(600)
Finance costs (interest payable)	(40)
Share of profit in associate	30
Profit before tax	690
Income tax expense (including tax on income from associate $10 million)	(210)
Profit for the period	480
Other comprehensive income:	
Foreign exchange difference of associate	(5)
Impairment losses on property, plant and equipment offset against revaluation surplus	(95)
Total comprehensive income	380
Attributable to:	
Equity holders of the parent	355
Non-controlling interest	25
Total comprehensive income	380

Draft statement of changes in equity for the year ended 30 June 2006

	$m
Total comprehensive income	355
Dividends paid	(446)
New shares issued	30
Total movement during the year	(61)
Shareholders' funds at 1 July 2005	495
Shareholders' funds at 30 June	434

The following relates to Zambeze:

(i)   Zambeze acquired a seventy per cent holding in Damp, a public limited company, on 1 July 2005. The fair values of the net assets acquired were as follows:

	$m
Property, plant and equipment	70
Inventories and work in progress	90
	160

The purchase consideration was $100 million in cash and $25 million (discounted value) deferred consideration which is payable on 1 July 2006. The difference between the discounted value of the deferred consideration ($25 million) and the amount payable ($29 million) is included in 'interest payable'. Zambeze wants to set up a provision for reconstruction costs of $10 million retrospectively on the acquisition of Damp. This provision has not yet been set up.

(ii) There had been no disposals of property, plant and equipment during the year. Depreciation for the period charged in cost of sales was $60 million.

(iii) Current liabilities comprised the following items:

	2006 $m	2005 $m
Trade payables	1,341	1,200
Interest payable	50	45
Taxation	190	185
	1,581	1,430

(iv) Non-current liabilities comprised the following:

	2006 $m	2005 $m
Deferred consideration – purchase of Damp	29	–
Liability for the purchase of Property, plant and equipment	144	–
Loans repayable	621	555
Provision for deferred tax	30	25
Retirement benefit liability	26	20
	850	600

(v) The defined benefit liability comprised the following:

	$m
Movement in year:	
Liability at 1 July 2005	20
Current and past service costs charged to profit or loss	13
Contributions paid to retirement benefit scheme	(7)
Liability 30 June 2006	26

There were no remeasurement gains or losses in the year.

(vi) Goodwill is calculated using the full goodwill method. At the date of acquisition, the fair value of the non-controlling interest was $50 million. Goodwill was impairment tested on 30 June 2006 and any impairment was included in the financial statements for the year ended 30 June 2006.

(vii)   The Finance Director has set up a company, River, through which Zambeze conducts its investment activities. Zambeze has paid $400 million to River during the year and this has been included in dividends paid. The money was invested in a specified portfolio of investments. Ninety-five per cent of the profits and one hundred per cent of the losses in the specified portfolio of investments are transferred to Zambeze. An investment manager has charge of the company's investments and owns all of the share capital of River. An agreement between the investment manager and Zambeze sets out the operating guidelines and prohibits the investment manager from obtaining access to the investments for the manager's benefit. An annual transfer of the profit/loss will occur on 30 June annually and the capital will be returned in four years' time. The transfer of $400 million cash occurred on 1 January 2006 but no transfer of profit/loss has yet occurred. The statement of financial position of River at 30 June 2006 is as follows:

River – statement of financial position at 30 June 2006

	$m
Investment at fair value through profit or loss	390
	–––––
	390
	–––––
Share capital	400
Retained earnings	(10)
	–––––
	390
	–––––

Required:

(a)   **Prepare a group cash flow statement for the Zambeze Group for the year ended 30 June 2006 using the indirect method.**   **(35 marks)**

(b)   **Discuss the issues which would determine whether River should be consolidated by Zambeze in the group financial statements.**   **(9 marks)**

(c)   **Discuss briefly the importance of ethical behaviour in the preparation of financial statements and whether the creation of River could constitute unethical practice by the finance director of Zambeze.**   **(6 marks)**

(Total: 50 marks)

SECTION B-TYPE QUESTIONS

REPORTING STANDARDS

20   YANONG (JUNE 15 EXAM) *Walk in the footsteps of a top tutor*

The directors of Yanong, a public limited company, have seen many different ways of dealing with the measurement and disclosure of the fair value of assets, liabilities and equity instruments. They feel that this reduces comparability among different entities' financial statements. They would like advice on several transactions where they currently use fair value measurement as they have heard that the introduction of IFRS 13 *Fair Value Measurement*, while not interfering with the scope of fair value measurement, will reduce the extent of any diversity and inconsistency.

(a)   Yanong owns several farms and also owns a division which sells agricultural vehicles. It is considering selling this agricultural retail division and wishes to measure the fair value of the inventory of vehicles for the purpose of the sale. Three markets currently exist for the vehicles. Yanong has transacted regularly in all three markets. At 30 April 2015, Yanong wishes to find the fair value of 150 new vehicles, which are identical. The current volume and prices in the three markets are as follows:

Market	Sales price – per vehicle $	Historical volume – vehicles sold by Yanong	Total volume of vehicles sold in market	Transaction costs – per vehicle $	Transport cost to the market – per vehicle
Europe	40,000	6,000	150,000	500	400
Asia	38,000	2,500	750,000	400	700
Africa	34,000	1,500	100,000	300	600

Yanong wishes to value the vehicles at $39,100 per vehicle as these are the highest net proceeds per vehicle, and Europe is the largest market for Yanong's product. Yanong would like advice as to whether this valuation would be acceptable under IFRS 13 *Fair Value Measurement*. **(6 marks)**

(b)   The company uses quarterly reporting for its farms as they grow short-lived crops such as maize. Yanong planted the maize fields during the quarter to 31 October 2014 at an operating cost of $10 million. The fields originally cost $20 million. There is no active market for partly grown fields of maize and therefore Yanong proposes to use a discounted cash flow method to value the maize fields.

As at 31 October 2014, the following were the cash flow projections relating to the maize fields:

	3 months to 31 January 2015 $ million	3 months to 30 April 2015 $ million	Total $ million
Cash inflows		80	80
Cash outflows	(8)	(19)	(27)
Notional rental charge for land usage	(1)	(1)	(2)
Net cash flows	(9)	60	51

In the three months to 31 January 2015, the actual operating costs amounted to $8 million and at that date Yanong revised its future projections for the cash inflows to $76 million for the three months to April 2015. At the point of harvest at 31 March 2015, the maize was worth $82 million and it was sold for $84 million (net of costs to sell) on 15 April 2015. In the measurement of fair value of the maize, Yanong includes a notional cash flow expense for the 'rent' of the land where it is self-owned.

The directors of Yanong wish to know how they should have accounted for the above biological asset at 31 October 2014, 31 January 2015, 31 March 2015 and when the produce was sold. Assume a discount rate of 2% per quarter as follows:

	Factor
Period 1	0.980
Period 2	0.961

(6 marks)

(c) On 1 May 2012, Yanong granted 500 share appreciation rights (SARs) to its 300 managers. All of the rights vested on 30 April 2014 but they can be exercised from 1 May 2014 up to 30 April 2016. At the grant date, the value of each SAR was $10 and it was estimated that 5% of the managers would leave during the vesting period. The fair value of the SARs is as follows:

Date	Fair value of SAR
30 April 2013	$9
30 April 2014	$11
30 April 2015	$12

All of the managers who were expected to leave employment did leave the company as expected before 30 April 2014. On 30 April 2015, 60 managers exercised their options when the intrinsic value of the right was $10.50 and were paid in cash.

Yanong is confused as to whether to account for the SARs under IFRS 2 *Share-based Payment* or IFRS 13 *Fair Value Measurement*, and would like advice as to how the SARs should have been accounted for from the grant date to 30 April 2015. **(6 marks)**

(d) Yanong uses the revaluation model for its non-current assets. Yanong has several plots of farmland which are unproductive. The company feels that the land would have more value if it were used for residential purposes. There are several potential purchasers for the land but planning permission has not yet been granted for use of the land for residential purposes. However, preliminary enquiries with the regulatory authorities seem to indicate that planning permission may be granted. Additionally, the government has recently indicated that more agricultural land should be used for residential purposes.

Yanong has also been approached to sell the land for commercial development at a higher price than that for residential purposes.

Yanong would like advice on how to measure the fair value of the land in its financial statements. **(5 marks)**

Required:

Advise Yanong on how the above transactions should be dealt with in its financial statements with reference to relevant International Financial Reporting Standards.

Note: The mark allocation is shown against each of the four issues above.

Professional marks will be awarded in this question for clarity and quality of presentation.

(2 marks)

Note: Ignore any deferred tax implications of the transactions above.

(Total: 25 marks)

21 **KLANCET (JUNE 15 EXAM)** *Walk in the footsteps of a top tutor*

Klancet, a public limited company, is a pharmaceutical company and is seeking advice on several financial reporting issues.

(a) Klancet produces and sells its range of drugs through three separate divisions. In addition, there are two laboratories which carry out research and development activities.

In the first of these laboratories, the research and development activity is funded internally and centrally for each of the three sales divisions. It does not carry out research and development activities for other entities. Each of the three divisions is given a budget allocation which it uses to purchase research and development activities from the laboratory. The laboratory is directly accountable to the division heads for this expenditure.

The second laboratory performs contract investigation activities for other laboratories and pharmaceutical companies. This laboratory earns 75% of its revenues from external customers and these external revenues represent 18% of the organisation's total revenues.

The performance of the second laboratory's activities and of the three separate divisions is regularly reviewed by the chief operating decision maker (CODM). In addition to the heads of divisions, there is a head of the second laboratory. The head of the second laboratory is directly accountable to the CODM and they discuss the operating activities, allocation of resources and financial results of the laboratory.

Klancet is uncertain as to whether the research and development laboratories should be reported as two separate segments under IFRS 8 *Operating Segments*, and would like advice on this issue. **(8 marks)**

(b) Klancet has agreed to sell a patent right to another pharmaceutical group, Jancy. Jancy would like to use the patent to develop a more complex drug. Klancet will receive publicly listed shares of the Jancy group in exchange for the right. The value of the listed shares represents the fair value of the patent. If Jancy is successful in developing a drug and bringing it to the market, Klancet will also receive a 5% royalty on all sales.

Additionally, Klancet won a competitive bidding arrangement to acquire a patent. The purchase price was settled by Klancet issuing new publicly listed shares of its own.

Klancet's management would like advice on how to account for the above transactions. **(7 marks)**

(c) Klancet is collaborating with Retto Laboratories (Retto), a third party, to develop two existing drugs owned by Klancet.

In the case of the first drug, Retto is simply developing the drug for Klancet without taking any risks during the development phase and will have no further involvement if regulatory approval is given. Regulatory approval has been refused for this drug in the past. Klancet will retain ownership of patent rights attached to the drug. Retto is not involved in the marketing and production of the drug. Klancet has agreed to make two non-refundable payments to Retto of $4 million on the signing of the agreement and $6 million on successful completion of the development.

Klancet and Retto have entered into a second collaboration agreement in which Klancet will pay Retto for developing and manufacturing an existing drug. The existing drug already has regulatory approval. The new drug being developed by Retto for Klancet will not differ substantially from the existing drug. Klancet will have exclusive marketing rights to the drug if the regulatory authorities approve it. Historically, in this jurisdiction, new drugs receive approval if they do not differ substantially from an existing approved drug.

The contract terms require Klancet to pay an upfront payment on signing of the contract, a payment on securing final regulatory approval, and a unit payment of $10 per unit, which equals the estimated cost plus a profit margin, once commercial production begins. The cost-plus profit margin is consistent with Klancet's other recently negotiated supply arrangements for similar drugs.

Klancet would like to know how to deal with the above contracts with Retto.

(8 marks)

Required:

Advise Klancet on how the above transactions should be dealt with in its financial statements with reference to relevant International Financial Reporting Standards.

Note: The mark allocation is shown against each of the three issues above.

Professional marks will be awarded in this question for clarity and quality of presentation. **(2 marks)**

(Total: 25 marks)

22 COATMIN (DEC 14 EXAM) *Walk in the footsteps of a top tutor*

(a) Coatmin is a government-controlled bank. Coatmin was taken over by the government during the recent financial crisis. Coatmin does not directly trade with other government-controlled banks but has underwritten the development of the nationally owned railway and postal service. The directors of Coatmin are concerned about the volume and cost of disclosing its related party interests because they extend theoretically to all other government-controlled enterprises and banks. They wish for general advice on the nature and importance of the disclosure of related party relationships and specific advice on the disclosure of the above relationships in the financial statements. **(5 marks)**

(b) At the start of the financial year to 30 November 2013, Coatmin gave a financial guarantee contract on behalf of one of its subsidiaries, a charitable organisation, committing it to repay the principal amount of $60 million if the subsidiary defaulted on any payments due under a loan. The loan related to the financing of the construction of new office premises and has a term of three years. It is being repaid by equal annual instalments of principal with the first payment having been paid. Coatmin has not secured any compensation in return for giving the guarantee, but assessed that it had a fair value of $1.2 million. The guarantee has been designated to be measured at fair value through profit or loss. The guarantee was given on the basis that it was probable that it would not be called upon. At 30 November 2014, Coatmin became aware of the fact that the subsidiary was having financial difficulties with the result that it has not paid the second instalment of principal. It is assessed that it is probable that the guarantee will now be called. However, just before the signing of the financial statements for the year ended 30 November 2014, the subsidiary secured a donation which enabled it to make the second repayment before the guarantee was called upon. It is now anticipated that the subsidiary will be able to meet the final payment. Discounting is immaterial. Coatmin wishes to know how the transaction would be accounted for in the financial records. **(7 marks)**

(c) Coatmin has entered into an interest rate swap agreement which acts as a hedge against a $2 million 2% bond issue which matures on 31 May 2016. The notional amount of the swap is $2 million with settlement every 12 months. The start date of the swap was 1 December 2013 and it matures on 31 May 2016. The swap is enacted for nil consideration. Coatmin receives interest at 1.75% a year and pays on the basis of the 12-month LIBOR rate. At inception, Coatmin designates the swap as a hedge in the variability in the fair value of the bond issue.

	Fair value 1 December 2013	Fair value 30 November 2014
	$000	$000
Fixed interest bond	2,000	2,030
Interest rate swap	Nil	203

The decline in Coatmin's creditworthiness has meant that, despite a reduction in LIBOR, the bond's fair value change has been negligible. The effect of credit risk is expected to continue to dominate the economic relationship between the bond and the swap in future accounting periods.

Coatmin wishes to know the circumstances in which it can use hedge accounting and needs advice on the use of hedge accounting for the above transactions. **(7 marks)**

(d) Coatmin provides loans to customers and funds the loans by selling bonds in the market. The liability is designated as at fair value through profit or loss. The bonds had an overall fair value increase of $50 million in the year to 30 November 2014 although the decline in Coatmin's creditworthiness has been calculated to have contributed to a fair value decline of $5 million. The directors of Coatmin would like advice on how to account for this movement. **(4 marks)**

Required:

Discuss, with suitable calculations where necessary, the accounting treatment of the above transactions in the financial statements of Coatmin.

Note: The mark allocation is shown against each of the questions above.

Professional marks will be awarded in this question for clarity and quality of presentation. **(2 marks)**

(Total: 25 marks)

23 KATYE (DEC 14 EXAM) *Walk in the footsteps of a top tutor*

(a) Kayte operates in the shipping industry and owns vessels for transportation. In June 2014, Kayte acquired Ceemone whose assets were entirely investments in small companies. The small companies each owned and operated one or two shipping vessels. There were no employees in Ceemone or the small companies. At the acquisition date, there were only limited activities related to managing the small companies as most activities were outsourced. All the personnel in Ceemone were employed by a separate management company. The companies owning the vessels had an agreement with the management company concerning assistance with chartering, purchase and sale of vessels and any technical management. The management company used a shipbroker to assist with some of these tasks.

Kayte accounted for the investment in Ceemone as an asset acquisition. The consideration paid and related transaction costs were recognised as the acquisition price of the vessels. Kayte argued that the vessels were only passive investments and that Ceemone did not own a business consisting of processes, since all activities regarding commercial and technical management were outsourced to the management company. As a result, the acquisition was accounted for as if the vessels were acquired on a stand-alone basis.

Additionally, Kayte had borrowed heavily to purchase some vessels and was struggling to meet its debt obligations. Kayte had sold some of these vessels but in some cases, the bank did not wish Kayte to sell the vessel. In these cases, the vessel was transferred to a new entity, in which the bank retained a variable interest based upon the level of the indebtedness. Kayte's directors felt that the entity was a subsidiary of the bank and are uncertain as to whether they have complied with the requirements of IFRS 3 *Business Combinations* and IFRS 10 *Consolidated Financial Statements* as regards the above transactions. **(12 marks)**

(b) Kayte's vessels constitute a material part of its total assets. The economic life of the vessels is estimated to be 30 years, but the useful life of some of the vessels is only 10 years because Kayte's policy is to sell these vessels when they are 10 years old. Kayte estimated the residual value of these vessels at sale to be half of acquisition cost and this value was assumed to be constant during their useful life. Kayte argued that the estimates of residual value used were conservative in view of an immature market with a high degree of uncertainty and presented documentation which indicated some vessels were being sold for a price considerably above carrying value. Broker valuations of the residual value were considerably higher than those used by Kayte. Kayte argued against broker valuations on the grounds that it would result in greater volatility in reporting.

Kayte keeps some of the vessels for the whole 30 years and these vessels are required to undergo an engine overhaul in dry dock every 10 years to restore their service potential, hence the reason why some of the vessels are sold. The residual value of the vessels kept for 30 years is based upon the steel value of the vessel at the end of its economic life. At the time of purchase, the service potential which will be required to be restored by the engine overhaul is measured based on the cost as if it had been performed at the time of the purchase of the vessel. In the current period, one of the vessels had to have its engine totally replaced after only eight years. Normally, engines last for the 30-year economic life if overhauled every 10 years. Additionally, one type of vessel was having its funnels replaced after 15 years but the funnels had not been depreciated separately. **(11 marks)**

Required:

Discuss the accounting treatment of the above transactions in the financial statements of Kayte.

Note: The mark allocation is shown against each of the elements above.

Professional marks will be awarded in this question for clarity and quality of presentation. **(2 marks)**

(Total: 25 marks)

24 ASPIRE (JUNE 14 EXAM) *Walk in the footsteps of a top tutor*

Aspire, a public limited company, operates many of its activities overseas. The directors have asked for advice on the correct accounting treatment of several aspects of Aspire's overseas operations. Aspire's functional currency is the dollar.

(a) Aspire has created a new subsidiary, which is incorporated in the same country as Aspire. The subsidiary has issued 2 million dinars of equity capital to Aspire, which paid for these shares in dinars. The subsidiary has also raised 100,000 dinars of equity capital from external sources and has deposited the whole of the capital with a bank in an overseas country whose currency is the dinar. The capital is to be invested in dinar denominated bonds. The subsidiary has a small number of staff and its operating expenses, which are low, are incurred in dollars. The profits are under the control of Aspire. Any income from the investment is either passed on to Aspire in the form of a dividend or reinvested under instruction from Aspire. The subsidiary does not make any decisions as to where to place the investments.

Aspire would like advice on how to determine the functional currency of the subsidiary. **(7 marks)**

(b) Aspire has a foreign branch which has the same functional currency as Aspire. The branch's taxable profits are determined in dinars. On 1 May 2013, the branch acquired a property for 6 million dinars. The property had an expected useful life of 12 years with a zero residual value. The asset is written off for tax purposes over eight years. The tax rate in Aspire's jurisdiction is 30% and in the branch's jurisdiction is 20%. The foreign branch uses the cost model for valuing its property and measures the tax base at the exchange rate at the reporting date.

Aspire would like an explanation (including a calculation) as to why a deferred tax charge relating to the asset arises in the group financial statements for the year ended 30 April 2014 and the impact on the financial statements if the tax base had been translated at the historical rate. **(6 marks)**

(c) On 1 May 2013, Aspire purchased 70% of a multi-national group whose functional currency was the dinar. The purchase consideration was $200 million. At acquisition, the net assets at cost were 1,000 million dinars. The fair values of the net assets were 1,100 million dinars and the fair value of the non-controlling interest was 250 million dinars. Aspire uses the full goodwill method.

Aspire wishes to know how to deal with goodwill arising on the above acquisition in the group financial statements for the year ended 30 April 2014. **(5 marks)**

(d) Aspire took out a foreign currency loan of 5 million dinars at a fixed interest rate of 8% on 1 May 2013. The interest is paid at the end of each year. The loan will be repaid after two years on 30 April 2015. The interest rate is the current market rate for similar two-year fixed interest loans.

Aspire requires advice on how to account for the loan and interest in the financial statements for the year ended 30 April 2014. **(5 marks)**

Aspire has a financial statement year end of 30 April 2014 and the average currency exchange rate for the year is not materially different from the actual rate.

Exchange rates	$1 = dinars
1 May 2013	5
30 April 2014	6
Average exchange rate for year ended 30 April 2014	5.6

Required:

Advise the directors of Aspire on their various requests above, showing suitable calculations where necessary.

Note: The mark allocation is shown against each of the four issues above.

Professional marks will be awarded in this question for clarity and quality of presentation. **(2 marks)**

(Total: 25 marks)

25 MINCO (JUNE 14 EXAM) *Walk in the footsteps of a top tutor*

(a) Minco is a major property developer which buys land for the construction of housing. One aspect of its business is to provide low-cost homes through the establishment of a separate entity, known as a housing association. Minco purchases land and transfers ownership to the housing association before construction starts. Minco sells rights to occupy the housing units to members of the public but the housing association is the legal owner of the building. The housing association enters into loan agreements with the bank to cover the costs of building the homes. However, Minco negotiates and acts as guarantor for the loan, and bears the risk of increases in the loan's interest rate above a specified rate. Currently, the housing rights are normally all sold out on the completion of a project.

Minco enters into discussions with a housing contractor regarding the construction of the housing units but the agreement is between the housing association and the contractor. Minco is responsible for any construction costs in excess of the amount stated in the contract and is responsible for paying the maintenance costs for any units not sold. Minco sets up the board of the housing association, which comprises one person representing Minco and two independent board members.

Minco recognises income for the entire project when the land is transferred to the housing association. The income recognised is the difference between the total sales price for the finished housing units and the total estimated costs for construction of the units. Minco argues that the transfer of land to the housing association means that its performance obligation is satisfied and that revenue can be recognised in accordance with IFRS 15 *Revenue from Contracts with Customers*. **(7 marks)**

(b) Minco often sponsors professional tennis players in an attempt to improve its brand image. At the moment, it has a three-year agreement with a tennis player who is currently ranked in the world's top ten players. The agreement is that the player receives a signing bonus of $20,000 and earns an annual amount of $50,000, paid at the end of each year for three years, provided that the player has competed in all the specified tournaments for each year. If the player wins a major tournament, she receives a bonus of 20% of the prize money won at the tournament. In return, the player is required to wear advertising logos on tennis apparel, play a specified number of tournaments and attend photo/film sessions for advertising purposes. The different payments are not interrelated. **(5 marks)**

(c) Minco leased its head office during the current accounting period and the agreement terminates in six years' time. There is a clause in the operating lease relating to the internal condition of the property at the termination of the lease. The clause states that the internal condition of the property should be identical to that at the outset of the lease. Minco has improved the building by adding another floor to part of the building during the current accounting period. There is also a clause which enables the landlord to recharge Minco for costs relating to the general disrepair of the building at the end of the lease. In addition, the landlord can recharge any costs of repairing the roof immediately. The landlord intends to replace part of the roof of the building during the current period. **(5 marks)**

(d) Minco acquired a property for $4 million and annual depreciation of $300,000 is charged on the straight line basis. At the end of the previous financial year of 31 May 2013, when accumulated depreciation was $1 million, a further amount relating to an impairment loss of $350,000 was recognised, which resulted in the property being valued at its estimated value in use. On 1 October 2013, as a consequence of a proposed move to new premises, the property was classified as held for sale. At the time of classification as held for sale, the fair value less costs to sell was $2.4 million. At the date of the published interim financial statements, 1 December 2013, the property market had improved and the fair value less costs to sell was reassessed at $2.52 million and at the year-end on 31 May 2014 it had improved even further, so that the fair value less costs to sell was $2.95 million. The property was sold on 5 June 2014 for $3 million. **(6 marks)**

Required:

Discuss how the above items should be dealt with in the financial statements of Minco.

Note: The mark allocation is shown against each of the four issues above.

Professional marks will be awarded in this question for clarity and quality of presentation. **(2 marks)**

(Total: 25 marks)

26 HAVANNA (DEC 13 EXAM) *Walk in the footsteps of a top tutor*

(a) Havanna owns a chain of health clubs and has entered into binding contracts with a number of organisations. The services rendered by Havanna include admission to health clubs, the provision of coaching and other similar benefits. These contracts are for periods of between 9 and 18 months. Havanna's accounting policy for revenue recognition is to recognise the contract income in full at the date when the contract was signed. **(6 marks)**

(b) In May 2013, Havanna decided to sell one of its regional business divisions through a mixed asset and share deal. The decision to sell the division at a price of $40 million was made public in November 2013 and gained shareholder approval in December 2013. It was decided that the payment of any agreed sale price could be deferred until 30 November 2015. The business division was presented as a disposal group in the statement of financial position as at 30 November 2013. At the initial classification of the division as held for sale, its net carrying amount was $90 million. In writing down the disposal group's carrying amount, Havanna accounted for an impairment loss of $30 million which represented the difference between the carrying amount and value of the assets measured in accordance with applicable International Financial Reporting Standards (IFRS).

In the financial statements at 30 November 2013, Havanna showed the following costs as provisions relating to the continuing operations. These costs were related to the business division being sold and were as follows:

(i) A loss relating to a potential write-off of a trade receivable which had gone into liquidation.

(ii) An expense relating to the discounting of the long-term receivable on the fixed amount of the sale price of the disposal group

(iii) A provision was charged which related to the expected transaction costs of the sale including legal advice and lawyer fees.

The directors wish to know how to treat the above transactions. **(9 marks)**

(c) Havanna has decided to sell its main office building to a third party and lease it back on a 10-year lease. The lease will be an operating lease. The current fair value of the property is $5 million and the carrying value of the asset is $4.2 million. The market for property is very difficult in the jurisdiction and Havanna therefore requires guidance on the consequences of selling the office building at a range of prices. The following prices have been achieved in the market during the last few months for similar office buildings:

(i) $5 million

(ii) $6 million

(iii) $4.8 million

(iv) $4 million

Assuming that the fair value of the property is $5 million, Havanna would like advice on how to account for the sale and leaseback, with an explanation of the effect which the different selling prices would have on the financial statements. **(8 marks)**

Required:

Advise Havanna on how the above transactions should be dealt with in its financial statements with reference to International Financial Reporting Standards where appropriate.

Note: The mark allocation is shown against each of the three issues above.

Professional marks will be awarded in this question for clarity and quality of presentation. **(2 marks)**

(Total: 25 marks)

27 BENTAL (DEC 13 EXAM) *Walk in the footsteps of a top tutor*

 Timed question with Online tutor debrief

(a) Bental, a listed bank, has a subsidiary, Hexal, which has two classes of shares, A and B. A-shares carry voting powers and B-shares are issued to meet Hexal's regulatory requirements. Under the terms of a shareholders' agreement, each shareholder is obliged to capitalise any dividends in the form of additional investment in B-shares. The shareholder agreement also stipulates that Bental agrees to buy the B-shares of the minority shareholders through a put option under the following conditions:

- The minority shareholders can exercise their put options when their ownership in B-shares exceeds the regulatory requirement, or

- The minority shareholders can exercise their put options every three years. The exercise price is the original cost paid by the shareholders.

In Bental's consolidated financial statements, the B-shares owned by minority shareholders are to be reported as a non-controlling interest. **(7 marks)**

(b) Bental had a number of highly probable future sales transactions that qualified for cash flow hedge accounting. The hedges were considered to be effective and gains on the hedging instruments had been recognised in accordance with *IFRS 9 Financial Instruments*. At 30 November 2013, it was decided that the hedged transactions were no longer highly probable, although they are still more likely than not to occur. Bental requires advice on how to deal with this.

Additionally, Bental has an investment in a foreign entity over which it has significant influence and therefore accounts for the entity as an associate. The entity's functional currency differs from Bental's and, in the consolidated financial statements, the associate's results fluctuate with changes in the exchange rate. Bental wishes to designate the investment as a hedged item in a fair value hedge in its individual and consolidated financial statements. **(6 marks)**

(c) On 1 September 2013, Bental entered into a business combination with another listed bank, Lental. The business combination has taken place in two stages, which were contingent upon each other. On 1 September 2013, Bental acquired 45% of the share capital and voting rights of Lental for cash. On 1 November 2013, Lental merged with Bental and Bental issued new A-shares to Lental's shareholders for their 55% interest.

On 31 August 2013, Bental had a market value of $70 million and Lental a market value of $90 million. Bental's business represents 45% and Lental's business 55% of the total value of the combined businesses.

After the transaction, the former shareholders of Bental excluding those of Lental owned 51% and the former shareholders of Lental owned 49% of the votes of the combined entity. The Chief Operating Officer (COO) of Lental is the biggest individual owner of the combined entity with a 25% interest. The purchase agreement provides for a board of six directors for the combined entity, five of whom will be former board members of Bental with one seat reserved for a former board member of Lental. The board of directors nominates the members of the management team. The management comprised the COO and four other members, two from Bental and two from Lental. Under the terms of the purchase agreement, the COO of Lental is the COO of the combined entity.

Bental proposes to identify Lental as the acquirer in the business combination but requires advice as to whether this is correct. **(10 marks)**

Required:

Discuss whether the accounting practices and policies outlined above are acceptable under International Financial Reporting Standards.

Note: The mark allocation is shown against each of the three issues above.

Professional marks will be awarded in this question for clarity and quality of presentation. **(2 marks)**

(Total: 25 marks)

 Calculate your allowed time, allocate the time to the separate parts

---

28 VERGE (JUNE 13 EXAM) *Walk in the footsteps of a top tutor*

(a) In its annual financial statements for the year ended 31 March 2013, Verge, a public limited company, had identified the following operating segments:

(i) Segment 1 local train operations

(ii) Segment 2 inter-city train operations

(iii) Segment 3 railway constructions

The company disclosed two reportable segments. Segments 1 and 2 were aggregated into a single reportable operating segment. Operating segments 1 and 2 have been aggregated on the basis of their similar business characteristics, and the nature of their products and services. In the local train market, it is the local transport authority which awards the contract and pays Verge for its services. In the local train market, contracts are awarded following a competitive tender process, and the ticket prices paid by passengers are set by and paid to the transport authority. In the inter-city train market, ticket prices are set by Verge and the passengers pay Verge for the service provided. **(5 marks)**

(b)   Verge entered into a contract with a government body on 1 April 2011 to undertake maintenance services on a new railway line. The total revenue from the contract is $5 million over a three-year period. The contract states that $1 million will be paid at the commencement of the contract but although invoices will be subsequently sent at the end of each year, the government authority will only settle the subsequent amounts owing when the contract is completed. The invoices sent by Verge to date (including $1 million above) were as follows:

Year ended 31 March 2012 $2.8 million

Year ended 31 March 2013 $1.2 million

The balance will be invoiced on 31 March 2014. Verge has only accounted for the initial payment in the financial statements to 31 March 2012 as no subsequent amounts are to be paid until 31 March 2014. The amounts of the invoices reflect the work undertaken in the period. Verge wishes to know how to account for the revenue on the contract in the financial statements to date.

Market interest rates are currently at 6%.   **(6 marks)**

(c)   In February 2012, an inter-city train did what appeared to be superficial damage to a storage facility of a local company. The directors of the company expressed an intention to sue Verge but in the absence of legal proceedings, Verge had not recognised a provision in its financial statements to 31 March 2012. In July 2012, Verge received notification for damages of $1.2m, which was based upon the estimated cost to repair the building. The local company claimed the building was much more than a storage facility as it was a valuable piece of architecture which had been damaged to a greater extent than was originally thought. The head of legal services advised Verge that the company was clearly negligent but the view obtained from an expert was that the value of the building was $800,000. Verge had an insurance policy that would cover the first $200,000 of such claims.

After the financial statements for the year ended 31 March 2013 were authorised, the case came to court and the judge determined that the storage facility actually was a valuable piece of architecture. The court ruled that Verge was negligent and awarded $300,000 for the damage to the fabric of the facility.   **(6 marks)**

(d)   Verge was given a building by a private individual in February 2012. The benefactor included a condition that it must be brought into use as a train museum in the interests of the local community or the asset (or a sum equivalent to the fair value of the asset) must be returned. The fair value of the asset was $1.5 million in February 2012. Verge took possession of the building in May 2012. However, it could not utilise the building in accordance with the condition until February 2013 as the building needed some refurbishment and adaptation and in order to fulfil the condition. Verge spent $1 million on refurbishment and adaptation.

On 1 July 2012, Verge obtained a cash grant of $250,000 from the government. Part of the grant related to the creation of 20 jobs at the train museum by providing a subsidy of $5,000 per job created. The remainder of the grant related to capital expenditure on the project. At 31 March 2013, all of the new jobs had been created.

(6 marks)

Required:

Advise Verge on how the above accounting issues should be dealt with in its financial statements for the years ending 31 March 2012 (where applicable) and 31 March 2013.

Note: The mark allocation is shown against each of the four issues above.

Professional marks will be awarded in this question for clarity and quality of presentation.   **(2 marks)**

(Total: 25 marks)

29   JANNE (JUNE 13 EXAM) *Walk in the footsteps of a top tutor*

(a)   Janne is a real estate company, which specialises in industrial property. Investment properties including those held for sale constitute more than 80% of its total assets.

It is considering leasing land from Maret for a term of 30 years. Janne plans to use the land for its own office development but may hold the land for capital gain. The title will remain with Maret at the end of the initial lease term. Janne can lease the land indefinitely at a small immaterial rent at the end of the lease or may purchase the land at a 90% discount to the market value after the initial lease term. Janne is to pay Maret a premium of $3 million at the commencement of the lease, which equates to 70% of the value of the land. Additionally, an annual rental payment is to be made, based upon 4% of the market value of the land at the commencement of the lease, with a market rent review every five years. The rent review sets the rent at the higher of the current rent or 4% of the current value of the land. Land values have been rising for many years.

Additionally, Janne is considering a suggestion by Maret to incorporate a clean break clause in the lease which will provide Janne with an option of terminating the agreement after 25 years without any further payment and also to include an early termination clause after 10 years that would require Janne to make a termination payment which would recover the lessor's remaining investment.   **(12 marks)**

(b)   Janne measures its industrial investment property using the fair value method, which is measured using the 'new-build value less obsolescence'. Valuations are conducted by a member of the board of directors. In order to determine the obsolescence, the board member takes account of the age of the property and the nature of its use. According to the board, this method of calculation is complex but gives a very precise result, which is accepted by the industry. There are sales values for similar properties in similar locations available as well as market rent data per square metre for similar industrial buildings.   **(5 marks)**

(c)   Janne operates through several subsidiaries and reported a subsidiary as held for sale in its annual financial statements for both 2012 and 2013. On 1 January 2012, the shareholders had, at a general meeting of the company, authorised management to sell all of its holding of shares in the subsidiary within the year. Janne had shown the subsidiary as an asset held for sale and presented it as a discontinued operation in the financial statements at 31 May 2012. This accounting treatment had been continued in Janne's 2013 financial statements.

Janne had made certain organisational changes during the year to 31 May 2013, which resulted in additional activities being transferred to the subsidiary. Also during the year to 31 May 2013, there had been draft agreements and some correspondence with investment bankers, which showed in principle only that the subsidiary was still for sale.   **(6 marks)**

Required:

Advise Janne on how the above accounting issues should be dealt with in its financial statements.

Note: The mark allocation is shown against each of the three issues above.

Professional marks will be awarded in this question for clarity and quality of presentation.   **(2 marks)**

(Total: 25 marks)

30 COATE (DEC 12 EXAM)

(a) Coate, a public limited company, is a producer of ecologically friendly electrical power (green electricity). Coate's revenue comprises mainly the sale of electricity and green certificates. Coate obtains green certificates under a national government scheme. Green certificates represent the environmental value of green electricity. The national government requires suppliers who do not produce green electricity to purchase a certain number of green certificates. Suppliers who do not produce green electricity can buy green certificates either on the market on which they are traded or directly from a producer such as Coate. The national government wishes to give incentives to producers such as Coate by allowing them to gain extra income in this way.

Coate obtains the certificates from the national government on satisfactory completion of an audit by an independent organisation, which confirms the origin of production. Coate then receives a certain number of green certificates from the national government depending on the volume of green electricity generated. The green certificates are allocated to Coate on a quarterly basis by the national government and Coate can trade the green certificates.

Coate is uncertain as to the accounting treatment of the green certificates in its financial statements for the period ended 30 November 2012. **(7 marks)**

(b) During the year ended 30 November 2012, Coate acquired an overseas subsidiary whose financial statements are prepared in a different currency to Coate. The amounts reported in the consolidated statement of cash flows included the effect of changes in foreign exchange rates arising on the retranslation of its overseas operations. Additionally, the group's consolidated statement of cash flows reported as a loss the effect of foreign exchange rate changes on cash and cash equivalents as Coate held some foreign currency of its own denominated in cash. **(5 marks)**

(c) Coate also sold 50% of a previously wholly owned subsidiary, Patten, to a third party, Manis. Manis is in the same industry as Coate. Coate has continued to account for the investment in Patten as a subsidiary in its consolidated financial statements. The main reason for this accounting treatment was the agreement that had been made with Manis, under which Coate would exercise general control over Patten's operating and financial policies. Coate has appointed three out of four directors to the board. The agreement also stated that certain decisions required consensus by the two shareholders.

Under the shareholder agreement, consensus is required with respect to:

- significant changes in the company's activities

- plans or budgets that deviate from the business plan

- accounting policies; acquisition of assets above a certain value; employment or dismissal of senior employees; distribution of dividends or establishment of loan facilities.

Coate feels that the consensus required above does not constitute a hindrance to the power to control Patten, as it is customary within the industry to require shareholder consensus for decisions of the types listed in the shareholders' agreement.

(6 marks)

(d)   In the notes to Coate's financial statements for the year ended 30 November 2012, the tax expense included an amount in respect of 'Adjustments to current tax in respect of prior years' and this expense had been treated as a prior year adjustment. These items related to adjustments arising from tax audits by the authorities in relation to previous reporting periods.

The issues that resulted in the tax audit adjustment were not a breach of tax law but related predominantly to transfer pricing issues, for which there was a range of possible outcomes that were negotiated during 2012 with the taxation authorities. Further at 30 November 2011, Coate had accounted for all known issues arising from the audits to that date and the tax adjustment could not have been foreseen as at 30 November 2011, as the audit authorities changed the scope of the audit. No penalties were expected to be applied by the taxation authorities.   **(5 marks)**

Required:

Discuss how the above events should be accounted for in the individual or, as appropriate, the consolidated financial statements of Coate.

Note: The mark allocation is shown against each of the four events above.

Professional marks will be awarded in this question for the clarity and quality of the presentation and discussion.   **(2 marks)**

(Total: 25 marks)

31   BLACKCUTT (DEC 12 EXAM)

Blackcutt is a local government organisation whose financial statements are prepared using International Financial Reporting Standards.

(a)   Blackcutt wishes to create a credible investment property portfolio with a view to determining if any property may be considered surplus to the functional objectives and requirements of the local government organisation. The following portfolio of property is owned by Blackcutt.

Blackcutt owns several plots of land. Some of the land is owned by Blackcutt for capital appreciation and this may be sold at any time in the future. Other plots of land have no current purpose as Blackcutt has not determined whether it will use the land to provide services such as those provided by national parks or for short-term sale in the ordinary course of operations.

The local government organisation supplements its income by buying and selling property. The housing department sells some of these properties in the ordinary course of its operations as a result of changing demographics. The rest of these properties are held to provide housing to low-income employees at below market rental. The rent paid by employees covers the cost of maintenance of the property.

(7 marks)

(b) Blackcutt has outsourced its waste collection to a private sector provider called Waste and Co and pays an annual amount to Waste and Co for its services. Waste and Co purchases the vehicles and uses them exclusively for Blackcutt's waste collection. The vehicles are painted with the Blackcutt local government organisation name and colours. Blackcutt can use the vehicles and the vehicles are used for waste collection for nearly all of the asset's life. In the event of Waste and Co's business ceasing, Blackcutt can obtain legal title to the vehicles and carry on the waste collection service. **(6 marks)**

(c) Blackcutt owns a warehouse. Chemco has leased the warehouse from Blackcutt and is using it as a storage facility for chemicals. The national government has announced its intention to enact environmental legislation requiring property owners to accept liability for environmental pollution. As a result, Blackcutt has introduced a hazardous chemical policy and has begun to apply the policy to its properties. Blackcutt has had a report that the chemicals have contaminated the land surrounding the warehouse. Blackcutt has no recourse against Chemco or its insurance company for the clean-up costs of the pollution. At 30 November 2012, it is virtually certain that draft legislation requiring a clean-up of land already contaminated will be enacted shortly after the year end. **(4 marks)**

(d) On 1 December 2006, Blackcutt opened a school at a cost of $5 million. The estimated useful life of the school was 25 years. On 30 November 2012, the school was closed because numbers using the school declined unexpectedly due to a population shift caused by the closure of a major employer in the area. The school is to be converted for use as a library, and there is no expectation that numbers using the school will increase in the future and thus the building will not be reopened for use as a school. The current replacement cost for a library of equivalent size to the school is $2.1 million. Because of the nature of the non-current asset, value-in-use and net selling price are unrealistic estimates of the value of the school. The change in use would have no effect on the estimated life of the building. **(6 marks)**

Required:

Discuss how the above events should be accounted for in the financial statements of Blackcutt.

Note: The mark allocation is shown against each of the four events above.

Professional marks will be awarded in this question for the clarity and quality of the presentation and discussion. **(2 marks)**

(Total: 25 marks)

32 WILLIAM (JUNE 12 EXAM)

William is a public limited company and would like advice in relation to the following transactions.

(a) William owned a building on which it raised finance. William sold the building for $5 million to a finance company on 1 June 2011 when the carrying amount was $3.5 million. The same building was leased back from the finance company for a period of 20 years, which was felt to be equivalent to the majority of the asset's economic life. The lease rentals for the period are $441,000 payable annually in arrears. The interest rate implicit in the lease is 7%. The present value of the minimum lease payments is the same as the sale proceeds.

William wishes to know how to account for the above transaction for the year ended 31 May 2012. **(7 marks)**

(b)   William operates a defined benefit scheme for its employees. The scheme was revised on 1 June 2011. This resulted in the benefits being enhanced for some members of the plan and, because benefits do not vest for these members for five years, William wishes to spread the increased cost over that period. During the current year, several highly paid employees left William to work for other companies.

William transferred plan assets with a fair value of $0.4 million to the employees' new pension schemes and in return extinguished its obligation to these employees with respect to pension benefits. The actuary estimates that the present value of the defined benefit obligation eliminated by this transaction was $0.3 million.

William requires advice on how to account for the above scheme under IAS 19 *Employee Benefits*. **(7 marks)**

(c)   On 1 June 2009, William granted 500 share appreciation rights to each of its 20 managers. All of the rights vest after two year's service and they can be exercised during the following two years up to 31 May 2013. The fair value of the right at the grant date was $20. It was thought that three managers would leave over the initial two-year period and they did so. The fair value of each right was as follows:

Year	Fair value at year end $
31 May 2010	23
31 May 2011	14
31 May 2012	24

On 31 May 2012, seven managers exercised their rights when the intrinsic value of the right was $21.

William wishes to know what the liability and expense will be at 31 May 2012.

(5 marks)

(d)   William acquired another entity, Chrissy, on 1 May 2012. At the time of the acquisition, Chrissy was being sued as there is an alleged mis-selling case potentially implicating the entity. The claimants are suing for damages of $10 million. William estimates that the fair value of any contingent liability is $4 million and feels that it is more likely than not that no outflow of funds will occur.

William wishes to know how to account for this potential liability in Chrissy's entity financial statements and whether the treatment would be the same in the consolidated financial statements. **(4 marks)**

Required:

Discuss, with suitable computations, the advice that should be given to William in accounting for the above events.

Note: The mark allocation is shown against each of the four events above.

Professional marks will be awarded for clarity and expression of your discussion. **(2 marks)**

(Total: 25 marks)

33 ETHAN (JUNE 12 EXAM)

Ethan, a public limited company, develops, operates and sells investment properties.

(a) Ethan focuses mainly on acquiring properties where it foresees growth potential, through rental income as well as value appreciation. The acquisition of an investment property is usually realised through the acquisition of the entity, which holds the property.

In Ethan's consolidated financial statements, investment properties acquired through business combinations are recognised at fair value, using a discounted cash flow model as approximation to fair value. There is currently an active market for this type of property. The difference between the fair value of the investment property as determined under the accounting policy, and the value of the investment property for tax purposes results in a deferred tax liability.

Goodwill arising on business combinations is determined using the measurement principles for the investment properties as outlined above. Goodwill is only considered impaired if and when the deferred tax liability is reduced below the amount at which it was first recognised. This reduction can be caused both by a reduction in the value of the real estate or a change in local tax regulations. As long as the deferred tax liability is equal to, or larger than, the prior year, no impairment is charged to goodwill. Ethan explained its accounting treatment by confirming that almost all of its goodwill is due to the deferred tax liability and that it is normal in the industry to account for goodwill in this way.

Since 2008, Ethan has incurred substantial annual losses except for the year ended 31 May 2011, when it made a small profit before tax. In year ended 31 May 2011, most of the profit consisted of income recognised on revaluation of investment properties. Ethan had announced early in its financial year ended 31 May 2012 that it anticipated substantial growth and profit. Later in the year, however, Ethan announced that the expected profit would not be achieved and that, instead, a substantial loss would be incurred. Ethan had a history of reporting considerable negative variances from its budgeted results.

than's recognised deferred tax assets have been increasing year-on-year despite the deferred tax liabilities recognised on business combinations. Ethan's deferred tax assets consist primarily of unused tax losses that can be carried forward which are unlikely to be offset against anticipated future taxable profits. **(11 marks)**

(b) Ethan wishes to apply the fair value option rules of IFRS *9 Financial Instruments* to debt issued to finance its investment properties. Ethan's argument for applying the fair value option is based upon the fact that the recognition of gains and losses on its investment properties and the related debt would otherwise be inconsistent. Ethan argued that there is a specific financial correlation between the factors, such as interest rates, that form the basis for determining the fair value of both Ethan's investment properties and the related debt. **(7 marks)**

(c) Ethan has an operating subsidiary, which has in issue A and B shares, both of which have voting rights. Ethan holds 70% of the A and B shares and the remainder are held by shareholders external to the group. The subsidiary is obliged to pay an annual dividend of 5% on the B shares. The dividend payment is cumulative even if the subsidiary does not have sufficient legally distributable profit at the time the payment is due.

In Ethan's consolidated statement of financial position, the B shares of the subsidiary were accounted for in the same way as equity instruments would be, with the B shares owned by external parties reported as a non-controlling interest. **(5 marks)**

Required:

Discuss how the above transactions and events should be recorded in the consolidated financial statements of Ethan.

Note: The mark allocation is shown against each of the three transactions above.

Professional marks will be awarded for clarity and expression of your discussion.

(2 marks)

(Total: 25 marks)

34 DECANY (DEC 11 EXAM)

Decany owns 100% of the ordinary share capital of Ceed and Rant. All three entities are public limited companies. The group operates in the shipbuilding industry, which is currently a depressed market. Rant has made losses for the last three years and its liquidity is poor. The view of the directors is that Rant needs some cash investment. The directors have decided to put forward a restructuring plan as at 30 November 2011. Under this plan:

(1) Ceed is to purchase the whole of Decany's investment in Rant. The purchase consideration is to be $98 million payable in cash to Decany and this amount will then be loaned on a long-term unsecured basis to Rant; and

(2) Ceed will purchase land with a carrying amount of $10 million from Rant for a total purchase consideration of $15 million. The land has a mortgage outstanding on it of $4 million. The total purchase consideration of $15 million comprises both five million $1 nominal value non-voting shares issued by Ceed to Rant and the $4 million mortgage liability which Ceed will assume; and

(3) A dividend of $25 million will be paid from Ceed to Decany to reduce the accumulated reserves of Ceed.

The Statements of Financial Position of Decany and its subsidiaries at 30 November 2011 are summarised below:

	Decany $m	Ceed $m	Rant $m
Non-current assets			
Tangible non-current assets at depreciated cost/valuation	600	170	45
Cost of investment in Ceed	130		
Cost of investment in Rant	95		
Current assets	155	130	20
	980	300	65
Equity and reserves			
Share capital	140	70	35
Retained earnings	750	220	5
	890	290	40
Non-current liabilities:			
Long-term loan	5		12
Current liabilities			

Trade payables	85	10	13
	980	300	65

As a result of the restructuring, several of Ceed's employees will be made redundant. According to the detailed plan, the costs of redundancy will be spread over two years with $4 million being payable in one year's time and $6 million in two years' time. The market yield of high quality corporate bonds is 3%. The directors feel that the overall restructure will cost $2 million.

Required:

(a) (i) **Prepare the individual entity statements of financial position after the proposed restructuring plan** **(13 marks)**

(ii) **Set out the requirements of IAS 27 *Separate Financial Statements* as regards the reorganisation and payment of dividends between group companies, discussing any implications for the restructuring plan.** **(5 marks)**

(b) **Discuss the key implications of the proposed plans for the restructuring of the group.** **(5 marks)**

Professional marks will be awarded in part (b) for clarity and expression of your discussion. **(2 marks)**

(Total: 25 marks)

35 SCRAMBLE (DEC 11 EXAM)

 Timed question with Online tutor debrief

Scramble, a public limited company, is a developer of online computer games.

(a) At 30 November 2011, 65% of Scramble's total assets were mainly represented by internally developed intangible assets comprising the capitalised costs of the development and production of online computer games. These games generate all of Scramble's revenue. The costs incurred in relation to maintaining the games at the same standard of performance are expensed to the statement profit or loss. The accounting policy note states that intangible assets are valued at historical cost. Scramble considers the games to have an indefinite useful life, which is reconsidered annually when the intangible assets are tested for impairment. Scramble determines value in use using the estimated future cash flows which include maintenance expenses, capital expenses incurred in developing different versions of the games and the expected increase in turnover resulting from the above mentioned cash outflows. Scramble does not conduct an analysis or investigation of differences between expected and actual cash flows. Tax effects were also taken into account.

(7 marks)

(b)   Scramble has two cash generating units (CGU) which hold 90% of the internally developed intangible assets. Scramble reported a consolidated net loss for the period and an impairment charge in respect of the two CGUs representing 63% of the consolidated profit before tax and 29% of the total costs in the period. The recoverable amount of the CGUs is defined, in this case, as value in use. Specific discount rates are not directly available from the market, and Scramble estimates the discount rates, using its weighted average cost of capital. In calculating the cost of debt as an input to the determination of the discount rate, Scramble used the risk-free rate adjusted by the company specific average credit spread of its outstanding debt, which had been raised two years previously. As Scramble did not have any need for additional financing and did not need to repay any of the existing loans before 2014, Scramble did not see any reason for using a different discount rate. Scramble did not disclose either the events and circumstances that led to the recognition of the impairment loss or the amount of the loss recognised in respect of each cash-generating unit. Scramble felt that the events and circumstances that led to the recognition of a loss in respect of the first CGU were common knowledge in the market and the events and the circumstances that led to the recognition loss of the second CGU were not needed to be disclosed.   **(7 marks)**

(c)   Scramble wished to diversify its operations and purchased a professional football club, Rashing. In Rashing's financial statements for the year ended 30 November 2011, it was proposed to include significant intangible assets which related to acquired players' registration rights comprising registration and agents' fees. The agents' fees were paid by the club to players' agents either when a player is transferred to the club or when the contract of a player is extended. Scramble believes that the registration rights of the players are intangible assets but that the agent's fees do not meet the criteria to be recognised as intangible assets as they are not directly attributable to the costs of players' contracts. Additionally, Rashing has purchased the rights to 25% of the revenue from ticket sales generated by another football club, Santash, in a different league. Rashing does not sell these tickets nor has any discretion over the pricing of the tickets. Rashing wishes to show these rights as intangible assets in its financial statements.   **(9 marks)**

Required:

Discuss the validity of the accounting treatments proposed by Scramble in its financial statements for the year ended 30 November 2011.

The mark allocation is shown against each of the three accounting treatments above.

Professional marks will be awarded for clarity and expression of your discussion.   (2 marks)

(Total: 25 marks)

 Calculate your allowed time, allocate the time to the separate parts

36   LOCKFINE (JUNE 11 EXAM)

Lockfine, a public limited company, operates in the fishing industry and has recently made the transition to International Financial Reporting Standards (IFRS). Lockfine's reporting date is 30 April 2011.

(a)   In the IFRS opening statement of financial position at 1 May 2009, Lockfine elected to measure its fishing fleet at fair value and use that fair value as deemed cost in accordance with IFRS *1 First Time Adoption of International Financial Reporting Standards.* The fair value was an estimate based on valuations provided by two independent selling agents, both of whom provided a range of values within which the valuation might be considered acceptable. Lockfine calculated fair value at the average of the highest amounts in the two ranges provided. One of the agents' valuations was not supported by any description of the method adopted or the assumptions underlying the calculation. Valuations were principally based on discussions with various potential buyers. Lockfine wished to know the principles behind the use of deemed cost and whether agents' estimates were a reliable form of evidence on which to base the fair value calculation of tangible assets to be then adopted as deemed cost. **(6 marks)**

(b)   Lockfine was unsure as to whether it could elect to apply IFRS 3 *Business Combinations* retrospectively to past business combinations on a selective basis, because there was no purchase price allocation available for certain business combinations in its opening IFRS statement of financial position.

As a result of a major business combination, fishing rights of that combination were included as part of goodwill. The rights could not be recognised as a separately identifiable intangible asset at acquisition under the local GAAP because a reliable value was unobtainable for the rights. The fishing rights operated for a specified period of time.

On transition from local GAAP to IFRS, the fishing rights were included in goodwill and not separately identified because they did not meet the qualifying criteria set out in IFRS 1, even though it was known that the fishing rights had a finite life and would be fully impaired or amortised over the period specified by the rights. Lockfine wished to amortise the fishing rights over their useful life and calculate any impairment of goodwill as two separate calculations. **(6 marks)**

(c)   Lockfine has internally developed intangible assets comprising the capitalised expenses of the acquisition and production of electronic map data which indicates the main fishing grounds in the world. The intangible assets generate revenue for the company in their use by the fishing fleet and are a material asset in the statement of financial position. Lockfine had constructed a database of the electronic maps. The costs incurred in bringing the information about a certain region of the world to a higher standard of performance are capitalised. The costs related to maintaining the information about a certain region at that same standard of performance are expensed. Lockfine's accounting policy states that intangible assets are valued at historical cost. The company considers the database to have an indefinite useful life which is reconsidered annually when it is tested for impairment. The reasons supporting the assessment of an indefinite useful life were not disclosed in the financial statements and neither did the company disclose how it satisfied the criteria for recognising an intangible asset arising from development. **(6 marks)**

(d)   The Lockfine board has agreed two restructuring projects during the year to 30 April 2011:

Plan A involves selling 50% of its off-shore fleet in one year's time. Additionally, the plan is to make 40% of its seamen redundant. Lockfine will carry out further analysis before deciding which of its fleets and related employees will be affected. In previous announcements to the public, Lockfine has suggested that it may restructure the off-shore fleet in the future.

Plan B involves the reorganisation of the headquarters in 18 months time, and includes the redundancy of 20% of the headquarters' workforce. The company has made announcements before the year end but there was a three month consultation period which ended just after the year end, whereby Lockfine was negotiating with employee representatives. Thus individual employees had not been notified by the year end.

Lockfine proposes recognising a provision in respect of Plan A but not Plan B. **(5 marks)**

Required:

Discuss the principles and practices to be used by Lockfine in accounting for the above valuation and recognition issues.

Professional marks will be awarded in this question for clarity and quality of discussion.   **(2 marks)**

(Total: 25 marks)

37   ALEXANDRA (JUNE 11 EXAM)

Alexandra, a public limited company, designs and manages business solutions and IT infrastructures.

(a)   In November 2010, Alexandra defaulted on an interest payment on an issued bond loan of $100 million repayable in 2015. The loan agreement stipulates that such default leads to an obligation to repay the whole of the loan immediately, including accrued interest and expenses. The bondholders, however, issued a waiver postponing the interest payment until 31 May 2011. On 17 May 2011, Alexandra felt that a further waiver was required, so requested a meeting of the bondholders and agreed a further waiver of the interest payment to 5 July 2011, when Alexandra was confident it could make the payments. Alexandra classified the loan as long-term debt in its statement of financial position at 30 April 2011 on the basis that the loan was not in default at the end of the reporting period as the bondholders had issued waivers and had not sought redemption.   **(6 marks)**

(b)   Alexandra enters into contracts with both customers and suppliers. The supplier solves system problems and provides new releases and updates for software. Alexandra provides maintenance services for its customers. In previous years, Alexandra recognised revenue and related costs on software maintenance contracts when the customer was invoiced, which was at the beginning of the contract period. Contracts typically run for two years.

During 2010, Alexandra had acquired Xavier Co, which recognised revenue, derived from a similar type of maintenance contract as Alexandra, on a straight-line basis over the term of the contract. Alexandra considered both its own and the policy of Xavier Co to comply with the requirements of IFRS 15 *Revenue from Contracts with Customers* but it decided to adopt the practice of Xavier Co for itself and the group. Alexandra concluded that the two recognition methods did not, in substance, represent two different accounting policies and did not, therefore, consider adoption of the new practice to be a change in policy.

In the year to 30 April 2011, Alexandra recognised revenue (and the related costs) on a straight-line basis over the contract term, treating this as a change in an accounting estimate. As a result, revenue and cost of sales were adjusted, reducing the year's profits by some $6 million. **(5 marks)**

(c) Alexandra has a two-tier board structure consisting of a management and a supervisory board. Alexandra remunerates its board members as follows:

- Annual base salary

- Variable annual compensation (bonus)

- Share options

In the group financial statements, within the related parties note under IAS 24 *Related Party Disclosures*, Alexandra disclosed the total remuneration paid to directors and non-executive directors and a total for each of these boards. No further breakdown of the remuneration was provided.

The management board comprises both the executive and non-executive directors. The remuneration of the non-executive directors, however, was not included in the key management disclosures. Some members of the supervisory and management boards are of a particular nationality. Alexandra was of the opinion that in that jurisdiction, it is not acceptable to provide information about remuneration that could be traced back to individuals. Consequently, Alexandra explained that it had provided the related party information in the annual accounts in an ambiguous way to prevent users of the financial statements from tracing remuneration information back to specific individuals. **(5 marks)**

(d) Alexandra's pension plan was accounted for as a defined benefit plan in 2010. In the year ended 30 April 2011, Alexandra changed the accounting method used for the scheme and accounted for it as a defined contribution plan, restating the comparative 2010 financial information. The effect of the restatement was significant. In the 2011 financial statements, Alexandra explained that, during the year, the arrangements underlying the retirement benefit plan had been subject to detailed review. Since the pension liabilities are fully insured and indexation of future liabilities can be limited up to and including the funds available in a special trust account set up for the plan, which is not at the disposal of Alexandra, the plan qualifies as a defined contribution plan under IAS 19 *Employee Benefits* rather than a defined benefit plan. Furthermore, the trust account is built up by the insurance company from the surplus yield on investments. The pension plan is an average pay plan in respect of which the entity pays insurance premiums to a third party insurance company to fund the plan. Every year 1% of the pension fund is built up and employees pay a contribution of 4% of their salary, with the employer paying the balance of the contribution. If an employee leaves Alexandra and transfers the pension to another fund, Alexandra is liable for, or is refunded the difference between the benefits the employee is entitled to and the insurance premiums paid.

(7 marks)

Required:

Discuss how the above transactions should be dealt with in the financial statements of Alexandra for the year ended 30 April 2011.

Professional marks will be awarded in this question for clarity and quality of discussion. **(2 marks)**

(Total: 25 marks)

38 MARGIE (DEC 10 EXAM) *Walk in the footsteps of a top tutor*

Margie, a public limited company, has entered into several share related transactions during the period and wishes to obtain advice on how to account for the transactions.

(a) Margie has entered into a contract with a producer to purchase 350 tonnes of wheat. The purchase price will be settled in cash at an amount equal to the value of 2,500 of Margie's shares. Margie may settle the contract at any time by paying the producer an amount equal to the current market value of 2,500 of Margie shares, less the market value of 350 tonnes of wheat. Margie has entered into the contract as part of its hedging strategy and has no intention of taking physical delivery of the wheat. Margie wishes to treat this transaction as a share based payment transaction under IFRS 2 'Share-based Payment'. **(7 marks)**

(b) Margie has acquired 100% of the share capital of Antalya in a business combination on 1 December 2009. Antalya had previously granted a share-based payment to its employees with a four-year vesting period. Its employees have rendered the required service for the award at the acquisition date but have not yet exercised their options. The fair value of the award at 1 December 2009 is $20 million and Margie is obliged to replace the share-based payment awards of Antalya with awards of its own.

Margie issues a replacement award that does not require post-combination services. The fair value of the replacement award at the acquisition date is $22 million. Margie does not know how to account for the award on the acquisition of Antalya.

(6 marks)

(c) Margie issued shares during the financial year. Some of those shares were subscribed for by employees who were existing shareholders, and some were issued to an entity, Grief, which owned 5% of Margie's share capital. Before the shares were issued, Margie offered to buy a building from Grief and agreed that the purchase price would be settled by the issue of shares. Margie wondered whether these transactions should be accounted for under IFRS 2. **(4 marks)**

(d) Margie granted 100 options to each of its 4,000 employees at a fair value of $10 each on 1 December 2007. The options vest upon the company's share price reaching $15, provided the employee has remained in the company's service until that time. The terms and conditions of the options are that the market condition can be met in either year 3, 4 or 5 of the employee's service.

At the grant date, Margie estimated that the expected vesting period would be four years which is consistent with the assumptions used in estimating the fair value of the options granted. The company's share price reached $15 on 30 November 2010.

(6 marks)

Required:

Discuss, with suitable computations where applicable, how the above transactions would be dealt with in the financial statements of Margie for the year ending 30 November 2010.

Professional marks awarded for the clarity and quality of discussion. **(2 marks)**

(Total: 25 marks)

39 GREENIE (DEC 10 EXAM) *Walk in the footsteps of a top tutor*

(a) Greenie, a public limited company, builds, develops and operates airports. During the financial year to 30 November 2010, a section of an airport collapsed and as a result several people were hurt. The accident resulted in the closure of the terminal and legal action against Greenie. When the financial statements for the year ended 30 November 2010 were being prepared, the investigation into the accident and the reconstruction of the section of the airport damaged were still in progress and no legal action had yet been brought in connection with the accident. The expert report that was to be presented to the civil courts in order to determine the cause of the accident and to assess the respective responsibilities of the various parties involved, was expected in 2011.

Financial damages arising related to the additional costs and operating losses relating to the unavailability of the building. The nature and extent of the damages, and the details of any compensation payments had yet to be established. The directors of Greenie felt that at present, there was no requirement to record the impact of the accident in the financial statements.

Compensation agreements had been arranged with the victims, and these claims were all covered by Greenie's insurance policy. In each case, compensation paid by the insurance company was subject to a waiver of any judicial proceedings against Greenie and its insurers. If any compensation is eventually payable to third parties, this is expected to be covered by the insurance policies.

The directors of Greenie felt that the conditions for recognising a provision or disclosing a contingent liability had not been met. Therefore, Greenie did not recognise a provision in respect of the accident nor did it disclose any related contingent liability or a note setting out the nature of the accident and potential claims in its financial statements for the year ended 30 November 2010. **(6 marks)**

(b) Greenie was one of three shareholders in a regional airport Manair. As at 30 November 2010, the majority shareholder held 60.1% of voting shares, the second shareholder held 20% of voting shares and Greenie held 19.9% of the voting shares. The board of directors consisted of ten members. The majority shareholder was represented by six of the board members, while Greenie and the other shareholder were represented by two members each. A shareholders' agreement stated that certain board and shareholder resolutions required either unanimous or majority decision. There is no indication that the majority shareholder and the other shareholders act together in a common way. During the financial year, Greenie had provided Manair with maintenance and technical services and had sold the entity a software licence for $5 million. Additionally, Greenie had sent a team of management experts to give business advice to the board of Manair. Greenie did not account for its investment in Manair as an associate, because of a lack of significant influence over the entity. Greenie felt that the majority owner of Manair used its influence as the parent to control and govern its subsidiary. **(10 marks)**

(c) Greenie has issued 1 million shares of $1 nominal value for the acquisition of franchise rights at a local airport. Similar franchise rights are sold in cash transactions on a regular basis and Greenie has been offered a similar franchise right at another airport for $2.3 million. This price is consistent with other prices given the market conditions. The share price of Greenie was $2.50 at the date of the transaction. Greenie wishes to record the transaction at the nominal value of the shares issued.

Greenie also showed irredeemable preference shares as equity instruments in its statement of financial position. The terms of issue of the instruments give the holders a contractual right to an annual fixed cash dividend and the entitlement to a participating dividend based on any dividends paid on ordinary shares. Greenie felt that the presentation of the preference shares with a liability component in compliance with IAS 32 *Financial instruments: Presentation* would be so misleading in the circumstances that it would conflict with the objective of financial statements set out in the IASB's *Conceptual Framework for Financial Reporting*. The reason given by Greenie for this presentation was that the shares participated in future profits and thus had the characteristics of permanent capital because of the profit participation element of the shares. **(7 marks)**

Required:

Discuss how the above financial transactions should be dealt with in the financial statements of Greenie for the year ended 30 November 2010.

Professional marks awarded for the clarity and quality of discussion. **(2 marks)**

(Total: 25 marks)

40 CATE (JUNE 10 EXAM) *Walk in the footsteps of a top tutor*

(a) Cate is an entity in the software industry. Cate had incurred substantial losses in the financial years 31 May 2004 to 31 May 2009. In the financial year to 31 May 2010 Cate made a small profit before tax. This included significant non-operating gains. In 2009, Cate recognised a material deferred tax asset in respect of carried forward losses, which will expire during 2012. Cate again recognised the deferred tax asset in 2010 on the basis of anticipated performance in the years from 2010 to 2012, based on budgets prepared in 2010. The budgets included high growth rates in profitability. Cate argued that the budgets were realistic as there were positive indications from customers about future orders. Cate also had plans to expand sales to new markets and to sell new products whose development would be completed soon. Cate was taking measures to increase sales, implementing new programs to improve both productivity and profitability. Deferred tax assets less deferred tax liabilities represent 25% of shareholders' equity at 31 May 2010. There are no tax planning opportunities available to Cate that would create taxable profit in the near future.

(5 marks)

(b) At 31 May 2010 Cate held an investment in and had a significant influence over Bates, a public limited company. Cate had carried out an impairment test in respect of its investment in accordance with the procedures prescribed in IAS 36 *Impairment of assets*. Cate argued that fair value was the only measure applicable in this case as value-in-use was not determinable as cash flow estimates had not been produced. Cate stated that there were no plans to dispose of the shareholding and hence there was no binding sale agreement. Cate also stated that the quoted share price was not an appropriate measure when considering the fair value of Cate's significant influence on Bates. Therefore, Cate estimated the fair value of its interest in Bates through application of two measurement techniques; one based on earnings multiples and the other based on an option–pricing model. Neither of these methods supported the existence of an impairment loss as of 31 May 2010. **(5 marks)**

(c)   At 1 April 2009 Cate had a direct holding of shares giving 70% of the voting rights in Date. In May 2010, Date issued new shares, which were wholly subscribed for by a new investor. After the increase in capital, Cate retained an interest of 35% of the voting rights in its former subsidiary Date. At the same time, the shareholders of Date signed an agreement providing new governance rules for Date. Based on this new agreement, Cate was no longer to be represented on Date's board or participate in its management.

As a consequence Cate considered that its decision not to subscribe to the issue of new shares was equivalent to a decision to disinvest in Date. Cate argued that the decision not to invest clearly showed its new intention not to recover the investment in Date principally through continuing use of the asset and was considering selling the investment. Due to the fact that Date is a separate line of business (with separate cash flows, management and customers), Cate considered that the results of Date for the period to 31 May 2010 should be presented based on principles provided by IFRS 5 *Non-current assets held for sale and discontinued operations*.   **(8 marks)**

(d)   In its 2010 financial statements, Cate disclosed the existence of a voluntary fund established in order to provide a post-retirement benefit plan (Plan) to employees. Cate considers its contributions to the Plan to be voluntary, and has not recorded any related liability in its consolidated financial statements. Cate has a history of paying benefits to its former employees, even increasing them to keep pace with inflation since the commencement of the Plan. The main characteristics of the Plan are as follows:

(i)   the Plan is totally funded by Cate

(ii)   the contributions for the Plan are made periodically

(iii)   the post retirement benefit is calculated based on a percentage of the final salaries of Plan participants dependent on the years of service

(iv)   the annual contributions to the Plan are determined as a function of the fair value of the assets less the liability arising from past services.

Cate argues that it should not have to recognise the Plan because, according to the underlying contract, it can terminate its contributions to the Plan, if and when it wishes. The termination clauses of the contract establish that Cate must immediately purchase lifetime annuities from an insurance company for all the retired employees who are already receiving benefit when the termination of the contribution is communicated.   **(5 marks)**

Required:

Discuss whether the accounting treatments proposed by the company are acceptable under International Financial Reporting Standards.

Professional marks will be awarded in this question for clarity and quality of discussion.

(2 marks)

The mark allocation is shown against each of the four parts above.   **(Total: 25 marks)**

41   SELTEC (JUNE 10 EXAM) *Walk in the footsteps of a top tutor*

Seltec, a public limited company, processes and sells edible oils and uses several financial instruments to spread the risk of fluctuation in the price of the edible oils. The entity operates in an environment where the transactions are normally denominated in dollars. The functional currency of Seltec is the dollar.

(a)   The entity uses forward and futures contracts to protect it against fluctuation in the price of edible oils. Where forwards are used the company often takes delivery of the edible oil and sells it shortly afterwards. The contracts are constructed with future delivery in mind but the contracts also allow net settlement in cash as an alternative. The net settlement is based on the change in the price of the oil since the start of the contract. Seltec uses the proceeds of a net settlement to purchase a different type of oil or purchase from a different supplier. Where futures are used these sometimes relate to edible oils of a different type and market than those of Seltec's own inventory of edible oil. The company intends to apply hedge accounting to these contracts in order to protect itself from earnings volatility. Seltec has also entered into a long-term arrangement to buy oil from a foreign entity whose currency is the dinar. The commitment stipulates that the fixed purchase price will be denominated in pounds sterling.

Seltec is unsure as to the nature of derivatives and hedge accounting techniques and has asked your advice on how the above financial instruments should be dealt with in the financial statements.   **(14 marks)**

(b)   Seltec has decided to enter the retail market and has recently purchased two well-known brand names in the edible oil industry. One of the brand names has been in existence for many years and has a good reputation for quality. The other brand name is named after a famous film star who has been actively promoting the edible oil as being a healthier option than other brands of oil. This type of oil has only been on the market for a short time. Seltec is finding it difficult to estimate the useful life of the brands and therefore intends to treat the brands as having indefinite lives.

In order to sell the oil, Seltec has purchased two limited liability companies from a company that owns several retail outlets. Each entity owns retail outlets in several shopping complexes. The only assets of each entity are the retail outlets. There is no operational activity and at present the entities have no employees.

Seltec is unclear as to how the purchase of the brands and the entities should be accounted for.   **(9 marks)**

Required:

Discuss the accounting principles involved in accounting for the above transactions and how the above transactions should be treated in the financial statements of Seltec.

Professional marks will be awarded in this question for clarity and quality of discussion.

(2 marks)

The mark allocation is shown against each of the two parts above.   **(Total: 25 marks)**

42   KEY (DEC 09 EXAM) *Walk in the footsteps of a top tutor*

(a)   Key, a public limited company, is concerned about the reduction in the general availability of credit and the sudden tightening of the conditions required to obtain a loan from banks. There has been a reduction in credit availability and a rise in interest rates. It seems as though there has ceased to be a clear relationship between interest rates and credit availability, and lenders and investors are seeking less risky investments. The directors are trying to determine the practical implications for the financial statements particularly because of large write downs of assets in the banking sector, tightening of credit conditions, and falling sales and asset prices. They are particularly concerned about the impairment of assets and the market inputs to be used in impairment testing. They are afraid that they may experience significant impairment charges in the coming financial year. They are unsure as to how they should test for impairment and any considerations which should be taken into account.

Required:

Discuss the main considerations that the company should take into account when impairment testing non-current assets in the above economic climate.   (8 marks)

Professional marks will be awarded in part (a) for clarity and expression.   (2 marks)

(b)   There are specific assets on which the company wishes to seek advice. The company holds certain non-current assets, which are in a development area and carried at cost less depreciation. These assets cost $3 million on 1 June 2008 and are depreciated on the straight-line basis over their useful life of five years. An impairment review was carried out on 31 May 2009 and the projected cash flows relating to these assets were as follows:

Year to	31 May 2010	31 May 2011	31 May 2012	31 May 2013
Cash flows ($000)	280	450	500	550

The company used a discount rate of 5%. At 30 November 2009, the directors used the same cash flow projections and noticed that the resultant value in use was above the carrying amount of the assets and wished to reverse any impairment loss calculated at 31 May 2009. The government has indicated that it may compensate the company for any loss in value of the assets up to 20% of the impairment loss.

Key holds a non-current asset, which was purchased for $10 million on 1 December 2006 with an expected useful life of 10 years. On 1 December 2008, it was revalued to $8.8 million. At 30 November 2009, the asset was reviewed for impairment and written down to its recoverable amount of $5.5 million.

Key committed itself at the beginning of the financial year to selling a property that is being under-utilised following the economic downturn. As a result of the economic downturn, the property was not sold by the end of the year. The asset was actively marketed but there were no reasonable offers to purchase the asset. Key is hoping that the economic downturn will change in the future and therefore has not reduced the price of the asset.

Required:

Discuss with suitable computations, how to account for any potential impairment of the above non-current assets in the financial statements for the year ended 30 November 2009. **(15 marks)**

Note: The following discount factors may be relevant

Year 1	0.9524
Year 2	0.9070
Year 3	0.8638
Year 4	0.8227

(Total: 25 marks)

43   ARON (JUNE 09 EXAM) *Walk in the footsteps of a top tutor*

The directors of Aron, a public limited company, are worried about the challenging market conditions which the company is facing. The markets are volatile and illiquid. The central government is injecting liquidity into the economy. The directors are concerned about the significant shift towards the use of fair values in financial statements. IFRS 9 requires the initial measurement of financial instruments to be at fair value. The directors are uncertain of the relevance of fair value measurements in these current market conditions.

Required:

(a)   Briefly discuss how the fair value of financial instruments is determined, commenting on the relevance of fair value measurements for financial instruments where markets are volatile and illiquid. **(4 marks)**

(b)   Further they would like advice on accounting for the following transactions within the financial statements for the year ended 31 May 2009:

(i)   Aron issued one million convertible bonds on 1 June 2006. The bonds had a term of three years and were issued with a total fair value of $100 million which is also the par value. Interest is paid annually in arrears at a rate of 6% per annum and bonds, without the conversion option, attracted an interest rate of 9% per annum on 1 June 2006. The company incurred issue costs of $1 million. If the investor did not convert to shares they would have been redeemed at par. At maturity all of the bonds were converted into 25 million ordinary shares of $1 of Aron. No bonds could be converted before that date. The directors are uncertain how the bonds should have been accounted for up to the date of the conversion on 31 May 2009 and have been told that the impact of the issue costs is to increase the effective interest rate to 9.38%.

(6 marks)

(ii)   Aron held 3% holding of the shares in Smart, a public limited company. The investment was designated upon recognition as fair value through other comprehensive income and as at 31 May 2009 was fair valued at $5 million. The cumulative gain recognised in equity relating to this investment was $400,000. On the same day, the whole of the share capital of Smart was acquired by Given, a public limited company, and as a result, Aron received shares in Given with a fair value of $5.5 million in exchange for its holding in Smart. The company wishes to know how the exchange of shares in Smart for the shares in Given should be accounted for in its financial records.   **(4 marks)**

(iii) The functional and presentation currency of Aron is the dollar ($). Aron has a wholly owned foreign subsidiary, Gao, whose functional currency is the zloti. Gao owns a debt instrument which is held for trading, and therefore accounted for at fair value through profit or loss. In Gao's financial statements for the year ended 31 May 2008, the debt instrument was carried at its fair value of 10 million zloti.

At 31 May 2009, the fair value of the debt instrument had increased to 12 million zloti. The exchange rates were:

	Zloti to $1
31 May 2008	3
31 May 2009	2
Average rate for year to 31 May 2009	2.5

The company wishes to know how to account for this instrument in Gao's individual financial statements and also the consolidated financial statements of the group.   **(5 marks)**

(iv) Aron granted interest free loans to its employees on 1 June 2008 of $10 million. The loans will be paid back on 31 May 2010 as a single payment by the employees. The market rate of interest for a two-year loan on both of the above dates is 6% per annum. The company is unsure how to account for the loan but wishes to classify the loans as being accounted for at amortised cost under IFRS 9 *Financial instruments.* Any loss allowance would be immaterial and can be ignored.   **(4 marks)**

Required:

Discuss, with relevant computations, how the above financial instruments should be accounted for in the financial statements for the year ended 31 May 2009.

Note: The mark allocation is shown against each of the transactions above.

Note: The following discount and annuity factors may be of use

	Discount factors			Annuity factors		
	6%	9%	9.38%	6%	9%	9.38%
1 year	0.9434	0.9174	0.9142	0.9434	0.9174	0.9174
2 years	0.8900	0.8417	0.8358	1.8334	1.7591	1.7500
3 years	0.8396	0.7722	0.7642	2.6730	2.5313	2.5142

Professional marks will be awarded in this question for clarity and quality of discussion.   **(2 marks)**

(Total: 25 marks)

44 MARRGRETT (DEC 08 EXAM) *Walk in the footsteps of a top tutor*

 Timed question with Online tutor debrief

Marrgrett, a public limited company, is currently planning to acquire and sell interests in other entities and has asked for advice on the impact of IFRS 3 (Revised) *Business combinations* and IFRS 10 *Consolidated financial statements*.

The company is considering purchasing additional shares in an associate, Josey, a public limited company. The holding will increase from 30% stake to 70% stake by offering the shareholders of Josey, cash and shares in Marrgrett. Marrgrett anticipates that it will pay $5 million in transaction costs to lawyers and bankers. Josey had previously been the subject of a management buyout. In order that the current management shareholders may remain in the business, Marrgrett is going to offer them share options in Josey subject to them remaining in employment for two years after the acquisition. Additionally, Marrgrett will offer the same shareholders, shares in the holding company which are contingent upon a certain level of profitability being achieved by Josey. Each shareholder will receive shares of the holding company up to a value of $50,000, if Josey achieves a pre-determined rate of return on capital employed for the next two years.

Josey has several marketing-related intangible assets that are used primarily in marketing or promotion of its products. These include trade names, internet domain names and non-competition agreements. These are not currently recognised in Josey's financial statements.

Marrgrett does not wish to measure the non-controlling interest in subsidiaries on the basis of the proportionate interest in the identifiable net assets, but wishes to use the 'full goodwill' method on the transaction. Marrgrett is unsure as to whether this method is mandatory, or what the effects are of recognising 'full goodwill'. Additionally the company is unsure as to whether the nature of the consideration would affect the calculation of goodwill.

To finance the acquisition of Josey, Marrgrett intends to dispose of a partial interest in two subsidiaries. Marrgrett will retain control of the first subsidiary but will sell the controlling interest in the second subsidiary which will become an associate. Because of its plans to change the overall structure of the business, Marrgrett wishes to recognise a re-organisation provision at the date of the business combination.

Required:

Discuss the principles and the nature of the accounting treatment of the above plans under International Financial Reporting Standards setting out any impact that IFRS 3 (Revised) *Business combinations* **and IFRS 10** *Consolidated financial statements* **might have on the earnings and net assets of the group.**

Note: This requirement includes 2 professional marks for the quality of the discussion.

(Total: 25 marks)

 Calculate your allowed time, allocate the time to the separate parts

45 NORMAN (JUN 08 EXAM) *Online question assistance*

(a) Norman, a public limited company, has three business segments which are currently reported in its financial statements. Norman is an international hotel group which reports to management on the basis of region. The results of the regional segments for the year ended 31 May 2008 are as follows:

Region	Revenue		Segment results	Segment	Segment
	External	Internal	profit/(loss)	assets	liabilities
	$m	$m	$m	$m	$m
Europe	200	3	(10)	300	200
South East Asia	300	2	60	800	300
North America	460	4	103	1,900	1,260
Central America	30	1	1	80	100
Others	10	–	1	20	40

There were no significant intercompany balances in the segment assets and liabilities. The hotels are located in capital cities in the various regions, and the company sets individual performance indicators for each hotel based on its city location.

Required:

Discuss the principles in IFRS 8 *Operating segments* for the determination of a company's reportable operating segments and how these principles would be applied for Norman plc using the information given above. **(11 marks)**

(b) In May 2008, Norman started issuing vouchers to customers when they stay in its hotels. The vouchers entitle the customers to a discount on a subsequent room booking in June, July or August 2008. Past experience of similar schemes suggests that only two in five vouchers are redeemed by the customer. Sales of rooms in May 2008 amounted to $30 million and have been fully paid for. Norman issued 250,000 vouchers entitling customers to discounts of $5 million. **(6 marks)**

Norman has obtained a significant amount of grant income for the development of hotels in Europe. The grants have been received from government bodies and relate to the size of the hotel which has been built by the grant assistance. The intention of the grant income was to create jobs in areas where there was significant unemployment. The grants received of $70 million will have to be repaid if the cost of building the hotels is less than $500 million. **(6 marks)**

Required:

Discuss how the above income would be treated in the financial statements of Norman for the year ended 31 May 2008.

Professional marks will be awarded in this question for clarity and quality of discussion. **(2 marks)**

(Total: 25 marks)

 Online question assistance

46   MACALJOY (DEC 07 EXAM)   *Online question assistance*

Macaljoy, a public limited company, is a leading support services company which focuses on the building industry. The company would like advice on how to treat certain items under IAS 19 *Employee benefits* and IAS 37 *Provisions, contingent liabilities and contingent assets*. The company operates the Macaljoy (2006) Pension Plan which commenced on 1 November 2006 and the Macaljoy (1990) Pension Plan, which was closed to new entrants from 31 October 2006, but which was open to future service accrual for the employees already in the scheme. The assets of the schemes are held separately from those of the company in funds under the control of trustees. The following information relates to the two schemes:

Macaljoy (1990) Pension Plan

The terms of the plan are as follows:

(i)   Employees contribute 6% of their salaries to the plan

(ii)   Macaljoy contributes, currently, the same amount to the plan for the benefit of the employees

(iii)   On retirement, employees are guaranteed a pension which is based upon the number of years service with the company and their final salary.

The following details relate to the plan in the year to 31 October 2007:

	$m
Present value of obligation at 1 November 2006	200
Present value of obligation at 31 October 2007	240
Fair value of plan assets at 1 November 2006	190
Fair value of plan assets at 31 October 2007	225
Current service cost	20
Pension benefits paid	19
Total contributions paid to the scheme for year to 31 October 2007	17

Macaljoy (2006) Pension Plan

Under the terms of the plan, Macaljoy does not guarantee any return on the contributions paid into the fund. The company's legal and constructive obligation is limited to the amount that is contributed to the fund. The following details relate to this scheme:

	$m
Fair value of plan assets at 31 October 2007	21
Contributions paid by company for year to 31 October 2007	10
Contributions paid by employees for year to 31 October 2007	10

The discount rates for the two plans are:

	1 November 2006	31 October 2007
Discount rate	5%	6%

The company would like advice on how to treat the two pension plans, for the year ended 31 October 2007, together with an explanation of the differences between a defined contribution plan and a defined benefit plan.

Warranties

Additionally the company manufactures and sells building equipment on which it gives a standard one year warranty to all customers. The company has extended the warranty to two years for certain major customers and has insured against the cost of the second year of the warranty. The warranty has been extended at nil cost to the customer. The claims made under the extended warranty are made in the first instance against Macaljoy and then Macaljoy in turn makes a counter claim against the insurance company. Past experience has shown that 80% of the building equipment will not be subject to warranty claims in the first year, 15% will have minor defects and 5% will require major repair. Macaljoy estimates that in the second year of the warranty, 20% of the items sold will have minor defects and 10% will require major repair.

In the year to 31 October 2007, the following information is relevant:

	Standard warranty (units)	Extended warranty (units)	Selling price per unit (both) ($)
Sales	2,000	5,000	1,000
		Major repair $	Minor defect $
Cost of repair (average)		500	100

Assume that sales of equipment are on 31 October 2007 and any warranty claims are made on 31 October in the year of the claim. Assume a risk adjusted discount rate of 4%.

Required:

Draft a report suitable for presentation to the directors of Macaljoy which:

(a) (i) **Discusses the nature of and differences between a defined contribution plan and a defined benefit plan with specific reference to the company's two schemes.** **(7 marks)**

   (ii) **Shows the accounting treatment for the two Macaljoy pension plans for the year ended 31 October 2007 under IAS 19 *Employee benefits*.** **(7 marks)**

(b) (i) **Discusses the principles involved in accounting for claims made under the above warranty provision.** **(6 marks)**

   (ii) **Shows the accounting treatment for the above warranty provision under IAS 37 *Provisions, contingent liabilities and contingent assets* for the year ended 31 October 2007.** **(3 marks)**

   Appropriateness of the format and presentation of the report and communication of advice. **(2 marks)**

(Total: 25 marks)

 Online question assistance

47   WADER (JUNE 07 EXAM)

Wader, a public limited company, has a year end of 31 May 20X7. The following information is relevant:

(a)   Wader's receivables are short-term and do not contain a significant financing component. Using historical observed default rates, updated for changes in forward-looking estimates, Wader estimates the following default rates for its trade receivables that are outstanding as at 31 May 20X7:

	Not overdue	1–30 days overdue	31–60 days overdue	61+ days overdue
Default rate	0.5%	1.5%	6.1%	16.5%

The trade receivables of Wader as at 31 May 20X7 are as follows:

	Gross carrying amount ($m)
Not overdue	10.1
1 – 30 days overdue	4.3
31 – 60 days overdue	1.6
61 + days overdue	1.0

Wader has recognised a loss allowance of $0.2 million in respect of its trade receivables.   **(6 marks)**

(b)   Wader is assessing the valuation of its inventory. It has a significant quantity of a product and needs to evaluate its value for the purposes of the statement of financial position. Sales of the product are high, but it incurs high production costs. The reason for its success is that a sales commission of 20% of the list selling price is paid to the sales force. The following details relate to this product:

	$ per unit
List price – normal selling price	50.0
Allocation of customer discounts on selling price	2.5
Warehouse overheads until estimated sale date	4.0
Basic salaries of sales team	2.0
Cost of product	35.0

The product is collected from the warehouses of Wader by the customer.   **(4 marks)**

(c)   Wader is reviewing the accounting treatment of its buildings. The company uses the 'revaluation model' for its buildings. The buildings had originally cost $10 million on 1 June 20X5 and had a useful economic life of 20 years. They are being depreciated on a straight line basis to a nil residual value. The buildings were revalued downwards on 31 May 20X6 to $8 million which was the buildings' recoverable amount. At 31 May 20X7 the value of the buildings had risen to $11 million which is to be included in the financial statements. The company is unsure how to treat the above events.   **(6 marks)**

(d) Wader has decided to close one of its overseas branches. A board meeting was held on 30 April 20X7 when a detailed formal plan was presented to the board. The plan was formalised and accepted at that meeting. Letters were sent out to customers, suppliers and workers on 15 May 20X7 and meetings were held prior to the year-end to determine the issues involved in the closure. The plan is to be implemented in June 20X7. The company wish to provide $8 million for the restructuring but are unsure as to whether this is permissible. Additionally there was an issue raised at one of the meetings. The operations of the branch are to be moved to another country from June 20X7 but the operating lease on the present buildings of the branch is non-cancellable and runs for another two years, until 31 May 20X9. The annual rent of the buildings is $150,000 payable in arrears on 31 May and the lessor has offered to take a single payment of $270,000 on 31 May 20X8 to settle the outstanding amount owing and terminate the lease on that date. Wader has additionally obtained permission to sublet the building at a rental of $100,000 per year, payable in advance on 1 June. The company needs advice on how to treat the above under IAS 37 *Provisions, contingent liabilities and contingent assets.* **(7 marks)**

Required:

Discuss, with suitable calculations, the accounting treatments of the above items in the financial statements for the year ended 31 May 20X7.

Note: A discount rate of 5% should be used where necessary.

Professional marks will be awarded in this question for clarity and quality of discussion.

(2 marks)

(Total: 25 marks)

48 ROUTER (JUNE 07 EXAM) *Online question assistance*

(a) Router, a public limited company operates in the entertainment industry. It recently agreed with a television company to make a film which will be broadcast on the television company's network. The fee agreed for the film was $5 million with a further $100,000 to be paid every time the film is shown on the television company's channels. It is hoped that it will be shown on four occasions. The film was completed at a cost of $4 million and delivered to the television company on 1 April 20X7. The television company paid the fee of $5 million on 30 April 20X7 but indicated that the quality of the film, whilst satisfactory, was not as good as expected. The directors of Router are unsure how much revenue should be recognised in the financial statements for the year ended 31 May 20X7. **(6 marks)**

(b) Router has a number of film studios and office buildings. The office buildings are in prestigious areas whereas the film studios are located in 'out of town' locations. At present both types of buildings are valued using the 'revaluation model'. The management of Router wish to apply the 'revaluation model' to the office buildings and the 'cost model' to the film studios in the year ended 31 May 20X7.

During the year, Router set up a theme park. In this case only, the land and buildings on the park are leased on a single lease from a third party. The lease term is for 30 years, which is the remaining useful economic life of the buildings. The directors are unsure whether the land element prevents the lease from being classified as a finance lease. **(6 marks)**

(c) At 1 June 20X6, Router held a 25% shareholding in a film distribution company, Wireless, a public limited company. On 1 January 20X7, Router sold a 15% holding in Wireless thus reducing its investment to a 10% holding. Router no longer exercises significant influence over Wireless. Immediately before that sale, the carrying value of the interest in Wireless in the group financial statements was $55 million. Router received $40 million for its sale of the 15% holding in Wireless. At 1 January 20X7, the fair value of the remaining investment in Wireless was $23 million and at 31 May 20X7 the fair value was $26 million.   **(6 marks)**

(d) Additionally Router purchased 60% of the ordinary shares of a radio station, Playtime, a public limited company, on 31 May 20X7. The remaining 40% of the ordinary shares are owned by a competitor company who owns a substantial number of warrants issued by Playtime which are currently exercisable. If these warrants are exercised, they will result in Router only owning 35% of the voting shares of Playtime.   **(5 marks)**

Required:

Discuss how the above items should be dealt with in the group financial statements of Router for the year ended 31 May 20X7.

Professional marks will be awarded in this question for clarity and quality of discussion.

(2 marks)

(Total: 25 marks)

 Online question assistance

---

49   EGIN (JUNE 06 EXAM)

On 1 June 20X5, Egin, a public limited company, was formed out of the re-organisation of a group of companies with foreign operations. The directors require advice on the disclosure of related party information but are reluctant to disclose information as they feel that such transactions are a normal feature of business and need not be disclosed.

Under the new group structure, Egin owns 80% of Briars, 60% of Doye, and 30% of Eye. Egin exercises significant influence over Eye. The directors of Egin are also directors of Briars and Doye but only one director of Egin sits on the management board of Eye. The management board of Eye comprises five directors. Originally the group comprised five companies but the fifth company, Tang, which was a 70% subsidiary of Egin, was sold on 31 January 20X6. There were no transactions between Tang and the Egin Group during the year to 31 May 20X6. 30% of the shares of Egin are owned by another company, Atomic, which exerts significant influence over Egin. The remaining 40% of the shares of Doye are owned by Spade.

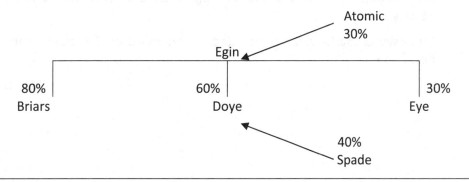

During the current financial year to 31 May 20X6, Doye has sold a significant amount of plant and equipment to Spade at the normal selling price for such items. The directors of Egin have proposed that where related party relationships are determined and sales are at normal selling price, any disclosures will state that prices charged to related parties are made on an arm's length basis.

The directors are unsure how to treat certain transactions relating to their foreign subsidiary, Briars. Egin purchased 80% of the ordinary share capital of Briars on 1 June 20X5 for 50 million euros when its net assets were fair valued at 45 million euros, with goodwill measured on a proportion of net assets basis. At 31 May 20X6, it is established that goodwill is impaired by 3 million euros. Additionally, at the date of acquisition, Egin had made an interest free loan to Briars of $10 million. The loan is to be repaid on 31 May 20X7. An equivalent loan would normally carry an interest rate of 6% taking into account Briars' credit rating.

The exchange rates were as follows:

	Euros to $
1 June 20X5	2.0
31 May 20X6	2.5
Average rate for year	2.3

Financial liabilities of the Group are normally measured at amortised cost.

One of the directors of Briars who is not on the management board of Egin owns the whole of the share capital of a company, Blue, that sells goods at market price to Briars. The director is in charge of the production at Briars and also acts as a consultant to the management board of the group.

Required:

(a)　(i)　Discuss why it is important to disclose related party transactions, explaining the criteria which determine a related party relationship.　**(4 marks)**

　　　(ii)　Describe the nature of any related party relationships and transactions which exists:

　　　　　–　within the Egin Group including Tang　**(4 marks)**

　　　　　–　between Spade and the Egin Group　**(3 marks)**

　　　　　–　between Atomic and the Egin Group　**(3 marks)**

　　　　　commenting on whether transactions should be described as being at 'arm's length'.

(b)　Describe with suitable calculations how the goodwill arising on the acquisition of Briars will be dealt with in the group financial statements and how the loan to Briars should be treated in the financial statements of Briars for the year ended 31 May 20X6.　**(9 marks)**

　　Professional marks will be awarded in this question for clarity and quality of discussion.　**(2 marks)**

(Total: 25 marks)

50   TYRE (JUNE 06 EXAM)

Tyre, a public limited company, operates in the vehicle retailing sector. The company is currently preparing its financial statements for the year ended 31 May 20X6 and has asked for advice on how to deal with the following items:

(i)   Tyre requires customers to pay a deposit of 20% of the purchase price when placing an order for a vehicle. If the customer cancels the order, the deposit is not refundable and Tyre retains it. If the order cannot be fulfilled by Tyre, the company repays the full amount of the deposit to the customer. The balance of the purchase price becomes payable on the delivery of the vehicle when the title to the goods passes. Tyre proposes to recognise the revenue from the deposits immediately and the balance of the purchase price when the goods are delivered to the customer. The cost of sales for the vehicle is recognised when the balance of the purchase price is paid. Additionally, Tyre had sold a fleet of cars to Hub and gave Hub a discount of 30% of the retail price on the transaction. The discount given is normal for this type of transaction. Tyre has given Hub a buyback option which entitles Hub to require Tyre to repurchase the vehicles after three years for 40% of the purchase price. The normal economic life of the vehicles is five years and it is believed that the customer has a significant economic inventive to exercise the buyback option.   **(8 marks)**

(ii)   The property of the former administrative centre of Tyre is owned by the company. Tyre had decided in the year that the property was surplus to requirements and demolished the building on 10 June 20X6. After demolition, the company will have to carry out remedial environmental work, which is a legal requirement resulting from the demolition. It was intended that the land would be sold after the remedial work had been carried out. However, land prices are currently increasing in value and, therefore, the company has decided that it will not sell the land immediately. Tyres uses the 'cost model' in IAS 16 *Property, plant and equipment* and has owned the property for many years.   **(7 marks)**

(iii)   Tyre has entered into two new long lease property agreements for two major retail outlets. Annual rentals are paid under these agreements. Tyre has had to pay a premium to enter into these agreements because of the outlets' location. Tyre feels that the premiums paid are justifiable because of the increase in revenue that will occur because of the outlets' location. Tyre has analysed the leases and has decided that one is a finance lease and one is an operating lease but the company is unsure as to how to treat this premium.   **(5 marks)**

(iv)   Tyre recently undertook a sales campaign whereby customers can obtain free car accessories, by presenting a coupon, which has been included in an advertisement in a national newspaper, on the purchase of a vehicle. The offer is valid for a limited time period from 1 January 20X6 until 31 July 20X6. The management are unsure as to how to treat this offer in the financial statements for the year ended 31 May 20X6.   **(5 marks)**

Required:

Advise the directors of Tyre on how to treat the above items in the financial statements for the year ended 31 May 20X6.

(The mark allocation is shown against each of the above items.)   **(Total: 25 marks)**

51   PROCHAIN (JUNE 06 EXAM)

Prochain, a public limited company, operates in the fashion industry and has a financial year-end of 31 May 20X6. The company sells its products in department stores throughout the world. Prochain insists on creating its own selling areas within the department stores which are called 'model areas'. Prochain is allocated space in the department store where it can display and market its fashion goods. The company feels that this helps to promote its merchandise. Prochain pays for all the costs of the 'model areas' including design, decoration and construction costs. The areas are used for approximately two years after which the company has to dismantle the 'model areas'. The costs of dismantling the 'model areas' are normally 20% of the original construction cost and the elements of the area are worthless when dismantled. The current accounting practice followed by Prochain is to charge the full cost of the 'model areas' against profit or loss in the year when the area is dismantled. The accumulated cost of the 'model areas' shown in the statement of financial position at 31 May 20X6 is $20 million. The company has estimated that the average age of the 'model areas' is eight months at 31 May 20X6.   **(7 marks)**

Prochain acquired 100% of a sports goods and clothing manufacturer, Badex, a private limited company, and on 1 June 20X5. Prochain incurred legal fees of $2 million in respect of the acquisition. Prochain intends to develop its own brand of sports clothing which it will sell in the department stores. The shareholders of Badex valued the company at $125 million based upon profit forecasts which assumed significant growth in the demand for the 'Badex' brand name. Prochain had taken a more conservative view of the value of the company and estimated the fair value to be in the region of $108 million to $120 million of which $20 million relates to the brand name 'Badex'. Prochain is only prepared to pay the full purchase price if profits from the sale of 'Badex' clothing and sports goods reach the forecast levels. The agreed purchase price was $100 million plus two potential further payments. The first being $10 million in two years on 31 May 20X7. This is a guaranteed payment of $10 million in cash with no performance conditions. The second payment is contingent on certain profits target being met. At the date of acquisition it was assessed that the fair value of such consideration was $5 million.   **(8 marks)**

After the acquisition of Badex, Prochain started developing its own sports clothing brand 'Pro'. The expenditure in the period to 31 May 20X6 was as follows:

Period from	Expenditure type	$m
1 June 20X5 – 31 August 20X5	Research as to the extent of the market	3
1 September 20X5	Prototype clothing and goods design	4
1 December 20X5 – 31 January 20X6	Employee costs in refinement of products	2
1 February 20X6 – 30 April 20X6	Development work undertaken to finalise design of product	5
1 May 20X6 – 31 May 20X6	Production and launch of products	6
		20

The costs of the production and launch of the products include the cost of upgrading the existing machinery ($3 million), market research costs ($2 million) and staff training costs ($1 million).

Currently an intangible asset of $20 million is shown in the financial statements for the year ended 31 May 20X6. **(6 marks)**

Prochain owns a number of prestigious apartments which it leases to famous persons who are under a contract of employment to promote its fashion clothing. The apartments are let at below the market rate. The lease terms are short and are normally for six months. The leases terminate when the contracts for promoting the clothing terminate. Prochain wishes to account for the apartments as investment properties with the difference between the market rate and actual rental charged to be recognised as an employee benefit expense.

(4 marks)

Assume a discount rate of 5.5% where necessary.

Required:

Discuss how the above items should be dealt with in the financial statements of Prochain for the year ended 31 May 20X6 under International Financial Reporting Standards.

(Total: 25 marks)

52 PANEL (DEC 05 EXAM)

The directors of Panel, a public limited company, are reviewing the procedures for the calculation of the deferred tax provision for their company. Panel is adopting International Financial Reporting Standards for the first time as at 31 October 20X5 and the directors are unsure how the deferred tax provision will be calculated in its financial statements ended on that date including the opening provision at 1 November 20X3.

Required:

(a) (i) **Explain how changes in reporting standards are likely to have an impact on the provision for deferred taxation under IAS 12 *Income taxes*.** **(5 marks)**

(ii) **Describe the basis for the calculation of the provision for deferred taxation on first time adoption of IFRSs including the provision in the opening IFRS statement of financial position.** **(4 marks)**

Additionally the directors wish to know how the provision for deferred taxation would be calculated in the following situations under IAS 12 *Income taxes*:

(i) On 1 November 20X3, the company had granted ten million share options worth $40 million subject to a two year vesting period. Local tax law allows a tax deduction at the exercise date of the intrinsic value of the options. The intrinsic value of the ten million share options at 31 October 20X4 was $16 million and at 31 October 20X5 was $46 million. The increase in the share price in the year to 31 October 20X5 could not be foreseen at 31 October 20X4. The options were exercised at 31 October 20X5. The directors are unsure how to account for deferred taxation on this transaction for the years ended 31 October 20X4 and 31 October 20X5.

(ii) Panel is leasing plant under a finance lease over a five year period. The asset was recorded at the present value of the minimum lease payments of $12 million at the inception of the lease which was 1 November 20X4. The asset is depreciated on a straight line basis over the five years and has no residual value. The annual lease payments are $3 million payable in arrears on 31 October and the effective interest rate is 8% per annum. The directors have not leased an asset under a finance lease before and are unsure as to its treatment for deferred taxation. The company can claim a tax deduction for the annual rental payment as the finance lease does not qualify for tax relief.

(iii) A wholly owned overseas subsidiary, Pins, a limited liability company, sold goods costing $7 million to Panel on 1 September 20X5, and these goods had not been sold by Panel before the year-end. Panel had paid $9 million for these goods. The directors do not understand how this transaction should be dealt with in the financial statements of the subsidiary and the group for taxation purposes. Pins pays tax locally at 30%.

(iv) Nails, a limited liability company, is a wholly owned subsidiary of Panel, and is a cash generating unit in its own right. The value of the property, plant and equipment of Nails at 31 October 20X5 was $6 million and purchased goodwill was $1 million before any impairment loss. The company had no other assets or liabilities. An impairment loss of $1.8 million had occurred at 31 October 20X5. The tax base of the property, plant and equipment of Nails was $4 million as at 31 October 20X5. The directors wish to know how the impairment loss will affect the deferred tax provision for the year. Impairment losses are not an allowable expense for taxation purposes.

Assume a tax rate of 30%.

Required:

(b) Discuss, with suitable computations, how the situations (i) to (iv) above will impact on the accounting for deferred tax under IAS 12 *Income taxes* in the group financial statements of Panel. (16 marks)

(The situations in (i) to (iv) above carry equal marks) (Total: 25 marks)

53 VIDENT (JUNE 05 EXAM)

The directors of Vident, a public limited company, are reviewing the impact of IFRS 2 *Share-based payment* on the financial statements for the year ended 31 May 20X5 as they will be applying the reporting standard for the first time. However, the directors of Vident are unhappy about having to apply the standard and have put forward the following arguments as to why they should not recognise an expense for share-based payments:

(i) They feel that share options have no cost to their company and, therefore, there should be no expense recognised in profit or loss.

(ii) They do not feel that the expense arising from share options under IFRS 2 actually meets the definition of an expense under the *Framework* document.

(iii) The directors are worried about the dual impact of the IFRS on earnings per share, as an expense is recognised in profit or loss and the impact of share options is recognised in the diluted earnings per share calculation.

(iv) They feel that accounting for share-based payment may have an adverse effect on their company and may discourage it from introducing new share option plans.

The following share option schemes were in existence at 31 May 20X5:

Director's name	Grant date	Options granted	Fair value of options at grant date $	Exercise price $	Performance conditions	Vesting date	Exercise date
J. Van Heflin	1 June 20X3	20,000	5	4.50	A	06/20X5	06/20X6
R. Ashworth	1 June 20X4	50,000	6	6	B	06/20X7	06/20X8

The price of the company's shares at 31 May 20X5 is $12 per share and at 31 May 20X4 was $12.50 per share.

The performance conditions which apply to the exercise of executive share options are as follows:

Performance Condition A

The share options do not vest if the growth in the company's earnings per share (EPS) for the year is less than 4%. The rate of growth of EPS was 4.5% (20X3), 4.1% (20X4), 4.2% (20X5). The directors must still work for the company on the vesting date.

Performance Condition B

The share options do not vest until the share price has increased from its value of $12.50 at the grant date (1 June 20X4) to above $13.50. The director must still work for the company on the vesting date.

No directors have left the company since the issue of the share options and none are expected to leave before June 20X7. The shares vest and can be exercised on the first day of the due month.

The directors are uncertain about the deferred tax implications of adopting IFRS 2. Vident operates in a country where a tax allowance will not arise until the options are exercised and the tax allowance will be based on the option's intrinsic value at the exercise date.

Assume a tax rate of 30%.

Required:

Draft a report to the directors of Vident setting out:

(a)   the reasons why share-based payments should be recognised in financial statements and why the directors' arguments are unacceptable   **(9 marks)**

(b)   a discussion (with suitable calculations) as to how the directors' share options would be accounted for in the financial statements for the year ended 31 May 20X5, including the adjustment to opening balances   **(9 marks)**

(c)   the deferred tax implications (with suitable calculations) for the company which arise from the recognition of a remuneration expense for the directors' share options.   **(7 marks)**

(Total: 25 marks)

54 ARTWRIGHT

Artwright, a public limited company, produces artefacts made from precious metals.

(i)   Artwright has entered into three derivative contracts during the year ended 30 November 20X4, details of which are as follows:

	Initial recognition at fair value	Fair value at the year-end	Reason
A	Nil	$20m (liability)	Artwright believes that oil prices are due to rise in the future so during the year has entered into oil futures contract to buy oil at a fixed price. Artwright has no exposure to oil prices in the course of its business. In fact, oil prices have fallen resulting in the loss at the year-end.
B	$1m	$9m (liability)	Artwright has an investment in equity designated to be measured at fair value through other comprehensive income. Artwright is concerned the investment will fall in value and it wishes to cover this risk. Thus during the year it has entered into derivative B to cover any fall in value and designated this as a hedging instrument as part of a fair value hedge. In fact, the asset has risen in value by $8.5 million.
C	Nil	$25m (asset)	Artwright is concerned about the potential for raw material prices to rise. It wishes to cover this risk that future costs will rise over the next two to three years. Thus it has entered into derivative C – a futures contract. This arrangement has been designated as a cash flow hedge. At the year-end the raw material prices have risen, potentially giving the company an increased future cost of $24 million.

All designated hedges meet the effectiveness criteria outlined in IFRS 9 *Financial Instruments*.

(ii)   On 1 December 20X3, Artwright purchased $10 million of bonds at par. These bonds had been issued by Winston, an entity operating in the video games industry. The bonds were due to be redeemed at a premium on 30 November 20X6, with Artwright also receiving 5% interest annually in arrears. The effective rate of interest on the bonds was 15%. Artwright often holds bonds until the redemption date, but will sell prior to maturity if investments with higher returns become available. Winston's bonds were deemed to have a low credit risk at inception.

On 30 November 20X4, Artwright received the interest due on the bonds. However, there were wider concerns about the economic performance and financial stability of the video games industry. As a result, there has been a fall in the fair value of bonds issued by Winston and similar companies. The fair value of the Artwright's investment at 30 November 20X4 was $9 million. Nonetheless, based on Winston's strong working capital management and market optimism about the entity's forthcoming products, the bonds were still deemed to have a low credit risk.

The financial controller of Artwright calculated the following expected credit losses for the Winston bonds as at 30 November 20X4:

12 month expected credit losses	$0.2m
Lifetime expected credit losses	$0.4m

Required:

(a) **Outline the hedge effectiveness criteria according to IFRS 9 *Financial Instruments* and discuss how each of the three derivatives would be accounted for in the financial statements for the year ended 30 November 20X4.** **(14 marks)**

(b) **Discuss how the investment in the bonds of Winston should be accounted for in the year ended 30 November 20X4.** **(9 marks)**

Professional marks will be awarded in this question for clarity and quality of discussion.

(2 marks)

(Total: 25 marks)

55   LUCKY DAIRY

The Lucky Dairy, a public limited company, produces milk for supply to various customers. It is responsible for producing twenty five per cent of the country's milk consumption. The company owns 150 farms and has a stock of 70,000 cows and 35,000 heifers (young female cows) which are being raised to produce milk in the future. The farms produce 2.5 million kilograms of milk per annum and normally hold an inventory of 50,000 kilograms of milk.

The herds comprise at 31 May 20X2:

70,000	–	3 year old cows (all purchased on or before 1 June 20X1)
25,000	–	heifers (average age 1½ years old – purchased 1 December 20X1)
10,000	–	heifers (average age 2 years – purchased 1 June 20X1)

There were no animals born or sold in the year. The per unit values less estimated costs to sell were as follows:

	$
2 year old animal at 1 June 20X1	50
1 year old animal at 1 June 20X1 and 1 December 20X1	40
3 year old animal at 31 May 20X2	60
1½ year old animal at 31 May 20X2	46
2 year old animal at 31 May 20X2	55
1 year old animal at 31 May 20X2	42

The company has had a difficult year in financial and operating terms. The cows had contracted a disease at the beginning of the financial year which had been passed on in the food chain to a small number of consumers. The publicity surrounding this event had caused a drop in the consumption of milk and as a result the dairy was holding 500,000 kilograms of milk in storage.

The government had stated, on 1 April 20X2, that it was prepared to compensate farmers for the drop in the price and consumption of milk. An official government letter was received on 6 June 20X2, stating that $1.5 million will be paid to Lucky on 1 August 20X2. Additionally on 1 May 20X2, Lucky had received a letter from its lawyer saying that legal proceedings had been started against the company by the persons affected by the disease.

The company's lawyers have advised them that they feel that it is probable that they will be found liable and that the costs involved may reach $2 million. The lawyers, however, feel that the company may receive additional compensation from a government fund if certain quality control procedures had been carried out by the company. However, the lawyers will only state that the compensation payment is 'possible'.

The company's activities are controlled in three geographical locations, Dale, Shire and Ham. The only region affected by the disease was Dale and the government has decided that it is to restrict the milk production of that region significantly. Lucky estimates that the discounted future cash income from the present herds of cattle in the region amounts to $1.2 million, taking into account the government restriction order. Lucky was not sure that the fair value of the cows in the region could be measured reliably at the date of purchase because of the problems with the diseased cattle. The cows in this region amounted to 20,000 in number and the heifers 10,000 in number. All of the animals were purchased on 1 June 20X1. Lucky has had an offer of $1 million for all of the animals in the Dale region (net of point of sale costs) and $2 million for the sale of the farms in the region. However, there was a minority of directors who opposed the planned sale and it was decided to defer the public announcement of sale pending the outcome of the possible receipt of the government compensation. The Board had decided that the potential sale plan was highly confidential but a national newspaper had published an article stating that the sale may occur and that there would be many people who would lose their employment. The Board approved the planned sale of Dale farms on 31 May 20X2.

The directors of Lucky have approached your firm for professional advice on the above matters.

Required:

Advise the directors on how the biological assets and produce of Lucky should be accounted for under IAS 41 _Agriculture_ and discuss the implications for the published financial statements of the above events.

You should produce a table which shows the changes in value of the cattle stock for the year to 31 May 20X2 due to price change and physical change excluding the Dale region as at 31 May 20X2. Ignore the effects of taxation. **(Total: 25 marks)**

56 SHIRES PROPERTY CONSTRUCTION

Shires Property Construction found itself in financial difficulty. The following is a trial balance at 31 December 2010 extracted from the books of the company.

	$
Land	156,000
Building (net)	27,246
Equipment (net)	10,754
Intangible asset – brand	60,000
Financial assets at fair value through profit or loss	27,000
Inventories	120,247
Trade receivables	70,692
Deficit on retained earnings	39,821
	511,760

	$
Equity shares of $1 each	200,000
5% Unsecured loan	70,000
8% Debenture loan 2013 (secured)	80,000
Interest payable on debenture	12,800
Trade payables	96,247
Loans from directors	16,000
Bank overdraft	36,713
	511,760

The authorised share capital is 200,000 equity shares of $1 each.

During a meeting of shareholders and directors, it was decided to carry out a scheme of internal reconstruction. The following scheme has been agreed:

(1)   Each equity share is to be redesignated as a share of $0.25.

(2)   The existing $70,000 unsecured loan is to be redeemed in part by an issue of 140,000 equity shares of $0.25 each at nominal value, with the balance of the loan having an increased rate of interest of 8%.

(3)   The equity shareholders are to accept a reduction in the nominal value of their shares from $1 to $0.25, and to subscribe for a new issue on the basis of 1 for 1 at a price of $0.30 per share.

(4)   The debenture loan is secured against the land and buildings owned by Shires Property Construction. The debenture holders are to accept 20,000 equity shares of $0.25 each in lieu of the interest payable. It is agreed that the value of the interest liability is equivalent to the nominal value of the shares issued. The interest rate is to be increased to 9.5%. A further $9,000 of this 9.5% debenture is to be issued and taken up by the existing holders at par value.

(5) $6,000 of directors' loans is to be cancelled. The balance is to be settled by issue of 10,000 equity shares of $0.25 each.

(6)   The brand and the deficit on retained earnings are to be written off.

(7)   The financial assets are to be sold at their fair value of $60,000.

(8)   The bank overdraft is to be repaid.

(9) $46,000 is to be paid to trade payables now and the balance at quarterly intervals.

(10)   10% of the trade receivables are to be written off.

(11)   The remaining assets were professionally valued and should be included in the books and accounts as follows:

	$
Land	90,000
Building	80,000
Equipment	10,000
Inventories	50,000

(12)   It is expected that, due to changed conditions and new management, operating profits will be earned at the rate of $50,000 p.a. after depreciation but before interest and tax. Due to losses brought forward and tax allowances it is unlikely that any tax liability will arise until 2013.

Required:

(a)   Prepare the statement of financial position of the Shires Property immediately after the reconstruction.   **(12 marks)**

(b)   Illustrate and explain how the anticipated operating profits will be divided amongst the interested parties before and after the reconstruction. (Ignore the deficit on retained earnings in determining whether any dividends are payable).   **(8 marks)**

(c)   Comment on the capital structure of the Shires Property subsequent to reconstruction.   **(5 marks)**

(Total: 25 marks)

57   BOOMERANG

Boomerang plc was incorporated as an importer of Australian decorations and ornaments which it customises and packages before selling in the UK. The company sells its products in the luxury market and had traded profitably until four years ago when the global financial crisis began to have an impact on the business. Since that date it has suffered continuous losses which have resulted in a negative balance on retained earnings.

The company has been developing a new market for its products in concession arrangements for floor space with high-quality retailers in selected locations. The directors expect that Boomerang will return to profit in 2013. They expect profit before interest and tax to be approximately $200,000 in each of the next three years. As a result of developing this new market, it is expected that additional working capital of $500,000 will be required in 2015. As a consequence of this new strategy, Boomerang will dispose of its freehold property imminently.

However the directors are concerned that even if Boomerang achieves an annual profit before interest and tax of $200,000 it will be a number of years before a dividend could be distributed to the equity shareholders and it would be difficult to raise fresh funds from the shareholders in 2015 if there was little prospect of a dividend payment for several years.

The bank overdraft is currently unsecured and the bank has expressed concern regarding the increase in the overdraft in recent months and has requested that Boomerang takes steps to address this situation.

The directors are considering whether it would be beneficial to implement a reconstruction scheme and, in particular, whether it would be likely to receive the necessary support from the various interested parties.

The 8% debenture is currently secured by a floating charge against the inventory and receivables of Boomerang. Employees' wages and professional fees are regarded as preferential creditors. Corporate tax liabilities are not regarded as preferential creditors.

The variation of the rights of the shareholders and creditors was to be effected under legislation which requires that the scheme should be approved by a majority in number and 75% in value of each class of shareholders, by a majority in number and 75% in value of each class of creditor affected, and by the court. The directors of Boomerang have had initial discussions with their auditors to ensure the legality of this proposal.

The key elements of the proposed scheme include:

- A capital reduction scheme to reduce the existing equity shares from $1 to $0.40 per share.

- The directors will subscribe for 750,000 equity shares of $0.40 at nominal value as demonstration of commitment to the success of the scheme.

- The 4% unsecured debenture due in 2013 will be repaid.

- Disposal of the freehold property for $700,000.

- Payment of the most urgent trade payables to ensure continuing supplies amounting to approximately $200,000, plus payment of the outstanding tax liability.

- Payment of professional fees of $40,000.

- Assessment of the recoverable values of assets to recognise impairments and write-offs as appropriate.

In the event of liquidation, professional fees of $40,000 would be payable.

Assume that Boomerang is subject to an income tax rate of 25% on profit after interest for the year; ignore any other tax issues, such as utilisation of tax losses against profits.

Draft statements of financial position at 31 October 2012 before and after the proposed reconstruction scheme were as follows:

ASSETS	Before reconstruction	After reconstruction
Non-current assets:	$	$
Property, plant & equipment:		
Freehold property	400,000	nil
Leasehold premises	394,000	370,000
Plant, equipment and vehicles	710,000	675,000
Current assets:		
Inventory	440,000	400,000
Receivables	290,000	225,000
	2,234,000	1,670,000
EQUITY AND LIABILITIES	$	$
Equity shares of $1 each/$0.40 each	1,350,000	840,000
Retained deficit	(1,346,000)	(340,000)
	4,000	500,000
Liabilities		
4% Debentures 2013 (unsecured)	170,000	nil
8% Debentures (secured by a floating charge)	540,000	540,000
Corporate tax liabilities	190,000	
Payables	576,000	326,000
Wages	260,000	160,000
Bank overdraft	494,000	144,000
	2,234,000	1,670,000

Required:

Draft a memorandum for the finance director of Boomerang which evaluates:

(a)   the outcome of liquidation of Boomerang, on the basis that the values following reconstruction are a reasonable approximation to realisable values upon liquidation. Your comments should make clear the order of settlement of liabilities.

(7 marks)

(b)   the outcome of the proposed reconstruction scheme from the perspective of each of the following parties, on the assumption that any necessary legal and regulatory compliance issues have been properly dealt with, and that the forecast profit before interest and tax for the year to 31 October 2013 is reasonable:

(i)   Holder of 10% of the equity prior to implementation of the scheme

(ii)   8% debenture holder

(iii)   The bank

(iv)   Trade creditors

Your evaluation should consider whether each of the above parties would be likely to support the reconstruction as outlined, together with any factors which may be necessary to induce or encourage them to support the scheme.   (15 marks)

As a separate issue, Boomerang is disputing a decision by the tax authorities regarding additional tax liabilities relating to earlier years, which are excluded from the statement of financial position at 31 October 2012 as currently stated. The tax authorities communicated their decision to Boomerang on 5 November and, following independent professional advice that an appeal is likely to be successful, Boomerang lodged an appeal against the decision on 28 November. As a result, Boomerang decided that the additional tax liabilities need not be included in the financial statements for the year ended 31 October 2012.

Required:

(c)   Evaluate how this information is likely to affect the preparation of the financial statements for the year ended 31 October 2012.   (3 marks)

(Total: 25 marks)

ESSAY STYLE QUESTIONS

58   IAS 1 AND INTEGRATED REPORTING (JUNE 15)

IAS 1 *Presentation of Financial Statements* defines profit or loss and other comprehensive income. The purpose of the statement of profit or loss and other comprehensive income is to show an entity's financial performance in a way which is useful to a wide range of users so that they may attempt to assess the future net cash inflows of an entity. The statement should be classified and aggregated in a manner which makes it understandable and comparable. However, the International Integrated Reporting Council (IIRC) is calling for a shift in thinking more to the long term, to think beyond what can be measured in quantitative terms and to think about how the entity creates value for its owners. Historical financial statements are essential in corporate reporting, particularly for compliance purposes, but it can be argued that they do not provide meaningful information. Preparers of financial statements seem to be unclear about the interaction between profit or loss and other comprehensive income (OCI) especially regarding the notion of reclassification, but are equally uncertain about whether the IIRC's Framework constitutes suitable criteria for report preparation. An Exposure Draft on the Conceptual Framework published by the International Accounting Standards Board (IASB) has tried to clarify what distinguishes recognised items of income and expense which are presented in profit or loss from items of income and expense presented in OCI.

Required:

(a)   (i)   Describe the current presentation requirements relating to the statement of profit or loss and other comprehensive income.   **(4 marks)**

(ii)   Discuss, with examples, the nature of a reclassification adjustment and the arguments for and against allowing reclassification of items to profit or loss.   **(5 marks)**

(iii)   Discuss the principles and key components of the IIRC's Framework, and any concerns which could question the Framework's suitability for assessing the prospects of an entity.   **(8 marks)**

(b)   Cloud, a public limited company, regularly purchases steel from a foreign supplier and designates a future purchase of steel as a hedged item in a cash flow hedge. The steel was purchased on 1 May 2014 for $8 million and, by that date, a cumulative gain on the hedging instrument of $3 million had been credited to other comprehensive income and was held within equity. At the year end of 30 April 2015, the steel had a net realisable value of $6 million. The steel was finally sold on 3 June 2015 for $6.2 million.

On a separate issue, Cloud purchased an item of property, plant and equipment for $10 million on 1 May 2013. The asset is depreciated over five years on the straight line basis with no residual value. At 30 April 2014, the asset was revalued to $12 million. At 30 April 2015, the asset's value has fallen to $4 million. The entity makes a transfer from revaluation surplus to retained earnings for excess depreciation, as the asset is used.

Required:

Show how the above transactions would be dealt with in the financial statements of Cloud from the date of the purchase of the assets.

Note: Candidates should ignore any deferred taxation effects.   **(6 marks)**

Professional marks will be awarded in this question for clarity and quality of presentation.   **(2 marks)**

(Total: 25 marks)

59   IMPAIRMENT OF ASSETS (DEC 14)

(a)   An assessment of accounting practices for asset impairments is especially important in the context of financial reporting quality in that it requires the exercise of considerable management judgement and reporting discretion. The importance of this issue is heightened during periods of ongoing economic uncertainty as a result of the need for companies to reflect the loss of economic value in a timely fashion through the mechanism of asset write-downs. There are many factors which can affect the quality of impairment accounting and disclosures. These factors include changes in circumstance in the reporting period, the market capitalisation of the entity, the allocation of goodwill to cash generating units, valuation issues and the nature of the disclosures.

Required:

Discuss the importance and significance of the above factors when conducting an impairment test under IAS 36 _Impairment of Assets_.   **(13 marks)**

(b)   (i)   Estoil is an international company providing parts for the automotive industry. It operates in many different jurisdictions with different currencies. During 2014, Estoil experienced financial difficulties marked by a decline in revenue, a reorganisation and restructuring of the business and it reported a loss for the year. An impairment test of goodwill was performed but no impairment was recognised.

Estoil applied one discount rate for all cash flows for all cash generating units (CGUs), irrespective of the currency in which the cash flows would be generated. The discount rate used was the weighted average cost of capital (WACC) and Estoil used the 10-year government bond rate for its jurisdiction as the risk free rate in this calculation. Additionally, Estoil built its model using a forecast denominated in the functional currency of the parent company. Estoil felt that any other approach would require a level of detail which was unrealistic and impracticable. Estoil argued that the different CGUs represented different risk profiles in the short term, but over a longer business cycle, there was no basis for claiming that their risk profiles were different.

(ii)   Fariole specialises in the communications sector with three main CGUs. Goodwill was a significant component of total assets. Fariole performed an impairment test of the CGUs. The cash flow projections were based on the most recent financial budgets approved by management. The realised cash flows for the CGUs were negative in 2014 and far below budgeted cash flows for that period. The directors had significantly raised cash flow forecasts for 2015 with little justification. The projected cash flows were calculated by adding back depreciation charges to the budgeted result for the period with expected changes in working capital and capital expenditure not taken into account.

Required:

Discuss the acceptability of the above accounting practices under IAS 36 _Impairment of Assets_.   **(10 marks)**

Professional marks will be awarded in this question for clarity and quality of presentation.   **(2 marks)**

(Total: 25 marks)

60   DEBT AND EQUITY (JUNE 14 EXAM)

(a)   The difference between debt and equity in an entity's statement of financial position is not easily distinguishable for preparers of financial statements. Some financial instruments may have both features, which can lead to inconsistency of reporting. The International Accounting Standards Board (IASB) has agreed that greater clarity may be required in its definitions of assets and liabilities for debt instruments. It is thought that defining the nature of liabilities would help the IASB's thinking on the difference between financial instruments classified as equity and liabilities.

Required:

(i)   **Discuss the rules that should be applied when deciding if a financial instrument should be classified as debt or equity.**

Note: Examples should be given to illustrate your answer.   **(9 marks)**

(ii)   **Explain why it is important for entities to correctly classify a financial instrument as debt or equity in the financial statements.**   **(5 marks)**

(b)   The directors of Avco, a public limited company, are reviewing the financial statements of two entities which are acquisition targets, Cavor and Lidan. They have asked for clarification on the treatment of the following financial instruments within the financial statements of the entities.

Cavor has two classes of shares: A and B shares. A shares are Cavor's ordinary shares and are correctly classed as equity. B shares are not mandatorily redeemable shares but contain a call option allowing Cavor to repurchase them. Dividends are payable on the B shares if, and only if, dividends have been paid on the A ordinary shares. The terms of the B shares are such that dividends are payable at a rate equal to that of the A ordinary shares. Additionally, Cavor has also issued share options which give the counterparty rights to buy a fixed number of its B shares for a fixed amount of $10 million. The contract can be settled only by the issuance of shares for cash by Cavor.

Lidan has in issue two classes of shares: A shares and B shares. A shares are correctly classified as equity. Two million B shares of nominal value of $1 each are in issue. The B shares are redeemable in two years' time at the option of Lidan. Lidan has a choice as to the method of redemption of the B shares. It may either redeem the B shares for cash at their nominal value or it may issue one million A shares in settlement. A shares are currently valued at $10 per share. The lowest price for Lidan's A shares since its formation has been $5 per share.

Required:

Discuss whether the above arrangements regarding the B shares of each of Cavor and Lidan should be treated as liabilities or equity in the financial statements of the respective issuing companies.   **(9 marks)**

Professional marks will be awarded in this question for clarity and quality of presentation.   **(2 marks)**

(Total: 25 marks)

61 ZACK (DEC 13 EXAM)

(a) Due to the complexity of International Financial Reporting Standards (IFRS), often judgements used at the time of transition to IFRS have resulted in prior period adjustments and changes in estimates being disclosed in financial statements. The selection of accounting policy and estimation techniques is intended to aid comparability and consistency in financial statements. However, IFRS also place particular emphasis on the need to take into account qualitative characteristics and the use of professional judgement when preparing the financial statements. Although IFRS may appear prescriptive, the achievement of all the objectives for a set of financial statements will rely on the skills of the preparer. Entities should follow the requirements of IAS 8 *Accounting Policies, Changes in Accounting Estimates and Errors* when selecting or changing accounting policies, changing estimation techniques, and correcting errors.

However, the application of IAS 8 is additionally often dependent upon the application of materiality analysis to identify issues and guide reporting. Entities also often consider the acceptability of the use of hindsight in their reporting.

Required:

(i) **Discuss how judgement and materiality play a significant part in the selection of an entity's accounting policies.**

(ii) **Discuss the circumstances where an entity may change its accounting policies, setting out how a change of accounting policy is applied and the difficulties faced by entities where a change in accounting policy is made.**

(iii) **Discuss why the current treatment of prior period errors could lead to earnings management by companies, together with any further arguments against the current treatment.**

Credit will be given for relevant examples.

Note: The total marks will be split equally between each part. (15 marks)

(b) In 2013, Zack, a public limited company, commenced construction of a shopping centre. It considers that in order to fairly recognise the costs of its property, plant and equipment, it needs to correct its accounting policies by capitalising borrowing costs incurred whilst the shopping centre is under construction. A review of past transactions suggests that there has been one other project involving assets with substantial construction periods where there would be a material misstatement of the asset balance if borrowing costs were not capitalised. This project was completed in the year ended 30 November 2012. Previously, Zack had incorrectly expensed the borrowing costs as they were incurred. The borrowing costs which could be capitalised are $2 million for the 2012 asset and $3 million for the 2013 asset.

A review of the depreciation schedules of the larger plant and equipment not affected by the above has resulted in Zack concluding that the basis on which these assets are depreciated would better reflect the resources consumed if calculations were on a reducing balance basis, rather than a straight-line basis. The revision would result in an increase in depreciation for the year to 30 November 2012 of $5 million, an increase for the year end 30 November 2013 of $6 million and an estimated increase for the year ending 30 November 2014 of $8 million.

Additionally, Zack has discovered that its accruals systems for year-end creditors for the financial year 30 November 2012 processed certain accruals twice in the ledger. This meant that expenditure services were overstated in the financial statements by $2 million. However, Zack has since reviewed its final accounts systems and processes and has made appropriate changes and introduced additional internal controls to ensure that such estimation problems are unlikely to recur.

All of the above transactions are material to Zack.

Required:

Discuss how the above events should be shown in the financial statements of Zack for the year ended 30 November 2013. **(8 marks)**

Professional marks will be awarded in this question for clarity and quality of presentation. **(2 marks)**

(Total: 25 marks)

62 LIZZER (JUNE 13 EXAM)

(a) Developing a framework for disclosure is at the forefront of current debate and there are many bodies around the world attempting to establish an overarching framework to make financial statement disclosures more effective, coordinated and less redundant. It has been argued that instead of focusing on raising the quality of disclosures, these efforts have placed their emphasis almost exclusively on reducing the quantity of information. The belief is that excessive disclosure is burdensome and can overwhelm users. However, it could be argued that there is no such thing as too much 'useful' information for users.

Required:

(i) **Discuss why it is important to ensure the optimal level of disclosure in annual reports, describing the reasons why users of annual reports may have found disclosure to be excessive in recent years.** **(9 marks)**

(ii) **Describe the barriers, which may exist, to reducing excessive disclosure in annual reports.** **(6 marks)**

(b) The directors of Lizzer, a public limited company, have read various reports on excessive disclosure in the annual report. They have decided to take action and do not wish to disclose any further detail concerning the two instances below.

(i) Lizzer is a debt issuer whose business is the securitisation of a portfolio of underlying investments and financing their purchase through the issuing of listed, limited recourse debt. The repayment of the debt is dependent upon the performance of the underlying investments. Debt-holders bear the ultimate risks and rewards of ownership of the underlying investments. Given the debt specific nature of the underlying investments, the risk profile of individual debt may differ.

Lizzer does not consider its debt-holders as being amongst the primary users of the financial statements and, accordingly, does not wish to provide disclosure of the debt-holders' exposure to risks in the financial statements, as distinct from the risks faced by the company's shareholders, in accordance with IFRS 7 *Financial Instruments: Disclosures.* **(4 marks)**

(ii)   At the date of the financial statements, 31 January 2013, Lizzer's liquidity position was quite poor, such that the directors described it as 'unsatisfactory' in the management report. During the first quarter of 2013, the situation worsened with the result that Lizzer was in breach of certain loan covenants at 31 March 2013. The financial statements were authorised for issue at the end of April 2013. The directors' and auditor's reports both emphasised the considerable risk of not being able to continue as a going concern.

The notes to the financial statements indicated that there was 'ample' compliance with all loan covenants as at the date of the financial statements. No additional information about the loan covenants was included in the financial statements. Lizzer had been close to breaching the loan covenants in respect of free cash flows and equity ratio requirements at 31 January 2013.

The directors of Lizzer felt that, given the existing information in the financial statements, any further disclosure would be excessive and confusing to users.

(4 marks)

Required:

Discuss the directors' view that no further information regarding the two instances above should be disclosed in the financial statements because it would be 'excessive'.

Note: The mark allocation is shown against each of the two instances above.

Professional marks will be awarded in this question for clarity and quality of presentation. **(2 marks)**

(Total: 25 marks)

63   JAYACH (DEC 12 EXAM)

(a)   IFRS 13 defines fair value, establishes a framework for measuring fair value and requires significant disclosures relating to fair value measurement. Fair value measurements are categorised into a three-level hierarchy, based on the type of inputs to the valuation techniques used. However, the guidance in IFRS 13 does not apply to transactions dealt with by certain specific standards.

Required:

(i)   **Discuss the main principles of fair value measurement as set out in IFRS 13.**
(7 marks)

(ii)   **Describe the three-level hierarchy for fair value measurements used in IFRS 13.** **(6 marks)**

(b)   Jayach, a public limited company, is reviewing the fair valuation of certain assets and liabilities.

It carries an asset that is traded in different markets and is uncertain as to which valuation to use. The asset has to be valued at fair value under International Financial Reporting Standards. Jayach currently only buys and sells the asset in the Australasian market. The data relating to the asset are set out below:

Year to 30 November 2012	Asian market	European market	Australasian market
Volume of market – units	4 million	2 million	1 million
Price	$19	$16	$22
Costs of entering the market	$2	$2	$3
Transaction costs	$1	$2	$2

Additionally, Jayach had acquired an entity on 30 November 2012 and is required to fair value a decommissioning liability. The entity has to decommission a mine at the end of its useful life, which is in three years' time. Jayach has determined that it will use a valuation technique to measure the fair value of the liability. If Jayach were allowed to transfer the liability to another market participant, then the following data would be used.

Input	Amount
Labour and material cost	$2 million
Overhead	30% of labour and material cost
Third party mark-up – industry average	20%
Annual inflation rate	5%
Risk adjustment – uncertainty relating to cash flows	6%
Risk-free rate of government bonds	4%
Entity's non-performance risk	2%

Jayach needs advice on how to fair value the liability.

Required:

Discuss, with relevant computations, how Jayach should fair value the above asset and liability under IFRS 13. (10 marks)

Professional marks will be awarded in this question for the clarity and quality of the presentation and discussion. (2 marks)

(Total: 25 marks)

64   IFRS FOR SME APPLIED (DEC 10 EXAM) *Walk in the footsteps of a top tutor*

(a)   The principal aim when developing accounting standards for small to medium-sized enterprises (SMEs) is to provide a framework that generates relevant, reliable, and useful information which should provide a high quality and understandable set of accounting standards suitable for SMEs. There is no universally agreed definition of an SME and it is difficult for a single definition to capture all the dimensions of a small or medium-sized business. The main argument for separate SME accounting standards is the undue cost burden of reporting, which is proportionately heavier for smaller firms.

Required:

(i)   **Comment on the different approaches which could have been taken by the International Accounting Standards Board (IASB) in developing the 'IFRS for Small and Medium-sized Entities' (IFRS for SMEs), explaining the approach finally taken by the IASB.** **(6 marks)**

(ii)   **Discuss the main differences and modifications to IFRS which the IASB made to reduce the burden of reporting for SME's, giving specific examples where possible.** **(8 marks)**

Professional marks will be awarded in part (a) for clarity and quality of discussion.

(2 marks)

(b)   Whitebirk has met the definition of a SME in its jurisdiction and wishes to comply with the 'IFRS for Small and Medium-sized Entities'. The entity wishes to seek advice on how it will deal with the following accounting issues in its financial statements for the year ended 30 November 2010. The entity currently prepares its financial statements in accordance with full IFRS.

(i)   Actuarial gains and losses arising on the defined benefit obligation are accounted for as part of the net remeasurement component for the year. The net remeasurement component is included within other comprehensive income for the year and within other components of equity on the statement of financial position.

(ii)   Whitebirk purchased 90% of Close, a SME, on 1 December 2009. The purchase consideration was $5.7 million and the value of Close's identifiable assets was $6 million. The value of the non-controlling interest at 1 December 2009 was estimated at $0.7 million. Whitebirk wishes to use the full goodwill method if allowed. The estimated life of goodwill cannot be reliably determined but management wish to use the highest possible estimate. Whitebirk wishes to know how to account for goodwill under the IFRS for SMEs.

(iii)   Whitebirk has incurred $1 million of research expenditure to develop a new product in the year to 30 November 2010. Additionally, it incurred $500,000 of development expenditure to bring another product to a stage where it is ready to be marketed and sold.

Required:

Discuss how the above transactions should be dealt with in the financial statements of Whitebirk, with reference to the 'IFRS for Small and Medium-sized Entities'. **(9 marks)**

(Total: 25 marks)

65 HOLCOMBE (JUNE 10 EXAM) *Walk in the footsteps of a top tutor*

(a) Leasing is important to Holcombe, a public limited company as a method of financing the business. The Directors feel that it is important that they provide users of financial statements with a complete and understandable picture of the entity's leasing activities. They believe that the current accounting model is inadequate and does not meet the needs of users of financial statements.

Holcombe has leased plant for a fixed term of six years and the useful life of the plant is 12 years. The lease is non-cancellable, and there are no rights to extend the lease term or purchase the machine at the end of the term. There are no guarantees of its value at that point. The lessor does not have the right of access to the plant until the end of the contract or unless permission is granted by Holcombe.

Fixed lease payments are due annually over the lease term after delivery of the plant, which is maintained by Holcombe. Holcombe accounts for the lease as an operating lease but the directors are unsure as to whether the accounting treatment of an operating lease is conceptually correct.

Required:

(i) **Discuss the reasons why the current lease accounting standards may fail to meet the needs of users and could be said to be conceptually flawed**

(7 marks)

(ii) **Discuss whether the plant operating lease in the financial statements of Holcombe meets the definition of an asset and liability as set out in the Conceptual Framework for Financial Reporting.** **(7 marks)**

Professional marks will be awarded in part (a) (i) and (ii) for clarity and quality of discussion. **(2 marks)**

(b) Holcombe also owns an office building with a remaining useful life of 30 years. The carrying amount of the building is $120 million and its fair value is $150 million. On 1 May 2009, Holcombe sells the building to Brook, a public limited company, for its fair value and leases it back for five years at an annual rental payable in arrears of $16 million on the last day of the financial year (30 April). This is a fair market rental. Holcombe's incremental borrowing rate is 8%.

On 1 May 2009, Holcombe has also entered into a short operating lease agreement to lease another building. The lease will last for three years and is currently $5 million per annum. However an inflation adjustment will be made at the conclusion of leasing years 1 and 2. Currently inflation is 4% per annum.

The following discount factors are relevant (8%).

	Single cash flow	Annuity
Year 1	0.926	0.926
Year 2	0.857	1.783
Year 3	0.794	2.577
Year 4	0.735	3.312
Year 5	0.681	3.993

Required:

(i) Show the accounting entries in the year of the sale and lease back assuming that the operating lease is recognised as an asset in the statement of financial position of Holcombe **(6 marks)**

(ii) State how the inflation adjustment on the short term operating lease should be dealt with in the financial statements of Holcombe. **(3 marks)**

(Total: 25 marks)

66 CORPORATE REPORTING (DEC 08 EXAM) *Walk in the footsteps of a top tutor*

Whilst acknowledging the importance of high quality corporate reporting, the recommendations to improve it are sometimes questioned on the basis that the marketplace for capital can determine the nature and quality of corporate reporting. It could be argued that additional accounting and disclosure standards would only distort a market mechanism that already works well and would add costs to the reporting mechanism, with no apparent benefit. It could be said that accounting standards create costly, inefficient, and unnecessary regulation. It could be argued that increased disclosure reduces risks and offers a degree of protection to users. However, increased disclosure has several costs to the preparer of financial statements.

Required:

(a) Explain why accounting standards are needed to help the market mechanism work effectively for the benefit of preparers and users of corporate reports. **(9 marks)**

(b) Discuss the relative costs to the preparer and benefits to the users of financial statements of increased disclosure of information in financial statements.

(14 marks)

Quality of discussion and reasoning. **(2 marks)**

(Total: 25 marks)

67 MANAGEMENT COMMENTARY

The International Accounting Standards Board issued IFRS Practice Statement 1 *Management Commentary* in December 2010 which provides a broad, non-binding framework for the presentation of management commentary which that relates to IFRS prepared financial statements.

Required:

(a) Explain the purpose of management commentary. **(5 marks)**

(b) Explain the principles and framework that should be applied when preparing a management commentary. **(10 marks)**

(c) Identify potential elements for inclusion within a management commentary, and explain why such items should be included in the management commentary.

(10 marks)

(Total: 25 marks)

68 REVENUE RECOGNITION

In May 2014, the International Accounting Standards Board (IASB) issued IFRS 15 *Revenue from Contracts with Customers*. This replaced IAS 11 *Construction Contracts* and IAS 18 *Revenue*. The new standard outlines a five step approach to revenue recognition.

Required:

(a) (i)   Discuss why a new International Financial Reporting Standard governing revenue recognition was required.   **(5 marks)**

(ii)   According to IFRS 15, what are the five steps for recognising revenue?
                                                                          (3 marks)

(iii) Discuss the role of judgement when accounting for revenue in accordance with IFRS 15.   **(7 marks)**

Amos enters into a contract with Lucas to construct a building. Construction started on 1 October 20X1. The contract price was agreed at $4 million, plus a bonus of $1 million that would be payable if construction is completed by 30 September 20X2. The building has been designed especially for Lucas and could not be sold to another entity without significant modifications. Although Amos believes that it is more likely than not that it will meet the bonus criteria, it has some doubt due to the unique nature of this particular project. The terms of the contract specify that Lucas must pay Amos within 30 days of the end of each quarter based on the progress of construction as at the end of each quarter. Amos measures progress to completion in terms of the contract costs incurred as a proportion of total estimated contract costs. Total contract costs are estimated at $2.5 million. If Lucas cancels the contract, then it is liable to pay Amos for the work completed.

By 31 December 20X1, Amos has incurred costs of $0.5 million on the contract. The estimate of total contract costs remains unchanged. Although progress on the contract has been satisfactory, there are still doubts about whether the $1 million bonus will be received.

Required:

(b)   Explain how Amos should account for the above transaction in accordance with IFRS 15 in the year ended 31 December 20X1.   **(8 marks)**

Professional marks will be awarded for clarity and quality of expression.   **(2 marks)**

(Total: 25 marks)

69 IMPAIRMENT OF FINANCIAL ASSETS

Under the new requirements of IFRS 9 *Financial Instruments*, allowances for expected credit losses are recognised in respect of investments in debt that are measured at amortised cost or at fair value through other comprehensive income.

Required:

(a) **Outline the accounting treatment of financial asset impairments according to IFRS 9 *Financial Instruments* and discuss the potential benefits and drawbacks of this approach.** **(15 marks)**

Glasgow is a provider of finance, whose year end is 31 October 2013. On 1 November 2012, it acquired a portfolio of financial assets that were debt instruments. These were made up of four year loans and were initially recognised at their nominal value $100,000 (which was also their fair value). They were classified to be measured at amortised cost. Each loan has a coupon rate of 8% as well as an effective rate of 8%.

By the 31 October 2013, no actual defaults had occurred. However, information emerged that the sector in which the borrowers operate is experiencing tough economic conditions. The directors of Glasgow therefore felt that the risk of default over the remaining loan period had increased substantially. After considering a range of possible outcomes, and weighting these for probability, the overall rate of return from the portfolio is expected to be approximately 2% of nominal value per annum for each of the next three years.

Required:

(b) **Explain how the above should be accounted for in the year ended 31 October 2013.** **(8 marks)**

Professional marks will be awarded in this question for the clarity and quality of the presentation and discussion. **(2 marks)**

(Total: 25 marks)

70 INTEGRATED REPORTING

(a) It is sometimes claimed that the primary financial statements and disclosure notes do not satisfy the information needs of user groups, particularly shareholders and other providers of financial capital. As a result, many entities now produce an array of non-financial reports. Integrated Reporting <IR>, in particular, has received increased international recognition. The International Integrated Reporting Framework outlines the purpose and proposed content of an Integrated Report. Although optional, it is hoped that the preparation of Integrated Reports by companies will address some of the problems associated with traditional financial reporting.

Required:

(i) **Identify and explain the limitations of financial reporting.** **(6 marks)**

(ii) **According to the International Integrated Reporting Framework, what is the purpose and suggested content of an Integrated Report?** **(6 marks)**

(iii) **Discuss the extent to which Integrated Reporting addresses the limitations of traditional financial reporting.** **(5 marks)**

(b)   TinCan is a company involved in developing and manufacturing scientific instruments. Its financial statements are prepared in accordance with International Financial Reporting Standards (IFRS) and it has a reporting date of 30 November 2014. TinCan has a large team of highly qualified research scientists. Employing these motivated and skilled members of staff enables TinCan to produce the most innovative and desirable products on the market, which are sold at high margins. Employee turnover is very low, with few employees leaving to work for its competitors. This is a result of TinCan's flexible working conditions, commitment to staff training, and high rates of pay.

Required:

In relation to the above issue, explain the likely benefits of TinCan producing an Integrated Report. (6 marks)

Professional marks will be awarded in this question for the clarity and quality of the presentation and discussion. (2 marks)

(Total: 25 marks)

71   FRAMEWORK

(a)   The *Conceptual Framework for Financial Reporting 2010* ('the Framework') sets out the concepts that underlie the preparation and presentation of financial statements for external users. In recent years, the IASB has been working to revise certain key areas of the Framework. This project resulted in the issue of an Exposure Draft on the Framework in July 2015.

Required:

(i)   **Explain the purpose of the Framework.** (5 marks)

(ii)   **Outline the definitions of the elements per the Framework.** (5 marks)

(iii)   **Explain why the IASB are seeking to amend the definitions of 'assets' and 'liabilities' and outline the amended definitions proposed in the recent Exposure Draft.** (5 marks)

(b)   One area that the existing Framework does not deal with is derecognition. This means that accounting standards differ in their approach to this area, which causes inconsistencies. This can create problems for the preparers of financial information.

Coyote is a public limited entity. It operates in the shipping industry and has a reporting date of 31 December 2015. It has entered into a number of transactions in the current year. The directors are unaware of the specific rules governing the following transactions and whether or not they involve asset derecognition:

- On 31 December 2015, Coyote sold receivables with a carrying amount of $3 million to a debt factor and received an immediate cash payment of $2.6 million. The terms of the factoring arrangement state that Coyote must reimburse the factor for any amounts not collected after six months. No accounting entries have been posted.

- Coyote has a number of ships that are classified as property, plant and equipment. The ships are split into components that are depreciated separately. The engines are depreciated over an estimated useful life of eight years. During the current period, one of the ships required its engine replacing after just five years. The only entry posted is to capitalise the cost of the replacement engine.

Required:

Discuss the correct accounting treatment of the above transactions in the financial statements of Coyote for the year ended 31 December 2015. **(8 marks)**

Professional marks will be awarded in this question for the clarity and quality of presentation and discussion. **(2 marks)**

(Total: 25 marks)

UK GAAP FOCUS

72 KUTCHEN (JUNE 15 EXAM) (UK GAAP FOCUS)

Kutchen has been considering purchasing a UK group of companies. The group is a qualifying entity for the purpose of applying FRS 102 *The Financial Reporting Standard applicable in the UK and Republic of Ireland*. However, the UK group has a complex structure and some of the subsidiaries are currently available for sale. As a consequence, the directors of Kutchen would like advice on the interaction of FRS 102 and the Companies Act 2006, and the requirements regarding exemptions from the preparation of group accounts and the exclusion of subsidiaries from consolidation.

Required:

Advise the directors of Kutchen regarding the requirements to prepare group accounts and the exclusion of subsidiaries from consolidation under FRS 102 and the Companies Act 2006. **(8 marks)**

73 KLANCET (JUNE 15 EXAM) (UK GAAP FOCUS)

Coact, a UK entity, is collaborating with Retto Laboratories (Retto), a third party, to develop two existing drugs owned by Coact.

In the case of the first drug, Retto is simply developing the drug for Coact without taking any risks during the development phase and will have no further involvement if regulatory approval is given. Regulatory approval has been refused for this drug in the past. Coact will retain ownership of the patent rights attached to the drug. Retto is not involved in the marketing and production of the drug. Coact has agreed to make the two non-refundable payments to Retto of $4 million on the signing of the agreement and $6 million on successful completion of the development.

Coact and Retto have entered into a second collaboration agreement in which Coact will pay Retto for developing and manufacturing an existing drug. The existing drug already has regulatory approval. The new drug being developed by Retto for Coact will not differ substantially from the existing drug. Coact will have exclusive marketing rights to the drug if the regulatory authorities approve it. Historically, new drugs of this kind receive approval if they do not differ substantially from an existing approved drug.

The contract terms require Coact to pay an upfront payment on signing of the contract, a payment on securing final regulatory approval, and a unit payment of $10 per unit, which equals the estimated cost plus a profit margin, once commercial production begins.

The cost-plus profit margin is consistent with Coact's other recently negotiated supply arrangements for similar drugs.

Coact would like to know how to deal with the above contracts with Retto.

Required:

Discuss the different ways in which the above contracts would be accounted for under FRS 102 *The Financial Reporting Standard applicable in the UK and Republic of Ireland,* **and the IFRS for SMEs.** **(8 marks)**

74 JOEY (DEC 14 EXAM) (UK GAAP FOCUS)

The directors of Joey have heard that the Financial Reporting Council in the UK has recently published a range of new Financial Reporting Standards (FRSs) in the UK and Republic of Ireland. They wish to know the nature of these standards and what companies qualify to use them.

Required:

Outline the scope of the UK standards and discuss the eligibility criteria for any UK operations of the Joey Group. **(8 marks)**

75 KATYE (DEC 14 EXAM) (UK GAAP FOCUS)

Kayte owns an entity, which used 'old' UK GAAP to prepare its financial statements. The directors of Kayte are unsure of the business implications of the new Financial Reporting Standards (new UK GAAP), and also how accounting for certain transactions differs from IFRS for SMEs. They are particularly concerned about the accounting for income tax.

Required:

Prepare a report to the Directors of Kayte, setting out the business implications of a change from 'old' to 'new' UK GAAP and an explanation as to how income tax would be accounted for under 'new' UK GAAP as compared to IFRS for SMEs. **(11 marks)**

76 TRAILER (JUNE 13 EXAM) (UK GAAP FOCUS)

Trailer is considering purchasing a local entity that currently uses UK Generally Accepted Accounting Practice (GAAP). Trailer feels that the use of UK GAAP will have had a major impact on the financial statements of the entity and that these may not be comparable to similar companies that use the IFRS for small and medium entities (IFRS for SME). Before continuing with the purchase of the entity, Trailer wishes to know whether there are any significant differences between UK GAAP and the IFRS for SME regarding business combinations.

Required:

Discuss any key differences between UK GAAP and IFRS for SME regarding business combinations, accounting for subsidiary undertakings and accounting for associates.

(6 marks)

77   IFRS FOR SME AND FRS 102 (DEC 10 EXAM) (UK GAAP FOCUS)

Note: this question has been taken from the December 2010 P2 INT exam. It has been amended to make it relevant for students sitting the P2 UK exam.

The principal aim when developing accounting standards for small to medium-sized enterprises (SMEs) is to provide a framework that generates relevant, reliable, and useful information which should provide a high quality and understandable set of accounting standards suitable for SMEs. There is no universally agreed definition of an SME and it is difficult for a single definition to capture all the dimensions of a small or medium-sized business. The main argument for separate SME accounting standards is the undue cost burden of reporting, which is proportionately heavier for smaller firms.

Required:

(a)   **Discuss the main differences and modifications to IFRS which the IASB made to reduce the burden of reporting for SME's, giving specific examples where possible.**

(8 marks)

Whitebirk wishes to seek advice on the differences between IFRS for SME and FRS 102 with respect to the following accounting issues which are of relevance to its financial statements for the year ended 30 November 2010. The entity currently prepares its financial statements in accordance with full IFRS.

(i)   Whitebirk has a defined benefit pension plan but has not yet calculated the pension deficit for inclusion in the financial statements for the year ended 30 November 2010. The defined benefit plan is relatively small, although still material to the entity, and Whitebirk believes that estimating the obligation using the projected unit credit method would involve undue cost and effort.

(ii)   Whitebirk purchased 90% of Close, a SME, on 1 December 2009. The purchase consideration was $5.7 million and the value of Close's identifiable assets was $6 million. The value of the non-controlling interest at 1 December 2009 was estimated at $0.7 million. Whitebirk wishes to use the full goodwill method if allowed. The estimated life of goodwill cannot be reliably determined but management wish to use the highest possible estimate.

(iii) Whitebirk has incurred $1 million of research expenditure to develop a new product in the year to 30 November 2010. Additionally, it incurred $500,000 of development expenditure to bring another product to a stage where it is ready to be marketed and sold.

Required:

(b)   **Outline the differences between IFRS for SME and FRS 102 in respect of the above three issues.** **(15 marks)**

Professional marks will be awarded in this question for the clarity and quality of the presentation and discussion. **(2 marks)**

(Total: 25 marks)

78 HERBIE (UK GAAP FOCUS)

Herbie is a medium sized company which has invested in several smaller companies. Draft total comprehensive income in the consolidated statement of profit or loss and other comprehensive income for the year ended 31 December 20X1 is $12m. The accountant is, however, unsure of the accounting treatment of the following transactions:

(i)   A new associate was acquired on 31 December 20X1. The cost of the shares was $4m, plus transaction costs of $0.2m were incurred. Herbie has recognised an investment in the associate at $4.2m in the consolidated statement of financial position.

(ii)   Herbie owns a licence, which is a type of intangible asset. On 1 January 20X1, the licence had a carrying amount of $3m and a remaining useful economic life of three years. The amortisation for the period ending 31 December 20X1 has been correctly calculated and accounted for. At 31 December 20X1, the licence was deemed to have a fair value of $3.1m by reference to an active market. Herbie would like to measure the licence at fair value, if permitted by the relevant accounting standard.

(iii)   On 1 January 20X1, Herbie received a $0.2m government grant. The cash has been correctly recorded, and the other side of the entry was posted to a suspense account. The grant was given on the condition that Herbie continues to employ at least twenty 16–18 year olds over the next 2 years. Herbie is virtually certain that this condition will be complied with. The directors of Herbie believe that the accruals model of accounting for government grants will result in the most relevant information for shareholders and would like to use this model if allowed.

Required:

(a)   Explain how the three transactions should be accounted for in accordance with IFRS for SME and FRS 102.   **(6 marks)**

(b)   Calculate the revised consolidated total comprehensive income for the Herbie group for the year ended 31 December 20X1 assuming that Herbie prepares its consolidated financial statements in accordance with:

(i)   IFRS for SME

(ii)   FRS 102.   **(3 marks)**

                                                                                                        (Total: 9 marks)

Section 2

ANSWERS TO PRACTICE QUESTIONS

SECTION A-TYPE QUESTIONS

GROUP FINANCIAL STATEMENTS

1   KUTCHEN (JUNE 15 EXAM) *Walk in the footsteps of a top tutor*

Key answer tips

There are some tricky issues in part (a) of this question. In particular, many students would have struggled to calculate the fair value of the non-controlling interests at the relevant acquisition dates. However, those calculations are worth very few marks. It is therefore important that you do not waste time on the bits of the question that you struggle with. Make sure that you manage your time carefully and that you concentrate on the issues and adjustments that you are happiest with.

(a)   **Consolidated statement of financial position at 31 March 2015**

Assets:	$m
Non-current assets	
Property, plant and equipment (W10)	314.00
Goodwill ($10.38 + $15.68) (W3)	26.06
Finance lease receivable	71.80
($50 + $14 + $8 – $3 (W8) + $2.8 (W8))	
	411.86
Current assets ($44 + $25 + $64)	133.00
Total assets	544.86

Equity and liabilities:

Share capital (43 + 20 (W3))	63.00
Retained earnings (W5)	50.05
Other components of equity (W5)	25.40
	138.45
Non-controlling interest (W4)	33.06
Total equity	171.51
Non-current liabilities (W11)	101.35
Current liabilities (W12)	272.00
Total equity and liabilities	544.86

Workings

(W1) Group structure

Tutorial note

Always start by drawing a group structure in order to establish the relationship between the investing company and its investments.

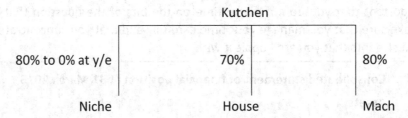

At the reporting date, Kutchen no longer has control over Niche. Therefore, the assets and liabilities of Niche are not consolidated.

(W2) Net assets

Tutorial note

If you are told the fair value of the net assets of the subsidiary at acquisition then you will need to work out the fair value adjustments as a balancing figure.

House

	Acq'n date	Rep date
	$m	$m
Share capital	13	13
Other components	3	5
Retained earnings	18	24
FVA – Land (bal. fig)	14	14
	48	56

Mach

	Acq'n date	Rep date
	$m	$m
Share capital	26	26
Other components	4	4
Retained earnings	12	15
FVA – Land (bal. fig)	13	13
	55	58

(W3) Goodwill

Tutorial note

Consideration must be included in the goodwill calculation at fair value. The fair value of contingent consideration should take into account the probability of payment occurring.

House

	$m
Fair value of share consideration (20m × $2)	40.00
Fair value of contingent consideration (5m × $2 × 20%)	2.00
NCI at acquisition (13m × $4.20 × 30%)	16.38
Fair value of identifiable net assets (W2)	(48.00)
Goodwill	10.38

The consideration of $42 million had not been accounted for. The nominal value of the shares issued of $20 million (20m × $1) should be recorded in share capital. The remaining $22 million should be recorded in other components of equity (W5).

Mach

	$m
Fair value of cash consideration	52.0
Fair value of land transferred	5.0
NCI at acquisition (see below)	13.68
Fair value of identifiable net assets (W2)	(55.0)
Goodwill	15.68

A profit on disposal of $2 million arises on the land for the difference between its fair value of $5 million and its carrying amount of $3 million. This will increase group retained earnings (W5)

The value of Mach can be determined by multiplying its profit for the period by an appropriate price-earnings ratio. Therefore, the value of Mach is $68.4 million ($3.6m × 19). The fair value of the non-controlling interest's holding is therefore $13.68 million ($68.4m × 20%).

(W4) Non-controlling interest

Tutorial note

There are very easy marks available for calculating the non-controlling interest. Make sure that you have memorised the standard workings.

	$m
NCI in House at acquisition (W3)	16.38
NCI % of House's post-acquisition net assets	2.40
30% × ($56m – $48m) (W2)	
NCI in Mach at acquisition (W3)	13.68
NCI % of Mach's post-acquisition net assets	0.60
20% × ($58m – $55m) (W2)	
	33.06

(W5) Reserves

Tutorial note

Any adjustments to profit must be included in your retained earnings working.

Retained earnings

	$m
Kutchen	41.00
Gain on land ($5m – $3m) (W3)	2.00
Group % of House's post-acquisition retained earnings	4.20
70% × (($56m – $48) – ($5m – $3m)) (W2))	
Group % of Mach's post-acquisition retained earnings	2.40
80% × (($58m – $55m) – ($4m – $4m)) (W2)	
Profit on Niche (W6)	10.00
Gain on curtailment (W7)	2.00
Loss on settlement (W7)	(1.60)
Restructuring (W7)	(6.00)
Finance lease correction (W8)	(3.00)
Finance lease residual value (W8)	2.80
Impairment (W9)	(5.00)
Deferred tax asset (W9)	1.25
	———
	50.05
	———

Tutorial note

Make sure that you deal with retained earnings and other components of equity separately.

Other components of equity

	$m
Kutchen	12.00
Share consideration (W3)	22.00
Group % of House's post-acquisition other components	1.40
70% × ($5m – $3m) (W2)	
Group % of Mach's post-acquisition other components	–
80% × ($4m – $4m) (W2)	
Transfer to retained earnings r.e. Niche (W6)	(10.00)
	———
	25.40
	———

(W6) Niche

The group's investment in Niche has been fully disposed of during the year.

Niche was purchased by the group for $40 million and was sold by the group for $50 million. Therefore, the total gain arising on the investment in Niche is $10 million and this must be transferred from other components of equity to retained earnings.

An alternative calculation of the $10 million gain is as follows:

	$m
Sale proceeds	50.0
Net assets at date of disposal	(60.0)
Goodwill ($40m – (80% of $44m) – impairment $2m)	(2.8)
NCI at disposal ($60m × 20%)	12.0
	———
Loss on sale of Niche	(0.8)
Post-acquisition profits	
(80% × ($60m – $44m)) – impairment $2m	10.8
	———
	10
	———

(W7) Restructuring

Tutorial note

This question tests pension curtailments and settlements. These issues are not commonly examined. You may wish to revisit the Complete Text if you are unfamiliar with these adjustments.

Pensions

After restructuring, the present value of the pension liability in location 1 is reduced to $8 million. Thus there will be a gain on curtailment of $2 million ($10m – $8m).

As regards location 2, there is a settlement because the liability will be extinguished by the payment of $4 million. Therefore there is a loss of $1.6 million ($2.4m – $4m).

The changes to the pension scheme in locations 1 and 2 require the following adjustments:

Location 1

Dr Pension obligation (non-current liab.)	$2.0m
Cr Profit or loss	$2.0m

Location 2

Dr Pension obligation (non-current liab.)	$2.4m
Dr Profit or loss	$1.6m
Cr Current liabilities	$4.0m

Provision

Tutorial note

Even though there has been no formal announcement of the restructuring, Kutchen has started implementing it and therefore it must be accounted for under IAS 37 Provisions, Contingent Liabilities and Contingent Assets.

A provision of $6 million should be made at the year end.

Dr Profit or loss	$6.0m
Cr Provisions (current liab.)	$6.0m

(W8) Finance lease

Kutchen should have shown the lease receivable at $47 million. Therefore an adjustment of $3 million will have to be made to profit or loss and the lease receivable.

The unguaranteed residual value should also have been recognised as part of the lease receivable.

The adjustments required are:

Dr Profit or loss	$3.0m
Cr Lease receivable	$3.0m
Dr Lease receivable	$2.8m
Cr Profit or loss	$2.8m

(W9) Impairment

Tutorial note

Items of property, plant and equipment are non-monetary assets. This means that they are recorded in an entity's functional currency using the spot (historic) exchange rate and are not retranslated.

A recoverable amount that has been determined in an overseas currency will need to be translated using the exchange rate on the day it was calculated.

The building would have been recorded at its cost of $12.5 million (D25m/2). By the year end, its carrying amount would be $12.0 million ($12.5m × 24/25).

The recoverable amount of the building is $7 million (D17.5/2.5). This gives rise to an impairment loss of $5 million ($12m – $7m) in profit or loss.

Dr Profit or loss	$5.0m
Cr PPE	$5.0m

Tutorial note

If the tax base of an asset or liability is higher than its carrying amount then a deferred tax asset is calculated. This asset is recognised if sufficient taxable profits will be available in the future against which the temporary difference can be utilised.

The tax base and carrying amount of the non-current assets were the same before the impairment charge. After the impairment charge, the carrying amount is $5 million lower than the tax base. This will create a deferred tax asset of $1.25 million ($5m × 25%). As Kutchen expects to make profits for the foreseeable future, this can be recognised in the financial statements.

Dr Deferred tax	$1.25m
Cr Profit or loss	$1.25m

(W10) Property, plant and equipment

Tutorial note

Remember to adjust the relevant balances for the fair value uplifts calculated in the net asset tables (W2). Many students forget to do this and therefore lose easy marks.

	$m
Kutchen	216.0
House	41.0
Mach	38.0
Increase in value of land – House (W2)	14.0
Increase in value of land – Mach (W2)	13.0
Sale of land as consideration for Mach (W3)	(3.0)
Impairment of building (W9)	(5.0)
	314.0

(W11) Non-current liabilities

Tutorial note

Many companies offset deferred tax assets and liabilities. Hence the deferred tax asset arising from the impairment has been netted off from non-current liabilities. It would be equally acceptable to show a deferred tax asset within non-current assets instead.

	$m
Kutchen	67.0
House	12.0
Mach	28.0
Reduction of pension obligation ($2m + $2.4m) (W7)	(4.4)
Deferred tax (W9)	(1.25)
	101.35

(W12) Current liabilities

	$m
Kutchen	199.0
House	26.0
Mach	37.0
Pension payment (W7)	4.0
Restructuring provision (W7)	6.0
	272.0

(b)   **Financial liabilities and equity**

IAS 32 *Financial Instruments: Presentation* establishes principles for presenting financial instruments as liabilities or equity. IAS 32 does not classify a financial instrument as equity or financial liability on the basis of its legal form but the substance of the transaction.

The key feature of a financial liability is that the issuer is obliged to deliver cash, another financial asset or a variable number of its own equity shares to the holder. An obligation to pay cash may arise from a requirement to repay principal or interest or dividends. In contrast, equity has a residual interest in the entity's assets after deducting all of its liabilities. An equity instrument includes no obligation to deliver cash, another financial asset or a variable number of its own equity shares to another entity.

The contract for contingent payments does meet the definition of a financial liability under IAS 32. Kutchen has an obligation to pay cash to the vendor of the NCI under the terms of a contract. It is not within Kutchen's control to be able to avoid that obligation.

The liability should be initially measured at fair value. Since the contingent payments relate to the acquisition of the NCI, the offsetting entry would be recognised directly in equity.

Contingent liabilities

The contingent payments should not be treated as contingent liabilities. IAS 37 *Provisions, Contingent Liabilities and Contingent Assets*, excludes from its scope contracts which are executory in nature.

(c) **Philosophies**

The IASB emphasises the fundamental importance of standards which focus on principles, drawn clearly from the IASB's Conceptual Framework, rather than on detailed rules. This approach requires both companies and their auditors to exercise professional judgement in the public interest, by requiring preparers to develop financial statements which provide a faithful representation of all transactions and requiring auditors to resist client pressures.

The US financial reporting model is based largely on principles, but supplemented by extensive rules and regulations. Companies want detailed guidance because those details eliminate uncertainties about how transactions should be structured, and auditors want specificity because those specific requirements limit the number of difficult disputes with clients and may provide defence in litigation.

The IASB has indicated that a body of detailed guidance encourages a rulebook mentality and it often helps those who are intent on finding ways around standards. The detailed guidance may obscure, rather than highlight, the underlying principles, since the emphasis is often on compliance with the 'letter' of the rule rather than on the 'spirit' of the accounting standard.

Ethical challenges

Moving from a rules-based system of accounting standards to a principles-based system could create ethical challenges for accountants. More professional judgement would be needed, which could be perceived as creating potential ethical grey areas. However, whilst IFRS tend to use more of a principles-based approach, this, in turn, requires accountants to have a complete understanding of ACCA's ethical principles and possess an ability to apply those principles effectively using a personal decision-making process. Accountants are required to appreciate the critical role ethics serves in the accounting profession and work continually in improving their process for recognising and thinking through ethical issues. The ethical conduct of an accountant should not be influenced by the nature of the accounting principles and practices, which are being complied with.

Convergence of accounting principles is an important part of the IASB's work plan and road map for adoption of a single set of high quality globally accepted accounting standards. It follows therefore that there should be global convergence on the subject of an independent accountant's ethical responsibility for assuring that financial statements do in fact fairly present economic reality.

There is no doubt that where a rules-based system has been in operation, there is likely to be an expansion of ethical challenges for both accountants and auditors involved with the financial statements of public companies if a principles-based approach was adopted. For example, the litigious atmosphere which businesses face in the US could lead to poor application of IFRS because of pressures relating to potential litigation. However, it is up to the accounting profession to ensure that ethical practices ensure high quality financial statements. Initially, accountants may face ethical pressures from management to develop and follow a rationale for seeing the financial results of their organisation in absolutely the most favourable light, because of the apparent elimination of accounting rules. However, IFRS are a robust set of accounting standards and it is unrealistic to assume that these standards could not replace those based around rules.

	ACCA Marking scheme		
			Marks
(a)	Property, plant and equipment		4
	Goodwill		7
	Non-current liabilities		2
	Finance lease		3
	Deferred tax		2
	Current assets		1
	Pensions		3
	Retained earnings		6
	Other components of equity		2
	Non-controlling interest		3
	Current liabilities		2
		Maximum	35
(b)	1 mark per point up to maximum		8
(c)	Philosophy		3
	Ethical considerations		4
Total			**50**

Examiner's comments

This question required the candidates to prepare a consolidated statement of financial position.

Candidates seemed to be able to calculate NCI using market prices but struggled with the calculation involving the PE ratio. The understanding of the PE ratio is fundamental to corporate reporting. Analysts use this ratio extensively and it is one of the simple ways to value an entity. In terms of the syllabus, it is dealt with at Paper F7 as well as being included in syllabus section C1(a) 'Prepare reports relating to corporate performance for external stakeholders'.

As stated above, candidates should be able to understand the principles of corporate reporting and be able to apply them. The calculation using the PE ratio to value a business is very straightforward and as such only carried one mark in the marking scheme but if candidates do not understand the meaning of the ratio, then it is understandable that they could not calculate the value of the entity. There was some comment in the media about the use of the own figure rule (OFR). The OFR is only used when a candidate has wrongly calculated a 'figure' which is subsequently used in another calculation. The candidate will lose the marks for the original calculation but, if the 'own figure' is subsequently used correctly, marks will then be given for the correct principle being used. It is unfair to penalise a candidate on more than one occasion for an incorrect calculation.

The holding company decided to restructure one of its business segments which affected the employees' pension benefits in two locations. Candidates were expected to show the impact on profit or loss of the restructuring. This part of the question was quite well done. Additionally the holding company leased out equipment under a finance lease but had incorrectly accounted for the lease. Again candidates performed quite well on this part of the question. Finally, the holding company impairment tested its non-current assets and it was decided that a building located overseas was impaired because of major subsidence. Candidates were expected to calculate the impairment loss and the deferred tax asset, which arose because of the impairment. This part of the question was quite well answered.

Question 1b required candidates to discuss the difference between equity and liabilities, and the proposed accounting treatment of the contingent payments on acquisition of NCI. The Framework and IAS 32 *Financial Instruments; Presentation* set out the fundamental differences between equity and liabilities and this question has been posed before in this examination paper. The definition is fundamental to the presentation of financial statements and performance reporting. Candidates however still struggle with this difference. Also, it would seem sensible that if the question required a discussion of the above then, the second part of the question might require the use of this distinction. Hence the contingent payment was in fact a financial liability, which very few candidates recognised.

Question 1c required a discussion of the philosophy behind 'rules based' and 'principles based' accounting standards together with a discussion of the ethical challenges faced by accountants if there were a switch in a jurisdiction from 'rules based' to 'principles based' accounting standards. This part of the question was well answered by candidates, which was very pleasing. It is important to realise in answering this type of question that there is a range of possible points, which could be raised by candidates, which may or may not be included in the model answer. Candidates were given due credit for relevant opinion on the subject matter of the question.

2   JOEY (DEC 14 EXAM)   *Walk in the footsteps of a top tutor*

Key answer tips

Remember to allocate your time carefully when attempting question 1 in the P2 exam. The examiner has consistently commented that over-running on this question is a key reason why people fail.

Spend some time upfront establishing the group structure (W1), as this is crucial in determining how the investments will be accounted for. A strong knowledge of consolidation technique, and the standard workings, should enable you to score high marks.

If you do get stuck with particular issues or adjustments then it is important to move on. Spend your time on the areas of the question that you are confident with.

(a) **Consolidated statement of financial position at 30 November 2014**

	$m
Assets:	
Non-current assets	
Property, plant and equipment (W8)	6,709
Goodwill (W3)	89
Intangible assets – franchise right ($20 – $5) (W2)	15
Investment in joint venture (W6)	0.75
	6,813.75
Current assets (W9)	2,011.3
Total assets	8,825.05
Equity and liabilities:	
Equity attributable to owners of parent	
Share capital	850
Retained earnings (W5)	3,450.25
Other components of equity (W5)	258.5
	4,558.75
Non-controlling interest (W4)	908.1
Non-current liabilities ($1,895 + $675 + $200)	2,770
Current liabilities (W10)	588.2
Total liabilities	3,358.2
Total equity and liabilities	8,825.05

Workings

(W1) Group structure

Tutorial note

Always start by drawing a group structure in order to establish the relationship between the investing company and its investments.

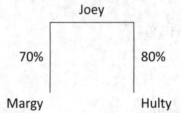

At the start of 1 December 2013, Joey increased its shareholding in Margy from 30% to 70%, thus gaining control. On this date, the previously held investment must be remeasured to fair value with any gain or loss being recorded in profit or loss.

The carrying amount of Margy at the date control was achieved was:

	$m
Consideration	600
Profit share	90
Revaluation share	10
Carrying amount	700

On the date control is achieved, the investment is remeasured from $700 million to its fair value of $705 million. The gain of $5 million is recorded in profit or loss.

(W2) Net assets

Tutorial note

Establishing the net assets of Margy at the acquisition date is tricky because the relevant information is spread over the first three notes in the question.

During the measurement period the acquirer in a business combination must retrospectively adjust the provisional amounts recognised at the acquisition date to reflect new information obtained about facts and circumstances that existed as of the acquisition date. The measurement period ends no later than twelve months after the acquisition date. It is important to note that the $2,250m fair value of the net assets at the acquisition date does not take into account the changes in estimates relating to the valuation of the provision and building that arise in the measurement period. Therefore, the $2,250m must be adjusted.

Margy

	Acq'n date	Rep date
	$m	$m
Share capital	1,020	1,020
Other components	70	80
Retained earnings	900	980
Contingent liability	(6)	–
Land (bal. fig)	266	266
	———	
Fair value of identifiable net assets before measurement period adjustments	2,250	
Provision (to adjust liability from $6m to $5m)	1	–
Buildings	(40)	(40)
Depreciation reduction ($40m/20)		2
	———	———
	2,211	2,308
	———	———

Hulty

	Acq'n date	Rep date
	$m	$m
Share capital	600	600
Other components	40	40
Retained earnings	300	350
FVA – franchise (bal. fig)	20	20
Franchise amortisation ($20m/(5 – 1)		(5)
	———	———
	960	1,005
	———	———

(W3) Goodwill

Tutorial note

When dealing with a step acquisition, the goodwill calculation must include the fair value of the consideration paid for the new shares plus the fair value of the previous shareholding.

Margy

	$m
Fair value of consideration	975
Fair value of previous shareholding	705
NCI at acquisition	620
Fair value of identifiable net assets (W2)	(2,211)
Goodwill	89

Tutorial note

Gains on a bargain purchase are rare, and normally arise from the use of inappropriate fair values as at the acquisition date. IFRS 3 says that the fair values used must be reviewed before a gain on bargain purchase can be recognised in profit or loss.

Hulty

	$m
Fair value of consideration	700
NCI at acquisition	250
Fair value of identifiable net assets (W2)	(960)
Gain on a bargain purchase	(10)

A gain on a bargain purchase is immediately credited to the statement of profit or loss.

(W4) Non-controlling interest

	$m
NCI in Margy at acquisition (W3)	620.0
NCI % of post-acquisition net assets	29.1
(30% × ($2,308m − $2,211m) (W2))	
NCI in Hulty at acquisition (W3)	250.0
NCI % of post-acquisition net assets	9.0
(20% × ($1,005m − $960m) (W2))	
	908.1

(W5) Reserves

Tutorial note

Remember to split group reserves into retained earnings and other components of equity.

Retained earnings

	$m
Joey	3,340.0
Gain on step acquisition (W1)	5.0
Margy:	60.9
70% × (($2,308m – $2,211m) – ($80m – $70m)) (W2))	
Hulty:	36.0
80% × ($1,005m – $960m) (W2))	
Gain on bargain purchase (W3)	10.0
Payable to CP (W6)	(0.7)
Removal of JCP profit (W6)	(1.5)
Joey's share of JCP profit (W6)	0.75
Depreciation (W7)	(0.1)
Impairment (W7)	(0.3)
PPE disposal (W7)	0.2
	3,450.25

Other components of equity

	$m
Joey	250.0
Margy: 70% × ($80m – $70m) (W2)	7.0
Hulty: 80% × ($40m – $40m) (W2)	–
Revaluation gain (W7)	1.5
	258.5

(W6) Joint arrangements

Tutorial note

A joint arrangement is an arrangement over which two or more parties have joint control. Remember that joint arrangements may take the form of joint operations or joint ventures. A joint venture, which normally involves the establishment of a separate entity, is accounted for using the equity method.

For the period to 31 May 2014, the requirement for unanimous key strategic decisions means this is a joint arrangement. Since there is no legal entity, it would be classified as a joint operation. Joey would account for its direct rights to the underlying results and assets.

Up until 31 May 2014, the joint operation had the following results:

	$m
Revenue (5m × 6/12)	2.5
Cost of sales (2m × 6/12)	(1.0)
Gross profit	1.5

The amount that belongs to Joey is therefore:

	$m
Sales (90% × 2.5m)	2.25
Cost of sales (printing, binding, platform – all by Joey)	(1.0)
Gross profit	1.25
Profit royalty to CP (calculated as 30% of $1.5m)	(0.45)
Net profit	0.8

Therefore Joey should adjust the accounting for the period to 31 May 2014 as follows:

Dr Profit or loss ($0.45m + ($2.5m × 10%))	$0.7 million
Cr Accounts payable CP	$0.7 million

From 1 June 2014, Joey has a share of the net assets rather than direct rights. This means that the joint arrangement would be classified as a joint venture and must be accounted for using the equity method. Therefore the adjustment to the current accounting will be:

Remove profit of new entity JCP:

Dr Profit or loss	$1.5 million
Cr JCP – profit for period	$1.5 million

Recognise Joey's equity-accounted share of JCP's profit:

Dr Investment in joint venture (($5m – $2m)/2 × 50%)	$0.75 million
Cr Profit or loss	$0.75 million

(W7) Asset held for sale

Tutorial note

IFRS 5 is very commonly tested in the P2 examination. Make sure that you know the key requirements of this standard.

The criteria in IFRS 5 *Non-current Assets Held for Sale and Discontinued Operations* are met at 31 March 2014. Therefore, Joey should depreciate the property until the date of reclassification as held for sale. Thus, the depreciation charge is $300,000 × 4/12 = $100,000. The carrying amount of the property is therefore $13.9 million.

The property should be revalued to its fair value at that date of $15.4 million as the difference between the property's carrying amount at that date and its fair value is deemed to be material. The revaluation increase of $1.5 million is recognised in other comprehensive income in accordance with IAS 16 *Property, Plant and Equipment*.

The property should then be reclassified as held for sale and remeasured to fair value less costs to sell ($15.1 million), which results in the recognition of a loss of $300,000 which should be recognised in profit or loss.

When the property is disposed of on 30 November 2014, a profit on disposal of $200,000 is recognised (net proceeds of $15.3 million less carrying amount of $15.1 million). Any remaining revaluation reserve relating to the property is not recognised in profit or loss, nor transferred to retained earnings in accordance with IAS 16 because of group policy.

Accounting entries

Dr Profit or loss $100,000

Cr Property $100,000

Being the depreciation up to the date of reclassification as held for sale.

Dr Property $1.5 million

Cr OCI $1.5 million

Being the increase in the value of the property to fair value at the date of the reclassification.

Dr Profit or loss $300,000

Cr Property $300,000

Being the loss arising on reclassification.

Dr Receivable $15.3 million

Cr Property $15.1 million

Cr Profit or loss $0.2 million

Being the disposal of the property at the year end. Note that an alternative treatment would be to show a receivable of $15.6 million for the proceeds due and a payable of $0.3 million for the costs to sell the asset.

(W8) Property, plant and equipment

Tutorial note

Try to reference your adjustments to your workings. This will help you to score marks even if your calculations contain errors.

	$m
Joey	3,295
Margy	2,000
Hulty	1,200
Decrease in value of building – Margy ($40m – $2m) (W2)	(38)
Increase in value of land – Margy (W2)	266
Depreciation (W7)	(0.1)
Revaluation (W7)	1.5
Loss on reclassification (W7)	(0.3)
Disposal (W7)	(15.1)
	6,709

(W9) Current assets

	$m
Joey	985
Margy	861
Hulty	150
Sale of property (W7)	15.3
	2,011.3

(W10) Current liabilities

	$m
Joey	320
Margy	106
Hulty	160
Joint operation – CP (W6)	0.7
Joint venture (W6)	1.5
	588.2

(b)

> **Tutorial note**
>
> *To score highly, this question requires a detailed knowledge of IFRS 2. However, solid marks can still be obtained for demonstrating a basic understanding of the standard. For instance: is the share-based payment scheme cash-settled or equity settled; when will it be accounted for; and what accounting entries will be posted?*

Share-based payment

IFRS 2 *Share-based Payment* includes within its scope the transfer of a parent entity's equity instruments for goods or services.

Group share-based payment transactions are treated as equity-settled when:

(i) the awards granted are the entity's own equity instruments, or

(ii) the entity has no obligation to settle the share-based payment transaction.

In the group accounts, the transaction is treated as equity-settled as the group is receiving all of the services in consideration for the group's equity instruments.

An expense is charged in the group statement of profit or loss for the fair value of the share-based payment at the grant date over the vesting period, with a corresponding credit in equity. In this case the shares vest immediately, therefore the expense recognised will be the full grant date fair value.

Subsidiary financial statements

In the subsidiaries' accounts, the grant is treated as an equity-settled transaction because the subsidiaries do not have an obligation to settle the award.

An expense is charged in the subsidiaries' statements of profit or loss for the fair value of the share-based payment at the grant date over the vesting period, with a corresponding credit in equity. In this case the shares vest immediately, therefore the expense recognised in Margy's and Hulty's statement of profit or loss will be the full grant date fair value.

The credit in equity is treated as a capital contribution as Joey is compensating the employees of Margy and Hulty with no expense to the subsidiaries.

Joey's individual financial statements

In the separate accounts of Joey, there is no share-based payment charge as there are no employees providing services to the parent. Joey would recognise an increase in its investment in the subsidiaries and a credit to equity.

Disclosures

The disclosure requirements of IAS 24 *Related Party Disclosures* should be applied if any of the employees are key management personnel.

(c)

Tutorial note

*When answering ethics questions, students have a tendency to simply recite and explain the ACCA ethical code. Do not fall into this trap, as you will score poorly. The question asks you about the ethical conflicts facing the accountant and the ethical principles which would guide how the accountant should respond **in this situation**. Your answer must therefore reference and discuss the specific situation outlined in the question.*

Ethical conflicts

Joey needs a significant injection of capital in order to modernise plant and equipment and the bank requires the company to demonstrate good projected cash flow and profitability. However, the projected cash flow statement does not satisfy the bank's criteria and the directors have told the bank that the financial results will meet the criteria. Thus there is pressure on the chief accountant to forward a financial report which meets the bank's criteria. The chief accountant cannot afford to lose his job because of his financial commitments and this in itself creates an ethical dilemma for the accountant, as not only is there self-interest of the accountant involved but also the interests of the company and its workforce. The accountant has to rely upon his moral and ethical judgement in these circumstances.

Ethical principles

Ethical standards are used by members of a profession to decide the right course of action in given circumstances. Ethics rely on logical and rational reasoning to reach a decision, morals are a behavioural code of conduct to which an individual ascribes and ethical rules create an obligation to undertake a particular course of action. Conflict can arise between personal and ethical values but when an individual becomes a member of a profession, there is a recognition that there is acceptance of the standards of that profession which include its code of ethics and values.

The ethical rules of the accounting profession represent an attempt to codify principles. A profession is distinguished by having a specialised body of knowledge, a social commitment, the ability to regulate itself and high social status. The profession should seek to promote or preserve public interest. Professional accountants make a bargain with society in which they promise to serve the public interest which may, at times, be at their own expense. Accountants, as professionals, cannot rely exclusively on rules to define how they will act ethically. Members of the profession have a responsibility to present the truth in a fair and honest fashion and in a spirit of public service. In such circumstances, accountants should think carefully before seeking creative accounting solutions to particular problems. Thus, in this case, the chief accountant should insist that the report to the bank is a true reflection of the current financial position, irrespective of the consequences for himself.

ACCA Marking scheme		Marks
(a)	Property, plant and equipment	5
	Goodwill	6
	Assets held for sale	5
	Current assets/total non-current liabilities	1
	Retained earnings	8
	Other components of equity	3
	Non-controlling interest	4
	Current liabilities	1
	Joint venture	2
	Maximum	**35**
(b)	Subjective assessment of discussion Up to 2 marks per element	8
(c)	Subjective assessment – 1 mark per point	7
Total		**50**

Examiner's comments

This question required candidates to prepare a consolidated statement of financial position for a group. Candidates had to deal with a step acquisition, an unrecognised contingent liability, a revision of the fair values on acquisition, 'negative' goodwill, a joint arrangement and an asset held for sale. Candidates dealt with the group structure quite well and the calculation of goodwill /'negative goodwill' arising on acquisition was generally accurate. Candidates invariably calculate retained earnings and non-controlling interest inaccurately but the marking guide gives credit for candidates own figures as long as the principle is correct. For example, marks are allocated for calculating NCI as long as candidates are using the correct share of the subsidiaries' post acquisition earnings. Additionally, if a candidate makes an error early in a calculation, then candidates can gain marks for their own figures. This latter point also enhances the importance of candidates showing full and clear workings.

The main area that candidates found difficult was dealing with the joint arrangement. For the first half of the year, the arrangement was a joint operation where the holding company only accounted for its direct rights to the underlying results and assets. In the second half of the year, the arrangement was a joint venture and the holding company accounted for the arrangement as a joint venture using equity accounting. It is important that where candidates meet an accounting problem, which is not familiar to them, they should realise that there are marks available for the correct identification of the issue even if their accounting treatment is not totally accurate. In other words, it is important that candidates attempt the element of the question as often a pass mark can be gained for a reasonable attempt.

In question 1(b), the holding company granted share options to the employees of the subsidiaries over its own shares and the awards vested immediately. Candidates were asked to show the accounting for this transaction in its own, the subsidiaries, and the group financial statements. The answer to this part of the question was relatively straightforward as it relied upon knowledge of group accounting principles and double entry bookkeeping. In the group accounts, there would be a debit for the expense in the group statement of profit or loss and a credit in equity. In the subsidiaries' accounts, there will be a debit for the expense charged in the subsidiaries' statements of profit or loss and a credit in equity. In the separate accounts of the holding company, there would be a debit to its investment in the subsidiaries and a credit to equity. The accounting for this part was not reliant upon detailed knowledge of IFRS 2 but on application of principles.

Part 1(c) required candidates to discuss the potential ethical conflicts where an accountant is placed under undue pressure by directors and to discuss the ethical principles, which would guide how a professional accountant should respond in this situation. Generally, in this type of question, marks are awarded for the principles and the application of those principles. If a candidate simply lists the ethical guidance then it is impossible to gain full marks. Candidates must apply the principles to the scenario.

3 MARCHANT (JUNE 14 EXAM) *Walk in the footsteps of a top tutor*

Key answer tips

The key starting point when producing a consolidated statement of profit or loss and other comprehensive income is to understand the group structure. Marchant disposed of shares in Nathan but did not lose control. Therefore, Nathan's incomes and expenses must be consolidated for the full year and there is no profit or loss on disposal. However, Marchant lost control over Option half way through the year. This means that Option's incomes and expenses must be consolidated for the first 6 months and then a profit on disposal calculated. Marchant retained significant influence over Option, so must account for the remaining holding using the equity method for the second half of the year.

In part (b), make sure that you answer the question. There are two requirements to address: does IFRS adopt a fair value model, and does IFRS accounting reflect the financial value of an entity? Simply reciting the rules from IFRS 13 *Fair Value Measurement* will score you limited marks.

There are easy marks to obtain in part (c), but make sure that your answer relates to the specifics of the scenario.

(a) **(i)** **Marchant Group: Statement of profit or loss and other comprehensive income for the year ended 30 April 2014**

	$m
Revenue ($400 + $115 + (6/12 × $70) – $12 (W6))	538.0
Cost of sales ($312 + $65 + (6/12 × $36) – $12 (W6))	(383.0)
Gross profit\\	155.0
Other income ($21 + $7 + (6/12 × $2) – $5.3 (W3))	23.7
Administrative costs ($15 + $9 + (6/12 × $12)	(30.0)
Other expenses ($35 + $19 + (6/12 × $8) + $5 (W2) + $7.2 (W7) + $2.36 (W8) + $2.13 (W9))	(74.7)
Operating profit	74.0
Share of profits of associates (20% × (6/12 × $15))	1.5
Profit on disposal of subsidiary (W4)	22.0
Finance costs ($5 + $6 + (6/12 × $4) – $3 (W10))	(10.0)
Finance income ($6 + $5 + (6/12 × $8))	15.0
Profit before tax	102.5
Income tax expense ($19 + $9 + (6/12 × $5)	(30.5)
Profit for the year	72.0

Other comprehensive income:
Items which will not be reclassified to profit or loss

Changes in revaluation surplus ($10 – $5 (W3) – $2.2 (W8))	2.8
Remeasurements – defined benefit plan (W7)	(2.0)
Total items which will not be reclassified subsequently to profit or loss	0.8

Items which may be reclassified subsequently to profit or loss

Losses on cash flow hedge (W10)	(3.0)
Other comprehensive loss for the year	(2.2)
Total comprehensive income for the year	69.8

Profit attributable to:

Owners of the parent (bal. fig.)	60.2
Non-controlling interest (W11)	11.8
	72.0

Total comprehensive income attributable to:

Owners of the parent (bal. fig.)	59.2
Non-controlling interest (W11)	10.6
	69.8

Workings

(W1) Group structure

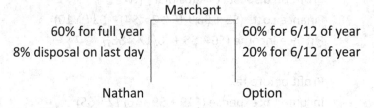

Marchant

60% for full year	60% for 6/12 of year
8% disposal on last day	20% for 6/12 of year

Nathan   Option

(W2) Nathan's goodwill

Tutorial note

Remember, impairments recorded against goodwill can never be reversed.

	$m
Fair value of consideration	80
Fair value of non-controlling interest	45
	125
Fair value of identifiable net assets acquired	(110)
	15
Goodwill at acquisition	15
Impairment (20%)	(3)
Goodwill	12

The goodwill has been increased to $17 million ($15m + $2m). However, impairments recorded against goodwill can never be reversed. Therefore, $5 million ($17m – $12m) needs to be charged to profit or loss to undo the reversal and to reduce the goodwill to the correct amount of $12 million.

(W3) Disposal of shares in Nathan

Tutorial note

Control over Nathan has not been lost. Therefore, no profit or loss on disposal should be recorded in the consolidated financial statements.

A profit on disposal will have been recorded in the individual accounts of Marchant, calculated as follows:

	$m
Proceeds	18.0
Carrying amount of investment disposed (8/60 × $95m)	(12.7)
Profit	5.3

This profit on disposal must be removed from other income. There will be no consolidated profit or loss on disposal because control over the subsidiary has not been lost.

The current year gain on the investment in Nathan of $5 million ($95m – $90m) must also be removed from other comprehensive income.

(W4) Disposal of Option

Tutorial note

If control over an investment has been lost, a profit or loss on disposal must be calculated and included in the consolidated statement of profit or loss. This calculation is normally worth a lot of marks so it is important to learn the proforma.

As Marchant has sold a controlling interest in Option, a gain or loss on disposal should be calculated. Additionally, the results of Option should only be consolidated in the statement of profit or loss and other comprehensive income for the six months to 1 November 2013. Thereafter Option should be accounted for using the equity method.

The gain recognised in profit or loss would be as follows:

	$m	$m
Fair value of consideration		50
Fair value of residual interest		40
		90
Less carrying amount of subsidiary:		
Net assets at disposal	90	
Goodwill at disposal (W5)	12	
Non-controlling interest at disposal	(34)	
		(68)
Gain on disposal to profit or loss		22

(W5) Goodwill of Option

	$m
Fair value of consideration	70
Fair value of non-controlling interest	28
Fair value of identifiable net assets acquired	(86)
Goodwill	12

(W6) Intra-group sale

Tutorial note

Intra-group trading must be eliminated from consolidated revenue and costs of sales. Any unrealised profits should also be eliminated by increasing cost of sales. However, if a loss is made on intra-group trading, it may suggest that the value of the goods have fallen and therefore that the loss is actually realised.

The loss on the sale of the inventory is not eliminated from group profit or loss. Because the sale is at fair value, the inventory value must have been impaired and therefore the loss on sale must remain realised. However, the revenue and cost of sales of $12 million will be eliminated.

(W7) Defined benefit plan

Tutorial note

For a defined benefit pension plan, the cost recorded in profit or loss is comprised of the service cost component and the net interest component. Any remeasurement gain or loss is recorded in other comprehensive income.

	$m
Current service cost	4.0
Net interest component (10% × ($50m – $48m))	0.2
Past service cost	3.0
	___
Net service cost recognised in profit or loss	7.2
Remeasurements in OCI	2.0
	___
Net cost for year recognised in total comprehensive income	9.2
	___

IAS 19 does not specify where the service cost and net interest component should be presented. Therefore it would be acceptable to include the net interest component in finance costs.

(W8) Property, plant and equipment

Tutorial note

A downwards revaluation of property, plant and equipment is firstly charged to other comprehensive income to the extent that a revaluation reserve exists for the specific asset. Any excess downwards revaluation is recorded in profit or loss.

	$m
Cost of PPE	12.0
Depreciation for y/e 30/4/13 ($12m/10)	(1.2)
	___
Carrying amount at 30 April 2013	10.8
Gain in revaluation surplus	2.2
	___
Fair value at 30 April 2013	13.0
Depreciation for y/e 30/4/14 ($13m/9)	(1.44)
	___
Carrying amount at 30 April 2014	11.56
Fall in value charged to OCI (balance on reval surplus)	(2.2)
Fall in value charged to profit or loss (bal. fig)	(2.36)
	___
Fair value at 30 April 2014	7
	___

(W9) Share options

Tutorial note

The expense of an equity-settled share-based payment scheme with employees is valued using the fair value of the option at the grant date. This expense is spread over the vesting period based on the number of options expected to vest. The other side of the double entry is recorded in equity.

Year	Expense for year	Cumulative expense	Calculation
	$m	$m	
30 April 2013	1.07	1.07	4 directors × $100 × 8,000 × 1/3
30 April 2014	2.13	3.2	6 directors × $100 × 8,000 × 2/3

(W10) Cash flow hedge

Tutorial note

Under an effective cash flow hedge, the gain or loss on the derivative is recorded in other comprehensive income.

The gain or loss on an effective cash flow hedge should be recorded in other comprehensive income, and therefore removed from finance costs.

(W11) Profit and TCI attributable to the NCI

Tutorial note

When calculating the NCI's share of Nathan's profit and TCI, it is important to think about the date of the share disposal. The 8% holding of Nathan was not sold to the NCI until the very last day of the year. Therefore, when the profits and OCI of Nathan were earned, the NCI share was 40% rather than 48%.

	Nathan	Option
	$m	$m
Profit (6/12 Option)	19.0	7.5
Adjustments		
Cash flow hedge (W10)	3.0	–
	22.0	7.5
× NCI % (40%)	8.8	3.0

The total profit attributable to the NCI is therefore $11.8 million ($8.8 + $3.0).

	Nathan	Option
	$m	$m
TCI	19.0	7.5
(6/12 Option)		
× NCI % (40%)	7.6	3.0

The TCI attributable to the NCI is therefore $10.6 million ($7.6m + $3.0m).

(ii)

Tutorial note

If control over an investment is retained, then a profit or loss on disposal is not included in the consolidated financial statements. Instead, equity is adjusted.

Note that part (ii) asks you to explain how the sale of the shares will be treated. Calculations by themselves are not sufficient to score a high mark.

Once control has been achieved, transactions whereby the parent entity acquires further equity interests from non-controlling interests, or disposes of equity interests but without losing control, are accounted for as equity transactions. Therefore:

- the carrying amounts of the controlling and non-controlling interests are adjusted to reflect the changes in their relative interests in the subsidiary

- any difference between the amount by which the non-controlling interests is adjusted and the fair value of the consideration paid or received is recognised directly in equity attributed to the owners of the parent; and

- there is no consequential adjustment to the carrying amount of goodwill, and no gain or loss is recognised in profit or loss or in other comprehensive income.

Tutorial note

The difference between the proceeds received and the increase in the non-controlling interest is recorded in equity (normally in 'other components of equity').

The increase in the non-controlling interest is calculated as the share of the Nathan's goodwill and net assets that the group has effectively sold to the minority shareholders.

Sale of equity interest in Nathan

	$m
Fair value of consideration received	18
Amount recognised as non-controlling interest (net assets per question at year end ($120m + fair value adjustment of $14m (see below) + goodwill of $12m) × 8%)	(11.7)
	―――
Positive movement in parent equity	6.3
	―――

The fair value adjustment at acquisition is calculated as follows:

	$m
Share capital	25
Retained earnings	65
Other components of equity	6
Fair value adjustment (bal. fig.)	14
	―――
Fair value of net assets	110
	―――

(b)

Tutorial note

If you have a good knowledge of the P2 examinable standards then you should be aware that lots of assets and liabilities are not measured at fair value. Can you give any examples?

The use of fair value

IFRSs utilise the 'fair value' concept and 'present value' more frequently than some other accounting frameworks. However, IFRSs do not require that all assets and liabilities are valued at fair value. The financial statements of many entities will measure many items using cost based models, except where entities grow through acquisition when acquired assets and liabilities are valued at fair value on the acquisition date.

IFRS 9 *Financial Instruments* uses two classification categories for financial assets: amortised cost and fair value. Classification under IFRS 9 is driven by the entity's business model for managing the financial assets and the contractual characteristics of the financial assets.

A financial asset is measured at amortised cost if two criteria are met:

(i) the objective of the business model is to hold the financial asset for the collection of the contractual cash flows; and

(ii) the contractual cash flows under the instrument solely represent payments of principal and interest.

Other standards also offer a choice of measurement basis. A revaluation through other comprehensive income is allowed provided it is carried out regularly under IAS 16 *Property, Plant and Equipment* and, in addition, IAS 40 *Investment Property* allows as an option the measurement of investment properties at fair value with corresponding changes in earnings as this better reflects the business model of some property companies. However, the historical cost basis is still regularly used by entities holding investment properties. IAS 38 *Intangible Assets* allows the measurement of intangible assets at fair value, with corresponding changes in equity, but only if there is an active market, and thus a reliable valuation, for these assets.

Fair values, when used in the financial statements, affect the performance measurement and the net assets position and improve the disclosure of risks and of value which may be realisable. Fair values can be subjective and therefore a fair value measurement may be influenced by bias. IFRS 13 *Fair Value Measurement* was developed to solve the problems in the application of the fair value concept. By formalising the definition of a fair value, and the ways in which it should be determined, IFRS 13 maximises faithful representation, comparability and verifiability.

IFRS and financial value

In some ways, fair value accounting will provide a more meaningful representation of the value of an entity. If derivative contracts were measured at cost, they would often be held at nil value. By requiring them to be measured at fair value, IFRS requires a better reflection of the benefits and risks that an entity is exposed to.

However, it is too simplistic to say that financial statements prepared under IFRSs reflect the aggregate financial value of an entity. The IASB identifies the objective of general purpose financial reporting as being the provision of financial information about the reporting entity which is useful to existing and potential investors, lenders and other creditors in making decisions about providing resources to the entity. The Conceptual Framework states that general purpose financial reports are not designed to show the value of a reporting entity. The purpose of IFRS financial statements is not to disclose the selling value of the entity, even when some of the identifiable assets and liabilities are recorded at fair value. As IFRSs do not allow an entity to recognise intangible assets generated internally by business operations, any attempt to state the aggregate value of the business would be incomplete.

(c)

Tutorial note

In part (c), do not just write down everything that you know about ethics. Your answer must be tailored to the scenario. Therefore, you should try and mention the subjective nature of lease accounting, the loan application, and the actions that the financial controller should take.

Financial reporting issues

A lease is classified as a finance lease if it transfers substantially all the risks and rewards incidental to ownership. All other leases are classified as operating leases and classification is made at the inception of the lease. Whether a lease is a finance lease or an operating lease depends on the substance of the transaction rather than the legal form.

Ethical and professional implications

The classification of a lease can be quite subjective. In the case of a lease of land, this is particularly subjective as the title to the land may not pass to the lessee at the end of the agreement but the lease may still be classed as a finance lease where the present value of the residual value of the land is negligible and the risks and rewards pass to the lessee. Thus, it appears that at first sight this is a difference in a professional opinion, which can be solved by the financial controller seeking advice.

If the features of the lease appear to meet IAS 17 Leases criteria for classification as a finance lease and the treatment used is part of a strategy to understate the liabilities of the entity in order to raise a loan, then an ethical dilemma arises. Professional accountants are capable of making judgements, applying their skills and reaching informed decisions in situations where the general public cannot. The judgements made by professional accountants should be independent and not affected by business pressures. The code of ethics is very important because it sets out boundaries outside which accountants should not stray. The financial director should not place the financial controller under undue pressure in order to influence his decisions. If the financial controller is convinced that the lease is a finance lease, then disclosure of this fact should be made to the internal governance authority. The financial controller will have the knowledge that his actions were ethical.

ACCA Marking scheme		Marks
(a)	Impairment adjustment	4
	Nathan	6
	Option	6
	Inventory	1
	Share options	4
	PPE	3
	Employee benefits	4
	NCI	2
	Sale of equity interest in Nathan	5
	Maximum	**35**
(b)	1 mark per point up to maximum	9
(c)	1 mark per point up to maximum	6
Total		**50**

Examiner's comments

This type of question is normally framed so as to test group accounting principles. Candidates dealt with the calculation of goodwill very well. However, any subsequent increase in the recoverable amount is likely to be internally generated goodwill rather than a reversal of purchased goodwill impairment. IAS 38 *Intangible Assets* prohibits the recognition of internally generated goodwill, thus any reversal of impairment is not recognised. Candidates did not deal particularly well with this point. Additionally there was some intra-group trading and the elimination of this element from Revenue and cost of sales. However, the loss on the sale of the inventory should not have been eliminated from group profit or loss. This is because the sale was at fair value, and therefore the inventory value must have been impaired with the loss on sale realised.

Because of the nature of the question, marks are given for the presentation of the consolidated statement of profit or loss and other comprehensive income. For example, marks were given for showing split between those items, which may or may not be reclassified and for showing the split between owners and NCI for profit/loss and total comprehensive income. These marks were allocated even if candidates showed their own figures.

When marking the paper, often marks are given for candidates own figures as it would be unfair to compound the effect of a candidate's mistake in, say a calculation. Thus it is important to ensure that candidates show all of their workings. Many candidates showed their workings on the face of the consolidated statement of profit or loss and other comprehensive income by bracketing a series of additions and subtractions of what could have been random numbers. Markers will look to see if there are recognisable figures in such a working but it is important to describe the calculation so that the marker can establish the principle. Marks are given for correct principles within accurate calculations.

In part (a)(ii) of the question candidates were asked to explain, with suitable calculations, how the sale of the 8% interest in a subsidiary should be dealt with in the group statement of financial position at 30 April 2014. Marks were allocated for the explanation and the calculation. Thus if a candidate simply showed the calculation, marks were lost. Candidates generally answered this part of the question quite well.

Part 1 (b) of the question required candidates to discuss the use of fair value in IFRSs and the fact that IFRSs do not reflect the financial value of an entity. This required candidates to answer across a range of standards and not just focus on IFRS 13. The question did not mention IFRS 13 specifically but rather an appreciation of the use of fair values in IFRS generally. The question carried 9 marks. Again, if a client asked an ACCA member about fair value in IFRS, the client would not simply expect an explanation of only IFRS 13. IFRS 13 was obviously relevant in answering this question but the marks were capped if candidates simply mentioned this IFRS. The question was not well answered as the nature of the discussion was often limited, which indicates a lack of reading by candidates and possibly an approach to learning which is individual standard based rather than principle based.

Part (c) of the question required a discussion of the ethical and professional issues which faced a financial controller who disagreed with a superior over the treatment of a finance lease where the correct treatment of the lease could jeopardise the loan application. Marks were given for a discussion of IAS 17 but they had to comment on the fact that subjectivity and professional judgement were involved. The remainder of the marks were allocated for the ethical discussion, which many candidates were quite poor at, choosing to spend a significant amount of time discussing the rules underlying IAS 17 rather than using professional and ethical insight.

4   ANGEL (DEC 13 EXAM) *Walk in the footsteps of a top tutor*

Key answer tips

Many students do not like statements of cash flows. However, there are lots of easy marks available. Make sure that you set up a pro-forma statement and slot in all the easy figures that you can find, such as opening and closing cash and cash equivalents. Look at the statement of changes in equity – there are many cash flows given here that can simply be placed in your proforma. Pay careful attention as to whether your figures need brackets or you will lose marks.

To answer part (b) it is essential to know the definition of a 'cash equivalent'. Make sure that you state this definition and then apply it to the two deposits in the question.

Always attempt the ethics requirement. There are very easy marks available in part (c).

(a)   Statement of cash flows for the year ended 30 November 2013

	$m
Profit for the year (W1)	197
Adjustments to operating activities	
Financial assets – profit on sale (W5)	(14)
Retirement benefit expense (W7)	10
Depreciation (W1)	29
Profit on sale of PPE (W1)	(14)
Associate's profit (W3)	(12)
Impairment of goodwill and intangible assets (W6)	116.5
Finance costs	10
	———
	322.5
Movements in working capital	
Decrease in trade receivables (125 – 180 – 3)	58
Decrease in inventories (155 – 190 – 6)	41
Decrease in trade payables (155 – 361 – 4)	(210)
	———
Cash generated from operating activities	211.5
Cash paid to retirement benefit scheme (W7)	(9)
Interest paid (11 – 1 capitalised)	(10)
Income taxes paid (W4)	(135.5)
	———
Net cash generated by operating activities	57
	———

Cash flows from investing activities	
Sale of financial assets (W5)	40
Purchase of financial assets	(57)
Purchase of property, plant and equipment (PPE) (W1)	(76)
Cash grant for PPE (W1)	1
Purchase of subsidiary (30 – 2) (W2)	(28)
Proceeds from sale of PPE (W1)	63
Dividend received from associate (W3)	3
Purchase of associate (W3)	(71)
	─────
Net cash flows used by investing activities	(125)
	─────
Cash flows from financing activities	
Proceeds of issue of share capital (SOCIE)	225
Repayment of long-term borrowings (26 – 57)	(31)
Dividends paid (SOCIE)	(10)
Non-controlling interest dividend (SOCIE)	(6)
	─────
Net cash generated by financing activities	178
	─────
Net increase in cash and cash equivalents	110
Cash and cash equivalents at beginning of period	355
	─────
Cash and cash equivalents at end of period	465
	─────

Workings

(W1) Property, plant and equipment

Tutorial note

Angel has made several accounting mistakes with regards to property, plant and equipment. This means that PPE additions and draft profit before tax must be corrected.

The following transactions would need to be made to recognise the asset in the entity's statement of financial position as of 30 November 2013.

Dr Property, plant and equipment $7m
Cr OCI $4m
Cr Retained earnings (to correct) $3m

The accounting policy of the Angel Group is to treat capital-based grants as deferred income.

However, the grant of $2m relates to capital expenditure and revenue. The grant should be split equally over revenue and capital.

The correcting entries should therefore be:

Dr PPE $2m

Cr Retained earnings $1m

Cr Deferred income $1m

Additions for PPE year before any adjustments are $66m ($80m – $14m from sub). However, this needs increasing by $3 million (refurbishment) + $2 million (grant) + $5 million (the construction costs and borrowing costs). Total additions are therefore $76 million.

Profit before tax was $188 million. This needs to be increased by $3 million (refurbishment) + $1 million (grant) + $5 million (construction costs and borrowing costs). Revised profit before tax is therefore $197 million.

(W2) Purchase of subsidiary

Tutorial note

The subsidiary's identifiable net assets are consolidated at fair value. This means that their carrying amount in the consolidated financial statements differs from their tax base, normally giving rise to a deferred tax liability.

The purchase of the subsidiary is adjusted for in the statement of cash flows by eliminating the assets and liabilities acquired, as they were not included in the opening balances. The fair values will be used, as they will be the values utilised on acquisition.

Calculation of deferred tax arising on acquisition:

	$m
Fair values of Sweety's identifiable net assets excluding deferred tax	20.0
Less tax base	(15.0)
Temporary difference arising on acquisition	5.0
Net deferred tax liability arising on acquisition (30% × $5m)	1.5

Calculation of goodwill:

	$m
Purchase consideration	30.0
Fair value of net assets (net of deferred tax)	(20.0)
Deferred taxation	1.5
Goodwill arising on acquisition	11.5

(W3) Associate

Tutorial note

Associates are accounted for using the equity method.

	$m
Balance at 1 December 2012	nil
Profit for period $40m × 30%	12
Dividend received $10m × 30%	(3)
Cost of acquisition (bal. fig.)	71
	___
Balance at 30 November 2013	80
	___

Therefore, cash paid for the investment is $71 million, and cash received from the dividend is $3 million.

(W4) Taxation

Tutorial note

When calculating the tax paid during the year, remember to include the opening and closing deferred tax balances in your workings. Also, you need to look out for deferred tax charges in the year that have been recorded in other comprehensive income.

	$m
Balance at 1 December 2012 ($31 + $138)	169
Charge for year (P/L)	46
Deferred tax on acquisition (W2)	1.5
Tax on revaluation PPE	2
Tax on financial assets	1
Cash paid (bal. fig.)	(135.5)
	___
Balance at 30 November 2013 ($35 + $49)	84
	___

(W5) Financial assets

The sale proceeds of the financial assets were $40 million. Thus, an adjustment for the profit of $14 million on the sale of the financial assets has to be made. The deferred tax of $1 million arose on the gain on revaluation.

(W6) Goodwill

Tutorial note

Reconcile the goodwill balance year-on-year to find the impairment charge. This is a non-cash expense so must be added back in the reconciliation between profit before tax and cash generated from operations.

	$m
Opening balance at 1 December 2012	120.0
Current year amount on subsidiary (W2)	11.5
Impairment (bal. fig.)	(26.5)
	————
Closing balance at 30 November 2013	105.0
	————

Impairments of other intangibles amount to $90m ($240m – 150m).

Total impairments are therefore $116.5m ($90m + $26.5m).

(W7) Retirement benefit

Tutorial note

The service cost component and net interest component are non-cash expenses. These must be added back to profit in the reconciliation between profit before tax and cash generated from operations.

	$m
Opening balance at 1 December 2012	74
Remeasurement – actuarial losses	4
Current year service cost plus interest	11
Contributions paid	(9)
	————
Closing balance at 30 November 2013	80
	————

An adjustment has to be made in the statement of cash flow for the current year expense. The $11 million service cost and interest figure above includes the carrying value of the subsidiary's defined benefit obligation at the acquisition date. Therefore, the actual expense is $10m ($11m – $1m).

(b) There are two classification principles which could be used to determine the classification of cash flows. Cash flows can be classified in accordance with the nature of the activity to which they relate which is most appropriate to the business of the entity, or cash flows can be classified consistently with the classification of the related or underlying item in the statement of financial position. Generally speaking, cash flows in IAS 7 should be classified in accordance with the nature of the activity to which they relate which is the most appropriate to the business of the entity.

The following elements could be used to help identify the nature of the cash flows being analysed:

- the cause or reason for which the cash flow is received or paid,

- the counterparty who receives or pays the cash flow,

- whether cash flows result from transactions which enter into the determination of profit or loss, or

- the predominant source of cash flows.

Tutorial note

State the definition of a 'cash equivalent' for some easy marks.

The statement of cash flows analyses changes in cash and cash equivalents during a period. Cash and cash equivalents comprise cash in hand and demand deposits, together with short-term, liquid investments which are readily convertible to a known amount of cash and which are subject to an insignificant risk of changes in value. IAS 7 does not define 'short term' but does state 'an investment normally qualifies as a cash equivalent only when it has a short maturity of, say, three months or less from the date of acquisition'.

Consequently, equity or other investments which do not have a maturity date are excluded from cash equivalents unless they are, in substance, cash equivalents. This three-month time limit is somewhat arbitrary but is consistent with the concept of insignificant risk of changes in value and a purpose of meeting short-term cash commitments.

Tutorial note

Remember to apply the definition of 'cash equivalents' to the scenario.

As regards the deposits, the following is the case:

(i) Although the principal ($3 million) will be recoverable with early withdrawal, the entity will lose all accumulated interest over the term, which seems to be a significant penalty. The cash is not needed to meet short-term cash commitments and so would not qualify as a cash equivalent.

(ii) Although the deposit is stated to have a 12-month maturity period, it can be withdrawn with 21 days' notice. Although this incurs a penalty, the reduction in the rate of interest from 3% to 2% is unlikely to be considered significant. The intention of management is to keep these funds available for short-term cash needs and so this deposit is likely to qualify as a cash equivalent.

(c)   The directors should be persuaded that professional ethics are an inherent part of the profession as well as other major professions such as law and engineering. Professional ethics are a set of moral standards applicable to all professionals. Each professional body has its own ethical code such as the ACCA's Code of Ethics and Conduct, which requires its members to adhere to a set of fundamental principles in the course of their professional duty, such as confidentiality, objectivity, professional behaviour, integrity and professional competence and due care.

The main aim of professional ethics is to serve as a moral guideline for professional accountants. By referring back to the set of ethical guidelines, the accountant is able to decide on the most appropriate course of action, which will be in line with the professional body's stance on ethics. The presence of a code of ethics is a form of declaration by the professional body to the public that it is committed to ensuring the highest level of professionalism amongst its members.

Often there may be ethical principles which conflict with the profit motive and it may be difficult to decide on a course of action. Ethical guidelines can help by developing ethical reasoning in accountants by providing insight into how to deal with conflicting principles and why a certain course of action is desirable. Individuals may hold inadequate beliefs or hold on to inadequate ethical values. An accountant has an ethical obligation to encourage the directors to operate within certain boundaries when determining the profit figure.

Users are becoming reactive to unethical behaviour by directors. This is leading to greater investment in ethical companies with the result that unethical practices can have a greater impact on the value of an entity than the reporting of a smaller profit figure.

Ethical guidelines enable individuals to understand the nature of one's own opinion and ethical values. Ethical guidelines help identify the basic ethical principles which should be applied. This will involve not only code-based decisions but also the application of principles which should enable the determination of what should be done in a given situation. This should not conflict with the profit motive unless directors are acting unscrupulously. Ethical guidance gives a checklist to be applied so that outcomes can be determined. Ethical issues are becoming more and more complex and it is critical to have an underlying structure of ethical reasoning, and not purely be driven by the profit motive.

ACCA Marking scheme		
		Marks
(a)	Net profit before taxation	4
	Net cash generated from operations	16
	Cash flow from investing activities	10
	Cash flow from financing activities	5
		———
	Maximum	35
		———
(b)	Subjective assessment of discussion	9
(c)	Subjective assessment – 1 mark per point	6
		———
Total		50
		———

Examiner's comments

This question required candidates to prepare a consolidated statement of cash flows using the indirect method for the Angel Group plc for the year ended 30 November 2013 in accordance with the requirements of IAS 7 *Statement of Cash Flows*. Questions requiring the preparation of consolidated statement of cash flows will always consist of fairly basic adjustments and more complex ones. The complex adjustments require candidates to determine how the statement of cash flows is affected by the information in the question. For example, in this question, a grant had been received by Angel but it had not recorded correctly in the financial statements. More basic adjustments would be the purchase of an associate, the implication of impairment of goodwill and the sale and purchase of financial assets. These latter adjustments just require candidates to show how these items are dealt with in the consolidated statement of cash flows. Invariably there will be a calculation of goodwill in the question so that candidates can demonstrate their group accounting skills. The impact on the cash flow statement will depend on the nature of the information given. In this case, a subsidiary was purchased and the balances had to be adjusted for in the consolidated statement of cash flows. Several candidates did not adjust for the purchase of the subsidiary. This of course affects several items in the consolidated statement of cash flows. However the marking scheme treated the non-adjustment of the various balances as a single error. Additionally, candidates had to show how a retirement benefit obligation as adjusted for the purchase of the subsidiary was dealt with and also PPE movement was complicated by the capitalisation of interest in the period as well as the above-mentioned grants.

Consolidated statement of cash flows questions will always have complex elements and this question was no different. However, there are some elements of the consolidated statement of cash flows which are quite basic and candidates always score well in this regard. Marks are awarded, for example, for simply showing the proceeds of the issue of share capital, which was simply the deduction of two figures in the statement of financial position. However, the difficulty with a consolidated statement of cash flows question is that it is more difficult to award marks for method as some of the items in the statement are either 'right' or 'wrong'. In consolidated statement of financial position questions, marks are allocated for method for such calculations as goodwill, NCI, Group reserves etc. In this type of question there are not as many of these types of calculations. Additionally, candidates often place the wrong sign on the correct figure. For example, a deduction is made in the statement rather than an addition. If this is a simple subtraction of two figures and the candidate puts the wrong sign on the resultant figure then it is difficult to award marks.

It is important as always to show all workings. For example, very few candidates correctly calculated the income taxes paid figure but there were several marks for this calculation, which were often awarded in the workings in the scripts. As intimated above, many of the figures in the statement do not need workings but where they do, it is important to show them.

5   TRAILER (JUNE 13 EXAM)   *Walk in the footsteps of a top tutor*

Key answer tips

This question involves a D-shaped group. It is therefore vital to spend time establishing the group structure and the group's effective interest in the sub-subsidiary. There are a number of accounting issues that need to be dealt with, such as provisions, a defined benefit pension plan and a loan that has been made to a charity at a lower than market rate of interest. If you find yourself struggling with any adjustments in the real exam then move on as this will help to maximise your marks in the limited time available.

(a)   **Trailer plc**

Consolidated Statement of Financial Position at 31 May 2013

	$m
Assets:	
Non-current assets:	
Property, plant and equipment (W11)	3,780.6
Goodwill (W3)	398
Financial assets (W12)	480.8
Current assets (W13)	1,726
Total assets	6,385.4
Equity and liabilities	
Equity attributable to owners of parent	
Share capital	1,750
Retained earnings (W5)	1,254.7
Other components of equity (W5)	170.1
	3,174.8
Non-controlling interest (W4)	892.6
Total non-current liabilities (W14)	1,906
Current liabilities (W15)	412
Total liabilities	2,318
Total equity and liabilities	6,385.4

Workings

(W1) Group structure

Tutorial note

When dealing with a complex group, it is vital to work out the group and NCI's effective interest in the sub-subsidiary. These percentages are used when calculating NCI and also group reserves.

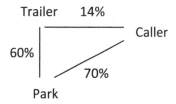

The group effective interest in Caller is:

Direct	14%
Indirect (60% × 70%)	42%
	———
Group effective interest	56%
	———

The NCI interest in Caller is therefore 44% (100% – 56%).

The acquisition date for Caller is 1 June 2012 as this is when Trailer gains control over Park and therefore gains indirect control over Caller.

(W2) Net assets

Tutorial note

If you are told the fair value of the net assets of the subsidiary at acquisition then you will need to work out the fair value adjustments as a balancing figure.

Park

	Acq'n date	Rep date
	$m	$m
Share capital	1,210	1,210
Other components	55	80
Retained earnings	650	930
FVA – Land (bal. fig)	35	35
	———	———
	1,950	2,255
	———	———

Caller

	Acq'n date	Rep date
	$m	$m
Share capital	800	800
Other components	70	95
Retained earnings	240	350
FVA – Land (bal. fig)	40	40
	1,150	1,285

(W3) Goodwill

Tutorial note

The cost of Caller has three elements: the cost of the direct holding, the cost of the indirect holding and the indirect holding adjustment.

Park

	$m
Fair value of consideration	1,250
NCI at acquisition (40% × $1,950m)	780
Fair value of identifiable net assets acquired (W2)	(1,950)
Goodwill at acquisition	80
Impairment (W6)	(80)
Goodwill at reporting date	–

Caller

	$m
Fair value of consideration:	
Direct holding (FV at date control achieved)	280
Indirect holding	1,270
Indirect holding adjustment (40% × $1,270m)	(508)
NCI at acquisition (44% × $1,150m)	506
Less fair value of identifiable net assets (W2)	(1,150)
Goodwill at reporting date	398

Trailer's investment in Caller was held at $310m at the reporting date. Therefore, the fair value increase of $30m ($310m – $280m) that has arisen since the date that control was achieved must be removed from the consolidated statements. Retained earnings must also be reduced by $30m.

(W4) Non-controlling interest

Tutorial note

You will need to process the other side of your indirect holding adjustment through the NCI working.

	$m
NCI in Park at acquisition (W3)	780
NCI % of post-acquisition net assets	122
(40% × ($2,255m − $1,950m) (W2))	
Indirect holding adjustment (W3)	(508)
NCI in Caller at acquisition (W3)	506
NCI % of post-acquisition net assets	59.4
(44% × ($1,285m − $1,150m) (W2))	
Impairment (40% × $167m (W6))	(66.8)
	892.6

(W5) Reserves

Retained earnings

	$m
Trailer	1,240
Park: 60% × ($930m − $650m (W2))	168
Caller: 56% × ($350m − $240m) (W2))	61.6
Gain on Caller investment (W3)	(30)
Impairment of goodwill (W6)	(80)
Impairment of other assets (60% × $167 (W6))	(100.2)
Interest charge (W7)	(4.0)
Interest credit (W7)	2.8
Reversal of impairment loss (W8)	11.6
Restructuring provision (W9)	(14)
Pension plan (W10)	(1.1)
	1,254.7

Other components of equity

	$m
Trailer	125
Park: 60% × ($80m – $55m) (W2)	15
Caller: 56% × ($95m – $70m) (W2)	14
Revaluation gain (W8)	21
Pension plan remeasurement (W10)	(4.9)
	170.1

(W6) Impairment of Park

Tutorial note

In note 3 of the question, we are told the recoverable amount of the net assets of Park. We therefore need to compare this to the carrying amount of Park's net assets.

Remember that goodwill has been calculated using the proportionate basis. This means that, when performing an impairment review, the goodwill must be grossed up to include the NCI's interest.

		$m
Goodwill (W3)	80	
Notional NCI ($80m × 40/60)	53.3	
Total notional goodwill		133.3
Net assets at reporting date (W2)		2,255
Total carrying amount of assets		2,388.3
Recoverable amount		(2,088.0)
Impairment		300.3

The impairment is firstly allocated to the total notional goodwill of $133.3m. However, only 60% of the total notional goodwill has been recognised in the statements and therefore only 60% ($80m) of the impairment is accounted for. This expense is all attributable to the owners of Trailer.

The remaining impairment of $167m ($300.3m – $133.3m) is allocated against PPE. This impairment loss is attributable to the owners of the Trailer and the NCI based on their respective shareholdings.

(W7) Loan to charity

Tutorial note

The reduced interest rate should be recognised as a reduction in the fair value of the asset when measured for the first time.

The fair value of the asset is determined by calculating the present value of all future cash receipts using the prevailing market interest rate for a similar instrument. This will result in a lower figure for fair value than the amount advanced. The difference is recognised as an expense in profit or loss.

Financial asset – fair value

	Cash flows $m	Discount factor	Present value $m
2013	1.5	0.94	1.4
2014	1.5	0.89	1.3
2015	51.5	0.84	43.3
			————
			46.0
			————

The advance of the loan should have been accounted for by posting the following:

Dr Financial assets	$46.0m
Cr Cash	$50.0m
Dr Profit or loss	$4.0m

The asset is then held at amortised cost:

1 June 2012 $m	Interest credit (6%) $m	Cash received $m	31 May 2013 $m
46.0	2.8	(1.5)	47.3

The correcting entries should therefore be:

Dr Retained earnings	$4.0m
Cr Financial asset	$4.0m
Dr Financial asset	$2.8m
Cr Retained earnings	$2.8m

(W8) The Office

Tutorial note

If no revaluation reserve exists for an item of PPE then a downwards revaluation is recognised in the statement of profit or loss.

In 2012, Trailer would have charged $3m for depreciation ($90m/30 years) leaving the office with a carrying value of $87m ($90m – $3m). Trailer would then have accounted for the remaining $12m ($87m – $75m) fall in value as a revaluation loss and charged this to profit or loss.

In 2013, Trailer would have charged depreciation of $2.6m ($75m/29 year remaining useful life), reducing the carrying amount of the asset to $72.4m ($75m – $2.6m). In order to bring the asset up to its current value of $105m at the end of the year, it must be increased by $32.6m ($105m – $72.4m).

Some of this reversal can be recognised in profit or loss, but this is capped at the amount needed to increase the asset to the value it would have been had no impairment occurred. If no impairment had occurred, the asset would have been held at $84m ($90m × (2 × $3m)). Therefore, the gain recorded in profit or loss is $11.6m ($84m – $72.4m). The remainder of the gain is recognised in other comprehensive income.

The entries will be:

Dr Property, plant and equipment $32.6m
Cr Profit or loss $11.6m
Cr Other comprehensive income $21m

(W9) Provision for restructuring

Tutorial note

Only those costs that result directly from and are necessarily entailed by a restructuring may be included in a restructuring provision. This includes costs such as employee redundancy costs or lease termination costs. Expenses that relate to ongoing activities, such as relocation and retraining, are excluded.

With regard to the service reduction, a provision should be recognised for the redundancy and lease termination costs of $14 million. The sites and details of the redundancy costs have been identified.

In contrast, Trailer should not recognise a provision for the finance and IT department's re-organisation. The re-organisation is not due to start for two years. External parties are unlikely to have a valid expectation that management is committed to the re-organisation as the time frame allows significant opportunities for management to change the details of the plan or even to decide not to proceed with it. Additionally, the degree of identification of the staff to lose their jobs is not sufficiently detailed to support the recognising of a redundancy provision.

(W10) Pension plan

Tutorial note

To calculate the remeasurement component, reconcile the opening and closing net pension deficit. The remeasurement component is accounted for in other comprehensive income.

The liability recognised in the financial statements will be $6m ($35 – $29m).

	$m
Net obligation at 1 June 2012 ($30m – $28m)	2.0
Net interest component ($2m × 5%)	0.1
Contributions	(2)
Service cost component	1
Remeasurement loss (bal. fig)	4.9
	___
Net obligation at 31 May 2013 ($35m – $29m)	6

The service cost component and net interest component will be charged to profit or loss ($1.1m) and the remeasurement loss to OCI ($4.9m). There will be no adjustment for the contributions, which have already been taken into account.

(W11) PPE

	$m
Trailer	1,440
Park	1,100
Caller	1,300
Increase in value of land – Park (W2)	35
Increase in value of land – Caller (W2)	40
Impairment (W6)	(167)
Increase in value of offices (W8)	32.6
	_____
	3,780.6

(W12) Financial assets

	$m
Trailer	320
Park	21
Caller	141
Interest charge (W7)	(4.0)
Interest credit (W7)	2.8
	_____
	480.8

(W13) Current assets

	$m
Trailer	895
Park	681
Caller	150
	1,726

(W14) Non-current liabilities

	$m
Trailer	985
Park	765
Caller	150
Defined benefit liability (W10)	6
	1,906

(W15) Current liabilities

	$m
Trailer	115
Park	87
Caller	196
Provision for restructuring (W9)	14
	412

(b)

Tutorial note

When calculating goodwill in this part of the question, you will not be penalised for any mistakes that you made in part (a).

*Remember that goodwill calculated under the fair value method **does not** need grossing up when performing an impairment review.*

Park

	$m
Fair value of consideration	1,250
Fair value of NCI	800
Fair value of identifiable net assets acquired (W2)	(1,950)
Goodwill	100

Caller

	$m
Direct holding	280
Indirect holding	1,270
Indirect holding adjustment (40% × $1,270m)	(508)
Fair value of NCI	530
Fair value of identifiable net assets acquired (W2)	(1,150)
Goodwill	422

Impairment of goodwill

Park

	$m
Goodwill	100
Identifiable net assets (W2)	2,255
Total	2,355
Recoverable amount	(2,088)
Impairment	267
Allocated to	
Goodwill	100
PPE (split $66.8m NCI/$100.2m retained earnings)	167
Total	267

Under the previous method used by Trailer, NCI was recognised at their share of net assets and did not include any goodwill. The full goodwill method means that non-controlling interest and goodwill are both increased by the goodwill that relates to the non-controlling interest.

It can be seen that goodwill is effectively adjusted for the change in the value of the non-controlling interest which represents the goodwill attributable to the NCI. In the case of Park, goodwill has increased from $80m to $100m, and the figure used for NCI under the proportionate method of $780m has moved to the fair value of $800m at 1 June 2012, that is an increase of $20m. In the case of Caller, goodwill has increased by $24m from $398m to $422m and the figure used for NCI (before adjustments) under the proportionate method of $506m has moved to its fair value of $530m at 1 June 2012, that is a rise of $24 million. The choice of method of accounting for NCI only makes a difference in an acquisition where less than 100% of the acquired business is purchased.

The full goodwill method increases reported net assets, which means that any impairment of goodwill will be greater. Thus in the case of Park, the impairment of goodwill will be $100m but this will be charged $60m to retained earnings and $40 million to NCI. PPE will be charged with $167m under either method. Both amounts are charged to retained earnings and NCI in the proportion 60/40, that is based upon the profit or loss allocation. Although measuring non-controlling interest at fair value may prove difficult, goodwill impairment testing is easier under full goodwill, as there is no need to gross up goodwill for partially owned subsidiaries.

(c)   There are several reasons why an accountant should study ethics. The moral beliefs that an individual holds may not be sufficient because often these are simple beliefs about complex issues. The study of ethics can sort out these complex issues by teaching the principles that are operating in these cases. Often there may be ethical principles which conflict and it may be difficult to decide on a course of action. The study of ethics can help by developing ethical reasoning in accountants by providing insight into how to deal with conflicting principles and why a certain course of action is desirable. Individuals may hold inadequate beliefs or hold on to inadequate ethical values. For example, it may be thought that it is acceptable to hold shares in client companies for business reasons, which, of course, is contrary to ethical guidance. Additionally, compliance with GAAP could be thought to be sufficient to meet the duty of an accountant. However, it can be argued that an accountant has an ethical obligation to encourage a more realistic financial picture by applying ethical judgement to the provisions of GAAP.

Another important reason to study ethics is to understand the nature of one's own opinion and ethical values. Ethical principles should be compatible with other values in life. For example, one's reaction to the following circumstances: the choice between keeping your job and violating professional and ethical responsibilities, the resolution of conflicts of interest if they involve family.

Finally, a good reason for studying ethics is to identify the basic ethical principles that should be applied. This will involve not only code-based decisions but also the application of principles that should enable the determination of what should be done in a given situation. The ethical guidance gives a checklist to be applied so that the outcome can be determined. Ethical issues are becoming more and more complex and it is critical to have knowledge of the underlying structure of ethical reasoning.

Professional ethics is an inherent part of the profession. ACCA's Code of Ethics and Conduct requires its members to adhere to a set of fundamental principles in the course of their professional duty, such as confidentiality, objectivity, professional behaviour, integrity and professional competence and due care. The main aim of professional ethics is to serve as a moral guideline for professional accountants. By referring back to the set of ethical guidelines, the accountant is able to decide on the most appropriate course of action, which will be in line with the professional body's stance on ethics. The presence of a code of ethics is a form of declaration by the professional body to the public that it is committed to ensuring the highest level of professionalism amongst its members.

Although the takeover does not benefit the company, its executives or society as a whole, the action is deceptive, unethical and hence unfair. It violates the relationship of trust, which the company has with society and the professional code of ethics. There are nothing but good reasons against the false disclosure of profits.

	ACCA Marking scheme		
			Marks
(a)	Property, plant and equipment		5
	Goodwill		6
	Financial assets		5
	Current assets/total non-current liabilities		1
	Retained earnings		6
	Other components of equity		3
	Non-controlling interest		3
	Current liabilities		1
	Pension plan		5
			──
		Maximum	35
			──
(b)	Subjective assessment of discussion		4
	Up to 2 marks per element		
	Calculations		5
			──
		Maximum	9
			──
(c)	Subjective assessment – 1 mark per point		6
			──
Total			50
			──

Examiner's comments

This question required candidates to prepare a group consolidated statement of financial position. The group was a complex group with candidates being required to determine the nature of the group holdings and the dates on which control occurred. The partial goodwill method was used by the entity and there was an impairment calculation required also. The group made a loan to a charitable organisation for the building of new sporting facilities and candidates had to deal with the financial asset, which had a subsidised rate of interest. The discounted interest rate was recognised as a reduction in the fair value of the asset when measured for the first time thus reflecting the economic substance of the transaction. There were additional adjustments required for the following:

- The acquisition of office accommodation where the fair value of the accommodation fell and was reflected in the financial statements but the market recovered unexpectedly quickly with the result that the offices should be valued upwards.

- The announcement of two major restructuring plans with no entries having been made in the financial statements for the plans.

- The accounting for the group pension plan where the figures had not been taken into account for the year except for the contributions paid which have been entered in cash and the defined benefit obligation.

Candidates generally score well on question 1. The goodwill calculations were invariably correct as was the nature of the group relationships. The treatment of the office accommodation was well answered as was the pension element.

Surprisingly the restructuring costs were not particularly well dealt with by candidates. Only those costs that result directly from and are necessarily entailed by the restructuring may be included, such as employee redundancy costs or lease termination costs. Expenses that relate to ongoing activities, such as relocation and retraining are excluded. With regard to the service reduction, a provision should have been recognised for the redundancy and lease termination costs. In contrast, the group should not have recognised a provision for the finance and IT department's re-organisation, as the re-organisation was not due to start for two years. Candidates had problems with the discounting of the loan to the charitable organisation. They often confused the principles involved, not realising that the fair value of the asset should be reduced for the subsidised rate of interest.

There are a significant number of marks attached to the retained earnings, OCI and NCI calculations. The marking scheme for these elements of the answer is based mainly around the candidates' own figures. This means that if the principles are applied correctly, then the candidate receives the marks allocated. This in turn means that the candidate should ensure that the workings are quite clear and labelled with an explanation of the figure. For example, post acquisition reserves of the subsidiary should always have an explanation of where the figure has been derived. Similarly if there is an impairment loss, the candidate will gain credit for charging this against retained earnings even if the candidate's calculation of the impairment loss is incorrect as the principle involved is correct.

6   MINNY (DEC 12 EXAM) *Walk in the footsteps of a top tutor*

Key answer tips

This consolidated statement of financial position involves a vertical group. Minny controls Bower, and Bower controls Heeny. Therefore, Minny controls Heeny through its interest in Bower. It is vital to establish the group and the NCI's effective interest in the sub-subsidiary. These percentages will be used when calculating NCI and group reserves. When consolidating a vertical group, you also need to remember to process the indirect holding adjustment.

(a)   Consolidated Statement of Financial Position at 30 November 2012

	$m
Assets:	
Non-current assets:	
Property, plant and equipment (W10)	1,606.0
Goodwill (W3)	190.0
Intangible assets (W11)	227.0
Investment in Puttin (W7)	50.5
Current assets (W12)	1,607.0
Disposal group (W9)	33.0
Total assets	3,713.5

Equity and liabilities

Equity attributable to owners of parent

Share capital	920.0
Retained earnings (W5)	936.1
Other components of equity (W5)	77.8
	1,933.9
Non-controlling interest (W4)	394.6
	2,328.5
Total non-current liabilities (W13)	711.0
Disposal group (W9)	3.0
Current liabilities (W14)	671.0
Total liabilities	1,385.0
Total equity and liabilities	3,713.5

Workings

(W1) Group structure

Tutorial note

When dealing with a complex group, it is vital to work out the group and NCI's effective interest in the sub-subsidiary. These percentages are used when calculating NCI and also group reserves.

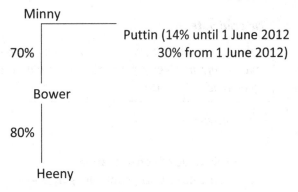

The group effective interest in Heeny is 56% (70% × 80%). The NCI holding is therefore 44% (100% − 56%).

(W2) Net assets

Tutorial note

If you are told the fair value of the net assets of the subsidiary at acquisition then you will need to work out the fair value adjustments as a balancing figure.

Bower

	Acq'n date $m	Rep date $m
Share capital	400	400
Other components	27	37
Retained earnings	319	442
FVA – Land (bal. fig)	89	89
	835	968

Heeny

	Acq'n date $m	Rep date $m
Share capital	200	200
Other components	20	25
Retained earnings	106	139
FVA – Land (bal. fig)	36	36
	362	400

(W3) Goodwill

Tutorial note

Heeny is a sub-subsidiary. You must remove the NCI's share of the cost of the investment in Heeny from the goodwill calculation. This is known as an indirect holding adjustment.

Bower

	$m
Fair value of consideration	730
Fair value of non-controlling interest	295
Fair value of identifiable net assets acquired (W2)	(835)
Goodwill at acquisition	190
Impairment (W6)	–
Goodwill at reporting date	190

Heeny

	$m
Fair value of consideration	320
Indirect holding adjustment (30% × $320)	(96)
FV of NCI at acquisition (a 44% holding)	161
Less fair value of identifiable net assets (W2):	(362)
Goodwill at acquisition	23
Impairment (W6)	(23)
Goodwill at reporting date	–

(W4) Non-controlling interest

Tutorial note

Process the other side of your indirect holding adjustment through the NCI working.

	$m
NCI in Bower at acquisition	295.0
NCI % of post-acquisition net assets	39.9
(30% × ($968 – $835) (W2))	
Indirect holding adjustment (W3)	(96.0)
NCI in Heeny at acquisition	161.0
NCI % of post-acquisition net assets	16.7
(44% × ($400 – $362) (W2))	
Impairment	(22.0)
(44% × $50 (W6))	
	394.6

(W5) Reserves

Retained earnings

	$m
Minny	895.0
Bower: 70% × ($442 – $319 (W2))	86.1
Heeny: 56% × ($139 – $106) (W2))	18.5
Impairment (56% × $50 (W6))	(28.0)
Puttin gain from OCE (W7)	3.0
Puttin dividend (W7)	2.0
Share of Puttin's post-acquisition retained earnings (W7)	2.5
Intangible assets (W8)	(9.0)
Impairment of disposal group (W9)	(34.0)
	936.1

Other components of equity

	$m
Minny	73.0
Bower: 70% × ($37 – $27) (W2)	7.0
Heeny: 56% × ($25 – $20) (W2)	2.8
Puttin gain to retained earnings (W7)	(3.0)
Puttin dividend (W7)	(2.0)
	77.8

(W6) Impairment

Tutorial note

*In note 3 of the question, we are told that the recoverable amount of each subsidiary has been determined 'without consideration of liabilities'. In other words, you are given the recoverable amounts of the assets only. Make sure that you compare this to the carrying value of each subsidiary's **assets** (rather than the net assets).*

	Bower $m	Heeny $m
Goodwill (W3)	190	23
Assets (per SFP)	1,130	595
Fair value adjustment (W2)	89	36
Total asset value	1,409	654
Recoverable amount	(1,425)	(604)
Impairment	n/a	50

There is no impairment in the case of Bower but Heeny's assets are impaired. Goodwill of $23 million plus $27 million of the intangible assets will be written off.

Group reserves will be debited with $28 million and NCI with $22 million, being the loss in value of the assets split according to the effective interests.

(W7) Puttin

Tutorial note

Minny has significant influence over Puttin. Puttin is therefore an associate and must be accounted for using the equity method.

The gain of $3 million ($21m – $18m) recorded within OCE up to 1 June 2012 would not be transferred to profit or loss for the year but can be transferred within equity and hence to retained earnings under IFRS *9 Financial Instruments.*

Dr OCE $3m

Cr Retained earnings $3m

The dividend should have been credited to Minny's profit or loss and not OCI.

Dr OCE $2m

Cr Retained earnings $2m

The amount included in the consolidated statement of financial position would be:

	$m
Cost ($21m + $27m)	48.0
Share of post-acquisition profits	4.5
($30 million × 6/12 × 30%)	
Less dividend received	(2.0)
	———
	50.5
	———

There is no impairment as the carrying amount of the investment in the separate financial statements does not exceed the carrying amount in the consolidated financial statements nor does the dividend exceed the total comprehensive income of the associate in the period in which the dividend is declared.

The group's share the post-acquisition retained earnings movement is $2.5m ($4.5m – $2.0m). This will be held within group retained earnings (W5).

(W8) Development

Tutorial note

There are strict criteria in IAS 38 governing the items that can be included in the cost of an intangible asset.

Minny should recognise the $10 million as an intangible asset plus the cost of the prototype of $4 million and the $3 million to get it into condition for sale. The remainder of the costs should be expensed including the marketing costs. This totals $9 million, which should be taken out of intangibles and expensed.

Dr Retained earnings $9m
Cr Intangible assets $9m

(W9) Disposal group

Tutorial note

A disposal group held for sale should be measured at the lower of its carrying value and the fair value less costs to sell.

	$m
PPE	49
Inventory	18
Current liabilities	(3)
Proceeds	(30)
Impairment loss	34

A plan to dispose of net assets is an impairment indicator. The assets and liabilities will be shown as single line items in the statement of financial position. Assets will be held at $33m ($49m + $18m − $34m) and liabilities at $3 million.

(W10) PPE

	$m
Minny	920
Bower	300
Heeny	310
Increase in value of land – Bower (W2)	89
Increase in value of land – Heeny (W2)	36
Disposal group (W9)	(49)
	1,606

(W11) Intangible assets

	$m
Minny	198
Bower	30
Heeny	35
Intangible expensed (W8)	(9)
Impairment of intangible (W6)	(27)
	227

(W12) Current assets

	$m
Minny	895
Bower	480
Heeny	250
Disposal group (W9)	(18)
	1,607

(W13) Non-current liabilities

	$m
Minny	495
Bower	123
Heeny	93
	711

(W14) Current Liabilities

	$m
Minny	408
Bower	128
Heeny	138
Disposal group (W9)	(3)
	671

(b)   An asset or disposal group is available for immediate sale in its present condition, if the entity has the intention and ability to transfer the asset or disposal group to a buyer.

There is no guidance in the standard on what constitutes available for immediate sale but the guidance notes set out various examples.

Tutorial note

Try and provide examples of what constitutes 'available for immediate sale'.

Customary terms of sale such as surveys and searches of property do not preclude the classification as held for sale. However, present conditions do not include any conditions that have been imposed by the seller of the asset or disposal group, such as if planning permission is required before sale. In this case, the asset is not held for sale. The problem is determining whether the entity truly intends to dispose of the group of assets.

Tutorial note

Make sure that you state relevant criteria from the accounting standard.

A sale is 'highly probable' where it is significantly more likely than probable that the sale will occur and probable is defined as 'more likely than not'. IFRS 5 attempts to clarify what this means by setting out the criteria for a sale to be highly probable. These criteria are:

- there is evidence of management commitment

- there is an active programme to locate a buyer and complete the plan

- the asset is actively marketed for sale at a reasonable price compared to its fair value

- the sale is expected to be completed within 12 months of the date of classification, and

- actions required to complete the plan indicate that it is unlikely that there will be significant changes to the plan or that it will be withdrawn.

Because the standard defines 'highly probable' as 'significantly more likely than probable', this creates a high threshold of certainty before recognition as held-for-sale. IFRS 5 expands on this requirement with some specific conditions but the uncertainty still remains. Thus, a number of issues has arisen over the implementation of the standard, mainly due to the fact that there is subjectivity over the requirements of the standard.

(c)   A company may distribute non-cash assets. The transfer of the asset from Bower to Minny amounts to a distribution of profits rather than a loss on disposal. The shortfall between the sale proceeds and the carrying amount is $1 million and this will be treated as a distribution. Bower has retained earnings of $442 million available at the year end plus the sale of the non-current asset will 'realise' an additional amount of $400,000 from the revaluation reserve. It is likely that the sale will be legal, depending upon the jurisdiction concerned. If the transaction meets the criteria of IFRS 5 Non-current Assets Held for Sale and Discontinued Operations, then the asset would be held in the financial statements of Bower in a separate category from plant, property and equipment and would be measured at the lower of carrying amount at held-for-sale date and fair value less costs to sell. If the asset is held for sale, IAS 16 Property, *Plant and Equipment* does not apply.

The boundary between ethical practices and legality is sometimes blurred. Questions would be asked of the directors as to why they would want to sell an asset at half of its current value, assuming that $2 million is the current value and that $1 million is not a fair approximation of fair value. It may raise suspicion. Corporate reporting involves the development and disclosure of information, which should be truthful and neutral. Both Bower and Minny would need to make related party disclosures so that the transaction is understood by stakeholders.

The nature of the responsibility of the directors requires a high level of ethical behaviour. Shareholders, potential shareholders, and other users of the financial statements rely heavily on the financial statements of a company as they can use this information to make an informed decision about investment. They rely on the directors to present a true and fair view of the company. Unethical behaviour is difficult to control or define. However, it is likely that this action will cause a degree of mistrust between the directors and shareholders unless there is a logical business reason for their actions. Shareholders in most jurisdictions who receive an unlawful dividend are liable to repay it to the company.

ACCA Marking scheme		
		Marks
(a)	Property, plant and equipment	5
	Goodwill	5
	Intangible assets	1
	Investment in Puttin	4
	Current assets	1
	Disposal group	5
	Retained earnings	6
	Other components of equity	4
	Non-controlling interest	3
	Current liabilities	1
		───
	Maximum	**35**
		───
(b)	1 mark per point up to maximum – definition	4
	Discussion	3
(c)	Accounting treatment	4
	Ethical considerations	4
		───
Total		**50**
		───

Examiner's comments

This question required candidates to prepare a consolidated statement of financial position for the Minny Group, as at 30 November 2012. The group structure was a complex group with a sub-subsidiary. Candidates also had to deal with an associate, which had originally been an investment within the group, impairment testing the holdings in the group companies, a disposal group and the capitalisation of development expenditure. Candidates dealt with the group structure quite well and the calculations of goodwill arising on acquisition were generally accurate. It is important to take time in the examination to determine the nature of the group structure as marks are allocated for this in the marking guide. Often candidates calculate retained earnings and non controlling interest inaccurately but the marking guide gives credit for candidates own figures as long as the principle is correct. This latter point also enhances the importance of candidates showing full and clear workings. Some candidates condense their workings into a disproportionately small space in the answer book. Clarity is more important than conciseness. In this question, there were marks allocated for the presentation of the disposal group on the face of the statement of financial position. Many candidates did not show the disposal group separately on the face.

The main problems that arose were the treatment of the impairment of goodwill, the gain arising on the accounting for the associate, and the treatment of the disposal group. Additionally, candidates often find it difficult to deal with the volume of information in the question. This skill can be improved by exam practice and technique.

7   **ROBBY (JUNE 12 EXAM)**   *Walk in the footsteps of a top tutor*

Key answer tips

This question involves a parent company achieving control over a subsidiary in stages (a step acquisition). Remember, goodwill is calculated on the date that control is achieved.

The parent company also has a share in a joint operation. This means that it must recognise its share of the assets, liabilities, incomes and expenses of the operation.

Included in parts (a) and (b) are issues regarding de-recognition of financial assets. A detailed knowledge of IFRS 9 is required. When answering discursive requirements, such as part (b), remember to state the relevant rules in the standard and then apply these rules to the scenario.

(a)   **Robby Consolidated Statement of Financial Position at 31 May 2012**

	$m
Assets	
Non-current assets:	
Property, plant and equipment (W10)	241.1
Goodwill (W3)	6.0
Financial assets (W11)	29.0
Current assets (W12)	36.0
Total assets	312.1
Equity and Liabilities	
Ordinary shares	25.0
Other components of equity (W5)	2.0
Retained earnings (W5)	81.5
Total equity	108.5
Non-controlling interest (W4)	27.6
Total equity	136.1
Non-current liabilities including provision (W14)	94.8
Current liabilities (W13)	81.2
Total equity and liabilities	312.1

Workings

(W1) Group structure

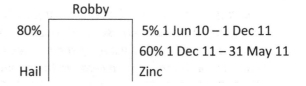

Robby

80% | 5% 1 Jun 10 – 1 Dec 11
| 60% 1 Dec 11 – 31 May 11

Hail | Zinc

(W2) Net assets

Tutorial note

Further information obtained about the fair value of the identifiable net assets of a subsidiary as at the acquisition date within the measurement period is accounted for retrospectively. The measurement period ends twelve months after the acquisition date.

Hail

	Acq'n date	Rep date
	$m	$m
Share capital	20	20
Retained earnings	16	27
FVA – Land (bal. fig)	24	24
	——	——
	60	71
	——	——

Zinc

	Acq'n date	Rep date
	$m	$m
Share capital	10	10
Retained earnings	15	19
PPE uplift ($26m – $10m – $15m)	1	1
Additional uplift	3	3
Excess depreciation (($4m/5 years) × 6/12)		(0.4)
	——	——
	29	32.6
	——	——

(W3) Goodwill

Tutorial note

Control over Zinc is achieved in stages. On the date that control is achieved, the previously held equity must be revalued to fair value with the gain or loss recorded in profit or loss. The fair value of the previously held equity is then included as part of the consideration when calculating the goodwill that arises on acquisition.

Hail

Since acquisition, the investment in Hail has been revalued upwards from $50m to $55m. This must be reversed. Moreover, dividend income has been incorrectly recognised in other comprehensive income. The adjusting entries are:

Dr Other comprehensive income	$5.0
Cr Investment in Hail	$5.0
Dr Other comprehensive income	$2.0
Cr Retained earnings	$2.0

Goodwill on acquisition of Hail

	$m
Fair value of consideration	50
Fair value of non-controlling interest	15
Fair value of identifiable net assets acquired (W2)	(60)
Goodwill at acquisition	5

Zinc

The total investment in Zinc is held in the SFP at $19m. This includes the $16m paid for the 55% holding, meaning that the 5% holding is held at $3m ($19m – $16m).

On the date that control is achieved, the previously held equity must be revalued to fair value with the gain recorded in profit or loss. A revaluation of $2m ($5m – $3m) is therefore required:

Dr Investment $2.0

Cr Profit or loss $2.0

Goodwill on acquisition of Zinc

	$m
Fair value of consideration	16
Fair value of previously held equity	5
Fair value of NCI at acquisition	9
Less fair value of identifiable net assets (W2):	(29)
Goodwill	1

Total goodwill at the reporting date is therefore $6m ($5m + $1m).

(W4) Non-controlling interest

	$m
Hail: NCI at acquisition (W3)	15.0
Hail: NCI % of net asset movement	2.2
(20% × ($71 – $60) (W2))	
Zinc: NCI at acquisition (W3)	9.0
Zinc: NCI % of net asset movement	1.4
(40% × ($32.6 – $29) (W2))	
	27.6

(W5) Reserves

Retained earnings

	$m
Robby	70.0
80% × Hail's post-acquisition retained earnings (80% × ($27 – $16) (W2))	8.8
60% × Zinc's post-acquisition retained earnings (60% × (($19 – $0.4) – $15) (W2))	2.16
Dividend adjustment (W3)	2.0
Control in stages adjustment (W3)	2.0
Joint operations profit share (W6)	0.7
Impairment (W7)	(0.7)
Transfer from equity (W7)	0.1
Receivables error (W8)	0.4
Land error (W9)	(4.0)
	81.5

Other components of equity

	$m
Robby	11.0
Hail revaluation adjustment (W3)	(5.0)
Dividend adjustment (W3)	(2.0)
Impairment (W7)	(1.9)
Transfer to retained earnings (W7)	(0.1)
	2.0

(W6) Joint operation

Tutorial note

If there is a joint operation, each operator should account for their share of the assets, liabilities, incomes and expenses.

SOFP	1 June 2011 $m	Dismantling cost $m	Depreciation $m	Unwinding of discount $m	31 May 2012 $m
PPE	6	2 × 40%	(6.8 × 1/10)		6.1
Trade receivables					8
Trade payables (0.2 + 6.4)/					6.6
Provision		0.8		0.04	0.84
Profit or loss					
Revenue (20.00 × 40%)					8
Cost of sales (16.00 × 40%)					(6.4)
Operating cost (0.50 × 40%)					(0.2)
Depreciation					(0.7)
Finance expense					(0.04)
					———
Net profit to retained earnings (W5)					0.7
					———

(W7) Impairment of PPE

Tutorial note

If a previously revalued asset is impaired, the impairment loss is firstly allocated against gains recorded for the same asset that are still held within equity. Any remaining impairment loss is then recognised in profit or loss.

The carrying amount of the PPE at 31 May 2011 was $9m ($10m – ($10m/20 × 2 years). The revaluation gain recorded was therefore $2m ($11m – $9m).

At 31 May 2012, the PPE would have been depreciated by $0.6m ($11m/18 years) giving a carrying amount of $10.4m ($11m – $0.6m).

If the asset had not been revalued, the depreciation would have been $0.5m ($10m/20 years). Therefore a reserve transfer is made for the excess depreciation of $0.1m ($0.6m – $0.5m).

Dr Other components of equity $0.1m

Cr Retained earnings $0.1m

The 'revaluation surplus' remaining in other components is therefore $1.9m ($2.0m – $0.1m).

The impairment loss on the PPE of $2.6m ($10.4m – $7.8m) will firstly be charged against the remaining revaluation surplus of $1.9m. The excess impairment of $0.7m ($2.6m – $1.9m) will be charged to profit or loss:

Dr Profit or loss $0.7m

Dr Other components of equity $1.9m

Cr PPE $2.6m

(W8) Trade receivables

Tutorial note

Financial assets should only be de-recognised if the risks and rewards of ownership have transferred.

The risks and rewards of ownership have not transferred. The correcting double entry is:

Dr Trade receivables $4.0m

Cr Secured borrowings $3.6m

Cr Retained earnings $0.4m

(W9) Land

The sale of land should not be recognised in the financial statements as the risks and rewards of ownership have not been transferred. The land can be repurchased at the sale price plus a premium, which represents effectively an interest payment. It is effectively manipulating the financial statements in order to show a better cash position. The land should be reinstated at its carrying amount before the transaction, so $12 million, a current liability recognised of $16 million and the profit on disposal of $4 million that was recorded reversed.

(W10) PPE

	$m
Robby	112.0
Hail	60.0
Zinc	26.0
Increase in value of land – Hail (W2)	24.0
Increase in value of PPE – Zinc (W2)	4.0
Excess depreciation in Zinc (W2)	(0.4)
Impairment loss (W7)	(2.6)
Joint operation (W6)	6.1
Land – option to repurchase (W9)	12.0
	241.1

(W11) Financial assets

	$m
Robby	9.0
Hail	6.0
Zinc	14.0
	29.0

(W12) Current assets

	$m
Robby	5.0
Hail	7.0
Zinc	12.0
Factoring trade receivables (W8)	4.0
Joint operation (W6)	8.0
	36.0

(W13) Current liabilities

	$m
Robby	47.0
Hail	6.0
Zinc	2.0
Secured borrowings (W8)	3.6
Joint operation (W6)	6.6
($6.40 trade payable + $0.20 operating costs)	
Land sale (W9)	16.0
	81.2

(W14) Non-current liabilities

	$m
Robby	53.0
Hail	20.0
Zinc	21.0
Joint operation (W6)	0.84
($0.80 provision + unwinding of discount $0.04)	
	94.84

(b)

> **Tutorial note**
>
> *Start off by stating the de-recognition rules from IFRS 9. You would not be expected to know the same level as detail as is provided below.*

(i)   The basic rules for the derecognition model in IFRS 9 Financial Instruments is to determine whether the asset under consideration for derecognition is:

(i)   an asset in its entirety, or

(ii)   specifically identified cash flows from an asset (or a group of similar financial assets), or

(iii)   a fully proportionate (pro rata) share of the cash flows from an asset (or a group of similar financial assets), or

(iv)   a fully proportionate (pro rata) share of specifically identified cash flows from a financial asset (or a group of similar financial assets).

Once the asset under consideration for de-recognition has been determined, an assessment is made as to whether the asset should be derecognised. Derecognition is required if either:

(i)   the contractual rights to the cash flows from the financial asset have expired, or

(ii)   financial asset has been transferred, and if so, whether the transfer of that asset is subsequently eligible for derecognition.

An asset is transferred if either the entity has transferred the contractual rights to receive the cash flows, or the entity has retained the contractual rights to receive the cash flows from the asset, but has assumed a contractual obligation to pass those cash flows on under an arrangement that meets the following three conditions:

(i)   the entity has no obligation to pay amounts to the eventual recipient unless it collects equivalent amounts on the original asset

(ii)   the entity is prohibited from selling or pledging the original asset (other than as security to the eventual recipient)

(iii)   the entity has an obligation to remit those cash flows without material delay.

Once an entity has determined that the asset has been transferred, it then determines whether or not it has transferred substantially all of the risks and rewards of ownership of the asset. If substantially all the risks and rewards have been transferred, the asset is derecognised. If substantially all the risks and rewards have been retained, derecognition of the asset is precluded.

If the entity has neither retained nor transferred substantially all of the risks and rewards of the asset, then the entity must assess whether it has relinquished control of the asset or not. If the entity does not control the asset then derecognition is appropriate; however, if the entity has retained control of the asset, then the entity continues to recognise the asset to the extent to which it has a continuing involvement in the asset.

Tutorial note

Now apply the rules that you have stated to the information in the scenario.

Robby has transferred its rights to receive cash flows and its maximum exposure is to repay $3.6 million. This is unlikely, but Robby has guaranteed that it will compensate the bank for all credit losses. Additionally, Robby receives the benefit of amounts received above $3.6 million and therefore retains both the credit risk and late payment risk. Substantially, all the risks and rewards remain with Robby and therefore the receivables should still be recognised.

(ii) Manipulation of financial statements often does not involve breaking rules, but the purpose of financial statements is to present a fair representation of the company's or group's position, and if the financial statements are misrepresented on purpose then this could be deemed unethical. The financial statements in this case are being manipulated to hide the fact that the group has liquidity problems. The Robby Group has severe problems with a current ratio of 0.44 ($36m/$81.2m) and a gearing ratio of 0.83 ($53 + 20 + 21 + factored receivables 3.6 + land option 16 = 113.6/equity interest including NCI $136.09m). The sale and repurchase of the land would make little difference to the overall position of the company, but would maybe stave off proceedings by the bank if the overdraft were eliminated. Robby has considerable PPE, which may be undervalued if the sale of the land is indicative of the value of all of the PPE.

Accountants have the responsibility to issue financial statements that do not mislead users as they assume that such professionals are acting in an ethical capacity, thus giving the financial statements credibility. Accountants should seek to promote or preserve the public interest. If the idea of a profession is to have any significance, then it must have the trust of users. Accountants should present financial statements that meet the qualitative characteristics set out in the Framework. Faithful representation and verifiability are two such concepts and it is critical that these concepts are applied in the preparation and disclosure of financial information.

ACCA Marking scheme		
		Marks
(a)	Property, plant and equipment	6
	Goodwill	6
	NCI	4
	Financial asset	1
	Current asset	3
	OCE	3
	Retained earnings	6
	Non-current liabilities	2
	Current liabilities	4
		──
	Maximum	35
		──
(b) (i)	1 mark per point up to max	9
(ii)	Manipulation	2
	Ethical discussion	4
		──
	Maximum	6
		──
Total		50
		──

Examiner's comments

Part 1 (a) required candidates to prepare a consolidated statement of financial position of a group in accordance with International Financial Reporting Standards. The question required candidates to deal with the acquisition of a subsidiary, the acquisition of another subsidiary that was formerly an investment, a joint operation, the impairment of PPE, the factoring of debts and a deliberate manipulation of the financial statements. Candidates are very good at preparing group accounts using the full goodwill method but not quite as good at accounting for the acquisition of a subsidiary that was formerly an investment. The main issue was determining the fair value of the consideration as some candidates did not take into account the increase in the fair value of the equity interest. Most of the accounting for the various transactions was quite well attempted. Candidates' answers to the impairment of PPE element of the question were often extremely accurate. However, the answers to the joint operation element of the question were quite poor. Candidates did not seem to have an understanding of the 'book-keeping' for such an arrangement. Candidates often understood the relationship but could not account for it.

Part 1 (b) (i) required candidates to describe the rules of IFRS 9 *Financial Instruments* relating to the de-recognition of a financial asset anyhow these rules affected the treatment of the portfolio of trade receivables accounted for in part 1 (a) of the question. Surprisingly few candidates seemed to know the de-recognition rules of IFRS 9 and often described the nature of a financial instrument, when a financial instrument should be recognised and the valuation methods utilised. Often this was correct but was not answering the question. The best way to demonstrate knowledge is in answering the question set on the exam paper not the question in a candidate's mind. Most candidates recognised that substantially, all the risks and rewards remained with the holding company and therefore the receivables should still be recognised.

In part (b) (ii), many candidates spent a disproportionate amount of time discussing the accounting treatment with little time spent on the ethical aspect of the transaction. This section of the paper is aimed at assessing the candidates' ethical viewpoints and therefore it is imperative that candidates give it due regard.

8   TRAVELER (DEC 11 EXAM) *Walk in the footsteps of a top tutor*

Key answer tips

This is a good question for testing knowledge of a number of consolidation issues. In particular, this group uses both the share of net assets method and the fair value method to value the non-controlling interest at acquisition. This has important implications for subsequent goodwill impairments – goodwill calculated under the share of net asset method must be grossed up to include the non-controlling interest's share when performing an impairment review.

This question also involves the parent company increasing its shareholding in a subsidiary from 60% to 80%. Goodwill is calculated on the date that control is achieved and is not re-calculated. Instead, this increase in the group's shareholding is accounted for within equity.

The examiner has said several times that a key reason why candidates fail P2 is because they over-run on question 1. Therefore, manage your time carefully. If you find yourself getting bogged down in an issue or an adjustment then leave it and move on.

(a)   Consolidated Statement of Financial Position at 30 November 2011

	$m
Assets:	
Non-current assets:	
Property, plant and equipment (W10)	1,842.3
Goodwill (W3)	69.2
Financial assets (W8)	130.1
Defined benefit surplus (W9)	52.0
Current assets (W11)	2,081.0
	_____
Total assets	4,174.6
	_____

Equity and liabilities	$m
Equity attributable to owners of parent	
Share capital	1,120
Retained earnings (W5)	992.4
Other components of equity (W5)	81.7
	_____
	2,194.1
Non-controlling interest (W4)	343.5
	_____
	2,537.6
	_____
Total non-current liabilities (W11)	851.0
Current liabilities (W11)	786.0
	_____
Total liabilities	1,637.0
	_____
Total equity and liabilities	4,174.6
	_____

Workings

(W1) Group structure

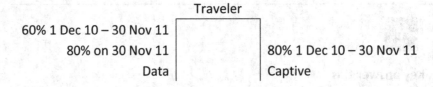

Traveler

60% 1 Dec 10 – 30 Nov 11
80% on 30 Nov 11
Data

80% 1 Dec 10 – 30 Nov 11
Captive

(W2) Net assets

Tutorial note

The identifiable net assets of a subsidiary are consolidated at fair value. Make sure that fair value adjustments are processed through your net asset workings.

Data

	Acq'n date	Rep date
	$m	$m
Share capital	600	600
Retained earnings	299	442
Other Equity	26	37
FVA – Land (bal. fig)	10	10
	————	————
	935	1,089
	————	————

Captive

	Acq'n date	Rep date
	$m	$m
Share capital	390	390
Retained earnings	90	169
Other Equity	24	45
FVA – Land (bal. fig)	22	22
	————	————
	526	626
	————	————

(W3) Goodwill

Tutorial note

Pay attention to whether the NCI at acquisition is being measured at its share of the subsidiary's identifiable net assets or at fair value.

Remember that goodwill is calculated at the date control is achieved over another company. It is not recalculated for any further share purchases.

Data

	$m
Fair value of consideration for 60% interest	600
Fair value of non-controlling interest	395
Fair value of identifiable net assets acquired (W2)	(935)
	———
Goodwill at acquisition	60
Impairment (W6)	(50)
	———
Goodwill at reporting date	10
	———

Captive

	$m
Fair value of consideration	541
NCI at acquisition ($526 × 20%)	105.2
Less fair value of identifiable net assets (W2):	(526)
	———
Goodwill	120.2
Impairment (W6)	(61)
	———
	59.2
	———

Total goodwill at the reporting date is therefore $69.2m ($10 + $59.2).

The assets transferred as part of the consideration need to be removed from non-current assets, and the gain on disposal needs to be calculated. The sale consideration of $64 million has been recorded in profit. The carrying amount of the asset is $56 million, giving a gain on disposal of $8 million. The adjustment required to arrive at the gain is:

Dr Retained earnings (W5) $56m

Cr PPE (W10) $56m

(W4) Non-controlling interest

	$m
NCI in Date pre additional share purchase (W7)	456.6
Reduction in NCI (W7)	(228.3)
Impairment of Data goodwill (W6)	(10)
NCI in Captive:	
NCI at acquisition (W3)	105.2
NCI % of post-acquisition net assets	20.0
(20% × ($626 – $526) (W2))	
	343.5

(W5) Reserves

Retained earnings

	$m
Traveler	1,066.0
Sale of non-current asset (W3)	(56.0)
Impairment of goodwill (W6) ($40 + $61)	(101.0)
Impairment of financial asset (W8)	(7.9)
Defined benefit cost (W9)	(55.0)
Depreciation for year factory (W10)	(2.7)
Post acquisition reserves:	
Data (60% × ($442 – $299) (W2))	85.8
Captive (80% × ($169 – $90) (W2))	63.2
	992.4

Other components of equity

	$m
Traveler	60.0
Data (60% × ($37 –$26) (W2))	6.6
Captive (80% × ($45 – $24) (W2))	16.8
Positive movement in equity (W7)	8.3
Remeasurement loss (W9)	(10.0)
	81.7

(W6) Impairment of goodwill

Tutorial note

Pay close attention to whether the non-controlling interest has been valued using the share of net assets method or the fair value method.

If the share of net assets method has been used, then only the goodwill attributable to the parent has been calculated. When performing an impairment review, this goodwill must be notionally grossed up to include the NCI's share.

Data

	$m
Goodwill (W3)	60
Identifiable net assets (W2)	1,089
Total	1,149
Recoverable amount	(1,099)
Goodwill impairment (W3)	50

The goodwill impairment relating to Data will be split 80%/20% between the group and the NCI. Thus retained earnings will be debited with $40 million (W5) and NCI with $10 million (W4).

Note: Given that the impairment review arose at the year end when Traveler's shareholding was 80%, this is now the basis of profit allocation and hence has been used in determining the split between group and NCI. It could be argued that a 60:40 allocation between group and NCI is also appropriate as this was how profits that arose in the year have been apportioned and the impairment is a loss that arose in the year, albeit calculated at the year end.

Captive

	$m	$m
Goodwill (W3)	120.2	
Notional NCI ($120.2 × 20/80)	30.1	
Total notional goodwill		150.3
Identifiable net assets (W2)		626.0
Total		776.25
Recoverable amount		(700.0)
Impairment		76.25

The impairment is allocated to the notional goodwill. However, only 80% of the notional goodwill has been recognised in the consolidated statements and so only 80% of the impairment is accounted for. This means that the goodwill impairment recognised (W3) is $61m ($76.25 × 80%). This expense is all attributable to the group and therefore retained earnings (W5) must be debited with $61m.

(W7) Increase in shareholding

Tutorial note

If the group increases its shareholding in a subsidiary, goodwill is not recalculated. Instead, this transaction is accounted for within equity. The difference between the cash paid and the decrease in the NCI is recorded in other components of equity.

	$m	$m
Fair value of consideration		220
NCI at acquisition (W3)	395	
NCI % of net assets movement		
($1,089 – $935) (W2) × 40%)	61.6	
NCI 30 November 2011	456.6	
Reduction in NCI (20/40 × $456.6)		228.3
Positive movement in equity (W5)		8.3

(W8) Financial asset

Tutorial note

Granting concessions to a borrower is an indication that a financial asset is credit impaired. The expected credit losses must therefore be calculated as the difference between the gross carrying amount of the asset and the present value of the estimated future cash flows when discounted at the original effective rate of interest.

		$m	$m
Carrying amount			30.00
PV of future cash flows:			
Year 1	8m × 1/1.067	7.50	
Year 2	8m × 1/1.067²	7.03	
Year 3	8m × 1/1.067³	6.59	
			(21.1)
Expected credit losses			8.9

The loss allowance must be increased by $7.9m ($8.9m – $1.0m), giving an impairment loss in profit or loss of $7.9m (W5).

The carrying amount of financial assets in the consolidated statements will be $130.1m ($108m + $10m + $20m – $7.9m).

(W9) Defined benefit pension fund

Tutorial note

The amount recognised in the statement of financial position in respect of a defined benefit pension scheme is the scheme's net deficit or surplus.

The net interest component and service cost component are recognised in profit or loss. The remeasurement component is recorded in other comprehensive income.

The entries for the pension scheme would be as follows:

Dr Profit or loss (W5) $55m
Cr Defined benefit asset $55m

Dr Defined benefit asset $45m
Cr Cash (W11) $45m

The re-measurement component is calculated at follows:

	$m
PV of obligation at 1 December 2010	250
Fair value of assets at 1 December 2010	(322)
Pension surplus at 1 December 2010	(72)
Pension costs	55
Contributions paid	(45)
Re-measurement loss	10
Pension surplus at 30 November 2011	(52)

($288m – $340m)

In order to recognise the re-measurement component, the entry is:

Dr OCI (W5) $10m

Cr defined benefit asset $10m

(W10) Property, plant and equipment

Tutorial note

According to IAS 16, different parts of an asset may have different useful economic lives. An entity should allocate the cost paid for property, plant and equipment to its significant parts and depreciate these separately.

The roof will be depreciated over five years at $1 million per annum ($5m/5 years).

The remainder will be depreciated over 25 years, taking into account the residual value, to give a charge of $1.7 million per annum (($45m − $2m)/25 years).

The total depreciation for the year is therefore $2.7 million.

	$m
Traveler	439
Data	810
Captive	620
Increase in value of land – Data (W2)	10
Increase in value of land – Captive (W2)	22
Less depreciation	(2.7)
Less disposal of asset (W3)	(56)
	1,842.3

(W11) Assets and liabilities

Current liabilities

	$m
Traveler	274
Data	199
Captive	313
	786

Non-current liabilities

	$m
Traveler	455
Data	323
Captive	73
	851

Current assets

	$m
Traveler	995
Data	781
Captive	350
Pension contributions (W9)	(45)
	2,081

(b) IFRS 8 does not prescribe how centrally incurred expenses and central assets should be allocated to segments. However, allocation of costs and expenses is an area where the basis chosen by an entity can have a significant effect on the segment results. IFRS 8, however, does require that amounts be allocated on a reasonable basis.

The head office management costs could be allocated on the basis of turnover or net assets. The basis of allocation will significantly affect the results. The pension expense may be allocated on the number of employees or salary expense of each segment. Allocating the expense to a segment with no pensionable employees would however not be reasonable. The costs of managing properties could be allocated on the basis of the type, value and age of the properties used by each segment. Different bases can be appropriate for each type of cost.

The standard does not require allocation of costs to be on a consistent basis. An entity may allocate interest to a segment profit or loss but does not have to allocate the related interest-bearing asset to the segment assets or liabilities. IFRS 8 calls this asymmetrical allocation.

IFRS 8 requires the information presented to be the same basis as it is reported internally, even if the segment information does not comply with IFRS or the accounting policies used in the consolidated financial statements. Examples of such situations include segment information reported on a cash basis (as opposed to an accruals basis), and reporting on a local GAAP basis for segments that are comprised of foreign subsidiaries. Although the basis of measurement is flexible, IFRS 8 requires entities to provide an explanation of:

(i) the basis of accounting for transactions between reportable segments

(ii) the nature of any differences between the segments' reported amounts and the consolidated totals.

For example, those resulting from differences in accounting policies and policies for the allocation of centrally incurred costs that are necessary for an understanding of the reported segment information. In addition, IFRS 8 requires reconciliations between the segments' reported amounts and the consolidated financial statements.

(c)

> *Tutorial note*
>
> *With a little bit of practice, you should score high marks on ethics. However, the P2 examiner has noted that many students do not attempt this part of the question.*

Traditional ethical conduct relating to disclosure is insufficient when applied to corporate social responsibility (CSR) disclosure because the role of company is linked with the role of citizen, which is held to a higher ethical standard. Corporate citizens are companies acting on behalf of a social interest, which may or may not affect revenues. These socially beneficial actions raise the ethical standard for such companies because of altruistic intentions, which is entirely different from the profit-generating purpose of a company. The ethical expectations of corporate citizens are thus more demanding than those for businesses without a social interest, especially in the way corporate citizens communicate their practices.

The ethics of corporate social responsibility disclosure are difficult to reconcile with shareholder expectations. Companies must remain profitable but there may be conflict. Maintaining integrity becomes more challenging when a company may report less profit and thus lower directors' bonuses. The problem that faces many companies is how to ethically, legally, and effectively disclose information while maintaining their market position.

It can be argued that increased CSR disclosure is in itself a form of socially responsible behaviour, and that by offering more information to the public, companies better meet their responsibilities to stakeholders. There are ethical implications of companies using CSR reporting for the sole purpose of improving revenue. The ethical implications are exacerbated if the desired effects of disclosing responsible conduct are solely to improve profitability. Disclosing good conduct solely for profit is unacceptable because it exploits something of much higher value (right conduct) to promote something which may be thought as being of lower value (profit).

ACCA Marking scheme		
		Marks
(a)	Property, plant and equipment	4
	Goodwill	7
	Financial assets	4
	Defined benefit asset	2
	Current assets/total non-current liabilities	3
	Share capital	1
	Retained earnings	7
	Other components of equity	3
	Non-controlling interest	3
	Current liabilities	1
		—
	Maximum	35
		—
(b)	Subjective assessment	
	Up to 2 marks per element	8
(c)	Subjective assessment	7
		—
Total		50
		—

Examiner's comments

This question required candidates to prepare a consolidated statement of financial position for the Traveler Group. The question included the calculation of goodwill arising on the acquisition of subsidiaries using both the full and partial goodwill methods. Additionally, goodwill was impairment tested, thus candidates had to determine whether goodwill was impaired in situations where goodwill had been calculated using both methods set out in IFRS3 Business Combinations.

On the whole candidates demonstrated a good knowledge of the consolidation process together with calculation skills for the accounting adjustments needed to the parent's financial statements. A range of different methods was used to perform the consolidation and candidates were not penalised for using a different method to the model answer. It is important however to lay out answers in a logical and understandable manner.

Candidates performed well in the calculation of full goodwill but many candidates did not complete the partial method of calculating goodwill successfully. This problem was exacerbated when candidates' impairment tested goodwill. Full goodwill was impairment tested correctly in most cases but the unrecognised goodwill on the non-controlling interest, which represents the grossing up of goodwill for the purpose of impairment testing partial goodwill, was not included in many candidates' answers.

The impairment loss on the financial asset was calculated by discounting the annual payments using the original effective interest rate. Most candidates recognised the need to discount the future cash flows but many used the incorrect discount rate. Candidates accounted for the defined benefit pension scheme very well.

Traveler had a factory that required component accounting. The entity could not treat the roof and the building as a single asset and therefore should treat them separately. This procedure was not carried out successfully in many cases. The confusion seemed to arise over the relative length of lives of the two components and over the treatment of the residual value.

Candidates are generally performing well on the group accounting question in the paper but still seem to be spending a disproportionate amount of time on the question. Full goodwill is well calculated but the adjustments to the financial statements require candidates to deal with situations which may not be familiar to them. Thus candidates are required to use the principles which they have learned. Application of principles seems to be an issue for some candidates.

Common weaknesses of answers included:

- Ignoring the change in ownership interest

- Calculating impairment by simply comparing goodwill to recoverable amount without considering the net assets or fair value adjustment

- Not calculating a movement in equity for the non controlling interest change

- Including OCI changes in retained earnings rather than other components of equity.

9 ROSE (JUNE 11 EXAM) *Walk in the footsteps of a top tutor*

Key answer tips

This question involves consolidating an overseas subsidiary.

When consolidating a subsidiary with a different functional currency to that of the group, its assets and liabilities are translated at the closing exchange rate. Translation differences arise on goodwill and the opening net assets and profit of the subsidiary. Current year exchange differences are recorded in other comprehensive income. The cumulative exchange gains and losses are held within equity.

This question also involves the parent company increasing its shareholding in a subsidiary from 70% to 80%. This results in a decrease in the NCI holding from 30% to 20%, a decline of one third. Such transactions are accounted for within equity and no adjustments are made to goodwill.

(a)

Tutorial note

Remember to state the rules (how is a functional currency determined) and then apply those rules to the scenario.

(i)   The functional currency is a matter of fact and is the currency of the primary economic environment in which the entity operates. It should be determined at the entity level. The primary economic environment in which an entity operates is normally the one in which it primarily generates and expends cash.

The following factors should be considered in determining Stem's functional currency:

(i)   the currency that mainly influences the determination of the sales prices

(ii)   the currency of the country whose competitive forces and regulations mainly influences operating costs.

The currency that dominates the determination of sales prices will normally be the currency in which the sales prices for goods and services are denominated and settled. In Stem's case, sale prices are influenced by local demand and supply, and are traded in dinars. Analysis of the revenue stream points to the dinar as being the functional currency. The cost analysis is variable as the expenses are influenced by the dinar and the dollar.

IAS 21 also requires entities to consider secondary factors when determining the functional currency. These factors include the degree of autonomy and the independence of financing. Stem operates with a considerable degree of autonomy both financially and in terms of its management. Stem does not depend on the group for finance.

In conclusion, the functional currency of Stem will be the dinar as the revenue is clearly influenced by the dinar, and although the expenses are mixed, secondary factors point to the fact that the functional currency is different to that of Rose.

(ii)   **Rose plc**

Consolidated Statement of Financial Position at 30 April 2011

Assets:

	$m
Non-current assets	
Property, plant and equipment (W11)	603.65
Goodwill ($16m + $6.2m) (W3)	22.2
Intangible assets ($4m – $1m) (W2)	3
Financial assets ($15m + $7m + D50m/5)	32
	660.85
Current assets ($118m + $100m + D330m/5)	284
Total assets	944.85
Equity and liabilities:	
Share capital	158
Retained earnings (W5)	267.12
Exchange reserve (W7)	10.27
Other components of equity (W6)	6.98
Non-controlling interest (W4)	89.83
Total equity	532.20

Non-current liabilities ($56m + $42m + D160m/5 + $0.65m (W12))	130.65
Current liabilities ($185m + $77m + D100m/5)	282
	———
Total liabilities	412.65
	———
Total equity and liabilities	944.85
	———

Workings

(W1) Group structure

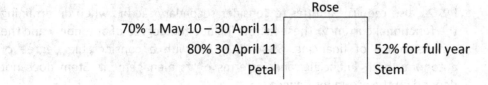

```
                                    Rose
70% 1 May 10 – 30 April 11  ┌──────────┐
        80% 30 April 11     │          │   52% for full year
              Petal         │          │   Stem
```

(W2) Net assets

Tutorial note

The identifiable net assets of a subsidiary are consolidated at fair value. Make sure that fair value adjustments are processed through your net asset workings.

Petal

	Acq'n date $m	Rep date $m
Share capital	38	38
Other equity	3	4
Retained earnings	49	56
FV adjustment – land (bal. fig)	30	30
	———	———
FV of recognised net assets	120	128
FV adjustment – patent	4	4
Amortisation ($4m/4 years)	–	(1)
	———	———
FV of identifiable net assets	124	131
	———	———

Stem

	Acq'n date	Rep date
	Dm	Dm
Share capital	200	200
Other equity	–	–
Retained earnings	220	300
FV adjustment – land (bal. fig)	75	75
	————	————
	495	575
	————	————

(W3) Goodwill

Tutorial note

Pay attention to whether the NCI at acquisition is being measured as its share of net assets or at fair value.

Goodwill in an overseas subsidiary should be translated each year at the closing exchange rate.

Petal

	$m
Fair value of consideration	94
Fair value of NCI at acquisition	46
Fair value of identifiable net assets acquired (W2):	(124)
	————
Goodwill	16
	————

Stem

	Dm
Fair value of consideration ($46m × 6 (acquisition rate))	276
Fair value of NCI at acquisition	250
Fair value of identifiable net assets acquired (W2):	(495)
	————
Goodwill	31
	————

Goodwill is deemed to be an asset of the subsidiary and is translated at the closing rate at each reporting date.

Goodwill in Stem is therefore $6.2m (D31m/5).

(W4) Non-controlling Interest

	$m
Petal at acquisition (W3)	46
NCI % of post-acquisition net assets (30% × ($131m – $124m)) (W2)	2.1
Reduction in NCI due to share purchase (W10)	(16.03)
Stem at acquisition (D250m/6) (W3)	41.67
NCI % of post-acquisition net assets (all comprised of current year profits) (48% × (D300m – D220m)/5.8) (W2)	6.62
Exchange gain – goodwill (W8)	0.49
Exchange gain on net assets (W9)	8.98
	———
	89.83
	———

(W5) Retained earnings

	$m
Rose	256
Current service cost – bonus scheme (W12)	(0.65)
Depreciation overcharged (W11)	0.4
Rose's share of post acquisition retained earnings:	
Petal (70% x (($56m – $1m) — $49m) (W2))	4.2
Stem (52% × (D300m – D220m) (W2)/5.8)	7.17
	———
	267.12
	———

(W6) Other components of equity

	$m
Rose	7
Petal – negative movement in equity (W10)	(2.97)
Revaluation surplus – overseas property (W11)	2.25
Rose's share of post-acquisition other components	0.7
Petal (70% × ($4m – $3m) (W2))	
	———
	6.98
	———

(W7) Exchange reserve

	$m
Exchange gain on goodwill (W8)	0.54
Exchange gain on net assets (W9)	9.73
	———
	10.27
	———

(W8) Exchange gain on Stem's goodwill

Tutorial note

If goodwill is calculated using the fair value method, the exchange gain or loss must be apportioned between the group and the NCI.

	Dm	Exchange rate	$m
Goodwill at 1 May 2010 (W3)	31	6.0	5.17
Impairment	–	5.8	–
Exchange gain (bal. fig)	–		1.03
Goodwill at 30 April 2011	31	5.0	6.2

Goodwill has been calculated under the fair value method. Therefore, the exchange gain must be allocated between the group and the NCI based on their respective shareholdings:

Group: $1.03m × 52% = $0.54m (W7)

NCI: $1.03m × 48% = $0.49m (W4)

(W9) Exchange gain on Stem's opening net assets and profit

Tutorial note

Exchange gains or losses arising on the opening net assets and profit of an overseas subsidiary are apportioned between the group and the NCI.

	Dm	Exchange rate	$m
Net assets at 1 May 2010 (W2)	495	6.0	82.5
Profit for the year (D300m – D220m)	80	5.8	13.79
Exchange gain (bal. fig)	–		18.71
Net assets at 30 April 2011	575	5.0	115.0

The exchange gain on the opening net assets and profit must be allocated between the group and the NCI based on their respective shareholdings:

Group: $18.71m × 52% = $9.73m (W7)

NCI: $18.71m × 48% = $8.98m (W4)

(W10) Increase in ownership

Tutorial note
Goodwill is not recalculated when the group increases its shareholding in a subsidiary. Instead, this is accounted for within equity. The difference between the consideration for the extra shares and the reduction in the NCI is accounted for in other components of equity.

	$m
Fair value of consideration	19
Reduction in NCI in Petal	(16.03)
(10/30 × ($46m + $2.1m) (W4))	
Negative movement (debit) in equity	2.97

(W11) Property, plant and equipment

Tutorial note
A company should review its depreciation method, depreciation rates and residual values on an annual basis. Amendments are changes in accounting estimates and so dealt with prospectively (the remaining carrying value of the asset must be written off over its remaining useful life using the new depreciation estimates).

	$m	$m
Rose		370
Petal		110
Stem (D380m/5)		76
Petal fair value adjustment (W2)		30
Stem fair value adjustment (D75m/5) (W2)		15
Change in residual value:		
Carrying value at 1 May 2010	10.7	
($20m – (($20m – $1.4m) × 3/6))		
Correct depreciation charge for year	2.7	
(($10.7m – $2.6m) × 1/3)		
Depreciation actually charged in year	3.1	
(($20m – $1.4m) × 1/6)		
Depreciation overcharged		0.4
Overseas property:		
Cost (D30m/6)	5.0	
Depreciation ($5m/20)	(0.25)	
Carrying value	4.75	
Fair value (D35m/5)	7.0	
Revaluation gain ($7m – $4.75m)		2.25
		603.65

(W12) Employee bonus scheme

The cumulative bonus payable will be $4.42 million (see calculation below).

The benefit allocated to each year will be this figure divided by five years. That is $884,000 per year. The current service cost is the present value of this amount at 30 April 2011. That is $884,000 divided by 1.08 for four years, i.e. $0.65m

	30 April 2011 $m	30 April 2012 $m	30 April 2013 $m	30 April 2014 $m	30 April 2015 $m
Benefit 2% of salary which increases at 5%	0.8	0.84	0.882	0.926	0.972
Bonus cumulative	0.8	1.64	2.522	3.448	4.42

(b)

Tutorial note

*Make sure that you discuss whether the accounting treatment is correct **and** also the ethical issues raised.*

Rose's allocation of the cost of acquisition of companies is not based on 'fair value' as defined in IFRS 13. Further the application of fair value in accordance with IFRS may result in the identification and allocation of the cost of the business combination to other types of intangible assets in addition to those recognised by Rose.

IFRS 3 requires an acquirer to allocate the cost of a business combination by recognising the acquiree's identifiable assets, liabilities and contingent liabilities that satisfy the recognition criteria at their fair values at the date of acquisition.

IFRS 13 defines fair value as the amount for which an asset would be sold in an orderly transaction between market participants at the measurement date.

Fair value is therefore not an amount that is specific to the acquirer, nor should it take into account the acquirer's intentions for the future of the acquired business.

If Rose plans to allocate the cost of business combination to assets based on the value that they have for Rose, this is not in compliance with IFRS.

The contract-based customer relationships are identifiable in accordance with IAS 38 and would probably have value. In order to be recognised separately, the identifiable assets, liabilities and contingent liabilities have to satisfy the probability and reliable measurement criteria of IFRS 3. For intangible assets acquired in business combinations the probability recognition criterion is always considered to be satisfied. Furthermore, IAS 38 states that the fair value of intangible assets acquired in business combinations can normally be measured sufficiently reliably to be recognised separately from goodwill. Part of the cost of the business combination of the company should be allocated to customer relationships, assuming there to be a positive value at the date of acquisition and notwithstanding the fact that many of the customers were already known to Rose. The fair value of the customer relationships should reflect what a well-informed buyer without previous customer relationships with these customers would be willing to pay for those assets.

Management often seeks loopholes in financial reporting standards that allow them to adjust the financial statements as far as is practicable to achieve their desired aim. These adjustments amount to unethical practices when they fall outside the bounds of acceptable accounting practice. Reasons for such behaviour often include market expectations, personal realisation of a bonus, and maintenance of position within a market sector. In most cases conformance to acceptable accounting practices is a matter of personal integrity. It is often a matter of intent and therefore if the management of Rose is pursuing such policies with the intention of misleading users, then there is an ethical issue.

ACCA Marking scheme			Marks
(a)	(i)	1 mark per point up to maximum	8
	(ii)	Amortisation of patent	1
		Acquisition of further interest	5
		Stem – translation and calculation of goodwill	7
		Retained earnings and other equity	8
		Non-controlling interest	3
		Property, plant and equipment	6
		Non-current liabilities	1
		Employee bonus scheme	4
		Maximum	**35**
(b)		Accounting treatment	4
		Ethical considerations	3
Total			**50**

Examiner's comments

This question required candidates to discuss and apply the principles set out in IAS 21 *The Effects of Changes in Foreign Exchange Rates* in order to determine the functional currency of an entity. It then required candidates to prepare a consolidated statement of financial position of the group at 30 April 2011 showing the exchange difference arising on the translation of the entity's net assets. Candidates had to show how to deal with an acquisition of a further interest from the non-controlling interest for a cash consideration and the revaluation of an overseas property Further a long-term bonus scheme for employees and a change in the residual value of property had to be dealt with by candidates.

The determination of the functional currency was well dealt with by candidates. The question set out all of the relevant detail for this determination but some candidates did not use this information and did not accrue marks as a result. The consolidation of the financial statements was again well carried out by candidates. There are alternative ways to arrive at the correct solution to this type of question and this was taken into account in the marking of the answers. Candidates seemed to generally understand the method used to translate the financial statements of an overseas subsidiary. Some candidates used incorrect exchange rates to translate the statement of financial position of the subsidiary but most candidates managed to compute goodwill correctly using the full goodwill method. The cumulative bonus payable on the long term bonus scheme was often incorrectly calculated with the main problem being the present value calculation.

Part (b) saw the company considering the acquisition of a service company which had contract-based customer relationships with well-known domestic and international companies. Candidates had to discuss the validity of the accounting treatment proposed by the entity and whether such proposed treatment raised any ethical issues. The main issue with the answers to this question was that candidates focussed on the accounting treatment at the expense of the ethical considerations. The contract-based customer relationships were identifiable in accordance with IAS 38 and would probably have value. In order to be recognised separately, the identifiable assets, liabilities and contingent liabilities have to satisfy the probability and reliable measurement criteria of IFRS 3. For intangible assets acquired in business combinations the probability recognition criterion is always considered to be satisfied. Many candidates failed to reach this conclusion.

10 JOCATT GROUP (DEC 10 EXAM) *Walk in the footsteps of a top tutor*

Key answer tips

As with many of the group accounting questions, much of the difficulty in part (a) lies in the accounting issues included rather than the preparation of the cash flow statement itself. In particular the question refers to 'draft financial statements' which is normally an indication that there are accounting errors within the statements as currently presented. The best way to approach a cash flow question is to have a sound knowledge and understanding of the standard format for the statement, and then to deal with the individual issues identified in the question, completing the statement as you deal with each issue. You should expect to deal with a change in group structure in an ACCA P2 statement of cash flows examination question; in this particular case, there is acquisition of a subsidiary during the year. In addition, this question includes the following accounting issues: financial assets, defined benefit scheme, investment property, property, plant and equipment, purchase of an interest in an associate during the year, together with payments for taxation and dividends. Ensure that you do not spend too much time on these issues to the exclusion of completing the cash flow statement itself. Start your workings with those issues you find quickest and easiest to deal with.

(a) **Jocatt Group: Statement of Cash flows for the year ended 30 November 2010**

	$m	$m
Cash flows from operating activities:		
Profit before tax	45	
Adjustments to operating activities:		
Retirement benefit current and past service cost (W7)	16	
Depreciation on PPE	27	
Loss on replacement of investment property component part	0.5	
Amortisation of intangible assets (W9)	17	
Profit on sale of land (W6)	(9)	
Gain on investment property (W8)	(1.5)	
Profit of associates	(6)	
Impairment of goodwill (W1)	31.5	
Gain on remeasurement of initial holding in Tigret (W1)	(1)	

Finance costs (inc net interest component on defined benefit plan)	8
Cash paid to retirement benefit scheme (W7)	(7)
Decrease in trade receivables (113 – 62 + 5)	56
Decrease in inventories (128 – 105)	23
Increase in trade payables (144 – 55)	89
Cash generated from operations	288.5
Interest paid (8 – 2 interest on defined benefit plan)	(6)
Income taxes paid (W4)	(16.5)
Cash flow from operating activities	266
Cash flows from investing activities:	
Purchase of associate (W3)	(48)
Purchase of PPE (W6)	(98)
Purchase of subsidiary (W2)	(8)
Purchase of investment property (W8)	(1)
Proceeds from sale of land	15
Purchase of intangible assets (W9)	(12)
Purchase of financial assets (W10)	(5)
	(157)
Cash flows from financing activities:	
Repayment of long-term borrowings (71 – 67)	(4)
Proceeds from rights issue to NCI (W5)	2
Non-controlling interest dividend (W5)	(13)
Dividends paid by Jocatt (per SOCIE)	(5)
	(20)
Net increase in cash and cash equivalents	89
Cash and cash equivalents at beginning of period	143
Cash and cash equivalents at end of period	232

Tutorial note

Note that the 'gains on property' in the statement of profit or loss of $10.5 million is made up of a $9 million profit on the sale of land (W6) and a $1.5 million gain on investment properties (W8). Make sure that you don't accidentally adjust for these gains twice.

Workings

(W1) Goodwill on acquisition of Tigret

Tutorial note

Fair value uplifts on consolidation create a deferred tax liability in the consolidated financial statements. This increases the amount of goodwill recognised at the acquisition date.

Goodwill calculation

	$m
Cash paid	15
Shares issued	15
Fair value of previous equity interest	5

Fair value of consideration paid to acquire control	35
Fair value of non-controlling interest	20
Fair value of net assets at acquisition	(45)
Deferred tax (45 – 40) × 30%	1.5

Goodwill on acquisition	11.5

The previous investment has been revalued from $4 million to its fair value of $5 million, thus creating a gain of $1 million in profit or loss.

Tutorial note

Having calculated goodwill in acquisition of the new subsidiary, you can now reconcile the movement in the carrying value of goodwill between the two reporting dates; there is likely to be impairment of goodwill during the year – this should be accounted for as an adjustment to profit in the statement of cash flows.

Goodwill reconciliation

	$m
Opening balance at 1 December 2009	68
On acquisition of Tigret (above)	11.5
Impairment (bal. fig.)	(31.5)

Closing balance at 30 November 2010	48.0

(W2) Net cash impact of acquisition of subsidiary in year

Tutorial note

The final element of accounting for the acquisition of a subsidiary during the year is to account for the net cash impact of the acquisition – this typically will result in a cash outflow to be classified as an investing activity.

	$m
Cash outflow as part of consideration paid to acquire control	(15)
Cash balance acquired	7
Net cash outflow arising from acquisition of subsidiary	(8)

(W3) Associate

Tutorial note

There has been a cash outflow to pay for the purchase of new shares in associate companies – this should be classified as an investing activity in the statement of cash flows. When reconciling the year-on-year associate balance, remember that associates are accounted for using the equity method – the investment is increased by the group's share of the associate's profit after tax and it is reduced by any dividends paid by the associate to the group.

	$m
Opening balance at 1 December 2009	Nil
New investments in associate (bal. fig.)	48
Share of assoc profit after tax for period	6
Dividend received	Nil
Closing balance at 30 November 2010	54

(W4) Taxation

Tutorial note

Reconcile the opening and closing balances for both the income tax liability and the deferred tax provision in a single working, ensuring that you include any charge for the year included in profit or loss and also in other comprehensive income. You should also ensure that you correctly deal with any tax-related balances on a subsidiary acquired or disposed of during the year.

	$m
Opening tax balances at 1 December 2009 (41 + 30)	71
Deferred tax on acquisition (W1)	1.5
Charge for year per profit or loss	11
Charge for year in OCI (note viii)	1
Tax paid (bal. fig.)	(16.5)
Closing tax balances at 30 November 2010 (35 + 33)	68

(W5) Non-controlling interest

Tutorial note

When reconciling the movement in non-controlling interest (NCI) between the two reporting dates make sure that you factor in any NCI arising on acquisition of a subsidiary and also any NCI derecognised on a subsidiary disposal.

	$m
Opening balance at 1 December 2009	36
On acquisition (W1)	20
NCI share of total comp. income for year	10
Dividend paid (per SOCIE)	(13)
Rights issue (5 × 40%)	2
Closing balance at 30 November 2010	55

The dividend paid of $13 million and the cash received from the NCI as a result of the rights issue of $2 million should both be disclosed separately and classified within financing activities. The remaining $3 million from the rights issue was paid by Jocatt To Tigrett – this is an intragroup cash flow and so is not disclosed in the consolidated statement of cash flows.

(W6) PPE

Tutorial note

The reconciliation of PPE should include recognition of PPE which is now controlled by the group on acquisition of the subsidiary. Note that the carrying amount of PPE disposed of is removed and any gain or loss on disposal accounted for as an adjustment within operating activities. The cash disposal proceeds received are classified as a cash inflow within investing activities.

	$m
Opening balance at 1 December 2009	254
Revaluation loss (per SOCIE)	(7)
Plant in exchange transaction	4
Sale of land	(10)
Depreciation	(27)
On acquisition of Tigret	15
Current year cash additions (bal. fig.)	98
Closing balance at 30 November 2010	327

The profit on the sale of the land is $9 million ($15m cash received + $4m plant received – $10m carrying amount).

(W7) Defined benefit scheme

Tutorial note

The movement on the defined benefit plan during the year comprises the current and past service cost for the year (i.e. service cost component), the net interest component, and the remeasurement component. Remember that the remeasurement component is taken to other comprehensive income for the year – it is therefore not an item that should be adjusted for within operating activities. The cash contributions paid into the plan are identified as a reconciling item – they would normally be disclosed as a cash outflow within operating activities.

	$m
Opening balance at 1 December 2009	22
Current and past service cost for the year (10 + 6)	16
Net interest component	2
Net remeasurement component gain for year	(8)
Contributions paid (bal. fig.)	(7)
Closing balance at 30 November 2010	25

(W8) Investment property

	$m
Opening balance at 1 December 2009	6
Acquisition	1
Disposal	(0.5)
Gain (bal. fig.)	1.5
Closing balance at 30 November 2010	8

(W9) Intangible assets

	$m
Opening balance at 1 December 2009	72
Acquisitions (8 + 4)	12
On acquisition of Tigret	18
Amortisation (bal. fig.)	(17)
Closing balance at 30 November 2010	85

(W10) Financial assets at FV through OCI

	$m
Opening balance at 1 December 2009	90
Cash purchases (bal. fig)	5
Tigret now accounted for as a subsidiary	(4)
Total gain ($2m per SOCIE plus $1m tax)	3
Closing balance at 30 November 2010	94

(W11) Share capital

	$m
Opening balance at 1 December 2009	275
On acquisition of Tigret	15
Cash received (bal. fig.)	Nil
Closing balance at 30 November 2010	290

(b) (i) The direct method presents separate categories of cash inflows and outflows whereas the indirect method is a reconciliation of profit before tax reported in the statement of profit or loss to the cash flow from operations. The adjustments include non-cash items in the statement of profit or loss plus operating cash flows that were not included in profit or loss.

A problem for users is the fact that entities can choose the method used. This limits comparability.

The majority of companies use the indirect method for the preparation of statements of cash flow. Most companies justify this on the grounds that the direct method is too costly.

Users often prefer the direct method because it shows the major categories of cash flows. The direct method allows for reporting operating cash flows by understandable categories as they can see the amount of cash collected from customers, cash paid to suppliers, cash paid to employees and cash paid for other operating expenses. Users can gain a better understanding of the major trends in cash flows and can compare these cash flows with those of the entity's competitors.

The complicated adjustments required by the indirect method are difficult to understand and provide entities with more leeway for manipulation of cash flows. The adjustments made to reconcile net profit before tax to cash from operations are confusing to users. In many cases these cannot be reconciled to observed changes in the statement of financial position. Thus users will only be able to understand the size of the difference between net profit before tax and cash from operations.

(ii)

Tutorial note

You should try to apply each of the fundamental ethical principles to the situation in the question. Try to avoid making general or vague comments, or referring to issues which are not relevant to the circumstances outlined in the question.

Although all entities will rely on financing to improve and expand, cash inflows from financing activities cannot continue indefinitely. It is therefore important that entities can generate sufficient cash flows from their trading activities to meet mandatory payments, such as interest and tax. Presenting loan proceeds as an operating cash flow will therefore make the entity look more liquid, sustainable, and financially secure.

Corporate reporting involves the development and disclosure of information, which the entity knows is going to be used. The information has to be truthful and neutral. The nature of the responsibility of the directors requires a high level of ethical behaviour. Shareholders, potential shareholders, and other users of the financial statements rely heavily on the financial statements of a company as they can use this information to make an informed decision about investment. They rely on the directors to present a true and fair view of the company.

Unethical behaviour is difficult to control or define. The directors must consider how to best apply accounting standards even when faced with issues that could cause them to lose income. The directors should not pursue self-interest or fail to maintain objectivity and independence, and must act with appropriate professional judgement. Therefore the proceeds of the loan should be reported as cash flows from financing activities.

ACCA Marking scheme			
			Marks
(a)		Net profit before tax	1
		Retirement benefit expense	2
		Depreciation on PPE	1
		Depreciation on investment property	1
		Amortisation of intangible assets	1
		Profit on sale of land	1
		Profit on investment property	1
		Associates profit	1
		Impairment of goodwill	4
		Fin assets at FV through OCI	1
		Finance costs	1
		Decrease in trade receivables	1
		Decrease in inventories	1
		Increase in trade payables	1
		Cash paid to defined benefit scheme	1
		Finance costs paid	1
		Income taxes paid	2
		Purchase of associate	1
		Purchase of PPE	2
		Purchase of subsidiary	1
		Additions – investment property	1
		Proceeds from sale of land	1
		Intangible assets	1
		Purchases of fin assets at FVTOCI	1
		Repayment of long-term borrowings	1
		Rights issue NCI	1
		Non-controlling interest dividend	1
		Dividends paid	1
		Net increase in cash and cash equivalents	1
		Maximum	35
(b)	(i)	Subjective	8
	(ii)	Subjective	7
Total			50

Examiner's comments

This question required candidates to prepare a consolidated statement of cash flows for a group using the indirect method. The question required candidates to calculate goodwill on the acquisition of an entity where the group already held an investment in the entity. The goodwill needed to be calculated in order to ascertain the impairment of goodwill which was an adjustment to the operating activities of the group. Candidates performed well on this part of the question but often failed to take account of the deferred taxation adjustment. The question also required candidates to deal with the acquisition of the subsidiary in preparing the cash flow statement and to calculate the cash flows relating to the associate, PPE, non-controlling interest, deferred taxation, a defined benefit scheme, investment property and intangible assets. This part of the question was well answered. There were some elements of a cash flow question which are relatively easy to answer and candidates generally obtained the marks in these areas.

The main areas where candidates found difficulties were:

(1)   Ensuring that the purchase of the subsidiary was dealt with in calculating cash flows across the range of assets and liabilities.

(2)   The treatment of the past service costs relating to the defined benefit scheme.

(3)   The calculation of the cash flows on taxation, although many candidates made a good attempt at this calculation.

Part (b) of the question required candidates to comment on the directors' view that the indirect method of preparing statements of cash flows is more useful and informative to users than the direct method and to discuss the reasons why the directors may wish to report the loan proceeds as an operating cash flow rather than a financing cash flow commenting on whether there are any ethical implications of adopting this treatment. The first part of this element of the question was often poorly answered. In fact often it was not attempted. Currently there is a debate over whether the direct method should be used in preference to the indirect method and thus candidates should be aware of the advantages and disadvantages of the methods. It shows that candidates are not reading widely enough and are focusing on a narrow range of topical issues. The ethical part of the question was quite well answered although many candidates did not read the question fully enough as it stated that the directors were to receive extra income if the operating cash flow exceeded a predetermined target for the year. Part of the answer to the question was therefore contained in the scenario.

11   ASHANTI (JUNE 10 EXAM) *Walk in the footsteps of a top tutor*

Key answer tips

As with many of the group accounting questions, the difficulty lies in the accounting issues included rather than the consolidation process itself. In this case there is an impairment of goodwill, unrealised profit in inventory, revenue issues, the revaluation of financial assets and property, plant and equipment, and a holiday pay accrual. There are also share transactions; one of which results in a loss of control and therefore a profit or loss on disposal. Parts (b) and (c) focus upon reclassification of financial assets, together with the ethical implications of earnings management.

(a)   **Consolidated statement of profit or loss and other comprehensive income**

	$m
Revenue	1,096.0
($810 + $235 + ($142 × 6/12) – $15 (W7) – $5 (W9))	
Cost of sales	(854.8)
($686 + $137 + ($84 × 6/12) + $2 (W2) – $15 (W7) + $1 (W7) +	
$1.6 (W10) + $0.21 (W11))	
Gross profit	241.2
Other income	49.0
($31 + $17 + ($12 × 6/12) – $5 (W8))	
Distribution costs	(64.0)
($30 + $21 + ($26 × 6/12))	
Administrative expenses	(95.2)
($55 + $29 + ($12 × 6/12) + $2.2 (W3) + $3 (W9))	

Profit from operations	131.0
Profit on disposal of subsidiary (W4)	3.8
Share of profit of associate (W6)	2.1
Finance costs	(18.0)
($8 + $6 + ($8 × 6/12))	
Profit before taxation	118.9
Taxation	(49.0)
($21 + $23 + ($10 × 6/12))	
Profit for the period	69.9

Other comprehensive income
Items that will not be reclassified to profit or loss in future periods

Remeasurement losses on defined benefit plan	(14.0)
Net gains on PPE revaluation	19.6
($12 + $6 + $1.6 (W10))	
Total comprehensive income for the period	75.5

Profit attributable to:	
Equity holders of Ashanti (bal. fig.)	55.5
Non-controlling interest (W12)	14.4
	69.9
Total comprehensive income attributable to:	
Equity holders of Ashanti (bal. fig.)	59.3
Non-controlling interest (W12)	16.2
	75.5

Workings

(W1) Group structure

Tutorial note

Include dates of share purchases and disposals for each member of the group. This will help you to identify any necessary pro-rating.

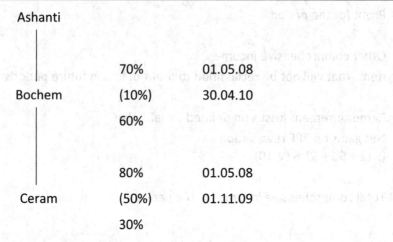

Ashanti		
	70%	01.05.08
Bochem	(10%)	30.04.10
	60%	
	80%	01.05.08
Ceram	(50%)	01.11.09
	30%	

The share disposal by Ashanti in respect of Bochem does not change control of that company by Ashanti. This is accounted for as a transaction between equity holders and so no profit or loss on disposal is calculated.

For the first six months of the year, Ashanti has an effective interest in Ceram of 56% (70% × 80%). The NCI interest in Ceram for this six month period is therefore 44% (100% – 56%).

The share disposal by Bochem in respect of Ceram results in a loss of control by the group. This means that a profit or loss on disposal must be accounted for at 1 November 2009. Ceram became an associate from the date that control was lost – i.e. the last six months of the year.

(W2) Net assets

Tutorial note

This requires knowledge of accounting for fair value adjustments, including accounting for depreciation on a fair value adjustment. Remember that a depreciation charge for one year on the fair value adjustment must be included in the consolidated statement of profit or loss.

Bochem	Acquisition date	Reporting date
	$m	$m
Equity shares	55	)
Retained earnings	85	) 210
Other equity components	10	)
FVA – plant (bal fig)	10	10
Dep'n on FVA (2/5)		(4)
	───	───
	160	216
	───	───

One year's depreciation charge on the fair value adjustment is charged in the consolidated statement of profit or loss – $2 million.

Ceram	Acquisition date	Reporting date
	$m	$m
Given in question	115	160
	───	───

(W3) Goodwill

Tutorial note

Deal with the impairments separately so that you clearly identify impairment in year – this needs to be included in the consolidated statement of profit or loss for the year to 30 April 2010.

Bochem	$m
Purchase consideration	150.0
Fair value of NCI at acquisition	54.0
	────
	204.0
Fair value of net assets at acquisition (W2)	(160.0)
	────
Goodwill at acquisition	44.0
Impairment in earlier year (15%)	(6.6)
Impairment in year (5%) to group P/L	(2.2)
	────
Goodwill at reporting date	35.2
	────

Tutorial note

Ashanti exercised control over Ceram via its controlling interest in Bochem. Therefore an indirect holding adjustment is required in the goodwill calculation.

Ceram	$m
Consideration	136.0
Indirect holding adjustment (30% × $136)	(40.8)
Fair value of NCI at acquisition	26.0
	121.2
Fair value of net assets at acquisition (W2)	(115.0)
Goodwill at acquisition/reporting date	6.2

(W4) Profit or loss on disposal of controlling interest in Ceram

Tutorial note

There is a loss of control in Ceram during the year because Bochem disposes of a 50% interest in the share capital of that company. A profit on disposal must be calculated for inclusion in the consolidated statement of profit or loss. Remember that this investment was held by Bochem and so the NCI must be allocated its share of this profit.

		$m
Proceeds		90.0
Fair value of residual holding at disposal date		45.0
		135.0
Carrying amount of Ceram at disposal:		
Net assets at disposal (W2)	160.0	
Goodwill at disposal (W3)	6.2	
NCI at disposal	(35.0)	
		(131.2)
Profit on disposal to Bochem		3.8

(W5) Disposal of shares in Bochem (no loss of control)

Tutorial note

Ashanti's sale of shares in Bochem does not lead to a loss of control. Consequently there is no gain or loss to the group arising on this transaction. Instead, it is regarded as a transaction between equity holders, which will result in an increase or decrease to other components of equity.

Note: This transaction is accounted for through equity. It does not feature in the statement of profit or loss and other comprehensive income. Therefore, this working is provided for information purposes only.

Bochem		$m
Proceeds of share disposal		34.0
CV of Bochem at transaction date:		
Net assets (W2)	216.0	
Unimpaired goodwill (W3)	35.2	
	———	
	251.2	
Change in NCI (10% × 251.2)		25.1
		———
Increase in equity		8.9
		———

(W6) Share of profit of associate

Tutorial note

Associates are accounted for using the equity method. This means that the group shows its share of the associate's profit after tax in the consolidated statement of profit or loss. Remember that Ceram has only been an associate for half of the year.

6/12 × $14m × 30% = $2.1m

(W7) Intra-group trading

Tutorial note

Most profit or loss questions involve intra-group trading. Make sure that you are happy with the required adjustments because they are a source of easy marks.

Ashanti has sold goods to both Bochem and Ceram. Group revenue and cost of sales will need to be adjusted by a total of $15 million ($10m + $5m).

The unrealised profit in inventory applies only to goods sold to Bochem during the year. The unrealised profit is $1 million ($10m × 20% × 50%).

(W8) Financial asset

Fair value at the reporting date can be determined by discounting the expected future cash flows using the current market rate of interest. Any change in fair value is taken to profit or loss for the year.

Date	Cashflow ($000)	10% discount factor	$000
30.04.11	1,600	0.909	1,454
30.04.12	1,400	0.826	1,156
30.04.13	16,500	0.751	12,391
			———
Fair value			15,001
Fall in FV to P/L			4,999
			———
Carrying amount			20,000
			———

(W9) Sale to restructuring customer

Tutorial note

A contract with a customer should only be accounted for where it is probable that the entity will receive the consideration that it is entitled to. Based upon the available information, this would not appear to be the case.

Revenue from the sale should not be included in the financial statements to 30 April 2010. Therefore, revenue and receivables should be reduced by $5 million. This also means that the loss allowance only needs to be increased by $3 million ($8 million – $5 million).

(W10) Property impairment

Tutorial note

When property, plant and equipment (PPE) is revalued, the annual depreciation charge is calculated by spreading the revised valuation over the remaining estimated useful life of the PPE. Remember to factor in the transfer of excess depreciation from the revaluation reserve to retained earnings.

		Property	Reval'n res
		$000	$000
01.05.08	Purchase	12,000	
Depreciation	(12,000/10)	(1,200)	
Revaluation (bal.)		2,200	2,200
CV at 30.04.09		13,000	2,200
Depreciation	(13,000/9)	(1,440)	
Reserve transfer	(1,440 – 1,200)		(240)
Revaluation (bal.)		(3,560)	(1,960)
CV at 30.04.10		8,000	Nil

Of the downward revaluation totalling $3.560 million, only $1.960 million should have been charged to other comprehensive income. The remaining $1.6 million needs to be charged to profit or loss.

(W11) Holiday pay accrual

At the reporting date, Ashanti should make an accrual for unused holiday entitlement as there is an obligation on Ashanti. It is measured based upon the probable amount of the claim as follows:

Cost per day: $19m/255 days = $74,510

Cost per day per employee = $74,510/900 = $83

Number of employee days to pay: 3 days × 900 employees × 95% = 2,565 days

Accrual required: 2,565 days × $83 = $0.21 million

(W12) Profit/TCI attributable to NCI

Tutorial note

The NCI interest in Bochem rose to 40% at the year end, but was 30% during the year.

	Profit $m	TCI $m
Per Bochem's F/S	36.0	42
Depreciation on FV adj (W2)	(2.0)	(2.0)
Goodwill impairment (W3)	(2.2)	(2.2)
Profit on disposal (W4)	3.8	3.8
Share of associate (W6)	2.1	2.1
Profit/TCI post-adjustment	37.7	43.7
Attributable to NCI (30%)	11.3	13.1

	Profit/TCI $m
Per Ceram's F/S ($14 × 6/12)	7.0
Attributable to NCI (44%) (W1)	3.1

The total profit attributable to the NCI is $14.4 million ($11.3m + $3.1m).

The total TCI attributable to the NCI is $16.2 million ($13.1m + $3.1m).

(b)

Tutorial note

This part of the question requires you to state and explain when reclassification of financial instruments may be possible. You should begin by identifying circumstances when this may be required, and then go on to explain how any reclassification is accounted for.

Classification of financial instruments is determined upon initial recognition. In some cases, there may only be one classification possible, as in the case of financial assets held for trading which must be accounted as fair value through profit or loss. Other financial assets, for example loans and receivables, may be accounted for either as fair value through profit or loss, or may be designated to be measured at amortised cost, provided they meet eligibility criteria.

In the case of financial assets, IFRS 9 requires a reassessment of whether any initial designation of classification remains appropriate when an entity changes its business model. IFRS 9 states that such reclassifications are expected to be 'very infrequent'. Whether the business model has changed is a decision made by the senior management of the entity, and may be a consequence of factors either internal to the entity, or from the external business environment. Such changes in business model would be demonstrable to external parties; i.e. a clear shift in strategy. One example of a change in business model would be if an entity closed down part of its business.

Examples which would not be regarded as changes in business model include:

*   The temporary disappearance of a particular market for financial assets.
*   The transfer of financial assets between parts of the entity with different business models.
*   A change of intention in respect of particular financial assets, even where there have been significant changes in market conditions.

Where reclassification is required, then all affected financial assets are reclassified from the first day of the next reporting period (the reclassification date), with no restatement of prior periods required. There should be disclosure of objectives and policies for managing risks from financial instruments, which would presumably include any changes to the business model during that period, even though reclassification does not take place until the beginning of the next accounting period.

Allowing reclassification, even in limited circumstances, may allow an entity to manage its reported profit or loss by avoiding future fair value gains or losses on the reclassified assets.

(c)

Tutorial note

This part of the question deals with one possible consequence of reclassification of financial assets, management of earnings, and requires you to discuss the nature of management of earnings, and whether such a process is ethically acceptable.

'Earnings management' has been defined in various ways. It can be described as the purposeful intervention in the external financial reporting process with the intent of obtaining some private gain. Alternatively it can be the use of judgment in financial reporting and in structuring transactions to alter financial reports to either mislead stakeholders about the underlying economic performance of the company, or to influence contractual outcomes that depend on reported accounting judgments.

Incentives lie at the heart of earnings management. Managers should make accounting judgments and decisions solely with the intention of fairly reporting operating performance. However, there are often economic incentives for managers to engage in earnings management, because the value of the firm and the wealth of its managers or owners are normally linked to reported earnings. Contractual incentives to manage earnings arise when contracts between a company and other parties rely upon financial statements to determine financial exchanges between them.

By managing the results of operations, managers can alter the amount and timing of those exchanges. Contractual situations could stimulate earnings management. These would include debt covenants, management compensation agreements, job security, and trade union negotiations. Market incentives to manage earnings arise when managers perceive a connection between reported earnings and the company's market value. Regulatory incentives to manage earnings arise when reported earnings are thought to influence the actions of regulators or government officials. By managing the results of operations, managers may influence the actions of regulators or government officials, thereby minimising political scrutiny and the effects of regulation.

One way in which directors can manage earnings is by manipulation of accruals with no direct cash flow consequences. Examples of accrual manipulation include under-stating receivables allowances, delaying of asset write-offs and opportunistic selection of accounting methods. Accrual manipulation is a convenient form of earnings management because it has no direct cash flow implications and can be done after the year-end when managers are better informed about earnings. However, managers also have incentives to manipulate real activities during the year with the specific objective of meeting certain earnings targets. Real activity manipulation affects both cash flows and earnings.

Where management does not try to manipulate earnings, there is a positive effect on earnings quality. The earnings data is more reliable because management is not influencing or manipulating earnings by changing accounting methods, or deferring expenses or accelerating revenues to bring about desired short-term earnings results.

The absence of earnings management does not, however, guarantee high earnings quality. Some information or events that may affect future earnings may not be disclosed in the financial statements. Thus, the concept of earnings management is related to the concept of earnings quality. One major objective of the IASB Framework is to assist investors and creditors in making investing and lending decisions. The Framework refers not only to the reliability of financial statements, but also to the relevance and predictive value of information presented in financial statements.

Entities have a social and ethical responsibility not to mislead stakeholders. Ethics can and should be part of a corporate strategy, but a company's first priority often is its survival and optimising its profits in a sustainable way. Management of earnings may therefore appear to have a degree of legitimacy in this regard but there is an obvious conflict. An ethical position that leads to substantial and long-term disadvantages in the market place will not be acceptable to an entity.

It is reasonable and realistic not to rely exclusively on personal morality. A suitable economic, ethical and legal framework attempts to ensure that the behaviour of directors conforms to moral standards. Stakeholders depend on the moral integrity of the entity's directors. Stakeholders rely upon core values such as trustworthiness, truthfulness, honesty, and independence although these cannot be established exclusively by regulation and professional codes of ethics. Thus there is a moral dilemma for directors in terms of managing earnings for the benefit of the entity, which might directly benefit stakeholders and themselves whilst at the same time possibly misleading the same stakeholders.

	ACCA Marking scheme		
			Marks
(a)	Consolidated P/L and OCI		5
	Bochem		8
	Ceram		6
	Inventory		2
	Bond		4
	PPE		3
	Customer restructuring		2
	Employee benefits		2
	NCI		3
		Maximum	35
(b)	Financial assets		8
(c)	Management of earnings		7
Total			50

Examiner's comments

Candidates generally performed well in this question. Candidates were required to calculate goodwill on the purchase of a subsidiary in order to determine the impairment of goodwill to be charged in profit or loss. Candidates seemed to have a good knowledge of the calculation of goodwill under the full goodwill method. Candidates had to deal with the sale of a controlling interest which resulted in the retention of an associate interest. Generally candidates performed well this part of the question. The question also required candidates to deal with the accounting for a financial asset. Candidates made a reasonable attempt at this element of the question. Other elements of the question included dealing with revenue recognition, revaluation gains/losses on property, plant and equipment, calculating non controlling interest and accruing holiday pay for the entity. In a question such as this, it is very easy to make a mistake in calculation. Thus it is always important to show workings in a clear concise manner so that marks can be allocated for the principles and method used by the candidate.

12   GRANGE (DEC 09 EXAM) *Walk in the footsteps of a top tutor*

Key answer tips

As with many of the group accounting questions, the difficulty in part (b) lies in the accounting issues included rather than the consolidation process itself. In this case there is revaluation and reclassification of non-current assets and determining whether a provision for environmental damage is required. There are also equity transfers between the group and non-controlling interest shareholders for two of the subsidiaries. Be careful not to spend too much time on these adjustments. If you are struggling then leave them and move on. Part (a) is a self-contained calculation of the gain or loss following loss of control of a subsidiary company. Part (c) should also be a source of easy marks.

(a)   **Disposal of equity interest in Sitin**

Tutorial note

The disposal of shares results in a loss of control in Sitin. This requires a calculation of the profit or loss on disposal to be included in the group financial statements.

The amount recognised in profit or loss would be as follows:

	$m	$m
Fair value of consideration received		23
Fair value of residual interest		13
Less: net assets derecognised	(35)	
Less: goodwill derecognised ($39m – $32m)	(7)	(42)
Loss on disposal		(6)

Notes:

- The Grange group is entitled to its share of post-acquisition retained earnings up to disposal date.

- The group still has significant influence after the share sale so must recognise an associate based upon the fair value of the residual holding at 30 November 2009 of $13 million.

(b)   **Consolidated Statement of Financial Position at 30 November 2009**

	$m
Assets	
Non-current assets	
Intangible assets: goodwill ($30 + $8) (W3)	38.00
Intangible assets: franchise ($10 – $3) (W2)	7.00
Property, plant and equipment (W12)	784.47
Investment property – land (W7)	8.00
Investment in associate (Part (a))	13.00
	850.47
Current assets ($475 + $304 + $141)	920.00
Total assets	1770.47
Equity and liabilities	
Equity share capital	430.00
Retained earnings (W5)	401.67
Other components of equity (W5)	57.98
	889.65
Non-controlling interest (W4)	140.82

Total equity of the group	1,030.47
Non-current liabilities ($172 + $124 + $38)	334.00
Current liabilities	
Trade and other payables ($178 + $71 + $105)	354.00
Provisions (W13)	52.00
	———
Total equity and liabilities	1,770.47
	———

Workings

Tutorial note

Include any accounting adjustments relating to subsidiaries in the net assets working, so that their impact upon the group reserves and non-controlling interest can be easily dealt with.

Workings

(W1) Group structure

Grange

Park	60%	Fence	100%	Sitin	100%
Purchase	20%	Disposal	(25%)	Disposal	(60%)
Subsidiary	80%	Subsidiary	75%	Associate	40%

The share transactions during the year in respect of Park and Fence do not change control of those companies by Grange. They are therefore accounted for as transactions between equity holders. The disposal transaction in relation to Sitin results in a loss of control by Grange; a gain or loss on disposal must be accounted for and an investment in an associate must be recognised.

(W2) Net assets

Tutorial note

This requires knowledge of accounting for fair value adjustments – in particular, criteria for recognition of the franchise as an intangible asset. You should also assess their impact at the reporting date, together with any other accounting adjustments required at the reporting date.

Park	Acquisition date	Reporting date	Post-acq'n
	$m	$m	$m
Equity shares	230	230	
Retained earnings	115	170	
Other equity components	10	14	4
FVA – land (bal fig)	5	5	
	___		
Per question	360		
FVA – franchise	10	10	
Franchise amortisation		(3)	
((10/5 years) × 1.5)			
	___	___	___
	370	426	56

Tutorial note

This requires knowledge of accounting for fair value adjustments. You should also assess the impact of the revised estimate of the contingent liability, together with depreciation on the fair value adjustment for 16 months to the reporting date.

Fence	Acquisition date	Reporting date	Post-acq'n
	$m	$m	$m
Equity shares	150	150	
Retained earnings	73	65	
Other equity components	9	17	8
Contingent liability	(30)	(25)	
	___		
Per question	202		
FVA – plant	4	4	
Plant dep'n (16/120 months)		(0.53)	
	___	___	___
	206	210.47	4.47

(W3) Goodwill

Tutorial note

Goodwill is calculated using the full goodwill method per IFRS 3 revised for all members of the group.

	Park	*Fence*
	$m	*$m*
Purchase consideration	250	214
Fair value of NCI at acquisition	150	n/a
	400	214
Fair value of net assets at acquisition (W2)	(370)	(206)
Goodwill to SFP	30	8

(W4) Non-controlling interest

Tutorial note

The NCI holding in Park was 40% until the last day of the period. They are therefore allocated 40% of the net asset movement.

Note also that there is a transfer between equity holders which must be accounted for.

Park	$m
FV of NCI at acquisition	150.0
NCI % of post-acq'n mvt in net assets	22.4
40% × ($426 − $370) (W2)	
Equity transfer on share purchase by group (W6)	(86.2)
Fence	
Equity transfer on sale of shares by group (W6)	54.62
	140.82

(W5) Group reserves

Tutorial note

The group owned 60% and 100% of Park and Fence respectively until the final day of the period. The group are therefore allocated 60% and 100% of Park and Fence's post-acquisition reserves.

Other components of equity	$m
Grange	22.0
Park 60% × (14 – 10) (W2)	2.4
Fence 100% × (17 – 9) (W2)	8.0
Equity movement re share transactions with NCI:	
Park (W6)	(3.8)
Fence (W6)	25.38
Revaluation of overseas property (W9)	4.0
	———
	57.98
	———

Retained earnings	$m
Grange	410.0
Park 60% × (56 – 4) (W2)	31.2
Fence 100% × (4.47 – 8.0) (W2)	(3.53)
Sitin 100% × (35 – 32) (part (a))	3.0
Sitin – loss on disposal (part (a))	(6.0)
Investment property – land revalued (W7)	2.0
Provision for environmental claims (W8)	(7.0)
Impairment (W11)	(28.0)
	———
	401.67
	———

(W6) Transactions between equity holders

Tutorial note

If a share purchase or sale does not result in the gain or loss of control then it is accounted for as a transaction amongst equity holders. The difference between the consideration transferred/received and the change in the non-controlling interest is recorded in other components of equity.

Park	Group buy additional 20%		$m	$m
	Cash paid			(90.0)
	Decrease in NCI			
	NCI at acquisition		150.0	
	NCI % of net asset increase (40% × 56 (W2))		22.4	
	NCI at date of share sale		172.4	
	Reduction by 20/40			(86.2)
	Net decrease in equity			(3.8)

Fence	Group sell 25%		$m
	Cash received		80.00
	Increase in NCI	25% × (210.47 (W2) + 8.0 (W3))	(54.62)
	Increase in equity		25.38

(W7) Land

The plot of land is not being used for operational purposes, and Grange has not yet decided what to do with this asset. IAS 40 *Investment property* requires that such land should be classified as an investment property, rather than property, plant and equipment per IAS 16. It will therefore be measured at fair value, with changes in fair value taken to profit or loss. The subsequent fall in value is a non-adjusting event per IAS 10.

Plot of land	$m
Initial recognition at cost within PPE (to be removed)	6.0
Increase in fair value to profit or loss	2.0
To group SFP as investment property	8.0

(W8) Environmental issues

Tutorial note

A provision can only be recognised if there is an obligation from a past event that will lead to a probable outflow of economic benefits which can be measured reliably. Remember that obligations can be legal or constructive.

The anticipated fines of $1 million, together with the expected payments to local residents of $6 million are unavoidable obligations arising from past events and must be recognised in the financial statements.

The request from the regulator to make changes to the manufacturing process does not amount to an unavoidable obligation arising from past event, and therefore should not be recognised.

(W9) Overseas property

Tutorial note

IAS 16 Property, plant and equipment requires that revaluation gains are recorded in other comprehensive income. As this is an overseas property, the exchange rate at the reporting date is used to translate the year-end valuation of 12 million dinars.

	Dinar/Exchange rate	$m
Cost at acquisition	$8m/2	4
Revaluation gain		4
		───
Fair value at reporting date	$12m/1.5	8
		───

(W10) Restructuring

There is not yet a detailed formal plan, together with communication to those likely to be affected by any restructuring. Consequently, there is no legal or constructive obligation and no provision can be made at the reporting date.

(W11) Impairment review – Grange

Tutorial note

In performing the impairment review, identify any accounting adjustments relating to Grange so that the correct carrying value of the entity, as a cash generating unit, is used.

	$m
Carrying amount of net assets per draft SFP	862.0
Investment property revaluation (W7)	2.0
Provision for environmental claims (W8)	(7.0)
Revaluation of overseas property (W9)	4.0
Sitin – restatement to fair value of residual holding ($13m – $16m)	(3.0)
	───
	858.0
Value in use before restructuring	830.0
	───
Impairment – against property, plant and equipment	28.0
	───

(W12) Property plant and equipment

Tutorial note

You could show your workings for PPE and provisions (below) on the face of your statement of financial position. However, due to the number of adjustments required to these balanes, the workings have been presented below to improve clarity.

	$m
Grange	257
Park	311
Fence	238
Fair value adjustment – Park (W2)	5
Fair value adjustment – Fence ($4m – $0.53m) (W2)	3.47
Revaluation of overseas property (W9)	4
Land reclassified as investment property (W7)	(6)
Impairment of Grange's PPE (W11)	(28)
	784.47

(W13) Provisions for liabilities

	$m
Grange	10
Park	6
Fence	4
Contingent liability re Fence (W2)	25
Environmental provision (W8)	7
	52

(c)   Rules are a very important element of ethics. Usually this means focusing upon the rules contained in the accounting profession's code of professional conduct and references to legislation and corporate codes of conduct. They are an efficient means by which the accounting profession can communicate its expectations as to what behaviour is expected.

A view that equates ethical behaviour with compliance to professional rules could create a narrow perception of what ethical behaviour constitutes. Compliance with rules is not necessarily the same as ethical behaviour. Ethics and rules can be different. Ethical principles and values are used to judge the appropriateness of any rule.

Accountants should have the ability to conclude that a particular rule is inappropriate, unfair, or possibly unethical in any given circumstance. Rules are the starting point for any ethical question and rules are objective measures of ethical standards. In fact, rules are the value judgments as to what is right for accountants and reflect the profession's view about what constitutes good behaviour. Accountants who view ethical issues within this rigid framework are likely to suffer a moral crisis when encountering problems for which there is no readily apparent rule.

An overemphasis on ethical codes of behaviour tends to reinforce a perception of ethics as being punitive and does not promote the positive aspects of ethics that are designed to promote the reputation of an accounting firm and its clients, as well as standards within the profession. The resolution of ethical problems depends on the application of commonly shared ethical principles with appropriate skill and judgment. Ethical behaviour is based on universal principles and reasoned public debate and is difficult to capture in 'rules'.

Accountants have to make accounting policy choices on a regular basis. Stakeholders rely on the information reported by accountants to make informed decisions about the entity at hand. All decisions require judgment, and judgment depends on personal values with the decision needing to be made on some basis such as following rules, obeying authority, caring for others, justice, or whether the choice is right. These values and several others compete as the criterion for making a choice. Such personal values incorporate ethical values that dictate whether any accounting value chosen is a good or poor surrogate for economic value. To maintain the faith of the public, accountants must be highly ethical in their work. The focus on independence (conflict of interest) and associated compliance requirements may absorb considerable resources and conceptual space in relation to ethics in practice. This response is driven by a strong commitment within the firms to meet their statutory and regulatory obligations. The primary focus on independence may have narrowed some firms' appreciation of what constitutes broader ethical performance. As a result it may be that the increasing codification and compliance focus on one or two key aspects of ethical behaviour may be in fact eroding or preventing a more holistic approach to enabling ethics in practice.

If the director tells Field about the liquidity problems of Brook, then a confidence has been betrayed but there is a question of honesty if the true situation is not divulged. Another issue is whether the financial director has a duty to several stakeholders including the shareholders and employees of Grange, as if the information is disclosed about the poor liquidity position of Brook, then the amounts owing to Grange may not be paid. However, there is or may be a duty to disclose all the information to Field but if the information is deemed to be insider information then it should not be disclosed.

The finance director's reputation and career may suffer if Brook goes into liquidation especially as he will be responsible for the amounts owing by Brook. Another issue is whether the friend of the director has the right to expect him to keep the information private and if the shareholders of Grange stand to lose as a result of not divulging the information there may be an expectation that such information should be disclosed. Finally, should Field expect any credit information to be accurate or simply be a note of Brook's credit history? Thus it can be seen that the ethical and moral dilemmas facing the director of Grange are not simply a matter of following rules but are a complex mix of issues concerning trust, duty of care, insider information, confidentiality and morality.

	ACCA Marking scheme		
			Marks
(a)	Fair value of consideration		1
	Fair value of residual interest		1
	Net assets		2
	Goodwill		2
		Maximum	**6**
(b)	Property plant & equipment		6
	Investment property		2
	Goodwill		3
	Retained earnings		8
	Other components of equity		5
	Non-controlling interest		2
	Non-current liabilities/trade and other payables		1
	Provisions for liabilities		3
	Intangible assets		2
	Current assets		1
	Investment in associate		2
		Maximum	**35**
(c)	Subjective – 1 mark per point		9
Total			**50**

Examiner's comments

This required candidates to calculate a gain or loss on the disposal of an equity interest in a subsidiary, to prepare a consolidated statement of financial position and to discuss the relationship of ethical behaviour to professional rules. Candidates generally performed well in this question. The calculation of the loss arising on the disposal of the equity interest was extremely well answered with many candidates scoring full marks on this part of the question. The second part of the question additionally dealt with an acquisition of a further interest in a subsidiary and the disposal of a partial interest in a subsidiary as well as the treatment of contingent liabilities on consolidation, investment property, provisions for environmental claims, restructuring provisions and impairment. The breadth of topic areas was quite large. The main issues that candidates had were the calculations of the negative and positive movements in equity arising from the sale and purchase of equity holdings. Additionally the calculation of post acquisition reserves was quite complex and candidates did not always score well in this regard. However although candidates found it difficult to calculate post acquisition reserves, markers gave credit for the method and workings shown. The treatment of the non-consolidation adjustments (investment property, provisions for environmental claims, restructuring provisions etc.) was generally well answered although a major failing often involved the non-recognition of the restructuring provision, as a constructive obligation did not exist. Part c of the question required candidates to discuss the relationship between ethical behaviour and professional rules. The question required candidates to comment on the ethical behaviour of a director where the director possessed confidential information. Candidates performed well on this part of the question but it must be emphasised that it is important to refer to the information in the question when writing the answer.

13   BRAVADO (JUNE 09 EXAM) *Walk in the footsteps of a top tutor*

Key answer tips

This question includes the following issues: step acquisition and contingent consideration, accounting for an associate, investments in financial assets, foreign currency issues and directors' loans. Ensure that you do not spend too much time on these issues to the exclusion of completing the statement of financial position itself. Start your workings with those issues you find quickest and easiest to deal with. Parts (b) and (c) of the question should be a good source of marks for a well-prepared student as they include ethical and other issues associated with misstatements in the accounts.

(a)   **Consolidated Statement of Financial Position at 31 May 2009**

Assets	$m	$m
Non-current assets		
Property, plant and equipment (W11)	708.00	
Goodwill (W3)	25.00	
Investment in associate (W6)	22.50	
Financial assets (51 + 6 + 5 – 17.4) (W7))	44.60	800.10
Current assets		
Inventories (135 + 55 + 73 – 18 (W8))	245.00	
Trade receivables (91 + 45 + 32)	168.00	
Loans to directors (W9)	1.00	
Cash and cash equivalents (102 + 100 + 8 – 1 (W9))	209.00	623.00
Total assets		1,423.10

Equity and liabilities	$m	$m
Equity attributable to owners of parent		
Share capital	520.00	
Retained earnings (W5)	272.22	
Other components of equity (W5)	(6.40)	785.82
Non-controlling interest (W4)		148.88
Total equity of the group		934.70

Non-current liabilities		
Long-term borrowings (120 + 15 + 5)	140.00	
Deferred tax (W12)	39.40	179.40
Current liabilities		
Trade and other payables (W10)	217.00	
Current tax payable (60 + 8 + 24)	92.00	309.00
Total equity and liabilities		1,423.10

Workings

(W1) Group structure

Tutorial note

This requires knowledge of IFRS 3 as there is a step acquisition relating to Mixted. The initial shareholding is remeasured to fair value at the date control is acquired. Any gain or loss on remeasurement is taken to profit or loss.

Bravado

Message	Mixted	Clarity
80% on 1 June 2008	6% on 1 June 2007	10% on 1 June 2007
	64% on 1 June 2008	15% on 1 June 2008
	───	───
	70%	25%
	───	───

When control over Mixted is achieved on 1 June 2008, the previously held shares are revalued to fair value and a gain of $5 million ($15m − $10m) is recognised in profit or loss.

Dr Investment $5m

Cr Profit or loss $5m

On 1 June 2008, Clarity becomes an associate. Associates are accounted for using the equity method (W6). On this date, the previously recognised gains of $1 million ($9m − $8m) on the FVOCI investment can be transferred within equity.

Dr Other components of equity $1m

Cr Retained earnings $1m

(W2) Net assets

Tutorial note

Ensure that you include fair value adjustments at the date of acquisition and that you also assess their impact at the reporting date. Fair value adjustments may also give rise to deferred tax. When the fair value adjustment is depreciated, the temporary difference gets smaller and the deferred tax balance starts to reverse.

Message	*Acq date*	*Rep date*	*Post-acq'n*
	$m	*$m*	*$m*
Ordinary shares	220	220	
Retained earnings	136	150	
Other equity	4	4	
FV adj – land (bal. fig.)	40	40	
Fair value (given in question)	400	414	14

Mixted	*Acq'n date*	*Rep date*	*Post-acq'n*
	$m	*$m*	*$m*
Ordinary shares	100	100	
Retained earnings	55	80	
Other equity	7	7	
FV adj – PPE (bal. fig.)	14	14	
Less: Dep'n (14 × 1/7)		(2)	
Fair value (170 + 6)	176	199	
Deferred tax liability*	(3)	(3)	
Deferred tax reversal (2 dep'n × 30%)		0.6	
	173	196.6	23.6

*Deferred tax		
Carrying amount in consol. F/S	176
Tax Base	166
Deferred tax liability (176 – 166) × 30%	3

(W3) Goodwill

Tutorial note

When dealing with a step acquisition, remember to include the fair value of the previously owned shares as well as the fair value of the consideration transferred to acquire the new shares.

Message	$m
Purchase consideration	300
FV of NCI at acquisition	86
	–––––
	386
FV of NA at acquisition (W2)	(400)
	–––––
Gain on bargain purchase	(14)
	–––––

Mixted	$m
Cash consideration for new shares	118
Contingent consideration for new shares	12
Fair value of previously held shares	15
FV of NCI at acquisition	53
	–––––
	198
FV of NA at acquisition (W2)	(173)
	–––––
Goodwill	25
	–––––

The gain on bargain purchase is recognised in profit or loss.

Goodwill in the consolidated statement of financial position is therefore $25m.

(W4) Non-controlling interest

	$m
Message:	
FV of NCI at acquisition	86.00
20% × (414 – 400) (W2)	2.80
Mixted:	
FV of NCI at acquisition	53.00
30% × (196.6 – 173) (W2)	7.08
	–––––
	148.88
	–––––

(W5) Group reserves

Tutorial note

Keep the workings for retained earnings and other components of equity separate.

Retained earnings

	$m
Bravado	240.00
Less: Inventory write-down (W8)	(18.00)
Gain on step acquisition (W1)	5.00
Message: 80% × (414 – 400) (W2)	11.20
Mixted: 70% × (196.6 – 173) (W2)	16.52
Gain on bargain purchase (W3)	14.00
Share of associate profit (W6)	2.50
Reclassification of Clarity (W1)	1.00
	——
	272.22
	——

Other components of equity

	$m
Bravado	12.0
Reclassification of Clarity (W1)	(1.0)
Financial asset loss (W7)	(17.4)
	——
	(6.4)
	——

(W6) Investment in associate

Tutorial note

Associates are accounted for using the equity method. This means that the investment is increased by the group's share of the associate's profit after tax from the date that significant influence is obtained.

	$m
Cost (9 + 11)	20.0
Share of post acq'n profit (25% × 10)	2.5
	——
	22.5
	——

(W7) Financial asset

Tutorial note

The overseas equity instrument has been designated to be measured at fair value through other comprehensive income. The fair value is denominated in dinars so must be translated into dollars using the rate at which the value is determined.

The carrying amount of the financial asset at 31 May 2008 was $51 million (10m dinar × 5.1). The carrying amount at 31 May 2009 needs to be reduced to $33.6 million (7m dinar × 4.8). Therefore financial assets must be written down by $17.4 million ($51m – $33.6m) and the loss recorded in other comprehensive income.

(W8) Inventory

Tutorial note

Inventory is valued at the lower of cost and net realisable value.

Cost of inventory	$m
200,000 units × $1,500	300
100,000 units × $1,000	100
	400

Net realisable value per unit	
Selling price	1,450
Less selling costs	(10)
Finished product NRV	1,440
Less Conversion costs	(500)
1st stage product NRV	940

NRV of inventory	$m
200,000 units × $1,440	288
100,000 units × $940	94
	382

Inventory write down required	$m
Cost	400
NRV	382
	18

(W9) Director loan

Showing the loan as cash and cash equivalents is misleading. It should be reclassified:

	$m
Dr Current assets – loans to directors	1
Cr Cash	1

(W10) Current liabilities – trade payables

Tutorial note

Remember to include the contingent consideration as a current liability.

	$m
Bravado	115
Message	30
Mixted	60
Contingent consideration (W3)	12
	217

(W11) Property, plant and equipment

Tutorial note

Remember to include the impact of the fair value adjustments at the reporting date.

	$m
Bravado	265
Message	230
Mixted	161
FVA adj – land (W2)	40
FVA adj – PPE (W2)	14
FVA adj – PPE dep'n (W2)	(2)
	708

(W12) Deferred tax

Tutorial note

Remember to include the deferred tax arising on the subsidiary acquisition.

	$m
Bravado	25
Message	9
Mixted	3
Arising on acquisition of Mixted (W2)	3
Movement to year-end (W2)	(0.6)
	39.4

(b) **Goodwill calculated on a proportionate basis**

Tutorial note

Part (b) requires goodwill to be calculated on a proportionate basis – the alternative basis to that adopted by Bravado – and to comment on the outcome.

	Message $m	Mixted $m
Consideration	300	145.0
NCI at acq'n (20% × 400)	80	
NCI at acq'n (30% × 173)		51.9
	380	196.9
FV of NA at acquisition (W2)	(400)	(173.0)
Gain on bargain purchase/Goodwill	(20)	23.9

In the case of Mixted, the proportionate method of calculating goodwill results in a smaller value for total assets on the group statement of financial position. Consequently, any write off for impairment of goodwill may have a smaller effect upon the group financial statements.

In the case of Message, it results in a higher gain on the bargain purchase which increases the reported income.

(c)

Tutorial note

Part (c) of the question requires comment on the ethical and other responsibilities of directors where there may be a misclassification or misstatement within the accounts. Any comments should be applied to the specific situation identified within the question.

Showing a loan as cash and cash equivalents is misleading. The Framework says that financial statements should have certain characteristics:

(a)   relevance

(b)   faithful representation

These concepts would preclude the showing of directors' loans in cash. Faithful representation requires information to be free from bias. Relevance is hindered if transactions are not correctly classified.

Directors are responsible for the statutory financial statements and if they believe that they are not complying with IFRS, they should take all steps to ensure that the error or irregularity is rectified.

Directors have a responsibility to act honestly and ethically and not be motivated by personal interest and gain. If the ethical conduct of the directors is questionable then other areas of the financial statements may need scrutiny.

A loan of this nature could create a conflict of interest as the directors' personal interests may interfere or conflict with those of the company's. The loan to a director is unlikely to be an efficient use of corporate assets.

	ACCA Marking scheme	
		Marks
(a)	Message	5
	Mixted	6
	Clarity	4
	Financial asset at FVTOCI	3
	Retained earnings	3
	Post acquisition reserves	2
	Other components of equity	2
	Current liabilities	1
	NCI	2
	Inventories	2
	PPE	2
	Financial asset at FVTOCI	1
	Deferred tax	1
	Trade receivables	1
	Maximum	35
(b)	Message	3
	Mixted	3
	Explanation	3
(c)	Subjective	6
Total		50

Examiner's comments

This question required the preparation of a consolidated statement of financial position using the full goodwill method, a calculation and explanation of the impact on the calculation of goodwill if the non-controlling interest was calculated on a proportionate basis and a discussion of the ethics of showing a loan to a director as cash and cash equivalents. The main body of the question required candidates to deal with the calculation of goodwill in a simple situation, the calculation of goodwill where there was a prior holding in the subsidiary, an investment in an associate, a foreign currency transaction, deferred tax and impairment of inventory. Generally speaking the basic calculation of goodwill under the full goodwill method was well done by candidates. However the calculation of goodwill in a more complex situation where there was a prior holding, contingent consideration and deferred taxation was less well done. Many candidates did not complete the retained earnings calculation and often there was doubt over where the gain on bargain purchase should be recorded. (Group retained profits) The calculation of the impairment of inventories was dealt with quite well by candidates, as was the increase in the value of PPE and land. Often the increase in the depreciation charge as a result of the revaluation of PPE was not calculated correctly, nor was the deferred taxation effect. The main problem for candidates in calculating the NCI was the determination of the correct figure for post acquisition reserves especially as many candidates did not treat the depreciation charge and deferred taxation correctly. In part b of the question, a surprising number of candidates could not calculate goodwill using the proportionate basis. Candidates often calculated goodwill correctly in the simple case but as soon as any complexity was introduced the calculations were inaccurate. Many candidates left out part c completely. This was a little disturbing as part c dealt with the ethics of showing loans to directors as cash. Those candidates who answered the question dealt with the issues quite well.

14 **WARRBURT (DEC 08 EXAM)** *Walk in the footsteps of a top tutor*

Key answer tips

As with many of the group accounting questions, much of the difficulty in part (a) lies in the accounting issues included rather than the preparation of the cash flow statement itself. In particular the question refers to 'draft financial statements' which is normally an indication that there are accounting errors within the statements as currently presented. The best way to approach a cash flow question is to have a sound knowledge and understanding of the standard presentation for the statement, and then to deal with the individual issues identified in the question, completing the statement as you deal with each issue. This question includes the following issues: financial assets, retirement benefits, non-current asset additions including foreign currency, purchase of an interest in an associate and payments for taxation and dividends. Ensure that you do not spend too much time on these issues to the exclusion of completing the cash flow statement itself. Start your workings with those issues you find quickest and easiest to deal with.

(a)   **Warrburt Group Statement of cash flows for year ended 30 November 2008**

	$m	$m
Loss before tax	(21)	
Adjustments to operating activities		
Gain on disposal of financial assets at FVTOCI (W1)	(7)	
Gain on assets destroyed (3 – 1) (W3)	(2)	
Other investment income (W1)	(22)	
Retirement benefit expense (W2)	10	
Depreciation	36	
Profit on sale of PPE (63 – 56)	(7)	
Exchange loss (W8)	2	
Associate's profit	(8)	
Impairment of goodwill and intangible assets	32	
Finance costs	9	
Decrease in trade receivables (92 – 163)	71	
Decrease in inventories (135 – 198)	63	
Decrease in trade payables (W7)	(86)	
	–––––	
	70	
Cash paid to retirement benefit scheme (W2)	(10)	
Interest paid (W6)	(8)	
Income taxes paid (W5)	(39)	13
	–––––	
Cash flows from investing activities:		
Proceeds from sale of financial assets	45	
Purchase of PPE (W8)	(57)	
Proceeds from sale of PPE	63	
Dividend received from associate (W4)	2	
Purchase of associate (W4)	(96)	
Investment income received (W1)	22	(21)
	–––––	
Cash flows from financing activities:		
Proceeds of issue of share capital (per SOCIE)	55	
Repayment of long term borrowings (64 – 20)	(44)	
NCI dividend paid (per SOCIE)	(5)	
Dividends paid (per SOCIE)	(9)	(3)
	–––––	–––––
Net decrease in cash and cash equivalents		(11)
Cash and cash equivalents at beginning of period		323
		–––––
Cash and cash equivalents at end of period		312
		–––––

Workings

(W1) Investments

The sale proceeds of the financial assets were $45 million thus creating a profit on disposal of $7 million. However, there is also realisation of a gain on earlier revaluations in equity and, because these financial assets are investments in equity, this has correctly been transferred to retained earnings.

The other income per the statement of comprehensive income must be broken down to its various elements to ensure that they are correctly accounted for within the statement of cash flows as follows:

	$m
Sale proceeds	45
Carrying amount	(38)
	───
Profit on disposal of financial assets	7
Gain on destroyed assets (3 – 1) (W3)	2
Other investment income	22
	───
Other income per P/L	31
	───

(W2) Pension scheme

Tutorial note

This requires knowledge of accounting for defined benefit obligations, so that the cash flow impact can be identified.

The pension expense (made up of the service cost component and the net interest component) is a non-cash expense and so must be added back to profit when calculating cash generated from operations.

The benefits paid to beneficiaries of the retirement benefit scheme are paid out of the scheme's assets and not the company's. Hence there is no cash flow effect for the benefits paid. Contributions paid into the scheme are a cash outflow of $10 million.

(W3) The destroyed assets

Tutorial note

This requires knowledge of accounting for non-current assets, so that the cash flow impact can be identified.

The difference between the carrying amount of the destroyed assets ($1 million) and the fair value of the replacement assets ($3 million) gives rise to a gain of $2 million in profit or loss. This must be eliminated in the reconciliation between the loss before tax and cash generated from operations.

(W4) Associate

Tutorial note

Associates are accounted for using the equity method.

	$m
Opening balance	nil
Add: Share of profit after tax for period $24m × 25%	8
Less: Share of tax ($8m × 25%) included within tax charge	(2)
Less: Dividend received $8m × 25%	(2)
Investment in associates (bal. fig)	96
	___
Closing balance	100
	___

The share of the profit of the associate before tax is $8 million and the tax thereon will therefore be $2 million. This has been wrongly included in the group tax charge and so needs to be adjusted in the tax working (W5).

(W5) Taxation

Tutorial note

When calculating tax paid, deal with current tax and deferred tax together in a single working.

	$m
Opening tax balances (26 + 42)	68
Charge for the year per P/L	31
Tax on associate profit (W4)	(2)
Deferred tax re financial asset at FVTOCI revaluation gain	3
Deferred tax on property revaluation gains	2
Cash paid (bal fig.)	(39)
	___
Closing tax balances (28 + 35)	63
	___

In the statement of profit or loss for the year, Warrburt has accounted for the associate's share of profit before tax in arriving at the group loss before tax. The share of associate's tax is therefore within the group income tax charge and must be removed.

(W6) Short term provisions

	$m
Opening balance	4
Finance costs per Group P/L	9
Cash paid (bal. fig.)	(8)
Closing balance	5

(W7) Trade payables

	$m
Opening balance	180
Payable relating to PPE (W8)	21
Decrease in trade payables (bal. fig.)	(86)
Closing balance	115

(W8) Payable relating to overseas PPE

	Dinar m	Rate	$m
30 June 2008 – PPE and payable recorded	380	5.0	76
31 Oct 2008 – payment	(280)	4.9	(57)*
Foreign exchange loss (bal. fig.)			2
Outstanding payable	100	4.8	21

The actual cash spent on PPE is $57 million. This will be disclosed within cash flows from investing activities.

The foreign exchange loss will be added back in the reconciliation between the loss before tax and cash generated from operations.

(b) Financial statement ratios can provide useful measures of liquidity but an analysis of the information in the cash flow statement, particularly cash flow generated from operations, can provide specific insights into the liquidity of Warrburt. It is important to look at the generation of cash and its efficient usage. An entity must generate cash from trading activity in order to avoid the constant raising of funds from non-trading sources. The 'quality of the profits' is a measure of an entity's ability to do this. The statement of cash flow shows that the company has generated cash in the period despite sustaining a significant loss. The problem is the fact that the entity will not be able to sustain this level of cash generation if losses continue.

Operating cash flow determines the extent to which Warrburt has generated sufficient funds to repay loans, maintain operating capability, pay dividends and make new investments without external financing. Operating cash flow appears to be healthy, partially through the release of cash from working capital. This cash flow has been used to pay contributions to the pension scheme, pay finance costs and income taxes.

These uses of cash generated would be normal for any entity. However, the release of working capital has also financed in part the investing activities of the entity which includes the purchase of an associate and property, plant and equipment. The investing activities show a net cash outflow of $21 million after accounting for investment income which has been financed partly out of working capital and partly out of cash generated from operations which include changes in working capital. It seems also that the issue of share capital has been utilised to repay the long term borrowings and pay dividends. Also a significant amount of cash has been raised through selling the financial assets at FVTOCI. This may not continue in the future as it will depend on the liquidity of the market. This action seems to indicate that the long term borrowings have effectively been 'capitalised'. The main issue raised by the cash flow statement is the use of working capital to partially finance investing activities. However, the working capital ratio and liquidity ratios are still quite healthy but these ratios will deteriorate if the trend continues.

(c)   Companies can give the impression that they are generating more cash than they are, by manipulating cash flow. The way in which acquisitions, loans and, as in this case, the sale of assets, is shown in the statement of cash flows, can change the nature of operating cash flow and hence the impression given by the financial statements. The classification of cash flows can give useful information to users and operating cash flow is a key figure. The role of ethics in the training and professional lives of accountants is extremely important. Decision-makers expect the financial statements to be true and fair and fairly represent the underlying transactions.

There is a fine line between deliberate misrepresentation and acceptable presentation of information. Pressures on management can result in the misrepresentation of information. Financial statements must comply with International Financial Reporting Standards (IFRS), the Framework and local legislation. Transparency, and full and accurate disclosure is important if the financial statements are not to be misleading. Accountants must possess a high degree of professional integrity and the profession's reputation depends upon it. Ethics describe a set of moral principles taken as a reference point. These principles are outside the technical and practical application of accounting and require judgement in their application. Professional accountancy bodies set out ethical guidelines within which their members operate covering standards of behaviour, and acceptable practice. These regulations are supported by a number of codes, for example, on corporate governance which assist accountants in making ethical decisions. The accountant in Warrburt has a responsibility not to mask the true nature of the statement of cash flow. Showing the sale of assets as an operating cash flow would be misleading if the nature of the transaction was masked. Users of financial statements would not expect its inclusion in this heading and could be misled. The potential misrepresentation is unacceptable. The accountant should try and persuade the directors to follow acceptable accounting principles and comply with accounting standards. There are implications for the truth and fairness of the financial statements and the accountant should consider his position if the directors insist on the adjustments by pointing the inaccuracies out to the auditors.

	ACCA Marking scheme		
			Marks
(a)	Net loss before tax		1
	Financial instruments		4
	Retirement benefit		3
	Property, plant and equipment		6
	Insurance proceeds		2
	Associate		4
	Goodwill and intangibles		1
	Finance costs		2
	Taxation		4
	Working capital		4
	Proceeds of share issue		1
	Repayment of borrowings		1
	Dividends		1
	Non-controlling interest		1
			___
		Maximum	35
			___
(b)	Discussion		10
(c)	Discussion		5
			___
Total			50
			___

Examiner's comments

This question required candidates to produce a statement of cash flows which involved adjusting for disposal of financial assets, dealing with the cash consequences of a retirement benefit liability, adjusting for the purchase of a subsidiary and the purchase of property, plant and equipment (PPE) from overseas as well as the normal adjustments required to produce a statement of cash flows. Candidates generally performed well on part (a) of the question producing good answers, which were rewarded with good marks on this part. The calculation of the exchange loss on the PPE was problematical for some candidates from the viewpoint of how to treat it in the statement of cash flows. Also the calculation of trade payables often failed to take into account the creditor for the purchase of plant.

Part (b) of the question required a discussion of the key issues which the cash flow highlighted. Candidates were required to use the information in their answers to part a of the question in order to determine the cash flow problems which the company had such as the use of working capital to finance the investing activities of the company. Many candidates did not use the information in the first part of the question in answering this part but gave general advantages and disadvantages of statements of cash flows. This did attract some credit but in questions such as this one, candidates answered part (b) before part (a) and then failed to gain marks for as they failed to relate their answers to part (a).

Part (c) of the question required candidates to discuss the ethical responsibilities of an accountant when the directors have made suggestions of unethical practices. Candidates needed to discuss the nature of technical good practice and integrity and what is acceptable practice in terms of deliberate misrepresentation and presentation. This part of the question was quite well answered. However, candidates should develop a greater understanding of ethical principles rather than simple the ability to reiterate the ethical codes.

15   RIBBY, HALL AND ZIAN (JUN 08 EXAM)   *Online question assistance*

Key answer tips

There are several technical issues to deal with in this question. There is a foreign subsidiary entity which requires that the goodwill calculation to be made in foreign currency, and then retranslated at the reporting date. There is also a loan from one subsidiary to the foreign subsidiary on which exchange differences need to be accounted for correctly. Other technical issues to deal with prior to completing the consolidation include employee benefits, share-based payments and intra-group trading.

The final part of the question deals with ethical and professional issues relating to the accounting profession.

(a)   The functional currency is the currency of the primary economic environment in which the entity operates (IAS 21). The primary economic environment in which an entity operates is normally the one in which it primarily generates and expends cash. An entity's management considers the following factors in determining its functional currency (IAS 21):

(i)   the currency that dominates the determination of the sales prices; and

(ii)   the currency that most influences operating costs.

The currency that dominates the determination of sales prices will normally be the currency in which the sales prices for goods and services are denominated and settled. It will also normally be the currency of the country whose competitive forces and regulations have the greatest impact on sales prices. In this case it would appear that currency is the dinar as Zian sells its products locally and the prices are determined by local competition. However, the currency that most influences operating costs is in fact the dollar, as Zian imports goods which are paid for in dollars although all selling and operating expenses are paid in dinars. The emphasis is, however, on the currency of the economy that determines the pricing of transactions, as opposed to the currency in which transactions are denominated.

Factors other than the dominant currency for sales prices and operating costs are also considered when identifying the functional currency. The currency in which an entity's finances are denominated is also considered. Zian has partly financed its operations by raising a $4 million loan from Hall but it is not dependent upon group companies for finance. The focus is on the currency in which funds from financing activities are generated and the currency in which receipts from operating activities are retained.

Additional factors include consideration of the autonomy of a foreign operation from the reporting entity and the level of transactions between the two. Zian operates with a considerable degree of autonomy both financially and in terms of its management. Consideration is given to whether the foreign operation generates sufficient functional cash flows to meet its cash needs which in this case Zian does as it does not depend on the group for finance.

It would be said that the above indicators give a mixed view but the functional currency that most faithfully represents the economic effects of the underlying transactions, events, and conditions is the dinar, as it most affects sales prices and is most relevant to the financing of an entity. The degree of autonomy and independence provides additional supporting evidence in determining the entity's functional currency.

(b)   **Consolidated Statement of Financial Position of Ribby Group at 31 May 2008**

Assets	$m
Non-current assets	
Goodwill (W3)	16.8
Property, plant and equipment (W9)	414.7
Financial assets at fair value (W14)	23.3
	———
	454.8
Current assets (W15)	51.0
	———
Total assets	505.8
	———

Equity and liabilities	$m
Equity shares	60.0
Other components of equity (W6)	31.8
Retained earnings (W5)	121.7
	———
Total shareholders' equity	213.5
Non-controlling interests (W4)	59.6
	———
Total equity	273.1
Non-current liabilities (W16)	89.7
Current liabilities (W17)	143.0
	———
	505.8
	———

Workings

(W1) Group structure

(W2a) Net assets – Hall

	Acq'n date $m	Rep date $m
Share capital	40	40
Retained earnings	60	80
Other Equity	10	10
FVA – Land	10	10
PURP (W13)		(4)
	120	136

(W2b) Net assets– Zian

	Acq'n date Dinar(m)	Rep date Dinar(m)
Equity capital	209	209
Pre-acq'n retained earnings	220	220
FVA – Land	66	66
Post acq'n RE (299 – 220)		79
Loan – FX loss (W8)		(8)
	495	566

(W3a) Goodwill – Hall

	$m
Cost of investment	98
NCI at acquisition (30% × $120m) (W2a)	36
	134
Less: FV of net assets at acquisition (W2a)	(120)
Goodwill	14

(W3b) Goodwill and retranslation schedule – Zian

	Dinar (m)
Cost of investment	330
NCI at acquisition (40% × 495m dinar (W2b))	198
	528
FV of net assets at acquisition (W2b)	(495)
Goodwill at acquisition – no impairment	33

Translated at closing rate of 12 = $2.8m

The exchange gain or loss on retranslation of goodwill at the reporting date must also be identified as follows:

	Dinar(m)	Rate	$m
Goodwill at acquisition	33	11	3.0
FX gain (loss) on retranslation (W5)		**Bal fig**	**(0.2)**
Goodwill at reporting date	33	12	2.8

As goodwill was calculated using the proportionate basis, all of the exchange gain or loss on retranslation is allocated to the parent in (W5).

(W4) Non-controlling Interest

	$m
Hall: NCI at acquisition (30% × $120m) (W2a)	36.0
NCI % of post acquisition net assets (30% ×($136m − $120m)) (W2a))	4.8
Zian: NCI at acquisition (D198m/11) (W3)	18.0
NCI % of post-acquisition net assets (40% × $2.2m) (W7)	0.8
	59.6

(W5) Group reserves

	$m
Ribby	120.0
Hall: (70% × (136 − 120) (W2a)	11.2
Zian (60% × 2.2) (W7)	1.3
Ribby – building impaired (W9)	(0.8)
Ribby – penalty re early loan repayment (W10)	(1.0)
Ribby – cash bonus (W11)	(3.0)
Ribby – share options (W11)	(1.8)
Ribby – past service cost – pension costs (W12)	(4.0)
Exchange loss on retranslation of goodwill (W3b)	(0.2)
	121.7

(W6) Other components of equity

	$m
Ribby	30.0
Ribby – equity re share options (W10)	1.8
	31.8

(W7) Net asset translation

	Dinar(m)	Rate	$m
Net assets at acquisition	495	11	45.0
Profit since acquisition	**71**	**Bal fig**	**2.2**
Net assets at reporting date	566	12	47.2

Be careful, profit earned during the year is translated at the average rate for that year. However, the D71m profit has been earned over two years. Without knowing how much profit is earned in each year, and the average rate for each year, it is not possible to split out the post-acquisition profit from the post-acquisition foreign exchange differences arising on the translation of the profit.

Therefore, the $2.2m balance above represents both post-acquisition profits and the foreign exchange on net assets and profit. The group's share of this is taken to group reserves.

(W8) Zian – Exchange loss on loan from Hall

Loans between subsidiaries cannot be treated as part of the holding company's net investment in a foreign subsidiary (IAS 21). Zian will recognise an exchange difference on the loan from Hall in profit or loss and the exchange difference will flow through to the consolidated statement of profit or loss and will not be reclassified as a separate component of equity.

	Dinar (m)
Loan at 1 June 2007 $4m at 10 dinars	40
Loan at 31 May 2008 $4m at 12 dinars	48
Exchange loss	8

The loan of $4 million should be eliminated on consolidation from both financial assets (W14) and non-current liabilities (W16).

(W9) Tangible assets (including building impaired)

	$m	$m
Ribby	250.0	
Hall (120 + 10(FVA) (W2a))	130.0	
Zian ((360 + 66(FVA) (W2b))/12)	35.5	
		415.5
Building – impairment loss		
1 June 2007 cost 40m dinar @ 10	4.0	
Depreciation (20 years)	(0.2)	
	3.8	
31 May 2008 36m dinar @12	3.0	(0.8)
		414.7

(W10) Early repayment of loan

As Ribby entered into an agreement to repay the debt early plus a penalty, it should adjust the carrying value of the financial liability to reflect actual and revised estimated cash flows (IFRS 9). Therefore, the carrying amount of the loan liability should be increased by $1 million and be transferred to current liabilities.

(W11) Cash bonus and share options to employees of Ribby

A liability of $3 million should be accrued for the bonus to be paid in cash to the employees of Ribby. The management should also recognise an expense of (12/18 × 90% × $3 million) $1.8 million, with a corresponding increase in equity. The terms of the share options have not been fixed and, therefore, the grant date becomes 30 November 2008 as this is the date that the terms and conditions will be fixed. However, IFRS 2 requires the entity to recognise the services when received and, therefore, adjustment is required to the financial statements. Once the terms are fixed, the fair value can be calculated and any adjustments made.

	$m
Dr Expense – in retained earnings (W5)	4.8
Cr Equity (W6)	1.8
Cr Current liabilities (W16)	3.0

(W12) Defined benefit plan – past service cost

A past service cost of $4 million should be recognised immediately as, part of the service cost component. Thus the following entries will be required to account for the past service costs.

Dr Retained earnings (W5)	$4.0m
Cr Non-current liabilities (defined benefit obligation) (W16)	$4.0m

(W13) Accounting for sale of inventory (see part (c))

The transaction should not be shown as a sale. Inventory should be reinstated at $2 million instead of $6 million and a decrease in retained earnings of $4 million should occur in the accounting records of Hall.

Cr Inventory (W15)	$4m
Dr Retained earnings of Hall (W2a)	$4m

The cash position should be reversed also by increasing Ribby's cash balance by $6m (W15) and also increasing Hall's overdraft by $6m (W17).

(W14) Financial assets at fair value

	$m
Ribby	10.0
Hall	5.0
Zian (148m dinar @ 12)	12.3
Elimination of loan from Hall to Zian (W16)	(4.0)
	23.3

(W15) Current assets

		$m
Ribby		22.0
Hall		17.0
Zian (120m dinar @ 12)		10.0
Inventory adjustment (W13)		(4.0)
Cash reinstated re window dressing transaction (W13)		6.0
		51.0

(W16) Non-current liabilities

		$m
Ribby	90.0	
Hall	5.0	
Zian (48 + 8 (W8) m dinar @ 12)	4.7	
		99.7
Increase carrying amount of loan liability (W10)		1.0
Eliminate of loan from Hall to Zian (W14)		(4.0)
Past service cost (W12)		4.0
Loan & penalty reclassified to current liabs (W10)(W17)		(11.0)
		89.7

(W17) Current liabilities

		$m
Ribby		110.0
Hall		7.0
Zian (72m dinar @ 12)		6.0
Cash bonus to Ribby employees (W11)		3.0
Cash reinstated re window dressing transaction (W13)		6.0
Loan & penalty reclassified from N-C liabs (W10)(W16)		11.0
		143.0

(c) **Accounting and ethical implications of sale of inventory**

Manipulation of financial statements often does not involve breaking laws but the purpose of financial statements is to present a fair representation of the company's position, and if the financial statements are misrepresented on purpose then this could be deemed unethical. The financial statements in this case are being manipulated to show a certain outcome so that Hall may be shown to be in a better financial position if the company is sold. The retained earnings of Hall will be increased by $4 million, and the cash received would improve liquidity. Additionally this type of transaction was going to be carried out again in the interim accounts if Hall was not sold. Accountants have the responsibility to issue financial statements that do not mislead the public as the public assumes that such professionals are acting in an ethical capacity, thus giving the financial statements credibility.

A profession is distinguished by having a:

(i)   specialised body of knowledge

(ii)   commitment to the social good

(iii)   ability to regulate itself

(iv)   high social status.

Accountants should seek to promote or preserve the public interest. If the idea of a profession is to have any significance, then it must make a bargain with society in which they promise conscientiously to serve the public interest. In return, society allocates certain privileges. These might include one or more of the following:

*   the right to engage in self-regulation

*   the exclusive right to perform particular functions

*   special status.

There is more to being an accountant than is captured by the definition of the professional. It can be argued that accountants should have the presentation of truth, in a fair and accurate manner, as a goal.

	ACCA Marking scheme (adjusted)		
			Marks
(a)	Consideration of factors		6
	Conclusion		2
		Maximum	**8**
(b)	Translation of Zian		6
	Loan		2
	Goodwill: Zian		4
	Non-controlling interest		4
	Building		3
	Early repayment of loan		1
	Pension		2
	Inventory		1
	Bonus		3
	Goodwill: Hall		2
	Retained earnings	Hall	2
		Zian	1
		Ribby	3
	Other reserves		1
		Maximum	**35**
(c)	Discussion		7
Total			**50**

Examiner's comments

This question required candidates to determine the functional currency of an overseas subsidiary, and prepare a consolidated statement of financial position for a simple group structure involving an overseas subsidiary and several adjustments for foreign currency loans, employee compensation, past service pension costs, intercompany profit elimination, and early repayment of long term loans. The final part required candidates to discuss the manipulation of financial statements and the nature of accountants' responsibilities to the profession and to society. The first part of the question was answered well by many candidates but at the same time many candidates discussed the method used to translate the financial statements of an overseas subsidiary, which was not answering the question set. The answer to this part of the question required candidates to use the information in the scenario and if candidates did use the information then they achieved a higher mark than those that simply quoted the accounting standard.

Part (b) of the question was quite well answered. Candidates seemed to generally understand the method used to translate the financial statements of an overseas subsidiary. Some candidates used incorrect exchange rates to translate the statement of financial position of the subsidiary but most candidates managed to compute goodwill correctly, which was encouraging. The adjustments to the financial statements were mainly to the holding company/group account, which meant that candidates could calculate any adjustment without worrying about the effect on the non-controlling interest. Thus many candidates scored well when discussing the adjustments. Although the question does not ask for a discussion of the adjustments, it is good practice for candidates to write a brief explanation of the accounting practice used in answering the particular part of the question. Many candidates dealt with the past service cost, the early repayment of the loan and the accounting for the sale of the inventory very well. However the bonus payable to the employees was not dealt with quite as well with candidates not time apportioning half of the bonus and expensing the other half.

Part (c) of the question was not well answered and many candidates did not attempt it. It required a discussion of the role of a profession and its responsibility to society. It was a little worrying that many candidates did not know the distinguishing features of a profession or the demands that society places on the profession.

16 ANDASH (DEC 06 EXAM)

Key answer tips

Group statements of cash flow are relatively straight forward to deal with. This one has a number of complications, with the purchase of associate, disposal of subsidiary and share based payment transactions. Deal with the individual items and put the answer into the cash flow. Always deal with the easy adjustments first. You should find parts (b) and (c) provide easy marks because these topics are central to the syllabus.

(a) **Andash Group statement of cash flows for year-ended 31 October 20X6**

	$m	$m
Cash flows from operating activities		
Profit before taxation (w(i))		323
Adjustments for profit on sale of subsidiary	(8)	
Depreciation	260	
Impairment of goodwill (w(iv))	78	
Associate's profit (w(iii))	(1)	
Finance costs	148	477
		800
Increase in trade rec'ables (2,400 – 1,500 + 4 (w(v)))	(904)	
Increase in inventories (2,650 – 2,300 + 8 (w(v)))	(358)	
Increase in trade payables (4,700 – 2,800 + 6 (w(v)))	1,906	644
Cash generated from operations		1,444
Interest paid (40 + 148 – 70)		(118)
Income taxes paid (w(vi))		(523)
Net cash from operating activities		803
Cash flows from investing activities		
Purchase of associate (w(iii))	(10)	
Purchase of property, plant and equipment (w(ii))	(1,320)	
Sale of subsidiary (32 – 5 (w(v)))	27	(1,303)
		(500)
Cash flows from financing activities:		
Proceeds of issue of share capital (w(vii))	10	
Dividend paid to non-controlling interests	(20)	
Proceeds from long term borrowings	400	
Dividends paid	(50)	340
Net decrease in cash and equivalents		(160)
Cash and equivalents at 1 November 20X5		300
Cash and equivalents at 31 October 20X6		140

Workings

		$m
(i)	Profit before tax per draft	400
	Associate's profit (iii)	1
	Impairment of goodwill (iv)	(78)
	Profit before tax as amended	323

(ii)   Property, plant and equipment

IFRS 2 *Share-based payment* says that the fair value of the goods and services received should be used as the value of the share options issued. Therefore, the plant should be valued at $9 million and the share options at the same amount. There is no need to adjust depreciation because of the date of purchase, but other reserves will fall by $1 million.

	$m
Property, plant and equipment – balance 31 October 20X5	4,110
Purchases – non-cash ⎫ above	9
Over valuation	1
Depreciation	(260)
Sale of subsidiary	(10)
Purchases in period (balancing figure)	1,320
	____
Property, plant and equipment per SOFP	5,170
	____

(iii)   Associate – Joma

The investment in the associate should be measured using the equity method.

	$m	$m
Cost of investment		
FV of shares issued		50
Cash paid		10
		____
		60
Share of post-acquisition reserves (25% × ($32 – $20))	3	
Inter company profit eliminated (25% × ($16 – $8))	(2)	1
	____	____
		61
		____

(iv)   Impairment of Goodwill-Broiler

	Goodwill	*Net assets*	*Total*
	$m	$m	$m
Carrying amount	90	240	330
Unrecognised NCI (90 × 40/60)	60	–	60
	____	____	____
	150	240	390
Recoverable amount			260
			____
Impairment loss			(130)

Goodwill will be reduced by 60% of 130, i.e. **$78 million.** Profit or loss will be charged with this amount.

(v) **Sale of subsidiary**

The sale of the subsidiary should be taken into account in the statement of cash flows as follows:

	Dr	Cr
	$m	$m
Plant, property and equipment		10
Inventory		8
Trade receivables		4
Cash and cash equivalents		5
Trade payables	6	
Current tax payable	7	
Cash proceeds	32	
Goodwill disposed of		10
Profit on sale		8
	——	——
	45	45
	——	——

(vi) **Income taxes paid**

	$m
Current and deferred tax 31/10/X5 (770 + 300)	1,070
Statement of comprehensive income charge	160
Cash paid (balancing figure)	(523)
Sale of subsidiary	(7)
	——
Current and deferred tax 31/10/X6 (300 + 400)	700
	——

(vii) **Shares issued**

Cash flow from the issue of shares is $(60 − 50) i.e. $10 million (from the statement of changes in equity). The shares issued for the purchase of Joma are taken out of the issue proceeds set out in the statement of changes in equity.

(b) In many cases, the business focus is solely on profitability, with interpretation of financial information focusing on traditional ratios such as gross margin, net margin, return on capital employed. However, a business cannot survive without cash and cash flows cannot be ignored when assessing the performance of an entity.

Statements of cash flows enable users of the financial statements to assess the liquidity, solvency and financial adaptability of a business. A statement of cash flows provides information that is not available from the statement of financial position and the statement of comprehensive income.

A statement of cash flows is believed to provide useful information to users of the financial statements for the following reasons:

- Unlike profits, cash flows are not affected by an entity's choice of accounting policies or by the exercise of judgement. Cash flows can be verified objectively and therefore they allow little scope for 'creative accounting'.

- Cash flow information is thought to have predictive value. It may assist users of financial statements in making judgements on the amount, timing and degree of certainty of future cash flows.

- It gives an indication of the relationship between profitability and cash generating ability, and thus of the quality of the profit earned. The reconciliation of operating profit to the net cash flow generated by operating activities is particularly useful in this context and highlights movements in working capital.

- Cash flow may be more easily understood than profit, particularly by users who are unfamiliar with the technical aspects of financial reporting.

- The statement of cash flows provides information that may be useful in interpreting the statement of comprehensive income and statement of financial position. For example, it shows cash flow from capital transactions as well as from revenue transactions. It may highlight a company's financial adaptability (for example, its ability to generate future profits and cash flows by selling non-current assets or by issuing shares).

However, statements of cash flows are based on historical information and therefore do not provide complete information for assessing future cash flows. Neither cash flow nor profit provide a complete picture of a company's performance when looked at in isolation.

Measuring cash flow performance

There are a number of different ways cash flow performance can be assessed.

Cash generation from operations

Cash from operations should be compared to the profit from operations (cash from operations/profit from operations). If the ratio is greater than 1 it means that all profits have been converted into cash, which is a good performance.

Overtrading may be indicated by:

- high profits and low cash generation

- large increases in inventory, receivables and payables.

Dividend and interest payments

These should be compared to cash generated from trading operations to see whether the normal operations can sustain such payments. In most years they should.

Capital expenditure and financial investment

The nature and scale of a company's investment in non-current assets is clearly shown in the cash flow. This may be a cause of a net cash outflow in the period, but this should pay benefits in the future with increased profits.

Cash flow

The statement clearly shows the end result in cash terms of the company's activities in the year. However, the importance of this figure alone must not be overstated. A decrease in cash in the year may be for very sound reasons (e.g. there was surplus cash last year) or may be mainly the result of timing (e.g. a new loan was raised just after the end of the accounting period).

Free cash flow

Free cash flow represents the cash that an entity has left after paying out the cash to maintain its asset base. It is calculated as:

Free cash flow = Net profit + depreciation/amortisation – change in working capital – capital expenditure

(Or FCF = operating cash flow – capital expenditure.)

This is the amount of cash left over after paying expenses and operating investments. It is the cash available to be used in investing in new projects or repaid to share holders. A negative free cash flow is not necessarily a bad thing, as an entity may be investing to provide increased cash inflows in the future.

(c)   Window dressing is the act of showing a better position in the financial statements than actually exists. It is a form of creative accounting and while the financial statements may have been prepared in accordance with accounting standards, there is bias in the way the figures are presented. If the intention is to deceive stakeholders, then the practice of window dressing is unethical.

Aims of window dressing

The aim of window dressing is to improve the financial statements and show them in a more favourable light than they should be. It can be used to hide liquidity problems or to make the financial statements look better to present to lenders of finance. It can also be used to make the accounts look better to encourage investors.

Methods of window dressing

There are a number of ways to window dress the financial statements.

- **Sale and leaseback** – sell an asset before the year-end but lease it back post year-end.

- **Short term borrowing** just before year-end shows a better ability to repay debts although it does increase liabilities.

- **Receipt of receivables** – asking customers to pay their debts early so the cash is received before the end of the reporting period. Discounts are usually offered to customers so they will agree to this. This makes the cash position look better and it does improve liquidity but it usually reduces profits.

- **Bringing sales forward** – asking customers to take sales early so they can be recognised before the year-end. This increases revenue and profits but not cash. Unfortunately it brings problems for following financial year as the sales cannot be recognised again, so effectively the company is taking next year's sales into the current year.

- **Changing depreciation policies** – if an entity decides to extend the useful life of non-current assets this will reduce the statement of comprehensive income depreciation charge and increase the non-current assets in the statement of financial position.

- **Recognising intangible assets** – if this can be done it improves asset values although if amortised this expense will be recognised in profit or loss. If the intangible is not amortised it will give higher asset values that are not necessarily true.

- **Changing valuation policies such as inventory and provisions**. Any change in valuation methods will affect profit. This is especially the case for inventory.

It is often argued that cash flows and balances cannot be manipulated because cash flow is a matter of fact. It is not subject to estimates and it can only be treated in one way. However, there is still some scope for manipulation of cash flows.

Cash balances are measured at a point in time. This means that it is possible to arrange receipts and payments of cash so that the cash balance is some particular amount. A business may make a special effort to collect debts just before the year-end; likewise, it may also delay paying creditors until just after the year-end.

A business may also structure transactions so that the cash balance is favourably affected. For example, if assets are acquired under leasing agreements cash outflows are spread over several accounting periods rather than one accounting period.

Ethical issues

Arranging transactions to window dress the financial statements and make them look better than actually is the case is not an ethical way of preparing financial statements.

In preparing financial statements, the preparer must ensure that the information is prepared honestly and fairly and that it can be relied upon by the users of those financial statements. If the financial statements are altered so that they do not present fairly the financial position and performance of the entity then they may be misleading to users.

ACCA Marking scheme		Marks
(a)	Cash flows from operating activities	2
	Adjustments	4
	Cash generated from operations	3
	Interest	2
	Tax	2
	Associate	3
	Plant, property and equipment	2
	Sale of subsidiary	3
	Non controlling interest	2
	Long term borrowings	1
	Dividend paid	1
	Goodwill	3
	Maximum	**28**
(b)	Cash flow discussion	10
(c)	Window dressing discussion	12
Total		**50**

17 PARSLEY

Key answer tips

Part (a) of this question is a group accounting question. Parsley lost control of Sage during the year. Sage is therefore consolidated until the disposal date and a profit or loss on disposal must be calculated. Saffron is an overseas subsidiary, which must be translated into the group's presentation currency. Exchange differences on the retranslation of Saffron's opening net assets, profit and goodwill are recorded in other comprehensive income.

(a) **Consolidated statement of profit or loss and other comprehensive income for the year ended 30 April 20X4**

	$m
Revenue ($143 + ($68 × 6/12) + (FR210/4.6))	222.7
Cost of sales ($61 + (42 × 6/12) + (FR126/4.6) – $0.3 (W4))	(109.1)
Gross profit	113.6
Distribution costs ($10 + ($6 × 6/12) + (FR14/4.6))	(16.0)
Administrative expenses (W11)	(36.3)
Operating profit	61.3
Share of profit of associates (W3)	1.2
Profit on disposal (W7)	4.4
Investment income ($1 + ($2 × 6/12) – $0.4 (W2))	1.6
Finance costs (W12)	(4.3)
Profit before taxation	64.2
Taxation ($11 + ($2 × 6/12) + (FR9/4.6))	(14.0)
Profit for the period	50.2
Other comprehensive income	
Items that may be reclassified to profit or loss in future periods	
Exchange gains on retranslation of overseas subsidiary	5.8
($1.4 (W8) + $4.4 (W9))	
Total comprehensive income for the period	56.0

Profit attributable to:

Equity holders of Parsley (bal. fig.)	47.4
Non-controlling interest (W10)	2.8
	50.2

Total comprehensive income attributable to:

Equity holders of Parsley (bal. fig.)	50.8
Non-controlling interest ($2.8 (profit) + $0.6 (W8) + $1.8 (W9))	5.2
	56.0

Workings

Group structure

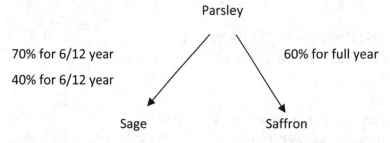

Parsley

70% for 6/12 year   60% for full year

40% for 6/12 year

Sage   Saffron

(W1) Saffron's brand

	FRm
Fair value of net assets	70
Carrying value of net assets	(60)
Fair value of brand	10

The excess amortisation on the brand is FR2m (FR10m/5 years)

(W2) Dividend

Parsley owned 40% of the ordinary shares of Sage when the dividend was paid.

Investment income of $0.4m ($1m × 40%) must be removed from consolidated profit or loss.

(W3) Associate

Parsley has significant influence over Sage for the second half of the year. The results of Sage for these six months must be equity accounted. The group's share of the associate's profit is $1.2m ($6m × 6/12 × 40%).

(W4) Finance lease

Parsley is leasing the asset for the majority of its useful economic life. The lease should be classified as a finance lease because the risks and rewards of ownership have transferred to Parsley.

An asset and liability should be recognised at the lower of the fair value and the present value of the minimum lease payments.

The cash payment of $1.3m should be removed from cost of sales. The depreciation on the asset of $1m ($5m/5 years) should be charged to cost of sales. The net impact is a reduction to cost of sales of $0.3m.

A finance cost of $0.5m should be charged ($5m × 9.5%) on the lease liability.

(W5) Borrowing costs

The weighted average cost of borrowings must be calculated. This is 9.4% (($14m × 10%) + ($6m × 8%)/$20m).

Interest relating to the 11 month construction period can be capitalised. This amount is:

$10m × 9.4% × (11/12) = $0.9m

The adjustment required is:

Dr PPE $0.9m

Cr Finance costs (P&L) $0.9m

(W6) Share options

The expense should be based on the number of shares that are expected to vest and the fair value of the options at the grant date. This expense is spread over the vesting period.

The expense in the year ended 30 April 20X4 is:

(100 employees − 5 − 5) × 10,000 options × $3.10 fair value × 6/24 = $0.7m.

The correcting entry is:

Dr Admin expenses (P&L) $0.7m

Cr Equity $0.7m

(W7) Profit on disposal

	$m	$m
Proceeds from disposal	6.5	
Fair value of interest retained	9.5	
		16.0
Goodwill disposed:		
Consideration	6.0	
NCI at acquisition ($5m × 30%)	1.5	
Net assets at acquisition	(5.0)	
Goodwill at disposal		(2.5)
Net assets at disposal:		
Share capital	1.0	
Retained earnings bfd	9.0	
Profit to disposal date ($6m × 6/12)	3.0	
Net assets at disposal		(13.0)
NCI at disposal:		
NCI at acquisition	1.5	
NCI % of post acquisition net assets (30% × ($13m – $5m))	2.4	
		3.9
Profit on disposal		4.4

(W8) Goodwill – Saffron

Calculation of goodwill in functional currency:

	FRm
Cost of acquisition	71
FV of NCI at acquisition	29
	100
Less FV net assets at acquisition	(70)
Goodwill at acquisition	30
Impairment	(4)
Goodwill at reporting date	26

FX gain on retranslation	FRm	Rate	$m
Acquisition	30	5.0	6.0
Impairment	(4)	4.6	(0.9)
FX gain on retranslation		**Bal fig**	**1.4**
Rep date	26	4.0	6.5

The forex gain attributable to the NCI is $0.6m ($1.4m × 40%).

(W9) Forex on opening net assets and profit

	FRm	Rate	$m
Opening net assets	70	5.0	14.0
Profit	27	4.6	5.9
(FR29m – FR2m (W1))			
FX gain on retranslation		**Bal fig**	**4.4**
Rep date	97	4.0	24.3

The forex gain attributable to the NCI is $1.8m ($4.4m × 40%).

(W10) Profit attributable to non-controlling interest

	$m
NCI share of Sage's profit	0.9
($6m × 6/12 × 30%)	
NCI share of Saffron's profit	2.3
((FR29 – 2 (W1))/4.6) × 40%)	
NCI share of goodwill impairment	(0.4)
($0.9m (W8) × 40%)	
Profit attributable to the NCI	2.8

(W11) Administrative expenses

	$m
Parsley	23.0
Sage ($10 × 6/12)	5.0
Saffron (FR29/4.6)	6.3
Excess amortisation (FR2 (W1)/4.6)	0.4
Goodwill impairment (W8)	0.9
Share-based payment (W6)	0.7
	36.3

(W12) Finance costs

	$m
Parsley	2.0
Sage ($4 × 6/12)	2.0
Saffron (FR3/4.6)	0.7
Lease (W4)	0.5
Borrowing costs (W5)	(0.9)
	4.3

(b) IAS 24 *Related party disclosures* states that a person or a close member of their family is related to the reporting entity if that person:

- has control, joint control or significant influence over the reporting entity

- is a member of key management personnel of the reporting entity or its parent.

The main circumstances that lead to an entity being related to the reporting entity are as follows:

- the entity and the reporting entity are members of the same group

- one entity is an associate or joint venture of the other

- both entities are joint ventures of the same third party

- the entity is controlled or jointly controlled by a person who is a related party of the reporting entity.

In the absence of related party disclosures, users of financial statements would assume that an entity has acted independently and in its own best interests. Most importantly, this assumes that all transactions have been entered into willingly and at arm's length (i.e. on normal commercial terms at fair value). Where related party relationships and transactions exist, this assumption may not be justified. These relationships and transactions lead to the danger that financial statements may have been distorted or manipulated, both favourably and unfavourably. The most obvious example of this type of transaction would be the sale of goods or rendering of services from one party to another on non-commercial terms (this may relate to the price charged or the credit terms given). Other examples of disclosable transactions are agency, licensing and leasing arrangements, transfer of research and development and the provision of finance, guarantees and collateral. Collectively this would mean there is hardly an area of financial reporting that could not be affected by related party transactions.

It is a common misapprehension that related party transactions need only be disclosed if they are not at arm's length. This is not the case. For example, a parent may instruct all members of its group to buy certain products or services (on commercial terms) from one of its subsidiaries. In the absence of the related party relationships, these transactions may not have occurred. If the parent were to sell the subsidiary, it would be important for the prospective buyer to be aware that the related party transactions would probably not occur in the future. Indeed even where there are no related party transactions, the disclosure of the related party relationship is still important as a subsidiary may obtain custom, receive favourable credit ratings, and benefit from a superior management team simply by being a part of a well respected group.

(c)   The subsidiaries of X are related parties to each other and to X itself as they are under common control.

One of the important aspects of related party relationships is that one of the parties may have its interests subordinated to those of another party, i.e. it may not be able to act in its own best interest. This appears to be the case in this situation. B (or at least one of its directors) believes that the price it is charging A is less than it could have achieved by selling the goods to non-connected parties. In effect these sales have not been made at an arm's length fair value. The obvious implication of this is that the transactions have moved profits from B to A. If the director's figures are accurate B would have made a profit on these transactions of $6 million (20 – 14) rather than the $1 million it has actually made. The transactions will also affect reported revenue and cost of sales and working capital in the individual financial statements of A and B. Some might argue that as the profit remains within the group, there is no real overall effect as, in the consolidated financial statements, intra-group transactions are eliminated. This is not entirely true. The implications of these related party sales are serious:

- B has a non controlling interest of 45% and they have been deprived of their share of the $5 million transferred profit. This could be construed as oppression of the minority and could be illegal.

- There is a similar effect on the profit share that the directors of B might be entitled to under the group profit sharing scheme as B's profits are effectively $5 million lower than they should be.

- Shareholders, independent analysts or even the (independent) managers of B would find it difficult to appraise the true performance of B. The related party transaction gives the impression that B is under-performing.

- This may lead to the minority selling their shares for a low price (because of poor returns) or calls for the company's closure or some form of rationalisation which may not be necessary.

- The tax authorities may wish to investigate the transactions under transfer pricing rules. The profit may have been moved to A's financial statements to avoid paying tax in B's tax jurisdiction which may have high levels of taxation.

- In the same way as B's results appear poorer due to the effect of the related party transactions, A's results would look better. This may have been done deliberately. X may intend to dispose of A in the near future and thus its more favourable results may allow X to obtain a higher sale price for A.

ACCA Marking scheme		
		Marks
(a)	P/L and OCI	35
(b)	Discussion	7
(c)	Discussion	8
		——
Total:		**50**
		——

18   MEMO

Key answer tips

Part (a) is a normal straightforward consolidation – there are a few adjustments to be dealt with but nothing too complicated, except perhaps accounting for the group exchange difference. It is a good question to test your understanding of the requirement of IAS 21 that goodwill arising should be treated as a foreign currency asset and retranslated at the end of each reporting period. Otherwise the consolidation proceeds as normal.

Part (b) of the question is mainly discussion of presentation and functional currency.

(a)   **Memo Group – Consolidated statement of financial position as at 30 April 20X4**

	$m
Goodwill (W3)	11.1
Property, plant and equipment (297 + (146/2.1))	366.5
Current assets (355 + (102/2.1) – 0.6 (W8))	403.0
	780.6

	$m
Equity shares of $1	60.0
Share premium account	50.0
Retained earnings (W5)	364.3
Foreign exchange reserve (W7)	8.8
	483.1
Non controlling interest (W4)	19.8
Total equity of the group	502.9
Non-current liabilities (30 + ((41 – 2 (W9))/2.1) – 5 (inter-co))	43.6
Current liabilities (205 + ((60 + 1.2 (W8))/2.1))	234.1
	780.6

Consolidated statement of profit or loss and other comprehensive income for the year ended 30 April 20X4

	$m
Revenue (200 + (142/2.0) – 6 (W8))	265.0
Cost of sales (120 + (96/2.0) + 1.3 (W3) – 6 + 0.6 (W8))	(163.9)
	————
Gross profit	101.1
Distribution and administrative expenses (30 + (20/2))	(40.0)
Finance costs (2/2)	(1.0)
Investment income	4.0
Net exchange gains on transactions (W8/W9) ((2.0 – 1.2)/2.0)	0.4
	————
Profit before taxation	64.5
Tax (20 + (9/2.0))	(24.5)
	————
Profit for the year	40.0
Other comprehensive income – items that may be reclassified to profit or loss in future periods:	
Exchange difference on translation of foreign subsidiary (W7)	11.7
	————
Total comprehensive income for the year	51.7
	————

Profit attributable to:	$m
Owners of the parent – bal fig	38.3
Non-controlling interest (W10)	1.7
	————
Profit for the year	40.0
	————

Total comprehensive income attributable to:	$m
Owners of the parent (bal fig)	47.1
Non-controlling interest (W10)	4.6
	————
Total comprehensive income for the year	51.7
	————

Workings

(W1) Group structure

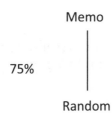

Memo

75%

Random

(W2) Net assets

	At acq'n Cr(m)	At rep date Cr(m)
Equity capital	32	32
Share premium	20	20
Pre-acquisition retained earnings	80	95
Ex loss on settled liability (W8)		(1.2)
Ex gain on restated foreign loan (W9)		2.0
	132	147.8

(W3) Goodwill in functional currency and retranslation schedule

	Cr(m)
Cost of acquisition	120.0
FV of NCI at acquisition	38.0
	158.0
Less: FV net assets acquired (W2)	(132.0)
Full goodwill at acquisition	26.0
Impairment in year – 10%	(2.6)
Unimpaired at reporting date	23.4

Gain or loss on retranslation of goodwill:

	Cr(m)	Rate	$m
At acquisition	26.0	2.5 acq'n rate	10.4
Impairment	(2.6)	2.0 ave	(1.3)
Exchange gain on retranslation		**Bal fig**	**2.0**
At rep date	23.4	2.1 cl rate	11.1

As the full goodwill method has been used, the impairment is allocated between the group and NCI based upon their respective shareholdings:

Group (75% × 1.3) = $1.0m (W5)

NCI (25% × 1.3) = $0.3 (W4)

As the full goodwill method has been used, the exchange gain on retranslation is allocated between the group and NCI based upon their respective shareholdings:

Group (75% × $2.0m) = $1.5m (W5)

NCI (25% × $2.0m) = $0.5m (W4)

(W4) Non-controlling Interest

	Cr(m)	Rate	$m
FV of NCI at acquisition	38.0	2.5	15.2
25% × (Cr147.8 – Cr132) (W2)	4.0	2.0	2.0
NCI share of goodwill impairment (W3)			(0.3)
NCI % of goodwill retranslation gain (W3)			0.5
NCI % of net assets retranslation gain (W6)			2.4
			─────
			19.8
			─────

(W5) Group retained earnings

	$m
Memo	360.0
(75% × (Cr147.8 – Cr132)/2.0 avg rate) (W2)	5.9
Unrealised profit on inventory (W8)	(0.6)
Group share of goodwill impairment (W3)	(1.0)
	─────
	364.3
	─────

(W6) Gain or loss on retranslation of net assets

	Cr(m)	Rate	$m
At acquisition	132.0	2.5 acq'n rate	52.8
Profit for year	15.8	2.0 av. rate	7.9
Exchange gain on retranslation		**Bal fig**	**9.7**
	─────		─────
At rep date	147.8	2.1 cl rate	70.4
	─────		─────

The exchange gain on retranslation of net assets is allocated between the group and NCI based upon their respective shareholdings:

Group (75% × $9.7m) = $7.3m (W7)

NCI (25% × $9.7m) = $2.4m (W4)

(W7) Summary of exchange gains on retranslation

	Total $m	Group $m	NCI $m
Goodwill (W3)	2.0	1.5	0.5
Net assets (W6)	9.7	7.3	2.4
	─────	─────	─────
At rep date	11.7	8.8	2.9
	─────	─────	─────

The total exchange gains on retranslation for the year of $11.7m are accounted for through other comprehensive income for the year. The group share of the gains is included as an item of other components of equity – it is effectively an unrealised amount. The NCI share of the gains on retranslation for the year is included in the NCI balance at the reporting date.

(W8) Intercompany purchases from Memo

	$m
Profit made by Memo $6 million × 20%	1.2
Profit remaining in inventory at year-end (½)	0.6

	CRm
Purchase from Memo in crowns ($6 million × 2)	12.0
Less payment made ($6 million × 2.2)	(13.2)
Exchange loss to profit or loss of Random	(1.2)

The exchange loss will be translated at the average rate (2 CR to $1) into dollars, i.e. $0.6 million. The fact that group cash flows have been affected by foreign currency fluctuations would mean that this loss will be reported in the group profit or loss.

The adjusting journal is:

Dr Profit or loss – exchange loss	CR 1.2m ($0.6m)
Cr Current liabilities	CR 1.2m ($0.6m)

This is adjusted in Random's accounts in Crowns (W2).

(W9) Intercompany loan

There is no exchange difference in the financial statements of Memo as the loan is denominated in dollars. However, there is an exchange gain arising in the financial statements of Random.

	CRm
Loan at 1 May 20X3 $5 million at 2.5	12.5
Loan at 30 April 20X4 $5 million at 2.1	10.5
Exchange gain to Random profit or loss	2.0

This will be translated into dollars at 30 April 20X4 and will appear in the consolidated profit or loss (2 million crowns ÷ 2, i.e. $1 million). The reason is that the loan was taken out in the currency of the holding company and the subsidiary was exposed to the foreign currency risk.

(W10) Allocation of profit for the year and total comprehensive income

	Cr(m)	Rate	$m
Profit aft tax (Cr147.8 – Cr132.0 (W2))	15.8		
Goodwill impaired	(2.6)		
NCI % of profit for year – 25%	**13.2**	**2.0**	**1.7**
NCI % of exchange gains on retranslation (W7)			2.9
NCI share of total comp income			**4.6**

(b) An environmental report allows an organisation to communicate with different stakeholders. The benefits of an environmental report include:

(i) evaluating environmental performance can highlight inefficiencies in operations and help to improve management systems. Memo could identify opportunities to reduce resource use, waste and operating costs.

(ii) communicating the efforts being made to improve social and environmental performance can foster community support for a business and can also contribute towards its reputation as a good corporate citizen. At present Memo has a poor reputation in this regard.

(iii) reporting efforts to improve the organisation's environmental, social and economic performance can lead to increased consumer confidence in its products and services.

(iv) commitment to reporting on current impacts and identifying ways to improve environmental performance can improve relationships with regulators, and could reduce the potential threat of litigation which is hanging over Memo.

(v) investors, financial analysts and brokers increasingly ask about the sustainability aspects of operations. A high quality report shows the measures the organisation is taking to reduce risks, and will make Memo more attractive to investors.

(vi) disclosing the organisation's environmental, social and economic best practices can give a competitive market edge. Currently Memo's corporate image is poor and this has partly contributed to its poor stock market performance.

(vii) the international trend towards improved corporate sustainability is growing and access to international markets will require increasing transparency, and this will help Memo's corporate image.

(viii) large organisations are increasingly requiring material and service suppliers and contractors to submit performance information to satisfy the expectations of their own shareholders. Disclosing such information can make the company a more attractive supplier than their competitors, and increase Memo's market share.

It is important to ensure that the policies are robust and effective and not just compliance based.

(c) Corporate social responsibility (CSR) is concerned with business ethics and the company's accountability to its stakeholders, and about the way it meets its wider obligations. CSR emphasises the need for companies to adopt a coherent approach to a range of stakeholders including investors, employees, suppliers, and customers. Memo has paid little regard to the promotion of socially and ethically responsible policies. For example, the decision to not pay the SME creditors on the grounds that they could not afford to sue the company is ethically unacceptable. Additionally, Memo pays little regard to local customs and cultures in its business dealings.

The stagnation being suffered by Memo could perhaps be reversed if it adopted more environmentally friendly policies. The corporate image is suffering because of its attitude to the environment. Environmentally friendly policies could be cost effective if they help to increase market share and reduce the amount of litigation costs it has to suffer. The communication of these policies would be through the environmental report, and it is critical that stakeholders feel that the company is being transparent in its disclosures.

Evidence of corporate misbehaviour (Enron, World.com) has stimulated interest in the behaviour of companies. There has been pressure for companies to show more awareness and concern, not only for the environment but for the rights and interests of the people they do business with. Governments have made it clear that directors must consider the short-term and long-term consequences of their actions, and take into account their relationships with employees and the impact of the business on the community and the environment. The behaviour of Memo will have had an adverse effect on their corporate image.

CSR requires the directors to address strategic issues about the aims, purposes, and operational methods of the organisation, and some redefinition of the business model that assumes that profit motive and shareholder interests define the core purpose of the company. The profits of Memo will suffer if employees are not valued and there is poor customer support.

Arrangements should be put in place to ensure that the business is conducted in a responsible manner. The board should look at broad social and environmental issues affecting the company and set policy and targets, monitoring performance and improvements.

ACCA Marking scheme		
		Marks
(a)	Consolidated statement of financial position	
	Translation of statement of financial position	6
	Goodwill	4
	Non controlling interest	4
	Group reserves	4
	Group statement of financial position	5
	Consolidated statement of P/L and OCI	5
	Unrealised profit	4
	Loan	3
		___
	Maximum	**35**
		___
(b)	Benefits of environmental report	8
(c)	Discussion of ethics and social responsibility	7
Total		___
		50
		___

19   ZAMBEZE

Key answer tips

There are lots of easy marks in a cash flow question. Set up a proforma and slot in any cash flows given to you in the questions. Make sure that you put brackets around any cash outflows. Then set up your reconciliation between profit before tax and cash generated from operations and adjust for any non-cash incomes and expenses given to you in the question. You will then need to work down the statement of financial position, reconciling the balances year-on-year using the information provided in the notes. Make sure that you show all workings so that you can be awarded partial marks if your end answers are wrong.

(a)   **Zambeze Group**

Group Statement of Cash Flows for the year ended 30 June 2006

	$m	$m
Cash flows from operating activities:		
Profit before taxation		690
Adjustments for:		
Share of profit in associate	(30)	
Depreciation	60	
Impairment of goodwill (W2)	8	
Interest expense	40	
Retirement benefit expense	13	
	———	
		91
		———
Operating profit before working capital changes:		781
Increase in trade receivables (610 – 530)	(80)	
Decrease in inventories (650 – 580 – 90)	20	
Increase in trade payables (1,341 – 1,200)	141	
	———	
		81
		———
Cash generated from operations:		862
Interest paid (W5)	(31)	
Income taxes paid (W4)	(190)	
Cash paid to retirement benefit scheme	(7)	
	———	
		(228)
		———
Net cash from operating activities:		634

Cash flows from investing activities

Acquisition of subsidiary	(100)	
Purchase of property, plant and equipment (W1)	(251)	
Dividends received from Associate (W3)	35	
Investment in River	(400)	
Net cash used in investing activities		(716)

Cash flows from financing activities:

Proceeds from issue of share capital	30	
Increase in long-term borrowings	66	
Dividends paid (W6)	(46)	
Non-controlling interest dividends (W2)	(58)	
Net cash used in financing activities		(8)
Net decrease in cash and cash equivalents		(90)
Cash and cash equivalents at beginning of period		140
Cash and cash equivalents at the end of period		50

Workings

(W1) Property, plant and equipment $m

Balance at 1 July 2005	1,005
Impairment losses	(95)
Depreciation	(60)
Purchases (bal. fig.)	395
Acquisition – Damp	70
Closing balance	1,315

Cash flow is $395 million minus the liability for Property, plant and equipment of $144 million, i.e. $251 million.

(W2) Goodwill and NCI

	$m
Purchase of subsidiary:	
Consideration paid (100 + 25)	125
Fair value of NCI at acquisition	50
	175
Fair value of net assets at acquisition	160
Goodwill at acquisition	15

	$m
Goodwill:	
Balance at 1 July 2005	25
Goodwill on acquisition of subsidiary	15
Impairment (bal. fig.)	(8)
Balance at 30 June 2006	32
Non-controlling interest	
Balance at 1 July 2005	45
FV of NCI at acquisition of Damp	50
Profit for year	25
Dividend (bal. fig.)	(58)
Balance at 30 June 2006	62

(W3) Associates

	$m
Balance at 1 July 2005	290
Income (net of tax) (30 – 10)	20
Foreign exchange loss	(5)
Dividends received (bal. fig.)	(35)
Balance at 30 June 2006	270

(W4) Taxation

	$m
Balance at 1 July 2005 (185 + 25)	210
Profit or loss (210 – 10)	200
Tax paid (bal. fig.)	(190)
Balance at 30 June 2006 (190 + 30)	220

(W5) Interest paid

	$m
Balance at 1 July 2005	45
Profit or loss	40
Unwinding of discount on purchase	(4)
Cash paid (bal. fig.)	(31)
Closing balance at 30 June 2006	50

(W6) Dividends

The cash payment to River should be shown as 'investing activities' of $400 million and the dividend paid will then be $46 million ($446m – $400m).

(b) The definition of 'control' underpins the definition of the parent and subsidiary relationship. IFRS 10 *Consolidated financial statements* identifies control as the sole basis for consolidation which comprises three elements as follows:

(i) power over the investee, where the investor has current ability to direct activities that significantly affect the investee's returns, and

(ii) exposure, or rights to, variable returns from involvement in the investee, and

(iii) the ability to use power over the investee to affect the amount of the investors returns.

IFRS 10 adopts a principles-based approach to determining whether or not control is exercised. As a result an entity has control over another entity when it has the ability to exercise that power, regardless of whether control is actively demonstrated or passive in nature.

Under IFRS 10 control of an entity effectively comprises the ability to control the entity's decision making with a view to obtaining benefits from the entity. The ability to control decision making alone is not normally sufficient to establish control for accounting purposes but would normally be accompanied by the objective of obtaining benefits from the entity's activities. If a company obtains the benefits of ownership, is exposed to the risks of ownership, and can exercise decision making powers to obtain those benefits, then the company must control the third party.

Consequently, IFRS 10 requires that Zambeze should consolidate River as Zambeze controls it through the operating guidelines. Zambeze also receives 95% of the profits and suffers all the losses of River. The guidelines were set up when River was formed and, therefore, the company was set up as a vehicle with the objective of keeping certain transactions off the statement of financial position of Zambeze. The investment manager manages the investments of River within the guidelines and incurs no risk and receives 5% of the profits for the management services.

(c) Ethics in accounting is of utmost importance to accounting professionals and those who rely on their services. Accounting professionals know that people who use their services, especially decision makers using financial statements, expect them to be highly competent, reliable, and objective. Those who work in the field of accounting must not only be well qualified but must also possess a high degree of professional integrity. A professional's good reputation is one of his or her most important assets.

Accounting plays a critical function in society. Accounting numbers affect human behaviour especially when it affects compensation, and to deliberately mask the nature of accounting transactions could be deemed to be unethical behaviour.

River was set up with the express purpose of keeping its activities off the statement of financial position. The Finance Director has an ethical responsibility to the shareholders of Zambeze and society not to mask the true nature of the transactions with this entity. Further, if the transaction has been authorised by the Finance Director without the authority or knowledge of the Board of Directors, then a further ethical issue arises. Showing the transfer of funds as a dividend paid is unethical and possibly illegal in the jurisdiction. The transfer should not be hidden and River should be consolidated.

			Marks
	ACCA Marking scheme		
(a)	Operating activities		6
	Retirement benefit		3
	Associate		3
	Subsidiary treatment		4
	Property, plant and equipment		3
	Goodwill		2
	Non-controlling interest		3
	Taxation		3
	Dividend paid		3
	Interest		2
	River		2
	Issue of shares		1
			―――
		Maximum	**35**
			―――
(b)	Issues		9
(c)	Ethics		6
			―――
Total			**50**
			―――

SECTION B-TYPE QUESTIONS

REPORTING STANDARDS

20   YANONG (JUNE 15 EXAM) *Walk in the footsteps of a top tutor*

Key answer tips

This question requires a strong knowledge of IFRS 13 *Fair Value Measurement*. It also tests IFRS 2 *Share-based Payment* and IAS 41 *Agriculture*. Revisit the relevant chapters in the Complete Text if your knowledge in these areas is lacking.

It would be easy to run out of time in this question. Use the mark allocation to manage your time effectively. If you do not complete all parts of the question then you will lose some of the available professional marks.

(a)

Tutorial note

Start off by stating the definition of fair value measurement and by outlining the markets in which it is determined. This is a source of easy marks.

IFRS 13 Fair Value Measurement

IFRS 13 says that fair value is an exit price in the principal market, which is the market with the highest volume and level of activity. It is not determined based on the volume or level of activity of the reporting entity's transactions in a particular market.

In the absence of a principal market, it is assumed that the transaction would occur in the most advantageous market. This is the market which would maximise the amount which would be received to sell an asset or minimise the amount which would be paid to transfer a liability, taking transaction costs into consideration. In either case, the entity must have access to the market on the measurement date.

If there is a principal market for the asset or liability, the fair value measurement represents the price in that market at the measurement date regardless of whether that price is directly observable or estimated using another valuation technique and even if the price in a different market is potentially more advantageous.

Tutorial note

Now apply those rules to the information and data in the question.

Application to Yanong

IFRS 13 makes it clear that the price used to measure fair value must not be adjusted for transaction costs, but should consider transportation costs. Yanong has currently deducted transaction costs in its valuation of the vehicles. Transaction costs are not deemed to be a characteristic of an asset or a liability but they are specific to a transaction and will differ depending on how an entity enters into a transaction.

In Yanong's case, Asia would be the principal market as this is the market in which the majority of transactions for the vehicles occur. As such, the fair value of the 150 vehicles would be $5,595,000 (($38,000 – $700) × 150).

(b)

Tutorial note

Fair value should be determined using level 1 or level 2 inputs whenever possible. However, an entity may sometimes have to use estimation techniques based on discounted cash flows. The examiner has stated that students at P2 are expected to be able to accurately discount cash flows to present value.

Fair value measurement techniques

Biological assets are measured at each reporting date at fair value less costs to sell.

Where reliable market-based prices or values are not available for a biological asset in its present location and condition, fair value should be measured using a valuation technique. In accordance with IFRS 13, relevant observable inputs should be maximised whilst unobservable inputs should be minimised.

An appropriate valuation technique would be the present value of expected net cash flows from the asset, discounted at a current market-based rate.

Application to maize

In the measurement of fair value of growing crops, a notional cash flow expense should be included for the 'rent' of the land where it is owned in order that the value is comparable to an entity which rents its land. The fair value of the biological asset is separate from the value of the land on which it grows.

	3 months to 31 January 2015	3 months to 30 April 2015	Total
	$ million	$ million	$ million
Cash inflows		80	80
Cash outflows	(8)	(19)	(27)
Notional rental charge for land	(1)	(1)	(2)
Net cash flows	(9)	60	51
Discounted at 2%	(8.82)	57.67	48.85

Thus in the quarterly accounts at 31 October 2014, the maize fields should be recognised at $68.85 million ($20 million land plus $48.85 million maize). A fair value gain of $48.85 million in respect of the Maize together with operating costs of $10 million should be shown in profit or loss.

At 31 January, Yanong has revised its projections for cash inflows to $76 million, which means that the net cash flows at that date were projected to be $56 million ($76m − $19m − $1m). Discounted at 2%, this amounts to $54.9 million. Thus a fair value gain of $6.05 million ($54.9m − $48.85m) together with the actual operating costs of $8 million should be shown in profit or loss.

Tutorial note

Harvested agricultural produce is initially measured at fair value less costs to sell. It is then immediately reclassified as inventories.

Harvest of maize

At the point of harvest, on 31 March 2015, the maize is valued at its fair value of $82 million which means that a fair value gain of $27.1 million ($82m − $54.9m) is recognised in profit or loss. The actual operating costs for the quarter would also be shown in profit or loss.

The maize is then classified as inventory. When the maize is sold, a further profit of $2 million ($84m − $82m) is made on sale.

(c)

Tutorial note

There are some key differences between the accounting treatment of cash-settled share-based payments and equity-settled share-based payments. Make sure that you learn the rules thoroughly.

The scope of IFRS 13

IFRS 13 applies when another IFRS requires or permits fair value measurements or disclosures about fair value measurements. IFRS 13 specifically excludes transactions covered by certain other standards including share-based payment transactions within the scope of IFRS 2 *Share-based Payment* and leasing transactions within the scope of IAS 17 *Leases*.

Thus share-based payment transactions are scoped out of IFRS 13.

Accounting for the SARs

For cash settled share-based payment transactions, the entity should recognise an expense and liability as service is rendered. The fair value of the liability is measured in accordance with IFRS 2 at each reporting date. Any changes in fair value are recognised in profit or loss in the period. Therefore, the SARs would have been accounted for during the vesting period as follows:

Year	Expense	Liability	Calculation
	$	$	
30 April 2013	641,250	641,250	(300 × 95%) × 500 × $9 × ½
30 April 2014	926,250	1,567,500	(300 × 95%) × 500 × $11

Until the liability is settled, the entity shall remeasure the fair value of the liability at the end of each reporting period and at the date of settlement, with any changes in fair value recognised in profit or loss for the period.

Liability 1 May 2014	$1,567,500
Cash paid (60 × 500 × $10.50)	($315,000)
Expense (bal. fig.)	$97,500
Liability 30 April 2015 ((285 – 60) × 500 × $12)	$1,350,000

The fair value of the liability would be $1,350,000 at 30 April 2015 and the expense for the year would be $97,500.

(d)

Tutorial note

There is not necessarily a right or a wrong answer to some P2 questions. What is more important is to apply the rules of the accounting standard to the specific scenario. You will get marks for reaching a sensible conclusion, even if this differs from the model answer.

The fair value of a non-financial asset

A fair value measurement of a non-financial asset takes into account a market participant's ability to generate economic benefits by using the asset in its highest and best use or by selling it to another market participant who would use the asset in its highest and best use. IFRS 13 presumes that the highest and best use is the current use.

IFRS 13 requires the entity to consider uses which are physically possible, legally permissible and financially feasible. For example, if the land is protected in some way by law and a change of law is required, then it cannot be the highest and best use of the land.

Application to Yanong

Yanong would need to have sufficient evidence to support its assumption about the potential for an alternative use, particularly in light of IFRS 13's presumption that the highest and best use is an asset's current use. Yanong's belief that planning permission was possible is unlikely to be sufficient evidence that the change of use is legally permissible. However, the fact the government has indicated that more agricultural land should be released for residential purposes may provide additional evidence as to the likelihood that the land being measured should be based upon residential value. Yanong would need to prove that market participants would consider residential use of the land to be legally permissible.

Provided there is sufficient evidence to support these assertions, alternative uses of the land should be considered. For example, it would seem that commercial development might provide greater value than residential development. Any costs required to transform the land (such as to obtain planning permission or to convert the land to its alternative use) should also be considered in the fair value measurement.

Since there are multiple types of market participants who would use the asset differently, these alternative scenarios must be considered before concluding on the asset's highest and best use. It appears that Yanong is not certain about what constitutes the highest and best use and therefore IFRS 13's presumption that the highest and best use is an asset's current use appears to be valid at this stage.

ACCA Marking scheme		Marks
(a)	1 mark per point up to maximum	6
(b)	1 mark per point up to maximum	6
(c)	1 mark per point up to maximum	6
(d)	1 mark per point up to maximum	5
	Professional marks	2
Total		**25**

Examiner's comments

This question dealt with the measurement and disclosure of the fair value of assets, liabilities and equity instruments. It did not focus specifically upon IFRS 13 *Fair Value Measurement*, but of course this standard is the basis of fair value measurement for many IFRSs.

Part (a) involved the application of principal and advantageous market definitions to a set of data. Candidates were awarded marks based upon the principles involved and the application of those principles. Answers were quite disappointing considering the fact that the market definitions are the cornerstone of IFRS 13. As mentioned above, the principles involved in this part of the question were quite basic and fundamental to the standard.

Part (b) of the question required candidates to apply a valuation technique to the valuation of short-lived crops where there was no active market for partly grown crops. A discounted cash flow method was used to value the crops and the entity wished to know how they should account for the biological asset at various quarterly dates and when the crops were sold. Candidates needed to use discounted cash flow techniques to value the crops. This part of the question was not well answered. Valuation techniques are used extensively in corporate reporting and therefore candidates must become accustomed to using such techniques in answering questions.

Part (c) of the question was well answered. It involved calculating and discussing the valuation of share appreciation rights (SARs) under IFRS 2 *Share-based Payment* and not IFRS 13.

However part (d) of the question was surprisingly poorly answered. One of the fundamental principles of IFRS 13 is that of 'highest and best use' as long as the alternate uses are physically, legally and financially permissible. In this question, the non-current asset had more value if it were used for residential purposes rather than for farmland providing that planning permission was granted. A discussion of this principle and its application was required but was seldom forthcoming from candidates.

21   KLANCET (JUNE 15 EXAM) *Walk in the footsteps of a top tutor*

Key answer tips

Students are often surprised by the lack of numbers and calculations in many Section B questions.

This question requires no calculations. To score well, it is important to be able to apply your accounting knowledge to the specific transactions. Do not simply knowledge dump. Instead, state the recognition and measurement rules from the relevant accounting standards before applying them to the scenario. If you struggle to identify which standards are relevant then think about the items involved. What accounting standard is used to account for an investment in shares? What accounting standard is used for purchases when consideration is in the form of shares?

(a)   **IFRS 8 *Operating Segments***

Tutorial note

Students often neglect IFRS 8 when studying but it has been tested several times in recent P2 exams. Make sure that you are familiar with the definition of an operating segment as well as the rules governing which operating segments must be disclosed.

IFRS 8 *Operating Segments* states that an operating segment is a component of an entity which engages in business activities from which it may earn revenues and incur costs. In addition, discrete financial information should be available for the segment and these results should be regularly reviewed by the entity's chief operating decision maker (CODM) when making decisions about resource allocation to the segment and assessing its performance. However, if a function is an integral part of the business, it may be disclosed as a segment even though it may not earn revenue.

According to IFRS 8, an operating segment should be reported if it meets any of the following quantitative thresholds:

(1)   Its reported revenue, including both sales to external customers and intersegment sales or transfers, is 10% or more of the combined revenue, internal and external, of all operating segments.

(2)   The absolute amount of its reported profit or loss is 10% or more of the greater, in absolute amount, of (i) the combined reported profit of all operating segments which did not report a loss and (ii) the combined reported loss of all operating segments which reported a loss.

(3)   Its assets are 10% or more of the combined assets of all operating segments.

Tutorial note

Apply the rules to each of the laboratories in turn. Make sure that you reach an explicit conclusion about whether or not they constitute operating segments.

The research and development laboratories

As regards the two research and development laboratories, qualitative and quantitative factors should be considered in determining the operating segments.

The qualitative factors will include whether the resultant operating segments are consistent with the principles of IFRS 8, whether the operating segments represent the level at which the CODM is assessing performance and allocating resources and whether the identified operating segments enable users of its financial statements to evaluate its activities and financial performance, and the business environment it operates in.

As a result of the application of the above criteria, the first laboratory will not be reported as a separate operating segment. The laboratory does not have a separate segment manager and the existence of a segment manager is normally an important factor in determining operating segments. Instead, the laboratory is responsible to the divisions themselves, which would seem to indicate that it is simply supporting the existing divisions and not a separate segment. Additionally, there does not seem to be any discrete performance information for the segment, which is reviewed by the CODM.

The second laboratory should be reported as a separate segment. It meets the quantitative threshold for percentage of total revenues and it meets other criteria for an operating segment. It engages in activities which earn revenues and incurs costs, its operating results are reviewed by the CODM and discrete information is available for the laboratory's activities. Finally, it has a separate segment manager.

(b)

Tutorial note

Take your time and think through which accounting standards are relevant to these transactions. Marks will only be given for discussion of the relevant accounting standards.

Sale of patent

All equity investments in the scope of IFRS 9 Financial Instruments are to be measured at fair value in the statement of financial position. Value changes are recognised in profit or loss, except for those equity investments for which the entity has elected to report value changes in 'other comprehensive income'.

Klancet should derecognise the patent which is transferred to Jancy. They should initially recognise the shares received at their fair value. The gain or loss is recorded in profit or loss.

Klancet should not yet recognise any asset relating to the future royalty stream from the potential sales of the drug, because this stream of royalties is contingent upon the successful development of the drug.

Purchase of patent

With regards to the purchase of the patent, this is an equity settled, share-based payment transaction. The rules from IFRS 2 Share-based Payment should be used. The entity should measure the goods purchased at the fair value of the goods received, unless that fair value cannot be estimated reliably. If Klancet cannot estimate reliably the fair value of the goods received, it should measure the value by reference to the fair value of the equity instruments granted.

(c)

Tutorial note

Many students are familiar with the rules in IAS 38 governing the accounting treatment of research and development expenditure. Make sure that you state these rules for easy marks.

IAS 38 *Intangible Assets*

IAS 38 Intangible Assets requires an entity to recognise an intangible asset if it is probable that the future economic benefits which are attributable to the asset will flow to the entity and the cost of the asset can be measured reliably. This requirement applies whether an intangible asset is acquired externally or generated internally.

The price which an entity pays to acquire an intangible asset reflects its expectations about the probability that the expected future economic benefits in the asset will flow to the entity. The effect of probability is reflected in the cost of the asset and so the probability recognition criterion above is always considered to be satisfied for separately acquired intangible assets.

The cost of a separately acquired intangible asset can usually be measured reliably. This is particularly so when the purchase consideration is in the form of cash or other monetary assets. The cost of a separately acquired intangible asset comprises its purchase price and any directly attributable cost of preparing the asset for its intended use.

IAS 38 includes additional recognition criteria for internally generated intangible assets. Development costs are capitalised only after technical and commercial feasibility of the asset for sale or use have been established. This means that the entity must intend and be able to complete the intangible asset be able to demonstrate how the asset will generate future economic benefits.

Tutorial note

Apply the recognition rules to each of the two projects. A sensible and methodical approach should lead to high marks being scored.

The first project

In the case of the first project, Klancet owns the potential new drug, and Retto is carrying out the development of the drug on its behalf. The payments to Retto therefore represent research and development by a third party.

Development costs are capitalised only after technical and commercial feasibility of the asset for sale or use have been established. This means that the entity must intend and be able to complete the intangible asset and either uses it or sells it and be able to demonstrate how the asset will generate future economic benefits. At present, this criterion does not appear to have been met as regulatory authority for the use of the drug has not been given and, in fact, approval has been refused in the past. Therefore, all costs should be expensed to profit or loss over the development period.

The second project

In the case of the second project, the drug has already been discovered and therefore the costs are for the development and manufacture of the drug and its slight modification. Regulatory approval has already been attained for the existing drug and therefore there is no reason to expect that this will not be given for the new drug. Therefore, Klancet should capitalise the upfront purchase of the drug and subsequent payments as incurred.

Klancet should consider impairment at each financial reporting date.

Amortisation should begin once regulatory approval has been obtained. Costs for the products have to be accounted for as inventory using IAS 2 *Inventories* and then expensed as a cost of sale once sold.

ACCA Marking scheme		
		Marks
(a)	1 mark per point up to maximum	8
(b)	1 mark per point up to maximum	7
(c)	1 mark per point up to maximum	8
	Professional marks	2
Total		25

22   COATMIN (DEC 14 EXAM) *Walk in the footsteps of a top tutor*

Key answer tips

This is a challenging question. To score a high mark, you would need some very detailed knowledge of both IAS 24 *Related Party Disclosures* and IFRS 9 *Financial Instruments*. However, as always, easy marks are available for demonstrating your knowledge of the relevant rules within the relevant accounting standards.

Remember to attempt every part of the question or you will not obtain the two professional marks available.

(a)

Tutorial note

This is a tricky requirement as few students are likely to be aware of the exemptions in IAS 24 for government related entities. However, you can still score solid marks for showing a basic knowledge of the contents and purpose of IAS 24.

Related party disclosures

Under IAS 24 *Related Party Disclosures*, disclosures are required in respect of an entity's transactions with related parties. Related parties include parents, subsidiaries, members of key management personnel of the entity or of a parent of the entity, and post-employment benefit plans.

Where there have been related party transactions during the period, management discloses the nature of the relationship, as well as information about the transactions and outstanding balances necessary for users to understand the potential impact of the relationship on the financial statements. Disclosure is made by category of related party and by major type of transaction. Management only discloses that related party transactions were made on terms equivalent to those which prevail in arm's length transactions if such terms can be substantiated.

Government related entities

Government-related entities are defined as entities which are controlled, jointly controlled or significantly influenced by the government. The financial crisis widened the range of entities subject to the related party disclosure requirements. The financial support provided by governments to financial institutions in many countries meant that the government controls significantly influenced some of those entities. A government-controlled bank would, in principle, be required to disclose details of its transactions, deposits and commitments with all other government-controlled banks and with the central bank.

However, IAS 24 has an exemption from all of the disclosure requirements of IAS 24 for transactions between government-related entities and the government, and all other government-related entities. Coatmin is exempt from the disclosure requirements in relation to related party transactions and outstanding balances, including commitments, with:

(a) a government which has control, joint control or significant influence over the reporting entity; and

(b) another entity which is a related party because the same government has control, joint control or significant influence over both the reporting entity and the other entity.

Those disclosures are replaced with a requirement to disclose:

(a) the name of the government and the nature of their relationship; and

(b) (i) the nature and amount of any individually significant transactions; and

    (ii) the extent of any collectively significant transactions qualitatively or quantitatively.

The disclosures provide more meaningful information about the nature of an entity's relationship with the government and material transactions.

(b)

> **Tutorial note**
>
> *Many students are likely to have discussed IAS 37 and the rules around provisions and contingencies. However, financial guarantee contracts are actually within the scope of IFRS 9 and so this would be technically incorrect. However, sensible discussion and application of IAS 37 would still score some marks.*

Financial guarantee contracts

IFRS 9 Financial Instruments says that an entity should classify all financial liabilities as subsequently measured at amortised cost using the effective interest method, unless it is a derivative, held for trading, or designated to be measured at fair value through profit or loss.

An entity shall present in profit or loss all gains and losses on financial guarantee contracts that are designated as at fair value through profit or loss.

The accounting entries on the assumption that discounting would not be material will therefore be:

1 December 2012

Dr Profit or loss	$1.2 million
Cr Financial liabilities	$1.2 million

To record the loss incurred in giving the guarantee.

30 November 2013

Dr Financial liabilities	$0.4 million
Cr Profit or loss	$0.4 million

To reduce the initial fair value over the life of the guarantee, reflecting the reduction in exposure as a result of the first repayment by the subsidiary.

30 November 2014

Dr Profit or loss	$39.2 million
Cr Financial liabilities	$39.2 million

To provide for the calling of the guarantee – the difference between the possible $40 million call and the carrying amount of the guarantee of $0.8 million.

Dr Financial liabilities	$39.6 million
Cr Profit or loss	$39.6 million

To move from the provision back to measurement at amortised initial value following event after the reporting period change in probabilities of the guarantee being called.

An event after the reporting period is an event, which could be favourable or unfavourable, which occurs between the end of the reporting period and the date when the financial statements are authorised for issue. The above is an adjusting event which is an event after the reporting period which provides further evidence of conditions which existed at the end of the reporting period.

(c)

Tutorial note

Students are typically weak at hedge accounting questions. However, the hedge accounting criteria can be learned off by heart and, therefore, easy marks can be scored.

Hedge accounting criteria

IFRS 9 *Financial Instruments* permits hedge provided that the hedging relationship meets the following criteria:

*   The hedging relationship consists only of eligible hedging instruments and hedged items
*   At the inception of the hedge there must be formal documentation identifying the hedged item and the hedging instrument
*   The hedging relationship meets all effectiveness requirements.

Hedge effectiveness

IFRS 9 requires hedge effectiveness to be assessed prospectively. The hedge effectiveness requirements are as follows

*   There must be an economic relationship between the hedged item and the hedging instrument
*   The effect of credit risk must not dominate the value changes that result from that economic relationship
*   The hedge ratio of the hedging relationship is the same as that resulting from the quantity of the hedged item that the entity actually hedges and the quantity of the hedging instrument that the entity actually uses to hedge that quantity of hedged item.

Coatmin's hedge

As variable interest rates fall, the fair value of the bond and the swap increase in value. Since the bond is a liability and the swap is an asset, these fair value movements should, theoretically, offset. As such, there is an economic relationship between the hedged item and the hedging instrument.

However, it would seem that credit risk is dominating changes in the economic relationship between the bond and the swap and that this is expected to continue in the future. As a result of credit risk, the fair value movements on the hedged item and the hedging instrument are unlikely to effectively offset.

The hedge fails the effectiveness criteria and, therefore, hedge accounting is not permitted. The swap is a derivative and so will be remeasured to its fair value of $203 million, with a corresponding gain in profit or loss. The bond will most likely be measured at amortised cost.

(d)

Tutorial note

*Read the question very carefully. Coatmin has issued a **financial liability**. Therefore, discussions of business models and contractual cash flows are irrelevant (they relate to the classification of financial assets).*

IFRS 9 rules

IFRS 9 requires gains and losses on financial liabilities designated as at fair value through profit or loss to be split into the amount of change in the fair value which is attributable to changes in the credit risk of the liability, which is shown in other comprehensive income, and the remaining amount of change in the fair value of the liability which is shown in profit or loss.

IFRS 9 allows the recognition of the full amount of change in the fair value in the profit or loss only if the recognition of changes in the liability's credit risk in other comprehensive income would create an accounting mismatch in profit or loss.

Amounts presented in other comprehensive income are not subsequently transferred to profit or loss, and the entity may only transfer the cumulative gain or loss within equity.

Application to Coatmin

Coatmin should increase the carrying amount of the liability by $50 million.

They should credit $5 million to OCI and charge $55 million to profit or loss.

ACCA Marking scheme		Marks
(a)	IAS 24	5
(b)	IFRS 9 explanation	3
	Guarantee calculations	4
(c)	Hedging discussion	4
	Effectiveness discussion	3
(d)	Credit risk entries	4
	Professional marks	2
Total		**25**

Examiner's comments

This question dealt with two main topic: financial instruments and related parties.

Part (a) of the question required candidates to discuss the general principles underpinning the accounting for related party transactions and then advise on the disclosure of related party relationships between government-related entities and the government. Inevitably, the model answers to the questions are more detailed than what is expected of candidates. There were only 5 marks available for this question. Therefore the number of marks available for the second part of the requirement was naturally quite small. Candidates who did not know the specific answer to this part of the question were given credit for discussion of the related principles and many candidates were scoring 4 out of 5 marks for this part of the question.

Part (b) of the question required candidates to show how a financial guarantee contract should be dealt with in the financial statements together with a discussion of the principles involved. The question was not well answered by candidates but a client would expect a qualified member of a profession to understand the difference between a provision and a financial guarantee. It appeared from the answers that this distinction was not understood by many candidates even though the question did say that the guarantee was being measured at fair value through profit or loss, which would tend to indicate that the guarantee was a financial instrument.

Part (c) set out a standard set of circumstances, which related to the use of hedge accounting. The entity required advice on the use of hedge accounting for the transactions in the question. This part was really quite textbook orientated and should have been well answered by candidates. However, it seems that hedging and hedge effectiveness are topics that candidates find quite difficult even in relatively straightforward situations.

The final part of the question dealt with a fair value increase in a financial liability, part of which related to the reduction in the entity's creditworthiness. This part of the question was quite well answered with candidates gaining marks for a discussion of the principles involved and for the accounting for the increase in the value of the liability.

23 KATYE (DEC 14 EXAM) *Walk in the footsteps of a top tutor*

Key answer tips

This question is split into two parts. Some depth is therefore required in your answers. Broadly speaking, you will be awarded one mark for every valid point that you make. Ensure that you are making enough points to achieve at least a pass mark.

As always, make sure that you thoroughly debrief the answer and make sure that you learn from any mistakes that you made.

(a)

Tutorial note

There are two parts to this question. Firstly, should Ceemone have been accounted for as a business combination or an asset acquisition? This requires knowledge of the definition of a business per IFRS 3 Business Combinations. Secondly, does the bank control the new entity to which some of the vessels have been transferred? Your starting point should be the definition of control as per IFRS 10 Consolidated Financial Statements.

Business combinations and Ceemone

In accordance with IFRS 3, an entity should determine whether a transaction is a business combination by applying the definition of a business in IFRS 3.

IFRS 3 defines a business as an integrated set of activities and assets which is capable of being conducted and managed for the purpose of providing a return in the form of dividends, lower costs or other economic benefits directly to investors or other owners, members or participants. A business consists of inputs and processes applied to those inputs which have the ability to create outputs. Although businesses usually have outputs, outputs are not required to qualify as a business.

When analysing the transaction, the following elements are relevant:

(i) Inputs: Shares in vessel owning companies, charter arrangements, outsourcing arrangements with a management company, and relationships with a shipping broker.

(ii) Processes: Activities regarding chartering and operating the vessels, financing the business, purchase and sales of vessels.

(iii) Outputs: Ceemone would generate revenue from charter agreements and has the ability to gain economic benefit from the vessels.

IFRS 3 states that whether a seller operated a set of assets and activities as a business or intends to operate it as a business is not relevant in evaluating whether it is a business. It is not relevant therefore that some activities were outsourced as Ceemone could choose to conduct and manage the integrated set of assets and activities as a business.

The accounting for the transaction as an asset acquisition therefore does not comply with the requirements of IFRS 3 *Business Combinations* because the acquisition included all the elements which constitute a business. This would mean that transaction costs should be expensed. The vessels should be consolidated at fair value A goodwill asset should be recognised for the difference between the consideration transferred and the fair value of the net assets at acquisition.

Control and the new entity

IFRS 10 *Consolidated Financial Statements* sets out the criteria for determining if an investor controls an investee. Control exists if the investor has all of the following elements:

(i) power over the investee, that is, the investor has existing rights which give it the ability to direct the relevant activities (the activities which significantly affect the investee's returns);

(ii) exposure, or rights, to variable returns from its involvement with the investee;

(iii) the ability to use its power over the investee to affect the amount of the investor's returns.

Where a party has all three elements, then it is a parent. Where at least one element is missing, then it is not.

The question arises in this case as to whether the entities created are subsidiaries of the bank. The bank is likely to have power over the investee, may be exposed to variable returns and certainly may have the power to affect the amount of the returns. Thus the bank is likely to have a measure of control. However, the extent will depend on the constitution of the entity.

(b)

Tutorial note

IAS 16 is an accounting standard that you would have first learned about when studying for F3 (or equivalent), and which you may have become unfamiliar with over time. If you have forgotten the detail of this standard, then revisit the Complete Text.

Be aware that this question requires very careful reading or you will not pull out all of the accounting issues.

Residual values

IAS 16 defines residual value as the estimated amount which an entity would currently obtain from disposal of the asset, after deducting the estimated costs of disposal, if the asset were already at the age and in the condition expected at the end of its useful life. IAS 16 requires the residual value to be reviewed at least at the end of each financial year end. If the estimated residual value is higher than an asset's carrying amount then no depreciation is charged.

Vessels with 10 year useful life

Kayte's calculation of the residual value of the vessels with a 10-year useful life is not acceptable under IAS 16 Property, Plant and Equipment. Undesirable volatility is not a convincing argument to support the use of a residual value equivalent to half of the acquisition cost. The residual value should be the value at the reporting date as if the vessel were already of the age and in the condition expected at the end of its useful life. Kayte should prepare a new model to determine residual value which would take account of broker valuations at the end of each reporting period.

Vessels with 30 year useful life

As regards the vessels which are kept for the whole of their economic life, a residual value based upon the scrap value of steel is acceptable. Therefore the vessels should be depreciated based upon the cost less the scrap value of steel over the 30-year period.

When major planned maintenance work is to be undertaken, the cost should be capitalised. The engine overhaul will be capitalised as a new asset which will then be depreciated over the 10-year period to the next overhaul. The depreciation of the original capitalised amount will typically be calculated such that it had a carrying amount of nil when the overhaul is undertaken.

This is not the case with one vessel, because work was required earlier than expected. In this case, any remaining carrying amount of the old engine and overhaul cost should be expensed immediately.

The initial carve out of components should include all major maintenance events which are likely to occur over the economic life of the vessel. Sometimes, it may subsequently be found that the initial allocation was insufficiently detailed, in that not all components were identified. This is the case with the funnels. In this situation it is necessary to determine what the carrying amount of the component would currently be had it been initially identified. This will sometimes require the initial cost to be determined by reference to the replacement cost and the associated accumulated depreciation charge determined using the rate used for the vessel. This is likely to leave a significant carrying amount in the component being replaced, which will need to be written off at the time the replacement is capitalised.

ACCA Marking scheme		
		Marks
(a)	IFRS 3/IFRS 10 – 1 mark per point	12
(b)	IAS 16 and application – 1 mark per point	11
	Professional marks	2
		———
Total		**25**
		———

Examiner's comments

This question was based upon a real scenario in the shipping industry and focused in the first part on IFRS 3 *Business Combinations* and IFRS 10 *Consolidated Financial Statements*. Candidates did not need to identify the relevant IFRSs as they were set out in this part of the question. The question examined two basic fundamental concepts in these two standards. Firstly, an entity should determine whether a transaction is a business combination by applying the definition of a business in IFRS 3. Secondly, IFRS 10 *Consolidated Financial Statements* sets out the situation where an investor controls an investee. The question required candidates to discuss and apply these two concepts to the scenario. As set out before in these reports, candidates can score well in these types of questions but only if they apply the principles to the information in the case study. The question was quite well answered with the main problem being the identification of the fact the acquisition included all the elements, that constitute a business.

The second part of the question dealt with accounting under IAS 16 *Property, Plant and Equipment*. In particular, it required candidates to apply their knowledge of IAS 16 to a scenario where there were differences in the estimates of residual value and to the componentisation of certain vessels. Generally candidates answered the question quite well. Componentisation regularly features in this examination as it is a major problem for entities worldwide. Marks were allocated on a basis of one mark per valid point which indicates that there is a minimum amount which candidates need to write in order to gain a pass mark in this question

24   ASPIRE (JUNE 14 EXAM)   *Walk in the footsteps of a top tutor*

Key answer tips

This question primarily tests the accounting treatment of overseas transactions. Part (a) is discursive, but the other parts are more numerical than seen in most of the recent P2 exams. If you struggle with the calculations, make sure you revisit the relevant chapters from the complete text.

Tutorial note

In section B questions, it is important to state the relevant rules from the accounting standard before applying them to the scenario. Make sure you begin your answer by identifying the factors that an entity should consider when determining a functional currency. If you do not know these rules, then you must learn them.

(a)   **Functional currency**

The functional currency is the currency of the primary economic environment in which the entity operates, which is normally the one in which it primarily generates and expends cash.

Primary indicators

An entity's management considers the following primary indicators in determining its functional currency:

(i)   the currency which mainly influences sales prices for goods and services

(ii)   the currency of the country whose competitive forces and regulations mainly determine the sales prices of goods and services; and

(iii)   the currency which mainly influences labour, material and other costs of providing goods and services.

Secondary factors and group factors

Further secondary indicators which may also provide evidence of an entity's functional currency are the currency in which funds from financing activities are generated and in which receipts from operating activities are retained.

Additional factors are considered in determining the functional currency of a foreign operation and whether its functional currency is the same as that of the reporting entity. These are:

(a)   the autonomy of a foreign operation from the reporting entity

(b)   the level of transactions between the two

(c)   whether the foreign operation generates sufficient cash flows to meet its cash needs; and

(d)   whether its cash flows directly affect those of the reporting entity.

When the functional currency is not obvious, management uses its judgement to determine the functional currency which most faithfully represents the economic effects of the underlying transactions, events and conditions.

Tutorial note

Apply the rules to the scenario and reach a conclusion. If your discussion is educated and balanced then you will still scores marks, even if your answer is incorrect.

Application to scenario

The operating costs are incurred in dollars. However, they are not material to any decision as to the functional currency. Therefore it is important to look at secondary factors to determine the functional currency.

The subsidiary has issued 2 million dinars of equity capital to Aspire. The subsidiary has also raised 100,000 dinars of equity capital from external sources. It therefore seems that dinar represents the currency in which the economic activities of the subsidiary are primarily carried out.

However, the subsidiary seems to operate with little autonomy. The income from investments is either remitted to Aspire or reinvested on instruction from Aspire. The subsidiary has a minimum number of staff and does not have any independent management. It would therefore seem that the subsidiary is simply a vehicle for the parent entity to invest in dinar related investments.

In conclusion, the subsidiary appears to be merely an extension of Aspire's activities. Therefore the functional currency of the subsidiary is the same as its parent's: the dollar.

Tutorial note

Deferred tax is accounted for on temporary differences between the accounting and tax treatment of a transaction. It is calculated by comparing the carrying amount of an asset or liability with its tax base. An important first step is to therefore work out these figures. Remember that the overseas property is a non-monetary item. Therefore, it is initially translated into the functional currency of Aspire at the historic rate but is not retranslated.

(b)   **Deferred tax**

According to IAS 12 Income Taxes, deferred tax is accounted for on temporary differences between the financial reporting treatment of a transaction and the tax treatment.

The property of the overseas branch is written down at different rates in the financial statements than it is for tax purposes, giving rise to a temporary difference. A temporary difference may also arise if the carrying amounts of the non-monetary assets of the overseas branch are translated at different rates to the tax base.

The property is a non-monetary asset and so is translated into Aspire's functional currency using the historic rate and is not retranslated. This means that the asset would initially be recorded at $1.2 million (D6m/5). The carrying amount of the asset at the reporting date is therefore $1.1 million ($1.2m × 11/12).

The tax base of the property at the reporting date is D5.25 million (D6m × 7/8). If translated at the closing rate, this gives $0.875 million (D5.25m/6).

The temporary difference is $0.225 million ($1.1m − $0.875m). The deferred tax balance will be calculated using the tax rate in the overseas country. The deferred tax liability arising is $45,000 ($0.225m × 20%), which will increase the tax charge in profit or loss.

If the tax base had been translated at the historic rate then it would have been $1.05 million (D5.25m/5). This would have led to a temporary difference of $50,000 ($1.1m − $1.05 m) and a deferred tax liability of $10,000 ($50,000 × 20%), which is significantly lower than when the closing rate is used.

Tutorial note

Goodwill in an overseas subsidiary is retranslated at each reporting date using the closing rate of exchange. It is therefore important to calculate goodwill in the overseas currency. Watch out for the purchase consideration – the examiner has given the dollar value so this must be translated back into dinar when calculating goodwill.

(c)   **Goodwill in an overseas subsidiary**

According to IAS 21 The *Effects of Changes* in Foreign Exchange Rates, goodwill arising on acquisition of foreign operations is treated as the foreign operation's asset. At each reporting date, it is translated at the closing rate of exchange. The exchange difference arising on the retranslation of the goodwill is recognised in other comprehensive income and accumulated as a separate component of equity.

	Dinars (m)
Purchase consideration ($200m × 5)	1,000
FV of NCI at acquisition	250
FV of net assets at acquisition	(1,100)
Goodwill at acquisition/reporting date	150

Goodwill at the reporting date is therefore $25m (D150m/6).

Goodwill at the acquisition date was $30m (D150m/5). An exchange loss of $5 million ($30m − $25m) will be charged to other comprehensive income together with any gain or loss on the retranslation of the net assets and profit of the operation.

The exchange loss should be split between the group and the NCI based on their respective shareholdings. Therefore, the exchange loss attributable to the group is $3.5 million ($5m × 70%) and the exchange loss attributable to the NCI is $1.5 million ($5m × 30%).

Tutorial note

There are two issues implicit in part (d): how to account for the loan, and how to translate the figures from dinars into dollars. Try and make sure that you address both of these issues.

(d)   **Overseas loan**

In accordance with IFRS 9 *Financial Instruments,* most financial liabilities are measured at amortised cost. They are initially recognised at fair value less transaction costs and the finance cost is calculated using the effective rate of interest. Because there are no transaction costs, the effective interest rate is 8%.

This loan is denominated in an overseas currency and so must be translated using the rules in IAS 21 The Effects of Changes in Foreign Exchange Rates. The overseas loan should initially be translated into the functional currency using the historic (spot) rate. The finance cost is translated at the average rate because it approximates to the actual rate. The cash payment should be translated at the historic (spot) rate (which, because the payment occurs at the reporting date, is the year-end rate). A loan is a monetary liability so is retranslated at the reporting date using the closing rate. Any exchange gain or loss is recognised in profit or loss.

	Dm	Rate	$m
1 May 2013	5.0	5	1.000
Finance cost (8%)	0.4	5.6	0.071
Payment	(0.4)	6	(0.067)
Foreign exchange gain (bal. fig.)			(0.171)
30 April 2014	5.0	6	0.833

The loan is initially recorded at $1 million. The finance cost recorded in the statement of profit or loss is $0.071 million, whilst the cash payment is recorded at $0.067 million. A foreign exchange gain of $0.171 million is recorded in the statement of profit or loss. The liability at the reporting date has a carrying amount of $0.833 million.

ACCA Marking scheme		
		Marks
(a)	1 mark per point up to maximum	7
(b)	1 mark per point up to maximum	6
(c)	1 mark per point up to maximum	5
(d)	1 mark per point up to maximum	5
	Professional marks	2
Total		**25**

Examiner's comments

This question required candidates to give advice on the correct accounting treatment of several aspects of an entity's overseas operations.

In part (a), the entity wished advice on how to determine the functional currency of the subsidiary and this carried 7 marks. Candidates scored well on this part of the question. The marks were allocated for knowledge of IAS 21 and for its application. It was important for candidates to use the information in the question. The decision as to the functional currency was subjective and was based upon the candidate's interpretation of the information in the question.

Part (b) required an explanation including a calculation as to why a deferred tax charge relating to a non-current asset arose in the group financial statements and the impact on the financial statements if the tax base had been translated at the historical rate. This part carried 6 marks. Marks were allocated for the discussion of deferred tax and for the impact on the financial statements. Many candidates ignored the fact that a discussion was required and simply calculated the deferred taxation amount. Many candidates found this part of the question quite difficult. There was an understanding of the nature of deferred tax but candidates found it difficult to apply those principles.

Part (c) of the question required candidates to deal with goodwill arising on the acquisition of an overseas subsidiary in the group financial statements. The question carried 5 marks. There again were marks for the discussion of the nature of the calculation. The treatment of goodwill on overseas subsidiaries is fundamental to the understanding of accounting for an overseas subsidiary. Goodwill arising on acquisition of foreign operations and any fair value adjustments are both treated as the foreign operation's assets and liabilities. They are expressed in the foreign operation's functional currency and translated at the closing rate. Exchange differences arising on the retranslation of foreign entities' financial statements are recognised in other comprehensive income and accumulated as a separate component of equity. Candidates often calculated goodwill correctly but found the retranslation of goodwill quite difficult. The majority of the marks on this part were allocated to the calculation.

The final part of the question required candidates to advise the directors on how to account for a foreign currency loan and interest in the financial statements. Again marks were allocated for discussion and calculation. Generally, candidates answered this part of the question satisfactorily.

25 MINCO (JUNE 14 EXAM) *Walk in the footsteps of a top tutor*

Key answer tips

This question is heavily discursive and provides good practice at applying accounting knowledge to real life scenarios. You may struggle to reach the correct conclusions, but you can still score well by demonstrating your awareness of the relevant rules from the relevant accounting standards.

It is important to attempt every part of the question, or you will lose the two professional marks that are available.

Tutorial note

Part (a) concerns whether Minco should have recognised revenue from transferring land to another entity. The sale of an asset is generally treated as a performance obligation satisfied at a point in time. Therefore, you need to assess whether control of the asset has been passed from Minco to the housing association. Remember to start your answer by discussing indicators of the transfer of control before then applying them to the scenario. Make sure that you reach an overall conclusion.

(a) **Revenue recognition**

According to IFRS 15 *Revenue from Contracts with Customers*, Minco has entered into a contract with the housing association to transfer land. This is a single performance obligation that is satisfied at a point in time. Revenue should be recognised when the housing association take control over the asset. Control of an asset means the ability to direct the use of, and obtain substantially all of the remaining benefits from, the asset.

The following are indications that control over the asset has passed:

- The customer has legal title
- The customer has physical possession
- The customer has accepted the asset
- The customer has the risks and rewards of ownership
- The entity has a right to payment

The housing association has legal title of the land. As a result, they are able to use the land to construct homes, which will bring them future benefits. These factors would suggest that control over the land has passed to the housing association.

However, it is important to consider whether the risks for the project have been transferred to the association. There are indications that the risks of ownership remain with Minco.

For instance:

- Minco enters into discussions with the housing contractors, suggesting continued control over the land.

- Minco determines the membership of the board of the housing association and thus there is a question mark over whether the board is independent from Minco. Minco guarantees that the housing association would not be liable if budgeted construction costs are exceeded, so the entity is exposed to financial risk in the construction process.

- Minco provides a guarantee as regards the maintenance costs, is liable for certain increases in the interest rate over expectations, and is responsible for financing variations in the procurement and construction contract which the contractor would not cover.

- Minco guarantees the payment for the housing association's debt on the building loan. Minco is exposed to risk as if it had built the housing units itself because it gives guarantees in respect of the construction process.

Tutorial note

Note: this question was originally set when IAS 18 Revenue was the examinable standard on revenue recognition. The new revenue standard, IFRS 15, involves much greater use of judgement in ascertaining the point in time at which revenue should be recognised. Therefore, alternative conclusions to the one presented below are potentially valid.

All things considered, it would seem that Minco has retained the significant risks. As such, it could also be argued to retain effective control of the land. Consequently, the revenue recognition criteria are not met on the transfer of the land. Revenue should be recognised when the housing units are finished and delivered to the buyer of the rights.

Tutorial note

Part (b) is actually much simpler than it first appears. Paying a sports personality to advertise a brand is not really any different from paying to advertise in a newspaper or a magazine. The potential extra performance-related payments will only be accounted for if there is a liability (i.e. an obligation) to pay them. Think about when the obligation to pay these amounts arises.

(b) **The signing bonus**

The signing bonus of $20,000, paid to the player on commencement of the contract, relates to advertising and promotional expenditure to improve Minco's brand image by the tennis player. Therefore, in accordance with IAS 38 Intangible Assets, the costs must be expensed when the entity has received the service.

The signing bonus relates to the full contract term so a prepayment of $20,000 is recognised on commencement. It should be expensed to profit or loss on a straight line basis over the three-year contract period.

Annual payment

A contractual obligation to deliver cash is a financial liability, which must be accounted for in accordance with *IFRS 9 Financial Instruments*. The liability is recognised at the point where Minco has an obligation. The obligation arises on the date when the player has competed in all the specified tournaments.

Bonuses

The player also receives additional performance-related payments for success in the tournaments. The bonus should be accrued and expensed when the player has won a tournament.

Tutorial note

It would seem that Minco needs to pay their landlord various amounts as a result of clauses in their lease contract. These clauses create obligations and, therefore, Minco needs to consider whether provisions are required and, if so, at what amount. Remember to begin your answer by stating the rules in the relevant accounting standard before applying these rules to the scenario.

(c)   **Provisions**

A provision must be recognised if:

- there is a present obligation from a past event

- an outflow of economic resources is probable

- the outflow of resources can be reliably measured.

The cost of building the floor should be capitalised as an item of property, plant and equipment. However, Minco has an obligation to remove the floor at the end of the lease. A provision should be made for the present value of the cost of removal of the floor in six years' time. The other side of the entry will be to property, plant and equipment. The total cost of the asset should be depreciated over the six-year period.

As regards the disrepair of the building, it would seem that Minco has a present obligation arising from the lease agreement because the landlord can recharge the costs of any repair to Minco. The obligating event is the wear and tear to the building which will arise gradually over the tenancy period and its repair can be enforced through the legal agreement. A provision should therefore be created at each year end for the estimated costs to repair the building for the wear and tear to date.

As regards the roof repair, it is clear from the lease that an obligation exists and therefore a provision should be made for the whole of the rectification work when the need for the repair was identified.

Tutorial note

Part (d) is the most technically demanding section of this question. The basic rule for assets held for sale is that they are measured at the lower of their carrying amount and the fair value less costs to sell with any decline in value charged to profit or loss as an impairment loss (unless a revaluation reserve exists). Impairment losses recorded against assets can be reversed (except for goodwill), but this reversal is capped.

Remember that the question asks you to 'discuss' how the issues should be treated. It is not sufficient to simply produce calculations.

(d)   **Held for sale**

In valuing the property, Minco should use the provisions of IFRS 5 *Assets held for Sale and Discontinued Operations*. Immediately before the initial classification of the asset as held for sale, the carrying amount of the asset should be measured in accordance with applicable IFRSs. After classification as held for sale, the property should be measured at the lower of carrying amount and fair value less costs to sell. Any impairment loss is recognised in profit or loss unless the asset has previously been measured at a revalued amount under IAS 16 or IAS 38, in which case the impairment is treated as a revaluation decrease.

A gain for any subsequent increase in fair value less costs to sell of an asset is recognised in the profit or loss to the extent that it is not in excess of the cumulative impairment loss which has been recognised in accordance with IFRS 5 or previously in accordance with IAS 36.

At the time of classification as held for sale, depreciation needs to be charged for the four months to 1 October 2013. This will be based upon the year end value at 31 May 2013 of $2.65 million. The property has 10 years life remaining based upon the depreciation to date and assuming a zero residual value, the depreciation for the four months will be approximately $0.1 million. Thus, at the time of classification as held for sale, the carrying amount is $2.55 million ($4m – $1 – $0.1 m – $0.35m) and fair value less costs to sell is assessed at $2.4 million. Accordingly, the initial write-down on classification as held for sale is $150,000 and the property is carried at $2.4 million.

IAS 34 *Interim Financial Reporting* says that the same financial reporting policies should be applied in the interim financial statements as are applied in the year-end financial statements. On 1 December 2013 in the interim financial statements, the property market has improved and fair value less costs to sell is reassessed at $2.52 million. The gain of $120,000 is less than the cumulative impairment losses of $500,000 recognised to date ($350,000 + $150,000). Accordingly, it is credited in profit or loss and the property is carried at $2.52 million.

On 31 May 2014, the property market has continued to improve, and fair value less costs to sell is now assessed at $2.95 million. The further gain of $430,000 is, however, in excess of the $380,000 cumulative impairment losses recognised to date ($350,000 + $150,000 – $120,000). Accordingly, a restricted gain of $380,000 is credited in profit or loss and the property is carried at $2.9 million.

Subsequently, the property is sold for $3 million at which point a gain of $100,000 is recognised. If deemed to be material, the sale would be disclosed as a non-adjusting event under IAS 10 *Events after the Reporting Period*.

ACCA Marking scheme		
		Marks
(a)	1 mark per point up to maximum	7
(b)	1 mark per point up to maximum	5
(c)	1 mark per point up to maximum	5
(d)	1 mark per point up to maximum	6
	Professional marks	2
		———
Total		**25**
		———

Examiner's comments

The scenarios set out in the question paper are based upon 'real life' examples and this question was a good example of this fact. An issue for candidates where questions are based upon real scenarios is that such questions will vary from diet to diet and will differ from textbook questions. Thus, to reiterate, in order to answer these questions candidates need to fully understand the principles embodied in IFRS.

Part (a) of the question dealt with a property developer who purchased land and transferred ownership to a housing association before construction starts. The developer argued that the transfer of land represented a sale of goods which fulfilled revenue recognition criteria. The facts were quite complicated but were very important to the determination of the correct treatment. The question carried 7 marks. Most candidates had knowledge of the accounting standard and many applied their knowledge satisfactorily.

In part (b), many candidates struggled to recognise the issues where a tennis player receives a signing bonus of $20,000, earns an annual amount of $50,000 and receives a bonus of 20% of the prize money won at a tournament. There was little discussion of the principles behind the accounting application.

In part (c) the entity leased its head office and improved the building but there was a clause in the lease, which stated that the building had to be returned in the same condition as at the beginning of the lease. There was also a clause which enabled the landlord to recharge the entity for costs relating to the general disrepair of the building and recharge any costs of repairing the roof immediately. The question carried 5 marks. This question required knowledge of two standards, IAS 16 and IAS 37. The scenarios that appear in this exam will often require multiple IFRSs to be applied to them.

Similarly, part (d) of the question required knowledge of IAS 34, IFRS 5 IAS 16 and IAS 38. In this part of the question, the entity acquired a property and an impairment loss was recognised, which resulted in the property being valued at its estimated value in use. The property was subsequently classified as held for sale but the property market improved and finally it was sold after the year-end. There was a need for candidates to calculate gains and losses at various stages of the question and thus the marks were allocated between discussion and calculation. This part of the question was quite well done in terms of the calculations but was quite weak on the discursive element. It is not possible to prepare for this type of question by simply reading a manual and learning notes or by listening to a lecture. It requires candidates to try and answer questions without reference to material and then comparing their efforts with a model answer, and not simply auditing the answer.

26   HAVANNA (DEC 13 EXAM) *Walk in the footsteps of a top tutor*

Key answer tips

This question requires a knowledge of revenue, disposal groups and sale-and-leaseback transactions. Make sure that you state the recognition rules from each standard for some easy marks. You should then try and apply the accounting standards to the specifics in the question.

Tutorial note

According to IFRS 15, revenue from satisfying a performance obligation should be recognised either at a point in time or over time. When answering this question, state the criteria for recognising revenue over time and then apply these to the scenario.

(a)   According to IFRS 15, revenue should be recognised over time if:

- the customer simultaneously receives and consumes the benefits provided by the entity's performance as the entity performs

- the entity's performance creates or enhances an asset (for example, work in progress) that the customer controls as the asset is created or enhanced, or

- the entity's performance does not create an asset with an alternative use to the entity and the entity has an enforceable right to payment for performance completed to date.

Health club services are simultaneously received and consumed by the customer. Therefore, Havanna's revenue recognition policy is incorrect and instead they should recognise revenue over time.

Tutorial note

Do not simply conclude that Havanna's current revenue recognition policy is wrong. Make sure that you also discuss how they should be recognising revenue.

When revenue is recognised over time, the amount of revenue recognised should be based on the progress to completion of the relevant performance obligation. Entities can use output or input methods to measure the progress to completion.

In Havanna's case, the time that has passed on a contract would seem to be the best measure of the stage of completion. Therefore, revenue should be recognised based on the proportion of each contract that has elapsed.

Tutorial note

Begin part (b) by stating the rules in IFRS 5 concerning the treatment of a disposal group that is held for sale. Of particular importance is the fact that assets or disposal groups that are classified as held for sale should be measured at the lower of their carrying amount and the fair value less costs to sell.

(b)   According to IFRS 5 *Non-current Assets Held for Sale and Discontinued Operations*, the carrying amounts of all the assets and liabilities in a disposal group are to be measured in accordance with applicable IFRSs immediately before the initial classification of the disposal group as held for sale. Any impairment loss is recognised in profit or loss unless the asset had been measured at a revalued amount under IAS 16 *Property, Plant and Equipment* or IAS 38 *Intangible Assets*, in which case the impairment is treated as a revaluation decrease.

After classification as held for sale, non-current assets or disposal groups which are classified as held for sale are measured at the lower of carrying amount and fair value less costs to sell.

Tutorial note

Apply the IFRS 5 rules. Notice that the division is being sold for $40m, so this is likely to be its fair value. If the disposal group is not held at the correct value, then a further impairment is required.

If it is assumed that the fair value of the division is $40 million (and ignoring costs to sell), the initial impairment loss of $30 million is insufficient. An additional impairment loss of $20 million is required.

Tutorial note

Disposal groups held for sale should be measured at the lower of carrying value and fair value less costs to sell. Think about the types of items that should have been incorporated into these values.

The treatment of the costs relating to the division being sold also appears to be incorrect.

The trade receivable should have been tested for impairment immediately before classification of the division as held for sale and the resulting loss should have been recognised against the net carrying amount of the disposal group at initial classification as held for sale.

As regards the expense relating to the discounting effect, the 'fair value less costs to sell' of the disposal group should have incorporated the effect of discounting given that payment will not take place until 2015. Similarly, with regards to the provision for transaction costs, the expected transaction costs should be considered as an additional cost of the transaction and, therefore, are a component of the costs to sell. Both of these items should therefore have been taken into account in the calculation of fair value less costs to sell and should not be presented as provisions relating to continuing operations in the statement of financial position.

Tutorial note

Begin part (c) by stating the basic treatment of a sale and operating leaseback.

(c)   As Havanna has decided that the leaseback is in substance an operating lease, then it recognises the lease payments as an expense in the statement of profit or loss over the life of the lease.

Tutorial note

The treatment of the gain or loss made on a sale and operating leaseback transaction depends on the relationship between the sales price and the fair value of the asset. Take each situation in turn and make sure that you explicitly state how the gain or loss will be treated.

With regards to the sale of the asset, Havanna will recognise the cash proceeds and derecognise the asset. They must consider how the sale price compares with the fair value of the asset in determining how to account for any gain or loss on disposal:

(i)   If the sale proceeds match the fair value of the asset, then the whole gain or loss on disposal is recognised immediately. Thus if the asset is sold for $5 million, a gain of $0.8 million will be recognised in profit or loss.

(ii)   If the sale proceeds are greater than the fair value of the asset, which is unlikely in the current market, this implies the creation of an artificial gain. The difference between the fair value of the asset and its carrying value is recognised immediately in profit or loss. The excess amount of the sale proceeds over the fair value of the asset is deferred and released to profit or loss over the life of the leaseback.

       Thus if the selling price were $6 million, a gain of $0.8 million would still be recorded but the balance of $1 million would be credited to profit or loss over the lease period of 10 years at $100,000 per annum.

(iii) Where the sale proceeds are less than the fair value of the asset, then any profit or loss is recognised immediately, unless it is clear that the loss is compensated for by lower lease rentals, in which case the loss is deferred and amortised to expenses over the life of the leaseback.

       As property valuations are, by their nature, estimates and therefore include a degree of tolerance, if the asset were sold for $4.8 million, the difference between the sale proceeds and the fair value of the asset is relatively small and probably indicates that the sale is genuinely at fair value. The sale proceeds would therefore be recognised in full and a gain of $0.6 million recorded.

(iv) If the sale proceeds were $4 million, there is a large difference between the fair value of the asset and the sale proceeds. It appears that the sale proceeds are artificially low which in turn is likely to be reflected in artificially low lease rentals charged. Therefore the sale proceeds of $4 million are recognised but the resulting $0.2 million loss on disposal is not recognised immediately. Instead, it is deferred and amortised to expenses over the 10-year life of the lease at $20,000 per annum.

ACCA Marking scheme		
		Marks
(a)	Revenue recognition up to	6
(b)	IFRS 5 explanation	9
(c)	Leases	8
	Professional marks	2
		—
Total		**25**
		—

Examiner's comments

Generally within each part of the question, marks are awarded for knowledge of the relevant standard(s) and for application of the standard(s) to the scenario. Thus it can be seen that if a candidate simply recites the IFRS, then it is unlikely that the candidate will score more than half marks. In fact, it is likely to be less than half marks.

In part (a) of the question the following sentence could be seen 'Havanna's accounting policy for revenue recognition is to recognise the contract income in full at the date when the contract was signed'. Therefore it should have been evident that the knowledge required was that of revenue. The level of knowledge needed to answer the question was quite basic but candidates had to apply that knowledge to gain the marks and again this was where any problem arose. However, this part of the question was answered quite well.

Part (b) of the question dealt with a disposal group with the relevant standard being IFRS 5 *Non current Assets Held for Sale and Discontinued Operations*. Again the marks were split between knowledge and application. The main issue with the answers to this question was that candidates found reasons as to why the disposal group was incorrectly classified as such, when there was no evidence in the question of this fact. The main problem was the measurement of the disposal group but many candidates failed to recognise this fact. It should be said that every question dealing with IFRS 5 will not be centred on the determination as to whether the non-current asset or disposal group is 'held for sale'. Again the knowledge level was basic and the application extremely important. The second part of part (b) required candidates to determine whether certain costs should be dealt with as part of continuing operations or as part of the disposal group. The marking of this section of the question was based upon the candidates reasoning and the treatment of the items involved. Obviously if the reasoning was inaccurate then few marks could be gained. The part of the question was not well answered and if candidates did not recognise that it was a measurement issue re IFRS 5 then they struggled to gain a pass mark in the part.

Part (c) of the question required candidates to give advice on accounting for a sale and lease back of property in four different price scenarios. This part of the question was answered quite well by candidates. The main issue was that some candidates simply showed the accounting entries without discussing the implications. However candidates scored well on this part.

27 BENTAL (DEC 13 EXAM) *Walk in the footsteps of a top tutor*

Key answer tips

This is a difficult question that tests some very technical areas. However, you can score highly if you have good exam technique.

Do make sure that you address the questions asked. For example, part (c) is about identifying the acquirer in the business combination. Start off by stating the rules per IFRS 3. You should then move on and evaluate whether Bental or Lental is the acquirer, using the specific information given to you in the scenario.

Tutorial note

Bental wants to report the B-shares as a non-controlling interest, which means that they will be held within the equity section of the statement of financial position. However, the B shareholders can demand payment (exercise their put options) every three years. It would seem that classification as equity might not be appropriate.

Begin this question by stating relevant definitions – when should a financial instrument be classified as equity and when should it be classified as a financial liability?

(a)   IAS 32 defines a financial liability as a contractual obligation to deliver cash, another financial asset, or a variable number of its own shares to another entity.

If there was an unconditional right to avoid delivering cash, another financial asset, or a variable number of its own shares then the instrument would be considered as an equity instrument.

A contingent settlement provision which requires settlement in cash or variable number of the entity's own shares only on the occurrence of an event which is very unlikely to occur is not considered to be genuine. An instrument including such a provision would, therefore, be an equity instrument.

Tutorial note

Apply the definitions that you have stated to the question. Bental is obliged to make cash payments to the B shareholders: does this mean that the B shares are equity or a financial liability?

Bental has classified the shares within equity. However, Bental does not have an unconditional right to avoid delivering cash to settle the obligation. Thus, the minority shareholders' holdings of B-shares should be treated as a financial liability in the consolidated financial statements.

Tutorial note

Part (b) tests some quite detailed hedge accounting rules. It is important to remember that the discontinuance of a hedge is accounted for prospectively. However, you need to think about the treatment of gains or losses previously recognised in other comprehensive income.

(b) **Cash flow hedge**

Hedge accounting must be discontinued if the hedging relationship no longer meets the qualifying criteria. If Bental's forecast transactions are no longer considered to be highly probable, then there is no qualifying item for hedge accounting and the hedge must be discontinued. The discontinuance of hedge accounting is accounted for prospectively.

If hedge accounting ceases for a cash flow hedge relationship because the forecast transaction is no longer expected to occur, gains and losses deferred in other comprehensive income must be taken to profit or loss immediately. If the transaction is still expected to occur and the hedge relationship ceases, the amounts accumulated in equity will be retained in equity until the hedged transaction occurs.

As the future transactions are still expected to occur, the previously recognised gains will remain in equity. They will be reclassified to profit or loss when the forecast sales occur.

Tutorial note

Remember that changes in the fair value of an associate do not impact consolidated profit or loss. Rather, an investment in an associate is accounted for using the equity method. This means that it is initially recognised at cost and then adjusted for the group's share of the post-acquisition movement in reserves.

Think about the definition of a fair value hedge and consider whether an investment in an associate would qualify as a hedged item. Make sure that you justify your conclusion.

Fair value hedge

A fair value hedge is a hedge of the exposure to changes in the fair value of a recognised asset or liability or a firm commitment that could affect profit or loss (or other comprehensive income for investments in equity that are measured at fair value through other comprehensive income).

The equity method recognises the investor's share of the associate's profit or loss, rather than changes in its fair value. Therefore, an associate in the consolidated financial statements does not qualify for fair value hedge accounting.

If the investment is held at fair value in the parent's individual financial statements, then fair value hedge accounting could be applied.

Tutorial note

Remember that the acquirer in a business combination is the entity that exercises control. Easy marks can be obtained for stating the definition of control in IFRS 10.

(c) IFRS 3 *Business Combinations* requires an acquirer to be identified in all business combinations, the acquirer being the combining entity which obtains control of the other combined entity.

IFRS 10 *Consolidated Financial Statements* says that an investor controls an investee when it is exposed, or has rights, to variable returns from its involvement with the investee and has the ability to affect those returns through its power over the investee. IFRS 10 states that power arises from rights.

Sometimes it is straightforward to assess power by looking at the voting rights obtained. When the parent acquires more than half of the voting rights of the entity, it normally has power if the relevant activities of the investee are directed by a vote or if a majority of the members of the governing body are appointed by a vote of the holder of the majority of the voting rights. Other rights which may give the investor power are:

- rights to appoint, reassign or remove members of key management personnel

- rights to appoint or remove another entity which directs the relevant activities

- rights to direct the investee to enter into or veto any changes to transactions for the benefit of the investor, and other rights (such as decision-making rights specified in a management contract).

There is a presumption that an entity achieves control over another entity by acquiring more than one half of the voting rights, unless it can be demonstrated that such ownership does not constitute control.

Tutorial note

In more complicated scenarios, like the one in this question, IFRS 3 sets out further rules for determining the acquirer in a business combination.

You may struggle to remember the rules off by heart. If this is the case, then use your common sense. Which company issued equity in the transaction? Which company is the bigger of the two? Which company seems to control the other? As always, try and reach a justified conclusion.

If the guidance in IFRS 10 does not clearly indicate which of the combining entities is the acquirer, IFRS 3 sets out other factors to be considered.

The acquirer is usually the entity which transfers cash or other assets. In this scenario, as Bental is the entity giving up a cash amount corresponding to 45% of the purchase price, this represents a significant share of the total purchase consideration.

When there is an exchange of equity interests in a business combination, the entity which issues the equity interests is normally the acquirer. In this case, as the majority of the purchase consideration is settled in equity instruments, Bental would appear to be the acquirer.

However, all pertinent facts and circumstances should be considered to determine which of the combining entities has the power to govern the financial and operating policies of the other entity.

The acquirer is usually the combining entity whose shareholders retain or receive the largest portion of the voting rights in the combined entity. The shareholders of Bental, the smaller of the two combining entities, appear to have obtained control since their share amounts to 51% of the voting rights after the transaction. A controlling ownership, however, does not necessarily mean that the entity has the power to govern the combined entity's financial and operating policies so as to obtain benefits from its activities.

Additionally, the acquirer could be deemed to be the entity whose owners have the ability to appoint or remove a majority of the members of the governing body of the combined entity. Five out of six members of the board here are former board members of Bental, which again suggests that Bental is the acquirer.

Additionally, the acquirer could be deemed the entity whose former management dominates the management of the combined entity. However, the management team consists of the COO plus two former employees of Lental as compared to two former employees of Bental. Therefore, the former management of Lental has a greater representation. Although the board nominates the management team, the COO will have significant influence through his share ownership and the selection of the team.

Other indications implying control may be the relative size of the combining entities in terms of, for example, assets, revenues or profit. As the fair value of Lental ($90 million) is significantly greater than Bental ($70 million), this would point towards Lental as the acquirer.

The arguments supporting Bental or Lental as the acquirer are finely balanced and therefore it is difficult to identify an acquirer in this case. It can be argued that Bental can be identified as the acquirer, on the basis that:

- Bental issued the equity interest
- Bental is the entity transferring the cash or other assets and
- Bental has the marginal controlling interest (51%).

ACCA Marking scheme		Marks
(a)	Financial instrument explanation up to	7
(b)	Hedged items	6
(c)	IFRS 3 explanation	10
	Professional marks	2
Total		**25**

Examiner's comments

Many of the scenarios set out in the question paper are based upon 'real life' examples and this question was a good example of this fact.

In part (a), an entity had a subsidiary which had two classes of shares, A and B, and the B-shares owned by minority shareholders were to be reported as a non-controlling interest. Candidates were required to determine whether this treatment was correct. The knowledge level required was simply the definition of equity and liability in IAS 32. The application however was given equal weighting in the marking. Candidates seemed to understand the definitions but could not apply them. If the application was not exactly correct, candidates scored marks for a sensible discussion. In answering this type of question, candidates should plan their answer by thinking of the knowledge required and how they are going to apply that knowledge as generally, both aspects are equally important. The question was generally answered reasonably well.

Part (b) of the question dealt with hedging relationships. It was a difficult question in many ways but candidates could score reasonably well if they approached the question sensibly. As set out above marks were awarded for knowledge and application. Therefore candidates could gain marks for knowledge of cash flow hedge accounting. The application to the scenario was quite difficult and required candidates to set out the accounting on termination of the specific hedging relationship. However, a pass mark in this part of the question was easily be gained by those candidates who applied their knowledge. The second element of part (b) again dealt with hedging and again the above principles applied. Knowledge of the equity method was required and its application in a hedging situation. This part of the question was not well answered.

Part (c) of the question dealt with the situation where the entity entered into a business combination with another listed bank. The question dealt with the situation where it was difficult to determine an acquirer. The knowledge required was that of IFRS 3 and IFRS 10. This type of question has been asked in the past and because of the introduction of IFRS 10, it was pertinent to ask candidates to apply the new standard. The key aspect of this question was the discussion of the principles and applying it to the scenario. The scenario contained a significant amount of information, which should have been used by candidates Marks were gained by discussing the various facts set out in the question. This part of the question was quite well answered.

In conclusion, although this question may have seemed difficult, parts (a) and (c) simply required basic knowledge of the IFRS and part (b) required knowledge of hedging relationships. At this level of a professional qualification, this knowledge level should be taken as granted. The application of this knowledge is where candidates were weakest. The question was not generally well answered by candidates.

28   VERGE (JUNE 13 EXAM) *Walk in the footsteps of a top tutor*

Key answer tips

This question covers a number of different standards. Some of these, such as revenue and provisions, are very common in the P2 exam and it is therefore vital that you learn these thoroughly. Make sure that you state the relevant accounting rules for easy marks, before applying them to the information in the scenario.

IFRS 8 *Operating Segments* is less commonly tested. However, it is easy to score solid marks in part (a) through using common sense.

Tutorial note

IFRS 8 Operating Segments is a standard applicable to listed entities. Its aim is to increase the usefulness of the information provided to the users by disaggregating the highly summarised information provided in the primary financial statements.

Even if you do not have a detailed knowledge of this standard, you should still be able to reach a sensible conclusion as to whether or not segments 1 and 2 should be aggregated.

(a)   IFRS *8 Operating Segments* states that reportable segments are those operating segments or aggregations of operating segments for which segment information must be separately reported. Aggregation of one or more operating segments into a single reportable segment is permitted (but not required) where certain conditions are met, the principal condition being that the operating segments should have similar economic characteristics. The segments must be similar in each of the following respects:

- the nature of the products and services

- the nature of the production processes

- the type or class of customer

- the methods used to distribute their products or provide their services

- the nature of the regulatory environment.

Segments 1 and 2 have different customers. The decision to award or withdraw a local train contract rests with the transport authority and not with the end customer, the passenger. In contrast, the decision to withdraw from a route in the inter-city train market would normally rest with Verge but would be largely influenced by the passengers' actions that would lead to the route becoming economically unviable. In view of the fact that the segments have different customers, the two segments do not satisfy the aggregation criteria above.

In the local train market, contracts are awarded following a competitive tender process, and, consequently, there is no exposure to passenger revenue risk. The ticket prices paid by passengers are set by a transport authority and not Verge. By contrast, in the inter-city train market, ticket prices are set by Verge and its revenues are, therefore, the fares paid by the passengers travelling on the trains. In this set of circumstances, the company is exposed to passenger revenue risk. This risk would affect the two segments in different ways but generally through the action of the operating segment's customer.

Therefore the economic characteristics of the two segments are different and so they should be reported as separate segments.

Tutorial note

If a customer is provided with a significant financing benefit, revenue is calculated by discounting the consideration receivable to present value.

Make sure that you pay careful attention to dates in this question. This is important for the discounting calculations as well as for determining that a prior period error has occurred.

(b) **Revenue recognition**

Maintenance services are simultaneously received and consumed. According to IFRS 15 *Revenue from Contracts with Customers,* this means that revenue should be recognised over time based on progress towards the satisfaction of the performance obligation. Thus Verge must recognise revenue as work is performed throughout the contract life.

The length of time between the transfer of the promised services and the payment date suggests that there is a significant financing component. Consideration should therefore be discounted to present value using the rate at which the customer could borrow. The difference between the discounted revenue and the payment received should be recognised as interest income.

The calculation of the revenue is as follows:

In the year ended 31 March 2012, Verge should have recorded revenue of $2.6 million ($1 million + ($1.8 million × (1/1.06^2))). Since Verge has received $1 million cash, a receivable of $1.6 million should be recognised.

In the year ended 31 March 2013, revenue should be recorded at $1.13 million ($1.2 million × (1/1.06)). In addition, the discount on the receivable recognised in the year ended 31 March 2012 must be unwound. Consequently, there will be interest income of $96,000 ($1.6 million × 6%).

Prior period error

Prior period errors are omissions from, and misstatements in, the entity's financial statements for one or more prior periods arising from a failure to use, or misuse of, reliable information that:

- was available when financial statements for those periods were authorised for issue, and

- could reasonably be expected to have been obtained and taken into account in the preparation and presentation of those financial statements.

Such errors include the effects of mathematical mistakes, mistakes in applying accounting policies, oversights or misinterpretations of facts and fraud. The fact that Verge only included $1 million of the revenue in the financial statements for the year ended 31 March 2012 is a prior period error.

Verge should correct the prior period errors retrospectively in the financial statements for the year ended 31 March 2013 by restating the comparative amounts for the prior period presented in which the error occurred.

Tutorial note

Provisions are a core standard at P2. Make sure that you know the criteria for recognising a provision off by heart.

(c) **Provisions**

Under IAS 37 *Provisions, Contingent Liabilities and Contingent Assets,* an entity must recognise a provision if, and only if:

- a present obligation (legal or constructive) has arisen as a result of a past event (the obligating event),

- payment is probable ('more likely than not'), and

- the amount can be estimated reliably.

An obligating event is an event that creates a legal or constructive obligation and, therefore, results in an entity having no realistic alternative but to settle the obligation. The obligating event took place in the year to 31 March 2012. A provision should be made on the date of the obligating event, which is the date on which the event takes place that results in an entity having no realistic alternative to settling the legal or constructive obligation. However, it is reasonable at 31 March 2012 to assess the need for a provision to be immaterial as no legal proceedings have been started and the damage to the building seemed superficial.

In the year to 31 March 2013, as a result of the legal arguments supporting the action, Verge will have to reassess its estimate of the likely damages and a provision is needed, based on the advice that it has regarding the likely settlement. Provisions should be reviewed at each year end for material changes to the best estimate.

Dr Profit or loss	$800,000
Cr Provision for damages	$800,000

The potential for reimbursements (e.g. insurance payments) to cover some of the expenditure required to settle a provision can be recognised, but only if receipt is virtually certain if the entity settles the obligation. IAS 37 requires that the reimbursement be treated as a separate asset. The amount recognised for the reimbursement cannot exceed the amount of the provision. IAS 37 permits the expense relating to a provision to be presented net of the amount. The company seems confident that it will satisfy the terms of the insurance policy and should accrue for the reimbursement:

Dr Other receivables	$200,000
Cr Profit or loss	$200,000

The court case was found against Verge but as this was after the authorisation of the financial statements, there is no adjustment of the provision at 31 March 2013. It is not an adjusting event.

Tutorial note

A good knowledge of accounting principles, from the Framework, would help with part (d) of this question. Remember that an asset is a resourced that is controlled by an entity as a result of a past event and which will lead to a probable inflow of economic benefits. At what point does Verge control the building?

(d)   **The asset**

In accordance with IAS *1 Presentation of Financial Statements,* all items of income and expense recognised in a period should be included in profit or loss for the period unless a standard or interpretation requires or permits otherwise.

IAS 16 Property, Plant and Equipment states that the recognition criteria for PPE are based on the probability that future benefits will flow to the entity from the asset and that cost can be measured reliably. The above normally occurs when the risks and rewards of the asset have passed to the entity.

Therefore at 31 March 2012, the building would not be recognised as the 'contract' is not unconditional and possession of the building has not been taken by Verge.

Once the conditions of the donated asset have been met in February 2013, the income of $1.5 million is recognised in the statement of profit or loss and other comprehensive income. The following transactions need to be made to recognise the asset in the entity's statement of financial position as of 31 March 2013.

Dr Property, plant and equipment	$2.5m
Cr Profit or loss	$1.5m
Cr Cash/trade payable	$1m

Depreciation of the building should also be charged for the period according to Verge's accounting policy.

Tutorial note

There are two types of government grants: revenue grants and capital grants. Whatever the type of grant, the income should be matched against the costs that it was intended to compensate.

The grant

IAS 20 Accounting for Government Grants and Disclosure of Government Assistance states that a government grant is recognised only when there is reasonable assurance that (a) the entity will comply with any conditions attached to the grant and (b) the grant will be received. Thus in this case the grant will be recognised.

The grant is recognised as income over the period necessary to match it with the related costs, for which it is intended to compensate, on a systematic basis. A grant receivable as compensation for costs already incurred or for immediate financial support, with no future related costs, should be recognised as income in the period in which it is receivable.

A grant relating to assets (capital based grant) may be presented in one of two ways:

* as deferred income

* by deducting the grant from the asset's carrying amount.

The grant of $250,000 relates to capital expenditure and revenue. It seems appropriate to account for the grant on the basis of matching the grant to the expenditure. Therefore $100,000 (20 × $5,000) should be taken to income and the remainder ($150,000) should be recognised as a capital based grant. The double entry would be:

Dr Cash	$250,000
Cr Profit or loss	$100,000
Cr Deferred income or PPE (depending on accounting policy)	$150,000

ACCA Marking scheme		
		Marks
(a)	Segment explanation up to	5
(b)	IFRS 15 explanation and calculation	6
(c)	IAS 37 explanation and calculation	6
(d)	IAS 1/16/20 explanation and calculation	6
	Professional marks	2
		——
Total		**25**
		——

Examiner's comments

The first scenario dealt with IFRS 8 *Operating Segments*. Candidates had to discuss how different segments should be treated in the financial statements. Candidates often set out the rules of aggregation of one or more operating segments into a single reportable segment. The principal condition being that the operating segments should have similar economic characteristics. Segments 1 and 2 had different customers and in view of the fact that the segments have different customers, the two segments did not satisfy one of the aggregation criteria. Many candidates came to this conclusion but not all used the information in the question, which was critical to scoring a good mark. The economic characteristics of the two segments were different and should be reported as separate segments.

In Part (b) the entity entered into a contract with a government body to undertake maintenance services on a new railway line. The total revenue from the contract was $5 million over a three-year period. Candidates had to discuss how the revenue was to be apportioned over the life of the contract. Candidates understood that the revenue should be measured at the fair value of the consideration received or receivable . The calculation of the revenue's fair value was not well done by candidates nor was the unwinding of the discount. Several candidates did not realise that this was a prior period error.

Part (c) of the question, required knowledge of IAS 37 *Provisions, Contingent Liabilities and Contingent Assets*, Candidates understood the requirements of IAS 37 but did not always apply them correctly. This question required the use of judgment and opinion and therefore candidates who did not fully answer in accordance with the model answer could still score well. The majority of the marks were for the application of IAS 37 and not for the reproduction of the standard.

Part (d) required knowledge of IAS 1 *Presentation of Financial Statements*, IAS 16 *Property, Plant and Equipment* and IAS 20 *Accounting for Government Grants and Disclosure of Government Assistance*. It involved the accounting for a donated asset and its recognition in the financial statements. Candidates needed to follow the scenario in a chronological sequence in order to answer the question correctly. IAS 16 states that the recognition criteria for PPE are based on the probability that future benefits will flow to the entity from the asset and that cost can be measured reliably. The above normally occurs when the risks and rewards of the asset have passed to the entity. Normally the risks and rewards are assumed to transfer when an unconditional and irrevocable contract is put in place. These facts were not known by several. The treatment of the government grant was well known by candidates.

On the whole the question was well answered but candidates should always show the accounting entries where this is possible from the question.

29   JANNE (JUNE 13 EXAM) *Walk in the footsteps of a top tutor*

Key answer tips

Part (a) is a very detailed test of the difference between an operating lease and a finance lease. The answer provided is very comprehensive and students would not be expected to replicate it. However, it is important to have a thorough knowledge of the situations that would normally be indicative of a finance lease. Make sure that, after stating these rules, you apply them to the question, explaining why each factor is suggestive of the existence of a finance or operating lease.

Part (b) tests IFRS 13 *Fair Value Measurement*. Make sure that you know the definition of 'fair value' per this standard and that you are aware of the three levels of inputs used to determine fair value.

Part (c) concerns whether a subsidiary meets the criteria to be 'held for sale'. Start off by stating the rules per IFRS 5 for classifying an asset, or group of assets, as held for sale. You should then apply these rules to the scenario.

Tutorial note

IAS 17 lists many factors that should be considered when determining whether a lease is a finance lease or an operating lease. You should begin your answer by stating as many of these as you can remember.

(a)   The lease of the land is subject to the general lease classification criteria of IAS 17 *Leases* and the fact that land normally has an indefinite economic life is an important consideration. Thus, if the lease of land transfers substantially all the risks and rewards incidental to ownership to the lessee, then the lease is a finance lease, otherwise it is an operating lease. A lease of land with a long term may be classified as a finance lease even if the title does not pass to the lessee. Situations set out in IAS 17 that would normally lead to a lease being classified as a finance lease include the following:

- the lease transfers ownership of the asset to the lessee by the end of the lease term

- the lease term is for the major part of the economic life of the asset, even if title is not transferred

- at the inception of the lease, the present value of the minimum lease payments amounts to at least substantially all of the fair value of the leased asset

- the lessee has the ability to continue to lease for a secondary period at a rent that is substantially lower than market rent.

> **Tutorial note**
>
> *You should now apply the criteria from IAS 17 to the question. Do not worry if some parts of the scenario are suggestive of a finance lease whilst others are suggestive of an operating lease. However, do try and reach a conclusion at the end as to what type of lease you think it is and therefore what the accounting treatment should be.*

A contingent rent is an amount that is paid as part of the lease payments but is not fixed or agreed in advance at the inception of the lease, rather the amount to be paid is dependent on some future event. Under IAS 17, contingent rents are excluded from minimum lease payments and are accounted as expense/income in the period in which they are incurred/earned. Contingent rents may indicate that a lease is an operating lease if the nature of the contingency provides evidence that the lessor has not transferred substantially all of the risks and rewards of ownership of the land. However, other factors have to be taken into account besides the contingent rental.

The presence of an option to extend the lease at substantially less than a market rent or purchase it at a discount of 90% on the market value implies that the lessor expects to achieve its return on investment mainly through the lease payments and therefore is content to continue the lease for a secondary period at an immaterial rental or sell it at a substantial discount to the market value. This is an indicator of a finance lease. It is reasonable to assume that the lessee will extend the lease or purchase the land in these circumstances. However, an option to extend it at a market rental without the purchase provision may indicate that the lessor has not achieved its return on investment through the lease rentals and therefore is relying on a subsequent lease or sale to do so. This is an indicator of an operating lease as there will be no compelling commercial reason why the lessee should extend the agreement. In this case, the lease term is not for the major part of the economic life of the asset as the asset is land.

However, it would appear that the minimum lease payments would equate to the fair value of the asset, given the fact that the lease premium is 70% of the current fair value and the rent is 4% of the fair value for 30 years. Additionally, if land values rise, then there is a revision of the rental every five years to ensure that the lessor achieves the return on the investment.

If a lease contains a clean break clause, where the lessee is free to walk away from the lease agreement after a certain time without penalty, then the lease term for accounting purposes will normally be the period between the commencement of the lease and the earliest point at which the break option is exercisable by the lessee. If a lease contains an early termination clause that requires the lessee to make a termination payment to compensate the lessor such that the recovery of the lessor's remaining investment in the lease is assured, then the termination clause would normally be disregarded in determining the lease term. However, the suggestions made by Maret do add substance to the conclusion that the lease is a finance lease, as the early termination clause requires a payment which recovers the lessor's investment and it would appear that Maret is happy to allow the termination of the agreement after 25 years which would imply that the lessor's return would have been achieved after that period of time.

As a result of the above, it would appear that the lease is a finance lease. The upfront premium plus the present value of the annual payments at the commencement of the lease would be capitalised as property, plant and equipment and the annual lease payments would be shown as a liability. The interest expense would be recognised over the lease term so as to produce a constant periodic rate of interest on the remaining balance of the liability.

Additionally, Janne plans to use the land in its business but may hold the land for capital gain. Thus the lease may meet the definition of an investment property if it is to be held for capital gain. In the latter case, IAS 40 *Investment Property* should be used to account for the land with the lessee's chosen model used to account for it.

Tutorial note

Part (b) is about whether the fair values of investment properties have been determined correctly. Therefore, begin your answer with the definition of fair value according to IFRS 13.

(b)   IFRS 13 *Fair Value Measurement* acts as a common framework on how to measure the fair value when its determination is required or permitted by another IFRS. The framework defines fair value and provides a single source of guidance for measuring fair value. IFRS 13 defines the fair value of an asset as an 'exit price', which is the price that would be received to sell an asset or paid to transfer a liability in an orderly transaction between market participants at the measurement date. Fair value is a market-based measurement, not an entity-specific measurement, and fair value reflects current market conditions.

Tutorial note

IFRS 13 uses a three-level hierarchy, prioritising valuation methods that use level 1 inputs. Give a brief description of each level of the hierarchy.

In IFRS 13, fair value measurements are categorised into a three-level hierarchy based on the type of inputs and are not based on a valuation method. The new hierarchy is defined as follows:

- Level 1 inputs are unadjusted quoted prices in active markets for items identical to the asset being measured.

- Level 2 inputs are inputs other than quoted prices in active markets included within Level 1 that are directly or indirectly observable.

- Level 3 inputs are unobservable inputs that are usually determined based on management's assumptions.

Tutorial note

Now it is time to apply your knowledge to the scenario. What level of input has Janne used? What level of input is available for them to use?

Due to the nature of investment property, which is often unique and not traded on a regular basis, and the subsequent lack of observable input data for identical assets, fair value measurements are likely to be categorised as Level 2 or Level 3 valuations.

Level 2 inputs are likely to be sale prices per square metre for similar properties in the same location, observable market rents and property yields from the latest transactions. Level 3 inputs may be yields based on management estimates, cash flow forecasts using the entity's own data, and assumptions about the future development of certain parameters such as rental income that are not derived from the market.

Management should maximise the use of relevant observable inputs and minimise the use of unobservable inputs. A valuation based on 'new-build value less obsolescence' does not reflect the level 2 inputs which are available, such as sale prices and market rent. As level 2 data is available, the entity should use this data in valuing the industrial property.

Tutorial note

Part (c) is about whether a subsidiary meets the criteria in IFRS 5 to be classified as 'held for sale'. Remember, a subsidiary is a group of assets and liabilities and therefore is a 'disposal group'.

Start your answer by outlining the criteria in IFRS 5 concerning when a disposal group can be classified as held for sale.

(c) Under IFRS *5 Non-current Assets Held for Sale and Discontinued Operations*, a disposal group is classified as held for sale where its carrying amount will be recovered principally through sale rather than continuing use.

To be classified as held for sale, the sale should highly probable and expected to be complete within one year from the date of classification. The asset or disposal group should be available for sale in its immediate location and condition and actively marketed at a price reasonable in relation to its fair value.

A disposal group can, exceptionally, be classified as held for sale/discontinued after a period of 12 months if it meets certain criteria, such as if circumstances arose that were previously considered unlikely and, as a result, a disposal group remained unsold.

Tutorial note

Apply your knowledge of IFRS 5 to the scenario. Does the subsidiary meet the criteria to be classified as held for sale? Make sure that you fully explain your answer.

The draft agreements with investment bankers appear not to be sufficiently detailed to prove that the subsidiary met the criteria at the point of classification as required by IFRS 5. This requires the disposal group to be available for immediate sale in its present condition subject only to terms that are usual and customary for sales of such disposal groups.

Also, Janne had made certain organisational changes during the year to 31 May 2013, which resulted in additional activities being transferred to the subsidiary. This confirms that the subsidiary was not available for sale in its present condition as at the point of classification.

Furthermore, the shareholders' authorisation to sell the subsidiary was only granted for one year and there is no indication that this was extended by the subsequent shareholders' meeting in 2013.

The subsidiary should have been treated as a continuing operation in the financial statements for both years ended 31 May 2012 and 31 May 2013.

ACCA Marking scheme			
			Marks
(a)	Leases explanation up to		12
(b)	Investment properties explanation		5
(c)	IFRS 5 explanation		6
	Professional marks		2
			——
Total			**25**
			——

Examiner's comments

Part (a) dealt with a complex lease situation. Candidates were required to discuss the general lease classification criteria of IAS 17 *Leases* and the lease of land. However, the treatment of contingent rent, the presence of an option to extend the lease at substantially less than a market rent or purchase it at a discount of 90% on the market value also required discussion. The latter implies that the lessor expects to achieve its return on investment mainly through the lease payments and therefore is content to continue the lease for a secondary period at an immaterial rental or sell it at a substantial discount to the market value. This is an indicator of a finance lease. There were other elements to the question, including the fact that lease term was not for the major part of the economic life of the asset as the asset is land and that it appeared that the minimum lease payments would equate to the fair value of the asset, given the fact that the lease premium was 70% of the current fair value and the rent was 4% of the fair value for 30 years. There was also revision of the rental every five years to consider. It seemed that the lease was a finance lease but the lease also contained a clean break clause, where the lessee was free to walk away from the lease agreement after a certain time without penalty.

The key aspect to answering this question was to discuss each of the separate elements of the lease and then to reach a conclusion. If a candidate reached the conclusion that it was an operating lease, then this was contrary to the model answer but if the discussions which preceded this conclusion were well founded, then the candidate would achieve a good score.

Part (b) dealt with IAS 40 *Investment Property*, and the fair valuation of such property. It also required the knowledge of IAS 13 *Fair Value Measurement*, which acts as a common framework on how to measure the fair value when its determination is required or permitted by another IFRS. This question was well answered by most candidates as regards knowledge of IFRS 13 but again the application of IFRS 13 to the scenario was generally not well done.

Part (c) dealt with IFRS 5 *Non-current Assets Held for Sale and Discontinued Operations*, and this was well answered by candidates. Again it is important to note that only a portion of the marks is allocated to knowledge of the standard itself and the rest to application. It then becomes obvious why candidates do not score well as many simply set out the requirements of the IFRS without application to the scenario.

30 COATE (DEC 12 EXAM)

Key answer tips

This is a typical multi-standard question. Part (a) involves quite a high level of application skills and some students may find it difficult to pick out the relevant standards. However, parts (b), (c), and (d) signpost the issues much more clearly. Therefore, you may prefer to start with these parts.

As soon as you identify the issue (for instance, part (c) is about whether Coate controls Patten), then state the rules from the relevant standard (in this case, IFRS 10) for easy marks.

(a) Coate should recognise the certificates under inventories in accordance with IAS *2 Inventories*, as they are held for sale in the ordinary course of business.

The benefit of receiving green certificates should be accounted for as government grants in accordance with IAS *20 Accounting for Government Grants and Disclosure of Government Assistance*. The receipt of green certificates qualify as government grants in accordance with IAS 20, as they represent assistance by government in the form of resources provided to an entity in return for past compliance with certain conditions relating to its operating activities.

A government grant is recognised only when there is reasonable assurance that the entity will comply with any conditions attached to the grant and the grant will be received. This will arise upon completion of an audit to confirm the origin of production.

Income from the receipt of the certificates should be recognised in profit or loss in such a way as to match it with the related costs which they were intended to compensate. This could be shown under a general heading, such as 'Other income', or deducted in reporting the related expense. The certificates compensate Coate for electricity that it has been produced and whose production has been audited. Therefore, the grant income should be matched against the costs of producing this electricity, which would arguably be best presented by reducing cost of sales in the period.

The journal entry to record the certificates would be:

| Dr | Certificates (SOFP) | $fair value of certificate at receipt |
| Cr | Cost of sales (P/L) | $fair value of certificate at receipt |

Selling the green certificates to other electricity suppliers falls under IFRS 15 *Revenue from Contracts with Customers*. Each contract contains a single performance obligation, which is to provide green certificates. Revenue should be recognised when control of the certificates passes to these other electricity suppliers, which is likely to be the trade date. The amount of revenue recognised will be the consideration received or receivable by Coate, which should be equivalent to the fair value of the certificates at the trade date.

On the sale of a certificate, the following entries will be posted:

| Dr | Cash/receivables (SOFP) | $fair value of certificate at trade |
| Cr | Revenue (P/L) | $fair value of certificate at trade |

| Dr | Cost of sales (p/L) | $fair value of certificate at receipt |
| Cr | Certificate (SOFP) | $fair value of certificate at receipt |

Any unsold certificates at the reporting date will be held within inventories on the statement of financial position.

The accounting policies relating to the accounting treatment of the green certificates should be disclosed in the financial statements as required by IAS 1 *Presentation of Financial Statements*.

(b) The method of translation for foreign operations in IAS 21 *The Effects of Changes in Foreign Exchange Rates* requires monetary and non-monetary assets and liabilities to be translated at the closing rate, and income and expense items to be translated at the rate ruling at the date of the transaction or an average rate that approximates to the actual exchange rates.

All exchange differences relating to the retranslation of a foreign operation's opening net assets to the closing rate will have been recognised in other comprehensive income and presented in a separate component of equity. As such exchange differences have no cash flow effect, However, the opening net assets of Coate include foreign currency cash and cash equivalents; therefore the exchange difference arising on their retranslation at the closing rate for the current period will have been reflected in the closing balances in the financial statements.

The effect of exchange rate changes on cash and cash equivalents held or due in a foreign currency is reported in the statement of cash flows in order to reconcile cash and cash equivalents at the beginning and the end of the period. This amount is presented separately from cash flows from operating, investing and financing activities and includes the differences had those cash flows been reported at the end of period exchange rates.

(c)   In accordance with IFRS 10 *Consolidated Financial Statements,* an investor considers all relevant facts and circumstances when assessing whether it controls an investee.

An investor controls an investee if and only if the investor has all of the following elements:

*   power over the investee, that is the investor has existing rights that give it the ability to direct the relevant activities (the activities that significantly affect the investee's returns)

*   exposure, or rights, to variable returns from its involvement with the investee

*   the ability to use its power over the investee to affect the amount of the investor's returns.

The shareholder agreement shows that Coate has influence over the company. However, as shareholder consensus is required in respect of many significant decisions, Coate is unable to utilise the position it has at board level where it has the power to cast the majority of votes. Therefore, Coate does not control Patten.

Such terms of the agreement indicate the existence of a joint arrangement in accordance with IFRS 11 *Joint Arrangements,* that is a joint venture, as decisions are made at entity level operations and not regarding individual assets and liabilities.

As such, Coate is required to deconsolidate Patten as a subsidiary from its group accounts as it does not control the entity. Further, Coate should account for Patten in accordance with IAS 28 *Associates and Joint Ventures.* This will require Coate to equity account for Patten within the consolidated financial statements.

(d)   A prior period error is an omission from or misstatement in the entity's financial statements arising from a failure to use or misuse of reliable information that was available at the time of authorisation of the financial statements and could reasonably be expected to have been obtained and taken into account at the time of their preparation and presentation.

Tax expenses are difficult to estimate correctly and tax computations are open for review or audit by taxation authorities for a number of years after the end of the reporting period. The audit adjustments did not arise from a failure to use reliable information, which was available during previous reporting periods, as Coate correctly applied the provisions of tax law. The issues that the adjustments related to were transfer pricing issues for which there was a range of possible outcomes that were negotiated during 2012 with the taxation authorities. This indicates that these adjustments were effectively a change in an accounting estimate.

Further at 31 May 2011, Coate had accounted for all known issues arising from the audits to that date and the adjustment could not have been foreseen as at 31 May 2011, as the audit authorities changed the scope of the audit. Thus, the adjustments could not have been made at 31 May 2011 as the information and conditions did not exist at that date. Further, no penalties were expected to be applied by the taxation authorities, which indicates that there were no errors in the provision of information to the authorities. This again points to a change in accounting estimate and not a prior period error.

The tax adjustments resulting from the taxation authority audits should therefore be treated as a change in an accounting estimate and not as a prior period adjustment.

IAS 8 Accounting Policies, Changes in Accounting Estimates and Errors provides that the effect of a change in an accounting estimate should be recognised prospectively by including it in profit or loss in the period of the change.

IAS *12 Income Taxes* requires separate disclosure of the major components of the tax expense. It states that such components may include any adjustments recognised in the period for current tax of prior periods and the deferred tax expense. Thus, separate disclosure of these elements of the tax adjustments is required.

ACCA Marking scheme		
		Marks
(a)	1 mark per point up to maximum	7
(b)	1 mark per point up to maximum	5
(c)	1 mark per point up to maximum	6
(d)	1 mark per point up to maximum	5
	Professional marks	2
Total		**25**

31 BLACKCUTT (DEC 12 EXAM)

Key answer tips

Make sure that you look out for key phrases in the section B scenarios, as these will help you to identify the relevant standards. For instance, in part (a), holding land for 'capital appreciation' would suggest IAS 40 *Investment Property* but selling assets 'in the ordinary course of operations' implies IAS 2 *Inventories*. Similarly, in part (b), the fact that the vehicles are used for 'nearly all of the asset's life' and the discussion of 'legal title' is suggestive of a lease agreement.

(a) IAS *40 Investment Property* sets out the accounting treatment for investment property and the related disclosure requirements. It deals with the recognition, measurement and disclosure of investment property. The scope includes property held for capital appreciation or to earn rentals. Investment property is defined as property held by the owner or held on a finance lease to earn rentals or for capital appreciation or both, rather than for:

- use in producing or supplying goods or services or for administrative purposes or

- sale in the ordinary course of business.

The definition excludes owner-occupied property, property intended for sale in the ordinary course of business, property being constructed on behalf of third parties and property that is leased to a third party under a finance lease.

Where the fair value model under IAS 40 is applied, such a property is measured at fair value. Where an entity provides ancillary services to occupants of a property owned by the entity, the property is an investment property if such ancillary services are a relatively insignificant portion of the arrangement as a whole. Where, however, such services are a more significant portion, such as in a hotel, the property is treated not as investment property, but as an owner-occupied property.

Investment property should be recognised as an asset when it is probable that the future economic benefits associated with the property will flow to the entity and the cost of the property can be reliably measured.

Thus, the land that is owned by Blackcutt for capital appreciation which may be sold at any time in the future and the land that has no current purpose are both considered to be investment property under IAS 40. If the land has no current purpose, it is considered to be held for capital appreciation.

Blackcutt supplements its income by buying and selling property, and the housing department regularly sells some of these properties. As these sales are in the ordinary course of its operations and are routinely occurring, then the housing stock held for sale will be classified as inventory. The other properties, which are held to provide housing to low-income employees at below market rental, will not be treated as investment property as the property is not held for capital appreciation and the income just covers the cost of maintaining the properties and thus is not for profit. The property is held to provide housing services rather than rentals. The rental revenue is incidental to the purposes for which the property is held. This property will be accounted for under IAS 16 Property, *Plant and Equipment.* The property is treated as owner occupied as set out above.

(b)   An entity may enter into an arrangement that does not take the legal form of a lease but conveys a right to use an asset. An entity should use the Conceptual Framework for Financial Reporting in conjunction with IAS *17 Leases* to determine whether such arrangements are, or contain, leases that should be accounted for in accordance with the standard. Determining whether an arrangement is, or contains, a lease is based on the substance of the arrangement and requires an assessment of:

- the risks and rewards of the arrangement and how best to recognise them

- the right to use the asset or direct others to use the asset

- the right to control the use of the underlying asset by operating the asset or directing others to operate the asset

- who obtains much of the benefit from the asset.

In this case, the private sector provider purchases the vehicles and uses them exclusively for the local government organisation. The vehicles are ostensibly those of Blackcutt as they are painted with the local government name and colours. Blackcutt can use the vehicles and the vehicles are used in this connection for nearly all of the asset's life. In the event of the private sector provider's business ceasing, Blackcutt can re-possess the vehicles and carry on the refuse collection service. Thus, the arrangement fits the terms of a lease and Blackcutt should account for the vehicles as a finance lease.

The value associated with the lease can be obtained by considering the fair value of acquiring the vehicle. This will also be the initial lease obligation. The payment made by Blackcutt to the leasing company may be two-fold, representing the cost of the lease obligation and the service element relating to the cost of the collection of the waste.

(c)   A provision shall be recognised under IAS 37 *Provisions, Contingent Liabilities and Contingent Assets* when:

- there is a present obligation (legal or constructive) as a result of a past event

- it is probable that an outflow of resources embodying economic benefits or service potential will be required to settle the obligation

- a reliable estimate can be made of the amount of the obligation.

If the above conditions are not met, no provision shall be recognised.

In this case, the obligating event is the contamination of the land because of the virtual certainty of legislation requiring the clean up. Additionally, there is probably going to be an outflow of resources embodying economic benefits, because Blackcutt has no recourse against the entity or its insurance company. Therefore a provision is recognised for the best estimate of the costs of the clean up. As Blackcutt has no recourse against Chemco, recovery of the costs of clean up is not likely and hence no corresponding receivable should be recorded.

(d)   An asset is impaired if its carrying amount exceeds its recoverable amount. At the end of each reporting period, an assessment should take place as to whether there is any indication that an asset may be impaired. If any indication exists, the recoverable amount should be estimated.

Impairment in this case is indicated because the purpose for which the building is used has changed significantly from a place for educating students to a library and this is not anticipated to change for the foreseeable future.

Replacement cost could be used to determine fair value. However, per IFRS 13, this would require adjustment to reflect the characteristics, such as age, of the building. Therefore, depreciated replacement cost could be used an alternative.

An impairment loss using a depreciated replacement cost approach would be determined as follows:

Asset	Cost/replacement cost $000	Accumulated depreciation $000 – 6/25	Carrying amount/ replacement cost $000 30 November 2012
School	5,000	(1,200)	3,800
Library	2,100	504	(1,596)
Impairment loss			2,204

Thus Blackcutt would record the impairment loss of $2.204m.

ACCA Marking scheme		
		Marks
(a)	1 mark per point up to maximum	7
(b)	1 mark per point up to maximum	6
(c)	1 mark per point up to maximum	4
(d)	1 mark per point up to maximum	6
	Professional marks	2
Total		**25**

32   WILLIAM (JUNE 12 EXAM)

Key answer tips

This is a good question for practicing your knowledge of a range of core P2 standards. Remember that you are not simply asked for calculations and adjustments, but rather to 'discuss' the accounting treatment of the four issues.

(a)   **Classifying the lease**

A lease is classified as a finance lease if it transfers substantially the risks and rewards incident to ownership. All other leases are classified as operating leases. Situations that would normally lead to a lease being classified as a finance lease include the following:

- the lease transfers ownership of the asset to the lessee by the end of the lease term

- the lessee has the option to purchase the asset at a price which is expected to be sufficiently lower than fair value at the date the option becomes exercisable that, at the inception of the lease, it is reasonably certain that the option will be exercised

- the lease term is for the major part of the economic life of the asset, even if title is not transferred

- at the inception of the lease, the present value of the minimum lease payments amounts to at least substantially all of the fair value of the leased asset

- the lease assets are of a specialised nature such that only the lessee can use them without major modifications being made.

In this case the lease back of the building is for the major part of the building's economic life and the present value of the minimum lease payments amounts to all of the fair value of the leased asset. Therefore the lease should be recorded as a finance lease.

Accounting for the sale and leaseback

The sale of the building at $5.0 million creates a gain of $1.5 million ($5m – $3.5m). This is deferred and released to profit or loss over the lease term. Therefore, $75,000 ($1.5m/20 years) of income will be recorded in profit or loss in the current period.

This is a finance lease, so an asset and lease liability will be recognised at $5 million.

The asset will be depreciated over the shorter of its useful life and the lease term. Therefore, the depreciation expense in profit or loss in the current year will be $250,000 ($5m/20 years). The asset will have a carrying amount of $4,750,000 ($5m – $0.25m) at the reporting date.

Interest will be charged on the lease liability at a rate of 7%. This gives an interest expense of $350,000 ($5m × 7%) in profit or loss and increases the lease liability by the same amount. The cash payment of $441,000 will reduce the lease liability. The carrying amount of the liability at the reporting date will be $4,909,000 ($5m + $0.35m – $0.441m).

(b)   **Defined benefit plans**

The expense in profit or loss for the defined benefit plan will include:

- the net interest component

- the service cost component.

Net interest component

The net interest component is calculated by applying the discount rate at the start of the year to the net defined benefit asset or liability at the start of the year. The discount rate used is a high-quality corporate bond rate where there is a deep market in such bonds, and a government bond rate in other markets.

The service cost component

The service cost component is charged to profit or loss. It comprises:

- the current service cost

- any past service cost

- any gain or loss on settlement or curtailment.

Past-service costs are recognised as part of the service cost component in the period of a plan amendment. The plan benefits which were enhanced on 1 June 2011 would have to be immediately recognised and the unvested benefits would not be spread over five years from that date.

The transaction with the former employees will produce a loss on settlement. This will be the difference between the assets transferred and the present value of the obligation extinguished. Therefore a loss of $0.1m ($0.4m – $0.3m) will be charged to profit or loss as part of the service cost component.

Recognition of remeasurements

Remeasurements gains and losses are recognised immediately in 'other comprehensive income' (OCI). Remeasurements recognised in OCI cannot be recycled through profit or loss in subsequent periods.

Presentation

The benefit cost will be split between (i) the cost of benefits accrued in the current period (service cost) and benefit changes (past-service cost, settlements and curtailments); and (ii) finance expense or income. This analysis can be in the statement of profit or loss or in the notes.

(c)   Expenses in respect of cash-settled share-based payment transactions should be recognised over the period during which goods are received or services are rendered, and measured at the fair value of the liability. The fair value of the liability should be remeasured at each reporting date until settled. Changes in fair value are recognised in profit or loss.

The fair value of each share appreciation right (SAR) is made up of an intrinsic value and its time value. The time value reflects the fact that the holders of each SAR have the right to participate in future gains. Although the scheme vested in the previous year, there is a liability to pay cash to the SAR holders who have not yet exercised their rights.

This liability must be remeasured at the year-end giving rise to an additional expense:

Liability 31 May 2011 (17 × 500 × $14)	$119,000
Cash paid (7 × 500 × $21)	($73,500)
Expense (bal. fig.)	$74,500
Liability 31 May 2012 (10 × 500 × $24)	$120,000

Therefore the expense for the year is $74,500 and the liability at the year end is $120,000.

(d) IAS 37 *Provisions, Contingent Liabilities and Contingent Assets* describes contingent liabilities in two ways.

- Firstly, as reliably possible obligations whose existence will be confirmed only on the occurrence or non-occurrence of uncertain future events outside the entity's control, and

- Secondly, as present obligations that are not recognised because:

    - it is not probable that an outflow of economic benefits will be required to settle the obligation, or

    - the amount cannot be measured reliably.

Treatment in the individual financial statements

In Chrissy's financial statements contingent liabilities are not recognised but are disclosed and described in the notes to the financial statements. The disclosure should include an estimate of their potential financial effect and uncertainties relating to the amount or timing of any outflow, unless the possibility of settlement is remote.

Treatment in the consolidated financial statements

In a business combination, a contingent liability is recognised at the acquisition date if it meets the definition of a liability and if it can be measured.

This means William would recognise a liability of $4 million in the consolidated accounts. This will increase the goodwill arising on the acquisition of Chrissy.

ACCA Marking scheme		Marks
(a)	Definition of lease	3
	Leaseback principle	1
	Accounting	3
(b)	Accounting treatment	7
(c)	Cash-based payments	2
	Calculation	3
(d)	Contingent liability – discussion	4
	Communication skills	2
Total		**25**

33   ETHAN (JUNE 12 EXAM)

Key answer tips

In part (a), the examiner mentions 'fair values', 'business combinations' and 'deferred tax'. Make sure that you discuss all of these issues, otherwise you are throwing away easy marks. Part (b) is tricky and requires a detailed knowledge of IFRS 9. However, part (c) involves a relatively simple discussion of whether some shares meet the definition of debt or equity. This latter issue has proved popular in recent P2 exams.

(a)   IFRS 13 *Fair Value Measurement* acts as a common framework on how to measure the fair value when its determination is required or permitted by another IFRS. IFRS 13 defines the fair value of an asset as an 'exit price', which is the price that would be received to sell an asset or paid to transfer a liability in an orderly transaction between market participants at the measurement date. Fair value is a market-based measurement, not an entity-specific measurement, and fair value reflects current market conditions.

In IFRS 13, fair value measurements are categorised into a three-level hierarchy based on the type of inputs and are not based on a valuation method. The new hierarchy is defined as follows:

- Level 1 inputs are unadjusted quoted prices in active markets for items identical to the asset being measured.

- Level 2 inputs are inputs other than quoted prices in active markets included within Level 1 that are directly or indirectly observable.

- Level 3 inputs are unobservable inputs that are usually determined based on management's assumptions.

The use of discounted cash flows to determine fair value is based on level 3 inputs and should not be used if level 1 or 2 inputs exists.

Ethan's methods for determining whether goodwill is impaired, and the amount it is impaired by, are not in accordance with IAS 36 *Impairment of Assets*. The standard requires assets (or cash generating units (CGU) if not possible to conduct the review on an asset by asset basis) to be stated at the lower of carrying amount and recoverable amount. The recoverable amount is the higher of fair value less costs to sell and value in use. Fair value less costs to sell is a post-tax valuation taking account of deferred taxes.

According to IAS 36, the deferred tax liability should be included in calculating the carrying amount of the CGU, since the transaction price also includes the effect of the deferred tax and the purchaser assumes the tax risk. Therefore, the impairment testing of goodwill should be based on recoverable amount, rather than on the relationship between the goodwill and the deferred tax liability as assessed by Ethan.

Ethan should disclose both the methodology by which the recoverable amount of the CGU, and therefore goodwill, is determined and the assumptions underlying that methodology under the requirements of IAS 36. The standard requires Ethan to state the basis on which recoverable amount has been determined and to disclose the key assumptions on which it is based.

In accordance with IAS 36, where impairment testing takes place, goodwill is allocated to each individual real estate investment identified as a cash-generating unit (CGU). Periodically, but at least annually, the recoverable amount of the CGU is compared with its carrying amount. If this comparison results in the carrying amount being greater than the recoverable amount, the impairment is first allocated to the goodwill. Any further difference is subsequently allocated against the value of the investment property.

The recognition of deferred tax assets on losses carried forward is not in accordance with IAS 12 *Income Taxes.* Ethan is not able to provide convincing evidence to ensure that Ethan would be able to generate sufficient taxable profits against which the unused tax losses could be offset. Historically, Ethan's activities have generated either significant losses or very minimal profits; they have never produced large pre-tax profits. Therefore, in accordance with IAS 12, there is a need to produce convincing evidence from Ethan that it would be able to generate future taxable profits equivalent to the value of the deferred tax asset recognised.

Any decision would be based mainly on the following:

- history of Ethan's pre-tax profits

- previously published budget expectations and realised results in the past

- Ethan's expectations for the next few years; and

- announcements of new contracts.

There have been substantial negative variances arising between Ethan's budgeted and realised results. Also, Ethan has announced that it would not achieve the expected profit, but rather would record a substantial loss. Additionally, there is no indication that the losses were not of a type that could clearly be attributed to external events that might not be expected to recur. Thus the deferred tax asset should not be recognised or at the very least reduced.

(b)   Normally debt issued to finance Ethan's investment properties would be accounted for using amortised cost model. However, Ethan may apply the fair value option in IFRS 9 Financial Instruments as such application would eliminate or significantly reduce a measurement or recognition inconsistency between the debt liabilities and the investment properties to which they are related. The provision requires there to be a measurement or recognition inconsistency that would otherwise arise from measuring assets or liabilities or recognising the gains and losses on them on different bases. An entity is required to determine whether an accounting mismatch is created when the financial liability is first recognised, and this determination is not reassessed.

The IASB concludes that accounting mismatches may occur in a wide variety of circumstances and that financial reporting is best served by providing entities with the opportunity of eliminating such mismatches where that results in more relevant information. Ethan supported the application of the fair value option with the argument that there is a specific financial correlation between the factors that form the basis of the measurement of the fair value of the investment properties and the related debt. Particular importance was placed on the role played by interest rates, although it is acknowledged that the value of investment properties will also depend, to some extent, on rent, location and maintenance and other factors. For some investment properties, however, the value of the properties will be dependent on the movement in interest rates.

Under IFRS 9, entities with financial liabilities designated as FVTPL recognise changes in the fair value due to changes in the liability's credit risk directly in other comprehensive income (OCI). There is no subsequent recycling of the amounts in OCI to profit or loss, but accumulated gains or losses may be transferred within equity. The movement in fair value due to other factors would be recognised within profit or loss. However, if presenting the change in fair value attributable to the credit risk of the liability in OCI would create or enlarge an accounting mismatch in profit or loss, all fair value movements are recognised in profit or loss.

(c)   Ethan's classification of the B shares as equity instruments does not comply with IAS 32 *Financial Instruments: Presentation.*

IAS 32 defines a financial liability to include, amongst others, any liability that includes a contractual obligation to deliver cash or financial assets to another entity.

An instrument is an equity instrument rather than a financial liability if, and only if, the instrument does not include a contractual obligation either to deliver cash or another financial asset to the entity or to exchange financial assets or liabilities with another entity under conditions that are potentially unfavourable.

IAS 32 explains that when classifying a financial instrument in consolidated financial statements, an entity should consider all the terms and conditions agreed between members of a group and holders of the instrument, in determining whether the group as a whole has an obligation to deliver cash or another financial instrument in respect of the instrument or to settle it in a manner that results in classification as a liability.

Therefore, since the operating subsidiary is obliged to pay an annual cumulative dividend on the B shares and does not have discretion over the distribution of such dividend, the shares held by Ethan's external shareholders should be classified as a financial liability in Ethan's consolidated financial statements and not non-controlling interest. The shares being held by Ethan will be eliminated on consolidation as intercompany.

ACCA Marking scheme		
		Marks
(a)	Impairment testing	5
	Deferred taxation	6
(b)	Fair value option – IFRS 9	7
(c)	Financial liability	5
	Communication skills	2
		—
Total		**25**
		—

34   DECANY (DEC 11 EXAM)

Key answer tips

This is an unusual question about a group reorganisation. If you found it difficult, make sure that you debrief the answer fully.

(a)   (i)   Cash purchase of Rant by Ceed

	Decany $m	Ceed $m	Rant $m
Non-current assets			
Tangible non-current assets at depreciated cost/valuation	600	185	35
Cost of investment in Ceed	130		11
Cost of investment in Rant		98	
Loan receivable	98		
Current assets (155 + 25)/(130 – 98)/(98 + 20)	180	32	118
	1,008	315	164
Equity and reserves			
Share capital	140	75	35
Share premium		6	
Retained earnings	776	185.5	10
(750 – 2 + 3 + 25)/(220 – 25 – 9.5)			
	916	266.5	45
Non-current liabilities			
Long-term loan (12 + 98 – 4 = 106)	5	4	106
Provisions	2	9.5	
Current liabilities			
Dividend payable		25	
Trade payables	85	10	13
	1,008	315	164

Redundancy costs and provision for restructuring

The communication of the restructuring creates a valid and constructive expectation and should be provided for in the company incurring the cost. It should be provided for in Ceed's financial statements as Ceed will incur these costs.

Redundancy costs should be recognised at the present value of the future cash flows:

	$m
$4m \times 1/1.03$	3.9
$6m \times 1/1.03^2$	5.6
	9.5

The provision for restructuring of $9.5m will be shown in Ceed's and overall restructuring provision in Decany's records ($2 million).

Purchase of Rant

The cost of the investment in Ceed's financial statements will be $98 million and current assets will be reduced by the same amount. Decany will record a loan receivable of $98 million and a profit of $3 million. The loan to Rant will be recorded in long-term loans and in current assets.

Transfer of land

Nominal value of shares allotted		5
Fair value of consideration received		
Value of land	$15m	
Less mortgage	($4m)	11
Premium on shares allotted		6

The value of the shares issued to Decany would be the land less the mortgage, which is $11 million.

(ii) IAS 27 allows the cost of an investment in a subsidiary, in limited reorganisations, to be based on the carrying amount of its share of the equity items shown in the separate financial statements of the original parent at the date of the reorganisation rather than its fair value. This relief is limited to reorganisations where a new parent is inserted above an existing parent of a group (or entity), and:

(i) The new parent obtains control of the original parent (or entity) by issuing equity instruments in exchange for existing equity instruments of the original parent (or entity)

(ii) The assets and liabilities of the new group and the original group are the same immediately before and after the reorganisation; and

(iii) The owners of the original parent (or entity) before the reorganisation have the same absolute and relative interests after the reorganisation.

It appears that the reorganisation meets these criteria as the shares issued for the purchase of the land are non-voting shares and all other conditions appear to be met. Any group reorganisation establishing new parent entities should be carefully assessed to establish whether it meets the conditions imposed to be effectively accounted for on a 'carry-over basis' rather than at fair value.

IAS 27 requires all dividends from a subsidiary, jointly controlled entity or associate to be recognised in profit or loss in its separate financial statement.

Per IAS 36, the payment of such dividends requires the entity to consider whether there is an indicator of impairment. An indicator of impairment exists if:

- The dividend exceeds the total comprehensive income of the subsidiary

- The carrying amount of the investment exceeds the amount of net assets (including associated goodwill) recognised in the consolidated financial statements.

None of the above criteria affect the payment of the dividend by Ceed.

Care will need to be taken as to what constitutes a dividend (defined as a distribution of profits). Management will also need to carefully consider the timing of the dividends, particularly as a detailed impairment test will be needed when dividends are declared.

(b) The plan has no impact on the group financial statements as all of the internal transactions will be eliminated on consolidation but does affect the individual accounts of the companies.

The reconstruction only masks the problem facing Rant. It does not solve or alter the business risk currently being faced by the group.

The proposed provision for restructuring has to meet the requirements of IAS 37 *Provisions, Contingent Liabilities and Contingent Assets* before it can be included in the financial statements. There must be a detailed formal plan produced and a valid expectation in those affected that the plan will be carried out. The provision appears to be large considering that the reconstruction does not involve major relocation of assets and there is a separate provision for redundancy.

The transactions outlined in the plans are essentially under common control and must be viewed in this light. This plan overcomes the short-term cash flow problem of Rant and results in an increase in the accumulated reserves. The plan does show the financial statements of the individual entities in a better light except for the significant increase in long-term loans in Rant's statement of financial position. The profit on the sale of the land from Rant to Ceed will be eliminated on consolidation.

In the financial statements of Rant, the investment in Ceed should be accounted for under IFRS 9. There is now cash available for Rant and this may make the plan attractive. However, the dividend from Ceed to Decany will reduce the accumulated reserves of Ceed but if paid in cash will reduce the current assets of Ceed to a critical level.

The purchase consideration relating to Rant may be a transaction at an overvalue in order to secure the financial stability of the former entity. A range of values are possible which are current value, carrying amount or possibly at zero value depending on the purpose of the reorganisation. Another question which arises is whether the sale of Rant gives rise to a realised profit. Further, there may be a question as to whether Ceed has effectively made a distribution. This may arise where the purchase consideration was well in excess of the fair value of Rant. An alternative to a cash purchase would be a share exchange. In this case, local legislation would need to be reviewed in order to determine the requirements for the setting up of any share premium account.

ACCA Marking scheme				
				Marks
(a)	(i)	Decany		5
		Ceed		5
		Rant		3
				———
			Maximum	13
				———
	(ii)	IAS 27		5
(b)		Discussion – subjective		5
		Professional marks		2
				———
Total				25
				———

35 SCRAMBLE (DEC 11 EXAM)

Key answer tips

This standard requires a detailed knowledge of IAS 38 *Intangible Assets* and IAS 36 *Impairment of Assets*. Impairments are a timely issue in the current economic climate. Therefore, if you struggled with this question, then you should use this answer to enhance your knowledge of this accounting standard.

(a) **IAS 38 *Intangible Assets***

The internally generated intangibles are capitalised in accordance with IAS 38, *Intangible Assets*. It appears that Scramble is correctly expensing the maintenance costs as these do not enhance the asset over and above original benefits.

The decision to keep intangibles at historical cost is a matter of choice and therefore policy. Scramble's accounting policy in this regard is acceptable.

An intangible asset can have a finite or indefinite life and IAS 38 states that an intangible asset shall be regarded by the entity as having an indefinite useful life when, based on an analysis of all of the relevant factors, there is no foreseeable limit to the period over which the asset is expected to generate net cash inflows for the entity.

An indefinite life does not mean infinite and IAS 38 comments that given the history of rapid changes in technology, computer software and many other intangible assets are susceptible to technological obsolescence and the useful life may be short.

If the life of an intangible is indefinite then, in accordance with IAS 36, an entity is required to test for impairment by comparing its recoverable amount with its carrying amount

(i)   annually, and

(ii)   whenever there is an indication that the intangible asset may be impaired.

The useful life of an intangible asset that is not being amortised shall be reviewed each period to determine whether events and circumstances continue to support an indefinite useful life assessment for that asset. To determine whether the asset is impaired, IAS 36 must be applied and the intangible asset's recoverable amount should be compared to its carrying amount.

IAS 36 *Impairment of Assets*

The way in which Scramble determines its value in use cash flows for impairment testing purposes does not comply with IAS 36 *Impairment of Assets*.

Cash flow projections should be based on reasonable and supportable assumptions, the most recent budgets and forecasts, and extrapolation for periods beyond budgeted projections. Management should assess the reasonableness of its assumptions by examining the causes of differences between past cash flow projections and actual cash flows. This process does not seem to have been carried out by Scramble.

Additionally, cash flow projections should relate to the asset in its current condition and future restructurings to which the entity is not committed and expenditures to improve or enhance the asset's performance should not be anticipated. The cash flows utilised to determine the value in use were not estimated for the asset in its current condition, as they included those which were expected to be incurred in improving the games and cash inflows expected as a result of those improvements.

Finally, estimates of future cash flows should not include cash inflows or outflows from financing activities, or income tax receipts or payments. Scramble has taken into account the tax effects of future cash flows.

(b) **The discount rate**

The calculation of the discount rate is not wholly in accordance with the requirements of IAS 36 because the discount rate applied did not reflect the market assessment of the contributing factors. According to IAS 36, the discount rate to be applied in these circumstances is a pre-tax rate that reflects the current market assessment of the time value of money and the risks specific to the assets for which the future cash flow estimated have not been adjusted. IAS 36 specifies that a rate that reflects the current market assessment of the time value of the money and the risks specific to the assets is the return that the investors would require if they chose an investment that would generate cash flows of amounts, timing and risk profile equivalent to those that the entity expects to derive from the assets.

If a market-determined asset-specific rate is not available, a surrogate must be used that reflects the time value of money over the asset's life as well as country risk, currency risk, price risk, and cash flow risk. This would include considering the entity's own weighted average cost of capital, the entity's incremental borrowing rate and other market borrowing rates. Therefore, the inputs to the determination of the discount rates should be based on current credit spread levels in order to reflect the current market assessment of the time value of the money and asset specific risks. The credit spread input applied should reflect the current market assessment of the credit spread at the moment of impairment testing, irrespective of the fact that Scramble did not intend taking any additional financing.

Disclosures

Scramble has not complied with the disclosure requirements of IAS 36, in that neither the events and circumstances that led to the impairment loss nor the amounts attributable to the two CGUs were separately disclosed. IAS 36 requires disclosure of the amount of the loss and as regards the cash-generating unit, a description of the amount of impairment loss by class of assets. The fact that the circumstances were common knowledge in the market is not a substitution for the disclosure of the events and circumstances.

(c)   According to IAS 38, the three critical attributes of an intangible asset are:

(1)   Identifiability

(2)   control (power to obtain benefits from the asset)

(3)   future economic benefits (such as revenues or reduced future costs).

An intangible asset is identifiable when it is separable or arises from contractual or other legal rights, regardless of whether those rights are transferable or separable from the entity or from other rights and obligations.

IAS 38 requires an entity to recognise an intangible asset if, and only if, it is probable that the future economic benefits that are attributable to the asset will flow to the entity; and the cost of the asset can be measured reliably.

Registration rights

The registration rights meet the definition and recognition criteria of IAS 38 because they arise from contractual rights. Scramble has control because the right can be transferred or extended and the economic benefits result from the fee income Scramble can earn as fans come to see the player play.

Under IAS 38 the cost of separately acquired assets comprises: (a) its purchase price, including import duties and non-refundable purchase taxes, after deducting trade discounts and rebates; and (b) any directly attributable cost of preparing the asset for its intended use. IAS 38 gives examples of directly attributable costs which include professional fees arising directly from bringing the asset to its working conditions. In this business, the players' registration rights meet the definition of intangible assets and the agents' fees represent professional fees incurred in bringing the asset into use.

The requirements above apply to costs incurred initially to acquire or internally generate an intangible asset and those incurred subsequently to add to, replace part of, or service it. Thus the agents' fees paid on the extension of players' contracts can be considered costs incurred to service the player registration rights and should be treated as intangible assets.

The right to revenue

Where an entity purchases the rights to a proportion of the revenue that a football club generates from ticket sales, it will generally have acquired a financial asset because it has a contractual right to receive cash. Note that If Rashing had purchased the rights to sell the tickets for a football club, and was responsible for selling the tickets, then this would create an intangible asset.

In this instance Rashing should recognise a financial asset in accordance with IFRS 9. The asset would be classed as either amortised cost or fair value depending on Rashing's model for managing the financial asset and the contractual cash flow characteristics of the financial asset. A financial instrument would be classed as amortised cost if both of the following conditions are met:

(a)   The asset is held within a business model whose objective is to hold assets to collect contractual cash flows.

(b)   The contractual terms of the financial asset give rise on specified dates to cash flows that are solely payments of principal and interest on the principal amount outstanding.

Rashing does not meet these criteria because Rashing's receipts are not solely payments of interest and capital but are based on ticket revenues and match attendance. As such, the fair value model is more appropriate.

36 LOCKFINE (JUNE 11 EXAM)

Key answer tips

Easy marks can be obtained in this question through stating your knowledge of IAS 38 *Intangible Assets,* IFRS 13 *Fair Value Measurement* and IAS 37 *Provisions, Contingent Liabilities and Contingent Assets.* Many students, however, would have a relatively weak knowledge of IFRS 1. If you struggled with this standard, make sure that you fully debrief the answer and learn from it.

(a) According to IFRS 1, assets carried at cost (e.g. property, plant and equipment) may be measured at their fair value at the date of the opening IFRS statement of financial position. Fair value becomes the 'deemed cost' going forward under the IFRS cost model. Deemed cost is an amount used as a surrogate for cost or depreciated cost at a given date.

Fair value is defined in IFRS 13 as the price that would be received to sell an asset or paid to transfer a liability in an orderly transaction between market participants at the measurement date.

In IFRS 13, fair value measurements are categorised into a three-level hierarchy based on the type of inputs. The hierarchy is defined as follows:

- Level 1 inputs are unadjusted quoted prices in active markets for items identical to the asset being measured.

- Level 2 inputs are inputs other than quoted prices in active markets included within Level 1 that are directly or indirectly observable.

- Level 3 inputs are unobservable inputs that are usually determined based on management's assumptions.

The selling agents' estimates provided very little information about the valuation methods and underlying assumptions. It may be that the valuations are comprised of level 2 inputs but, dependent on the level of adjustment made to observable prices, they may be based on level 3 inputs. Level 3 inputs should not be used if level 1 or 2 inputs are available. It is therefore vital to understand more clearly the valuation methods adopted.

It may not be prudent to value the boats at the average of the higher end of the range of values, particularly if these values involve a large degree of judgement.

Therefore, Lockfine was not in breach of IFRS 1 but it is unclear whether fair value has been determined in accordance with IFRS 13.

(b)   In accordance with IFRS 1, an entity which, during the transition process to IFRS, decides to retrospectively apply IFRS 3 to a certain business combination must apply that decision consistently to all business combinations occurring between the date on which it decides to adopt IFRS 3 and the date of transition. The decision to apply IFRS 3 cannot be made selectively.

The entity must consider all similar transactions carried out in that period; and when allocating values to the various assets (including intangibles) and liabilities of the entity acquired in a business combination to which IFRS 3 is applied, an entity must necessarily have documentation to support its purchase price allocation. If there is no such basis, alternative or intuitive methods of price allocation cannot be used unless they are based on the strict application of the standards.

IAS 38 requires an entity to recognise an intangible asset, whether purchased or self-created (at cost) if, and only if:

- it is probable that the future economic benefits that are attributable to the asset will flow to the entity; and

- the cost of the asset can be measured reliably.

Lockfine was unable to obtain a reliable value for the fishing rights, and thus it was not possible to them to be separately recognised. The rights have therefore been correctly subsumed within goodwill.

The goodwill arising on acquisition should be accounted for in accordance with IAS 36 which requires an annual impairment test.

(c)   An intangible asset is an identifiable non-monetary asset without physical substance. Thus, the three critical attributes of an intangible asset are:

(a)   identifiability

(b)   control (power to obtain benefits from the asset)

(c)   future economic benefits (such as revenues or reduced future costs)

The electronic maps meet the above three criteria for recognition as an intangible asset as they are identifiable, Lockfine has control over them and future revenue will flow from the maps. The maps will be recognised because there are future economic benefits attributable to the maps and the cost can be measured reliably. After initial recognition the benchmark treatment is that intangible assets should be carried at cost less any amortisation and impairment losses and thus Lockfine's accounting policy is in compliance with IAS 38.

An intangible asset has an indefinite useful life when there is no foreseeable limit to the period over which the asset is expected to generate net cash inflows for the entity. The term indefinite does not mean infinite.

An important underlying assumption in assessing the useful life of an intangible asset is that it reflects only the level of future maintenance expenditure required to maintain the asset 'at its standard of performance assessed at the time of estimating the asset's useful life'. The indefinite useful life should not depend on planned future expenditure in excess of that required to maintain the asset. The company's accounting practice in this regard seems to be in compliance with IAS 38.

IAS 1 *Presentation of Financial Statements* requires that an entity discloses accounting policies relevant to an understanding of its financial statements. Given that the internally generated intangible assets are a material amount of total assets, more information should have been disclosed.

(d)   The restructuring plans should be considered separately as they relate to separate and different events.

According to IAS 37, *Provisions, Contingent Liabilities and Contingent Assets,* a constructive obligation to restructure arises only when an entity:

(a)   Has a detailed formal restructuring plan identifying at least:

(i)   the business activities, or part of the business activities, concerned

(ii)   the principal locations affected

(iii)   the location, function and approximate number of employees who will be compensated for terminating their services

(iv)   the expenditure that will be undertaken

(v)   the implementation date of the plan; and, in addition,

(b)   Has raised a valid expectation among the affected parties that it will carry out the restructuring by starting to implement that plan or announcing its main features to those affected by it.

For a plan to be sufficient to give rise to a constructive obligation when communicated to those affected by it, its implementation needs to be planned to begin as soon as possible and to be completed in a timeframe that makes significant changes to the plan unlikely.

In the case of Plan A, a provision for restructuring should not be recognised. A constructive obligation arises only when a company has a detailed formal plan and makes an announcement of the plan to those affected by it. However, neither the specific fleet nor employees have been identified as yet. The plan to date does not provide sufficient detail that would permit Lockfine to recognise a constructive obligation.

In the case of Plan B, a public announcement constitutes a constructive obligation to restructure if it is made in such a way and in such detail that it gives rise to a valid expectation. It is not necessary that the individual employees of Lockfine be notified as the employee representatives have been notified. However, It will be necessary to look at the nature of the negotiations and if the discussions are about the terms of the redundancy or a change in plans. Assuming the former, then a provision can be recognised.

ACCA Marking scheme		
		Marks
(a)	1 mark per point maximum	6
(b)	1 mark per point maximum	6
(c)	1 mark per point maximum	6
(d)	1 mark per point maximum	5
	Professional marks	2
Total		**25**

37 ALEXANDRA (JUNE 11 EXAM)

Key answer tips

This is a mixed-standards question. Do not be put off by the level of detail in the answer as this would not be expected from even the most well-prepared of students. Solid marks can be obtained by stating your knowledge of the relevant standards, even if you then reach an incorrect conclusion about the accounting treatment.

(a)   The loan should have been classified as short-term debt.

According to IAS *1, Presentation of financial statements,* a liability should be classified as current if it is due to be settled within 12 months after the date of the statement of financial position. If an issuer breaches an undertaking under a long-term loan agreement on or before the date of the statement of financial position, such that the debt becomes payable on demand, the loan is classified as current even if the lender agrees, after the statement of financial position date, not to demand payment as a consequence of the breach.

It follows that a liability should also be classified as current if a waiver is issued before the date of the statement of financial position, but does not give the entity a period of grace ending at least 12 months after the date of the statement of financial position. The default on the interest payment in November represented a default that could have led to a claim from the bondholders to repay the whole of the loan immediately, inclusive of incurred interest and expenses.

As a further waiver was issued after the date of the statement of financial position, and only postponed payment for a short period, Alexandra did not have an unconditional right to defer the payment for at least 12 months after the date of the statement of financial position as required by the standard in order to be classified as long-term debt.

Alexandra should also consider the impact that a recall of the borrowing would have on the going concern status. If the going concern status is questionable then Alexandra would need to provide additional disclosure surrounding the uncertainty and the possible outcomes if waivers are not renewed. If Alexandra ceases to be a going concern then the financial statements would need to be prepared on a break-up basis.

(b)   IFRS 15 *Revenue from Contracts with Customers* requires entities to decide whether revenue from satisfying a performance obligation is recognised at a point in time or over time. Maintenance services are simultaneously provided and consumed and so revenue should be recognised over time based on progress towards the satisfaction of the performance obligation at the date of the statement of financial position.

The previous policy applied of recognising revenue on invoice at the commencement of the contract did not comply with IFRS 15. The subsequent change in policy to one which recognised revenue over the contract term, therefore, was the correction of an error rather than a change in estimate and should have been presented as such in accordance with IAS 8 *Accounting Policies, Changes in Accounting Estimates and Errors* and been effected retrospectively.

Given that the maintenance contract with the customer involved the rendering of services over a two-year period, the income from maintenance contracts that has been recognised in full in the year ended 30 April 2010, needs to be split between that occurring in the year and that to be recognised in future periods. This will result in a net debit to opening retained earnings as less income will be recognised in the prior year. Comparative figures for the statement of profit or loss require restatement accordingly.

In the current year, the maintenance contracts have already been dealt with following the correct accounting policy. The income from the maintenance contracts deferred from the revised opening balance will be recognised in the current year as far as they relate to that period. As the maintenance contracts only run for two years, it is likely that most of the income deferred from the prior year will be recognised in the current period. The outcome of this is that there will be less of an impact on the statement of profit or loss as although this year's profits have reduced by $6m, there will be an addition of profits resulting from the recognition of maintenance income deferred from last year.

(c)   The exclusion of the remuneration of the non-executive directors from key management personnel disclosures did not comply with the requirements of IAS 24 *Related Party Disclosures* which defines key management personnel as those persons having authority and responsibility for planning, directing and controlling the activities of the entity, directly or indirectly, including any director (whether executive or otherwise) of that entity.

Additionally, Alexandra did not comply with the requirement for key management personnel remuneration to be analysed by category. The explanation of Alexandra is not acceptable.

IAS 24 states that an entity should disclose key management personnel compensation in total and for each of the following categories:

(a)   short-term employee benefits

(b)   post-employment benefits

(c)   other long-term benefits

(d)   termination benefits; and

(e)   share-based payment.

Providing such disclosure will not give information on what individual board members earn as only totals for each category need be disclosed, hence will not breach any cultural protocol. However legislation from local government and almost certainly local corporate governance will require greater disclosure for public entities such as Alexandra.

(d)   A defined contribution plan is one where an entity pays fixed contributions to a fund and has no further obligation to pay further contributions if the fund does not have sufficient assets to pay the employee benefits. Alexandra's pension arrangement does not meet the criteria as outlined in IAS 19 *Employee Benefits* for defined contribution accounting on the grounds that the risks, although potentially limited, remained with Alexandra.

The following factors support this:

- The premium for the employee is fixed and the balance of the required premium rests with Alexandra, exposing the entity to changes in premiums depending on the return on the investments by the insurer and changes in actuarial assumptions.

- The insurance contract states that when an employee leaves Alexandra and transfers his pension to another fund, Alexandra is liable for or is refunded the difference between the benefits the employee is entitled to based on the pension formula and the entitlement based on the insurance premiums paid. Alexandra is therefore exposed to actuarial risks, i.e. a shortfall or over funding as a consequence of differences between returns compared to assumptions or other actuarial differences.

- The agreement between Alexandra and the employees does not include any indication that, in the case of a shortfall in the funding of the plan, the entitlement of the employees may be reduced. Consequently, Alexandra has a legal or constructive obligation to pay further amounts if the insurer did not pay all future employee benefits relating to employee service in the current and prior periods.

Since the risks of the plan remain with Alexandra, it should be accounted for as a defined benefit plan.

ACCA Marking scheme		
		Marks
(a)	1 mark per point maximum	6
(b)	1 mark per point maximum	5
(c)	1 mark per point maximum	5
(d)	1 mark per point maximum	7
	Professional marks	2
		——
Total		**25**
		——

38 MARGIE (DEC 10 EXAM) *Walk in the footsteps of a top tutor*

Key answer tips

This is a multi-part question which focuses upon application of IFRS 2 and other reporting standards. Each part is self-contained, so can be answered in the order you prefer. Remember to clearly identify which part you are answering, particularly if you are answering them out of order. The marks attributable for each part of the question give a good indication of how to allocate your time.

Tutorial note

Determine whether or not the transaction falls within the scope of IFRS 2. If not, explain why not and then continue by explaining the required accounting treatment.

(a)   The arrangement is not within the scope of IFRS 2 *Share-based payment* because the contract may be settled net and has not been entered into in order to satisfy Margie's expected purchase, sale or usage requirements.

Margie appears to have entered into a derivative contract to pay or receive a cash amount. IFRS 9 *Financial Instruments* requires derivatives to be measured at fair value through profit or loss, unless it is part of a hedging arrangement.

Contracts to buy or sell non-financial items are within the scope of IFRS 9 if they can be settled net in cash or another financial asset and are not entered into and held for the purpose of the receipt or delivery of a non-financial item in accordance with the entity's expected purchase, sale, or usage requirements. Contracts to buy or sell non-financial items are inside the scope if net settlement occurs. The following situations constitute net settlement:

(a)   the terms of the contract permit either counterparty to settle net

(b)   there is a past practice of net settling similar contracts

(c)   there is a past practice, for similar contracts, of taking delivery of the underlying and selling it within a short period after delivery to generate a profit from short-term fluctuations in price, or from a dealer's margin; or

(d)   the non-financial item is readily convertible to cash.

The contract will be accounted for as a derivative and should be valued at fair value (asset or liability at fair value) through profit or loss. Initially the contract should be valued at nil as under the terms of a commercial contract the value of 2,500 shares should equate to the value of 350 tonnes of wheat. At each period end the contract would be remeasured to fair value and it would be expected that differences will arise between the values of wheat and Margie shares as their respective market values will be dependent on a number of differing factors. The net difference should be taken to profit or loss.

This arrangement cannot be hedge accounted for because the purchase of wheat is not highly probable or a firm commitment.

Tutorial note

Determine how the award should be accounted for on acquisition of Antalya. You should consider both the original award made by Antalya and also the award made by Margie upon acquisition of the subsidiary.

(b)   Share-based payment awards exchanged for awards held by the acquiree's employees are measured in accordance with IFRS 2 *Share-based payment*. If the acquirer is obliged to replace the awards, some or all of the fair value of the replacement awards must be included in the consideration. The amount not included in the consideration will be recognised as a compensation expense. If the acquirer is not obliged to exchange the acquiree's awards, the acquirer does not adjust the consideration even if the acquirer does replace the awards.

A portion of the fair value of the award granted by Margie is accounted for under IFRS 3 and a portion under IFRS 2, even though no post-combination services are required. The amount included in the cost of the business combination is the fair value of Antalya's award at the acquisition date ($20 million). Any additional amount, which in this case is $2 million, is accounted for as a post-combination expense under IFRS 2. This amount is recognised immediately as a post-combination expense because no post-combination services are required.

Tutorial note

This part of the question contains two separate issues – ensure that you address both issues in turn.

(c)　The shares issued to the employees were issued in their capacity as shareholders and not in exchange for their services. The employees were not required to complete a period of service in exchange for the shares. Thus the transaction is outside the scope of IFRS 2.

As regards the purchase of the building, Grief did not act in its capacity as a shareholder. Instead, Margie approached the company with the proposal to buy the building. Grief was a supplier of a building and as such the transaction comes under IFRS 2. The building is valued at fair value with equity being credited with the same amount.

Tutorial note

This part of the question considers how to account for a share-based payment scheme when the vesting period is uncertain at the grant date. When the scheme is measured for the first time for inclusion in the financial statements, the cost should be spread over the expected vesting period at that date. Subsequent treatment will depend upon whether the actual vesting period is shorter or longer than the expected vesting period.

(d)　Where the vesting period is linked to a market performance condition, an entity must estimate the expected vesting period. If the actual vesting period is shorter than estimated, the charge should be accelerated in the period that the entity delivers the cash or equity instruments to the counterparty. When the vesting period is longer, the expense is recognised over the originally estimated vesting period.

Margie expects the market condition to be met in 2011 and thus anticipates that it will charge $1 million per annum until that date (100 × 4,000 × $10 divided by 4 years). As the market condition has been met in the year to 30 November 2010, the expense charged in the year would be $2 million ($4 million – $2 million already charged) as the remaining expense should be accelerated and charged in the year.

ACCA Marking scheme		Marks
(a)	Discussion IFRS 9	5
	Conclusion	2
(b)	Discussion of IFRS 3/IFRS 2	4
	Calculation	2
(c)	Discussion	4
(d)	Discussion	4
	Calculation	2
	Professional	2
		―
Total		**25**
		―

Examiner's comments

This question was a case study type question based around share-based transactions. The question was not totally related to IFRS 2 but also to other standards where shares are exchanged in a transaction.

The first scenario dealt with a contract to purchase a commodity with shares. The purchase price was to be settled in cash at an amount equal to the value of an amount of the entity's shares. The entity wished to treat the transaction as a share based payment transaction under IFRS 2 *Share-based Payment*. Many candidates did not recognise the fact that the transaction should be dealt with under IFRS 9. This type of transaction has been examined recently but candidates did not seem to recognise the nature of the transaction.

In part (b) the entity acquired 100% of the share capital of another entity in a business combination and this entity had previously granted a share-based payment to its employees. A replacement award was issued a replacement award that did not require post-combination services. Candidates had to understand the interaction of IFRS 2 and IFRS 3 in order to answer the question. The question was not well answered although candidates did seem to realise that there was a post combination expense to be taken into account.

In part (c), the entity issued shares during the financial year which were subscribed for by employees who were existing shareholders, and some were issued to an entity for the purchase of a building. Candidates often felt that the first transaction was within the scope of IFRS 2 and the second was not. Unfortunately this assumption was incorrect with the correct answer being that the first transaction was outside the scope and the second was within scope.

In part (d) the entity granted share options to each of its employees with the options vesting in the future provided the employee has remained in the company's service until that time. The terms and conditions of the options had a market condition. Candidates generally seemed to understand the effect of a market condition and answered this part of the question very well. Overall this question was not as well answered as the other questions on the paper.

39   GREENIE (DEC 10 EXAM) *Walk in the footsteps of a top tutor*

Key answer tips

As this is a discussion question dealing with several issues, you should deal with each in turn, clearly identifying which part of the question requirement you are dealing with, particularly if you answer the various parts out of order. Whilst some marks will be available for stating definitions from reporting standards, additional credit will be earned for application of the definitions to the circumstances outlined within the question. As a final point, remember that you will earn appropriate credit for discussing relevant issues and points, even if you arrive at a different conclusion to the suggested answer, so ensure that you apply good exam technique and answer all parts of the question requirement.

Tutorial note

A good starting point is a definition from a relevant reporting standard, which can then be applied to the scenario within the question.

(a)   IAS 37 states that an entity must recognise a provision if, and only if:

(i)   a present obligation (legal or constructive) has arisen as a result of a past event (the obligating event),

(ii)   payment to settle the obligation is probable ('more likely than not'), and

(iii)   the amount can be estimated reliably.

An obligating event is an event that creates a legal or constructive obligation and, therefore, results in an enterprise having no realistic alternative but to settle the obligation.

At the date of the financial statements, there was no current obligation for Greenie. In particular, no action had been brought in connection with the accident. It was not yet probable that an outflow of resources would be required to settle the obligation. Thus no provision is required.

Tutorial note

Again, state the relevant definition and apply it to the circumstances within the question.

Greenie may need to disclose a contingent liability. IAS 37 defines a contingent liability as:

(a)   a possible obligation that has arisen from past events and whose existence will be confirmed by the occurrence or not of uncertain future events; or

(b)   a present obligation that has arisen from past events but is not recognised because:

(i)   it is not probable that an outflow of resources will occur to settle the obligation; or

(ii)   the amount of the obligation cannot be measured with sufficient reliability.

IAS 37 requires that entities should not recognise contingent liabilities but should disclose them, unless the possibility of an outflow of economic resources is remote. It appears that Greenie should disclose a contingent liability. The fact that the real nature and extent of the damages, including whether they qualify for compensation and details of any compensation payments remained to be established all indicated the level of uncertainty attaching to the case. The degree of uncertainty is not such that the possibility of an outflow of resource could be considered remote. Had this been the case, no disclosure under IAS 37 would have been required.

Thus the conditions for establishing a liability are not fulfilled. However, a contingent liability should be disclosed as required by IAS 37.

The possible recovery of these costs from the insurer gives rise to consideration of whether a contingent asset should be disclosed. Given the status of the expert report, any information as to whether judicial involvement is likely will not be available until 2011. Thus this contingent asset is more possible than probable. As such no disclosure of the contingent asset should be included.

Tutorial note

This part of the question deals with application of knowledge relating to circumstances when significant influence or control may be exercised. You should state and apply relevant definitions within your answer. As the question requirement is for a discussion, you should try to consider all relevant circumstances, and try to avoid writing a 'one-sided' justification of your conclusion.

(b)   Greenie appears to have significant influence over Manair, and therefore, it should be accounted for as an associate. According IAS 28 *Investments in Associates*, significant influence is the power to participate in the financial and operating decisions of the investee but is not control or joint control over the policies.

Where an investor holds 20% or more of the voting power of the investee, it is presumed that the investor has significant influence unless it can be clearly demonstrated that this is not the case. If the investor holds less than 20% of the voting power of the investee, it is presumed that the investor does not have significant influence, unless such influence can be clearly demonstrated.

In certain cases, whether significant influence exists should also be assessed when an investor holds less than 20% especially where it appears that the substance of the arrangement indicates significant influence. Greenie holds 19.9% of the voting shares and it appears as though there has been an attempt to avoid accounting for Manair as an associate. The fact that one investor holds a majority share of the voting power can indicate that other investors do not have significant influence. A substantial or majority ownership by an investor does not, however, necessarily preclude other investors from having significant influence. IAS 28 states that the existence of significant influence by an investor is usually evidenced in one or more of the following ways:

(i)   representation on the board of directors or equivalent governing body of the investee

(ii)   participation in the policy-making process

(iii)   material transactions between the investor and the investee

(iv)   interchange of managerial personnel; or

(v)   provision of essential technical information.

The shareholders' agreement allows Greenie to participate in some decisions. It needs to be determined whether these include financial and operating policy decisions of Manair, although this is very likely. The representation on the board of directors combined with the additional rights Greenie had under the shareholders' agreement, give Greenie the power to participate in some policy decisions. Additionally, Greenie had sent a team of management experts to give business advice to the board of Manair.

In addition, there is evidence of material transactions between the investor and the investee and indications that Greenie provided Manair with maintenance and technical services. Both these facts are examples of how significant influence might be evidenced.

Based on an assessment of all the facts, it appears that Greenie has significant influence over Manair and that Manair should be considered an associate and accounted for using the equity method of accounting.

Finally as it is likely that Manair is an associated undertaking of Greenie the transactions themselves would be deemed related party transactions. Greenie would need to disclose within its own financial statements the relationship, an outline of the transactions including their total value, outstanding balances including any debts deemed irrecoverable or doubtful.

Tutorial note

This part of the question requires discussion of two issues – recognition of the franchise right and classification of irredeemable preference shares. You should ensure that you address both issues to maximise the marks earned. Remember that, even if you arrive at the wrong conclusion, you will still earn marks for discussion of relevant issues within your answer.

(c)   **Franchise rights**

The purchase of the franchise is an equity-settled share-based payment within the scope of IFRS 2 *Share-based payment.* This is because a good has been purchased in exchange for shares or share options.

The fair value of the asset acquired can be reliably measured. Therefore, the franchise right should be recorded at $2.3 million, with a corresponding entry to equity.

Note that if the fair value had not been reliably measurable then the franchise right would have been recorded at the fair value of the equity instruments issued i.e. $2.5 million.

Irredeemable preference shares

Normally irredeemable preference shares would be classified as equity because there is no obligation to pay cash.

However, Greenie should treat its preference shares as compound financial instruments with both an equity and liability component. The contractual obligation to pay the fixed cash dividend creates a liability component and the right to participate in ordinary dividends creates an equity component. The value of the equity component is the residual amount after deducting the separately determined liability component from the fair value of the instrument as a whole.

IAS 1 *Presentation of financial statements* requires departure from a requirement of a standard only in the extremely rare circumstances where management conclude that compliance would be so misleading that it would conflict with the objective of financial statements set out in the Framework. Greenie's argument that the presentation of the preference shares in accordance with IAS 32 would be misleading is not acceptable. The fact that it would not reflect the nature of the instruments as having characteristics of permanent capital providing participation in future profits is not a valid argument.

IAS 1 requires additional disclosures when compliance with the specific requirements in IFRS is insufficient to enable a user to understand the impact of particular transactions or conditions on financial position and financial performance. A fair presentation would be achieved by complying with IAS 32 and providing additional disclosures to explain the characteristics of the preference shares.

ACCA Marking scheme		
		Marks
(a)	Provision discussion	3
	Contingent liability discussion	3
(b)	Significant influence discussion and application	10
(c)	Intangible assets	3
	Preference shares	4
	Professional	2
		—
Total		**25**
		—

Examiner's comments

This question dealt with real world scenarios taken from corporate financial statements. It is important that the exam paper reflects actual issues in financial statements and those candidates can apply their knowledge to these scenarios.

A public limited company which developed and operated airports was involved in litigation over an accident at one of the airports and the issues was whether a provision or contingent liability should be provided for. In this case it was important for candidates to justify their conclusion by discussing the nature of a provision and contingency. This part of the question was well answered although many candidates came to the incorrect conclusion.

In part (b), candidates had to determine the relationship between an entity and a company that it had invested in. There was a need to discuss the relationship between the two entities in order to determine what the relationship constituted. Many candidates did not again use the scenario and in this question it was critical to discuss the facts in the question. However the question was well answered.

In part (c) the entity issued shares for the acquisition of franchise rights at a local airport and showed irredeemable preference shares as equity instruments in its statement of financial position. Candidates had to determine the correct accounting treatment for these items. This part of the question was not well answered with candidates not understanding how to account for the irredeemable preference shares. Understanding the nature of equity and liability is a key element of the syllabus. Overall the question was well answered.

40 CATE (JUNE 10 EXAM) *Walk in the footsteps of a top tutor*

Key answer tips

This multi-topic question has a mark allocation against each topic to help you allocate your time. Normally, each element of the multi-topic question is independent of each other, and can therefore be attempted in any order. You should apply good exam technique and attempt each part in the order which you find easiest to deal with. Remember to clearly identify which order you attempted each part of the question so that the examiner can clearly follow what you have done.

Tutorial note

A good starting point is to state and explain the criteria for recognition of a deferred tax asset. Develop your answer to apply this information to the scenario. You should then be able to identify and explain whether this complies with IAS 12. If it does not, you should state this clearly, and explain the appropriate accounting treatment in the circumstances.

(a)   **Deferred tax assets**

A deferred tax asset should be recognised for deductible temporary differences, unused tax losses and unused tax credits to the extent that it is probable that taxable profit will be available against which the deductible temporary differences can be utilised. The recognition of deferred tax assets on losses carried forward does not seem to be in accordance with IAS 12 *Income taxes*. Cate is not able to provide convincing evidence that sufficient taxable profits will be generated against which the unused tax losses can be offset.

According to IAS 12 the existence of unused tax losses is strong evidence that future taxable profit may not be available against which to offset the losses. Therefore when an entity has a history of recent losses, the entity recognises deferred tax assets arising from unused tax losses only to the extent that the entity has sufficient taxable temporary differences or there is convincing other evidence that sufficient taxable profit will be available. As Cate has a history of recent losses and as it does not have sufficient taxable temporary differences, Cate needs to provide convincing other evidence that sufficient taxable profit would be available against which the unused tax losses could be offset. The unused tax losses in question did not result from identifiable causes, which were unlikely to recur as the losses are due to ordinary business activities. Additionally there are no tax planning opportunities available to Cate that would create taxable profit in the period in which the unused tax losses could be offset.

Thus at 31 May 2010 it is unlikely that the entity would generate taxable profits before the unused tax losses expired. The improved performance in 2010 would not be indicative of future good performance as Cate would have suffered a net loss before tax had it not been for the non-operating gains.

Cate's anticipation of improved future trading could not alone be regarded as meeting the requirement for strong evidence of future profits. When assessing the use of carry-forward tax losses, weight should be given to revenues from existing orders or confirmed contracts rather than those that are merely expected from improved trading. Estimates of future taxable profits can rarely be objectively verified.

Thus the recognition of deferred tax assets on losses carried forward is not in accordance with IAS 12 as Cate is not able to provide convincing evidence that sufficient taxable profits would be generated against which the unused tax losses could be offset.

Tutorial note

A good starting point is to set out the definition of recoverable amount as used in an impairment test. It should then be applied as far as practicable to the situation in the question. As with part (a), if the accounting treatment does not comply with a reporting standard, this should be identified and explained.

(b) **Investment**

Cate's position for an investment where the investor has significant influence and its method of calculating fair value can be challenged.

An asset's recoverable amount represents its greatest value to the business in terms of its cash flows that it can generate i.e. the higher of fair value less costs to sell (which is what the asset can be sold for less direct selling expenses) and value in use (the cash flows that are expected to be generated from its continued use including those from its ultimate disposal). The asset's recoverable amount is compared with its carrying value to indicate any impairment. Both net selling price (NSP) and value in use can be difficult to determine. However it is not always necessary to calculate both measures, as if the NSP or value in use is greater than the carrying amount, there is no need to estimate the other amount.

It should be possible in this case to calculate a figure for the recoverable amount. Cate's view that market price cannot reflect the fair value of significant holdings of equity such as an investment in an associate is incorrect. IFRS 13 *Fair Value Measurement* prioritises the use of level 1 inputs when determining fair value. A level 1 input is defined as a quoted price for an identical asset in an active market. The quoted price of a Bates share is a level 1 input and should be used. Management estimates, such as earnings multiples, are unobservable and are therefore classified as level 3 inputs.

Additionally the compliance with IAS 28, *Investments* in associates is in doubt in terms of the non-applicability of value in use when considering impairment. IAS 28 explains that in determining the value in use of the investments, an entity estimates:

(i)   its share of the present value of the estimated future cash flows expected to be generated by the associate, including the cash flows from the operations of the associate and the proceeds on the ultimate disposal of the investment; or

(ii)   the present value of the estimated future cash flows expected to arise from dividends to be received from the investment and from its ultimate disposal.

Estimates of future cash flows should be produced. These cash flows are then discounted to present value hence giving value in use.

It seems as though Cate wishes to avoid an impairment charge on the investment.

Tutorial note

This part of the question deals mainly with IFRS 5; you should state and apply the criteria for a disposal group to be regarded as 'held for sale'.

(c)   **Disposal group 'held for sale'**

Cate should stop consolidating Date on a line-by-line basis from the date that control was lost. The loss of control will create a profit or loss in the statement of profit or loss.

The retained interest would be recognised at fair value. Further investigation is required into whether this holding is treated as an associate or trade investment. IAS 28 *Investments in associates and joint ventures* defines significant influence as the power to participate in financial and operating decision-making, but not control or joint control. The agreement that Cate is no longer represented on the board or able to participate in management would suggest loss of significant influence despite the 35% of voting rights retained.

An entity classifies a disposal group as held for sale if its carrying amount will be recovered mainly through selling the asset rather than through usage and intends to dispose of it in a single transaction.

The conditions for a non-current asset or disposal group to be classified as held for sale are as follows:

(i)   The assets must be available for immediate sale in their present condition and its sale must be highly probable.

(ii)   The asset must be currently marketed actively at a price that is reasonable in relational to its current fair value.

(iii)   The sale should be completed or expected to be so, within a year from the date of the classification.

(iv)   The actions required to complete the planned sale will have been made and it is unlikely that the plan will be significantly changed or withdrawn.

(v)   Management is committed to a plan to sell.

Cate has not met all of the conditions of IFRS 5 but it could be argued that the best presentation in the financial statements was that set out in IFRS 5 for the following reasons.

The issue of dilution is not addressed by IFRS and the decision not to subscribe to the issue of new shares of Date is clearly a change in the strategy of Cate. Further, by deciding not to subscribe to the issue of new shares of Date, Cate agreed to the dilution and the loss of control which could be argued is similar to a decision to sell shares while retaining a continuing interest in the entity. Also Date represents a separate line of business, which is a determining factor in IFRS 5, and information disclosed on IFRS 5 principles highlights the impact of Date on Cate's financial statements. Finally, the agreement between Date's shareholders confirms that Cate has lost control over its former subsidiary.

Therefore, in the absence of a specific Standard or Interpretation applying to this situation, IAS 8 *Accounting policies*, changes in accounting estimates and errors states that management should use its judgment and refer to other IFRS and the Framework.

Thus considering the requirements of IFRS 10 and the above discussion, it could be concluded that the presentation based on IFRS 5 principles selected by the issuer was consistent with the accounting treatment required by IFRS 10 when a parent company loses control of a subsidiary.

Tutorial note

This part of the question deals mainly with determining whether or not an obligation exists in relation to a post-retirement benefit plan, and, if there is, how it should be accounted for.

(d)   **Pension plan**

A defined contribution plan is one where an entity has no legal or constructive obligation to pay further contributions if the fund does not have sufficient assets to pay all employee benefits relating to employee service in the current and prior periods. All other post-employment benefit plans that do not qualify as a defined contribution plan are, by definition, defined benefit plans.

There are various indications that the Plan should be accounted for as a defined benefit plan:

- Cate has a history of paying these pension benefits and has therefore created a constructive obligation that it will continue to do so.

- The benefits payable are linked to final salaries, thus potentially creating a plan deficit. Cate would therefore have a constructive obligation to increase its contributions.

- Cate has an obligation to purchase annuities for retired employees if it terminates its contributions into the plan.

Cate should account for the Plan as a defined benefit plan in accordance with IAS 19. Cate has to recognise, at a minimum, its net present liability for the benefits to be paid under the Plan.

ACCA Marking scheme		
		Marks
(a)	Deferred tax	5
(b)	Investment in associates	5
(c)	IFRS 5 discussion and conclusion	8
(d)	IAS 19 discussion and conclusion	5
Professional marks		2
		—
Total		**25**
		—

Examiner's comments

The question dealt with real world scenarios taken from corporate financial statements. It is important that the exam paper reflects actual issues in financial statements and that candidates can apply their knowledge to these scenarios. The first scenario dealt with deferred tax assets and their recognition in the financial statements. This part of the question was well answered. Part b dealt with impairment of assets where an entity wished to use a method not in accordance with the standard. It required candidates to apply their knowledge to the situation and not just repeat the rules in the standard. This part of the question was well answered.

Part (c) looked at a situation where a company had a direct holding of shares which were not subscribed for by the holding company with the result that the interest was reduced to that of an associate. The question required candidates to determine whether the results should be presented based on the principles provided by IFRS 5 *Non-current assets held for sale and discontinued operations*. Candidates performed quite well on this part. The key to success is to set out the principles in the standard and then to apply each one to the case in point.

The final part dealt with the existence of a voluntary fund established in order to provide a post-retirement benefit plan to employees. The entity considered its contributions to the plan to be voluntary, and had not recorded any related liability in its consolidated financial statements. The entity had a history of paying benefits to its former employees, and there were several other pieces of information in the question. Candidates had to apply their knowledge of defined benefit schemes to the scenario. It did not require an in-depth knowledge of the accounting standard but an ability to apply the principles. The question was answered satisfactorily by candidates.

41   SELTEC (JUNE 10 EXAM) *Walk in the footsteps of a top tutor*

Key answer tips

This two-part question is set in a scenario of an entity operating in the edible oils sector. Part (a) deals with derivatives and hedge accounting for 14 marks. The use and application of definitions will help in a technically demanding area of the syllabus. Part (b) deals with accounting for brands and the purchase of two companies for 9 marks. You should apply your knowledge of IAS 38 *Intangible assets* and IFRS 3 (revised) *Business combinations* to deal with each issue separately to gain as many marks as possible. There are also 2 professional marks available for clarity and quality of discussion within your answer, so ensure that you use appropriate presentation and professional language in your answer.

Tutorial note

Begin with stating the criteria for recognition and measurement criteria in relation to derivative financial instruments.

(a)   **Derivatives**

IFRS 9 *Financial instruments* states that a derivative is a financial instrument:

(i)   whose value changes in response to the change in an underlying variable such as an interest rate, commodity or security price, or index; such as the price of edible oil,

(ii)   that requires no initial investment, or one that is smaller than would be required for a contract with similar response to changes in market factors; in the case of the future purchase of oil, the initial investment is nil, and

(iii)   that is settled at a future date.

However, when a contract's purpose is to take physical delivery in the normal course of business, then normally the contract is not considered to be a derivative contract, unless the entity has a practice of settling the contracts on a net basis. Even though Seltec sometimes takes physical delivery, the entity has a practice of settling similar contracts on a net basis and taking delivery, only to sell shortly afterwards. In this case the contracts will be considered to be derivative contracts and should be accounted for at fair value through profit and loss, unless designated as a hedging instrument within a hedge accounting relationship.

Hedge accounting

Hedge accounting techniques may be used if the following conditions in IFRS 9 are met.

- The hedging relationship must only consist of eligible items and instruments

- At the inception of the relationship, there must be formal documentation, which identifies the hedged item, the hedging instrument, and the nature of the risk being hedged. The entity must also document how they will assess if the hedge effectiveness criteria are met.

- The hedging relationship must meet the hedge effectiveness requirements.

The hedge effectiveness requirements are as follows:

- There must be an economic relationship between the hedged item and the hedging instrument

- The effect of credit risk must not dominate the value changes that result from the relationship

- The hedge ratio of the hedging relationship is the same as that resulting from the quantity of the hedged item that the entity actually hedges and the quantity of the hedging instrument that the entity actually uses to hedge that quantity of hedged item.

Assuming that the criteria are met, Seltec could use cash flow or fair value hedge accounting.

Fair value hedge

A fair value hedge is a hedge of the exposure to changes in fair value of a recognised asset or liability or firm commitment to buy that is attributable to a particular risk and could affect profit or loss (or other comprehensive income if the hedged item is an investment in equity that has been designated to be measured at fair value though other comprehensive income (FVOCI)).

As long as the hedged item is not an investment in equity measured at FVOCI, then the gain or loss from the change in fair value of the hedging instrument is recognised immediately in profit or loss. At the same time the carrying amount of the hedged item is adjusted for the corresponding gain or loss with respect to the hedged risk, which is also recognised immediately in profit or loss.

Cash flow hedge

A cash flow hedge is a hedge of the exposure to variability in cash flows that is attributable to a particular risk associated with a recognised asset or liability or a highly probable forecast transaction, and could affect profit or loss.

The portion of the gain or loss on the hedging instrument that is determined to be an effective hedge is recognised in OCI and reclassified to profit or loss when the hedged cash transaction affects profit or loss.

Embedded derivatives

IFRS 9 defines an embedded derivative as a component of a hybrid instrument that also includes a non-derivative host contract, with the effect that some of the cash flows of the instrument vary in a way similar to a stand-alone derivative.

A foreign currency denominated contract contains an embedded derivative unless it meets one of the following criteria:

(i)   the foreign currency denominated in the contract is that of either party to the contract,

(ii)   the currency of the contract is that in which the related good or service is routinely denominated in commercial transactions,

(iii)   the currency is that commonly used in such contracts in the market in which the transaction takes place.

In the case of the commitment to buy oil in sterling, the pound sterling is not the functional currency of either party, oil is not routinely denominated in sterling, and the currency is not that normally used in business transactions in the environment in which Seltec carries out its business.

With regards to the accounting treatment of an embedded derivative, if the host contract is within the scope of IFRS 9 then the entire contract must be classified and measured in accordance with that standard.

If the host contract is not within the scope of IFRS 9, then the embedded derivative can be separated out and measured at fair value through profit or loss if:

(i)   the economic risks and characteristics of the embedded derivative are not closely related to those of the host contract

(ii)   a separate instrument with the same terms as the embedded derivative would meet the definition of a derivative; and

(iii)   the entire instrument is not measured at fair value with changes in fair value recognised in profit or loss.

The economic risks are not closely related as currency fluctuations and changes in the price of oil have different risks. The currency derivative can therefore be separated out and accounted for at fair value through profit or loss. Alternatively, because of the complexity involved in this, IFRS 9 permits the contract as a whole to be measured at fair value through profit or loss instead.

Tutorial note

Begin by stating the definition of an intangible asset, together with factors to be considered in determining whether recognition is appropriate, which can then be applied to the circumstances in the scenario.

(b)   **Intangible assets**

Intangible assets are classified as having:

(i)   an indefinite life (no foreseeable limit to the period over which the asset is expected to generate net cash inflows for the entity), or

(ii)   a definite life (a limited period of benefit to the entity).

Factors that should be considered when determining this classification are:

(i)   The entity's commitment to support the brand

(ii)   The extent to which the brand has long-term potential that is not underpinned by short-term fashion or trends. That is, the brand has had a period of proven success

(iii) The extent to which the products carrying the brand are resistant to changes in the operating environment. These products should be resistant to changes in legal, technological and competitive environments.

The brand of oil, which has been in existence for many years, is likely to have an indefinite life as it has already proven its longevity having been successful for many years. An intangible asset with an indefinite useful life should not be amortised. Its useful life should be reviewed each reporting period to determine whether events and circumstances continue to support an indefinite useful life assessment for that asset. If they do not, the change in the useful life assessment from indefinite to finite should be accounted for as a change in an accounting estimate. The asset should also be assessed for impairment in accordance with IAS 36.

The oil named after a famous film star is likely to decline in popularity as the popularity of the film star declines. It is a new product and its longevity has not been proven and therefore it is likely to have a finite life. The cost less residual value of an intangible asset with a finite useful life should be amortised on a systematic basis over that life. The amortisation method should reflect the pattern of benefits but if the pattern cannot be determined reliably, it should be amortised by the straight-line method.

Purchase of companies

A business combination is a transaction or event in which an acquirer obtains control of one or more businesses. A business is defined as an integrated set of activities and assets that is capable of being conducted and managed for the purpose of providing a return directly to investors or other owners, members or participants in the form of dividends, lower costs or other economic benefits to investors or owners.

The two entitles do not meet the definition of a business in IFRS 3 (Revised) *Business combinations* as they do not have any processes such as real estate management which are applied to the retail space that they own. The entities do not generate any outputs such as rental income. Therefore the acquisition should be treated as a purchase of assets.

ACCA Marking scheme	
	Marks
Hedge accounting	5
Futures	5
Embedded derivative	4
Brands	5
Business combinations	4
Professional marks	2
	——
Total	**25**
	——

Examiner's comments

The question was a case study type question based around a company in the edible oil industry. The company processed and sold edible oils and used several financial instruments to spread the risk of fluctuation in the price of edible oils. Additionally, the company was unclear as to how the purchase of the brands and certain entities should be accounted for. It involved knowledge of derivatives, hedging and embedded derivatives at a fundamental level. Candidates did not have to apply their knowledge to any degree but simply had to recognise the nature of various financial instruments involved and discuss their accounting treatment. This knowledge is essential knowledge and will be examined in future diets. Candidates' answers were satisfactory in the main but few candidates recognised the embedded derivative. The accounting for the brands was quite well answered with many students gaining high marks. The final part required candidates to apply IFRS 3 *Business combinations* to a scenario. The answers were often quite poor with the main weakness being the application of the knowledge and the understanding of the nature of the purchase of the entities.

42 KEY (DEC 09 EXAM) *Walk in the footsteps of a top tutor*

Key answer tips

This two-part question deals with non-current assets and impairment. Part (a) requires a general discussion of factors relevant when impairment testing during a period of limited availability of credit from banks. Part (b) develops this theme and requires specific impairment testing and supporting discussion of a particular scenario. This requires the use of present value information and extracts of discount tables have been provided in the question.

Tutorial note

A good starting point is to state and explain the definition of impairment and to outline when an impairment test may be required.

(a)   IAS 36 *Impairment of assets* states that an asset is impaired when its carrying amount will not be recovered from its continuing use or from its sale. An entity must determine at each reporting date whether there is any indication that an asset is impaired. If an indicator of impairment exists then the asset's recoverable amount must be determined and compared with its carrying amount to assess the amount of any impairment.

Accounting for the impairment of non-financial assets can be difficult as IAS 36 *Impairment of assets* is a complex accounting standard. The turbulence in the markets and signs of economic downturn will cause many companies to revisit their business plans and revise financial forecasts. As a result of these changes, there may be significant impairment charges.

Indicators of impairment may arise from either the external environment in which the entity operates or from within the entity's own operating environment. Thus the current economic downturn is an obvious indicator of impairment, which may cause the entity to experience significant impairment charges.

Assets should be tested for impairment at as low a level as possible, at individual asset level where possible. However, many assets do not generate cash inflows independently from other assets and such assets will usually be tested within the cash-generating unit (CGU) to which the asset belongs. Cash flow projections should be based on reasonable assumptions that represent management's best estimate of the range of economic conditions that will exist over the remaining useful life of the asset. The discount rate used is the rate, which reflects the specific risks of the asset or CGU.

Tutorial note

Here is the basic principle for the carrying value of assets in the statement of financial position, together with a definition of recoverable amount.

The basic principle is that an asset may not be carried in the statement of financial position at more than its recoverable amount. An asset's recoverable amount is the higher of:

- fair value less costs to sell and

- the present value of the future cash flows that are expected to be derived from the asset (value in use). The expected future cash flows include those from the asset's continued use in the business and those from its ultimate disposal.

This measurement basis reflects the economic decisions that a company's management team makes when assets become impaired from the viewpoint of whether the business is better off disposing of the asset or continuing to use it.

Note that, where a fair value measurement is required, IFRS 13 will normally apply unless specifically excluded. IFRS 13 formalises the procedure to determine a fair value measurement when required, so that observable inputs are used as far as possible to support a fair value measurement. As such, it is a market-based measurement based upon the value at which an asset would be disposed of or a liability transferred in an orderly transaction between market participants.

Therefore, the assumptions used in arriving at the recoverable amount need to be 'reasonable and supportable' regardless of whether impairment calculations are based on fair value less costs to sell or value in use. The acceptable range for such assumptions will change over time and forecasts for revenue growth and profit margins are likely to have fallen in the economic climate. The assumptions made by management should be in line with the assumptions made by industry commentators or analysts. Variances from market will need to be justified and highlighted in financial statement disclosures.

Tutorial note

This part of the answer considers market evidence and the reaction of the market to when impairment losses may or may not have been recognised.

Whatever method is used to calculate the recoverable amount; the value needs to be considered in the light of available market evidence. If other entities in the same sector are taking impairment charges, the absence of an impairment charge have to be justified because the market will be asking the same question.

It is important to inform the market about how it is dealing with the conditions, and be thinking about how different parts of the business are affected, and the market inputs they use in impairment testing. Impairment testing should be commenced as soon as possible as an impairment test process takes a significant amount of time. It includes identifying impairment indicators, assessing or reassessing the cash flows, determining the discount rates, testing the reasonableness of the assumptions and benchmarking the assumptions with the market. Goodwill does not have to be tested for impairment at the year-end; it can be tested earlier and if any impairment indicator arises at the reporting date, the impairment assessment can be updated. Also, it is important to comply with all disclosure requirements, such as the discount rate and long-term growth rate assumptions in a discounted cash flow model, and describe what the key assumptions are and what they are based on.

It is important that the cash flows being tested are consistent with the assets being tested. The forecast cash flows should make allowance for investment in working capital if the business is expected to grow. When the detailed calculations have been completed, the company should check that their conclusions make sense by comparison to any market data, such as share prices and analysts reports. Market capitalisation below net asset value is an impairment indicator, and calculations of recoverable amount are required. If the market capitalisation is lower than a value-in-use calculation, then the VIU assumptions may require reassessment. For example, the cash flow projections might not be as expected by the market, and the reasons for this must be scrutinised. Discount rates should be scrutinised in order to see if they are logical. Discount rates may have risen too as risk premiums rise. Many factors affect discount rates in impairment calculations. These include corporate lending rates, cost of capital and risks associated with cash flows, which are all increasing in the current volatile environment and can potentially result in an increase of the discount rate.

Tutorial note

Here is the application of the impairment review, including discounting of expected future cashflows to their present value at the date of the impairment review.

(b)   Wherever indicators of impairment exist, an impairment review should be carried out. Where impairment is identified, a write-down of the carrying value to the recoverable amount should be charged as an immediate expense in profit or loss. Using a discount rate of 5%, the value in use of the non-current assets is:

Year to 31 May:	2010	2011	2012	2013	Total
Discounted cash flows ($000)	267	408	431	452	1,558

The carrying value of the non-current assets at 31 May 2009 is $2.4 million ($3 million – depreciation of $600,000). Therefore the assets are impaired by $842,000 ($2.4m – $1.558m).

IAS 36 requires an assessment at each reporting date whether there is an indication that an impairment loss may have decreased. This does not apply to goodwill or to the unwinding of the discount. In this case, the same cash flows have been used in the calculation and so the increase in value is due to the unwinding of the discount (i.e. the cash flows are now closer to occurring and so are discounted less heavily).

Compensation received in the form of reimbursements from governmental indemnities is recorded in the statement of profit or loss when the compensation becomes receivable according to IAS 37 *Provisions, contingent liabilities and contingent assets*. It is treated as separate economic events and accounted for as such. At this time the government has only stated that it may reimburse the company and therefore credit should not be taken of any potential government receipt.

Tutorial note

Having identified the extent of any impairment, accounting for it depends upon whether the asset is carried at cost or at revalued amount.

For a revalued asset, the impairment loss is treated as a revaluation decrease. The loss is first set against any revaluation surplus and the balance of the loss is then treated as an expense in profit or loss. The revaluation gain and the impairment loss would be treated as follows:

	Depreciated historical cost $m	Revalued carrying value $m
1 December 2006	10.0	10.0
Depreciation (2 years)	(2.0)	(2.0)
Revaluation		(0.8)
	8.0	8.8
Depreciation	(1.0)	(1.1)
Impairment loss	(1.5)	(2.2)
30 November 2009 after impairment loss	5.5	5.5

The impairment loss of $2.2 million is charged to equity until the carrying amount reaches depreciated historical cost and thereafter it goes to profit or loss. It is assumed that the company will transfer an amount from revaluation surplus to retained earnings to cover the excess depreciation of $0.1 million as allowed by IAS 16. Therefore the impairment loss charged to equity would be $(0.8 – 0.1) million i.e. $0.7 million and the remainder of $1.5 million would be charged to profit or loss.

Tutorial note

Consideration now turns to IFRS 5 and whether the asset may be classified as held for sale.

A plan by management to dispose of an asset or group of assets due to under utilisation is an indicator of impairment. Therefore an impairment review should be conducted.

An asset should be classified as held for sale if its carrying amount will be recovered through a sales transaction and:

- the sale is highly probable and expected to take place within one year

- the asset is available for immediate sale in its present condition

- there is an active programme to locate a buyer

- the asset is being marketed at a price that is reasonable compared to its fair value, and

- it is unlikely that significant changes to the plan to sell will be made.

IFRS 5 requires an asset held for sale to be measured at the lower of its carrying amount and its fair value less costs to sell.

The fact that the asset is being marketed at a price in excess of its fair value may mean that the asset is not available for immediate sale and therefore may not meet the criteria for 'held for sale'.

	ACCA Marking scheme	
		Marks
(a)	Impairment process	4
	General considerations	4
	Professional marks	2
(b)	Non-current asset at cost	6
	Non-current asset at valuation	6
	Non-current assets held for sale	3
		——
Total		**25**
		——

43 ARON (JUNE 09 EXAM) *Walk in the footsteps of a top tutor*

Key answer tips

This question deals with recognition and measurement of financial instruments. Part (a) is concerned with the use of fair values, particularly if there is no reliable or active market to help determine fair value. Part (b) of the requirement deals with accounting for four financial instruments, including a convertible bond and an interest-free loan, together with supporting calculations, comment and explanation. Accounting for one of the financial instruments also required knowledge of accounting for foreign currency transactions.

(a) **Discussion of fair value and its relevance**

IFRS 13 *Fair value measurement* now formalises the basis upon which a fair value measurement is determined. This should help to bring consistency to the determination of a fair value measurement, both by an entity over time, and also between entities, to enhance constancy and comparability of information. It should also enhance transparency and understanding.

The fair value of an asset is defined as the price that would be received to sell and asset, or paid to transfer a liability in an orderly transaction between market participants at the measurement date. If available, a quoted market price in an active market for an identical asset or liability is the best evidence of fair value and should be used as the basis for the measurement. IFRS 13 refers to this as 'Level 1 inputs'. Level 2 inputs comprise observable inputs, other than those within Level 1, such as prices in an active market for similar, though not identical, assets or liabilities. Such fair value measurements will require assessment as to whether they require any adjustment to arrive at a reliable fair value measurement. Level 3 inputs are not directly observable and will typically comprise management estimates and judgements, including the use of pricing or other appropriate models, to arrive at a fair value measurement.

Fair values should also reflect the assumption that market entrants have had adequate time to undertake reasonable marketing activity. In addition, it is also assumed that any transaction is not based upon a distress or forced basis. Transactions costs are ignored as they are regarded as a feature of the transaction, not of the asset or liability to be measured.

The IASB has concluded that fair value is the most relevant measure for most financial instruments. Fair value measurements provide more transparency than historical cost based measurements. Reliability is as important as relevance because relevant information that is not reliable is of no use to an investor. Fair value measurements should be reliable and computed in a manner that is faithful to the underlying economics of the transaction. Measuring financial instruments at fair value should not necessarily mean abandoning historical cost information.

However, market conditions will affect fair value measurements. In many circumstances, quoted market prices are unavailable. As a result, difficulties occur when making estimates of fair value. It is difficult to apply fair value measures in illiquid markets and to decide how and when models should be used for fair valuation. Fair value information can provide a value at the point in time that it is measured but its relevance will depend on the volatility of the market inputs and whether the instruments are actively traded or are held for the long term. Fair value provides an important indicator of risk profile and exposure but to fully understand this and to put it into context, the entity must disclose sufficient information. IFRS 13 requires significant disclosures relating to how fair value measurements have been determined for inclusion in the financial statements, including the categorisation of inputs used to determine such measurements.

(b)   (i)   **Convertible bond**

Some compound instruments have both a liability and an equity component from the issuer's perspective. In this case, IAS 32 *Financial instruments: presentation* requires that the component parts be accounted for and presented separately according to their substance based on the definitions of liabilities and equity. The split is made at issuance and not revised for subsequent changes in market interest rates, share prices, or other events that changes the likelihood that the conversion option will be exercised.

A convertible bond contains two components. One is a financial liability, namely the issuer's contractual obligation to pay cash in the form of interest or capital, and the other is an equity instrument, which is the holder's option to convert into shares. When the initial carrying amount of a compound financial instrument is required to be allocated to its equity and liability components, the equity component is assigned the residual amount after deducting from the fair value of the instrument as a whole the amount separately determined for the liability component.

In the case of the bond, the liability element will be determined by discounting the future stream of cash flows which will be the interest to be paid and the final capital balance assuming no conversion. The discount rate used will be 9% which is the market rate for similar bonds without the conversion right. The difference between cash received and the liability component is the value of the option.

	$000
Present value of interest at end of:	
Year 1 (31 May 2007) ($100m × 6%) ÷ 1.09	5,505
Year 2 (31 May 2008) ($100m × 6%) ÷ 1.09^2	5,050
Year 3 (31 May 2009) ($100m + ($100m × 6%)) ÷ 1.09^3	81,852
Total liability component	92,407
Total equity element	7,593
Proceeds of issue	100,000

The issue cost will have to be allocated between the liability and equity components in proportion to the above proceeds.

	$000 Liability	$000 Equity	$000 Total
Proceeds	92,407	7,593	100,000
Issue cost	(924)	(76)	(1,000)
	91,483	7,517	99,000

The credit to equity of $7,517 would not be re-measured. The liability component of $91,483 would be measured at amortised cost using the effective interest rate of 9.38%, as this spreads the issue costs over the term of the bond. The interest payments will reduce the liability in getting to the year end. The initial entries would have been:

Financial instrument	$000	Issue costs	$000
Dr Cash	100,000	Cr Cash	1,000
Cr Liability	92,407	Dr Liability	924
Cr Equity	7,593	Dr Equity	76

The liability component balance on 31 May 2009 becomes $100,000 as a result of the effective interest rate of 9.38% being applied and cashflows at 6% based on nominal value.

B/fwd	Eff int 9.38%	Cashflow 6%	C/fwd
91,483	8,581	(6,000)	94,064
94,064	8,823	(6,000)	96,887
96,887	9,088	(6,000)	(100,000)

On conversion of the bond on 31 May 2009, Aron would issue 25 million ordinary shares of $1 and the original equity component together with the balance on the liability will become the consideration.

	$000
Share capital – 25 million at $1	25,000
Share premium	82,517
Equity and liability components (100,000 + 7,593 – 76)	107,517

(ii) **Shares in Smart**

In this situation Aron has to determine if the transfer of shares in Smart qualifies for derecognition. The criteria are firstly to determine that the asset has been transferred, and then to determine whether or not the entity has transferred substantially all of the risks and rewards of ownership of the asset. If substantially all the risks and rewards have been transferred, the asset is derecognised. If substantially all the risks and rewards have been retained, derecognition of the asset is precluded.

In this case the transfer of shares qualifies for derecognition as Aron no longer retains any risks and rewards of ownership. In addition Aron obtains a new financial asset which is the shares in Given which should be recognised at fair value. The transaction will be accounted for as follows:

	$m
Proceeds – FV of shares received in Given	5.5
Carrying amount of shares in Smart	5.0
	―――
Gain to profit or loss	0.5
	―――

The shares in Given should be recognised at fair value of $5.5 million; presumably there will be a designation upon initial recognition to account for this new financial asset at fair value through other comprehensive income if it is to be held on a continuing basis.

In addition, Aron may choose to make a transfer within equity of the cumulative gain recognised up to disposal date of $400,000.

(iii) **Foreign subsidiary**

In this situation, IFRS 9 will apply to the debt instrument in the foreign subsidiary's financial statements and IAS 21 *The effects of changes in foreign exchange rates* will apply in translating the financial statements of the subsidiary for inclusion in the group financial statements. Under IAS 21, all exchange differences resulting from translation are recognised in equity until disposal of the subsidiary, when they are recycled to profit or loss as part of the gain or loss on disposal of the subsidiary.

As the debt instrument is held for trading it will be carried at fair value through profit or loss in Gao's financial statements. Thus at 31 May 2009, there will be a fair value gain of 2 million zloti which will be credited to profit or loss of Gao. In the consolidated financial statements, the carrying value of the debt at 1 June 2008 would have been $3.3 million (10 million zloti ÷ 3). At the year end this carrying value will have increased to $6 million (12 million zloti ÷ 2). Aron will translate the statement of profit or loss of Gao using the average rate of 2.5 zloti to the dollar. Although the fair value of the debt instrument has increased by $2.7 million, Aron will only recognise 2 million zloti ÷ 2.5, i.e. $800,000 of this in the consolidated statement of profit or loss with the remaining increase in value of ($2.7 – $0.8) million, i.e. $1,900,000 being classified as other comprehensive income and taken to equity until the disposal of the foreign subsidiary.

	$m
Opening balance at 1 December 2008	3.3
Increase in year	2.7
Closing balance at 30 November 2009	6.0
Dr Debt instrument	2.7
Cr Consolidated profit or loss	0.8
Cr Equity	1.9

(iv) **Interest Free Loans**

When a financial asset is recognised initially, IFRS 9 requires it to be measured at fair value, plus transaction costs in certain situations. Normally the fair value is the fair value of the consideration given. However, the fair value of an interest free loan may not necessarily be its face amount.

In this case, the fair value may be estimated as the discounted present value of future receipts using the market interest rate. If the interest-free loans are to be measured at amortised cost, they must comply with the requirements of both the business model test and the cash flow characteristics test. The first test requires that the financial asset is held to collect the contractual cash flows associated with the asset. The second test requires that the cash flows consist solely of repayment of interest and capital relating to the financial asset. This would appear to be the case; if this was not the case, the financial asset would need to be accounted for as fair value through profit or loss.

The difference between the fair value of the loan and the face value of the loan will be treated as employee remuneration under IAS 19 *Employee benefits*.

	$m
Fair value of loan at 1 June 2008 ($10/(1.06^2)$)	8.9
Employee compensation (bal. fig.)	1.1
Cash paid	10.0

The employee compensation would be charged to profit or loss over the two-year period.

The loan asset will then be measured at amortised cost using the effective interest method. In this case the effective interest rate will be 6% and the value of the loan in the statement of financial position will be ($8.9 million × 1.06) i.e. $9.43 million. Interest of $0.53 million will be credited to profit or loss.

At 1 June 2008:
Dr Loan	8.9
Dr Employee compensation	1.1
Cr Cash	10.0

At 31 May 2009:
Dr Loan	0.53
Cr Profit or loss – interest	0.53

	ACCA Marking scheme		
			Marks
(a)	Fair value – IFRS 13 subjective		4
(b)	Convertible bond	explanation	2
		calculation	4
	Shares in Smart	explanation	2
		calculation	2
	Foreign subsidiary	explanation of principle	2
		accounting treatment	3
	Interest free loan	explanation of principle	2
		Accounting treatment	2
	Quality of explanation		2
			–––
		Maximum	**21**
			–––
Total			**25**
			–––

Examiner's comments

This question required a brief discussion of how the fair value of financial instruments is determined with a comment on the relevance of fair value measurements for financial instruments where markets are volatile and illiquid. This part of the question was quite well answered although the answers were quite narrow and many candidates simply described the classification of financial instruments in loans and receivables, available for sale etc. The second part of the question required candidates to discuss the accounting for four different financial instruments. The requirement was to discuss the accounting but many candidates simply showed the accounting entries without any discussion. If the accounting entries were incorrect then it was difficult to award significant marks for the attempt. If however there is a discussion of the principles, then it is easier to award marks for a discussion which has a subjective element to it rather than a calculation which is normally correct or incorrect. The financial instruments ranged from a convertible bond to transfer of shares to a debt instrument in a foreign subsidiary to interest free loans. The treatment of the convertible bond was quite well done except for the treatment of the issue costs and the conversion of the bond. This part of the question often gained good marks. Again the treatment of the transfer of shares and interest free loans was well done but the exchange and fair value gains were often combined and not separated in the case of the debt instrument of the foreign subsidiary. Generally speaking this was the best-answered question in part B of the paper.

44 MARRGRETT (DEC 08 EXAM) *Walk in the footsteps of a top tutor*

Key answer tips

This question requires discussion and application of accounting treatments to proposed transactions, specifically IFRS 3 (Revised) and IFRS 10. Although there is a single requirement for twenty-five marks, there are several issues to be considered. The best way to approach this question is to deal with each issue separately and to identify the specific accounting requirements for each issue. Having done that, the accounting treatment should then be applied to the specific information in the question.

The principles of consolidation

The principles to be applied are that:

(a)   a business combination occurs only in respect of the transaction that gives one entity control of another

(b)   the identifiable net assets of the acquiree are re-measured to their fair value on the date of the acquisition

(c)   NCI are measured on the date of acquisition under one of the two options permitted by IFRS 3 (Revised).

IFRS 10 identifies three elements to determine whether one entity has control over as follows:

(a)   power over the investee, where one party has the current ability to direct activities that significantly affect its returns, and

(b)   exposure, or rights to, variable returns from involvement in the investee, and

(c)   the ability to use power over the investee to affect the level of returns.

In most cases, this will be quite evident from one entity owning the majority of the equity capital of another entity. However, the approach to determining whether or not control is exercised is principles-based, which recognises that control may be exercised in a range of circumstances, other than by ownership of equity capital. IFRS 10 requires that the judgement of whether or not one entity controls another should be subject to regular review.

Consideration

IFRS 3 (Revised) says that the consideration paid to acquire a business is measured at fair value. Consideration will include cash, assets, contingent consideration, equity instruments, options and warrants. It also includes the fair value of all equity interests that the acquirer may have held previously in the acquired business.

An equity interest previously held in the acquiree which qualified as an associate under IAS 28 *Investments in associates and joint ventures* is similarly treated as if it were disposed of and reacquired at fair value on the acquisition date. Accordingly, it is re-measured to its acquisition date fair value, and any resulting gain or loss compared to its carrying amount under IAS 28 is recognised in profit or loss for the year. Thus the 30% holding in the associate previously held will be included in the consideration. If the carrying amount of the interest in the associate is not held at fair value at the acquisition date, the interest should be measured to fair value and the resulting gain or loss should be recognised in profit or loss. The business combination has effectively been achieved in stages.

Thus the 30% holding in the associate previously held will be included in the consideration. If the carrying amount of the interest in the associate is not held at fair value at the acquisition date, the interest should be measured to fair value and the resulting gain or loss should be recognised in profit or loss. The business combination has effectively been achieved in stages.

The fees payable in transaction costs are not deemed to be part of the consideration paid to the seller of the shares. They are not assets of the purchased business that are recognised on acquisition. Therefore, they should be expensed as incurred and the services received. Transaction costs relating to the issue of debt or equity, if they are directly attributable, will not be expensed but deducted from debt or equity on initial recognition.

It is common for part of the consideration to be contingent upon future events. Marrgrett wishes some of the existing shareholders/employees to remain in the business and has, therefore, offered share options as an incentive to these persons. The issue is whether these options form part of the purchase consideration or are compensation for post-acquisition services. The conditions attached to the award will determine the accounting treatment. In this case there are employment conditions and, therefore, the options should be treated as compensation and valued under IFRS 2 *Share-based payment*. Thus a charge will appear in post-acquisition earnings for employee services as the options were awarded to reward future services of employees rather than to acquire the business.

The additional shares to a fixed value of $50,000 are contingent upon the future returns on capital employed. Marrgrett only wants to make additional payments if the business is successful. All consideration should be fair valued at the date of acquisition, including the above contingent consideration. The contingent consideration payable in shares where the number of shares varies to give the recipient a fixed value ($50,000) meets the definition of a financial liability under IAS 32 *Financial instruments: presentation*. As a result the liability will have to be fair valued and any subsequent remeasurement will be recognised in profit or loss. There is no requirement under IFRS 3 (Revised) for the payments to be probable.

Identifiable net assets

Intangible assets should be recognised on acquisition under IFRS 3 (Revised). These include trade names, domain names, and non-competition agreements. Thus these assets will be recognised and goodwill effectively reduced. As a result of this, the post-combination statement of profit or loss may have charges for amortisation of the intangibles.

Marrgrett has a maximum period of 12 months to finalise the acquisition accounting but will not be able to recognise the re-organisation provision at the date of the business combination. The ability of the acquirer to recognise a liability for reducing or changing the activities of the acquiree is restricted. A restructuring provision can only be recognised in a business combination when the acquiree has at the acquisition date, an existing liability which complies with IAS 37 *Provisions, contingent liabilities and contingent assets*. These conditions are unlikely to exist at the acquisition date. A restructuring plan that is conditional on the completion of a business combination is not recognised in accounting for the acquisition but the expense will be charged against post-acquisition earnings.

Non-controlling interests

The standard gives entities the option, on a transaction by transaction basis, to measure non-controlling interests (NCI) at the fair value of the proportion of identifiable net assets or at full fair value. The standard gives entities a choice for each separate business combination of recognising full or partial goodwill.

Recognising full goodwill will increase reported net assets and may result in any future impairment of goodwill being of greater value. Measuring NCI at fair value may have some difficulties but goodwill impairment testing may be easier under full goodwill as there is no need to gross-up goodwill for partly-owned subsidiaries. The type of consideration does not affect goodwill regardless of how the payment is structured. Consideration is recognised in total at its fair value at the date of acquisition. The form of the consideration will not affect goodwill but the structure of the payments can affect post-acquisition profits. Contingent payments which are deemed to be debt instruments will be remeasured at each reporting date with the change going to profit or loss.

Disposals

A partial disposal of an interest in a subsidiary in which control is still retained does not result in a gain or loss in consolidated profit or loss but is instead accounted for within equity. This will arise by comparison of the disposal proceeds received from the share disposal with the increased interest that non-controlling interest shareholders have in the subsidiary at that date.

If the sale of shares causes control over a subsidiary to be lost then there will be a profit or loss on disposal. The remaining interest will be recognised at its fair value and, assuming it meets the criteria to be recognised as an associate, will be accounted for using the equity method.

Note that for an interest in another entity to be accounted for as an associate, it must meet the definition of an associate from IAS 28. An entity is regarded as an associate if an investor is able to exercise significant influence over it. IAS 28 defines significant influence as power to participate in the financial and operating policy decisions of an investee, but which is not control or joint control as defined by IFRS 10 and IFRS 11 respectively.

ACCA Marking scheme	
	Marks
Consideration	6
IFRS 3 and consideration	5
Consideration	2
Intangible assets	2
Non-controlling interests	5
Finalisation and reorganisation provision	2
IFRS 10 and IAS 28 (revised)	3
Total	**25**

45 NORMAN (JUN 08 EXAM) *Online question assistance*

Key answer tips

This is an important question for practicing your knowledge of operating segment disclosures. Make sure that you are able to state the quantitative tests for determining reportable segments and that you are able to apply this to the information in the question.

(a) **IFRS 8 *Operating Segments***

The core principle of IFRS 8 *Operating Segments* is that the entity should disclose information to enable users to evaluate the nature and financial effects of the types of business activities in which it engages and the economic environments in which it operates.

IFRS 8 *Operating segments* defines an operating segment as follows. An operating segment is a component of an entity:

- that engages in business activities from which it may earn revenues and incur expenses (including revenues and expenses relating to transactions with other components of the same entity)

- whose operating results are reviewed regularly by the entity's chief operating decision makers to make decisions about resources to be allocated to the segment and assess its performance; and for which discrete financial information is available.

As the key performance indicators are set on a city by city basis, there may be information within the internal reports about the components of the entity which has been disaggregated further. However, operating segments can be aggregated if they have similar economic characteristics. Therefore, the internal reports of Norman will need to be examined to assess if the nature of the operating segment aggregation is appropriate.

Quantitative tests

IFRS 8 requires an entity to report financial and descriptive information about its reportable segments. Reportable segments are operating segments that meet specified criteria:

- the reported revenue, from both external customers and intersegment sales or transfers, is 10% or more of the combined revenue, internal and external, of all operating segments; or

- the absolute measure of its reported profit or loss is 10% or more of the greater, in absolute amount, of (i) the combined reported profit of all operating segments that did not report a loss, and (ii) the combined reported loss of all operating segments that reported a loss; or

- its assets are 10% or more of the combined assets of all operating segments.

If the total external revenue reported by operating segments constitutes less than 75% of the entity's revenue, additional operating segments must be identified as reportable segments (even if they do not meet the quantitative thresholds set out above) until at least 75% of the entity's revenue is included in reportable segments. There is no precise limit to the number of segments that can be disclosed.

The revenue test

Total revenue is $1,010m ($200m + $300m + $460m + $30m + $10m + $3m + $2m + $4m + $1m). Any operating segments with revenue exceeding $101 million ($1,010m × 10%) must therefore be reported.

Europe, South East Asia and North America pass this test.

The asset test

Total segment assets are $3,100 million ($300m + $800m + $1,900m + $80m + $20m). Therefore, operating segments with total assets exceeding $310 million ($3,100 × 10%) must be reported.

South East Asia and North America both pass the assets test.

Results test

The total profit of the profit making segments is $165 million ($60m + $103m + $1m + $1m). The total loss of the loss making segments is $10 million. Therefore, any segment with a result that exceeds $16.5m ($165m × 10%) must be reported.

South East Asia and North America pass this test.

The 75% test

Europe, South East Asia and North America have all passed at least one of the 10% tests and so must be reported.

Together, their external revenue is $960m ($200m + $300m + $460m), representing 96% of external revenue. The reportable segments identified exceed 75% of external revenue, so no further operating segments need to be identified.

(b)   **Revenue recognition**

When entering into a contract with a customer, IFRS 15 *Revenue from Contracts with Customers* says that separate performance obligations must be identified.

Two performance obligations can be identified in this specific contract:

*   The promise to provide a hotel room

*   The promise to provide a discount on future bookings.

The total transaction price must therefore be allocated between these two performance obligations based on their relative standalone selling prices.

The selling price of the rooms of $30 million can be directly observed. Norman must estimate the standalone selling price of the vouchers, taking the likelihood of redemption into account. Therefore, the vouchers can be deemed to have a standalone selling price of $2m (2/5 × $5m).

The total transaction price of $30 million will therefore be allocated to the performance obligations as follows:

The rooms: $30m × $30m/($30m + $2m) = $28.1m

The vouchers: $30m × $2m/($30m + $2m) = $1.9m

Revenue should then be recognised as, or when, a performance obligation is satisfied.

The rooms have already been provided to customers, so the performance obligation has been satisfied and the $28.1 million can be recognised as revenue.

The $1.9m allocated to the vouchers should be recognised as revenue when the vouchers are redeemed or when they expire.

A contract liability of $1.9m should be recognised for the difference between the cash received and the revenue recognised ($30m – $28.1m).

Government grants

The recognition of government grants is covered by IAS 20 *Accounting for government grants and disclosure of government assistance*. Grants should not be recognised until there is reasonable assurance that the company can comply with the conditions relating to their receipt and the grant will be received.

Government grants are recognised in profit or loss on a systematic basis over the periods in which the entity recognises as expenses the related costs for which the grants are intended to compensate. IAS 20 says that capital grants should be matched against the depreciation of the hotels by using a deferred income approach or deducting the grant from the carrying amount of the asset.

There may be difficulties of matching costs and revenues when the terms of the grant do not specify precisely the expense towards which the grant contributes. In this case the grant appears to relate to both the building of hotels and the creation of employment. However, if the grant was related to revenue expenditure, then the terms would have been related to payroll or a fixed amount per job created. Additionally the grant is only to be repaid if the cost of the hotel is less than $500 million. Hence it would appear that the grant is capital based.

If the company feels that the cost of the hotel will not reach $500 million, a provision should be made for the estimated liability if the grant has been recognised.

ACCA Marking scheme			
			Marks
(a)	Identification of segments		2
	Definition		2
	Reporting information		2
	Norman applicability		5
			___
		Maximum	**11**
			___
(b)	Vouchers		6
	Grant income		6
	Quality of discussion		2
			___
		Maximum	**14**
			___
Total			**25**
			___

46 MACALJOY (DEC 07 EXAM)   *Online question assistance*

Key answer tips

Provisions and pension schemes are frequently examined topics in the P2 examination, within both section A and section B. The rules from these core standards must be learned and it is important that you can apply them to real-life scenarios. If you have identified gaps in your knowledge then fully debrief the following answer and revisit the relevant chapters in the Complete Text.

Report to the Directors of Macaljoy plc

Terms of reference

This report sets out the differences between a defined contribution and defined benefit plan, and the accounting treatment of the company's pension plans. It also discusses the principles involved in accounting for warranty claims, and the accounting treatment of those claims.

(a)   **Pension plans – IAS 19**

A defined contribution plan is a pension plan whereby an employer pays fixed contributions into a separate fund and has no legal or constructive obligation to pay further contributions (IAS 19). Payments or benefits provided to employees may be a simple distribution of total fund assets, or a third party (an insurance company) may, for example, agree to provide an agreed level of payments or benefits. Any actuarial (i.e. remeasurement) and investment risks of defined contribution plans are assumed by the employee or the third party. The employer is not required to make up any shortfall in assets and all plans that are not defined contribution plans are deemed to be defined benefit plans. Actuarial risk is the risk that the assumptions and estimations made when accounting for the defined benefit plan differ from what subsequently occurs in practice.

Defined benefit, therefore, is the residual category whereby, if an employer cannot demonstrate that all actuarial and investment risk has been shifted to another party and its obligations limited to contributions made during the period, then the plan is a defined benefit plan. Any benefit formula that is not solely based on the amount of contributions, or that includes a guarantee from the entity or a specified return, means that elements of risk remain with the employer and must be accounted for as a defined benefit plan. An employer may create a defined benefit obligation where no legal obligation exists if it has a practice of guaranteeing the benefits. An employer's obligation under a defined benefit plan is to provide the agreed amount of benefits to current and former employees. The differentiating factor between defined benefit and defined contribution schemes is in determining where the risks lie.

In a defined benefit scheme it is the employer that underwrites the vast majority of costs so that if investment returns are poor or costs increase the employer needs to either make adjustments to the scheme or to increase levels of contribution. Alternatively, if investment returns are good, then contribution levels could be reduced. In a defined contribution scheme the contributions are paid at a fixed level and, therefore, it is the scheme member who is shouldering these risks. If they fail to take action by increasing contribution rates when investment returns are poor or costs increase, then their retirement benefits will be lower than they had planned for.

For defined contribution plans, the cost to be recognised in the period is the contribution payable in exchange for service rendered by employees during the period. The accounting for a defined contribution plan is straightforward because the employer's obligation for each period is determined by the amount to be contributed for that period. Often, contributions are based on a formula that uses employee compensation in the period as its base. No actuarial or remeasurement assumptions are required to measure the obligation or the expense, and there are no remeasurement gains or losses to account for.

The employer should account for the contribution payable at the end of each period based on employee services rendered during that period, reduced by any payments made during the period. If the employer has made payments in excess of those required, the excess is a prepaid expense to the extent that the excess will lead to a reduction in future contributions or a cash refund.

For defined benefit plans, the amount recognised in the statement of financial position should be the present value of the defined benefit obligation (that is, the present value of expected future payments required to settle the obligation resulting from employee service in the current and prior periods), and reduced by the fair value of plan assets at the statement of financial position date. If the balance is an asset, the amount recognised may be limited under IAS 19 by application of the asset ceiling test.

In the case of Macaljoy, the 1990 plan is a defined benefit plan as the employer has the investment risk as the company is guaranteeing a pension based on the service lives of the employees in the scheme. The employer's liability is not limited to the amount of the contributions. There is a risk that if the investment returns fall short the employer will have to make good the shortfall in the scheme. The 2006 plan, however, is a defined contribution scheme because the employer's liability is limited to the contributions paid.

A curtailment occurs when there is a significant reduction in the number of employees covered by the plan. This gives rise to past service costs which are recognised at the earlier of:

- when the related restructuring costs are recognised, or

- when the related termination benefits are recognised, or

- when the curtailment occurs.

Curtailments, by definition, have a material impact on the entity's financial statements. The fact that no new employees are to be admitted to the 1990 plan does not constitute a curtailment because future service qualifies for pension rights for those in the scheme prior to 31 October 2006.

The accounting for the two plans is as follows. The company does not recognise any assets or liabilities for the defined contribution scheme but charges the contributions payable for the period ($10 million) to operating profit. The contributions paid by the employees will be part of the wages and salaries cost and when paid will reduce cash. The accounting for the defined benefit plan results in a liability of $15 million as at 31 October 2007, a charge in profit or loss of $20.5m for both the net interest component ($$0.5m) and the service cost component ($20m), and a net charge of $$1.5m in other comprehensive income for the remeasurement component (see Appendix 1).

(b) **Provisions – IAS 37**

An entity must recognise a provision under IAS 37 if, and only if:

(i) a present obligation (legal or constructive) has arisen as a result of a past event (the obligating event)

(ii) it is probable ('more likely than not'), that an outflow of resources embodying economic benefits will be required to settle the obligation

(iii) the amount can be estimated reliably.

An obligating event is an event that creates a legal or constructive obligation and, therefore, results in an enterprise having no realistic alternative but to settle the obligation. A constructive obligation arises if past practice creates a valid expectation on the part of a third party. If it is more likely than not that no present obligation exists, the enterprise should disclose a contingent liability, unless the possibility of an outflow of resources is remote.

The amount recognised as a provision should be the best estimate of the expenditure required to settle the present obligation at the statement of financial position date, that is, the amount that an enterprise would rationally pay to settle the obligation at the statement of financial position date or to transfer it to a third party. This means provisions for large populations of events such as warranties, are measured at a probability weighted expected value. In reaching its best estimate, the entity should take into account the risks and uncertainties that surround the underlying events.

Expected cash outflows should be discounted to their present values, where the effect of the time value of money is material using a risk adjusted rate (it should not reflect risks for which future cash flows have been adjusted). If some or all of the expenditure required to settle a provision is expected to be reimbursed by another party, the reimbursement should be recognised as a separate asset when, and only when, it is virtually certain that reimbursement will be received if the entity settles the obligation. The amount recognised should not exceed the amount of the provision. In measuring a provision future events should be considered. The provision for the warranty claim will be determined by using the expected value method.

The past event which causes the obligation is the initial sale of the product with the warranty given at that time. It would be appropriate for the company to make a provision for the Year 1 warranty of $280,000 and Year 2 warranty of $350,000, which represents the best estimate of the obligation (see Appendix 2). Only if the insurance company have validated the counter claim will Macaljoy be able to recognise the asset and income. Recovery has to be virtually certain. If it is virtually certain, then Macaljoy may be able to recognise the asset. Generally contingent assets are never recognised, but disclosed where an inflow of economic benefits is probable.

The company could discount the provision if it was considered that the time value of money was material. The majority of provisions will reverse in the short term (within two years) and, therefore, the effects of discounting are likely to be immaterial. In this case, using the risk adjusted rate (IAS 37), the provision would be reduced to $269,000 in Year 1 and $323,000 in Year 2. The company will have to determine whether this is material.

Appendix 1 – Statement of financial position at 31 October 2007:

	$m
Net defined benefit obligation	15.0

Statement of comprehensive income – year ended 31 October 2007:

Profit or loss:	$m
Net interest component	0.5
Service cost component	20.0
	20.5
Other comprehensive income:	
Net remeasurement component	1.5
Total comprehensive income charge for the year	22.0

The accounting for the defined benefit plan is as follows:

	Plan assets – FV	Plan obligation – PV	Net obligation
	$m	$m	$m
Balance b/fwd	(190.0)	200	10.0
Interest @5%	(9.5)	10	0.5
Service cost		20	20.0
Benefits paid	(19.0)	(19)	–
Contributions into plan	17.0		(17.0)
Remeasurement component (bal fig)	27.5	29	1.5
Balance c/fwd	225.0	240	15.0

Appendix 2 – Warranty

Year 1 warranty

	Expected value	Discounted expected value (4%)
	$000	$000
80% × Nil	0	
15% × 7,000 × $100	105	
5% × 7,000 × $500	175	
	280	269

Year 2 extended warranty

	Expected value	Discounted expected value (4%)
	$000	$000
70% × Nil	0	
20% × 5,000 × $100	100	
10% × 5,000 × $500	250	
	350	323

ACCA Marking scheme			
			Marks
(a)	Pensions		
	(i)	Explanation	7
	(ii)	Calculation	7
		Maximum	**14**
(b)	Provisions		
	(i)	Explanation	6
	(ii)	Calculation	3
	Structure of report		2
Total			**25**

Examiner's comments

This question required candidates to discuss the differences between a defined benefit and defined contribution scheme, to show the accounting entries for such schemes and to discuss the principles and accounting for warranty claims. The question examined the fundamental principles behind certain employee benefits and provisioning. It was surprising that several candidates confused the two types of scheme. Also at this level, it is important that candidates have an in depth knowledge of the differences between the two schemes rather than just a general view of the differences. The question was quite well answered and candidates often produced good quality answers. Professional marks were awarded for the structure of the report and consideration of certain factors, that is:

(i)   the intended purpose of the document

(ii)   its intended users and their needs

(iii)   the appropriate type of document

(iv)   logical and appropriate structure/format

(v)   nature of background information and technical language

(vi)   detail required

(vii)   clear, concise and precise presentation.

47   WADER (JUN 07 EXAM)

Key answer tips

This question tests in detail the way impairments of current and non-current assets have to be dealt with and when reorganisation provisions should be recognised. Receivables are a financial asset and the rules around the impairment of financial assets have recently been revised. As such, this is a highly examinable topic that requires attention. If you struggled with part (a), revisit the Financial Instruments chapter in the Complete Text.

(a)   Trade receivables are financial assets normally designated to be measured at amortised cost, provided both the business model test and cash flow characteristics test can be complied with per IFRS 9 *Financial instruments*.

A loss allowance is required for investments in debt instruments that are measured at amortised cost. For trade receivables that do not have a significant financing component, this loss allowance should always be equal to lifetime expected credit losses.

A credit loss is the difference between the contractual cash flows from an asset and what the entity expects to receive. These credit losses should be discounted to present value and weighted by the risks of a default occurring. Lifetime losses are the expected credit losses that arise from all possible default events over the life of the instrument.

Wader's expected credit losses can be calculated by multiplying the carrying amount of its receivables with the expected risk of default over their life. Calculation of credit losses must use information about past events and current economic conditions as well as forecasts of future economic conditions and therefore Wader is correct to have adjusted its historical default rates for future estimates. Discounting will not be required as the receivables are short-term.

The lifetime expected credit losses on the trade receivables are:

	Lifetime expected credit losses
	$m
Not overdue ($10.1m × 0.5%)	0.05
1 – 30 days overdue ($4.3m × 1.5%)	0.06
31 – 60 days overdue ($1.6m × 6.1%)	0.10
More than 60 days overdue ($1.0m × 16.5%)	0.17
	0.38

The allowance required is therefore $0.38 million. The current allowance of $0.2 million must be increased by $0.18 million and this will be charged as an impairment loss to the statement of profit or loss.

(b) IAS 2 *Inventories* requires inventory to be valued at the lower of cost and net realisable value (NRV).

NRV is the estimated selling price in the ordinary course of business, less the estimated cost of completion and the estimated costs necessary to make the sale. Any write-down should be recognised in profit or loss in the period in which the write down occurs.

When calculating NRV, the list selling price should be reduced by the customer discounts as this represents the proceeds to be received when the sale is made. The warehouse overhead costs will be incurred regardless of how long the inventory is held and are not necessarily incurred to enable the sale. It is appropriate to include personnel costs in the estimate of NRV but only where they are necessary. In this case the variable component of personnel salaries (commissions) will be taken into account but not the fixed salaries as they are normal overheads and do not influence the sale of the product.

	$
List price	50
Customer discounts	(2.5)
Commissions – sale	(10.0)
Net realisable value	37.5
Cost	35.0

The cost of the inventory is already lower than the NRV. No write down of this product is, therefore, required.

(c) IAS 16 *Property, plant and equipment* requires the increase in the carrying amount of an asset to be recognised in other comprehensive income and accumulated in equity under the heading 'revaluation surplus'. The increase should be recognised in profit or loss to the extent that it reverses a revaluation decrease of the same asset previously recognised in profit or loss. If an asset's carrying amount is decreased as a result of a revaluation, the decrease shall be recognised in profit or loss. However, the decrease is recognised in other comprehensive income as a reduction in the revaluation surplus accumulated within equity to the extent of any credit balance existing in revaluation surplus in respect of that asset. The buildings would be accounted for as follows:

	Year-ended	
	31 May 20X6	31 May 20X7
	$m	$m
Cost/valuation	10.0	8.00
Depreciation	(0.5)	(0.42)
($10m/20)		
($8m/19)		
	9.5	7.58
Impairment to profit or loss	(1.5)	
Reversal of impairment loss to profit or loss		1.42
Gain on revaluation – revaluation surplus		2.00
Carrying amount	8.0	11.00

The gain on revaluation in 20X7 has been recognised in profit or loss to the extent of the revaluation loss charged in 20X6 as adjusted for the additional depreciation ($1.5 \div 19$, i.e. $0.08m) that would have been recognised in 20X7 had the opening balance been $9.5 million, and the loss of $1.5 million not been recognised. This adjustment for depreciation is not directly mentioned in IAS 16, but is a logical consequence of the application of the matching principle and would be against the principle of IAS 16 if not carried out.

(d) A provision under IAS 37 *Provisions, contingent liabilities and contingent assets* can only be made in relation to the entity's restructuring plans where there is both a detailed formal plan in place and the plans have been announced to those affected. The plan should identify areas of the business affected, the impact on employees and the likely cost of the restructuring and the timescale for implementation. There should be a short timescale between communicating the plan and starting to implement it. A provision should not be recognised until a plan is formalised.

A decision before the end of the reporting period to restructure is not sufficient in itself for a provision to be recognised. A formal plan should be announced prior to the end of the reporting period. A constructive obligation should have arisen. It arises where there has been a detailed formal plan and this has raised a valid expectation in the minds of those affected. The provision should only include direct expenditure arising from the restructuring. Such amounts do not include costs associated with ongoing business operations. Costs of retraining staff or relocating continuing staff or marketing or investment in new systems and distribution networks, are excluded. It seems as though in this case a constructive obligation has arisen as there have been detailed formal plans approved and communicated thus raising valid expectations. The provision can be allowed subject to the exclusion of the costs outlined above.

Onerous contracts can result from restructuring plans or on a standalone basis. A provision should be made for the best estimate of the excess unavoidable costs under the onerous contract. This estimate should assess any likely level of future income from new sources. Thus in this case, the rental income from sub-letting the building should be taken into account. The provision should be recognised in the period in which it was identified and a cost recognised in profit or loss. Recognising an onerous contract provision is not a change in accounting policy under IAS 8 *Accounting policies, changes in accounting estimates and errors*.

The provision will be the lower of:

Scenario 1

	20X8	20X9	Total
	$	$	
Rent	150,000	150,000	
Discount rate	1/1.05	$1/1.05^2$	
Present value	142,857	136,054	
Sub-let income	(100,000)	(95,238)	
	42,857	40,816	83,673

Scenario 2

	20X8	20X9	Total
Rent	270,000		
Discount rate	1/1.05		
Present value	257,142		
Sub-let income	(100,000)		
	157,142		

Therefore, the provision would be $83,673 as this course of action would be more beneficial to the company.

ACCA Marking scheme	
	Marks
Impairment	7
Inventory	4
Property, plant & equipment	7
Restructuring	7
Total	**25**

48   ROUTER (JUN 07 EXAM) *Online question assistance*

Key answer tips

Part (a) tests revenue recognition. This is a common topic in the P2 exam, and should be considered highly examinable, particularly with the recent issue of IFRS 15 *Revenue from Contracts with Customers.*

(a)   **Revenue recognition**

Router's contract with its customer contains a single performance obligation, which is to make and transfer a film.

When determining the transaction price, IFRS 15 *Revenue from Contracts with Customers* says that the existence of variable consideration must be considered. Router's contract contains both fixed consideration (the $5 million fee), and variable consideration (the $100,000 fee each time the film is shown on television).

If a contract contains variable consideration, then an entity must estimate the amount that it will be entitled to for satisfying the performance obligation. If it is believed that the film will be shown four times, then the expected value of the variable consideration is $400,000.

However, variable consideration should only be included in the transaction price if it is highly probable that a significant reduction in the amount of cumulative revenue recognised will not occur. Estimates of usage fees are always going to be highly subjective. This uncertainty will be increased as a result of the film's quality issues. Therefore, the variable consideration should not be included in the transaction price.

Tutorial note

Note that paragraph B63 of IFRS 15 explicitly says that revenue from usage fees should not be recognised until both the original performance obligation has been satisfied and the usage occurs.

Therefore, revenue of $5 million should be allocated to the sale of the film and should be recognised when control of the film is passed to the customer. The fact that delivery and payment have occurred suggests that control has transferred and that the $5 million can be recognised. The cost of sale of $4 million should also be recognised in profit or loss. Revenue of $100,000 should be recognised each time the film is shown on television.

(b) **Office buildings and film studios**

IAS 16 *Property, plant and equipment* permits assets to be revalued on a class by class basis. A class of assets is a grouping of assets with a similar nature and use. The different characteristics of the buildings allow them to be classified separately. Different measurement models can, therefore, be used for the office buildings and the film studios.

However, IAS 8 *Accounting policies, changes in accounting estimates and errors* says that once an entity has decided on its accounting policies, it should apply them consistently from period to period and across all relevant transactions. An entity can change its accounting policies but only in specific circumstances. These circumstances are:

(i) where there is a new accounting standard or interpretation or changes to an accounting standard

(ii) where the change results in the financial statements providing reliable and more relevant information about the effects of transactions, other events or conditions on the entity's financial position, financial performance, or cash flows.

Voluntary changes in accounting policies are quite uncommon but may occur when an accounting policy is no longer appropriate. Router will have to ensure that the change in accounting policy meets the criteria in IAS 8. Additionally, depreciated historical cost will have to be calculated for the film studios at the commencement of the period and the opening balance on the revaluation reserve and any other affected component of equity adjusted. The comparative amounts for each prior period should be presented as if the new accounting policy had always been applied. There are limits on retrospective application on the grounds of impracticability.

Theme park lease

IAS 17 *Leases* says that if an entity leases land and buildings together then each element has to be assessed as a finance or operating lease separately. When determining the classification of the land element, it is important to remember that land has an indefinite economic life.

The fact that the building's useful life is the same as the lease term suggests that the building element of the lease should be classified as a finance lease. Based on the information available, the land element probably qualifies as an operating lease, because its useful economic life is so much longer than the lease term. However, the terms of the lease will need to be inspected in more detail. There could be other factors which may indicate that the land element is a finance lease, such as the relationship between the fair value and the present value of the minimum lease payments, as well as any options to buy or to continue to lease the land at below market rates.

(c) **Disposal of associate**

The investment in Wireless is currently accounted for using the equity method of accounting under IAS 28 (revised) *Investments in associates and joint ventures*. On the sale of a 15% holding, the interest in an associate will be derecognised, with a gain or loss on derecognition calculated for inclusion in profit or loss for the year. Router should recognise a gain on the sale of the holding in Wireless of $8 million (W1). The gain comprises the following:

(i) the disposal value or proceeds on the shares sold, plus

(ii) the fair value of the residual shareholding in Wireless, less

(iii) the carrying value of the associate at the date of disposal.

The residual holding of a 10% interest will be accounted for in accordance with IFRS 9. An equity instrument must be measured at fair value at the point of initial recognition, and thereafter at each reporting date until derecognition occurs. Normally, equity investments are classified as fair value through profit or loss (FVTPorL), with any change in fair value taken to profit or loss each year.

Alternatively, it is possible to designate the investment to be classified as fair value through other comprehensive income (FVTOCI) upon initial recognition. If this is the case, all movements in fair value, including the impact of any impairment, will be taken to other comprehensive income each year.

Therefore, at 1 January 20X7, the investment will be recorded at fair value. At 31 May 20X7 a further gain of $(26 – 23) million, i.e. $3 million will be recorded. The gain of $3 million will be recorded in either profit or loss or other comprehensive income for the year, depending upon how the investment was classified at initial recognition.

(d) **Control**

IFRS 10 *Consolidated financial statements*, identifies three elements of determining whether one entity has control of another as follows:

(i)   power over the investee, and

(ii)   exposure, or rights, to variable returns from its investment with the investee, and

(iii) ability to use its power over the investee to affect the amount of the investor's returns.

IFRS 10 identifies that any power by one entity to control another must be based upon current ability to direct activities which affect variable returns. At first sight, it would therefore appear that Router currently controls Playtime as it owns 60% of the issued equity capital of that entity.

However, IFRS 10 also states that potential voting right must be considered if the holder has the current and practical ability to exercise them. A competitor entity holds warrants which are currently exercisable and which, if exercised, would result in the competitor gaining control of Playtime. As the warrants are currently exercisable, this means that they should be factored into the assessment of control.

It would therefore seem that Router does not control Playtime and therefore should not consolidate it. Further information is required to assess whether Router exercises significant influence over Playtime. If this is the case, then Playtime is an associate and should be accounted for using the equity method. If significant influence does not exist, then the investment in the shares of Playtime is a financial asset that must be accounted for in accordance with IFRS 9 *Financial Instruments*.

Working

(W1) **Gain on sale of Wireless**

	$m
Sale proceeds	40
Plus the fair value of the residual investment	23
	63
Less: CV of interest in associate at disposal date	(55)
	8

ACCA Marking scheme	
	Marks
Revenue recognition	6
Studios and office	6
Film distribution company	6
Playtime	5
Presentation	2
	——
Available/maximum	**25**
	——

49 EGIN (JUNE 06 EXAM)

Key answer tips

This question covers related party transactions so a good knowledge of the standard is required. Part (a) of the question covers IAS 24 in detail – and there are a lot of easy marks to be gained here. Part (b) is not too difficult and could be attempted first.

(a) (i) **Importance and criteria determining a related party relationship**

Related party transactions form part of the normal business process. Companies operate their businesses through complex group structures and acquire interests in other entities for commercial or investment purposes. Control or significant influence is exercised by companies in a wide range of situations. These relationships affect the financial position and results of a company and can lead to transactions that would not normally be undertaken. Similarly those transactions may be priced at a level which is unacceptable to unrelated parties.

It is possible that even where no transactions occur between related parties, the operating results and financial position can be affected. Decisions by a subsidiary company can be heavily influenced by the holding company even though there may be no intercompany transactions. Transactions can be agreed upon terms substantially different from those with unrelated parties. For example the leasing of equipment between group companies may be at a nominal rental.

The assumption in financial statements is that transactions are carried out on an arm's length basis and that the entity has independent discretionary power over its transactions. Even if transactions are at terms equivalent to those in an arm's length, disclosure of related party transactions is useful information as future transactions may be affected. The *Framework* says that information contained in financial statements must be neutral, that is free from bias. Additionally the document says that information must represent faithfully the transactions it purports to represent. Without the disclosure of related party information, it is unlikely that these qualitative characteristics can be achieved.

IAS 24 *Related party disclosures* gives the following scenarios where a person or an entity is related to the reporting entity:

(a) A person or a close member of that person's family is related to a reporting entity if that person:

    (i) has control or joint control of the reporting entity

    (ii) has significant influence over the reporting entity

    (iii) is a member of the key management personnel of the reporting entity or of a parent of the reporting entity.

(b) An entity is related to a reporting entity if any of the following conditions applies:

    (i) The entity and the reporting entity are members of the same group (which means that each parent, subsidiary and fellow subsidiary is related to the others).

    (ii) One entity is an associate or joint venture of the other entity (or an associate or joint venture of a member of a group of which the other entity is a member).

    (iii) Both entities are joint ventures of the same third party.

    (iv) One entity is a joint venture of a third entity and the other entity is an associate of the third entity.

    (v) The entity is a post-employment benefit plan for the benefit of employees of either the reporting entity or an entity related to the reporting entity. If the reporting entity is itself such a plan, the sponsoring employers are also related to the reporting entity.

    (vi) The entity is controlled or jointly controlled by a person identified in (a).

    (vii) A person identified in (a)(i) has significant influence over the entity or is a member of the key management personnel of the entity (or of a parent of the entity).

Control is the power to govern the financial and operating policies of an entity so as to obtain benefits from its activities. The power does not need to be used for control to exist. Entities subject to common control from the same source are related parties because of the potential effect on transactions between them. Common control will exist where both entities are subject to control from management boards having a controlling nucleus of directors in common. Significant influence is the power to participate in the financial and operating policy decisions of the entity without controlling those policies. Significant influence can occur by share ownership, statute or agreement.

(ii)　**Egin Group**

Group structure:

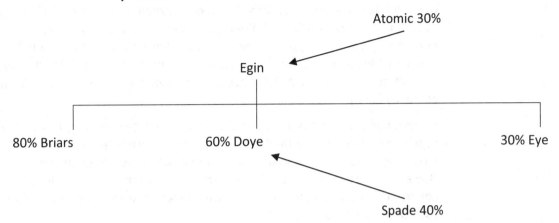

Briars and Doye and Egin are all related parties because they are members of the same group.

Egin and Eye are related parties because Egin has significant influence over Eye.

Briars and Doye are related parties of Eye. This is because they are under the control or significant influence of the same parent company.

Relationships between parents and subsidiaries should be disclosed even if there have not been any transactions between them. Therefore there should be disclosure of the relationship between Tang and Egin during the period even though Tang has now been sold.

The company, Blue, is a related party of Briars as the director controls Blue and is a member of the key management personnel of Briars. If the director is considered to be a related party of Egin, i.e. because the director acts as a consultant to the group, then this information should be disclosed in the group financial statements.

(iii)　**Spade and the Group**

Spade, being an investor in Doye, is a related party of that company and disclosure of the sale of plant and equipment will have to be made. The fact that Egin and Spade have an investment in the same company, Doye, does not itself make them related parties. The Egin group and Spade will only be related parties if there is the necessary control or influence. For example if Spade persuaded Egin to sell plant and equipment at significantly below its retail value then Egin would have subordinated its interests in agreeing to the transaction.

(iv) **Atomic and the Group**

IAS 24 says that all mentions of 'associates' within the standard also include the subsidiaries of the associate. Therefore, Atomic is a related party to Egin, over which is has significant influence, as well as Briars and Doye. The same does not necessarily apply to Eye. It would have to be proven that Atomic could significantly influence Eye because of its holding in Egin. It may be difficult to exercise such influence in an associate (Eye) of an associated company (Egin).

Related party transactions are between parties where one party has control or significant influence and by definition are not at arm's length. Therefore, the transactions between related parties should not be described as arm's length. However, Disclosures that related party transactions were made on terms equivalent to those that prevail in arm's length transactions can be made if such terms can be substantiated.

(b) **Purchase of Briars**

IAS 21 *The effects of changes in foreign exchange rates* requires goodwill arising on the acquisition of a foreign operation and fair value adjustments to acquired assets and liabilities to be treated as belonging to the foreign operation. They should be expressed in the functional currency of the foreign operation and translated at the closing rate at the end of each reporting period. Effectively goodwill is treated as a foreign currency asset which is retranslated at the closing rate.

In this case the goodwill arising on the acquisition of Briars would be treated as follows:

	Euros m	Rate	$m
Cost of acquisition	50		
FV NCI (20% × 45)	9		
	59		
Less: FV of net assets at acquisition	(45)		
Goodwill at 1 June 20X5	14	2.0	7.0
Impairment	(3)	2.3	(1.3)
Exchange loss (difference)			(1.3)
Goodwill at 31 May 20X6	11	2.5	4.4

At 31 May 20X6, the goodwill will be retranslated at 2.5 euros to the dollar to give a figure of $4.4 million. Therefore this will be the figure for goodwill in the statement of financial position and an exchange loss of $1.3 million will be recorded in other comprehensive income (translation reserve). The impairment of goodwill will be expensed in profit or loss to the value of $1.3 million.

Loan to Briars

The loan to Briars will be classed as a financial liability measured at amortised cost. When a financial liability is recognised initially in the statement of financial position, the liability is measured at fair value. IFRS 13 defines fair value as the price paid to transfer a liability in an orderly transaction between market participants at the measurement date.

Since fair value is a market transaction price, it will often be equal to the amount of consideration paid or received for the financial asset or financial liability. However, the loan has been made on an interest free basis, whereas normal market loans would attract an interest rate of 6%. This means that the transaction between Egin and Briars is not one between normal market participants. Therefore, the fair value of the loan must be calculated as the present value of the cash flows to be received or paid discounted using a market rate of interest.

Date	$000	Exchange rate	Euros 000
		Loan amount	
01/06/05 ($10m/1.06^2)	8,900	$1: 2 euros	17,800
Interest (6%)	534	$1: 2.3 euros	1,228
Forex (bal. fig.)			4,557
	9,434	$1: 2.5 euros	23,585

In profit or loss in the individual accounts of Briars there will be an interest expense of 1,228,000 euros and a foreign exchange loss of 4,557,000 euros.

ACCA Marking scheme				*Marks*
(a)	(i)	Reasons and explanation		4
	(ii)	Egin		4
		Spade		3
		Atomic		3
(b)	Goodwill			5
	Loan			4
Professional				2
Total				**25**

50   TYRE (JUNE 06 EXAM)

Key answer tips

This is a typical discussion question where you are asked to deal with a number of accounting issues. The first three are relatively straightforward and you will have come across them before. The last one is trickier, but you need to think of it in terms of IAS 37 and whether or not a provision is required.

(i)   **Sale to customers**

Tyre enters into contracts with customers that are within the scope of IFRS 15 *Revenue from Contracts with Customers*. The contracts contain a single performance obligation, which is the sale of a car. The total transaction price (the deposit plus the final balance) is allocated to this performance obligation and recognised as revenue when/as the performance obligation is satisfied.

The sale of a car is a performance obligation satisfied at a point in time. Therefore revenue should not be recognised until control of the car is transferred to the customer. Indicators that control has passed would include:

- The entity has a present right to payment

- The customer has legal title to the asset

- The entity has transferred physical possession of the asset

- The customer has the significant risks and rewards of ownership of the asset

- The customer has accepted the asset.

It would therefore seem that control does not pass to the customer until the car has been delivered.

When the deposit is received, it should be recognised as a liability. The deposit and the final payment will be recognised as revenue upon delivery of the car. If the customer does cancel the order, then the non-refundable deposit would be recognised in revenue at the date of the cancellation of the order.

Sale of fleet cars

The customer has an economic incentive to exercise the buyback option. Consequently, the customer is essentially paying for the right to use the asset over three years. Therefore, this is a lease agreement that should be accounted for in accordance with IAS 17 *Leases*.

Ownership of the assets are not expected to be transferred to Hub, the lease term is arguably not for the major part of the assets' life, and the present value of the minimum lease payments will not be substantially equivalent to the fair value of the asset. Therefore it is an operating lease.

No 'outright sale profit' will be recognised as the risks and rewards of ownership have been retained and no sale has occurred. The vehicles will be shown in property, plant and equipment and depreciated over their estimated useful economic life. The lease income should be recognised in the statement of profit or loss on a straight line basis over the lease term of three years unless some other basis is more representative.

(ii) **Former administrative building**

The land and buildings of the former administrative centre are accounted for as separate elements. The demolition of the building is an indicator of the impairment of the property under IAS 36. The building will not generate any future cash flows and its recoverable amount is zero. Therefore, the carrying value of the building will be written down to zero and the loss charged to profit or loss in the year to 31 May 20X6 when the decision to demolish the building was made. The land value will be in excess of its carrying amount as the company uses the cost model and land prices are rising. Thus no impairment charge is recognised in respect of the land.

The demolition costs will be expensed when incurred and a provision for environmental costs recognised when an obligation arises, i.e. in the financial year to 31 May 20X7. It may be that some of these costs could be recognised as site preparation costs and be capitalised under IAS 16.

The land will not meet the criteria set out in IFRS 5 *Non-current assets held for sale and discontinued operations* as a non-current asset that is held for sale. IFRS 5 says that a non-current asset should be classified as held for sale if its carrying amount will be recovered principally through a sale transaction rather than through continuing use. However, the non-current asset must be available for immediate sale and must be actively marketed at its current fair value (amongst other criteria) and these criteria have not been met in this case.

When the building has been demolished and the site prepared, the land could be considered to be an investment property and accounted for under IAS 40 *Investment property* where the fair value model allows gains (or losses) to be recognised in profit or loss for the period.

(iii) **Retail outlets**

The lease premium paid for a finance lease should be capitalised and recognised as an asset under the lease. The premium will be depreciated as part of the asset's value over the shorter of the lease term and the asset's useful life.

The operating lease premium will be spread over the lease term on a straight line basis unless some other method is more representative. The premium will be effectively treated as a prepayment of rent and is amortised over the life of the agreement.

(iv) **Car accessories**

A provision should only be recognised if there is a present obligation (legal or constructive), an outflow of economic resources is probable, and the entity can reliably estimate the amount of the obligation.

These conditions do not seem to have been met. Until the vehicle is purchased, there is no obligation to provide the accessories and therefore no provision should be created.

When the car is purchased and the accessories are transferred to the customer, the accessories become part of the cost of the sale. The revenue recognised will be the amount received from the customer (the total transaction price).

ACCA Marking scheme	
	Marks
Revenue recognition	8
Administrative building	7
Lease agreements	5
Car accessories	5
	—
Total	**25**
	—

51   PROCHAIN (JUN 06 EXAM)

Key answer tips

This is a multi-standard question covering many core topics. You are given marks for each segment of the question, so always answer the part of the question you are most comfortable with first. You don't need to attempt the question in order.

Model areas

The cost of the model areas should be accounted for as property, plant and equipment in accordance with IAS 16 *Property, plant and equipment* (PPE). PPE are tangible assets that are held for use in the production or supply of goods or services, for rental to others or for administrative purposes, and are expected to be utilised in more than one period. The model areas meet this definition because they are used in more than one accounting period, and customers will be able to view the fashion goods in those areas. The costs of the model areas should be depreciated over their expected useful life to their expected residual value which in this case is zero.

Prochain, after initial recognition, could use the cost model or revaluation model for the measurement of the model areas. However, it would be difficult to adopt the revaluation model as it would not be possible to measure fair value reliably.

Prochain has an obligation to dismantle the model areas after two years. The company should assess whether it has a present obligation as a result of a past event. The assessment should be carried out in accordance with IAS 37 *Provisions, contingent liabilities and contingent assets*. In this case it would seem that a provision should be set up and the amount added to the cost of the asset.

The provision recognised should be $3.6 million ($20m × 20% × $1/1.055^2$) and this would be added to the construction cost of the asset, giving a total cost of $23.6 million.

The asset would be depreciated over its useful life, with accumulated depreciation of $7.9 million ($23.6 million × 8/24) by the reporting date.

The discount on the provision must be unwound, giving rise to a finance cost of $0.13 million ($3.6m × 5.5% × 8/12). The provision will therefore have a carrying amount at the reporting date of $3.73 million ($3.6m + $0.13m).

Purchase of Badex

IFRS 3 *Business Combinations* requires that purchase consideration transferred to obtain control over a subsidiary is measured at its fair value. This includes any share consideration, deferred consideration, or contingent consideration. However, legal and professional costs must be expensed to the statement of profit or loss. Accordingly the legal fees of $2 million are not part of the cost of the investment.

The cash payment of $100 million should be recognised as part of the cost of the investment. The deferred consideration should be discounted to present value and recognised at $9m ($10m × $1/1.055^2$), with a corresponding credit to liabilities. The discount on the liability will be unwound over the year, with a $0.5m ($9m × 5.5%) charge recognised in finance costs in the statement of profit or loss in the current year. The contingent consideration is recognised at its fair value of $5m, with a corresponding credit to provisions. Total purchase consideration is therefore $114 million ($100 + $9m + $5m).

With regard to changes in the fair value of any contingent consideration after the acquisition date, if the change is due to additional information obtained after the acquisition date that affects the facts or circumstances as they existed at the acquisition date this is treated as a 'measurement period adjustment' and the liability (and goodwill) are remeasured. However, what is more likely, is that changes will be due to events after the acquisition date and therefore any remeasurement of the provision for contingent consideration will be charged to profit or loss.

The acquirer is required to recognise separately an intangible asset of the acquiree company at the acquisition date if it meets the definition of an intangible asset in IAS 38 *Intangible assets* and its fair value can be measured reliably. As the fair value of the brand name appears to be capable of reliable measurement, then it should be recognised in the consolidated statements at $20 million.

Research and development expenditure

IAS 38 *Intangible assets* provides guidance on the recognition of internally generated intangible assets, particularly on the expenditure on research and development of products. During the research phase, a project is not deemed to be far enough advanced for an entity to be able to demonstrate that it is probable that economic benefits will be generated. Therefore all expenditure incurred during this phase should be expensed immediately in the statement of profit or loss. Where economic benefits can realistically be expected to be generated from development activities, then an intangible asset can be recognised subject to meeting the following recognition criteria:

(i)   technical feasibility of project

(ii)   intention to complete the intangible asset and use or sell it

(iii)   the ability to use or sell the intangible

(iv)   generation of probable future economic benefits

(v)   availability of adequate technical, financial and other resources to complete the development and to use or sell it

(vi)   ability to reliably measure the expenditure attributable to the intangible.

For a company to recognise an intangible asset in the statement of financial position, it should be probable that the expected future economic benefits generated from the asset will flow to the entity and the cost of the asset should be capable of reliable measurement. Costs that should be recognised as part of the intangible asset are those that are directly attributable to preparing the asset for its intended use. These costs will include employee costs and design costs. Work undertaken to establish whether there is a market for a product is deemed not to be directly attributable to bringing the intangible asset into a condition for its intended use. Staff training costs are specifically excluded from the component costs of an internally generated intangible asset. The costs of upgrading the existing machinery can be capitalised as property, plant and equipment. IAS 36 *Impairment of assets* will be used to establish whether future economic benefits will be generated. Thus the costs incurred will be dealt with as follows:

	Profit or loss	SOFP	
		Intangible assets	Tangible assets
	$m	$m	$m
Research as to extent of market	3		
Prototype clothing and goods design		4	
Employee costs		2	
Development work		5	
Production and launch – machinery			3
market research	2		
training costs	1		
	——	——	——
	6	11	3
	——	——	——

Intangible assets should be carried using either the cost model or the revaluation model.

There is an element of subjectivity involved in determining the value of any intangible asset to arise from the above expenditure and it is up to the company to demonstrate that the recognition criteria are explicitly met. In this case, it would appear that the company would recognise $11 million. The project has advanced to a stage where it is probable that future economic benefits will arise.

Apartments

The apartments are occupied by persons who are contracted to the company and are essentially employees. The apartments should therefore be classified as property, plant and equipment. The apartments could be measured using the cost model or the revaluation model.

The difference between market rents and the actual rents charged cannot be recognised as an employee benefit expense.

ACCA Marking scheme	
	Marks
Model areas	7
Purchase of Badex	8
Research and development	6
Apartments	4
	——
Total	**25**
	——

52 PANEL (DEC 05 EXAM)

Key answer tips

This question requires you to be able to understand how various accounting treatments affect the deferred tax provision and to be able to apply that understanding.

(a) (i) IAS 12 *Income taxes* adopts a statement of financial position approach to accounting for deferred taxation. The IAS adopts a full provision approach to accounting for deferred taxation. It is assumed that the recovery of all assets and the settlement of all liabilities have tax consequences and that these consequences can be estimated reliably and are unavoidable. IFRSs recognition criteria are generally different from those embodied in tax law, and thus temporary differences will arise which represent the difference between the carrying amount of an asset and liability and its basis for taxation purposes (tax base). The principle is that a company will settle its liabilities and recover its assets over time and at that point the tax consequences will crystallise.

Thus a change in an accounting standard will often affect the carrying value of an asset or liability which in turn will affect the amount of the temporary difference between the carrying value and the tax base. This in turn will affect the amount of the deferred taxation provision which is the tax rate multiplied by the amount of the temporary differences (assuming a net liability for deferred tax).

(ii) A company has to apply IAS 12 to the temporary differences between the carrying amount of the assets and liabilities in its opening IFRS statement of financial position (1 November 20X3) and their tax bases (IFRS 1 *First time adoption of IFRS*). The deferred tax provision will be calculated using tax rates that have been enacted or substantially enacted by the end of the reporting period. The carrying values of the assets and liabilities at the date of the opening statement of financial position will be determined by reference to IFRS 1 and will use the applicable IFRSs in the first IFRS financial statements. Any adjustments required to the deferred tax balance will be recognised directly in retained earnings.

Subsequent statements of financial position (at 31 October 20X4 and 31 October 20X5) will be drawn up using the IFRSs used in the financial statements to 31 October 20X5. The deferred tax provision will be adjusted as at 31 October 20X4 and then as at 31 October 20X5 to reflect the temporary differences arising at those dates.

(b) (i) The tax deduction is based on the option's intrinsic value which is the difference between the market price and exercise price of the share option. It is likely that a deferred tax asset will arise which represents the difference between the tax base of the employee's service received to date and the carrying amount which will effectively normally be zero.

The recognition of the deferred tax asset should be dealt with on the following basis:

(a) if the estimated or actual tax deduction is less than or equal to the cumulative recognised expense then the associated tax benefits are recognised in the profit or loss

(b) if the estimated or actual tax deduction exceeds the cumulative recognised compensation expense then the excess tax benefits are recognised in other comprehensive income and held in a separate component of equity.

As regards the tax effects of the share options in the year to 31 October 20X4, the tax deduction is nil and the estimated future tax deduction is $8 million ($16m × 1/2). These are less than the cumulative recognised expense of $20 million ($40m × 1/2) so the tax benefit will be recognised in profit or loss

The tax benefit is 30% × $8 million = $2.4 million, which will be recognised within the deferred tax provision.

At 31 October 20X5, the options have been exercised. Tax receivable will be 30% × $46 million, i.e. $13.8 million. The deferred tax asset of $2.4 million is no longer recognised as the tax benefit has crystallised at the date when the options were exercised.

For a tax benefit to be recognised in the year to 31 October 20X4, the provisions of IAS 12 should be complied with as regards whether the deferred tax asset should be recognised.

(ii) Plant acquired under a finance lease will be recorded as property, plant and equipment and a corresponding liability for the obligation to pay future rentals. Rents payable are apportioned between the finance charge and a reduction of the outstanding obligation. A temporary difference will arise between the carrying value of the lease and its tax base. The tax base is nil because the tax relief is only obtained when payments are made.

	PPE in FS $m		Liability in FS $m
Initial	12	Initial	12
Depreciation (1/5)	(2.4)	Repaid	(3)
		Interest	(0.96)
		(8% × 12)	
	9.6		9.96

The carrying value of the lease in the financial statements is therefore a net liability $0.36m ($9.6m – $9.96). The tax base, as noted above, is nil.

A deferred tax asset of $108,000 ($0.36m × 30%) will arise.

(iii)   The subsidiary, Pins, has made a profit of $2 million on the transaction with Panel. These goods are held in inventory at the year-end and a consolidation adjustment of an equivalent amount will be made against profit and inventory.

Pins will have provided for the tax on this profit as part of its current tax liability. This tax will need to be eliminated at the group level and this will be done by recognising a deferred tax asset of $2 million × 30%, i.e. $600,000.

IAS 12 does not specifically address the issue of which tax rate should be used calculate the deferred tax provision. IAS 12 does generally say that regard should be had to the expected recovery or settlement of the tax. This would be generally consistent with using the rate applicable to the transferee company (Panel) rather than the transferor (Pins).

(iv)   The recognition of the impairment loss by Nails reduces the carrying value of the property, plant and equipment of the company and hence the taxable temporary difference. The deferred tax liability will, therefore, be reduced accordingly. No deferred tax would have been recognised on the goodwill in accordance with IAS 12 and, therefore, the impairment loss relating to the goodwill does not cause an adjustment to the deferred tax position.

	Goodwill $m	PP & E $m	Tax base $m
Balance at 31 October 20X5	1	6	
Impairment loss	(1)	(0.8)	
	–	5.2	4

The deferred tax liability before the impairment loss is (6 − 4) at 30%, i.e. $0.6 million. After the impairment loss it is (5.2 − 4) at 30%, i.e. $0.36 million, thus reducing the liability by $0.24 million.

ACCA Marking scheme			Marks
(a)	(i)	Discussion	5
	(ii)	IFRS 1	4
(b)	(i)	Share options	4
	(ii)	Leased asset	4
	(iii)	Unrealised profit	4
	(iv)	Impairment loss	4
Total			**25**

53 VIDENT (JUN 05 EXAM)

Key answer tips

This question requires a detailed knowledge of accounting for share-based payments as per IFRS 2. This is a key area of the syllabus so you should spend plenty of time on this question. Make sure that as well as calculating the effect of a share-based payment transaction, you can deal with the deferred tax effect as well. This question also includes a prior period adjustment as it deals with accounting for share-based payments for the first time by the company.

Report to the Directors of Vident, a public limited company

(a)   **IFRS 2 *Share-based payment***

The arguments put forward by the Directors for not recognising the remuneration expense have been made by many opponents of the IFRS.

The argument that the share options do not have a cost to the company and, therefore, should not be recognised, is not one which is consistent with the way that other share issues are dealt with. An accounting entry is required to recognise the resources received as consideration for the shares issued, just as occurs when shares are issued in a business acquisition. The expense recognised represents the consumption of the resources received, just as depreciation will be charged on the non-current assets acquired in a business acquisition. The consumption of the resources in the case of share options is immediate and may be spread over a period of time.

The question as to whether the expense arising from share options meets the definition of an expense as set out in the *Framework* is problematical. The *Framework* requires an outflow of assets or a liability to be incurred before an expense is created. Services do not normally meet the definition of an asset and, therefore, consumption of those services does not represent an outflow of assets. However, share options are issued for valuable consideration, that is the employee services and the benefits of the asset received results in an expense. The main reason why the creation of the expense is questioned is that the receipt of the asset and its consumption in the form of employee services occur at virtually the same time. The conclusion must, therefore, be that the recognition of the expense arising from share-based payment transactions is consistent with the *Framework*.

The argument that any cost from share-based payment is already recognised in the dilution of earnings per share (EPS) is not appropriate as the impact of EPS reflects the two economic events that have occurred. The company has issued share options with the subsequent effect on the diluted EPS and it has consumed the resources that it received for awarding those options, thereby decreasing earnings. Those two different effects on EPS are counted once each.

It is probably true that IFRS 2 may discourage companies from introducing or continuing with employee share plans. However, the main reason for the non-continuation of such schemes could be that the true economic consequences of such plans are being revealed rather than the situation where resources are consumed by issuing share options without accounting properly for those transactions. The role of accounting is to report in a neutral manner and not to distort the financial position.

(b) **Accounting in the financial statements for the year-ended 31 May 20X5**

IFRS 2 requires an expense to be recognised for the share options granted to the directors with a corresponding amount shown in equity. Where options do not vest immediately but only after a period of service, then there is a presumption that the services will be rendered over the vesting period. The fair value of the services rendered will be measured by reference to the fair value of the equity instruments at the date that the equity instruments were granted. Fair value should be based on market prices. The treatment of vesting conditions depends on whether or not the conditions relate to the market price of the instruments. Market conditions are effectively taken into account in determining the fair value of the instruments and therefore can be ignored for the purposes of estimating the number of equity instruments that will vest. For other conditions such as remaining in the employment of the company, the calculations are carried out based on the best estimate of the number of instruments that will vest. The estimate is revised when subsequent information is available.

Note that the requirements of IFRS 13 *Fair value measurement* do not apply to situations where IFRS 2 applies.

The share options are valued as follows:

	Prior to 1 June 20X4 Remuneration expense	Year-ended 31 May 20X5 Remuneration expense
	$	$
J. Van Heflin		
20,000 options × $5 × ½	50,000	50,000
R. Ashworth		
50,000 options × $6 × 1/3		100,000
	50,000	150,000

The conditions set out in performance condition A and the service conditions by the director have been met. The expense is spread over two years up to the vesting date of 1 June 20X5.

The increase in the share price to above $13.50 in condition B has not been met but IFRS 2 says that the services received should be recognised irrespective of whether the market condition is satisfied. Additionally the director has to work for the company for three years for the options to vest and, therefore, the expense is spread over three years.

The opening balance of retained earnings at 1 June 20X4 would be reduced by $50,000 and equity (separate component) increased by $50,000.

Directors' remuneration relating to share options of $150,000 would be recognised in profit or loss in the year ended 31 May 20X5 and equity (separate component) would be increased by the same amount.

(c)   **Deferred tax implications**

IAS 12 (para 58) requires the deferred tax on the share options to be recognised in profit or loss for the period. The difference between the tax base of the services received (that is the amount of the tax allowance in future periods) and the carrying value of zero will be a deductible temporary difference that results in a deferred tax asset. IFRS 2 says that the estimated future tax deduction should be based on the option's intrinsic value at the year-end as the value at the exercise date will not be known. The intrinsic value is the difference between the fair value (market price) of the share and the exercise price of the option.

Prior to 1 June 20X4

Deferred tax asset and income

20,000 options × ($12.50 – $4.50) (intrinsic value) × 1/2 (first year) × 30% tax rate i.e. $24,000

All of this deferred tax income will be recognised in the opening statement of financial position (subject to the rules of IAS 12 *Income taxes*).

If the amount of the tax deduction exceeds the amount of the accumulated remuneration expense, then this indicates that the tax deduction relates to equity as well as to the remuneration expense. The remuneration expense is $50,000 prior to 1/06/04 and the eligible tax deduction will be 20,000 × intrinsic value ($8) × 1/2 i.e. $80,000. Therefore of the deferred tax income ($80,000 – $50,000) × 30% will go to equity, i.e. $9,000.

	Year to 31 May 20X5
	$
Deferred tax asset at year-end	
20,000 options × ($12 – $4.50) × 30%	45,000
50,000 options × ($12 – $6) × 30% × 1/3	30,000
	75,000
Less recognised in opening balance	(24,000)
Deferred tax income for year to profit or loss	51,000

As above the total remuneration expense to date must be compared to the amount of the tax deduction. The total remuneration expense is $200,000 and the eligible tax deduction is $150,000 (20,000 × $12 – $4.50) + $100,000 (50,000 × $6 × 1/3) i.e. $250,000. Therefore of the deferred tax income $50,000 × 30%, i.e. $15,000 should go to equity. In 20X4, $9,000 of this figure has already gone to equity and therefore of the deferred tax income for 20X5 ($51,000), $6,000 should go to equity.

Thus a deferred tax asset will arise in your first financial statements using IFRS 2.

It is hoped that the above is useful.

ACCA Marking scheme		Marks
(a)	Discussion	9
(b)	Computation and discussion	9
(c)	Computation and discussion	7
Total		**25**

54 ARTWRIGHT

Key answer tips

This question requires a detailed knowledge of IFRS 9. This is a complex standard that is frequently examined, so make sure you review this question carefully.

(a) **Hedge effectiveness**

If an entity chooses to hedge account, then it must assess at inception and at each reporting date whether the hedge meets all effectiveness criteria. These criteria are as follows:

- There must be an economic relationship between the hedged item and the hedging instrument

- The effect of credit risk does not dominate the value changes that arise from that relationship

- The hedged ratio should be the same as that resulting from the quantity of the hedged item that the entity actually hedges and the quantity of the hedging instrument that the entity actually uses.

IFRS 9 *Financial Instruments* says that hedge effectiveness relates to expectations and therefore the assessment of effectiveness must be forwards-looking.

Derivatives

All derivatives have to be initially recognised at fair value, i.e. at the consideration given or received at inception of the contract. Derivatives A and C appear to have no purchase price, so are initially recognised at nil. Derivative B will be initially recognised at its fair value of $1m.

Derivative A: Artwright has entered into this derivative for speculative purposes. IFRS 9 requires that all derivatives not designated as part of a hedge accounting arrangement are accounted for at fair value through profit or loss. The loss of $20 million that has been incurred has to be immediately recognised profit or loss.

Derivative B: If a fair value hedge is effective, then the movement in the fair value of the item and the instrument since the inception of the hedge are normally recognised in profit or loss. However, if the hedged item is an investment in shares that has been designated to be measured at fair value through other comprehensive income (FVOCI), then the fair value movement on the hedged item and the hedging instrument are recognised in other comprehensive income.

The hedged item is an investment of shares designated to be measured at FVOCI. Therefore, the following entries are required at the reporting date:

Dr Financial asset $8.5m

Cr Other comprehensive income $8.5m

Dr Other comprehensive income $10m

Cr Derivative $10m.

Derivative C: If a cash flow hedge is effective, then the movement in the fair value of the instrument is accounted for through other comprehensive income. However, if the movement on the instrument exceeds the movement on the item, then the excess is recognised in profit or loss.

The following entry is required:

Dr Derivative $25m

Cr Other comprehensive income $24m

Cr Profit or loss $1m

When the raw materials are purchased, the gains recognised in other comprehensive income can be reclassified against the carrying amount of the inventory.

(b) **Investment in bonds**

Financial assets are initially measured at fair value, so the investment in the bond will be initially recognised at $10m.

It would seem that the entity's business model involves both holding debt instruments to collect their contractual cash flows and also selling the assets. As a debt instrument, it would appear that the contractual terms of the asset comprise the repayment of the principal and interest on the principal amount outstanding. Therefore, the asset should be measured at fair value through other comprehensive income.

Interest income should be recognised in profit or loss using the effective rate of interest. At the reporting date, the asset should be revalued to fair value with the gain or loss recognised in other comprehensive income. These gains or losses will be recycled to profit or loss if the asset is disposed of.

Interest income of $1.5 million (W1) should be recognised in profit or loss. Revaluing the asset to its fair value of $9.0 million will lead to a loss of $2.0 million (W1) being recorded in other comprehensive income.

Loss allowance

IFRS 9 *Financial Instruments* requires a loss allowance to be recognised on investments in debt that are measured at amortised cost or fair value through other comprehensive income.

If credit risk has not increased significantly since initial recognition, the loss allowance should be equal to 12-month expected credit losses. If credit risk has increased significantly, the loss allowance must be equal to lifetime expected credit losses.

The credit risk of Winston's bonds remains low at the reporting date, suggesting that there has not been a significant increase in credit risk. The loss allowance should therefore be equal to the 12-month expected credit losses of $0.2m.

When the financial asset is measured at fair value though other comprehensive income, the loss allowance is not adjusted against the asset's carrying amount (otherwise the asset will be held below fair value). Therefore, the loss allowance is charged to profit or loss, with the credit entry being recorded in other comprehensive income (essentially, this adjustment reclassifies $0.2m of the earlier downwards revaluation from other comprehensive income to profit or loss).

Working

(W1) Financial asset

	1/12/X3	Interest (15%)	Cash received	Total	Loss.	30/11/X4
	$m	$m	$m	$m	$m	$m
	10.0	1.5	(0.5)	11.0	(2.0)	9.0

ACCA Marking scheme				
				Marks
(a)	Hedge effectiveness			4
	Discussion A			3
	Discussion B			4
	Discussion C			3
(b)	Investment in bond			9
	Professional marks			2
Totak				**25**

55   LUCKY DAIRY

Key answer tips

IAS 41 *Agriculture* is a relatively simple accounting standard: biological assets are measured at initial recognition and at each year end at fair value less costs to sell with gains and losses recognised in profit or loss. However, there are lots of other issues within the scenario, such as the accounting treatment of provisions, contingencies, and held for sale assets, that are also worth many marks.

Biological assets

IAS 41 *Agriculture* prescribes the accounting treatment, financial statement presentation and disclosures related to agricultural activity. A biological asset such as a dairy herd should be measured at each reporting date at its fair value less estimated costs to sell except where fair value cannot be measured reliably. The fair value of cattle is the price in the relevant market less the transport and other costs of getting the cattle to that market. Any gains or losses arising from a change in the fair value should be included in profit or loss for the period in which it arises.

The standard encourages companies to separate the change in fair value less estimated point of sale costs between that due to physical changes and the portion attributable to price changes. Table 1 calculates these changes in fair value, excluding Dale region, which are $300,000 due to price change and $350,000 due to physical change. Again the company is encouraged by the standard to provide a quantified description of each group of biological assets. Thus the cows and the heifers should be shown and quantified separately in the statement of financial position.

Agricultural produce

Milk should be valued under IAS 41 at its fair value at the time of milking less estimated costs to sell. However, due to the bad publicity, the inventory of milk has risen tenfold from 50,000 kilograms to 500,000 kilograms. There is a need to ascertain whether this milk is fit for consumption and whether there will be a need to dispose of some of the milk. The quantity of milk which will not be sold should be determined and written off the value of the inventory.

Government grant

Unconditional government grants should be recognised as income under IAS 41 when and only when the government grant becomes receivable. Although there had been a statement on 1 April 20X2 that the grant/compensation was to be paid, it was only on 6 June 20X2 that an official letter was received stating the amount to be paid to Lucky and, therefore, the $1.5 million should be recognised as income in the year to 31 May 20X3.

Provisions and contingencies

IAS 37 *Provisions, Contingent Liabilities and Contingent Assets* indicates that where there is a present obligation as a result of a past obligating event which will probably result in an outflow of resources, then a provision should be recognised for the best estimate to settle the obligation. In this case the lawyers have indicated that it is probable that Lucky will become liable for the illness of consumers of the milk and, therefore, a provision for $2 million should be made.

IAS 37 is quite specific on expected reimbursement of costs. Such reimbursement should only be recognised when it is virtually certain that it will be received. In this case, the reimbursement is only possible, and therefore, an asset will not be recognised for the compensation which may be paid by the government. No disclosure should be made, as the payout is not probable.

Impairment

Given the various events that have affected the company during the period, it would seem that consideration should be given to impairment of the herd's value in the Dale region as it is the only one affected by the disease. Where a biological asset's fair value is not reliable it should be valued at cost less any impairment losses. This value should be $1.2 million (W1).

The planned sale

A disposal group should be classified as held for sale it its carrying amount will be recovered principally through a sales transaction and:

- The sale is highly probable
- The assets are available for immediate sale in their current condition
- The sale is expected within 12 months of the classification date
- The assets are being actively marketed at a price that is reasonable compared to their fair value.

The sale of farms in the Dale region was only approved on 31 May 20X2. This means that it is unlikely that the sale was being actively marketed at the year end and therefore the assets cannot be classified as held for sale.

No provision is required for any possible redundancies resulting from the sale. There is no constructive obligation to make the redundancies because a detailed plan has not yet been made and those affected by it have not been informed.

Table 1 – Based on cattle stock, excluding Dale region

	$000	$000
Fair value at 1 June 20X1 50,000 × $50		2,500
Purchase 1 December 20X1 25,000 × $40		1,000
Increase in fair value less estimated point of sale costs due to price change:		
50,000 × $(55 – 50)	250	
25,000 × $(42 – 40)	50	
	———	300
Increase in fair value less estimated point of sale costs due to physical change:		
50,000 × $(60 – 55)	250	
25,000 × $(46 – 42)	100	
	———	350
Fair value less estimated point of sale costs at 31 May 20X2:		
50,000 × 60	3,000	
25,000 × 46	1,150	
	———	
		———
		4,150
		———

Working

(W1) Dale region

In the Dale region, it was felt that the fair value could not be reliably measured on initial recognition. Therefore, the cows and heifers should be measured at cost less any accumulated depreciation (information not provided) and impairment losses until the fair value of the asset becomes measurable. It is considered that this is not yet the case with these animals.

	$000
20,000 cows at cost ($50) 1 June 20X1	1,000
10,000 heifers at cost ($40) 1 June 20X1	400
	———
	1,400
	———
Net selling price	1,000
	———
Value in use (discounted value of milk)	1,200
	———

Therefore the value of the cows is impaired and should be valued at the value in use of $1,200,000.

The value of the herd at 31 May 20X2 in the Dale region would have been 20,000 cows at $60 + 10,000 heifers at $55 i.e. $1.75m but for the unreliability of the herd's fair value.

ACCA Marking scheme	
	Marks
Discussion – subjective 1 mark per point	20
Table 1	5
	—
Total	**25**
	—

56   SHIRES PROPERTY CONSTRUCTION

Key answer tips

This three-part question is a good question to help you work through the process of applying a reconstruction scheme. It is unlikely that you would be asked to prepare journal entries, but this may help you to work through the process logically and they are provided for reference. Much of the revised statement of financial position can be compiled from information provided about new carrying values, without necessarily preparing a reconstruction account, although this may be required as part of your workings for the finished answer. The last two parts of the question involve explanation and comment, so don't regard this type of question as purely a 'number crunching' exercise; questions in part (b) of the exam paper invariably have a written element.

(a)   Shires Property Construction

Statement of financial position at 1 January 2010 (after reconstruction)

		$
Non-current assets:		
Land at valuation		90,000
Building at valuation		80,000
Equipment at valuation		10,000
		180,000
Current assets:		
Inventories at valuation	50,000	
Trade receivables ($70,692 × 90%)	63,623	
Cash at bank (W5)	46,287	159,910
		339,910
Equity and liabilities		
Equity shares @ $0.25 (W4)		142,500
Share premium		17,500
Retained earnings		nil
Capital reconstruction reserve (W1)		5,663
		165,663
Non-current liabilities:		
9.5% Debenture 2013	89,000	
8.0% Unsecured loan	35,000	
		124,000
Current liabilities:		
Trade payables		50,247
		339,910

(b)   Division of pre-tax profit

Interested parties		Before reconstruction	After reconstruction
Debenture holders		$	$
Gross interest	(W2)	6,400	8,455
5,000 equity shares	(W4)		1,360
		6,400	9,815
Unsecured loan			
Gross interest	(W3)	3,500	2,800
35,000 equity shares	(W4)		9,516
			12,316
Directors	(W4)		680
Balance to equity shareholders	(W4)	40,100	27,189
		50,000	50,000

The allocation of profit, both before and after the reconstruction, reflects respective interests of those who provide the long-term finance or the entity: the debenture holders, the unsecured loan holders and providers of equity finance.

The providers of loan finance will increase their share of available profit after the reconstruction. This could be regarded as reasonable as their continued support is required if the reconstruction is to be successful. Similarly, the proportion of available profit to which equity holders would be entitled has fallen, reflecting their relatively weak position before the reconstruction is implemented.

(c)   Comments on the capital structure

Gearing is: ($35,000 + $89,000)/($165,663 + $124,000) = 42.8%

Whether gearing is viewed as high or not depends upon the current economic climate. It will however reduce when the debenture loan is paid off in 2013. Indeed, dividends on equity shares will have to be very restrained if cash is to be available to redeem the debentures. Alternatively, debenture holders might agree to exchange them for equity shares.

The shareholders' equity almost covers approximately 92% of the carrying value of the non-current assets. The capital structure is reasonably satisfactory.

The debenture holders have done very well. Their interest has been increased by 1.5% and the redemption date has not been changed.

The providers of the unsecured loan have also received an increase in the rate of interest to be charged on that loan.

Workings

(W1) Trial balance after reconstruction

	$	$
Land	90,000	
Buildings	80,000	
Equipment	10,000	
Inventories	50,000	
Trade receivables	63,623	
Cash	46,287	
Equity shares @ $0.25		142,500
Share premium		17,500
8% Unsecured loan		35,000
9.5% debenture loan 2013		89,000
Trade payables		50,247
Reconstruction account (bal fig)		5,663
	339,910	339,910

Reconstruction account:	$	$
Retained earnings deficit	39,821	
Brand w/off	60,000	
Receivables w/off	7,069	
Redesignation of equity shares to $0.25		150,000
Land revalued	66,000	
Building revalued		52,754
Equipment revalued	754	
Inventory revalued	70,247	
Deb interest arrears cancelled		7,800
Directors loans cancelled		6,000
Gain on disposal of financial assets		33,000
Capital reconstruction reserve (bal fig)	5,663	
	249,554	249,554

(W2) Debenture loan interest gross

Before　　　8% × $80,000 = $6,400

After　　　9.5% × $89,000 = $8,455

This does, of course, include interest on capitalised interest.

(W3) Unsecured loan interest gross

Before　　　5% × $70,000 = $3,500

After　　　8% × $35,000 = $2,800

(W4) **The balance of the retained earnings of $50,000 belongs to the equity shareholders**

	$	$		$	$
Before		50,000	**After**	50,000	
Less: Deb interest	(6,400)			(8,455)	
Unsecured loan interest	(3,500)			(2,800)	
		(9,900)			(11,255)
Available for equity shareholders		40,100			38,745

After reconstruction:	Shares @ $0.25	Shares @ $0.25	Share premium
	No.	$	$
Debenture holders	20,000	5,000	
Unsecured loan	140,000	35,000	
Directors' shares	10,000	2,500	7,500
Other shareholders	400,000	100,000	10,000
	570,000	142,500	17,500

Profits available to pay dividends		$
Debenture holders	20,000/570,000 × $38,745	1,360
Unsecured loan	140,000/570,000 × $38,745	9,516
Directors	10,000/570,000 × $38,745	680
Original equity holders	400,000/570,000 × $38,745	27,189
		38,745

(W5) **Bank balance:**

Note ref		$
	Overdraft brought forward	(36,713)
3	Share issue @ $0.30	60,000
4	Additional debenture loan	9,000
7	Disposal proceeds of financial assets	60,000
9	Payment to trade payables	(46,000)
	Closing bank balance	46,287

Journal entries (for reference only)

			Dr	Cr
			$	$
(1)	Equity shares of $1 each		200,000	
	Equity shares of $0.25 each			50,000
	Reconstruction account			150,000

Re-designation of issued equity share capital as $0.25 shares (formerly $1 shares) and transferring excess nominal value to reconstruction account.

(2)	5% unsecured loan		70,000	
	8% unsecured loan			35,000
	Equity shares of $0.25 each			35,000

Exchange of 5% unsecured loan for 8% unsecured loan and 140,000 equity shares of $0.25 each.

(3)	Cash		60,000	
	Equity shares of $0.25 each – 200,000			50,000
	Share premium account $0.05 – 200,000			10,000

Issue of 200,000 $0.25 equity shares at an issue price of $0.30 to the original equity shareholders.

(4)(a)	Interest payable on debentures		12,800	
	Equity shares of $0.25 each – 20,000			5,000
	Reconstruction account			7,800

Issue of shares and capitalisation of unpaid debenture interest

(4)(b)	8% Debenture loan 2013		80,000	
	9.5% Debenture loan 2013			80,000

Increase in interest rate on 2013 Debenture loan to 9.5%.

(4)(c)	Cash		9,000	
	9.5% Debenture 2013			9,000

Issue of $9,000 debentures at par value for cash.

(5)	Loans from directors		16,000	
	Equity shares of $0.25 each – 10,000			2,500
	Share premium			7,500
	Reconstruction account			6,000

Capitalisation and writing off of directors' loans.

(6)	Reconstruction account		99,821	
	Intangible asset – brand			60,000
	Retained earnings			39,821

Brand and deficit on retained earnings written off.

(7)	Cash		60,000	
	Financial assets at FVTPorL			27,000
	Reconstruction account			33,000

Sale of financial assets at a profit of $33,000.

(8)	No journal entry required.			

(9)	Trade payables		46,000	
	Cash			46,000

Payment made to trade payables.

(10)	Reconstruction account	7,069	
	Trade receivables		7,069
	Write-off of bad debts.		
(11)	Land		66,000
	Building	52,754	
	Equipment		754
	Inventories		70,247
	Reconstruction account	84,247	
	Revaluation of non-current assets.		
		137,001	137,001

ACCA Marking scheme		
		Marks
(a)	Statement of financial position	12
(b)	Division of operating profits	8
(c)	Comments on capital structure	5
Total		**25**

57 BOOMERANG

Key answer tips

The question format within Section B of the examination paper will be mainly narrative. The answer to this question is perhaps longer than could reasonably be produced under examination conditions; however, the comprehensive answer is a good learning tool. You should try to answer each part of the question requirement, applying the respective legal rights of the various interest groups to ensure appropriate allocation of assets and profits based upon their respective legal entitlement.

(a) **MEMORANDUM**

To: Finance Director – Boomerang

From: Advisor

Re: Draft proposals for scheme of capital reduction and reorganisation of Boomerang

('the scheme') as at 31 October 2012

Thank you for a copy of the draft scheme.

In our view, one of the key considerations for the court and the various parties whose rights are being varied is whether the scheme is fair to all parties.

We have therefore reviewed the scheme as a whole and particularly from the perspective of each of the interested parties, including whether they would be likely to approve the scheme as required.

Liquidation:

Upon liquidation, the assets are realised and liabilities settled, with any surplus remaining going to the equity shareholders. If the company is insolvent, they are unlikely to receive any payment upon liquidation.

Creditors are paid off based upon their relative priority. A fixed charge holder is paid from the proceeds of the asset(s) subject to that charge. If the fixed charge asset(s) are insufficient to repay the charge holder, the charge holder becomes an unsecured creditor the balance still outstanding.

Floating charge holders are paid from the proceeds of the assets subject to that charge, subject to first paying out preferential creditors such as unpaid wages. If the floating charge holder has not been repaid in full, that charge-holder becomes an unsecured creditor for the balance outstanding.

If the amounts following reconstruction are used as a guide to realisable values of the various assets and liabilities (this many not necessarily be the case), the following is an indication of the likely outcome:

	$	$
Freehold property disposed of		700,000
Leasehold property		370,000
Plant and equipment		675,000
Inventory – subject to floating charge	400,000	
Receivables – subject to floating charge	225,000	
Less: preferential creditors – wages	(260,000)	
Less: preferential creditors – professional fees	(40,000)	
Balance –available to floating charge holder	325,000	
8% debenture	(540,000)	
Balance as unsecured creditor	(215,000)	1,745,000
Other unsecured creditors:		
4% debenture	(170,000)	
Corporate tax liabilities	(190,000)	
Trade payables	(576,000)	
Bank overdraft	(494,000)	(1,645,000)
Available for equity holders		100,000

The preferential creditors for unpaid wages and professional fees associated with liquidation would be paid in full from realisation of inventory and receivables. However, there would be insufficient funds from those assets to fully repay the 8% debenture holder. The unpaid balance would then be classified as an unsecured creditor.

All of the unsecured creditors would rank equally for repayment from the remaining assets – there would appear to be just enough realisable proceeds from the remaining assets. In effect, there would be a negligible dividend (i.e. return of capital) to the equity shareholders. Note that if any of the realisable values of the assets were significantly less than the amounts used above, the unsecured creditors would bear the loss on a pro rata basis.

(b) **Overview of the scheme**

One of the principal issues facing Boomerang at present is the accumulated deficit on retained earnings following several years of unprofitable trading. This means that, even if Boomerang were to commence trading profitably, the deficit would need to be cleared before there was any possibility of a dividend being paid to the equity shareholders. How long this may take would depend upon profitability and would require the continued patience of equity shareholders.

Another principal issue is the extent of the bank overdraft which is approximately $500,000 and which the bank has requested that steps be taken to reduce it. As the 8% debenture is secured against the inventory and receivables, the overdraft would only be repaid if there were sufficient assets to meet all claims of unsecured creditors. If the 8% debenture could not be repaid from the proceeds of realising the inventory and receivables, any unpaid amount would rank as an unsecured creditor and potentially increase the risk of less than full recovery of the overdraft by the bank.

Additionally, the 4% debenture is due for repayment in early 2013 and there is currently little prospect of being able to repay this as the bank is unwilling to increase the overdraft facility and there are likely to be problems finding significant additional sources of equity finance.

The immediate future:

If the profit forecast by Boomerang is reliable, the following is likely to result:

	$
Profit before interest and tax	200,000
Less: interest 8% × $540,000	(43,200)
Profit before tax	156,800
Tax @ 25%	(39,200)
Profit after tax for the year	117,600

The consequences of implementing the scheme can be summarised as follows:

(i) The bank overdraft would be reduced, but not cleared in the short term.

(ii) The 4% debenture due for repayment in 2013 would be paid in full.

(iii) There is a significant commercial risk that trade creditors and other providers of finance may not be willing to continue supporting the business if they are unlikely to receive repayment of interest and/or capital on normal due dates.

(iv) The possibility of raising additional finance for working capital in 2015, whether in the form of an issue of shares or increased loan finance, would be subject to considerable uncertainty.

(v) At this level of annual profit, all other factors remaining unchanged, it would take approximately (340,000/117,600) three years to clear the deficit on retained earnings and offer the possibility of a dividend from profits to equity shareholders.

(vi) This This level of profit equates to earnings per share of (117,600/2,100,000) 5.6 cents per share.

Holder of 10% of the equity before reconstruction

Following reconstruction, the shareholder will own (135,000/2,100,000) approximately 6.4% of the equity shares in issue. The proportionate voting power will be reduced if the reconstruction scheme is implemented. In addition, due to the increase in the number of shares in issue, profits available for distribution in the form of a dividend will need to be spread across an increased number of shareholders.

Even if the scheme is implemented, as there is still a deficit on retained earnings, this will need to be cleared before dividends could be paid. If the forecast level of profit is reliable, it would take three years before shareholders would potentially receive a dividend.

If Boomerang was liquidated, equity shareholders would receive a minimal amount. Arguably, the shareholder has nothing to lose by approving the reconstruction. They may benefit from some future return for no further outlay.

8% debenture holder

If Boomerang was liquidated, the 8% debenture holder would be repaid in full if the estimate of realisable values was reliable. The assets subject to the floating charge are, on their own, insufficient to ensure recovery of the amount due to the debenture holder. The debenture holder would rank as an unsecured creditor for part of the amount due, as preferential creditors must be paid in priority to floating charge holders.

The debenture holder may be tempted to take full recovery now, rather than risk less than full recovery at some later date if future trading is less profitable than expected. The debenture holder may be encouraged to support the scheme if the floating charge is extended to cover the business as a whole, providing more security to the debenture holder. Another factor that may encourage the debenture holder to support the scheme would be to increase the rate of interest they receive so as to counteract any increase in risk they are accepting.

The bank

The bank is a primary source of working capital for Boomerang, and it is likely that Boomerang would not be able to continue in business without this support.

The bank, as an unsecured creditor, is in a relatively weak position to recover the amount outstanding in the event of liquidation or upon breach of the terms and conditions of the overdraft agreement.

Based upon the available information, in the event of liquidation, the bank would fully recover the amounts advanced to Boomerang. In common with the position of the debenture holder as an unsecured creditor, full recovery is dependent upon realisation of assets for at least the values expected. If this did not happen, unsecured creditors would bear any shortfall on a pro rata basis.

The bank overdraft would be substantially reduced if the scheme was implemented. This would ease some of the concerns raised by the bank, but would still leave it exposed to potential future losses if future trading following reconstruction was not profitable or did not generate sufficient cash inflows to pay liabilities.

The bank may be willing to consider reclassifying part of their overdraft as a long-term loan, with an agreed schedule of repayments. This would also ease part of the immediate pressure on liquidity currently faced by Boomerang, with a beneficial impact upon liquidity ratios and short-term working capital management.

The bank may be encouraged to support any reconstruction scheme by having a charge against some or all of the assets not already subject to a charge. This could be problematical as there are only limited assets available and numerous competing interests (debenture holder, preferential creditors, other unsecured creditors) who would all like to reduce their exposure to risk by having amounts due to them secured.

Trade creditors

Currently, all trade creditors, who will be unsecured creditors, would be repaid in full if Boomerang was to be liquidated.

Whether they can be persuaded to support the scheme, rather than simply recovering what is due to them now, may not be a straightforward judgement for them to make.

Clearly, if Boomerang were to continue trading and make a profit, that would mean continued sales revenue for the suppliers. If future trading was not profitable, trade creditors would be at risk of not recovering all of the amounts due to them.

As individual creditors, they could take protective action, such as selling to Boomerang on a cash basis only, or by factoring receivables where sales have been made to Boomerang on credit. They could also impose lower credit limits than has previously been the case and strictly enforce the terms of business with Boomerang to minimise their risk of loss.

(c) **Additional tax liabilities**

The decision of the tax authorities is an adjusting event as defined by IAS 10 *Events after the reporting period*. Therefore, at the reporting date, it would appear that a provision is required in accordance with IAS 37 *Provisions, contingent liabilities and contingent assets* for the additional tax liabilities as they relate to past transactions and events and it is probable that they cannot be avoided.

If the decision to appeal is considered, application of IAS 10 suggests that this is a non-adjusting event as the decision to appeal only arises following the decision of the tax authorities communicated on 5 November - it does not affect the situation at the reporting date. As a non-adjusting event, the financial statements should not be adjusted to reflect this information. It is not relevant that an independent professional advisor considers that it is likely the decision of the tax authorities will be overturned.

There should be disclosure only of the decision to appeal, unless the ability to continue as a going concern is threatened.

ACCA Marking scheme		
		Marks
(a)	Liquidation of Boomerang	7
(b)	Reconstruction – overview and interested parties	15
(c)	Additional tax liabilities	3
		——
Total		**25**
		——

ESSAY STYLE QUESTIONS

58   IAS 1 AND INTEGRATED REPORTING (JUNE 15 EXAM)

Key answer tips

Question 4 in the P2 exam is the essay style question. The P2 examining team published articles on both IAS 1 and the International Integrated Reporting Framework prior to the June 2015 exam. This demonstrates the importance of wider reading when preparing for P2.

Part (b) normally involves application of theoretical issues to transactional examples. Student performance tends to be weaker here. Practising questions under exam conditions will help you to develop and hone your application skills.

(a)   (i)   **Presentation requirements**

IFRS currently requires the statement of profit or loss and other comprehensive income to be presented as either one statement, being a combined statement of profit or loss and other comprehensive income or two statements, being the statement of profit or loss and the statement of comprehensive income.

IAS 1 *Presentation of Financial Statements* defines profit or loss as 'the total of income less expenses, excluding the components of other comprehensive income'.

Other comprehensive income is defined as comprising 'items of income and expense (including reclassification adjustments) that are not recognised in profit or loss as required or permitted by other IFRSs'.

An entity has to show separately in OCI those items which might be reclassified (recycled) to profit or loss and those items which would never be reclassified (recycled) to profit or loss. The related tax effects have to be allocated to these sections.

(ii)   **Reclassification adjustments**

Reclassification adjustments are amounts recycled to profit or loss in the current period which were recognised in OCI in the current or previous periods.

Examples of items recognised in OCI which may be reclassified to profit or loss are foreign currency gains on the disposal of a foreign operation and realised gains or losses on cash flow hedges.

Examples of items recognised in OCI which may not be reclassified to profit or loss are changes in a revaluation surplus under IAS 16 *Property, Plant and Equipment*, and remeasurement gains and losses on a defined benefit plan under IAS 19 *Employee Benefits*.

Arguments for and against reclassification

There are several arguments for and against reclassification. If reclassification ceased, then there would be no need to define profit or loss, or any other total or subtotal in profit or loss, and any presentation decisions can be left to specific IFRSs. It is argued that reclassification protects the integrity of profit or loss and provides users with relevant information about a transaction which occurred in the period. Additionally, it can improve comparability where IFRS permits similar items to be recognised in either profit or loss or OCI.

Those against reclassification argue that the recycled amounts add to the complexity of financial reporting because reclassification is not understood by users of the financial statements. Others argue that reclassification may lead to earnings management. It can also be said that reclassification adjustments may not meet the definitions of income or expense in the period as the change in the asset or liability may have occurred in a previous period.

The lack of a consistent basis for determining how items should be presented has led to an inconsistent use of OCI in IFRS. Opinions vary but there is a feeling that OCI has become a home for anything controversial because of a lack of clear definition of what should be included in the statement. Many users are thought to ignore OCI, as the changes reported are not caused by the operating flows used for predictive purposes.

An exposure draft on the Conceptual Framework is seeking to clarify what distinguishes recognised items of income and expense which are presented in profit or loss from items of income and expense presented in OCI. It proposes a rebuttable assumption that all incomes and expenses recognised in OCI should be subsequently reclassified to profit or loss.

(iii) **Principles and key components of the IIRC's Framework**

The International Integrated Reporting Council (IIRC) has released a framework for integrated reporting. The Framework establishes principles and concepts which govern the overall content of an integrated report. The IIRC has set out a principles-based framework rather than specifying a detailed disclosure and measurement standard. This enables each company to set out its own report rather than adopting a checklist approach.

An integrated report sets out how the organisation's strategy, governance, performance and prospects can lead to the creation of value. The integrated report aims to provide an insight into the company's resources and relationships, which are known as the capitals and how the company interacts with the external environment and the capitals to create value. These capitals can be financial, manufactured, intellectual, human, social and relationship, and natural capital but companies need not adopt these classifications. Integrated reporting is built around the following key components:

(i) Organisational overview and the external environment under which it operates

(ii) Governance structure and how this supports its ability to create value

(iii) Business model

(iv) Risks and opportunities and how they are dealing with them and how they affect the company's ability to create value

(v)   Strategy and resource allocation

(vi) Performance and achievement of strategic objectives for the period and outcomes

(vii) Outlook and challenges facing the company and their implications.

(viii) The basis of presentation needs to be determined including what matters are to be included in the integrated report and how the elements are quantified or evaluated.

The Framework does not require discrete sections to be compiled in the report but there should be a high level review to ensure that all relevant aspects are included. An integrated report should provide insight into the nature and quality of the organisation's relationships with its key stakeholders, including how and to what extent the organisation understands, takes into account and responds to their needs and interests. Further, the report should be consistent over time to enable comparison with other entities.

The IIRC considered the nature of value and value creation. These terms can include the total of all the capitals, the benefit captured by the company, the market value or cash flows of the organisation and the successful achievement of the company's objectives. However, the conclusion reached was that the Framework should not define value from any one particular perspective because value depends upon the individual company's own perspective. It can be shown through movement of capital and can be defined as value created for the company or for others. An integrated report should not attempt to quantify value as assessments of value are left to those using the report.

The IIRC has stated that the prescription of specific measurement methods is beyond the scope of a principles-based framework. The Framework contains information on the principles-based approach and indicates that there is a need to include quantitative indicators whenever practicable and possible. Additionally, consistency of measurement methods across different reports is of paramount importance. There is outline guidance on the selection of suitable quantitative indicators.

Concerns

There are concerns over the ability to assess future disclosures, and there may be a need for confidence intervals to be disclosed. The preparation of an integrated report requires judgement but there is a requirement for the report to describe its basis of preparation and presentation, including the significant frameworks and methods used to quantify or evaluate material matters. Also included is the disclosure of a summary of how the company determined the materiality limits and a description of the reporting boundaries.

A company should consider how to describe the disclosures without causing a significant loss of competitive advantage. The entity will consider what advantage a competitor could actually gain from information in the integrated report, and will balance this against the need for disclosure.

The report does not contain a statement from those 'charged with governance' acknowledging their responsibility for the integrated report. This may undermine the reliability and credibility of the integrated report.

(b) **Cash flow hedge**

In accordance with IFRS 9, if a cash flow hedge results in the recognition of a non-financial asset then the previous gains or losses recognised in the cash flow hedge reserve must be removed and included in the initial carrying amount of the asset or liability.

Therefore, the gains of $3 million are removed from equity and are deducted from the initial cost of the inventory. Consequently, the inventory will be recorded at $5 million ($8m – $5m) on the purchase date.

The carrying amount of the inventory is already lower than its net realisable value, so no further write down is required.

When the inventory is sold for $6.2 million, a profit of $1.2 million ($6.2m – $5m) is recorded in profit or loss.

Property, plant and equipment

At 30 April 2014, there was a revaluation gain of $4 million being the difference between the carrying amount of $8 million ($10m × 4/5) and the revalued amount of $12 million. This revaluation gain would have been recognised in other comprehensive income and held within a revaluation surplus in equity.

At 30 April 2015 the carrying amount of the asset is $9 million ($12 million × 3/4). The entity will have transferred $1 million from revaluation surplus to retained earnings (being the difference between historical cost depreciation of $2 million and the $3m depreciation charged on the revalued amount), thus reducing the revaluation reserve to $3 million ($4m – $1m).

The revaluation loss is $5 million ($9m – $4m). Of this, $3 million will be charged to other comprehensive income because that is the balance remaining in the revaluation surplus. The remaining loss of $2 million will be charged against profit or loss.

ACCA Marking scheme			
			Marks
(a)	(i)	1 mark per point up to maximum	4
	(ii)	1 mark per point up to maximum	5
	(iii)	1 mark per point up to maximum	8
(b)		1 mark per point up to maximum	6
		Professional marks	2
			——
Total			**25**
			——

59   IMPAIRMENT OF ASSETS (DEC 14 EXAM)

Key answer tips

IAS 36 *Impairment of Assets* is an accounting standard that companies often fail to apply properly and which has been highlighted as an issue for regulators. The P2 examiner has regularly said that students should read widely if they wish to score well on the essay-style question.

(a)

Tutorial note

Ensure that you answer the requirement. The examiner states five key factors for impairment accounting (changes in circumstance in the reporting period, the market capitalisation of the entity, the allocation of goodwill to cash generating units, valuation issues and the nature of the disclosures) and asks for a discussion of their importance. Use the five factors as a way of structuring your answer, and make sure that you say something about each one.

All assets, including goodwill and intangible assets, have to be tested for impairment at the end of each reporting period, if there are indicators of impairment. The main issues in relation to IAS 36 *Impairment of Assets* are as follows:

Changes in circumstances

Changes in circumstances between the date of the impairment test and the next reporting period end may give rise to impairment indicators. If so, more than one impairment test may be required in an annual period. Where an annual impairment test is required for goodwill and certain other intangible assets, IAS 36 allows the impairment test to be performed at any time during the period, provided it is performed at the same time every year.

Many entities test goodwill at an interim period in the year. In times of high uncertainty, goodwill may have to be tested for impairment at year end and at a subsequent interim reporting date as well, if indicators of impairment arise after the annual test has been performed.

If an entity has to test for impairment at the end of the reporting date as well as at the scheduled annual date, it does not necessarily mean that the whole budget process needs to be redone, as top-down adjustments may be sufficient to assess any changes in the period since the latest goodwill impairment review.

Volatility in financial statements may indicate impairment. For example, falls or rises in commodity prices may affect impairment indicators for energy and mining entities, and require those assets to be tested for impairment in the next interim financial statements.

Market capitalisation as a special impairment indicator

Market capitalisation is a powerful indicator as, if it shows a lower figure than the book value of net assets, it inescapably suggests the market considers that the business is overvalued. However, the market may have taken account of factors other than the return which the entity is generating on its assets. A market capitalisation below book equity will not necessarily lead to an equivalent impairment loss. Entities should examine their cash generating units (CGUs) in these circumstances and may have to test goodwill for impairment. IAS 36 does not require a formal reconciliation between market capitalisation of the entity, fair value less costs to sell (FVLCS) and value in use (VIU). However, entities need to be able to understand the reason for the shortfall.

Allocating and reallocating goodwill to cash generating unit (CGU)

Given the complexity, sensitivity and need for significant judgement, companies experience issues assessing goodwill for impairment. The identification of CGUs and the allocation of acquired goodwill is unique to each entity and requires significant judgement. This allocation process in itself determines the appropriate carrying amount to test and should be a reasonable and supportable method.

Acquired goodwill is allocated to each of the acquirer's CGUs, or to a group of CGUs, which are expected to benefit from the synergies of the combination. If CGUs are subsequently revised or operations disposed of, IAS 36 requires goodwill to be reallocated, based on 'relative values', to the units affected. However, the standard does not expand on what is meant by 'relative value'. It does not mandate FVLCS as the basis, but it might mean that the entity has to carry out a valuation process on the part retained. There could be reasonable ways of estimating relative value by using an appropriate industry or business surrogate (for example, revenue, profits, industry KPIs).

Valuation issues

IAS 36 requires the recoverable amount of an asset or CGU to be measured as the higher of the asset's or CGU's FVLCS and VIU. Measuring the FVLCS and VIU of an asset or CGU requires the use of assumptions and estimates.

The following issues are proving particularly troublesome:

(a)   The use of a discounted cash flow (DCF) methodology to estimate FVLCS.

(b)   Determining the types of future cash flows which should be included in the measurement of VIU, in particular, those relating to restructuring programmes. IAS 36 requires an asset or CGU to be tested in its current status, not the status which management wishes it was in or hopes to get it into in the near future. Therefore, the standard requires VIU to be measured at the net present value of the future cash flows the entity expects to derive from the asset or CGU in its current condition over its remaining useful life. This means ignoring many management plans for enhancing the performance of the asset or CGU.

(c)   Determining the appropriate discount rate to apply. Unlike the cash flows used in an impairment test which are entity-specific, the discount rate is supposed to appropriately reflect the current market assessment of the time value of money and the risks specific to the asset or CGU.

When a specific rate for an asset or CGU is not directly available from the market, which is usually the case, the entity's weighted average cost of capital (WACC) can be used as a starting point. While not prescribed, WACC is by far the most commonly used base for the discount rate. However, the appropriate way to calculate the WACC is a complex subject, but the objective must be to obtain a rate, which is sensible and justifiable. In any event the rate can be subjective.

(d)   The impact of taxation on the impairment test, given the requirement in IAS 36 to measure VIU using pre-tax cash flows and discount rates. VIU, as defined by IAS 36, is primarily an accounting concept and not necessarily a business valuation of the asset or CGU. For calculating VIU, IAS 36 requires pre-tax cash flows and a pre-tax discount rate.

WACC is a post-tax rate, as are most observable equity rates used by valuers. Because of the issues in calculating an appropriate pre-tax discount rate and because it aligns more closely with their normal business valuation approach, some entities attempt to perform a VIU calculation based on a post-tax rate and post-tax cash flows.

(e)   Ensuring that the recoverable amount and carrying amount which are being compared are consistently determined. For example, pensions are mentioned by IAS 36 as items which might be included in the recoverable amount of a CGU. In practice, this could be fraught with difficulty, and entities will have to reflect the costs of providing pensions to employees and may need to make a pragmatic allocation to estimate a pension cost as part of the employee cost cash flow.

(f)   The incorporation of corporate assets into the impairment test. If possible, the corporate assets are to be allocated to individual CGUs on a 'reasonable and consistent basis'. This is not expanded upon in IAS 36 and affords some flexibility, but can lead to inconsistency. The same criteria must be applied at all times.

Impairment disclosures

Disclosure is a key communication to investors by management. Disclosures which describe the factors which could result in impairment become even more important when value has been eroded. Goodwill impairment disclosures are a requirement, but can be a problem. The key question is whether sufficient disclosure has been made about the uncertainty of the impairment calculation. Sensitivity disclosures about adverse situations, such as those triggered by volatile prices, provide useful information and whether a possible change in a key assumption, such as the discount rate, could lead to recoverable amount being equal to carrying amount, or result in impairment losses.

(b)

Tutorial note

You can score solid marks in this part using common sense. Does it sound reasonable that Estoli has used one discount rate for all CGUs, or that the directors of Fariole have significantly raised cash flow projections with little justification? Do not be afraid to state the obvious – that is where many of the easy marks come from.

(i) **Estoil**

The discount rate used by Estoil has not been calculated in accordance with the requirements of IAS 36 *Impairment of Assets*.

According to IAS 36, the future cash flows should be estimated in the currency in which they will be generated and then discounted using a discount rate appropriate for that currency. IAS 36 requires the present value to be translated using the spot exchange rate at the date of the value in use calculation.

Furthermore, the currency in which the estimated cash flows are denominated affects many of the inputs to the WACC calculation, including the risk free interest rate. Estoil has used the 10-year government bond rate for its jurisdiction as the risk free rate in the calculation of the discount rate. As government bond rates differ between countries due to different expectations about future inflation, value in use could be calculated incorrectly due to the disparity between the expected inflation reflected in the estimated cash flows and the risk free rate.

According to IAS 36, the discount rate should reflect the risks specific to the asset. Accordingly, one discount rate for all the CGUs does not represent the risk profile of each CGU. The discount rate generally should be determined using the WACC of the CGU or of the company of which the CGU is currently part. Using a company's WACC for all CGUs is appropriate only if the specific risks associated with the specific CGUs do not diverge materially from the remainder of the group. In the case of Estoil, this is not apparent.

(ii) **Fariole**

It appears that the cash flow forecasts were not prepared based on the requirements of IAS 36.

IAS 36 states that cash flow projections used in measuring value in use shall be based on reasonable and supportable assumptions which represent management's best estimate of the range of economic conditions which will exist over the remaining useful life of the asset. IAS 36 also states that management must assess the reasonableness of the assumptions by examining the causes of differences between past cash flow projections and actual cash. Management should ensure that the assumptions on which its current cash flow projections are based are consistent with past actual outcomes.

Despite the fact that the realised cash flows for 2014 were negative and far below projected cash flows, the directors had significantly raised budgeted cash flows for 2015 without justification. There are serious doubts about Fariole's ability to establish realistic budgets.

According to IAS 36, estimates of future cash flows should include:

(i) projections of cash inflows from the continuing use of the asset

(ii) projections of cash outflows which are necessarily incurred to generate the cash inflows from continuing use of the asset; and

(iii) net cash flows to be received (or paid) for the disposal of the asset at the end of its useful life.

IAS 36 states that projected cash outflows should include those required for the day-to-day servicing of the asset which includes future cash outflows to maintain the level of economic benefits expected to arise from the asset in its current condition. It is highly unlikely that no investments in working capital or operating assets would need to be made to maintain the assets of the CGUs in their current condition. Therefore, the cash flow projections used by Fariole are not in compliance with IAS 36.

ACCA Marking scheme		
		Marks
(a)	Subjective issues – 1 mark per point	13
(b)	Subjective	10
	Professional marks	2
		——
Total		**25**
		——

60 DEBT AND EQUITY (JUNE 14 EXAM)

Key answer tips

This question tests the rules around whether to classify a financial instrument as a financial liability or as equity. In its simplest terms, a financial liability involves an obligation to repay cash whilst equity includes no such obligation. However, there are additional details needed to score well in part (a) and to reach the correct conclusions in part (b). If you do not know relevant the rules, make sure that you fully debrief this answer and, if necessary, revisit the financial instruments chapter in the Complete Text.

(a) (i) To determine whether a financial instrument should be classified as debt or equity, IAS 32 uses principles-based definitions of a financial liability (debt) and of equity.

The key feature of debt is that the issuer is obliged to deliver either cash or another financial asset to the holder. The contractual obligation may arise from a requirement to repay principal or interest or dividends. For example, a bond which requires the issuer to make interest payments and redeem the bond for cash is classified as debt.

In contrast, equity is any contract which evidences a residual interest in the entity's assets after deducting all of its liabilities. A financial instrument is normally an equity instrument if the instrument includes no contractual obligation to deliver cash or another financial asset to another entity. For example, ordinary shares, where all the payments are at the discretion of the issuer, are classified as equity of the issuer.

However, a contract may involve the receipt or delivery of the entity's own equity instruments. The classification of this type of contract as debt or equity is dependent on whether there is variability in either the number of equity shares delivered or variability in the amount of cash or financial assets received. A contract which will be settled by the entity receiving or delivering a fixed number of its own equity instruments in exchange for a fixed amount of cash or another financial asset is an equity instrument. However, if there is any variability in the amount of cash or own equity instruments which will be delivered or received, then such a contract is a financial asset or liability as applicable.

For example, where a contract requires the entity to deliver as many of the entity's own equity instruments as are equal in value to a certain amount of cash, the holder of the contract would be indifferent as to whether it received cash or shares to the value of that amount. Thus this contract would be treated as debt.

(ii)   Reporting a financial instrument as debt rather than equity would lead to a deterioration in the gearing ratio. This may make the company appear more risky to potential investors or lenders, potentially creating problems when raising further finance.

Liability classification normally results in the servicing of the finance being treated as interest and charged to profit or loss. This will reduce retained earnings and may therefore affect the entity's ability to pay dividends on its equity shares.

Moreover, finance costs in profit or loss will reduce earnings per share, which may lower investor confidence in the entity. Lower profits may also lead to a breach of loan covenants, potentially triggering the need to repay borrowings.

Equity classification may avoid these impacts, but could be perceived negatively if seen to be diluting existing equity interests.

(b)   Cavor

The B shares of Cavor should be classified as equity as there is no contractual obligation to pay the dividends or to call the instrument. Dividends can only be paid on the B shares if dividends have been declared on the A shares. However, there is no contractual obligation to declare A share dividends.

The classification of the B share options in Cavor is dependent on whether there is variability in either the number of equity shares delivered or variability in the amount of cash or financial assets received. As the contract will be settled by the entity issuing a fixed number of its own equity instruments in exchange for a fixed amount of cash, then the share options are classified as an equity instrument.

Lidan

An obligation to settle in cash can be established indirectly through the terms and conditions of the financial instrument.

In this case, the value of the own share settlement alternative substantially exceeds that of the cash settlement option, meaning that the entity is implicitly obliged to redeem the option for a cash amount of $1 per share. The B shares of Lidan will therefore be classified as a liability.

ACCA Marking scheme			
			Marks
(a)	(i)	1 mark per point up to maximum	9
	(ii)	Effects	5
(b)		1 mark per point up to maximum	9
		Professional marks	2
Total			**25**

61 ZACK (DEC 13 EXAM)

Key answer tips

IAS 8 is a standard that you should have a good knowledge of from prior studies. The P2 examiner has said that 'question 4' can be on current issues or existing standards. Rote learning accounting rules will not help in a question such as this. Instead, it is important to engage with the accounting standards that you are learning about and to think through potential criticisms of them.

Relatively easy marks could, however, be obtained in part (b) by applying the rules of IAS 8 to some simple scenarios.

(a) (i) The selection of accounting policy and estimation techniques is intended to aid comparability and consistency in financial statements.

Entities should follow the requirements of IAS 8 *Accounting Policies, Changes in Accounting Estimates and Errors*, when selecting or changing accounting policies, changing estimation techniques, and correcting errors. An entity should determine the accounting policy to be applied to an item with direct reference to IFRS but accounting policies need not be applied if the effect of applying them would be immaterial.

Where IFRS does not specifically apply to a transaction, judgement should be used in developing or applying an accounting policy, which results in financial information which is relevant to the decision-making and assessment needs of users. In making that judgement, entities must refer to guidance in IFRS, which deals with similar issues and then subsequently to definitions, and criteria in the Framework. Additionally, entities can refer to recent pronouncements of other standard setters who use similar conceptual frameworks.

Entities should select and apply their accounting policies consistently for similar transactions. If IFRS specifically permits different accounting policies for categories of similar items, an entity should apply an appropriate policy for each of the categories in question and apply these accounting policies consistently for each category. For example, for different classes of property, plant and equipment, some may be carried at fair value and some at historical cost.

(ii) A change in accounting policy should only be made if the change is required by IFRS, or it will result in the financial statements providing reliable and more relevant financial information. Significant changes in accounting policy other than those specified by IFRS should be relatively rare. IFRS specifies the accounting policies for a high percentage of the typical transactions which are faced by entities. There are therefore limited opportunities for an entity to choose an accounting policy, as opposed to a basis for estimating figures which will satisfy such a policy.

IAS 8 states that the introduction of an accounting policy to account for transactions where circumstances have changed is not a change in accounting policy. Similarly, an accounting policy for transactions which did not occur previously or which were immaterial is not a change in accounting policy and therefore would be applied prospectively.

For example, where an entity changes the use of a property from an administration building to a residential space and therefore an investment property, this would result in a different treatment of revaluation gains and losses. However, this is not a change in accounting policy and so no restatement of comparative amounts should be made.

A change in accounting policy is applied retrospectively unless there are transitional arrangements in place. Transitional provisions are often included in new or revised standards and may not require full retrospective application.

Sometimes it is difficult to achieve comparability of prior periods with the current period where, for example, data might not have been collected in the prior periods to allow retrospective application. Restating comparative information for prior periods often requires complex and detailed estimation. This, in itself, does not prevent reliable adjustments.

When making estimates for prior periods, the basis of estimation should reflect the circumstances which existed at the time and it becomes increasingly difficult to define those circumstances with the passage of time. Estimates and circumstances might be influenced by knowledge of events and circumstances which have arisen since the prior period.

IAS 8 does not permit the use of hindsight when applying a new accounting policy, either in making assumptions about what management's intentions would have been in a prior period or in estimating amounts to be recognised, measured or disclosed in a prior period.

When it is impracticable to determine the effect of a change in accounting policy on comparative information, the entity is required to apply the new accounting policy to the carrying amounts of the assets and liabilities as at the beginning of the earliest period for which retrospective application is practicable. This could actually be the current period but the entity should attempt to apply the policy from the earliest date possible.

(iii) IAS 8 *Accounting Policies, Changes in Accounting Estimates and Errors* requires prior period errors to be amended retrospectively by restating the comparatives as if the error had never occurred. Hence, the impact of any prior period errors is shown through retained earnings rather than being included in the current period's profit or loss. Managers could use this treatment for prior period errors as a method for manipulating current period earnings. Restatements due to errors and irregularities can be considered to indicate poor earnings quality, and to threaten investor confidence, particularly if they occur frequently. Thus, it might appear that the factors associated with earnings corrections could be linked to earnings management.

Arguments against the approach in IAS 8 are:

- that the standard allows inappropriate use of hindsight

- that the treatment renders errors less prominent to users

- that it allows amounts to be debited or credited to retained profits without ever being included in a current period profit or loss.

Managers have considerable discretion regarding the degree of attention drawn to such changes. The information content and prominence to users of disclosures regarding prior period errors are issues of significance, with potential economic and earnings quality implications. Expenses could be moved backward into a prior period, with the result that managers are given a possible alternative strategy with which to manage earnings. It is possible to misclassify liabilities, for example, as non-current rather than current, or even simply miscalculate reported earnings per share. Under IAS 8, the prior period error can then be amended the following year, with no lingering effects on the statement of financial position as a result of the manipulation.

(b) IAS 23 *Borrowing Costs* states that such costs which are directly attributable to the acquisition, construction or production of a qualifying asset form part of the cost of that asset and, therefore, should be capitalised. Other borrowing costs are recognised as an expense. Thus the change in accounting policy actually only brings Zack in line with IFRS, with the result that there is an accounting error which will require a prior period adjustment.

In applying the new accounting policy, Zack has identified that there is another asset where there is a material impact if borrowing costs should have been capitalised during the construction period. This contract was completed during 2012. Thus, the financial statements for the year ended 30 November 2012 should be restated to apply the new policy to this asset. The effects of the restatement are as follows: at 30 November 2012, the carrying amount of property, plant and equipment is restated upwards by $2 million less depreciation for the period and this would result in an increase in profit or loss for the period of the same amount. Disclosures relating to prior period errors include: the nature of the prior period error for each prior period presented, to the extent practicable; the amount of the correction for each financial statement line item affected; and for basic and diluted earnings per share, the amount of the correction at the beginning of the earliest prior period presented. The disclosure would include the nature of the prior period error.

The line items in the statement of profit or loss and other comprehensive income would also change. For the current period, Zack would disclose the impact of the prior period error of $3 million. It can be assumed that, because the asset is under construction, there will be no depreciation on the asset.

The change in the depreciation method is not a change in an accounting policy but a change in an accounting estimate. For changes in accounting estimates, Zack should disclose the nature and the amount of the change which affects the current period or which it is expected to have in future periods. It should be noted that IAS 8 does permit an exception where it is impracticable to estimate the effect on future periods. Where the effect on future periods is not disclosed because it is impracticable, that fact should be disclosed. The revision results in an increase in depreciation for 2013 of $6m and the disclosure of an estimated increase for 2014 of $8m.

The systems error has resulted in a prior period error. In order to correct this error, Zack should restate the prior year information for the year ended 30 November 2012 for the $2m in the statement of profit or loss and other comprehensive income. Additionally, the trade creditors figure in the statement of financial position is overstated by $2 million and should be restated. The movement in reserves note will also require restating. This is not a correction of an accounting estimate.

ACCA Marking scheme		
		Marks
(a)	Subjective	15
(b)	Subjective	8
	Professional marks	2
		——
Total		**25**
		——

62   LIZZER (JUN 13 EXAM)

Key answer tips

The examiner wrote an article about the problems of excessive disclosure in the run up to the June 2013 exam. This shows the importance of wider reading when preparing for P2. Examiner articles can be accessed on the ACCA website.

Part (b) covered the disclosure requirements of IFRS 7. Whilst this might sound dauntingly technical, high marks could be obtained through the use of common sense. Imagine that you were a user of Lizzer's financial statements: what information would you want to know?

(a)   (i)   Excessive disclosure can obscure relevant information and make it harder for users to find the key points about the performance of the business and its prospects for long-term success. It is important that financial statements are relevant, reliable and can be understood. Additionally, it is important for the efficient operation of the capital markets that annual reports do not contain unnecessary information.

It is equally important that useful information is presented in a coherent way so that users can find what they are looking for and gain an understanding of the company's business and the opportunities, risks and constraints that it faces.

A company, however, must treat all of its shareholders equally in the provision of information. It is for each shareholder to decide whether they wish to make use of that information. It is not for a company to pre-empt a shareholder's rights in this regard by withholding the information.

A significant cause of excessive disclosure in annual reports is the vast array of requirements imposed by laws, regulations and financial reporting standards. Regulators and standard setters have a key role to play in cutting clutter, both by cutting the requirements that they themselves already impose and by guarding against the imposition of unnecessary new disclosures. A listed company may have to comply with listing rules, company law, international financial reporting standards, the corporate governance codes and, if it has an overseas listing, any local requirements, such as those of the SEC in the US. Thus a major source of excessive disclosure is the fact that different parties require differing disclosures for the same matter. For example, an international bank in the UK may have to disclose credit risk under IFRS 7 *Financial Instruments: Disclosures,* the Companies Acts and the Disclosure and Transparency Rules, the SEC rules and Industry Guide 3 as well as the requirements of Basel II Pillar 3. A problem is that different regulators have different audiences in mind for the requirements they impose on annual reports. Regulators attempt to reach wider ranges of actual or potential users and this can lead to a loss of focus and structure in reports.

Shareholders are increasingly unhappy with the substantial increase in the length of reports that has occurred in recent years. This, often, has not resulted in better information but more confusion as to the reason for the disclosure. A review of companies' published accounts will show that large sections such as 'Statement of Directors Responsibilities' and 'Audit Committee report' can be almost identical.

Preparers now have to consider many other stakeholders including employees, unions, environmentalists, suppliers, customers, etc. The disclosures required to meet the needs of this wider audience have contributed to the increased volume of disclosure. The growth of previous initiatives on going concern, sustainability, risk, the business model and others that have been identified by regulators as 'key' has also expanded the annual report size.

A problem that seems to exist is that disclosures are being made because a disclosure checklist suggests it may need to be made, without assessing whether the disclosure is necessary in a company's particular circumstances. It is inherent in these checklists that they include all possible disclosures that could be material.

The length of the annual report is not necessarily the problem but the way in which it is organised. The inclusion of 'immaterial' disclosures will usually make this problem worse but, in a well organised annual report, users will often be able to bypass much of the information they consider unimportant especially if the report is online. It is not the length of the accounting policies disclosure that is itself problematic, but the fact that new or amended policies can be obscured in a long note running over several pages. A further problem is that accounting policy disclosure is often 'boilerplate', providing little specific detail of how companies apply their general policies to particular transactions. Many disclosure requirements have been introduced in new or revised international accounting standards over the last ten years without any review of their overall impact on the length or usefulness of the resulting financial statements.

(ii) There are behavioural barriers to reducing disclosure. It may be that the threat of criticism or litigation could be a considerable limitation on the ability to cut disclosure. The threat of future litigation may outweigh any benefits to be obtained from eliminating 'catch-all' disclosures. Preparers of annual reports are likely to err on the side of caution and include more detailed disclosures than are strictly necessary to avoid challenge from auditors and regulators. Removing disclosures is perceived as creating a risk of adverse comment and regulatory challenge. Disclosure is the safest option and is therefore often the default position. Preparers and auditors may be reluctant to change from the current position unless the risk of regulatory challenge is reduced. The prospect of internal firm review and/or external review can induce auditors to take a 'tick-box' compliance approach to avoid challenge and adverse publicity. Companies have a tendency to repeat disclosures because they were there last year. Preparers wish to present balanced and sufficiently informative disclosures and may be unwilling to change.

A reassessment of the whole model will take time and may necessitate changes to law and other requirements. The IASB has recently issued a request for views regarding its forward agenda in which it acknowledges that stakeholders have said that disclosure requirements are too voluminous and not always focused in the right areas. In 2014, the IASB issued an Exposure Draft on the 'Disclosure Initiative'. This has suggested amendments to IAS 1 *Presentation of Financial Statements* with the aim of improving the quality of the disclosure information provided.

(b) (i) Lizzer's perception of who could reasonably be considered to be among the users of its financial statements is too narrow, being limited to the company's shareholders rather than including debt-holders; and the risk disclosures required by IFRS 7 should be enhanced to include those relating to the debt-holders, by individual series of debt where practicable, so as to ensure that significant differences between the various series of debt are not obscured. IAS 1 states that the objective of financial statements is to provide information about the financial position, financial performance and cash flows of an entity that is useful to a wide range of users in making economic decisions. The standard also states that omissions or misstatements of items are material if they could, individually or collectively, influence the economic decisions that users make on the basis of the financial statements.

The objective of IFRS 7 is to require entities to provide disclosures in their financial statements that enable users to evaluate the significance of financial instruments for the entity's financial position and performance. IFRS 7 states that, amongst other matters, for each type of risk arising from financial instruments, an entity shall disclose:

(a) the exposures to risk and how they arise

(b) its objectives, policies and processes for managing the risk and the methods used to measure the risk.

Thus the risks attached to the debt should be disclosed.

(ii)   Lizzer should have disclosed additional information about the covenants relating to each loan or group of loans, including the amount of headroom, as deemed appropriate under IFRS 7. The subsequent breach of the covenants represented a material event after the reporting period and should have given rise to relevant disclosures required by IAS 10 *Events after the reporting period* in relation to material non-adjusting events after the reporting period.

According to IFRS 7, an entity should disclose information that enables users of its financial statements to evaluate the nature and extent of risks arising from financial instruments to which the entity is exposed at the end of the reporting period. Disclosure of information about covenants is necessary to a greater extent in situations where the entity is close to breaching its covenants, and in situations where uncertainty is expressed in relation to the going concern assumption. Given the fact that, at 31 January 2013, there was a considerable risk of breach of covenants in the near future, Lizzer should have given additional information relating to the conditions attached to its loans, including details on how close the entity was to breaching the covenants.

A breach of covenants after the date of the financial statements, but before the financial statements were authorised for issue, constitutes a material non-adjusting event after the end of the reporting period which requires further disclosure in accordance with IAS 10. Additionally, there appears to be an apparent inconsistency between the information provided in the directors' and auditors' reports and that which is included in the financial statements. If balances are affected in the SOFP, then there would need to be some adjustment.

ACCA Marking scheme			
			Marks
(a)	Subjective	disclosure	9
		barriers	6
(b)	Subjective		8
	Professional marks		2
			—
Total			**25**
			—

63   JAYACH (DEC 12 EXAM)

Key answer tips

IFRS 13 *Fair Value Measurement* has proved popular with the P2 examiner. Make sure that you are very familiar with the definitions provided in this standard as well as the three-level hierarchy used.

Remember that part (b) required you to **discuss** how Jayach should determine the fair value of an asset and liability. If you are only producing calculations, then you are not fully answering the question and this means that you are throwing away easy marks.

(a)   (i)   Fair value is the price that would be received to sell an asset or paid to transfer a liability in an orderly transaction between market participants at the measurement date.

Fair value is focused on the assumptions of the market place and is not entity specific. It therefore takes into account any assumptions about risk. Fair value is measured using the same assumptions and taking into account the same characteristics of the asset or liability as market participants would. Such conditions would include the condition and location of the asset and any restrictions on its sale or use. Further, it is not relevant if the entity insists that prices are too low relative to its own valuation of the asset and that it would be unwilling to sell at low prices.

Prices to be used are those in 'an orderly transaction'. An orderly transaction is one that assumes exposure to the market for a period before the date of measurement to allow for normal marketing activities and to ensure that it is not a forced transaction. If the transaction is not 'orderly', then there will not have been enough time to create competition and potential buyers may reduce the price that they are willing to pay. Similarly, if a seller is forced to accept a price in a short period of time, the price may not be representative. It does not follow that a market in which there are few transactions is not orderly. If there has been competitive tension, sufficient time and information about the asset, then this may result in a fair value for the asset.

IFRS 13 does not specify the unit of account for measuring fair value. This means that it is left to the individual standard to determine the unit of account for fair value measurement. A unit of account is the single asset or liability or group of assets or liabilities. The characteristic of an asset or liability must be distinguished from a characteristic arising from the holding of an asset or liability by an entity. An example of this is that if an entity sold a large block of shares, it may have to do so at a discount to the market price. This is a characteristic of holding the asset rather than of the asset itself and should not be taken into account when fair valuing the asset.

Fair value measurement assumes that the transaction to sell the asset or transfer the liability takes place in the principal market for the asset or liability or, in the absence of a principal market, in the most advantageous market for the asset or liability. The principal market is the one with the greatest volume and level of activity for the asset or liability that can be accessed by the entity.

The most advantageous market is the one which maximises the amount that would be received for the asset or minimises the amount that would be paid to transfer the liability after transport and transaction costs.

An entity does not have to carry out an exhaustive search to identify either market but should take into account all available information. Although transaction costs are taken into account when identifying the most advantageous market, the fair value is not after adjustment for transaction costs because these costs are characteristics of the transaction and not the asset or liability. If location is a factor, then the market price is adjusted for the costs incurred to transport the asset to that market. Market participants must be independent of each other and knowledgeable, and able and willing to enter into transactions.

IFRS 13 sets out a valuation approach, which refers to a broad range of techniques, which can be used. These techniques are threefold. The market, income and cost approaches.

(ii)   When measuring fair value, the entity is required to maximise the use of observable inputs and minimise the use of unobservable inputs. To this end, the standard introduces a fair value hierarchy, which prioritises the inputs into the fair value measurement process.

Level 1 inputs are quoted prices (unadjusted) in active markets for items identical to the asset or liability being measured. As with current IFRS, if there is a quoted price in an active market, an entity uses that price without adjustment when measuring fair value. An example of this would be prices quoted on a stock exchange. The entity needs to be able to access the market at the measurement date. Active markets are ones where transactions take place with sufficient frequency and volume for pricing information to be provided. An alternative method may be used where it is expedient. The standard sets out certain criteria where this may be applicable. For example, where the price quoted in an active market does not represent fair value at the measurement date. An example of this may be where a significant event takes place after the close of the market such as a business reorganisation or combination.

The determination of whether a fair value measurement is level 2 or level 3 inputs depends on whether the inputs are observable inputs or unobservable inputs and their significance.

Level 2 inputs are inputs other than the quoted prices in level 1 that are directly or indirectly observable for that asset or liability. They are quoted assets or liabilities for similar items in active markets or supported by market data. For example, interest rates, credit spreads or yield curves. Adjustments may be needed to level 2 inputs and if this adjustment is significant, then it may require the fair value to be classified as level 3.

Level 3 inputs are unobservable inputs. The use of these inputs should be kept to a minimum. However, situations may occur where relevant inputs are not observable and therefore these inputs must be developed to reflect the assumptions that market participants would use when determining an appropriate price for the asset or liability. The entity should maximise the use of relevant observable inputs and minimise the use of unobservable inputs. The general principle of using an exit price remains and IFRS 13 does not preclude an entity from using its own data. For example, cash flow forecasts may be used to value an entity that is not listed. Each fair value measurement is categorised based on the lowest level input that is significant to it.

(b)

Year to 31 December 2012	Asian market	European market	Australasian market	
Volume of market – units	4 million	2 million	1 million	
Price	$19	$16	$22	
Costs of entering the market	($2)	($2)	(n/a)	see note
Potential fair value	$17	$14	$22	
Transaction costs	($1)	($2)	($2)	
Net profit	$16	$14	$20	

Note: As Jayach buys and sells in Australasia, the costs of entering the market are not relevant as these would not be incurred. Further transaction costs are not considered as these are not included as part of the valuation.

The principal market for the asset is the Asian market because of the fact that it has the highest level of activity due to the highest volume of units sold.

The most advantageous market is the Australasian market because it returns the best profit per unit.

If the information about the markets is reasonably available, then Jayach should base its fair value on prices in the Asian market due to it being the principal market, assuming that Jayach can access the market. The pricing is taken from this market even though the entity does not currently transact in the market and is not the most advantageous. The fair value would be $17, as transport costs would be taken into account but not transaction costs.

If the entity cannot access the Asian or European market, or reliable information about the markets is not available, Jayach would use the data from the Australasian market and the fair value would be $22. The principal market is not always the market in which the entity transacts. Market participants must be independent of each other and knowledgeable, and able and willing to enter into transactions.

The fair value of a liability assumes that it is transferred to a market participant at the measurement date. In many cases there is no observable market to provide pricing information. In this case, the fair value is based on the perspective of a market participant who holds the identical instrument as an asset. If there is no corresponding asset, then a valuation technique is used. This would be the case with the decommissioning activity. The fair value of a liability reflects any compensation for risk and profit margin that a market participant might require to undertake the activity plus the non-performance risk based on the entity's own credit standing. Thus the fair value of the decommissioning liability would be $3,215,000 (W1).

Working

(W1) Fair value of liability

	$000
Labour and material cost	2,000
Overhead (30%)	600
Third party mark-up – industry average (20% of 2,600)	520
	———
Total	3,120
Annual inflation rate (3,120 × 5% compounded for three years)	492
	———
Total	3,612
Risk adjustment – 6%	217
	———
Total	3,829
	———
Discounted at risk free rate of government bonds plus entity's non-performance risk – 6%	3,215

ACCA Marking scheme			
			Marks
(a)	(i)	1 mark per point up to maximum	9
	(ii)	IFRS 13 hierarchy	4
(b)		1 mark per point up to maximum	6
		Calculations	4
		Professional marks	2
Total			25

64 IFRS FOR SME APPLIED (DEC 10 EXAM) *Walk in the footsteps of a top tutor*

Key answer tips

This question is typical of the format of recent current issues questions. It requires technical knowledge and understanding, together with an applied element. Part (a) included discussion of the development of IFRS for SME, together with examples from that reporting standard of some key reporting requirements. Part (b) included application of two different accounting policies, together with explanation and comment upon the results of comparing the two treatments.

Tutorial note

Focus on the key requirements of the question, including definitions and explaining the accounting treatment required.

(a) (i) There were several approaches, which could have been taken in developing standards for SMEs. One course of action would have been for GAAP for SMEs to be developed on a national basis, with IFRS focusing on accounting for listed company activities. The main issue would have been that the practices developed for SMEs may not have been consistent and may have lacked comparability across national boundaries. Additionally, if a SME had wished to list its shares on a capital market, the transition to IFRS would have been more difficult.

Another approach would have been to detail the exemptions given to smaller entities in the mainstream IFRS. In this case, an appendix would have been included within the standard detailing the exemptions given to smaller enterprises.

A third approach would have been to introduce a separate set of standards comprising all the issues addressed in IFRS, which are relevant to SMEs.

However, the IFRS for SMEs is a self-contained set of accounting principles that are based on full IFRSs, which have been simplified so that they are suitable for SMEs. The Standard is organised by topic with the intention that the standard would be helpful to preparers and users of SME financial statements. The IFRS for SMEs and full IFRSs are separate and distinct frameworks. Entities that are eligible to apply the IFRS for SMEs, and that choose to do so, must apply that Standard in full and cannot choose the most suitable accounting policy from full IFRS or IFRS for SMEs.

However, the IFRS for SMEs is naturally a modified version of the full standards, and not an independently developed set of standards. It is based on recognised concepts and principles which should allow easier transition to full IFRS if the SME decides to become a public listed entity.

Note that the intention is for IFRS for SME to be updated at periodic intervals, approximately every three years. When this occurs, it is likely to increase the extent of comparability with full IFRS within which individual standards are revised, withdrawn or issued based upon the IASB work programme.

(ii)   In deciding on the modifications to make to IFRS, the needs of the users have been taken into account, as well as the costs and other burdens imposed upon SMEs by IFRS. Relaxation of some of the measurement and recognition criteria in IFRS has been made in order to achieve the reduction in these costs and burdens. Some disclosure requirements in full IFRS are intended to meet the needs of listed entities, or to assist users in making forecasts of the future. Users of financial statements of SMEs often do not need such detailed information.

Tutorial note

Make specific comments regarding which accounting requirements are excluded from IFRS for SME.

Small companies have different strategies, with survival and stability rather than profit maximisation being their goals. The stewardship function is often absent in small companies thus there are a number of accounting practices and disclosures which may not provide relevant information for the users of SME financial statements. As a result the standard does not address the following topics:

(i)   earnings per share

(ii)   interim financial reporting

(iii)   segment reporting

(iv)   insurance (because entities that issue insurance contracts are not eligible to use the standard); and

(v)   assets held for sale.

In addition there are certain accounting treatments, which are not allowable under the standard. An example of a disallowable treatment is the revaluation model for intangible assets. Generally there are simpler and more cost effective methods of accounting available to SMEs than those accounting practices, which have been disallowed.

Tutorial note

Make specific comments regarding which accounting requirements have been simplified by IFRS for SME.

Additionally the IFRS for SMEs makes numerous simplifications to the recognition, measurement and disclosure requirements in full IFRSs. Examples of these simplifications are:

(i) goodwill is amortised over its useful life. If the useful life cannot be reliably determined, then management must use an estimate of ten years or less. In comparison, IFRS 3 *Business Combinations* does not permit the amortisation of goodwill but instead requires an annual impairment review.

(ii) a simplified calculation is allowed if measurement of defined benefit pension plan obligations (under the projected unit credit method) involves undue cost or effort

(iii) the cost model is permitted for investments in associates and joint ventures.

As a result of the above, SMEs do not have to comply with over 90% of the volume of accounting requirements applicable to listed companies. If an entity opts to use the IFRS for SMEs, it must follow the standard in its entirety and it cannot cherry pick between the requirements of the IFRS for SMEs and those of full IFRSs.

Tutorial note

Part (b) tests your knowledge in relation to three specific accounting issues. You should deal with each situation in turn, explaining the requirements from the appropriate reporting standard(s).

(b) (i) **Defined benefit scheme**

The accounting policy currently applied by Whitebirk is consistent with IFRS for SME. Note that IFRS for SME also permits actuarial gains and losses to be recognised in profit or loss; this is not permitted by IAS 19. The entity shall apply its chosen accounting policy consistently to all of its defined benefit plans and all of its actuarial gains and losses. Actuarial gains and losses recognised in other comprehensive income shall also be presented within other components of equity on the statement of financial position.

(ii) **Business combination**

The IFRS states that the acquirer shall, at the acquisition date:

(a) recognise goodwill acquired in a business combination as an asset, and

(b) initially measure that goodwill at its cost, being the excess of the cost of the business combination over the acquirer's interest in the net fair value of the identifiable assets, liabilities and contingent liabilities.

After initial recognition, the acquirer shall measure goodwill acquired in a business combination at cost less accumulated amortisation and accumulated impairment losses. If an entity is unable to reliably determine the useful life of goodwill, the estimate used must be ten years or less. There is no choice of accounting method for non controlling interests and therefore the partial goodwill method would be used.

Goodwill will be $5.7 million less 90% of $6 million i.e. $0.3 million. Assuming the maximum estimate of useful life is used, the goodwill will then be amortised over ten years at a value of $30,000 per annum.

(iii) **Research and development expenditure**

The IFRS states that an entity shall recognise expenditure incurred internally on an intangible item, including all expenditure for both research and development activities, as an expense when it is incurred unless it forms part of the cost of another asset that meets the recognition criteria in this IFRS. Thus the expenditure of $1.5 million on research and development should all be written off to profit or loss.

ACCA Marking scheme			
			Marks
(a)	(i)/(ii)	Subjective assessment including professional	16
(b)	(i)	Defined benefit scheme	3
	(ii)	Business combination	4
	(iii)	Research and development expenditure	2
			___
Total			**25**
			___

Examiner's comments

In part (a), candidates had to comment on the different approaches which could have been taken by the International Accounting Standards Board in developing the 'IFRS for Small and Medium-sized Entities' explaining the approach finally taken by the IASB. Additionally candidates had to discuss the main differences and modifications to IFRS which the IASB made to reduce the burden of reporting for SME's. Specific examples had to be given and also a discussion of how the Board had dealt with the problem of defining an SME. This part of the question was very well answered. The subject had been very topical and been the subject of articles in the accountancy press.

In part (b) candidates had to discuss how the certain transactions should be dealt with in the financial statements of an entity with reference to the 'IFRS for Small and Medium-sized Entities'. The answers to this part of the question were quite variable. The three topic areas chosen were defined benefit, the purchase of an entity and research and development expenditure. Candidates were generally unclear about how to account for the transactions and many used full IFRS.

65 **HOLCOMBE (JUN 10 EXAM)** *Walk in the footsteps of a top tutor*

Key answer tips

This two-part question considers theoretical and conceptual issues associated with accounting for leases. Part (a) comprises two discussion-based elements; the first relates to whether the current reporting standard is conceptually flawed, and the second deals with whether the operating lease in the scenario meets the definition of an asset and liability from the Framework document. A sound knowledge of the reporting standard, together with logical application of the definition of an asset and liability should enable you to achieve a good mark for part (a) of the question. Part (b) of the question requires accounting for a sale and leaseback transaction if the operating lease was to be accounted for as an asset, together with accounting for an inflation adjustment. The last element of part (b) may put some students off, but the first element for six marks, should be a source of marks for most students for straight-forward application of accounting for derecognition of the office building and recognition of an operating lease asset and obligation. Within this question, there are also 2 professional marks available for clarity and quality of discussion within your answer, so ensure that you use appropriate presentation and professional language to gain these marks.

Tutorial note

Begin by identifying and explaining the weaknesses with the current accounting standard dealing with leasing. IAS 17; specific criticisms will earn more marks than vague or general comments.

(a) (i) The existing accounting model for leases has been criticised for failing to meet the needs of users of financial statements. It can be argued that operating leases give rise to assets and liabilities that should be recognised in the financial statements of lessees. Consequently, users may adjust the amounts recognised in financial statements in an attempt to recognise those assets and liabilities and reflect the effect of lease contracts in profit or loss. The information available to users in the notes to the financial statements is often insufficient to make reliable adjustments to the financial statements.

The existence of two different accounting methods for finance leases and operating leases means that similar transactions can be accounted for very differently. This affects the comparability of financial statements. Also current accounting standards provide opportunities to structure transactions so as to achieve a specific lease classification. If the lease is classified as an operating lease, the lessee obtains a source of financing that can be difficult for users to understand, as it is not recognised in the financial statements.

Existing accounting methods have been criticised for their complexity. In particular, it has proved difficult to define the dividing line between the principles relating to finance and operating leases. As a result, standards use a mixture of subjective judgments and rule based criteria that can be difficult to apply.

The existing accounting model can be said to be conceptually flawed. On entering an operating lease contract, the lessee obtains a valuable right to use the leased item. This right meets the Framework's definition of an asset. Additionally the lessee assumes an obligation to pay rentals that meet the Framework's definition of a liability. However, if the lessee classifies the lease as an operating lease, that right and obligation are not recognised.

There are significant and growing differences between the accounting methods for leases and other contractual arrangements. This has led to inconsistent accounting for arrangements that meet the definition of a lease and similar arrangements that do not. For example leases are financial instruments but they are scoped out of IAS 32/IFRS 9.

In 2013, the IASB issued an Exposure Draft on leases. In this document, the IASB proposed that an asset and a liability should be recognised for all leases which are longer than one year. This would address many of the criticisms of IAS 17 *Leases* that are outlined above.

Tutorial note

Begin by stating the definition of an asset and liability from the Framework document. This can then be applied to the specific information in the question, before coming to an opinion on whether or not the lease meets the definition of an asset or liability.

(ii) An asset is a resource controlled by the entity as a result of past events and from which future economic benefits are expected to flow to the entity. Holcombe has the right to use the leased plant as an economic resource because the entity can use it to generate cash inflows or reduce cash outflows. Similarly, Holcombe controls the right to use the leased item during the lease term because the lessor is unable to recover or have access to the resource without the consent of the lessee or unless there is a breach of contract. The control results from past events, which is the signing of the lease contract and the receipt of the plant by the lessee. Holcombe also maintains the asset.

Unless the lessee breaches the contract, Holcombe has an unconditional right to use the leased item. Future economic benefits will flow to the lessee from the use of the leased item during the lease term. Thus it could be concluded that the lessee's right to use a leased item for the lease term meets the definitions of an asset in the Framework.

A liability is a present obligation of the entity arising from past events, the settlement of which is expected to result in an outflow from the entity of resources embodying economic benefits. The obligation to pay rentals is a liability.

Unless Holcombe breaches the contract, the lessor has no contractual right to take possession of the item until the end of the lease term. Equally, the entity has no contractual right to terminate the lease and avoid paying rentals. Therefore the lessee has an unconditional obligation to pay rentals. Thus the entity has a present obligation to pay rentals, which arises out of a past event, which is the signing of the lease contract and the receipt of the item by the lessee. Finally the obligation is expected to result in an outflow of economic benefits in the form of cash.

Thus the entity's obligation to pay rentals meets the definition of a liability in the Framework.

Tutorial note

This part of the question requirement deals with accounting for a sale and leaseback arrangement; in particular, derecognition of an office building and capitalising rights and obligations under an operating lease, with the gain on disposal deferred and released over the operating lease term.

(b)   (i)   On sale of the building, Holcombe will recognise the following in the financial statements to 30 April 2010:

Dr   Cash $150m

Cr   Office building $120m

Cr   Deferred Income (SOFP) $30m

Recognition of gain on the sale of the building

Dr   Deferred Income (SOFP) $6m

Cr   Deferred Income (P/L) $6m

Release of the gain on sale of the building ($30m/5 years)

Dr   Right-of-use asset $63.89m

Cr   Lease obligation $63.89m

Recognition of the leaseback at the present value of lease payments using 8% discount rate ($16m × 3.993).

In the first year of the leaseback, Holcombe will recognise the following:

Dr   Lease obligation $16m

Cr   Cash $16m

Recognition of payment of rentals

Dr   Interest expense $5.11m

Cr   Lease obligation $5.11m

Recognition of interest expense ($63.89m × 8%)

Dr   Depreciation expense $12.78m

Cr   Right-of-use asset $12.78m

Recognition of depreciation of operating lease asset over five years ($63.89m/5 years).

The statement of financial position will show a carrying value of $51.11m being cost of $63.89m less depreciation of $12.78m.

(ii)   Inflation adjustments should be recognised in the period in which they are incurred as they are effectively contingent rent and are not included in any minimum lease calculations. A contingent rent according to IAS 17 is 'that part of the rent that is not fixed in amount but is based on the future amount of a factor that changes other than with the passage of time.' Thus in this case, Holcombe would recognise operating rentals of $5 million in year 1, $5 million in year 2 plus the inflation adjustment at the beginning of year 2, and $5 million in year 3 plus the inflation adjustment at the beginning of year 2 plus inflation adjustment at the beginning of year 3. Based on current inflation, the rent will be $5.2 million in year 2 and $5.408 million in year 3.

		ACCA Marking scheme	
			Marks
(a)	(i)	Subjective	7
	(ii)	Subjective	7
		Professional marks	2
(b)	(i)	Recognition of gain	1
		Recognition of the leaseback	1
		Recognition of the payment of rentals	2
		Recognition of interest expense and depreciation	2
	(ii)	Contingent rentals	3
Total			**25**

Examiner's comments

This question required candidates to discuss the reasons why the current lease accounting standards may fail to meet the needs of users and could be said to be conceptually flawed. The second part of the question required a discussion of a plant operating lease in the financial statements met the definition of an asset and liability as set out in the Conceptual Framework for Financial Reporting. Candidates' answers were quite narrow in their discussion of the weaknesses in the accounting standards. The definitions of asset and liability were well rehearsed and candidates scored well on this part of the question. It is apparent that very few candidates read widely. This question always deals with current issues which mean that a wider reading base is required to achieve a good mark. Accounting and Business, and the student accountant are just two examples of magazines that provide wider exposure to current issues.

The final part of the question required candidates to show the accounting entries in the year of the sale and lease back assuming that an operating lease was recognised as an asset in the statement of financial position and to state how an inflation adjustment on a short term operating lease should be dealt with in the financial statements of an entity. The purpose of this question was to show how a change in the current accounting standards (by recognising operating leases in the statement of financial position) would affect their accounting treatment. The question was well answered and candidates scored well generally on this question.

Walk in the footsteps of a top tutor

Key answer tips

This question requires explanation of the importance of accounting standards together with discussion of costs and benefits to users of increased disclosure in financial statements. The question requirement is separated into two specific parts, each with a mark allocation which should help you with time management during the examination, plus two marks for quality of discussion and reasoning. The best way to approach this question is to deal with each requirement separately and to make specific, supported, comments.

(a)   It could be argued that the marketplace already offers powerful incentives for high-quality reporting as it rewards such by easing or restricting access to capital or raising or lowering the cost of borrowing capital depending on the quality of the entity's reports. However, accounting standards play an important role in helping the market mechanism work effectively.

Tutorial note

Several reasons regarding the need for accounting standards can be identified – focus upon fundamental issues such as comparability, reliability and cost-benefit factors.

Accounting standards are needed because they:

- Promote a common understanding of the nature of corporate performance and this facilitates any negotiations between users and companies about the content of financial statements. For example, many loan agreements specify that a company provide the lender with financial statements prepared in accordance with generally accepted accounting principles or International Financial Reporting Standards. Both the company and the lender understand the terms and are comfortable that statements prepared according to those standards will meet certain information needs. Without standards, the statements would be less useful to the lender, and the company and the lender would have to agree to create some form of acceptable standards which would be inefficient and less effective.

- Assist neutral and unbiased reporting. Companies may wish to portray their past performance and future prospects in the most favourable light. Users are aware of this potential bias and are sceptical about the information they receive. Standards build credibility and confidence in the capital marketplace to the benefit of both users and companies.

- Improve the comparability of information across companies and national boundaries. Without standards, there would be little basis to compare one company with others across national boundaries which is a key feature of relevant information.

- **Create credibility in financial statements.** Auditors verify that information is reported in accordance with standards and this creates public confidence in financial statements.

- **Facilitate consistency of information by producing data in accordance with an agreed conceptual framework.** A consistent approach to the development and presentation of information assists users in accessing information in an efficient manner and facilitates decision-making.

(b)   **Increased information disclosure benefits users by reducing the likelihood that they will misallocate their capital.** This is obviously a direct benefit to individual users of corporate reports. The disclosure reduces the risk of misallocation of capital by enabling users to improve their assessments of a company's prospects.

Tutorial note

Benefits of increased information disclosure can also be identified from the earlier points made – focus upon cost-benefit factors and fundamental issues.

This creates three important results.

(i)   Users use information disclosed to increase their investment returns and by definition support the most profitable companies which are likely to be those that contribute most to economic growth. Thus, an important benefit of information disclosure is that it improves the effectiveness of the investment process.

(ii)   The second result lies in the effect on the liquidity of the capital markets. A more liquid market assists the effective allocation of capital by allowing users to reallocate their capital quickly. The degree of information asymmetry between the buyer and seller and the degree of uncertainty of the buyer and the seller will affect the liquidity of the market as lower asymmetry and less uncertainty will increase the number of transactions and make the market more liquid. Disclosure will affect uncertainty and information asymmetry.

(iii)   Information disclosure helps users understand the risk of a prospective investment. Without any information, the user has no way of assessing a company's prospects. Information disclosure helps investors predict a company's prospects. Getting a better understanding of the true risk could lower the price of capital for the company. It is difficult to prove however that the average cost of capital is lowered by information disclosure, even though it is logically and practically impossible to assess a company's risk without relevant information. Lower capital costs promote investment, which can stimulate productivity and economic growth.

However although increased information can benefit users, there are problems of understandability and information overload.

Tutorial note

Several reasons regarding costs and benefits of information disclosure can be identified.

Information disclosure provides a degree of protection to users. The benefit is fairness to users and is part of corporate accountability to society as a whole.

The main costs to the preparer of financial statements are as follows:

(i)   the cost of developing and disseminating information,

(ii)   the cost of possible litigation attributable to information disclosure,

(iii)   the cost of competitive disadvantage attributable to disclosure.

The costs of developing and disseminating the information include those of gathering, creating and auditing the information.

Additional costs to the preparers include training costs, changes to systems (for example on moving to IFRS), and the more complex and the greater the information provided, the more it will cost the company.

Although litigation costs are known to arise from information disclosure, it does not follow that all information disclosure leads to litigation costs. Cases can arise from insufficient disclosure and misleading disclosure. Only the latter is normally prompted by the presentation of information disclosure. Fuller disclosure could lead to lower costs of litigation as the stock market would have more realistic expectations of the company's prospects and the discrepancy between the valuation implicit in the market price and the valuation based on a company's financial statements would be lower. However, litigation costs do not necessarily increase with the extent of the disclosure. Increased disclosure could reduce litigation costs.

Disclosure could weaken a company's ability to generate future cash flows by aiding its competitors. The effect of disclosure on competitiveness involves benefits as well as costs. Competitive disadvantage could be created if disclosure is made relating to strategies, plans, (for example, planned product development, new market targeting) or information about operations (for example, production-cost figures). There is a significant difference between the purpose of disclosure to users and competitors. The purpose of disclosure to users is to help them to estimate the amount, timing, and certainty of future cash flows. Competitors are not trying to predict a company's future cash flows, and information of use in that context is not necessarily of use in obtaining competitive advantage. Overlap between information designed to meet users' needs and information designed to further the purposes of a competitor is often coincidental. Every company that could suffer competitive disadvantage from disclosure could gain competitive advantage from comparable disclosure by competitors. Published figures are often aggregated with little use to competitors.

Companies bargain with suppliers and with customers, and information disclosure could give those parties an advantage in negotiations. In such cases, the advantage would be a cost for the disclosing entity. However, the cost would be offset whenever information disclosure was presented by both parties, each would receive an advantage and a disadvantage.

There are other criteria to consider such as whether the information to be disclosed is about the company. This is both a benefit and a cost criterion. Users of corporate reports need company-specific data, and it is typically more costly to obtain and present information about matters external to the company. Additionally, consideration must be given as to whether the company is the best source for the information. It could be inefficient for a company to obtain or develop data that other, more expert parties could develop and present or do develop at present.

There are many benefits to information disclosure and users have unmet information needs. It cannot be known with any certainty what the optimal disclosure level is for companies. Some companies through voluntary disclosure may have achieved their optimal level. There are no quantitative measures of how levels of disclosure stand with respect to optimal levels. Standard setters have to make such estimates as best they can, guided by prudence, and by what evidence of benefits and costs they can obtain.

ACCA Marking scheme			Marks
(a)	Common understanding		2
	Neutral, unbiased		2
	Comparability		1
	Credibility		2
	Consistency		2
		Maximum	9
(b)	Investment process		4
	Risk		2
	Protection		2
	Costs		2
	Competitive disadvantage		2
	Other criteria		2
		Maximum	14
	Professional marks		2
Total			25

Examiner's comments

This question required candidates to discuss the reason why accounting standards are required to keep the market mechanism working effectively and additionally to discuss the costs and benefits to users of financial information of increased disclosure in financial statements. There were a variety of answers from candidates, which were quite good, but very few candidates made reference to the Framework. The Framework is always a useful reference point for answers to discursive questions. In answering the part of the question dealing with the costs and benefits of disclosure, very few candidates mentioned possible litigation and competitive disadvantage and advantage. Also information asymmetry and its link with the liquidity of the market were seldom mentioned. Particularly in these current times, this point has particular relevance. Future questions in this area may have a calculation element. Candidates answered this question very well producing answers which demonstrated a good understanding of the usefulness of accounting standards and the cost and benefits of disclosure.

67 MANAGEMENT COMMENTARY

Key answer tips

This question should be straight forward if you have studied this topic. If you lack knowledge, revisit the chapter in the Complete Text on non-financial reporting.

(a) **Purpose of the Management Commentary (MC)**

The Management Commentary (MC) is a narrative report that provides a context within which to interpret the financial position, financial performance and cash flows of an entity. Management are able to explain its objectives and its strategies for achieving those objectives. Users routinely use the type of information provided in management commentary to help them evaluate an entity's prospects and its general risks, as well as the success of management's strategies for achieving its stated objectives.

For many entities, management commentary is already an important element of their communication with the capital markets, supplementing as well as complementing the financial statements.

The MC is a Practice Statement (PS), rather than a mandatory reporting standard. The reason for this is that, not every entity may be required to prepare such a statement, due to factors such as:

- national business law

- relevant business practice regulation, such as corporate governance requirements

- the size of the entity, in financial terms and/or the nature and extent of business activities.

No two entities will be alike in all respects, so it would be difficult to be prescriptive or definitive on issues which will vary considerably between different entities.

This PS helps management to provide useful commentary to financial statements prepared in accordance with IFRS information. The users are identified as existing and potential members, together with lenders and creditors, which is similar to the principal users of annual financial reports.

It can be adopted by entities, where applicable, any time from the date of issue in December 2010.

(b) **Framework for presentation of management commentary**

The following principles should be applied when a management commentary is prepared:

1 to provide management's view of the entity's performance, position and progress; and

2 to supplement and complement information presented in the financial statements.

Consequently, the MC should include information which is both forward-looking and adheres to the qualitative characteristics of information as described in the 2010 Conceptual Framework for Financial Reporting. The fundamental qualitative characteristics are identified as relevance and faithful representation, which are supported by further enhancing characteristics of comparability, verifiability, timeliness and understandability.

The MC should provide information to help users of the financial reports to assess the performance of the entity and the actions of its management relative to stated strategies and plans for progress.

That type of commentary will help users of the financial reports to understand risk exposures and strategies of the entity, relevant non-financial factors and other issues not otherwise included within the financial statements. This clearly indicates that the MC should consist of information which is additional to information already contained within the IFRS financial statements, rather than simply a repeat or rearrangement of such information.

The MC should provide management's perspective of the entity's performance, position and progress. MC should derive from the information that is important to management in managing the business. This will typically include both backward-looking information and supporting commentary, together with forward-looking information and commentary. This latter component is often deficient or lacking within narrative components of financial statements as they are prepared at present as it is normally regarded as being commercially sensitive.

It could be argued that some of the content to be included within a MC is already included within the directors' report or, for examples, the chief executive's review. However, PS 1 provides a consistent basis for relevant commentary and supporting data which may not be included elsewhere within the annual financial statements. Additionally, the content of the MC should be linked to previous, and future, MC by identifying and explaining changes in strategy, expected and actual results and other issues supported by financial and non-financial measures and indicators of performance.

(c)   **Elements of management commentary**

Although the particular focus of MC will depend on the facts and circumstances of each individual entity, it should include information that is essential to an understanding of:

(i)   the nature of the business – this may include not only the nature and extent of current activities, but changes that may take place at some future date, together with factors that may influence whether such changes are implemented.

(ii)   management's objectives and its strategies for meeting those objectives – the objectives may include both financial objectives (such as growth in the equity dividend paid or earnings per share) and non-financial factors (such as improving health and safety performance or minimising environmental damage). The important issue is that they should be clearly stated, measurable and evaluated over time for performance or achievement of targets. This is likely to include information which may not have been published in the past.

As such, it may take time for managers to determine which information they should provide within the MC and how that information should be reported.

(iii)   the entity's most significant resources, risks and relationships – this may include information relating to relationships with principal customers and/or suppliers. Other factors which may be relevant include whether there are any factors which may undermine those relationships, such as volatility of exchange rates, government policy or regulation which may affect the entity, or even its customers and suppliers

(iv)   the results of operations and prospects; and

(v)   the critical performance measures and indicators that management uses to evaluate the entity's performance against stated objectives. This will include financial and non-financial information. There is likely to be qualitative information, together with supporting narrative and disclosures. The performance measures and indicators should be reported consistently each year, to enable comparison and evaluation to take place. Where performance measures and indicators are amended, this should be made clear within the commentary, including reasons for any amendment, together with restated information to enable evaluation of the revised data.

ACCA Marking scheme		
		Marks
(a)	Purpose of MC	5
(b)	Principles and framework	10
(c)	Elements to include	10
		——
Total		25
		——

68   REVENUE RECOGNITION

Key answer tips

Revenue recognition continues to be an important issue that is regularly tested in the P2 exam. It is important that you engage with the standards that you are learning about and that you think about potential criticisms of them.

(a)   (i)   There were a number of issues identified with IAS 11 *Construction Contracts* and IAS 18 *Revenue*. These included the following:

Limited guidance

It had been perceived that IAS 18 and IAS 11 offered limited guidance on some topics. In particular, there was a lack of guidance for transactions involving the delivery of more than one good or service. IAS 18 stated that, in certain circumstances, revenue recognition criteria had to be applied to the separately identifiable components of a single transaction in order to reflect the substance of the transaction. However, the standard did not state clearly when or how an entity should separate a single transaction into components.

There was also limited guidance on the real difference between the selling of a good and the provision of a service. This meant that some companies recognised revenue when risks and rewards transferred whilst other entities recognised revenue from the same transaction according to the stage of completion. Comparability was reduced as a result.

Conversion

The IASB and FASB wanted to converge their revenue standards but the US GAAP standard included numerous industry and transaction specific requirements. Therefore a new standard was required.

Disclosures

The disclosure requirements of the older standards were deemed to be inadequate, particularly in terms of providing information about key judgements applied by entities when recognising revenue.

(ii)   The five steps for recognising revenue are as follows:

    1   Identify the contract with the customer

    2   Determine the transaction price

    3   Identify the performance obligations within the contract

    4   Allocate the transaction price to each of the performance obligations

    5   Recognise revenue as or when a performance obligation is satisfied.

(iii)   Throughout all five steps of revenue recognition, entities are required to exercise judgement. For example:

- Contracts with customers do not need to be in writing but may arise through customary business practice. An entity must therefore ascertain whether it has a constructive obligation to deliver a good or service to a customer.

- A contract can only be accounted for if it is probable that the entity will collect the consideration that it is entitled to. Whether benefits are probable is, ultimately, a judgement.

- The entity must identify distinct performance obligations in a contract. However, past performance may give rise to expectations in a customer that goods or services not specified in the contract will be transferred. The identification of distinct performance obligations thus relies on management judgement about both contract terms, and the impact of the entity's past behaviour on customer expectations.

- Variable consideration should be included in the transaction price if it is highly probable that a significant reversal in the amount of cumulative revenue recognised to date will not occur. This may involve making judgements about whether performance related targets will be met.

- The transaction price must be allocated to distinct performance obligations, based on observable, standalone selling prices. However, estimates must be used if observable prices are not available.

- If a performance obligation is satisfied over time, revenue is recognised based on progress towards the completion of the performance obligation. There are various ways to measure completion, using either input or output methods, and the entity must determine which one most faithfully represents the transaction.

- If a performance obligation is satisfied at a point in time, the entity must use judgement to ascertain when control of the asset passes to the customer.

(b) Amos has entered into a contract with a customer that contains a single performance obligation: to construct a building.

The contract includes $4 million of fixed consideration and $1 million of variable consideration. The entity must estimate the variable consideration to which it is entitled. Using a most likely approach (since there are only two outcomes), Amos expects to receive $1 million. However, variable consideration should only be included in the transaction price if it is highly probable that a significant reversal in revenue recognised would not occur when the uncertainty is resolved. Due to the bespoke nature of this building, and the doubts expressed by Amos, the variable consideration should be excluded from the transaction price. The transaction price is therefore $4 million, all of which relates to the construction of the building.

Revenue from the construction should be recognised as or when the performance obligation is satisfied. Amos must therefore consider whether it satisfies the performance obligation over time, or at a point in time. Amos is creating an asset with no alternative use and has a right to payment for performance completed to date. Therefore, per IFRS 15, this should be accounted for as a performance obligation satisfied over time.

For performance obligations satisfied over time, revenue should be recognised based on progress towards the completion of the performance obligation. Based on costs incurred, the performance obligation is 20% ($0.5m/$2.5m) complete. Therefore, revenue of $0.8m ($4m × 20%) should be recognised.

Amos should show a corresponding receivable for $0.8m because they have an unconditional right to receive the money.

ACCA Marking scheme		Marks
(a)	Reasons for IFRS 15	5
	5 steps	3
	Judgement	7
(b)	Revenue recognition	8
	Professional marks	2
Total		**25**

69   IMPAIRMENT OF FINANCIAL ASSETS

Key answer tips

Question 4 is always an essay-style question requirement, which can include a small computation element. It may focus upon current issues in financial reporting, or upon a theoretical or conceptual issue.

If the focus is upon current issues, you should be prepared to explain the current financial reporting treatment based upon existing reporting standards, weaknesses in the required accounting treatment, and how any proposed replacement reporting standard will improve the situation.

(a)   **Financial asset impairment rules**

IFRS 9 *Financial Instruments* states that loss allowances must be recognised for financial assets that are debt instruments and which are measured at amortised cost or at fair value through other comprehensive income.

If the credit risk on the financial asset has not increased significantly since initial recognition, the loss allowance should be equal to 12-month expected credit losses. If the credit risk on the financial asset has increased significantly since initial recognition then the loss allowance should be equal to the lifetime expected credit losses. IFRS 9 simplifies the accounting treatment of the impairment of trade receivables and contract assets (recognised in accordance with IFRS 15 *Revenue from Contracts with Customers*) that do not have a significant financing component by saying that the loss allowance on these should always be equal to lifetime expected credit losses.

If a financial asset is credit impaired when purchased, then interest income is calculated using a credit adjusted effective interest rate. This incorporates expected lifetime credit losses at the inception date and therefore the allowance recorded against such assets should only be the change in the lifetime expected credit losses since inception.

An entity's estimate of expected credit losses must reflect an unbiased and probability-weighted amount that is determined by evaluating a range of possible outcomes, the time value of money, and reasonable and supportable information about past events and current conditions as well as forecasts of future economic conditions.

If an asset is credit impaired at the reporting date, then the expected credit losses should be measured as the difference between the asset's gross carrying amount and the present value of the estimated future cash flows when discounted at the original effective rate of interest.

Adjustments to the loss allowance are charged (or credited) to the statement of profit or loss. The loss allowance will reduce the net carrying amount of the financial asset, unless it is a debt instrument held at fair value through other comprehensive income (FVOCI). If an allowance is calculated for an asset measured at FVOCI then the increase (or decrease) in the allowance is still charged (or credited) to profit or loss but the other side of the entry is recorded in other comprehensive income.

Benefits and drawbacks

Anticipating credit losses is a prudent approach, meaning it is less likely that assets will be over-stated. Users of the financial statements are also provided with timely information, because they are warned about potential impairment issues before actual defaults have occurred.

However, judgement is required when ascertaining whether credit risk has increased significantly and also as to the value of expected credit losses. This could be argued to reduce verifiability and also to increase the scope for the manipulation of profits.

The IASB and the FASB differ in their approach to financial asset impairments, potentially creating material differences and thus reducing comparability between companies.

(b) **Impairment of Glasgow's financial assets**

The financial asset is measured at amortised cost and therefore investment income of $8,000 ($100,000 × 8%) would have been recognised in the statement of profit or loss in the first accounting period and the asset would have a gross carrying value of $100,000.

At year-end, there has been a significant increase in credit risk. An allowance equal to lifetime expected credit losses must now be provided for. This is the present value of the contractual cash flow shortages, weighted by the risks of default.

Glasgow were expecting an annual return of $8,000 a year ($100,000 × 8%) but, based on the evaluation of a range of possible outcomes and weighting these for probabilities, the expected return is now $2,000 a year ($100,000 × 2%). There is therefore an expected contractual cash shortfall of $6,000 per year, which needs to be discounted to present value using the original effective rate of 8%.

Date	Contractual cash flow shortfall ($)	Discount rate	Present value ($)
31 October 2014	6,000	$1/1.08$	5,556
31 October 2015	6,000	$1/1.08^2$	5,144
31 October 2016	6,000	$1/1.08^3$	4,763
			——
			15,463
			——

Glasgow will therefore need to recognise a loss allowance of $15,463. This will be netted off the value of the asset to reduce it to $84,537 in the statement of financial position. An impairment loss of $15,463 will be recognised in the statement of profit or loss.

ACCA Marking scheme		
		Marks
(a)	IFRS 9 rules	10
	Benefits and drawbacks	5
(b)	Impairment explanation and calculations	8
	Professional marks	2
		——
Total		**25**
		——

70   INTEGRATED REPORTING

Key answer tips

The Integrated Reporting Framework is a relatively new examinable document in the P2 syllabus. Students are therefore advised to ensure that they are familiar with the purpose and contents of an integrated report.

(a)   (i)   There are many limitations of financial reporting. These include the following:

Historical information

The statement of profit or loss shows the performance of the entity over the past reporting period. This offers little insight into the future. Moreover by the time financial statements are published, the information presented will be several months out of date.

Unrecognised assets/liabilities

Some assets and liabilities are not recognised in IFRS financial statements, thus limiting usefulness. Operating leases are a form of off-balance sheet finance that may make a company appear less geared and less risky than is really the case. Internally generated goodwill is not recognised under IFRS. This means that no asset is recognised in respect of the company's reputation or employee skills even though these may play a pivotal role in its success.

Clutter

Financial reports have been criticised in recent years for becoming increasingly cluttered as a result of extensive IFRS disclosure requirements. These disclosures are often generic and boilerplate in nature and make it more difficult for the users to find relevant information.

Financial/non-financial information

Current and past profits and cash flows are not the only determinate of future success. Long-term success is also dependent on how an entity is governed, the risks to which it is exposed and how well these are managed, and whether its business activities are sustainable into the medium and long-term. Financial statements prepared in accordance with IFRS say little about these areas.

Estimates

Financial reporting uses many estimates (for instance, depreciation rates). Estimates are subjective and could be manipulated in order to achieve particular profit targets. The subjective nature of estimates reduces comparability between companies.

The statement of cash flows somewhat compensates for the impact of accounting estimates. However, the cash position of an entity can also be window-dressed (such as by delaying payments to suppliers).

Professional judgement

Financial reporting requires judgement. For instance, judgement is required when classifying a lease as a finance lease or an operating lease. Judgement involves subjectivity, which reduces comparability.

Use of historical cost

Some accounting standards, such as IAS 16 *Property, Plant and Equipment*, permit assets to be measured at historical cost. In times of rising prices, the statement of profit or loss will not show a sustainable level of profit. Some standards, such as IAS 16 and IAS 40 *Investment Properties*, allow entities to choose between cost and fair value models. This may hinder the ability of users to compare companies.

(ii) **Purpose**

An Integrated Report is defined as a 'concise communication about how an organisation's strategy, governance, performance and prospects, in the context of its external environment, lead to the creation of value in the short, medium and long term'. Value is conceptualised in terms of a range of capitals, not just financial. Integrated Reporting is therefore based on the premise that maximizing financial capital at the expense of other capitals (such as human, social and natural) is not sustainable in the longer term.

The key users of an Integrated Report are deemed to be the providers of financial capital. The Integrated Report will help these users to assess the long-term performance and continuation of the entities that they invest in.

Content

The Framework for Integrated Reporting is principles based and therefore it does not prescribe KPIs to be disclosed.

An Integrated Report should cover the following elements:

- Organisational overview and external environment – 'What does the organisation do and what are the circumstances under which it operates?'

- Governance – 'How does the organisation's governance structure support its ability to create value in the short, medium and long term?'

- Opportunities and risks – 'What are the specific opportunities and risks that affect the organisation's ability to create value over the short, medium and long term, and how is the organisation dealing with them?'

- Strategy and resource allocation – 'Where does the organisation want to go and how does it intend to get there?'

- Business model – 'What is the organisation's business model and to what extent is it resilient?'

- Performance – 'To what extent has the organisation achieved its strategic objectives and what are its outcomes in terms of effects on the capitals?'

- Future outlook – 'What challenges and uncertainties is the organisation likely to encounter in pursuing its strategy, and what are the potential implications for its business model and future performance?'

- Basis of presentation – 'How does the organisation determine what matters to include in the integrated report and how are such matters quantified or evaluated?'

The exact content of these elements is judgemental. Management should include material issues and justify their decisions.

(iii) Integrated Reports focus on value creation in the medium and long-term. They are much more forward-looking than financial reporting and will therefore help user groups in the decision making process. Financial reporting conceptualises value in terms of profits and cash. Integrated Reporting takes a much wider more holistic view of an entity than financial reporting. This may be of particular use for those who wish to invest in 'sustainable' entities.

Issues of governance and risk are very prominent within Integrated Reports, but are often missing from financial reports. These are key determinants of future success.

Employee skills and expertise are often neglected in financial reporting, but form a prominent part of Integrated Reports.

However, there are still issues not addressed by Integrated Reporting: Assessments of materiality and KPIs are subjective. Therefore, once again, it will be difficult to compare the Integrated Reports of two different companies. Prepares of Integrated Reports may still let bias influence the content of their reports. This is particularly true if no assurance is provided on the report. Some may also view Integrated Reports as another form of 'clutter' and feel overwhelmed by the quantity of information that they are presented with.

(b) According to IAS 38 *Intangible Assets*, an entity usually has insufficient control over the expected future economic benefits arising from a team of skilled staff and from training to meet the definition of an intangible asset. This means that money spent on employee training is expensed to profit or loss. Because no asset is therefore recognised in relation to employee expertise, users are not fully aware of its value.

Employees are likely to be TinCan's greatest asset and details of this will be pivotal to any assessment of TinCan's long-term success. An Integrated Report conceptualises value in terms of a range of capitals, including human capital (i.e. employees). Therefore TinCan would make extensive disclosures about its staff.

TinCan's commitment to staff training would be disclosed as leading to a net increase in human capital. This human capital should eventually lead to an even greater increase in financial capital. KPIs, such as details of expenditure on staff training, would enable users to assess and compare TinCan's commitment to its staff over time. TinCan could also include KPIs covering staff turnover and staff pay to help the users compare these to industry averages. Disclosure of its investment in employees in an Integrated Report is likely to lead to stakeholder confidence about TinCan's likely performance in the medium to long-term.

TinCan should also disclose any risks that may threaten the sustainability of its business model and how those risks are being managed. For instance, TinCan faces the risk that other companies may try to recruit its employees through offers of higher pay. Similarly, it is possible that TinCan will lose market share as its competitors, who may pay lower staff salaries, develop cheaper alternative products.

These disclosures in the Integrated Report will help users to ascertain the sustainability of TinCan's business model. This may act to encourage the providers of financial capital to invest in TinCan.

ACCA Marking scheme			Marks
(a)	(i)	Limitations of financial reporting	6
	(ii)	Integrated Reports	6
	(iii)	Integrated Reporting and Financial Reporting	5
(b)		Employee skills	6
		Professional marks	2
			—
Total			**25**
			—

71 FRAMEWORK

Key answer tips

The P2 examiner has indicated that students are expected to be able to critique existing standards. A good knowledge of the Framework is therefore essential.

(a) (i) The purpose of the *Conceptual Framework* is:

- to assist the IASB when developing or reviewing IFRSs

- to assist the Board in promoting harmonisation of regulations, accounting standards and procedures relating to the presentation of financial statements by providing a basis for reducing the number of alternative accounting treatments permitted by IFRSs

- to assist national standard-setting bodies in developing national standards;

- to assist preparers of financial statements in applying IFRSs and in dealing with topics that have yet to form the subject of an IFRS

- to assist auditors in forming an opinion on whether financial statements comply with IFRSs

- to assist users of financial statements in interpreting the information contained in financial statements prepared in compliance with IFRSs

- to provide those who are interested in the work of the IASB with information about its approach to the formulation of IFRSs

Nothing in the Framework over-rides the requirements of a specific IFRS.

(ii) An asset is a resource controlled by the entity as a result of past events and from which future economic benefits are expected to flow to the entity.

A liability is a present obligation of the entity arising from past events, the settlement of which is expected to result in an outflow from the entity of resources embodying economic benefits.

Equity is the residual interest in the assets of the entity after deducting all its liabilities.

Incomes are increases in economic benefits during the accounting period in the form of increases in assets or decreases in liabilities that will result in an increase in equity (excluding contributions from equity participants).

Expenses are decreases in economic benefits during the accounting period in the form of decreases in assets or increases in liabilities that will result in a decrease in equity (excluding distributions to equity participants).

(iii)   **Reasons for revision**

The following reasons have been given for revising the definitions of the elements:

- The IASB believe that revised definitions would provide greater clarity.

- The current definitions are inconsistently applied across the range of IFRSs.

- The notion of an 'expectation' of a flow of economic benefits is vague. Does it refer to the probability of an inflow/outflow or to a mathematical 'expected value'?

- The current definitions have led some users to incorrectly believe the asset or liability to be the ultimate inflow or outflow of economic benefits rather than the actual underlying resource or obligation.

- The current definitions do not offer enough practical guidance as to the difference between a liability and equity. Further guidance here would benefit users, particularly when applying these concepts to financial instruments.

Proposed definitions

The proposed definition of an asset is that it is 'a present economic resource controlled by an entity as a result of past events'.

The proposed definition of a liability is that it is 'a present obligation of the entity to transfer an economic resource as a result of past events'.

(b)   **Receivables**

An entity has transferred a financial asset if it has transferred the contractual rights to receive the cash flows of the asset. If an entity has transferred an asset, it must evaluate the extent to which it has retained the significant risks and rewards of ownership. If the entity transfers substantially all the risks and rewards of ownership of the financial asset, the entity must derecognise the financial asset. Even if the financial asset has been legally transferred, it will not be derecognised if the entity retains the significant risks and rewards of ownership.

An asset has been transferred because Coyote has transferred the contractual rights to receive the cash flows. Coyote has guaranteed that it will compensate the factor for all losses and therefore retains credit risk. Substantially, all the risks remain with Coyote. The receivable should not be derecognised.

A current liability should be recognised for the cash received of $2.6 million. Over the life of the factoring relationship, the liability will be increased to $3 million with $0.4 million charged to profit and loss as a finance cost.

Property, plant and equipment

According to IAS 16, the carrying amount of an item of property, plant and equipment should be derecognised when disposed of or when no future economic benefits are expected. A disposal occurs when the recipient obtains control over the asset.

The engine that required replacement will provide no further economic benefits and so should be derecognised. A loss equal to the engine's remaining carrying amount will be charged to profit or loss. Management should review the eight year useful life attributed to the engines to ascertain if this is still relevant.

ACCA Marking scheme			
			Marks
(a)	(i)	Purpose of the Framework	5
	(ii)	Element definitions	5
	(iii)	Criticisms and proposed definitions	5
(b)		Transactions	8
		Professional marks	2
			——
Total			**25**
			——

UK GAAP FOCUS

72   KUTCHEN (JUNE 15 EXAM) (UK GAAP FOCUS)

Key answer tips

The additional examinable UK content for those sitting the P2 UK paper is not solely concerned with the differences between IFRS for SME and UK GAAP. Students are also expected to have knowledge of the Companies Act 2006 requirements in relation to the preparation of group accounts and the grounds on which a subsidiary can be excluded from consolidation. This question provides excellent practice at this syllabus area.

Requirements to prepare group accounts

The requirements in the Companies Act 2006 to prepare group accounts are largely mirrored in FRS 102, which states that consolidated financial statements (group accounts in the Companies Act) are prepared by all parent entities unless one of the following exemptions which are derived from the Companies Act applies:

(i)   The parent company is subject to the small companies regime (see ss.383 to 384 of the Companies Act).

(ii)   The parent company is a subsidiary included in a larger group which prepares consolidated financial statements and meets the requirements of ss.400 or 401 of the Companies Act, including:

(a)   The parent is itself a subsidiary whose immediate parent is established in an EEA state, and whose results are consolidated into the group financial statements of an undertaking established in an EEA state (not necessarily the immediate parent). Section 400 sets out further conditions for this exemption, including that a company which has any of its securities admitted to trading on a regulated market in an EEA state is not eligible for this exemption.

(b)   The parent is itself a subsidiary, its immediate parent is not established in an EEA state, and its results are consolidated into the group accounts of an undertaking (either the same parent or another) drawn up in accordance with the EU Seventh Directive or in an equivalent manner (for example, EU-IFRS accounts).

Section 401 sets out further conditions for this exemption, including that a company which has any of its securities admitted to trading on a regulated market in an EEA state is not eligible for this exemption.

(iii)   All of the parent's subsidiaries are excluded from consolidation under FRS 102.

If an entity is not a parent at the year end, then it is not required to prepare consolidated accounts.

Exclusion of subsidiaries from consolidation

Consolidated financial statements provide information about the group as a single economic entity. They include all subsidiaries of the parent except those excluded on one of the following grounds:

(a)   severe long-term restrictions substantially hinder the exercise of the rights of the parent over the assets or management of the subsidiary. These rights are the rights held by or attributed to the company in the absence of which it would not be the parent company; or

(b)   the subsidiary is held exclusively for resale and has not previously been included in the consolidation.

A subsidiary excluded from consolidation due to severe long-term restrictions is, if the parent still exercises significant influence, equity accounted and treated as an associate. Otherwise, the parent has a choice of accounting policy to measure the subsidiary either at cost less impairment, or at fair value through other comprehensive income (OCI) with movements below cost recorded in profit or loss or at fair value through profit or loss.

A subsidiary excluded from consolidation on the basis of not previously having been consolidated and being held exclusively for resale is accounted for in accordance with FRS 102, which gives a choice of accounting policy of either cost less impairment, fair value through OCI with movements below cost recorded in profit or loss or fair value through profit or loss unless it is held as part of an investment portfolio. If it is held as part of an investment portfolio, it is held at fair value through profit or loss.

Section 405 of the Companies Act states that a subsidiary may be excluded from consolidation if the necessary information to prepare the group accounts cannot be obtained without disproportionate expense or undue delay. FRS 102, however, states that this does not justify non-consolidation, effectively closing off the statutory option. Subsidiaries are not excluded from consolidation because the subsidiary has dissimilar business activities to the rest of the group.

ACCA Marking scheme	
	Marks
Subjective assessment – 1 mark per point	8
	—
Total	**8**
	—

73   KLANCET (JUNE 15 EXAM) (UK GAAP FOCUS)

Key answer tips

This question requires candidates to apply their knowledge of FRS 102 and IFRS for SMEs to a scenario involving research and development. It therefore requires more than a short description of the differences between the two standards. Make sure that you read the question carefully or you risk losing a large proportion of the marks available.

Under IFRS for SMEs, all research and development costs are recognised as an expense. No intangible assets would therefore be recognised in respect of either of these contracts during the research and development stage.

However, FRS 102 takes a different approach. In assessing whether the recognition criteria are met for an internally generated intangible asset, research and development costs are split into a research phase and a development phase. If an entity cannot distinguish between the two phases, then all expenditure on the project is treated as relating to the research phase. Expenditure relating to the research phase of a project is expensed as incurred. An entity makes an accounting policy choice to capitalise expenditure in the development phase as an intangible asset or recognise it as an expense. If it adopts a policy of capitalisation, this applies to a development if, and only if, the entity can demonstrate that a series of criteria have all been met. These are:

(a)   the project is technically feasible

(b)   the entity intends to complete the project and use or sell the intangible asset; the entity is able to sell or use the asset

(c)   it is probable that the asset will generate future economic benefits

(d)   the entity has sufficient resources to complete the project; and

(e)   the entity can measure reliably the directly attributable expenditure.

From the date that these criteria are met, all costs that are directly attributable to creating, producing, and preparing the asset to be capable of operating in the manner intended by management are capitalised.

FRS 102 permits an entity to recognise an intangible asset when it is probable that the entity will receive the expected future economic benefits attributable to the asset, and its cost or value can be measured reliably. The price which an entity pays to acquire an intangible asset reflects its expectations about the probability that the expected future economic benefits in the asset will flow to the entity. The effect of probability is reflected in the cost of the asset and the probability recognition criterion above is always considered to be satisfied for separately acquired intangible assets. The cost of a separately acquired intangible asset can usually be measured reliably. This is particularly so when the purchase consideration is in the form of cash or other monetary assets. The cost of a separately acquired intangible asset comprises its purchase price and any directly attributable cost of preparing the asset for its intended use.

FRS 102 and the first project

In the case of the first project, Coact owns the potential new drug, and Retto is carrying out the development of the drug on its behalf. The payments to Retto therefore represent research and development by a third party.

Development costs are capitalised only after technical and commercial feasibility of the asset for sale or use have been established. This means that the entity must intend and be able to complete the intangible asset and either uses it or sells it and be able to demonstrate how the asset will generate future economic benefits. At present, this criterion does not appear to have been met as regulatory authority for the use of the drug has not been given and, in fact, approval has been refused in the past. Therefore, all costs should be expensed to profit or loss over the development period.

FRS 102 and the second project

In the case of the second project, the drug has already been discovered and therefore the costs are for the development and manufacture of the drug and its slight modification. Regulatory approval has already been attained for the existing drug and therefore there is no reason to expect that this will not be given for the new drug. Therefore, Coact should capitalise the upfront purchase of the drug and subsequent payments as incurred.

ACCA Marking scheme	
	Marks
Subjective assessment – 1 mark per point	8
Total	8

74   JOEY (DEC 14 EXAM) (UK GAAP FOCUS)

Key answer tips

The UK specific syllabus content is very factual and needs to be learned by students sitting the UK P2 exam. This past exam question concerns the scope of the UK standards FRS 100, FRS 101, FRS 102 and FRS 105. This is core knowledge. If you struggled with this question, revisit the UK content in the Complete Text.

UK standards

The Financial Reporting Council in the UK has published:

(1)   FRS 100, *Application of financial reporting requirements*

(2)   FRS 101, *Reduced disclosure framework*; and

(3)   FRS 102, *The Financial reporting standard applicable in the UK and Republic of Ireland*.

(4)   FRS 105, *The Financial reporting standard applicable to the micro-entities regime.*

FRS 100

FRS 100 sets out the overall financial reporting requirements, giving many entities a choice depending on factors such as size, and whether or not they are part of a listed group.

FRS 100 identifies whether entities need to produce their consolidated or individual financial statements in accordance with EU IFRS or FRS 102.

FRS 101

FRS 101 provides companies with an opportunity to take advantage of reduced disclosures. However, companies should consider the advantages and disadvantages of the options before making a decision as to which regime to adopt.

Entities which are not required to use IFRS but wish to use its recognition and measurement requirements can choose to apply FRS 101 in their individual financial statements. FRS 101 permits UK subsidiaries to adopt EU IFRS for their individual financial statements but within the reduced disclosure framework (RDF). This option is also available for the parent company's individual financial statements.

To qualify for FRS 101, an entity must be a member of a group where the parent of that group prepares publicly available consolidated financial statements, and that member is included in the consolidation. In order to use RDF, the shareholders should have been notified in writing and those holding a certain percentage of shares have not objected, EU adopted IFRS have been applied and the financial statements make specified disclosures relating to the exemptions. A shareholder may object to the use of the disclosure exemptions only if the shareholder is the immediate parent of the entity, if the shareholder or shareholders hold more than half of the allotted shares in the entity which are not held by the immediate parent, or if the shareholder or shareholders hold 5% or more of the total allotted shares in the entity.

FRS 102

FRS 102 adopts an IFRS-based framework with proportionate disclosure requirements and improves the accounting and reporting for financial instruments. It is based on the IFRS for SMEs but with significant changes in order to address company law and to include extra accounting options.

FRS 105

The Financial Reporting Council has withdrawn the Financial Reporting Standard for Smaller Entities (FRSSE). Micro-entities can now choose to prepare their financial statements in accordance with FRS 105.

FRS 105 is based on FRS 102 but with some amendments to satisfy legal requirements and to reflect the simpler nature of micro-entities. For example, FRS 105:

- Prohibits accounting for deferred tax

- Prohibits accounting for equity-settled share-based payments before the issue of the shares

- Simplifies the rules around classifying a financial instrument as debt or equity

- Removes the distinction between functional and presentation currencies.

ACCA Marking scheme	
	Marks
Subjective assessment – 1 mark per point	8
	—
Total	**8**
	—

75   KATYE (DEC 14 EXAM) (UK GAAP FOCUS)

Key answer tips

This question has two requirements: what are the business implications of moving to a new set of accounting standards, and what are the differences between IFRS for SME and FRS 102 in relation to deferred tax. Always make sure that you answer all parts of the examiner's questions.

Deferred tax is one of the areas where there are numerous differences between FRS 102 and IFRS for SME. If you are studying for the UK P2 exam, these differences must be learned.

Business implications of new UK GAAP

For many entities, there may be a cash tax impact as a result of the transition away from current UK and Irish GAAP, which will impact the tax payable to or receivable from HM Revenue and Customs. UK tax liabilities are based upon local entity accounting profits. It is important that stakeholders understand this. Differing treatments of goodwill, lease incentives and intangible assets can affect tax outcomes.

Where accounting adjustments are made on transition, these may impact the amount of distributable reserves.

Changes to the accounting and financial reporting requirements will often require information not previously compiled. Entities will need to consider whether their existing systems and reporting structures can provide all of the information required under the new accounting framework.

Employee remuneration packages are often linked to accounting performance through profit-related bonus arrangements and share option arrangements and these remuneration arrangements will need to be assessed to understand the potential impact. It may be necessary to agree revised financial terms.

Often banking covenants or other finance arrangements are linked to key financial reporting measures. It may be necessary to renegotiate borrowing arrangements.

Entities will need to consider how they will manage the transition and consider how they will approach the training of the necessary finance team members under a new accounting framework.

A challenge for groups is the rolling out of the new accounting frameworks across a number of companies. It may be useful to consider entity rationalisation in order to simplify their structure to ensure the most efficient transition.

It is essential to manage the expectations of those affected across the business. The board of directors must fully understand the extent of the changes and determine a communications strategy to address the need of all stakeholders.

Income tax

The section on income tax in IFRS for SMEs has been replaced completely in FRS 102 *The Financial Reporting Standard applicable in the UK and Republic of Ireland.*

Under FRS 102, deferred taxation should be recognised in respect of all timing differences at the reporting date, subject to certain exceptions and for differences arising in a business combination. Under the IFRS for SMEs, a 'balance sheet' approach is taken, based on temporary differences. Temporary differences are differences between the tax base of an asset or liability and its carrying amount in the statement of financial position. It is probable that the result will be similar to that under IFRS for SMEs, except in rare circumstances.

ACCA Marking scheme	
	Marks
Subjective assessment – 1 mark per point	11
	—
Total	**11**
	—

76 TRAILER (JUN 13 EXAM) (UK GAAP FOCUS)

Key answer tips

This question requires knowledge of the differences between FRS 102 and IFRS for SME with regards to group accounting. These differences need to be learned. If you put the time into memorising these, then easy marks are available.

Under IFRS for SME, negative goodwill is recognised immediately in profit or loss. According to FRS 102, negative goodwill should be recognised on the statement of financial position as a deduction against goodwill. The subsequent treatment of negative goodwill under FRS 102 is that any amount up to the fair value of non-monetary assets acquired is recognised in profit or loss in the periods in which the non-monetary assets are recovered. Any amount exceeding the fair value of non-monetary assets acquired must be recognised in profit or loss in the periods expected to be benefited.

In accordance with FRS 102, if no reliable estimate of the useful life of goodwill can be made, then the life must not exceed five years. If the useful life of goodwill cannot be reliably determined under IFRS for SME, then the estimate used must not exceed ten years.

FRS 102, permits the reversal of an impairment loss recognised against goodwill if the reasons for the impairment have ceased to exist. IFRS for SME prohibits the reversal of impairment losses recognised against goodwill.

FRS 102 requires the cost of an associate to include transaction costs. These are excluded from the cost of the investment under IFRS for SME and are instead written off to profit or loss.

ACCA Marking scheme	
	Marks
Subjective assessment	6
	—
Total	**6**
	—

77 IFRS FOR SME AND FRS 102 (DEC 10 EXAM) (UK GAAP FOCUS)

Key answer tips

This requires technical knowledge and understanding, together with an applied element. Part (b) concerns the differences between IFRS for SME and FRS 102. Knowledge of these differences is vital for those candidates who are sitting the UK variant of the P2 exam.

Tutorial note

Make specific comments regarding which accounting requirements are excluded from IFRS for SME.

(a)   Small companies have different strategies, with survival and stability rather than profit maximisation being their goals. The stewardship function is often absent in small companies thus there are a number of accounting practices and disclosures which may not provide relevant information for the users of SME financial statements. As a result the standard does not address the following topics:

- earnings per share

- interim financial reporting

- segment reporting

- insurance (because entities that issue insurance contracts are not eligible to use the standard), and

- assets held for sale.

In addition there are certain accounting treatments, which are not allowable under the standard. An example of a disallowable treatment is the revaluation model for intangible assets. Generally there are simpler and more cost effective methods of accounting available to SMEs than those accounting practices, which have been disallowed.

Tutorial note

Make specific comments regarding which accounting requirements have been simplified by IFRS for SME.

Additionally the IFRS for SMEs makes numerous simplifications to the recognition, measurement and disclosure requirements in full IFRSs. Examples of these simplifications are:

- goodwill is amortised over its useful life, but if the useful life cannot be reliably determined then the estimate used must be ten years or less

- a simplified calculation is allowed if measurement of defined benefit pension plan obligations (under the projected unit credit method) involves undue cost or effort

- the cost model is permitted for investments in associates and joint ventures.

As a result of the above, SMEs do not have to comply with over 90% of the volume of accounting requirements applicable to listed companies. If an entity opts to use the IFRS for SMEs, it must follow the standard in its entirety and it cannot cherry pick between the requirements of the IFRS for SMEs and those of full IFRSs.

Tutorial note

Part (b) tests your knowledge in relation to three specific accounting issues. You should deal with each situation in turn, explaining both the IFRS requirement and the FRS 102 requirement.

(b) The following details the key differences of relevance to Whitebait.

(i) **Defined benefit scheme**

IFRS for SME allows some simplified estimation techniques if an entity is not able, without undue cost or effort, to use the projected unit credit method to measure its obligation and cost under defined benefit plans. Entities are permitted to:

– Ignore estimated future salary increases

– Ignore future service of current employees

– Ignore possible in-service mortality of current employees between the reporting date and the date employees are expected to begin receiving post-employment benefits.

Under FRS 102, the projected unit credit method must be used to estimate the defined benefit obligation.

(ii) **Business combination**

IFRS for SME states that the acquirer shall, at the acquisition date:

(a) recognise goodwill acquired in a business combination as an asset, and

(b) initially measure that goodwill at its cost, being the excess of the cost of the business combination over the acquirer's interest in the net fair value of the identifiable assets, liabilities and contingent liabilities.

After initial recognition, the acquirer shall measure goodwill acquired in a business combination at cost less accumulated amortisation and accumulated impairment losses. If an entity is unable to reliably determine the useful life of goodwill, then it must be estimated at ten years or less. There is no choice of accounting method for non controlling interests and therefore the partial goodwill method would be used.

Goodwill will be $5.7 million less 90% of $6 million i.e. $0.3 million. Assuming the maximum estimate of useful life is used, the goodwill will then be amortised over ten years at a value of $30,000 per annum.

Under FRS 102, if an entity is unable to make a reliable estimate of the useful life of goodwill, the life is presumed to be five years. The amortisation would therefore be $60,000 ($300,000/5) per annum.

(iii) Research and development expenditure

IFRS for SME states that an entity shall recognise expenditure incurred internally on an intangible item, including all expenditure for both research and development activities, as an expense when it is incurred unless it forms part of the cost of another asset that meets the recognition criteria in this IFRS. Thus the expenditure of $1.5 million on research and development should all be written off to profit or loss.

Under FRS 102, the $1 million spent on research would still be written off to profit or loss. However, development expenditure can be capitalised if it meets certain criteria (similar to those in IAS 38). Therefore, under FRS 102 and assuming the criteria have been met, Whitebait could choose to recognise the $500,000 development expenditure as an intangible asset. This would then be amortised over the asset's estimated useful economic life.

ACCA Marking scheme			
			Marks
(a)	Subjective assessment		8
(b)	(i)	Defined benefit scheme	4
	(ii)	Business combination	6
	(iii)	Research and development expenditure	5
	Professional marks – subjective assessment		2
			—
Total			**25**
			—

78   HERBIE (UK GAAP FOCUS)

Key answer tips

This is not a past exam question. However, it does provide a good opportunity to practice the differences between IFRS for SME and FRS 102. It is difficult to score well in these questions without a specific and detailed knowledge of these differences. Candidates sitting the UK version of the P2 paper must ensure that they spend sufficient time learning the examinable differences between the two reporting frameworks.

(a)   (i)   Transaction costs are excluded from the cost of an associate under IFRS for SME. Therefore, under IFRS for SME, the transaction costs of $0.2m must be written off to profit or loss, thus reducing total comprehensive income. The associate will have a carrying value of $4m.

Under FRS 102, the cost of an associate should include transaction costs. If Herbie accounted under FRS 102, no adjustments are required to the carrying value of the associate.

(ii)   IFRS for SME does not permit the revaluation model for intangible assets. This means that Herbie's licence could not be revalued to fair value and would instead be measured at cost less amortisation.

The revaluation model for intangible assets is allowed under FRS 102. The carrying amount of the licence at the revaluation date was $2.0m ($3m × 2/3). The license will be revalued to $3.1m giving a gain of $1.1m ($3.1m − $2.0m) that will be recorded in other comprehensive income. This will increase total comprehensive income by $1.1m.

(iii)   IFRS for SME only allows government grants to be accounted for under the performance model. This means that grants with conditions attached are only recognised as income when all conditions have been met. The conditions attached to Herbie's grant have not yet been met (the employees have not been employed for 2 years) so no income can be recognised. The grant should instead be recognised as a liability.

If an entity accounts under FRS 102, they can account for government grants under the performance model or the accruals model. Using the accruals model will allow Herbie to recognise the grant as income as the associated costs (employee salaries) are incurred.

Half of the employee costs will have been incurred (One of the two years has passed), so FRS 102 allows Herbie to recognise half of the grant as income. This will increase profits, and therefore total comprehensive income, by $0.1m ($0.2m × ½).

(b)

	(i) IFRS for SME	(ii) FRS 102
	$m	$m
Draft TCI	12	12
Issue (i)	(0.2)	–
Issue (ii)	–	1.1
Issue (iii)	–	0.1
Revised TCI	11.8	13.2

ACCA Marking scheme			
			Marks
(a)	(i)	Associate	2
	(ii)	Revaluation	2
	(iii)	Grant	2
(b)	Revised TCI		3
Total			**9**

Section 3

SEPTEMBER/DECEMBER 2015 EXAM QUESTIONS

SECTION A

1 BUBBLE

The following draft financial statements relate to Bubble, a public limited company and two other companies in which it owns investments.

Draft statements of financial position as at 31 October 2015

	Bubble $m	Salt $m	Tyslar Dinars m
Assets			
Non-current assets			
Property, plant and equipment	280	105	390
Investment in Salt	110	–	–
Investment in Tyslar	46	–	–
Financial assets	12	9	98
	448	114	488
Current assets			
Inventories	20	12	16
Trade and other receivables	30	25	36
Cash and cash equivalents	14	11	90
	64	48	142
Total assets	512	162	630
Equity and liabilities			
Equity shares	80	50	210
Retained earnings	230	74	292
Other components of equity	40	12	–
Total equity	350	136	502

Non-current liabilities	95	7	110
Current liabilities	67	19	18
	162	26	128
Total equity and liabilities	512	162	630

The following information is relevant to the preparation of the group statement of financial position:

1   Bubble acquired 80% of the equity shares of Salt on 1 November 2013 when Salt's retained earnings were $56 million and other components of equity were $8 million. The fair value of the net assets of Salt was $120 million at the date of acquisition. This does not include a contingent liability which was disclosed in Salt's financial statements as a possible obligation of $5 million. The fair value of the obligation was assessed as $1 million at the date of acquisition and remained unsettled as at 31 October 2015. $5 million is still disclosed as a possible obligation with no change in its fair value. Any remaining difference in the fair value of the net assets at acquisition relates to non-depreciable land. The fair value of the non-controlling interest at acquisition was estimated as $25 million. Bubble always adopts the full goodwill method under IFRS 3 *Business Combinations*.

2   Bubble also owns 60% of the equity shares of Tyslar, a company located overseas which uses the dinar as its functional currency. The shares in Tyslar were acquired on 1 November 2014 at a cost of 368 million dinars. At the date of acquisition, retained earnings were 258 million dinars and Tyslar had no other components of equity. No fair value adjustments were deemed necessary in relation to the acquisition of Tyslar. The fair value of the non-controlling interest was estimated as 220 million dinars at acquisition.

An impairment review of goodwill was undertaken as at 31 October 2015. No impairment was necessary in relation to Salt, but the goodwill of Tyslar is to be impaired by 20%. Neither Bubble, Salt nor Tyslar has issued any equity shares since acquisition.

3   On 1 February 2015, Bubble gave a loan to Tyslar for $10 million. Tyslar recorded this correctly in its financial statements using the spot rate of exchange. Tyslar repaid $5 million on 1 July 2015 when the spot exchange rate was $1 to 10 dinars. Tyslar therefore reduced its non-current liabilities by 50 million dinars. No further entries were made in Tyslar's financial statements. The remaining balances remain within the financial assets of Bubble and the non-current liabilities of Tyslar.

4   Bubble wished to expand its overseas operations and on 1 May 2015 acquired an overseas property with a fair value of 58.5 million dinars. In exchange for the building, Bubble paid the supplier with land which Bubble had held but had yet to determine its use. The carrying amount of the land was $5 million but it had an open market value of $7 million. Bubble was unsure as to how to deal with this transaction and so has transferred $5 million from investment properties to property, plant and equipment. The transaction has commercial substance.

In addition, Bubble spent $0.5 million to help relocate staff to the new property and added this amount to the cost of the asset. Bubble has made no other entries in its financial statements in relation to the property. Bubble has a policy of depreciating properties over 35 years and follows the revaluation model under IAS 16 *Property, Plant & Equipment*. Due to a surge in the market, it is estimated that the fair value of the property is 75 million dinars as at 31 October 2015.

5   Bubble operates a defined benefit scheme for its employees but has yet to record anything for the current year except to expense the cash contributions which were $6 million. The opening position was a net liability of $15 million which is included in the non-current liabilities of Bubble in its draft financial statements. Current service costs for the year were $5 million and interest rates on good quality corporate bonds fell from 8% at the start of the year to 6% by 31 October 2015. In addition, a payment of $3 million was made out of the cash of the pension scheme in relation to employees who left the scheme. The reduction in the pension scheme liability as a result of the curtailment was $4 million. The actuary has assessed that the scheme is in deficit by $17 million as at 31 October 2015.

6   The following exchange rates are relevant for the preparation of the group financial statements:

	Dinars to $
1 November 2014	8
1 February 2015	9
1 May 2015	9
31 October 2015	9.5
Average for the year to 31 October 2015	8.5

Required:

(a)   **Prepare the consolidated statement of financial position of the Bubble Group at 31 October 2015 in accordance with International Financial Reporting Standards.**

(35 marks)

(b)   The directors of Bubble are not fully aware of the requirements of IAS 21 *The Effects of Changes in Foreign Exchange Rates* in relation to exchange rate differences. They would like advice on how exchange differences should be recorded on both monetary and non-monetary assets in the financial statements and how these differ from the requirements for the translation of an overseas entity. The directors also wish advice on what would happen to the exchange differences if Bubble were to sell all of its equity shares in Tyslar, and any practical issues which would arise on monitoring exchange differences if the remaining balance on the loan from Bubble to Tyslar was not intended to be repaid.

Required:

Provide a brief memo for the directors of Bubble which identifies the correct accounting treatment for the various issues raised.   **(9 marks)**

(c) The directors of Bubble are thinking of acquiring further overseas investments in the near future but the entity currently lacks sufficient cash to exploit such opportunities. They would prefer to raise finance from an equity issue as Bubble already has significant loans within non-current liabilities and they do not wish to increase Bubble's gearing any further. They are therefore keen to maximise the balance on the group retained earnings in order to attract the maximum level of investment possible.

One proposal is that they may sell 5% of the equity interest in Tyslar during 2016. This will improve the cash position but will enable Bubble to maintain control over Tyslar. In addition, the directors believe that the shares can be sold profitably to boost the retained earnings of Bubble and of the group. The directors intend to transfer the relevant proportion of the exchange differences on translation of the subsidiary to group retained earnings, knowing that this is contrary to accounting standards.

Required:

Discuss why the proposed treatment of the exchange differences by the directors is not in compliance with International Financial Reporting Standards, explaining any ethical issues which may arise. **(6 marks)**

(Total: 50 marks)

2   CHEMCLEAN

(a) Chemclean trades in the chemical industry. The entity has development and production operations in various countries. It has entered into an agreement with Jomaster under which Chemclean will licence Jomaster's know-how and technology to manufacture a chemical compound, Volut. The know-how and technology has a fair value of $4 million. Chemclean cannot use the know-how and technology for manufacturing any other compound than Volut. Chemclean has not concluded that economic benefits are likely to flow from this compound but will use Jomaster's technology for a period of three years. Chemclean will have to keep updating the technology in accordance with Jomaster's requirements. The agreement stipulates that Chemclean will make a non-refundable payment of $4 million to Jomaster for access to the technology. Additionally, Jomaster will also receive a 10% royalty from sales of the chemical compound.

Additionally, Chemclean is interested in another compound, Yacton, which is being developed by Jomaster. The compound is in the second phase of development. The intellectual property of compound Yacton has been put into a newly formed shell company, Conew, which has no employees. The compound is the only asset of Conew. Chemclean is intending to acquire a 65% interest in Conew, which will give it control over the entity and the compound. Chemclean will provide the necessary resources to develop the compound. **(8 marks)**

(b)   In the year to 30 June 2015, Chemclean acquired a major subsidiary. The inventory acquired in this business combination was valued at its fair value at the acquisition date in accordance with IFRS 3 *Business Combinations*. The inventory increased in value as a result of the fair value exercise. A significant part of the acquired inventory was sold in the post-acquisition period but before 30 June 2015, the year end.

In the consolidated statement of profit or loss and other comprehensive income, the cost of inventories acquired in the business combination and sold by the acquirer after the business combination was disclosed on two different lines. The inventory was partly shown as cost of goods sold and partly as a 'non-recurring item' within operating income. The part presented under cost of goods sold corresponded to the inventory's carrying amount in the subsidiary's financial statements. The part presented as a 'non-recurring item' corresponded to the fair value increase recognised on the business combination. The 'non-recurring item' amounted to 25% of Chemclean's earnings before interest and tax (EBIT).

Chemclean disclosed the accounting policy and explained in the notes to the financial statements that showing the inventory at fair value would result in a fall in the gross margin due to the fair value increase. Further, Chemclean argued that isolating this part of the margin in the 'non-recurring items', whose nature is transparently presented in the notes, enabled the user to evaluate the structural evolution of its gross margin.   **(6 marks)**

(c)   In the consolidated financial statements for 2015, Chemclean recognised a net deferred tax asset of $16 million, which represented 18% of its total equity. This asset was made up of $3 million taxable temporary differences and $19 million relating to the carry-forward of unused tax losses. The local tax regulation allows unused tax losses to be carried forward indefinitely. Chemclean expects that within five years, future taxable profits before tax would be available against which the unused tax losses could be offset. This view was based on the budgets for the years 2015-2020. The budgets were primarily based on general assumptions about the development of key products and economic improvement indicators. Additionally, the entity expected a substantial reduction in the future impairment of trade receivables and property which the entity had recently suffered and this would result in a substantial increase in future taxable profit.

Chemclean had recognised material losses during the previous five years, with an average annual loss of $19 million. A comparison of Chemclean's budgeted results for the previous two years to its actual results indicated material differences relating principally to impairment losses. In the interim financial statements for the first half of the year to 30 June 2015, Chemclean recognised impairment losses equal to budgeted impairment losses for the whole year. In its financial statements for the year ended 30 June 2015, Chemclean disclosed a material uncertainty about its ability to continue as a going concern. The current tax rate in the jurisdiction is 30%.   **(9 marks)**

Required:

Discuss how the above items should be dealt with in the financial statements of Chemclean under International Financial Reporting Standards.

Note: The mark allocation is shown against each of the three issues above.

Professional marks will be awarded in question 2 for clarity and quality of presentation.
                                                                                    (2 marks)

                                                                                    (Total: 25 marks)

3   GASNATURE

(a)   Gasnature is a publicly traded entity involved in the production and trading of natural gas and oil. Gasnature jointly owns an underground storage facility with another entity, Gogas. Both parties extract gas from offshore gas fields, which they own and operate independently from each other. Gasnature owns 55% of the underground facility and Gogas owns 45%. They have agreed to share services and costs accordingly, with decisions regarding the storage facility requiring unanimous agreement of the parties. The underground facility is pressurised so that the gas is pushed out when extracted. When the gas pressure is reduced to a certain level, the remaining gas is irrecoverable and remains in the underground storage facility until it is decommissioned. Local legislation requires the decommissioning of the storage facility at the end of its useful life.

Gasnature wishes to know how to treat the agreement with Gogas including any obligation or possible obligation arising on the underground storage facility and the accounting for the irrecoverable gas.   **(9 marks)**

(b)   Gasnature has entered into a 10-year contract with Agas for the purchase of natural gas. Gasnature has made an advance payment to Agas for an amount equal to the total quantity of gas contracted for 10 years which has been calculated using the forecasted price of gas. The advance carries interest of 6% per annum, which is settled by way of the supply of extra gas. Fixed quantities of gas have to be supplied each month and there is a price adjustment mechanism in the contract whereby the difference between the forecasted price of gas and the prevailing market price is settled in cash monthly. If Agas does not deliver gas as agreed, Gasnature has the right to claim compensation at the current market price of gas. Gasnature wishes to know whether the contract with Agas should be accounted for under IFRS 9 *Financial Instruments*.   **(6 marks)**

(c)   Additionally, Gasnature is finalising its financial statements for the year ended 31 August 2015 and has the following issues:

(i)   Gasnature purchased a major refinery on 1 January 2015 and the directors estimate that a major overhaul is required every two years. The costs of the overhaul are approximately $5 million which comprises $3 million for parts and equipment and $2 million for labour. The directors proposed to accrue the cost of the overhaul over the two years of operations up to that date and create a provision for the expenditure.   **(4 marks)**

(ii)   From October 2014, Gasnature had undertaken exploratory drilling to find gas and up to 31 August 2015 costs of $5 million had been incurred. At 31 August 2015, the results to date indicated that it was probable that there were sufficient economic benefits to carry on drilling and there were no indicators of impairment. During September 2015, additional drilling costs of $2 million were incurred and there was significant evidence that no commercial deposits existed and the drilling was abandoned.   **(4 marks)**

Required:

Discuss, with reference to International Financial Reporting Standards, how Gasnature should account for the above agreement and contract, and the issues raised by the directors.

Note: The mark allocation is shown against each of the items above.

Professional marks will be awarded in question 3 for clarity and quality of presentation.

(2 marks)

(Total: 25 marks)

4   REVENUE FROM CONTRACTS WITH CUSTOMERS

There has been significant divergence in practice over recognition of revenue mainly because International Financial Reporting Standards (IFRS) have contained limited guidance in certain areas. The International Accounting Standards Board (IASB) as a result of the joint project with the US Financial Accounting Standards Board (FASB) has issued IFRS 15 *Revenue from Contracts with Customers*. IFRS 15 sets out a five-step model, which applies to revenue earned from a contract with a customer with limited exceptions, regardless of the type of revenue transaction or the industry. Step one in the five-step model requires the identification of the contract with the customer and is critical for the purpose of applying the standard. The remaining four steps in the standard's revenue recognition model are irrelevant if the contract does not fall within the scope of IFRS 15.

Required:

(a)   (i)   **Discuss the criteria which must be met for a contract with a customer to fall within the scope of IFRS 15.   (5 marks)**

(ii)   **Discuss the four remaining steps which lead to revenue recognition after a contract has been identified as falling within the scope of IFRS 15.   (8 marks)**

(b)   (i)   Tang enters into a contract with a customer to sell an existing printing machine such that control of the printing machine vests with the customer in two years' time. The contract has two payment options. The customer can pay $240,000 when the contract is signed or $300,000 in two years' time when the customer gains control of the printing machine. The interest rate implicit in the contract is 11.8% in order to adjust for the risk involved in the delay in payment. However, Tang's incremental borrowing rate is 5%. The customer paid $240,000 on 1 December 2014 when the contract was signed.   **(4 marks)**

(ii)   Tang enters into a contract on 1 December 2014 to construct a printing machine on a customer's premises for a promised consideration of $1,500,000 with a bonus of $100,000 if the machine is completed within 24 months. At the inception of the contract, Tang correctly accounts for the promised bundle of goods and services as a single performance obligation in accordance with IFRS 15. At the inception of the contract, Tang expects the costs to be $800,000 and concludes that it is highly probable that a significant reversal in the amount of cumulative revenue recognised will occur. Completion of the printing machine is highly susceptible to factors outside of Tang's influence, mainly issues with the supply of components.

At 30 November 2015, Tang has satisfied 65% of its performance obligation on the basis of costs incurred to date and concludes that the variable consideration is still constrained in accordance with IFRS 15. However, on 4 December 2015, the contract is modified with the result that the fixed consideration and expected costs increase by $110,000 and $60,000 respectively. The time allowable for achieving the bonus is extended by six months with the result that Tang concludes that it is highly probable that the bonus will be achieved and that the contract still remains a single performance obligation. Tang has an accounting year end of 30 November.   **(6 marks)**

Required:

Discuss how the above two contracts should be accounted for under IFRS 15. (In the case of (b)(i), the discussion should include the accounting treatment up to 30 November 2016 and in the case of (b)(ii), the accounting treatment up to 4 December 2015.)

Note: The mark allocation is shown against each of the items above.

Professional marks will be awarded in question 4 for clarity and quality of presentation.

(2 marks)

(Total: 25 marks)

Section 4

ANSWERS TO SEPTEMBER/DECEMBER 2015 EXAM QUESTIONS

1   BUBBLE

Key answer tips

Remember to allocate your time carefully when attempting question 1 in the P2 exam. The examiner has consistently commented that over-running on this question is a key reason why candidates fail the paper.

A strong knowledge of consolidation technique, and the standard workings, should enable you to score high marks. This is particularly the case when consolidating an overseas subsidiary.

If you do get stuck with a particular issue or adjustment then move on. Make sure that you spend your time on the areas of the question that you are confident with.

(a)   **Consolidated statement of financial position at 31 October 2015**

	$m
Assets:	
Non-current assets	
Property, plant and equipment (W12)	434.5
Goodwill ($16 + $10.1) (W3)	26.1
Financial assets ($12 + $9 + D98/9.5 – $5 (W6))	26.3
	———
	486.9
Inventories ($20 + $12 + D16/9.5)	33.7
Trade and other receivables ($30 + $25 + D36/9.5)	58.8
Cash and cash equivalents ($14 + $11 + D90/9.5)	34.5
	———
Total assets	613.9
	———

Equity and liabilities:

Equity attributable to owners of parent

Equity shares	80.0
Retained earnings (W5)	246.8
Other components of equity (W5)	41.4
Translation reserve (W7)	(7.0)
	361.2
Non-controlling interest (W4)	52.4
	413.6
Total equity	413.6
Non-current liabilities (W13)	111.4
Current liabilities ($67 + $19 + D18/9.5 + $1 (W2))	88.9
Total equity and liabilities	613.9

Workings

(W1) Group structure

Tutorial note

Always start by drawing a group structure in order to establish the relationship between the investing company and its investments.

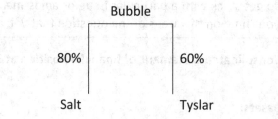

(W2) Net assets

Tutorial note

The identifiable net assets of a subsidiary must be recognised at their fair value at the acquisition date. This includes contingent liabilities. Be careful: a liability will reduce the total net asset figure.

Salt

	Acq'n date	Rep date
	$m	$m
Share capital	50	50
Other components	8	12
Retained earnings	56	74
Contingent liability	(1)	(1)
Land (bal. fig)	6	6
	———	———
($120 – $1)	119	141
	———	———

Tyslar

	Acq'n date	Rep date
	Dm	Dm
Share capital	210	210
Retained earnings	258	292
Forex loss on loan (W6)	–	(7.5)
	———	———
	468	494.5
	———	———

(W3) Goodwill

Tutorial note

Goodwill relating to an overseas subsidiary is retranslated at each reporting date using the closing rate of exchange.

Salt

	$m
Fair value of consideration	110
NCI at acquisition	25
Fair value of identifiable net assets (W2)	(119)
Goodwill at reporting date	16

Tyslar

	Dm
Fair value of consideration	368
NCI at acquisition	220
Fair value of identifiable net assets (W2)	(468)
Goodwill at acquisition	120
Impairment (20%)	(24)
Goodwill at reporting date	96

The goodwill of Tyslar is therefore $10.1 million (D96m/9.5).

(W4) Non-controlling interest

	$m
NCI in Salt at acquisition (W3)	25.0
NCI % of post-acquisition net assets	4.4
20% × ($141m – $119m) (W2))	
NCI in Tyslar at acquisition (D220m/8) (W3)	27.5
NCI % of post-acquisition net assets	1.2
40% × (($494.5m – $468m) (W2)/8.5)	
NCI % of goodwill impairment (W8)	(1.1)
NCI % of goodwill forex (W8)	(0.8)
NCI % of forex on net assets and profit (W9)	(3.8)
	52.4

(W5) Group reserves

Tutorial note

Remember to split group reserves into retained earnings and other components of equity.

Retained earnings

	$m
Bubble	230.0
Group % of Salt's post-acquisition profits 80% × (($141m − $119m) − ($12m − $8m)) (W2))	14.4
Group % of Tyslar's post-acquisition profits 60% × (($494.5m − $468m) (W2)/8.5)	1.9
Group % of goodwill impairment (W8)	(1.7)
Profit on PPE disposal (W10)	2.0
PPE error (W10)	(0.5)
Depreciation (W10)	(0.1)
Interest component (W11)	(1.2)
Current service cost (W11)	(5.0)
Reversal of cash contributions error (W11)	6.0
Curtailment gain (W11)	1.0
	————
	246.8
	————

Other components of equity

	$m
Bubble	40.0
Group % of Salt's post-acquisition other components 80% × ($12m − $8m) (W2)	3.2
PPE revaluation (W10)	1.0
Remeasurement component (W11)	(2.8)
	————
	41.4
	————

(W6) Intra-group loan

Tutorial note

A loan is a monetary liability and so must be retranslated at the reporting date. This will give rise to a foreign exchange gain or loss that is reported in profit or loss. If this arises in a subsidiary, then the profit adjustment needs to be made in the net assets table (W2).

Tyslar would have initially recorded the loan at 90 million dinars ($10m × 9). The settlement was recorded at 50 million dinars. At the year end, Tyslar should retranslate the outstanding loan of $5 million to 47.5 million dinars ($5m × 9.5). Therefore a foreign exchange loss of 7.5 million dinars (47.5m – (90m – 50m)) arises in Tyslar's financial statements. The entry required to record this is:

Dr Profit or loss (W2) D7.5m

Cr Non-current liabilities D7.5m

The intra-group balances then need to be eliminated in the consolidated financial statements:

Dr Non-current liabilities $5m

Cr Financial assets $5m

(W7) Translation reserve

Tutorial note

The translation reserve contains the group's share of the foreign exchange differences arising on the translation of the goodwill, opening net assets and profit of the overseas subsidiary.

	$m
Group share of goodwill forex (W8)	(1.3)
Group share of net asset and profit forex (W9)	(5.7)
	(7.0)

(W8) Exchange difference and impairment on Tyslar's goodwill

Tutorial note

If goodwill is calculated using the fair value method, the exchange gain or loss and any impairment must be apportioned between the group and the NCI.

	Dm	Exchange rate	$m
Opening goodwill (W3)	120	8.0	15.0
Impairment (W3)	(24)	8.5	(2.8)
Exchange loss (bal. fig)			(2.1)
	___		___
Closing goodwill	96	9.5	10.1
	___		___

Goodwill has been calculated under the fair value method. Therefore, the exchange loss and the impairment must be allocated between the group and the NCI based on their respective shareholdings.

Impairment

Group: $2.8m × 60% = $1.7m

NCI: $2.8m × 40% = $1.1m

Exchange loss

Group: $2.1m × 60% = $1.3m

NCI: $2.1m × 40% = $0.8m

(W9) Exchange loss on Tyslar's opening net assets and profit

Tutorial note

Exchange gains or losses arising on the opening net assets and profit of an overseas subsidiary are apportioned between the group and the NCI.

	Dm	Exchange rate	$m
Net assets at 1 Nov 14 (W2)	468	8.0	58.5
Profit for the year (D494.5m – D468m) (W2)	26.5	8.5	3.1
Exchange loss (bal. fig)			(9.5)
Net assets at 31 Oct 2015 (W2)	494.5	9.5	52.1

The exchange loss on the opening net assets and profit must be allocated between the group and the NCI based on their respective shareholdings:

Group: $9.5m × 60% = $5.7m

NCI: $9.5m × 40% = $3.8m

(W10) Overseas property

The property should have been recognised at $7 million, which is the fair value of the consideration transferred to acquire it. A profit on the disposal of the land of $2 million ($7m – $5m) should also have been recorded. The correcting entry is:

Dr PPE $2m

Cr P/L $2m

The staff relocation costs should not have been capitalised. The correcting entry is:

Dr P/L $0.5m

Cr PPE $0.5m

The building should be depreciated over its useful life, giving a charge of $0.1 million ($7m/35 × 6/12):

Dr P/L $0.1m

Cr PPE $0.1m

At the reporting date, the building should be revalued from its carrying amount of $6.9 million ($7m – $0.1m) to its fair value of $7.9 million (D75m/9.5). The entry required to record the $1 million gain is:

Dr PPE $1.0m

Cr OCI $1.0m

(W11) Pension plan

Tutorial note

To calculate the remeasurement component, reconcile the opening and closing net pension deficit. The remeasurement component is recognised in other comprehensive income.

The net interest component is calculated using the rate on good quality corporate bonds at the start of the year.

The liability to be recognised at the reporting date is $17 million. Therefore, non-current liabilities must be increased by $2 million ($17m – $15m).

The remeasurement component is calculated as follows:

	$m
Net obligation at 1 Nov. 2014	15.0
Net interest component ($15m × 8%)	1.2
Current service cost	5.0
Cash contributions	(6.0)
Curtailment gain ($4m – $3m)	(1.0)
Remeasurement loss (bal. fig)	2.8
	——
Net obligation at 31 Oct. 2015	17.0
	——

The net interest component and the current service cost are charged to profit or loss. The cash contributions have been incorrectly charged to profit or loss so must be removed. The gain on the curtailment of $1 million is recorded in profit or loss.

The remeasurement loss is recorded in other comprehensive income.

(W12) Property, plant and equipment

	$m
Bubble	280.0
Salt	105.0
Tyslar (D390/9.5)	41.1
Fair value uplift (W2)	6.0
PPE cost adjustment (W10)	2.0
Removal of incorrect costs (W10)	(0.5)
Depreciation (W10)	(0.1)
Revaluation (W10)	1.0
	——
	434.5
	——

(W13) Non-current liabilities

	$m
Bubble	95.0
Salt	7.0
Tyslar (D110/9.5)	11.6
Foreign exchange loss (D7.5/9.5) (W6)	0.8
Intra-group elimination (W6)	(5.0)
Increase in pension deficit (W11)	2.0
	———
	111.4

(b)

> *Tutorial note*
>
> *To score highly, this question requires a detailed knowledge of IAS 21. However, solid marks can still be obtained for demonstrating a basic understanding of the standard.*

Monetary items

Monetary items are units of currency held and assets and liabilities to be received or paid in a fixed or determinable number of units of currency. This would include foreign bank accounts, receivables, payables and loans. Non-monetary items are other items which are in the statement of financial position. For example, non-current assets, inventories and investments.

Monetary items are retranslated using the closing exchange rate (the year-end rate). The exchange differences on retranslation of monetary assets must be recorded in profit or loss. IAS 21 *The Effects of Changes in Foreign Exchange Rates* is not specific under which heading the exchange gains and losses should be classified.

Non-monetary items

Non-monetary items which are measured in terms of historical cost in a foreign currency are translated using the exchange rate at the date of the transaction. If non-monetary items are measured at fair value in a foreign currency then this amount must be translated using exchange rates at the date when the fair value was measured. Exchange differences on such items are recorded consistently with the recognition of the movement in fair values. For example, exchange differences on an investment property, a fair value through profit and loss financial asset, or arising on an impairment, will be recorded in profit or loss. Exchange differences on property, plant and equipment arising from a revaluation gain would be recorded in other comprehensive income.

Overseas subsidiaries

When translating a foreign subsidiary, the exchange differences on all the net assets, including goodwill, are recorded within other comprehensive income and are held within equity. The proportion belonging to the shareholders of the parent will usually be held in a separate translation reserve. The proportion belonging to the non-controlling interest is not shown separately but subsumed within the non-controlling interest figure in the consolidated financial statements.

If Bubble were to sell all of its equity shares in Tyslar, the cumulative exchange differences belonging to the equity holders of Bubble will be reclassified from equity to profit or loss. In addition, the cumulative exchange differences attributable to the non-controlling interest shall be derecognised but shall not be reclassified to profit or loss.

When a monetary item relating to a foreign operation is not intended to be settled, the item is treated as part of the entity's net investment in its subsidiary. There will be no difference in the accounting treatment in the individual accounts of Tyslar and hence exchange differences on the loan would remain in profit or loss. However, in the consolidated financial statements such differences should initially be recorded in other comprehensive income. These will be reclassified from equity to profit or loss on subsequent disposal of the subsidiary. This can cause practical issues in terms of monitoring all of the individual exchange differences to ensure that they are all correctly classified in the consolidated financial statements.

(c)

Tutorial note

When answering ethics questions, students have a tendency to simply recite and explain the ACCA ethical code. Do not fall into this trap, as you will score poorly. Your answer must therefore reference and discuss the specific situation in the question.

The accounting issue

If Bubble were to sell the shares profitably a gain would arise in its individual financial statements which would boost retained earnings.

However, if only 5% of the equity shares in Tyslar were sold, it would still hold 55% of the equity and presumably control would not be lost. The International Accounting Standards Board views this as an equity transaction (i.e. transactions with owners in their capacity as owners). This means that, in the consolidated financial statements, the relevant proportion of the exchange differences should be re-attributed to the non-controlling interest rather than to the retained earnings. The directors appear to be motivated by their desire to maximise the balance on the group retained earnings. It would appear that the directors' actions are unethical by overstating the group's interest in Tyslar at the expense of the non-controlling interest.

Ethical issues

The purpose of financial statements is to present a fair representation of the company's position and if the financial statements are deliberately falsified, then this could be deemed unethical. Accountants have a social and ethical responsibility to issue financial statements which do not mislead the public. Any manipulation of the accounts will harm the credibility of the profession since the public assume that professional accountants will act in an ethical capacity. The directors should be reminded that professional ethics are an integral part of the profession and that they must adhere to ethical guidelines such as the ACCA's *Code of Ethics and Conduct*. Deliberate falsification of the financial statements would contravene the guiding principles of integrity, objectivity and professional behaviour. The directors' intended action appears to be in direct conflict with the code by deliberating overstating the parent company's ownership interest in the group in order to maximise potential investment in Bubble.

Stakeholders are becoming increasingly reactive to the ethical stance of an entity. Deliberate falsification would potentially harm the reputation of Bubble and could lead to severe, long-term disadvantages in the market place. The directors' intended action will therefore not be in the best interests of the stakeholders in the business. There can be no justification for the deliberate falsification of an entity's financial statements.

ACCA Marking scheme		
		Marks
(a)	Share capital	1
	Goodwill Salt	1
	Intra-group loan	2
	Translation and exchange differences Tyslar	6
	Pension	4
	Property, plant and equipment	3
	Inventories	1
	Intra-group balances	2
	Other components of equity	3
	Retained earnings	6
	Non-controlling interest	3
	Non-current liabilities	2
	Current liabilities	1
	Maximum	**35**
(b)	1 mark per sensible comment	9
(c)	1 mark per sensible comment	6
Total		**50**

2   CHEMCLEAN

Key answer tips

This is a challenging question that requires a high level of application skills. Remember to attempt every part of the question or you will not obtain the two professional marks available.

(a)   **Intangible assets**

IAS 38 *Intangible Assets* requires an entity to recognise an intangible asset, whether purchased or self-created (at cost) if, and only if:

(i)   It is probable that the future economic benefits which are attributable to the asset will flow to the entity, and

(ii)   the cost of the asset can be measured reliably.

This requirement applies whether an intangible asset is acquired externally or generated internally.

The probability of future economic benefits must be based on reasonable and supportable assumptions about conditions which will exist over the life of the asset. The price an entity pays to acquire an intangible asset reflects expectations about the probability that the expected future economic benefits from the asset will flow to the entity. This means that the effect of probability is reflected in the cost of the asset and so the probability recognition criterion is always considered to be satisfied for intangible assets that are acquired separately or in a business combination.

In this case, Chemclean should recognise an intangible asset for the use of Jomaster's technology. The right should be measured at its cost of $4 million. The intangible asset should be amortised from the date it is available for use. The technology is available for use when the manufacturing of the compound begins. At the end of each reporting period, Chemclean is required to assess whether there is any indication that the asset may be impaired.

Due to the nature of intangible assets, subsequent expenditure will rarely meet the criteria for being recognised in the carrying amount of an asset. Thus Chemclean continues to expense its own internal development expenditure until the criteria for capitalisation are met and economic benefits are expected to flow to the entity from the capitalised asset. When the drug is sold, the royalty payments are presented in profit or loss.

Business combinations

IFRS 10 *Consolidated Financial Statements* says that: 'An investor controls an investee when the investor is exposed, or has rights, to variable returns from its involvement with the investee and has the ability to affect those returns through its power over the investee'. Therefore it appears that Chemclean will control Conew.

Any transaction in which an entity obtains control of one or more businesses qualifies as a business combination and is subject to the measurement and recognition requirements of IFRS 3.

IFRS 3 *Business Combinations* defines a 'business' as 'an integrated set of activities and assets that is capable of being conducted and managed for the purpose of providing a return in the form of dividends, lower costs or other economic benefits directly to investors or other owners, members or participants'. A business consists of inputs and processes applied to those inputs which have the ability to create outputs. Processes are included in the acquired group when intellectual property (IP) is accompanied by other resources such as assets or employees or other elements such as protocols and plans which will further help develop the IP to the next phase.

Conew does not meet the definition of a business. This means that the acquisition of an interest in Conew should be accounted for as an asset acquisition under IAS 38 *Intangible Assets*.

(b)   **Disclosure of the impact of fair value uplifts**

IAS 2 *Inventories* requires the carrying amount of inventories sold to be recognised as an expense in the period in which the related revenue is recognised. Cost of sales are costs previously included in the measurement of inventory which has now been sold plus unallocated production overheads and abnormal amounts of production costs of inventories.

IFRS 3 *Business Combinations* requires an acquirer to measure the identifiable assets acquired in a business combination at their fair values at the date of acquisition. Therefore, the carrying amount of the inventories originating from the acquisition of the subsidiary is their acquisition-date fair value. Consequently, the entire carrying amount of inventory, including the effects of the fair value step-up, should be presented as cost of sales.

IAS 1 *Presentation of Financial Statements* provides little specific guidance on the presentation of line items in financial statements, such as the level of detail or number of line items that should be presented in the financial statements. Furthermore, IAS 1's objective is to set out 'the overall requirements for the presentation of financial statements, guidelines for their structure and minimum requirements for their content'. In doing so, IAS 1 sets out minimum levels of required items in the financial statements by requiring certain items to be presented on the face of, or in the notes to, the financial statements and in other required disclosures. The current requirements in IFRS do not provide a definition of 'gross profit' or 'operating results' or many other common subtotals. The absence of specific requirements arises from the fact that the guidance in IAS 1 relies on management's judgement about which additional line items, headings and subtotals:

(a)   are relevant to an understanding of the entity's financial position/financial performance; and

(b)   should be presented in a manner which provides relevant, reliable, comparable and understandable information.

IAS 1 allows entities to include additional line items, amend descriptions and the ordering of items in order to explain the elements of financial performance due to various activities, which may differ in frequency and predictability.

Transactions like business combinations may have a significant impact on profit or loss and these transactions are not necessarily frequent or regular. However, the practice of presenting non-recurring items may be interpreted as a way to present 'extraordinary items' in the financial statements despite the fact that 'extraordinary items' are not allowed under IAS 1. It can also be argued that additional lines and subtotals, as permitted by IAS 1, may add complexity to the analysis of the financial statements, which may become difficult to understand if entities use sub-totals and additional headings to isolate the effects of non-recurring transactions from classes of expense or income.

In the case of Chemclean, the cost of the inventories sold should be presented as cost of goods sold and not split in the manner set out by Chemclean.

(c) **Deferred tax assets**

IAS 12 *Income Taxes* states that a deferred tax asset shall be recognised for the carry-forward of unused tax losses to the extent that it is probable that future taxable profit will be available against which unused tax losses can be utilised.

IAS 12 explains that the existence of unused tax losses is strong evidence that future taxable profit may not be available. Therefore, when an entity has a history of recent losses, the entity recognises a deferred tax asset arising from unused tax losses only to the extent that the entity has sufficient taxable temporary differences or when there is convincing other evidence that sufficient taxable profit will be available against which the unused tax losses can be utilised by the entity. IAS 12 states that in assessing the probability that taxable profit will be available against which the unused tax losses or unused tax credits can be utilised, a consideration is whether the unused tax losses result from identifiable causes which are unlikely to recur.

Chemclean recognised losses during the previous five years. In order to use the deferred tax asset of $16 million, Chemclean would have to recognise a profit of $53.3 million at the existing tax rate of 30%. In comparison, the entity recognised an average loss of $19 million per year during the five previous years.

A comparison of the budgeted results to its actual results for the previous two years indicated material differences relating to impairment losses. In the interim financial statements for the first half of the financial year to 30 June 2015, Chemclean recognised impairment losses equal to budgeted impairment losses for the whole year. The unused tax losses appear to result from identifiable causes, which are likely to recur.

Chemclean's budgets and assumptions are not convincing other evidence because the entity does not appear to have been capable of making accurate forecasts in the past and there were material differences between the amounts budgeted and realised for the previous two years. Chemclean had presented future budgets primarily based on general assumptions about the development of key products and economic improvement indicators, rather than what was expected to influence the future income and therefore enable the use of the deferred tax asset.

Finally, in its financial statements, Chemclean disclosed a material uncertainty about its ability to continue as a going concern. This would be a key factor when considering the recognition of a deferred tax asset.

Therefore no deferred tax asset or liability should be recognised. The liability of $3 million relating to temporary differences can be offset against $3 million of unused tax losses. No further tax losses should be recognised.

ACCA Marking scheme		
		Marks
(a)	1 mark per point up to maximum	8
(b)	1 mark per point up to maximum	6
(c)	1 mark per point up to maximum	9
	Professional marks	2
		—
Total		**25**
		—

3 GASNATURE

Key answer tips

Broadly speaking, you will be awarded one mark for every valid point that you make. Ensure that you are making enough points to achieve a pass mark. As always, make sure that you thoroughly debrief the answer and that you learn from any mistakes that you made.

(a) **Joint arrangements**

A joint arrangement occurs where two or more parties have joint control. The contractually agreed sharing of control of an arrangement exists only when decisions about the relevant activities require the unanimous consent of the parties sharing control.

The classification of a joint arrangement as a joint operation or a joint venture depends upon the rights and obligations of the parties to the arrangement.

A joint arrangement which is not structured through a separate vehicle is a joint operation. A joint operator accounts for the assets, liabilities, revenues and expenses relating to its involvement in a joint operation in accordance with the relevant IFRSs.

The arrangement with Gogas is a joint operation as there is no separate vehicle involved and they have agreed to share services and costs with decisions regarding the platform requiring unanimous agreement of the parties. This means that Gasnature should recognise its share of the asset as property, plant and equipment.

Dismantling

Under IAS 16 *Property, Plant and Equipment* (PPE), the cost of an item of property, plant and equipment includes the initial estimate of the costs of dismantling and removing the item and restoring the site on which it is located.

IAS 37 *Provisions, Contingent Liabilities and Contingent Assets* contains requirements on how to measure decommissioning, restoration and similar liabilities. Where the effect of the time value of money is material, the amount of a provision should be the present value of the expenditures expected to be required to settle the obligation.

Thus Gasnature should recognise 55% of the cost of decommissioning the underground storage facility. However, because Gasnature is a joint operator, there is also a contingent liability for 45% of the decommissioning costs and there is a possible obligation for the remainder of the costs depending on whether some uncertain future event occurs, that is Gogas goes into liquidation and cannot fund the decommissioning costs. Therefore Gasnature should also disclose a contingent liability relating to the Gogas's share of the obligation to the extent that it is contingently liable for Gogas's share.

Irrecoverable gas

IAS 16 states that property, plant and equipment are tangible items which:

(a) are held for use in the production or supply of goods or services, for rental to others, or for administrative purposes; and

(b) are expected to be used during more than one period.

The irrecoverable gas is necessary for the storage facility to perform its function as a gas storage facility. It is therefore part of the storage facility and should be capitalised as a component of the storage facility asset. Thus Gasnature should classify and account for its share of the irrecoverable gas as PPE. The irrecoverable gas should be depreciated to its residual value over the life of the storage facility.

When the storage facility is decommissioned and the cushion gas extracted and sold, the sale of the irrecoverable gas is accounted for as the disposal of an item of PPE in accordance with IAS 16 and the gain or loss recognised in profit or loss. The natural gas in excess of the irrecoverable gas which is injected into the facility should be treated as inventory in accordance with IAS 2 *Inventories*.

(b) **Financial instruments**

IFRS 9 *Financial Instruments* applies to those contracts to buy or sell a non-financial item which can be settled net in cash with the exception of contracts which are held for the purpose of the receipt or delivery of a non-financial item in accordance with the entity's expected purchase, sale or usage requirements. In other words, it will result in physical delivery of the commodity. Contracts which are for an entity's 'own use' are exempt from the requirements of IFRS 9.

There are various ways in which a contract to buy or sell a non-financial item can be settled net in cash or another financial instrument or by exchanging financial instruments. These include:

(a) when the terms of the contract permit either party to settle it net in cash

(b) when the ability to settle net in cash is not explicit in the terms of the contract, but the entity has a practice of settling similar contracts net in cash

(c) when, for similar contracts, the entity has a practice of taking delivery of the underlying and selling it within a short period after delivery, for the purpose of generating a profit

(d) when the non-financial item which is the subject of the contract is readily convertible to cash.

Contracts to buy or sell a non-financial item, such as a commodity, which can be settled net in cash or another financial instrument, or by exchanging financial instruments, are within the scope of IFRS 9. They are accounted for as derivatives.

It could be argued that the contract is net settled because the penalty mechanism requires Agas to compensate Gasnature at the current prevailing market price. Further, if natural gas is readily convertible into cash in the location where the delivery takes place, the contract could be considered net settled.

However, the contract will probably still qualify as 'own use' as long as it has been entered into and continues to be held for the expected counterparties' sales/usage requirements. This means that it falls outside IFRS 9 and therefore would be treated as an executory contract.

(c) (i) **Overhaul**

It is not acceptable to accrue the costs of the overhaul because the entity does not have a constructive obligation to undertake the overhaul.

Under IFRS, costs related to major inspection and overhaul are recognised as part of the carrying amount of property, plant and equipment if they meet the asset recognition criteria in IAS 16 *Property, Plant and Equipment*. The major overhaul component will then be depreciated on a straight-line basis over its useful life (i.e. over the period to the next overhaul) and any remaining carrying amount will be derecognised when the next overhaul is performed. Costs of the day-to-day servicing of the asset (i.e. routine maintenance) are expensed as incurred.

Therefore the cost of the overhaul should have been identified as a separate component of the refinery at initial recognition and depreciated over a period of two years. This will result in the same amount of expense being recognised in profit or loss over the same period as the proposal to create a provision.

(ii) **Drilling**

Since there were no indicators of impairment at the period end, all costs incurred up to 31 August 2015 amounting to $5 million should remain capitalised by the entity in the financial statements for the year ended on that date.

If material, disclosure should be provided in the financial statements of the additional activity during the subsequent period which determined the exploratory drilling was unsuccessful. This represents a non-adjusting event as defined by IAS 10 *Events after the Reporting Period* as an event which is indicative of a condition which arose after the end of the reporting period.

The asset of $5 million and additional drilling costs of $2 million incurred subsequently would be expensed in the following year's financial statements.

ACCA Marking scheme			
			Marks
(a)	1 mark per point up to maximum		9
(b)	1 mark per point up to maximum		6
(c)	(i)	1 mark per point up to maximum	4
	(ii)	1 mark per point up to maximum	4
	Professional marks		2
Total			25

4   REVENUE FROM CONTRACTS WITH CUSTOMERS

Key answer tips

The P2 examining team had written an article on IFRS 15 *Revenue from Contracts with Customers* shortly before this question was set. This demonstrates the importance of wider reading to scoring well on the essay-style question.

(a)   (i)   **Contracts**

A contract exists when an agreement between two or more parties creates enforceable rights and obligations between those parties. The agreement does not need to be in writing to be a contract but the decision as to whether a contractual right or obligation is enforceable is considered within the context of the relevant legal framework of a jurisdiction. Thus, whether a contract is enforceable will vary across jurisdictions. The performance obligation could include promises which result in a valid expectation that the entity will transfer goods or services to the customer even though those promises are not legally enforceable.

The first criteria set out in IFRS 15 is that the parties should have approved the contract and are committed to perform their respective obligations. It would be questionable whether that contract is enforceable if this were not the case. In the case of oral or implied contracts, this may be difficult but all relevant facts and circumstances should be considered in assessing the parties' commitment. The parties need not always be committed to fulfilling all of the obligations under a contract. IFRS 15 gives the example where a customer is required to purchase a minimum quantity of goods but past experience shows that the customer does not always do this and the other party does not enforce their contract rights. However, there needs to be evidence that the parties are substantially committed to the contract.

It is essential that each party's rights and the payment terms can be identified regarding the goods or services to be transferred. This latter requirement is crucial when determining the transaction price.

The contract must have commercial substance before revenue can be recognised, as without this requirement, entities might artificially inflate their revenue and it would be questionable whether the transaction has economic consequences.

Further, it should be probable that the entity will collect the consideration due under the contract. An assessment of a customer's credit risk is an important element in deciding whether a contract has validity but customer credit risk does not affect the measurement or presentation of revenue. The consideration may be different to the contract price because of discounts and bonus offerings. The entity should assess the ability of the customer to pay and the customer's intention to pay the consideration. If a contract with a customer does not meet these criteria, the entity can continually re-assess the contract to determine whether it subsequently meets the criteria.

Two or more contracts which are entered into around the same time with the same customer may be combined and accounted for as a single contract, if they meet the specified criteria. The standard provides detailed requirements for contract modifications. A modification may be accounted for as a separate contract or a modification of the original contract, depending upon the circumstances of the case.

(ii)   **Revenue recognition**

Step one in the five-step model requires the identification of the contract with the customer. After a contract has been determined to fall under IFRS 15, the following steps are required before revenue can be recognised.

Step two requires the identification of the separate performance obligations in the contract. This is often referred to as 'unbundling', and is done at the beginning of a contract. The key factor in identifying a separate performance obligation is the distinctiveness of the good or service, or a bundle of goods or services. A good or service is distinct if the customer can benefit from the good or service on its own or together with other readily available resources and is separately identifiable from other elements of the contract. IFRS 15 requires a series of distinct goods or services which are substantially the same with the same pattern of transfer, to be regarded as a single performance obligation. A good or service, which has been delivered, may not be distinct if it cannot be used without another good or service which has not yet been delivered. Similarly, goods or services which are not distinct should be combined with other goods or services until the entity identifies a bundle of goods or services which is distinct. IFRS 15 provides indicators rather than criteria to determine when a good or service is distinct within the context of the contract. This allows management to apply judgement to determine the separate performance obligations which best reflect the economic substance of a transaction.

Step three requires the entity to determine the transaction price, which is the amount of consideration which an entity expects to be entitled to in exchange for the promised goods or services. This amount excludes amounts collected on behalf of a third party, for example, government taxes. An entity must determine the amount of consideration to which it expects to be entitled in order to recognise revenue.

The transaction price might include variable or contingent consideration. Variable consideration should be estimated as either the expected value or the most likely amount. Management should use the approach which it expects will best predict the amount of consideration and should be applied consistently throughout the contract.

An entity can only include variable consideration in the transaction price to the extent that it is highly probable that a subsequent change in the estimated variable consideration will not result in a significant revenue reversal. If it is not appropriate to include all of the variable consideration in the transaction price, the entity should assess whether it should include part of the variable consideration. However, this latter amount still has to pass the 'revenue reversal' test.

Additionally, an entity should estimate the transaction price taking into account non-cash consideration, consideration payable to the customer and the time value of money if a significant financing component is present. The latter is not required if the time period between the transfer of goods or services and payment is less than one year. If an entity anticipates that it may ultimately accept an amount lower than that initially promised in the contract due to, for example, past experience of discounts given, then revenue would be estimated at the lower amount with the collectability of that lower amount being assessed. Subsequently, if revenue already recognised is not collectable, impairment losses should be taken to profit or loss.

Step four requires the allocation of the transaction price to the separate performance obligations. The allocation is based on the relative standalone selling prices of the goods or services promised and is made at inception of the contract. It is not adjusted to reflect subsequent changes in the standalone selling prices of those goods or services. The best evidence of standalone selling price is the observable price of a good or service when the entity sells that good or service separately. If that is not available, an estimate is made by using an approach which maximises the use of observable inputs. For example, expected cost plus an appropriate margin or the assessment of market prices for similar goods or services adjusted for entity-specific costs and margins or in limited circumstances a residual approach. When a contract contains more than one distinct performance obligation, an entity allocates the transaction price to each distinct performance obligation on the basis of the standalone selling price.

Where the transaction price includes a variable amount and discounts, consideration needs to be given as to whether these amounts relate to all or only some of the performance obligations in the contract. Discounts and variable consideration will typically be allocated proportionately to all of the performance obligations in the contract. However, if certain conditions are met, they can be allocated to one or more separate performance obligations.

Step five requires revenue to be recognised as each performance obligation is satisfied. An entity satisfies a performance obligation by transferring control of a promised good or service to the customer, which could occur over time or at a point in time. The definition of control includes the ability to prevent others from directing the use of and obtaining the benefits from the asset. A performance obligation is satisfied at a point in time unless it meets one of three criteria set out in IFRS 15. Revenue is recognised in line with the pattern of transfer.

If an entity does not satisfy its performance obligation over time, it satisfies it at a point in time and revenue will be recognised when control is passed at that point in time. Factors which may indicate the passing of control include the present right to payment for the asset or the customer has legal title to the asset or the entity has transferred physical possession of the asset.

(b)   (i)   The contract contains a significant financing component because of the length of time between when the customer pays for the asset and when Tang transfers the asset to the customer, as well as the prevailing interest rates in the market. A contract with a customer which has a significant financing component should be separated into a revenue component (for the notional cash sales price) and a loan component.

An entity should use the discount rate which would be reflected in a separate financing transaction between the entity and its customer at contract inception. IFRS 15 would therefore dictate that the rate which should be used in adjusting the promised consideration is 5%, which is the entity's incremental borrowing rate, and not 11.8%.

Tang would account for the significant financing component as follows:

Recognise a contract liability for the $240,000 payment received on 1 December 2014 at the contract inception:

Dr Cash $240,000

Cr Contract liability $240,000

During the two years from contract inception (1 December 2014) until the transfer of the printing machine, Tang adjusts the amount of consideration and accretes the contract liability by recognising interest on $240,000 at 5% for two years.

Year to 30 November 2015

Dr Interest expense $12,000

Cr Contract liability $12,000

The contract liability would stand at $252,000 ($240,000 + $12,000) at 30 November 2015.

Year to 30 November 2016

Dr Interest expense $12,600

Cr Contract liability $12,600

The entity would recognise contract revenue on the transfer of the printing machine at 30 November 2016 of $264,600 ($252,000 + $12,600) by debiting contract liability and crediting revenue with this amount.

(ii)   Tang accounts for the promised bundle of goods and services as a single performance obligation satisfied over time in accordance with IFRS 15.

At contract inception, Tang excludes the $100,000 bonus from the transaction price because it cannot conclude that it is highly probable that a significant reversal in the amount of cumulative revenue recognised will not occur. Completion of the printing machine is highly susceptible to factors outside the entity's influence. The transaction price is therefore $1,500,000.

By the end of the first year, the entity has satisfied 65% of its performance obligation on the basis of costs incurred to date. Costs incurred to date are therefore $520,000. Tang reassesses the variable consideration and concludes that the amount is still constrained. Therefore at 30 November 2015, the following would be recognised:

Revenue (65% × $1.5m) $975,000

Costs $520,000

Gross profit $455,000

On 4 December 2015, the contract is modified. As a result, the fixed consideration and expected costs increase by $110,000 and $60,000, respectively. In addition, the allowable time for achieving the bonus is extended by six months with the result that Tang concludes that it is highly probable that including the bonus in the transaction price will not result in a significant reversal in the amount of cumulative revenue recognised in accordance with IFRS 15. The transaction price is now therefore $1,710,000 ($1,500,000 + $100,000 + $110,000).

Tang has satisfied 60.5% of its performance obligation ($520,000 actual costs incurred compared to $860,000 total expected costs). The entity recognises additional revenue of $59,550 ((60.5% of $1,710,000) − $975,000 revenue recognised to date) at the date of the modification as a cumulative catch-up adjustment. As the contract amendment took place after the year end, the additional revenue would not be treated as an adjusting event.

ACCA marking scheme			
			Marks
(a)	(i)	1 mark per point up to maximum	5
	(ii)	1 mark per point	8
(b)	(i)	1 mark per point up to maximum	4
	(ii)	1 mark per point up to maximum	6
		Professional marks	2
Total			**25**